Planting Paradise

Planting Paradise

Cultivating the Garden 1501–1900

S T E P H E N   H A R R I S

Bodleian Library
UNIVERSITY OF OXFORD

First published in 2011 by

The Bodleian Library
Broad Street, Oxford OX1 3BG
www.bodleianbookshop.co.uk

ISBN   978 1 85124 343 3

Cover design by Dot Little
Text designed and typeset in 10.5 on 15 Monotype Baskerville,
based on a design by Dot Little,
by illuminati, Grosmont
Printed and bound by Great Wall Printing, China
on 157 gsm Go Ching matt art

A CIP record of this publication is available from
the British Library and the Library of Congress

Contents

Preface

---

the Glory of the Garden lies in more than meets the eye
'The Glory of the Garden', Rudyard Kipling, 1911

ONE DAY, many years ago, my sceptical grandmother was disturbed, in her kitchen, by a pair of Christian proselytisers knocking at her door. When they asked who had made her large, beautiful garden, she responded characteristically, 'my husband and his bloody hard work'. The 'bloody hard work' of my grandfather has been the hallmark of gardeners for centuries. Gardeners have transformed habitats and brought together plants from across the globe to produce imitations of natural environments and fantasies of their own devising. However, not only have landscapes been transformed but, less obviously, the plants themselves have been altered by generations of amateur and professional horticulturalists. The 'bloody hard work' of altering plants includes collecting and transporting them from their regions of origin, acclimatising, growing and propagating them in foreign climates and then, perhaps, selecting and manipulating them to create whimsical forms, which are unlikely to survive in the wild. The most popular of these plants survive, even if the gardens themselves disappear: today, my grandfather's 'bloody hard work' is covered with a house.

The original inspiration behind this book was the poem *Vertumnus* written by Abel Evans in 1713 in praise of Jacob Bobart the Younger, who, in the early eighteenth century, was in charge of the Oxford Botanic Garden, which had been established in 1621. The poem was an attempt to describe Bobart's role as a manipulator of plants. Using images published between 1501 and 1900, this book looks at the vast range of plants that we grow, whether in gardens, fields or plantations, and how our understanding of them changed over four centuries. The starting point of 1501 marks the time when the earliest printed botanical books were being published, as well as representing something of a turning point when educated people began to observe the natural world directly rather than relying on previous authority. The year 1900 marks the point at which we started to investigate plants through genetics, and our understanding of plants and how they worked once again changed dramatically. While the advances made by genetic investigations over the past century have been impressive, it was between 1501 and 1900 that much of our basic understanding of how plants can be moved, manipulated and cultivated was established. Inevitably our understanding of plants was a gradual process, developing over many centuries – stretching back long before our main period of reference. Consequently, this book is not chronological but is organised thematically.

Chapter 1 explores the importance of plants for life on earth, especially for humans, and looks at plant diversity, our knowledge of which increased dramatically during the period 1501–1900.

The following chapter discusses how we expanded our knowledge of plants through the botanical exploration of unknown regions, the cultivation of plants in living collections and the preservation of knowledge in books, manuscripts and herbaria. Knowledge of plant use has also been handed down the generations orally. Living plants, which change with the seasons, could be appreciated and investigated, and, perhaps, even evolve. The pressed, dried plants of the herbarium, the 'winter garden', were readily studied but did not change. Together, the library, garden and herbarium supported – and still support – our understanding of botanical novelty.

Chapter 3 considers some of the more curious byways that have contributed to or detracted from botanical understanding. The seventeenth-century diarist and arboriculturalist John Evelyn considered gardens, and their contents, to be allegories of the Garden of Eden. This was not an original view but had gradually developed, as the boundaries of European perceptions of the natural world expanded. The Church had argued for centuries over the nature of Eden and the consequences of the Fall, with the certainty, derived from the Ancients, that the physical limits of the earth were known. However, Columbus's discovery of the New World in the late fifteenth century shattered both ecclesiastical certainties and the faith of intellectuals in the veracity of Ancient Greek and Roman writers. Our understanding of plants has been marked by some very curious ideas that have an echo even today.

In Chapter 4 the utilitarian role of gardens is discussed. Botanic gardens, often associated with medical teaching, had the twin utilitarian objectives of providing access to medicine and food. Medicine and food, together with economics and politics, fuelled Europe's global ambitions from the early sixteenth century, which reached their zenith in the mid-nineteenth century. The investigation of new crops and medicines, using the global network of botanic gardens established by European colonial powers, became integral to imperial policies.

The theme of plants as power is developed further in Chapter 5; we see how the discovery of the New World challenged botanical hypotheses based on limited knowledge, half-truths and ancient authority. As the physical and intellectual worlds opened up during the Renaissance and Enlightenment, so the diversity of known plants increased, as did our knowledge and understanding of the natural world. Methods for the successful transport of plants were discovered and diverse plants became commonplace in the garden. However, the process of plant exploration and introduction has not always been benign. Numerous dubious practices have, in some cases, led to species extermination and the destruction of local economies.

We consider some of the practicalities of getting plants to grow away from their natural environments in Chapter 6; in particular, the need to manipulate light and temperature, together with soil nutrients and the means by which plants were propagated. Garden plant novelties provided more than mere food and medicine; they provided the opportunity to experiment and test fundamental biological ideas, which are explored in Chapter 7. For example, until the late seventeenth century it was thought plant sex was restricted to a few very special cases. The discovery, and experimental proof, that sex was almost universal among plants was a revelation that demolished the persistent belief in plant purity. Sex was the basis of Linnaeus's influential mid-eighteenth-century classification of the botanical world and led to a century of scientific and (misplaced) moral arguments. Scientific investigation enabled plants to be manipulated for agricultural production on a rational basis, provided Charles Darwin with evidence for the origin of species, and led the monk Gregor Mendel to his first understanding of the then unnamed science of genetics.

It is a curious feeling to have written much of this book in a city (Brasília) that was built in the middle of the twentieth century, in a country that was discovered by Western adventurers at the beginning of the sixteenth century. As I look from an apartment window onto a maze of housing blocks, most of the trees that line the streets are not native to Central Brazil; many are not even native to South America. The discovery, movement and acclimatisation of plants to human surroundings are not European or North American phenomena that stopped in the nineteenth century; they continue across the globe to the present day. Using images published between 1501 and 1900, this book explores the roles of gardens, in their widest sense, as laboratories for the investigation of botanical diversity. As people's ideas and knowledge of the world altered, so the plants grown in gardens changed. As the geography of plant discovery widened, the limits of Europe gave way to the exotica of the tropics. As technology advanced, more plants could be grown from Asia, Africa, South America and Australia. The range of new discoveries highlighted the tremendous diversity of plants, and is a testament to the rational understanding of plant biology.

It has been a privilege to work in the libraries of the University of Oxford and to be able to draw upon the expertise of those who have stewardship of these collections. I would like to thank especially Anne Marie Townsend of the Plant Sciences Library for all of her invaluable help with bringing this book together. I want to thank editor Caroline Brooke Johnson for her work on the manuscript and trying to keep me focused on the period between 1501 and 1900; to Deborah Susman for producing the book and Dot Little and Lucy Morton for the design. Finally, as always, I thank Carolyn for having lived, on two continents, through the conception, gestation and birth of this book.

CHAPTER I

People and plant diversity

———

When Garden Plants shall dye, yours most shall thrive
And shall preserve, themselves, and you alive.

William Hawkins, in Stephens & Brown,
Catalogus horti botanici Oxoniensis, 1658

PLANTS colonised the planet long before we evolved from our ape ancestors, and are the longest-lived organisms on earth. As the Ancient Egyptians started to construct the pyramids at Giza around 2500 BC, on another continent, individual Californian bristlecone pines (*Pinus longaeva*) were mere saplings. By the time William Caxton (*c.* 1415–1492) had printed his first page and Christopher Columbus (*c.* 1451–1506) had set foot in the Caribbean towards the end of the fifteenth century, these trees had been producing seed for thousands of years. Today, these same trees are at least 4,800 years old and continue to produce seed. Great cultures have arisen and empires fallen during the lives of these trees, yet we have no idea how long they can live.

The bristlecone pine is the Methuselah of the plant kingdom, although many plants are long-lived by the measure of our lives. In the Padua Botanic Garden, a specimen of the dwarf palm (*Chamaerops humilis*)

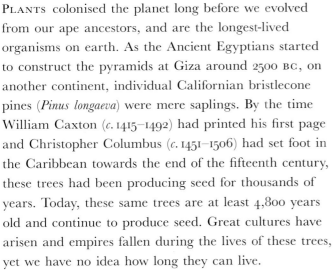

planted in 1585 still survives. In Paris, a Cretan maple (*Acer sempervirens*) survives which was raised from seed collected by Joseph Pitton Tournefort (1656–1708) in 1701. In the Oxford Botanic Garden,[1] which until 1840 was known as the Oxford Physic Garden, there is a yew tree (*Taxus baccata*) that was planted by the Garden's first Keeper, Jacob Bobart the Elder (*c.* 1599–1680), in 1645, during the English Civil War.

In the eighteenth century these gardens were also well known for the efforts gardeners and curators made to fill them with plants from across the known world. One of this active band of gardeners was Jacob Bobart the Younger (1641–1719) in Oxford. Bobart's three-acre domain was surrounded by a high stone wall, within which he cultivated a great variety of plants that he acquired from across the globe. Indeed, such was the reputation of Bobart as a cultivator of the rare and the exotic that Bobart's friend, the clergyman and academic

I

Abel Evans (1679–1737), wrote the poem *Vertumnus*, published in 1713; he did not spare his praise of Bobart. The poem not only highlighted Bobart's practical skills but his skills as an academic botanist interested in understanding plant diversity and how plants worked.

Plants for all seasons

In the West, the importance of plants, and the wide range of uses that humans make of them, was recorded as early as 300 BC by the Greek philosopher Theophrastus (*c.* 372–287 BC) in *Enquiry into Plants* and *Causes of Plants*. However, humans had used plants for thousands of years before Theophrastus formally recorded the fact. Indeed, human evolution, survival and cultural development have always been, and are, intimately associated with plants. Wars have been fought over plant products, whether it be nutmeg (*Myristica fragrans*) in the seventeenth century, tea (*Camellia sinensis*) and opium (*Papaver somniferum*) in the eighteenth and nineteenth centuries or cocaine (*Erythroxylum coca*) today. Human societies have been transformed through plant exploitation; for example, slaves transported from the Old World to the New World were used to grow tobacco and sugar, which fed the changing tastes of seventeenth- and eighteenth-century Europe.

Despite the vast number of ways in which plants have been used by humans, and many of these will be covered in later chapters, we exploited and continue to exploit only a small proportion of total plant diversity. The domestication of wheat some 10,000 years ago was a spur to the development of civilisation in the Near East. Of the approximately 350,000 flowering plants,

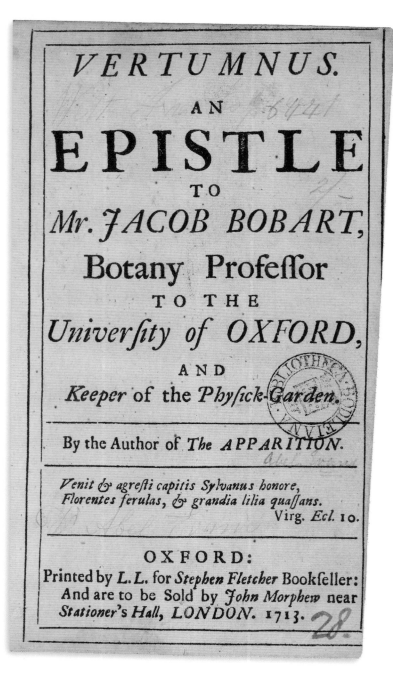

VERTUMNUS.

AN

EPISTLE

TO

Mr. JACOB BOBART,

Botany Professor

TO THE

University of OXFORD,

AND

Keeper of the *Physick-Garden.*

By the Author of *The* APPARITION.

Venit & agresti capitis Sylvanus honore,
Florentes ferulas, & grandia lilia quassans.
Virg. *Ecl.* 10.

OXFORD:

Printed by *L. L.* for *Stephen Fletcher* Bookseller: And are to be Sold by *John Morphew* near *Stationer's Hall,* LONDON. 1713.

FIGURE 1 (*left*) Abel Evans's poem *Vertumnus* (1713) praised Jacob Bobart the Younger's stewardship of the Oxford Botanic Garden. The poem is reminiscent of John Milton's work, and draws an image of Bobart as ruling his botanical subjects, and having ultimate control over their fates, just as Queen Anne ruled her subjects. In it Evans describes the garden, the diversity of species that the Bobarts, father and son, had introduced from Europe, Asia, Africa and the Americas. However, the difficulties the Bobarts experienced in getting some of these plants to grow in foreign soil are not ignored.

FIGURE 2 (*right*) The chromolithographs in Berthe van Nooten's *Fleurs, fruits et feuillages choisis de la flore et de la pomone de l'Ile de Java* (1866), a book 'particularly addressed to women', revealed the physical peculiarities of the durian and other native and introduced Javanese fruits.

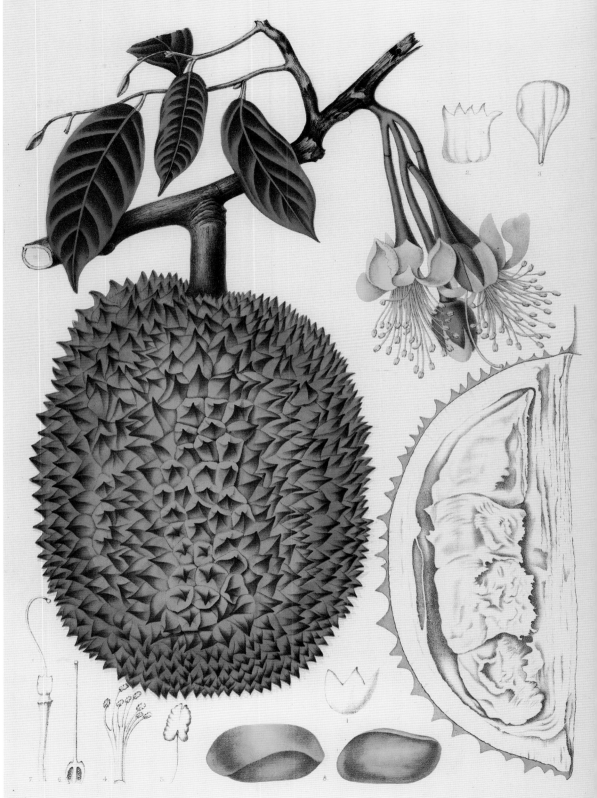

Peint d'après nature par Mme Berthe Hoola van Nooten, à Batavia.

Chromolith par G. Severeyns Lith de l'Acad Roy de Belgique.

today 60 per cent of the human population's calorie intake is provided by only four species of grass (wheat, maize, rice and sugar); this figure is unlikely to have changed significantly over the past five centuries. Besides essential foods, plants also provided beverages, spices, fruits, vegetables and oils. Worldwide, medicines have been derived from up to 70,000 plant species, and until the twentieth century plants were the only sources of effective remedies. Plants provided timber and bamboo for building, cotton and jute for cloth, rubber for tyres and contraceptives, sunflower and palm oils for cooking, frankincense and myrrh for incense, ylang-ylang and rose for perfumes, and indigo and woad for dyes. Plants also had and continue to have immense aesthetic value, and fortunes were made and lost in the seventeenth and eighteenth centuries through fashions for particular types of plant. Tulips became immensely popular in Holland in the early seventeenth century, which led to 'tulipomania' and vast amounts of money spent on bulbs. In Britain, florists' societies emerged, where the focus was on breeding different colours and forms of plants such as hyacinths and auriculas.

Newly discovered plants were often the cause of great enthusiasm. However, other discoveries were greeted with more ambivalence. In 1621, the botanist John Goodyer (1592–1664) was far from impressed with the Jerusalem artichoke (*Helianthus tuberosus*), which had been sent to him from North America in 1617:

> these roots are dressed divers waies; some boile them in water, and after stew them with sacke and butter, adding a little Ginger: others bake them in pies, putting Marrow, Dates, Ginger, Raisons of the Sun, Sacke, … But in my judgement, which way soever they be drest and eaten they

stirre and cause a filthie loathsome stinking winde within the bodie, thereby causing the belly to bee pained and tormented, and are a meate more fit for swine, than men.[2]

In contrast, the durian, one of many extraordinary fruits discovered by European palates in the tropics, is infamous for combining a heavenly taste with a mephitic odour. The biogeographer and evolutionary biologist Alfred Russel Wallace (1823–1913) was a durian enthusiast:

> pulp is the eatable part, and its consistence and flavor are indescribable. A rich butter-like custard highly flavoured with almonds gives the general idea of it, but intermingled with it come wafts of flavor that call to mind cream-cheese, onion-sauce, brown-sherry, and other incongruities.… It is neither acid, nor sweet, nor juicy, yet one feels the want of none of these qualities, for it is perfect as it is. It produces no nausea or other bad effect, and the more you eat of it the less inclined you feel to stop. In fact, to eat durions, is a new sensation worth a voyage to the East to experience.[3]

Plant diversity and novelty

Approximately 430,000 green plant species have been scientifically described since the early sixteenth century. This figure reflects the exploration, the accumulation and synthesis of knowledge about plants over the past five centuries. The main groups of plants, in their broadest senses, have been recognised since the earliest printed herbals. However, thanks to complex changes in group definition between the sixteenth and nineteenth centuries, it is easier to consider the groups as they are defined today: green algae through the mosses, liverworts, ferns and fern allies to the gymnosperms

FIGURE 3 The *Phycologia Australica* (1858–63) was published in five volumes and contained 300 coloured plates, including this one of the green alga *Caulerpa obscura*. All the illustrations were made by Harvey and show the reader 'to his or her eye a coloured drawing, accompanied when necessary with such magnified dissections as will enable any one possessed of a microscope to refer with certainty the figure before him to the plant which it represents'. It is one of the most important and beautiful books on seaweeds ever published.

and flowering plants. While new plant species were continually being discovered as botanical exploration continued, many species were also driven to extinction without ever becoming known to science. People have tended to prefer the conifers and the flowering plants, with periodic enthusiasms for the true ferns. Plant diversity drove horticulturalists to enrich European gardens and scientists to try to understand how plants functioned and how such diversity arose.

Green algae

The green algae comprise some 12,000 species, although they are not a single evolutionary group in the plant tree of life. The majority of green algae are found in freshwater habitats, although some are found in the sea, yet others are found in terrestrial habitats or as part of lichens.

The Irish botanist William Henry Harvey (1811–1866) was attracted to the study of algae, 'some of the most beautiful and delicate of Nature's vegetable productions',[4] because 'to be useless, various, and abstruse is a sufficient recommendation of a science to make it pleasing to me.'[5] Harvey had extensive practical botanical experience in South Africa, where he was Treasurer-General between 1836 and 1842, or 'Her Majesty's Pleasurer-General', as he feared his collecting fervour would be viewed by his colleagues. On returning to Dublin he became curator of the Trinity College Herbarium. Between 1853 and 1856 he went on a voyage that would see him collecting and studying algae from the Indian Ocean, the Australian colonies and the evocative Friendly Islands. During the eighteen months he explored Australian shores, Harvey 'collected,

prepared and dried upwards of 20,000 specimens of 600 species of Algae'.[6] Many of these specimens were later sold to offset the cost of the journey. Harvey proposed to write a book that would catalogue his dispersed collections and promote interest in the marine biology of 'our Australian dependencies' among amateur and professional naturalists. Harvey was convinced that 'our fellow-countrymen, wherever they go, bring or send home specimens of natural objects, and there is, perhaps, no country where collections of botanical … specimens are more widely dispersed than in England among the population'.[7]

Mosses and liverworts

There are approximately 24,000 moss and liverwort species, although most species are very small and fail to attract great attention. However, peatlands, which cover about 1 per cent of the earth's surface, are dominated by the moss genus *Sphagnum*. Like Harvey, the German botanist Johann Dillenius (1684–1747) was another explorer of the botanically obscure. In 1721 Dillenius came to England, with a prodigious botanical reputation, through the patronage of the botanist and diplomat William Sherard (1659–1728). In his *Historia Muscorum* (1741), Dillenius was the first to try seriously to enumerate all of the 'lower plants' known. In total, 661 species were recognised, including fungi, lichens, algae, mosses and liverworts. The species described in the *Historia* are associated with specimens in Dillenius's herbarium, the majority of which were probably collected by Dillenius himself. However, there were numerous contributors from the most prominent botanical luminaries of the early eighteenth

6

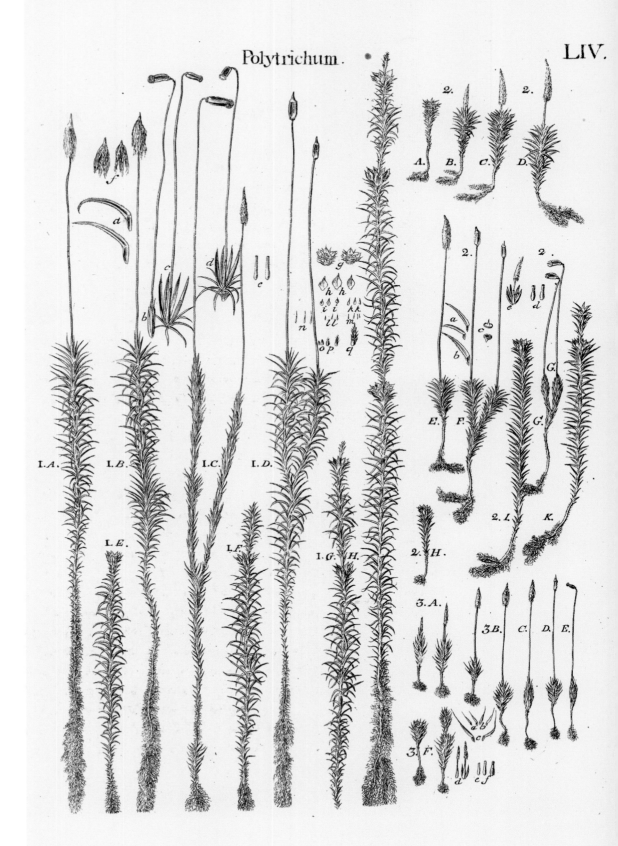

FIGURE 4 Hairmosses (*Polytrichum*) are among the largest mosses in Europe. As with the much more famous *Hortus Elthamensis* (1732), the 85 plates of the *Historia Muscorum* (1741) were drawn and engraved by Dillenius. Two hundred and fifty copies of the *Historia* were published and cost one guinea each but the book sold poorly and was a financial failure. Dillenius attempted to recoup his loses by preparing an abridged version to sell for half a guinea; it was never published. The *Historia* is perhaps Dillenius's most scientifically enduring work, and was used extensively by Linnaeus in his *Species Plantarum* (1753).

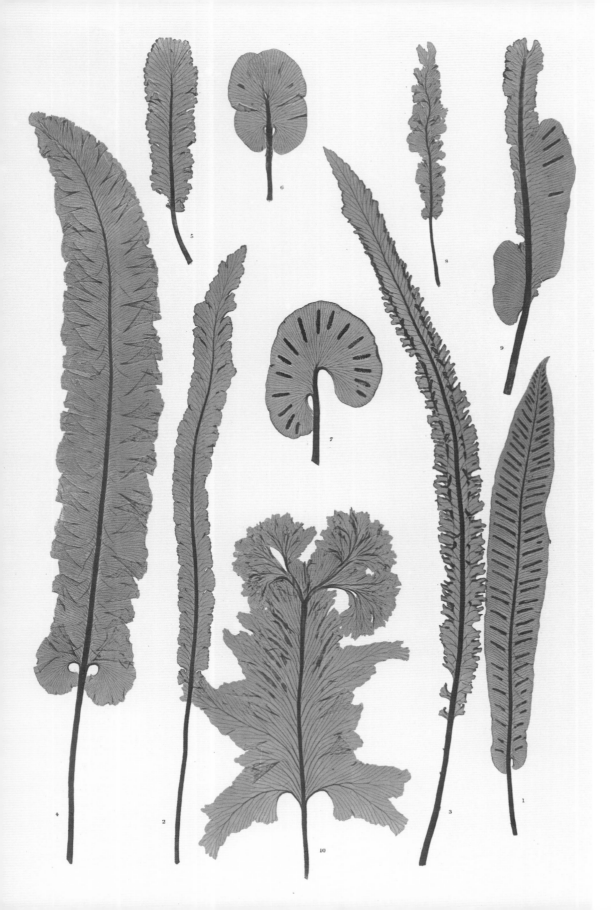

FIGURE 5 Thomas Moore's *Ferns of Great Britain and Ireland* (1857) was an elaborate publication based on nature printing. Nature printing was invented in the fifteenth century and, at it simplest, involves applying ink to a plant and then pressing it against a piece of paper, often in a printing press. This technique of producing an image of a plant is suited to objects that are naturally flat, such as the *Scolopendrium vulgare* shown here. However, the technique in slow and destructive, so Moore's publisher Henry Bradbury modified the method by making an impression of the specimen in soft lead, which was then copied by an electroplate process to produce a printing block.

century, including John Bartram (1699–1777), Hermann Boerhaave (1668–1738), Mark Catesby (1682–1749), Olof Celsius (1670–1756), Peter Collinson (1694–1768), Carolus Linnaeus (1707–1778), Richard Richardson (1663–1741), Hans Sloane (1660–1753) and Albert von Haller (1708–1777). Furthermore, specimens came from places as far apart as Britain, Russia, Carolinas, Bahamas, Greenland, Patagonia and Australia.

Fern and fern allies

There are approximately 13,000 ferns and fern allies, the majority of which are tropical. The ferns and their allies, which are usually found in damp, shaded areas, became popular as both garden and house plants, especially for their delicate, complex and highly diverse leaves. Indeed, so popular was fern collecting in Victorian England that the Irishman Patrick Bernard O'Kelly (*c.*1852–1937) made a living collecting plants, especially ferns from the Burren, and selling them to gardeners. With enthusiasm came the possibilities of publishing elaborate works. One elaborate work on ferns, Thomas Moore's *Ferns of Great Britain and Ireland* (1857), was published by Henry Bradbury.

Gymnosperms

The gymnosperms comprise some 800 species and are most familiar as the conifers such as pines, larches and cypresses. Gymnosperms (literally 'naked seed') are usually cone-bearing trees and are particularly diverse in the fossil record. They are found on all continents, except Antarctica, but are particularly diverse on mountains and dominate northern coniferous forests. Gardeners, especially the wealthy with land and gardens

to fill, were attracted by the landscape possibilities of conifers in the eighteenth and nineteenth centuries. The ginkgo (*Ginkgo biloba*) was first encountered by Europeans as a temple tree in China in the late seventeenth century and was introduced to Britain in the mid-eighteenth century. Monkey puzzle trees from South America and the Pacific became Victorian favourites, as did the tallest of all living organisms, the towering Californian redwood (*Sequoia sempervirens*), which can reach 115 metres. The botanical and evolutionary curiosity welwitschia (*Welwitschia mirabilis*), with its two huge leaves and very short stem, is found only in the deserts of Angola and Namibia. When this plant was discovered in 1859 it was a botanical sensation, and considerable efforts were made to bring it into cultivation. However, the plant's unusual environmental needs mean that it remains a species that is difficult to cultivate.

Aylmer Bourke Lambert (1761–1842) was an amateur member of the late-eighteenth-century British botanical aristocracy, with the private fortune and the appetites to match. He collected together one of the most important private herbaria and botanical libraries of the early nineteenth century. Lambert was a friend of the botanical patriarchs Sir Joseph Banks (1743–1820) and Sir James Edward Smith (1759–1828), and, when Smith purchased all of Linnaeus's library and herbarium, he became one of the founder members of the Linnean Society of London (1788). When Lambert died, his collections were sold to try to pay the staggering debts he accrued during his extravagant life. Lambert is perhaps best known for his magnificently illustrated folio *A Description of the genus Pinus* (1803–24), which included almost all of the pines

then known. Lambert's concept of the economically and horticulturally important genus *Pinus* was broader than today, so included many species which we today regard as belonging to different genera.

Flowering plants

The group of plants that have attracted most attention in the past five centuries is the flowering plants (angiosperms). Flowering plants comprise some 350,000 species. Flowers are complex structures whose origin was described by Charles Darwin (1809–1882) as an 'abominable mystery'; the mystery remains to the present day. We now know that the majority of flowers ensure sexual reproduction; although this was not always the case and there were often acrimonious disputes about whether plants had sex, which will be discussed in the final chapter. Flowers are associated with methods of moving pollen from the male to the female floral parts, whilst seeds show numerous dispersal strategies that ensure the next generation is carried away from its parents. These features, plus factors such as seed dormancy, mean flowering plants are capable of travelling in both space and time and exploiting numerous, diverse ecological habitats. Flowering plants are adapted to freshwater and marine habitats, through temperate and tropical forests, savannahs and grasslands to deserts, high altitudes and the polar regions.

Particular groups of flowering plants have inspired exploration, study and obsession. Orchids are one such group, although perhaps more interesting is the enthusiasm for palms expressed by the German botanist Carl Friederich Philipp von Martius (1794–1868). Von Martius transformed our knowledge of Brazilian plants through the extensive journeys he made in the country between 1817 and 1820. He initiated the forty-volume *Flora Brasiliensis* (1840–1906), the most complete Flora of Brazil ever written, but it was the grandeur of palms, which he studied in the field, which caught his imagination. Indeed, the inscription on Martius's tomb emphasises his affinity with palms: *In palmis semper virens resurgo!* (Among ever green palms, I revive).

FIGURE 6 (*left*) Aylmer Lambert's *A Description of the genus Pinus* (1842) has the distinction of being one of the earliest plant monographs illustrated with coloured plates. Monographs focus on particular groups of plants rather than geographical areas. The hand-coloured engravings were based on illustrations by some of the finest botanical artists the period could boast. The majority were by Ferdinand Bauer, such as the larch shown here, but other artists included Georg Ehret, Sydney Parkinson and James Sowerby.

FIGURE 7 (*overleaf*) The three-volume *Historia Naturalis Palmarum* (1823–50) revealed Carl Friedrich Philipp von Martius's qualities as a botanist and laid the foundations of modern palm taxonomy. The illustrations in these volumes show the form and diversity of palms and place each species within a landscape, such as the *Desmoncus orthacanthos* shown here.

Martius palm. ad nat. del.

C. Hefs in lap. del.

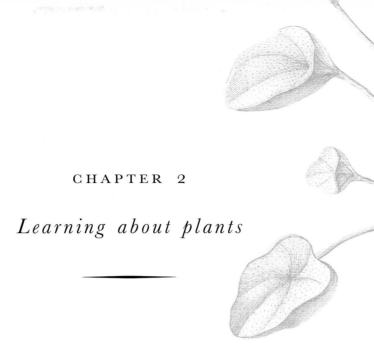

CHAPTER 2

Learning about plants

If you have a garden and a library, you have everything you need.
Cicero

GARDENERS and botanists crave diversity, for their gardens or in the wider natural world. Before 1492, Western European botanical thought was concentrated in northern Europe and the Mediterranean. Knowledge of the strange plants to be found in the lands beyond the eastern fringes of the Mediterranean Sea and the Ottoman Empire was cursory at best. The discovery of the New World shattered botanical edifices based on limited knowledge, half truths and ancient authority. As the world opened up during the Renaissance and Enlightenment, there was a dramatic increase in the diversity of known plants and knowledge about these plants.

Exploring the world for plants produced the diversity that was amassed in living collections found in gardens or in the field, preserved as dried specimens in herbaria and recorded in libraries. It is from the four basic working sources of the field, garden, herbarium and library that our understanding of plants has emerged. New places and new environments created new challenges to understanding and making sense of plant diversity.

Mark Catesby (1682–1749), the English naturalist, artist and explorer of Florida and the Carolinas, was captivated by North American plants and he wanted the English to benefit from knowledge about plants:

> a [North American] forest of a thousand miles in length
> … must afford a plentiful variety of trees and shrubs, that
> may be usefully employed to inrich [*sic*] and adorn our
> woods by their valuable timber and delightful shade; or
> to embellish and perfume our gardens with the elegance
> of their appearance and the fragrancy of their odours; in
> both which respects they greatly excel our home produc-
> tions of the like kind.

He went on to observe that

> a small spot of land in America has, within less than half
> a century, furnished England with a greater variety of trees
> than has been procured from all the other parts of the
> world for more than a thousand years past.[8]

FIGURE 8 The elaborate title page of Georg Markgraf and Willem Piso's *Historia Naturalis Brasiliae* (1648) shows two European-looking Amerindians at the head of an avenue of tropical trees that focus the eye onto a village scene with people dancing. In the foreground, a wreathed Neptune slouches behind a shell, his left elbow on a turtle and his right hand on a vase that overflows with the animal bounty of the sea. An anteater in the lower right laps from a clam shell, a sloth climbs a tree on the left and a snake coils around a palm. Behind Neptune is a row of plants; the enigmatic pineapple, the Brazilian staple manioc and a costus. Passion flowers twine around the trunks of the trees, which include a monkey pot and a palm. The swag beneath the title is replete with tropical fruits. The female Amerindian holds a bunch of cashew fruits, which are also shown on the tree behind her.

FIGURE 9   The title page of Willem Piso's *De Indiae Utriusque* has an extraordinary combination of Asian and South American influences, and is clearly based on the title page of Markgraf and Piso's *Historia Naturalis Brasiliae* (1648); the main structure, plants and man on the left are identical. Neptune has been replaced by a relative of the pig from the Moluccas, the babirusa, and a leopard, and behind them is an engraving based on Durer's famous sketch of the rhinoceros and an engraving of a dodo; the latter would be extinct by 1700. On the right of the image is an Asian man, holding what appears to be a nutmeg branch, a tree only found in the Moluccas of Southeast Asia.

Plant exploration

The most famous of the early-seventeenth-century plant collectors were the John Tradescants, father (1570s–1638) and son (1608–1662). The father took the opportunity to collect plants in Archangel, Russia in 1618, whilst the son travelled to Virginia in 1637. In 1699, the English privateer William Dampier (?1651–1715) spent a few hours at Sharks Bay, on the west coast of Australia, grabbing botanical curiosities that would be the most complete collection of Australian flora until Joseph Banks (1743–1820) and Daniel Solander (1736–1782) collected more comprehensively from eastern Australia in 1770. In contrast, the Englishman Richard Spruce (1817–1893) spent approximately fifteen years, between 1849 and 1864, in Amazonia and the Andes collecting and researching the area's plant life.

There are multifarious reasons for, and means of, discovering new plants. Motives may be selfish or selfless, and exploration undertaken by the maverick or the institutionalised. There were those for whom plants were merely another spoil of adventure; some were interested in personal fame and fortune, yet others wanted to whitewash their reputations. There were those who were motivated by a desire to know or were inspired by an idea. Expeditions were financed by personal fortunes, the generosity of private sponsors or institutions, the largesse of governments or monarchs, or the rewards of crime or personal obsession. Explorers travelled individually, or as members of ad hoc expeditions or commissioned enterprises. Explorers' rewards were the plaudits of nations, recognition by the few during life or after death, but more often botanical

explorers are merely footnotes remembered through the deeds of others and the plants around us.

The young Dutch physician Willem Piso (1611–1678) and the German astronomer Georg Markgraf (1610–1644) were encouraged to explore Brazil by the German Dutchman Johan Maurits van Nassau-Siegen (1604–1679) during his governorship of Dutch Brazil (1638–1644). Piso, from his medical practice in Recife, investigated tropical medicine, whilst Markgraf ventured across the colony to investigate natural history and cartography. Piso returned to Holland in 1644 and became a rich, prominent member of the Dutch scientific and medical establishment. In contrast, Markgraf was sent to Angola by the West India Company, where he died. Piso published their joint investigations as *Historia Naturalis Brasiliae* (1648). Piso contributed four books on Brazilian medicine, which established him as an authority on tropical medicine. Markgraf, one of the most important early natural historians of Brazil, contributed posthumously eight books on natural history. The elaborate frontispiece of *Historia Naturalis Brasiliae* gives an impression of abundance in a tropical paradise.

This impression is maintained in the frontispiece of Piso's *De Indiae Utriusque re naturali et medica* (1658), essentially a second edition of *Historia Naturalis Brasiliae*. The relationship between Piso and Markgraf has been a subject of considerable study, primarily because of this publication. Piso was attacked because of careless and inaccurate treatment of Markgraf's work. Linnaeus severely criticised the work, while others, including Markgraf's brother, accused Piso of diminishing Markgraf's reputation by referring to him as 'his servant' and accusing him of drunkenness and financial irregularities.[9] When Linnaeus named the genus *Pisonia* after Piso, he added, characteristically, the barbed comment that the plant's spines were as unpleasant as Piso's reputation. In contrast, Linnaeus commemorated Markgraf's name in the extraordinary genus *Marcgravia*, in the astonishing tropical plant family Marcgraviaceae.

To the right mind, exploration of the natural world can be a transforming encounter. Few scientists have summed up the overwhelming experience of collecting in a new area more clearly than Alexander von Humboldt (1769–1859) when he wrote of his friend and colleague Aimé Bonpland (1773–1858): 'Bonpland assured me that he would go stark mad if the excitement didn't stop soon.'[10] Humboldt's five-year expedition was one of the great journeys of the nineteenth century, and he returned to Europe with results that were to transform the study of tropical biology. Humboldt's journey was also one of the stimuli for that other nineteenth-century biological odyssey, Charles Darwin's voyage on the *Beagle* (1831–36). The long gestation of Darwin's observations from this expedition finally resulted in the publication of *On the Origin of Species* in 1859.

Exploration may also be undertaken vicariously through financing others to do it. Thus, Mark Catesby's explorations of the Carolinas and Bahamas in the early eighteenth century were funded by a cartel of scientists and gentlemen that included notables such as the botanist and diplomat William Sherard and James Brydges (1673–1744), first Duke of Chandos, the owner of a renowned garden at his estate, Cannons. For those with fewer financial resources but a desire to have the first plant of a particular sort growing in their garden,

people could be hired to undertake specific commissions. Thus, the apothecary and gardener John Parkinson (1567–1650) regularly employed 'roote gatherers' and even sent the physician William Boel to Spain to collect plants in 1608. Boel's expedition produced bulbs and seeds of more than a hundred species for Parkinson. However, the vicissitudes of the English climate meant most of them died. As if losing most of the plants by natural means was not enough for Parkinson, Boel had also passed some of the seed on to one of Parkinson's rivals:

> going into Spaine almost wholly on my charge hee [Boel] brought mee little else for my mony, but while I beate the bush another catcheth and eateth the bird: so while I with care and cost sowed them [perennial peas] yearely hoping first to publish them, another [Mr Coys] that never saw them unlesse in my Garden, nor knew of them but by a collateral friend, prevents me whom they knew had their descriptions ready for the Presse.[11]

Parkinson had even lost the cachet of having the only examples in Britain of those plants which had survived: 'Master William Coys … a great and ancient lover and cherisher of these delights [a perennial pea], and of all other rare plants, in his lifetime assured me he had growing in his garden at Stubbers.'[12]

Botanical exploration is a perilous activity; disaster, disease and death are ever-present concerns. Yet the explorer need not travel far from home for such experiences. The Pyrenees proved very attractive as a plant hunting ground to the provident French botanist Joseph Pitton Tournefort:

> he found in these vast solitudes a subsistence similar to one of the most austere Anchorites, and the unfortunate

FIGURE 10 Hipólito Ruiz and José Pavón's *Flora Peruviana et Chilensis* (1798–1802) contains 325 metal engravings by numerous artists and many of the plants had never been illustrated before. Furthermore, many were destined to become familiar garden and house plants, such as the *Gunnera tinctoria* and *Peperomia scutellaefolia* shown here.

inhabitants, provided with what they were able, not many others than he had thieves to fear. Also it was repeatedly plundered by Spanish Miquelets. They imagined a stratagem to steal some money on these kinds of occasions. He put the Réaux in bread that he carried on him, and that was so black and so hard, that although the thieves were strong & scorned not people who had nothing, they treated him with contempt.[13]

However, such adventures were minor compared to the botanical explorers killed whilst collecting plants. At least five of Linnaeus's most prominent students 'perished in the Cause of Science'[14] during fieldwork: Pehr Löfling (1729–1756) died in Venezuela, Fredric Hasselquist (1722–1752) in Turkey, Pehr Forsskål (1732–1763) in Yemen, Carl Fredrik Adler (1720–1761) in Java and Christopher Tärnström (1711–1746) in Vietnam. Between 1768 and 1771, Joseph Banks's expedition on the *Endeavour* killed all but two of the nine men he took with him. In Hawaii, David Douglas (1799–1834), responsible for introducing some of the most familiar conifers to our gardens, was killed by a bull trapped in a pit.

In the field, minor irritations and absurdities often take on a life of their own. In 1787, during his short exploration of Cyprus, John Hawkins (1761–1841) emphasised some of the minor inconveniences of an explorer's life:

> we drew out some straw mattrasses on the pavement ... I lay stretched out on a hard mattrass before the altar of an old Monastery which was perched on the summit of one of the highest mountains of Cyprus. ... Weary as I was I enjoyed only a few short intervals of repose while my botanical fellow traveller [John Sibthorp] blew his snoring horn the whole night. The next morning I escaped early from my cold & uncomfortable bed room.[15]

In his mid-twenties the Scottish botanist George Gardner (1810–1849) spent five years (1836–41) collecting plants in the interior of Brazil and summed up his experience of tropical field work thus:

> the privations which the traveller experiences in these uninhabited, and often desert countries, can scarcely be appreciated by those who have never ventured into them, where he is exposed at times to a burning sun, at others to torrents of rain, such as are only to be witnessed within the tropics, separated for years from all civilized society, sleeping for months together in the open air, in all seasons, surrounded by beasts of prey and hordes of more savage Indians, often obliged to carry a supply of water on horseback over the desert tracts, and unfrequently passing two or three days without tasting solid food, not even a monkey coming in the way to satisfy the cravings of hunger.[16]

The English explorer Henry Bates (1825–1892), who spent eleven years (1848–59) in Amazonia, suffered all manner of depravations but

> suffered most inconvenience from the difficulty of getting news from the civilised world down river, from the irregularity of receipt of letters, parcels of books and periodicals, and towards the latter part of my residence from ill health arising from bad and insufficient food. The want of intellectual society, and of the varied excitement of European life, was also felt most acutely, and this, instead of becoming deadened by time, increased until it became almost insupportable. I was obliged, at last, to come to the conclusion that the contemplation of Nature alone is not sufficient to fill the human heart and mind. ... I was worst off in the first year, 1850, when twelve months elapsed without letters or remittances. Towards the end of this time my clothes had worn to rags; I was barefoot, a great inconvenience in tropical forests, notwithstanding statements to the contrary that have been published by travellers; my servant ran away, and I was robbed of nearly all my copper money.[17]

For many botanical explorers it is the loss of their collections and notes that is most feared. The expedition of Hipólito Ruiz López (1754–1816), José Antonio Pavón (1754–1840) and Joseph Dombey (1742–1794) to Chile and Peru between 1777 and 1788 seemed to be cursed with bad luck. When the 'charming and extravagant' Dombey landed in Cadiz with his share of their botanical haul in February 1785, after narrowly escaping shipwreck around Cape Horn, his collection was impounded; the Spanish wanted half since Ruiz and Pavón's part had been lost in a shipwreck. Dombey got back to Paris in October 1785, where his collection was further damaged by sloppy handling. Ruiz and Pavón remained in Peru and lost most of their remaining collections and notes in a fire which destroyed their camp. The pair returned to Spain in 1788 and started to publish their results, as *Flora Peruviana, et Chilensis Prodromus* (1794), but with little recognition of Dombey's role. In 1852, Alfred Russel Wallace lost the whole of his South American collections when the ship taking him and his specimens back to England caught fire. Humboldt summed up the plight of the collector and his collections: 'in seas infested with pirates a traveller can only be sure of what he takes with him'.[18]

Legal and modern ethical concerns rarely inconvenienced botanical explorers of the past. The need to obtain permits to travel safely, in sometimes hostile lands, was a necessity but once the collector was safely in an area any specimens were fair game. For example, in 1865, the English businessman Charles Ledger (1818–1906) illegally collected quinine tree seeds from Bolivia and sold the seed to the British and the Dutch. Export of quinine was illegal since it was a government monopoly. In the twentieth century, Kew's reputation suffered through its involvement with the acquisition of rubber tree seeds from Brazil, and the destruction of that country's rubber-based economy, in the nineteenth century. Quinine and rubber are discussed in more detail in Chapters 4 and 5 respectively. The botanical and economic rewards of plant exploration have been high but the social costs, including poverty, warfare, slavery and other forms of exploitation, have been enormous. The presence of a species in a garden or a herbarium is a summary of these often overlooked social costs which occur at all levels of the introduction process, from the initial plant collection through its initial successful growth in its new home to its widespread acceptance by the populace. These activities have led some historians and politicians to produce monochrome caricatures of plant collecting as 'ecological imperialism'.

The library

Libraries are where ghosts, the restless concerns of the living and the thoughts and observations of the long dead are found. They provide information exchange between cultures and across generations. One of the records contained within a library is that of an apparently uneventful, poorly attended scientific meeting held in February 1865, in Brno. At this meeting, an obscure 43-year-old priest presented a paper on plant hybridisation. The priest was Gregor Mendel (1822–1884) and the simplicity of his ideas on inheritance would shatter old speculations when the significance of his work was finally recognised at the start of the next

FIGURE II   Rembert Dodoens's *Histoire des plantes* (1557) was a sensation for two centuries. The title page of the *Histoire* is an elaborate allegory associated with medicinal plants and a garden as paradise. The god Apollo, in his Roman form with a radiant halo, could bring ill health and plague but he also had the ability to cure. His son Asclepius, the Greek god of medicine, was instructed in the art of medicine by the centaur Chiron. Gentius (ruled 180–168 BC) was the last king of Illyria and according to Pliny the Elder discovered the healing properties of gentians. Arthemisia (Artemis; Diana in her Roman form), the Greek goddess of virginity and the hunt, is represented here by a rather matronly lady and is strongly associated with wormwood (*Artemisia*). Mithridates (132–63 BC), king of Pontus in northern Turkey, apparently increased his tolerance to poisons and created a complex, universal antidote to all poisons. During the Renaissance, a complex mixture called mithridate was used to cure poisoning, whilst theriac was used for about 1,900 years after Mithridates' death. Lysimachus (360–281 BC), a successor of Alexander the Great, ruled Thrace, Asia Minor and Macedonia. At the bottom of the title page is a representation of Hercules, killing the dragon Ladon, when he went to steal 'apples' from the garden of the Hesperides. It is this Herculean parody that has come to plague some discussions of plant collecting in the twentieth century.

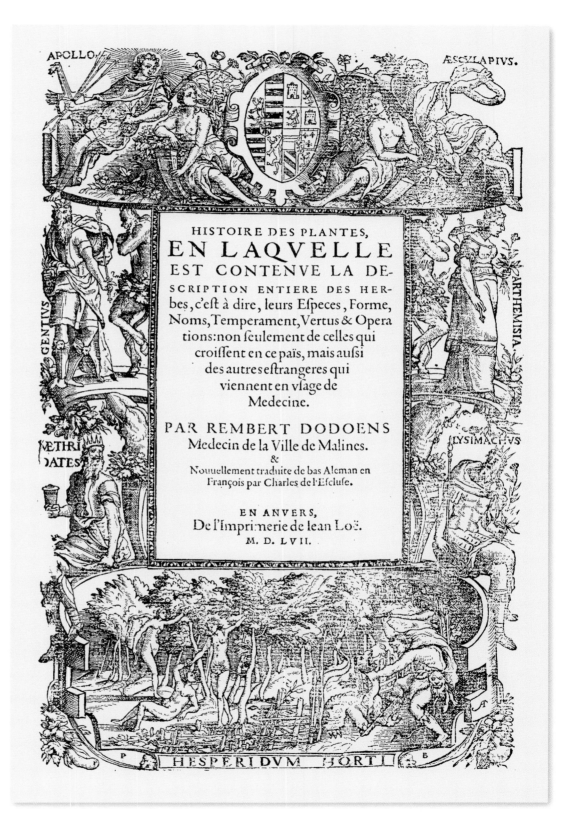

century. At about the same time Darwin's great idea of natural selection was shaking society. However, unlike Darwin, Mendel had no great promoter or articulator of his ideas. Mendel's ideas would languish in an apparently unread or at least poorly understood journal article for about thirty years until they were rediscovered.

The earliest botanical books are the herbals of the fifteenth century, which provide names, illustrations, descriptions, properties and virtues of the herbs. They are the first printed plant identification guides. Herbals took advantage of much earlier manuscripts, notably in *De materia medica* by the Greek physician Dioscorides (AD 40–90). *De materia* was the ultimate authority on plants for over 1,500 years until the Renaissance. In the 1930s, Arthur Hill, director of the Royal Botanic Gardens at Kew, described the practical value of Dioscorides' work for an elderly monk on Mount Athos:

> He was a remarkable old Monk with an extensive knowledge of plants and their properties. Though fully gowned in a long black cassock he travelled very quickly, usually on foot and sometimes on a mule, carrying his 'Flora' with him in a large, black, bulky bag. Such a bag was necessary since his 'Flora' was nothing less than four manuscript folio volumes of Dioscorides, which apparently he himself had copied out. This Flora he invariably used for determining any plant which he could not name at sight.[19]

The earliest surviving copy of *De materia* is the magnificently illustrated *Codex Vindobonensis* (*c.* AD 512), with its illustrations and descriptions of 580 plants, made in Byzantium for the noble woman Anicia Juliana (AD 462–?527). For over a millennium the *Codex* passed through countless hands until it finally

arrived in the Imperial Library, Vienna in 1569. In the late eighteenth century, the Imperial Library also contained the *Codex Neapolitanus*, another illustrated manuscript copy of Dioscorides' text, made in the Apennine peninsula approximately a century after the *Codex Vindobonensis*. Laborious rote copying of these texts and their illustrations had introduced errors that were blindly propagated through multiple manuscripts and on into printed form, since few people could check facts against the original documents and, more importantly, few people bothered to look at the plants in the world around them. Introspection and recursive copying was changed by the European Renaissance of the fifteenth and sixteenth centuries, whilst the introduction of moveable type, from the mid-fifteenth century, had a dramatic impact on the availability of information about plants, albeit to the elite defined by either money or education.

These two Vienna manuscripts were essential reference material for anyone seriously interested in medicinal plants. Their importance led the influential eighteenth-century physician Gerard van Swieten (1700–1772) to support an ambitious project to reproduce all the illustrations in these two manuscripts, at their original sizes, as copper engravings. Ultimately this project was not completed, although the botanist Nikolaus von Jacquin (1727–1817) owned two proof copies from 410 of the plates. One copy was sent to Linnaeus in 1763 and eventually went to the Linnean Society in London. The other, *Plantarum Dioscoridis Icones*, 412, is in the University of Oxford, and was obtained by the Oxford botanist John Sibthorp (1758–1796), although it is unclear from Sibthorp's words 'by the Friendship of

FIGURE 12 *Plantarum Dioscoridis Icones* 412, of which *Peganum hamale* is shown, was considered by Joseph Franz Jacquin to be the only perfect copy of the ill-fated publishing enterprise to reproduce the original illustrations in the *Codex Vindobonensis* and *Codex Neapolitanus*. The possession of these illustrations proved crucial to Sibthorp on his eastern Mediterranean journeys, since he could show people the images and ask where the plants grew, what they were called, and compare contemporary Greek names with Byzantine names.

Jacquin procured' whether these illustrations were given or lent.

In the case of *De materia medica* there had been a flurry of sixteenth-century publications trying to identify Dioscorides' medicinal plants. The Italian physician Pier Andrea Matthiolus (1501–77) is most famous for his *Commentarii in Sex Libros Pedacii Dioscorides* that was first published in 1544. The *Commentarii* was a sensation, sold some 32,000 copies in the early editions and eventually went to sixty editions. Yet Matthiolus never travelled to the eastern Mediterranean, where Dioscorides wrote, and equated Greek plant names with plants he knew. Thus, to Matthiolus, the Strawberry Tree of Dioscorides was *Arbutus unedo*, but had he visited the eastern Mediterranean it would have been obvious the tree was Andrachne, another *Arbutus* species characteristic of the eastern Mediterranean.

Furthering the study of natural history

Until the seventeenth century, books were primarily the trophies and tools of the wealthy and of scholars. As private individuals became more interested in horticulture and the general populace became wealthier and more educated, they wanted plants to show off in their gardens and books about plants and how to grow them. By the eighteenth century, a great wealth of books was being published, although it is not always clear at whom they were aimed. Book publishing was also aided by the Georgian fashion for having libraries in houses and the need to stock them. Cynically, books gave an air of learning to a household and even attracted scholars, which would add lustre; the owner did not have to read the books. Books and, by analogy, libraries

could promote the study of natural history and make it more accessible to a literate public, thirsty for scientific knowledge of the world around them. In the mid-1850s, in the advertisement to his *Phycologia Australica*, the botanist William Harvey claimed that 'in England, the publication of serial works, accompanied by plates or woodcuts, and confined to separate branches either of Zoology or of Botany, has been found greatly to promote the study of Natural History in general.'[20] In the case of Harvey's volume, as with so many illustrated books on plants and animals, his public also had to be wealthy.

One reviewer's enthusiasm for Lambert's *Description of the genus Pinus* (1803–24) came with a sting in its tail:

> The magnitude of the plates …, the excellent execution of the engravings, and the elegant stile in which the letter press part of the work is finished, have so greatly enhanced its cost, as to render it unattainable to many who would wish to be in the number of its purchasers. These luxuries must be reserved for those who can spare as many guineas as are specified in its advertised price.[21]

The costs associated with publishing the large illustrated works of the early nineteenth century was a continual problem for both purchasers and authors alike. The young, idealistic botanist John Lindley (1799–1865) was forced to abandon the publication of his *Collectanea Botanica* (1821):

> It was his [Lindley's] determination that neither care nor cost should be spared in making it worthy of public support: and, as pecuniary remuneration was never expected, the price was only calculated to defray the actual expenses incurred in the course of its publication. A variety of circumstances, which it is not necessary to mention here,

FIGURE 13 Georg Rumphius's *Herbarium Amboinensis* (1741) is one of a host of botanical publications which were finally published long after the death of the original author. During the Dutch Golden Age, Amboyna, in the heart of the Spice Islands of the Far East, was a source of great wealth because of the nutmeg and clove trade. This allegory shows the botanical wealth of the islands being presented to Europe, over an image of the fort on Amboyna.

G.E.RUMPHII HERBARIUM AMBOINENSE.

HET *AMBOINSCHE KRUYD-BOEK* VAN *G.E.RUMPHIUS.*

have, however, induced him to swerve from his original designs and resolve upon abandoning the undertaking altogether after the publication of four more numbers.[22]

Georg Eberhard Rumphius (1628–1702), the 'blind seer of Ambon', was a German–Dutch botanist employed by the Dutch East India Company. He is best known for his authorship of *Herbarium Amboinensis*, a catalogue of the plants of Ambon (now part of Indonesia) which provided the basis for all future studies of the Moluccan flora. However, the genesis and publication of this book was fraught with difficulties. Rumphius started his investigations of the Moluccan flora in about 1666 but went blind in 1670, shortly before his wife and daughter were killed in an earthquake. However, he continued to work on the manuscript with the help of assistants. In 1686, a manuscript was sent to Holland for printing but the ship carrying the manuscript was attacked by the French. In 1687, the illustrations were consumed by fire. Finally, in 1690, the first three volumes of the book were complete. By 1696, the *Herbarium Amboinensis* had arrived safely in Holland but was lost to the archives of the Dutch East India Company until the professor of botany at the University of Amsterdam, Johannes Burman (1707–1780), edited and published the work. The complete manuscript was finally published in 1741, thirty-nine years after Rumphius's death and seventy-five years after he started the project.

Specimens and notes can be lost or become separated from each other, collections may be allowed to decay or are destroyed, and results may not be published because of conflicting priorities, personal idiosyncrasies or, most tragically, the collector's premature death. In the early 1790s, Professor John Sibthorp commented on Tournefort's botanical legacy and told his students in Oxford that,

> had he [Tournefort] lived to have executed his Descriptions of the Plants of y^e. East it would have been a great Work, & would probably have thrown much Light upon the obscure Passages of y^e. ancient Authors attentive to the Traditions of the Country.[23]

These words were prophetic. Six years later, following Sibthorp's early death, they summarised many commentators' views on his legacy. The *Flora Graeca* (1806–40), together with the *Florae Graecae Prodromus* (1806–16), present the botanical results of the two expeditions that John Sibthorp made to the eastern Mediterranean in 1786–87 and 1794–95 and was completed long after Sibthorp's death in 1796. The *Flora Graeca* is one of the world's rarest Floras; only twenty-five copies of the first printing were made. It is one of the most magnificent; being best known for the 966 hand-painted, folio-sized plants by the artist Ferdinand Bauer (1760–1826). Bauer was one of the world's finest botanical artists and worked in Oxford to produce watercolours from pencil sketches that he had made whilst he was in the field with Sibthorp. The sketches are surrounded by numbers that correspond to a colour-coding system devised by Bauer. Bauer worked very fast, and completed each watercolour in approximately one and a half days. The sumptuousness of the publication imposed by the conditions of Sibthorp's will meant that the *Flora Graeca* was expensive. Subscribers paid £254 for the ten volumes; the true cost was £620. This cost meant that Sibthorp had placed a serious inconvenience

FLORA GRÆCA Sibthorpiana.

CENTURIA SEXTA.

1826.

ATHENÆ.

FIGURE 14 Frontispiece of Sibthorp and Smith's *Flora Graeca*, Volume 6 (1826). The *Flora Graeca* (1806–40), together with the *Florae Graecae Prodromus* (1806–16), present the results of two expeditions that John Sibthorp made to the eastern Mediterranean in 1786–87 and 1794–95 and was completed long after Sibthorp's early death in 1796. This frontispiece is one of seven completed by Ferdinand Bauer. The plant species in the garland (labelled from top left clockwise) are: *Consolida tenussima, Nigella arvensis* var. *glauca, Peganum harmala, Glinus lotoides, Geum coccineum, Cistus monspeliensis, Cistus parviflorus, Euphorbia chamaesyce, Capparis* sp., *Fumana arabica*. The vignette shows Athens.

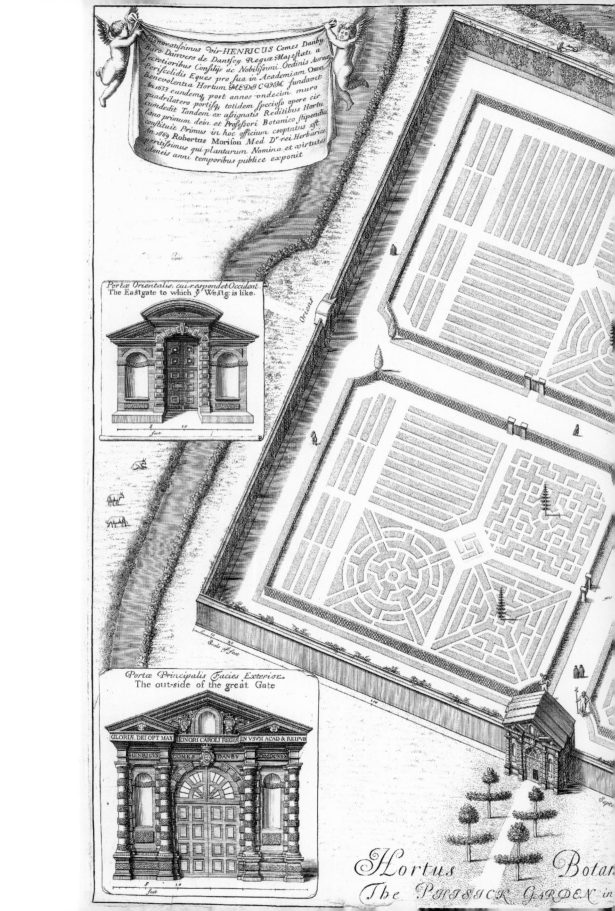

Honoratissimus Vir HENRICUS Comes Danby, Baro Danvers de Dantsey, Regiæ Majestati a Secretioribus Consilijs ac Nobilissimi Ordinis Auræ Periscelidis Eques pro sua in Academiam Oxon benevolentia Hortum MEDICUM fundavit An 1633 eundemq, post annos undecim muro quadrilatero portisq, totidem speciose opere circumdedit Tandem ex assignatis Reditibus Hortulano primum dein et Professori Botanico stipendia constituit Primus in hoc officium cooptatus est An 1669 Robertus Morison Med Dr rei Herbariæ peritissimus qui plantarum Nomina et virtutes idoneis anni temporibus publice exponit

Portæ Orientalis, cui respondet Occident.
The Eastgate to which y^e Westg: is like.

Portæ Principalis Facies Exterior.
The out-side of the great Gate

GLORIÆ. DEI OPT. MAX   HONORI CAROLI REGIS   IN VSVM ACAD & REIPVB

HENRICVS   COMES   DANBY   DCXXXII

Hortus   Botan...
The PHYSICK GARDEN in...

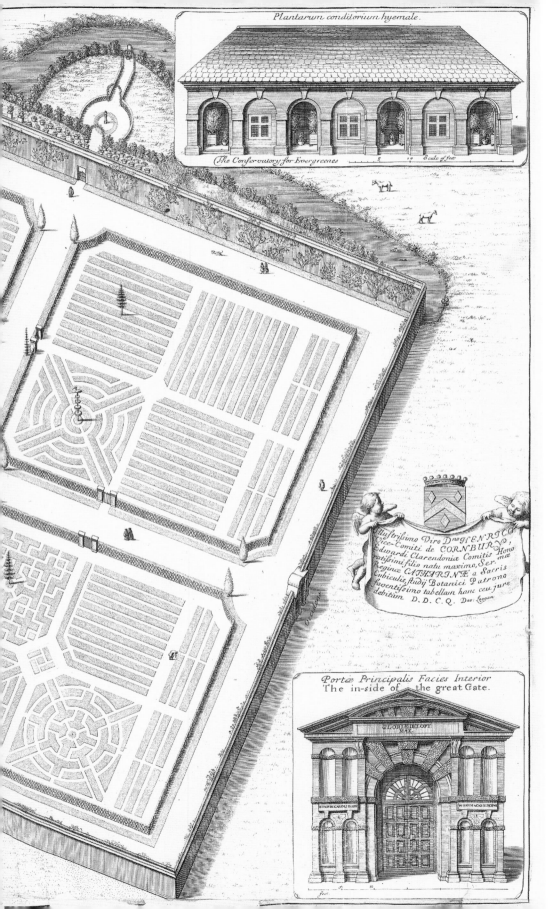

FIGURE 15 David Loggan's *Oxonia Illustrata* (1675) shows a plan of 'Oxford Physick Garden', less than thirty years after the first catalogue of the garden was published. At the entrance of the garden, 'Old Jacob [Bobart the Elder] some years past got two yew trees wch being formed by his skill are now grown up to be Gigantick bulkey fellows, one holding a Bill, th'other a Club on his shoulder.' Gentlemen, dons and two dogs are shown wandering around the garden, whilst two gardeners weed the paths and tend the beds. At the top of Loggan's plate is a 'Conservatory for Evergreenes'; evergreens, especially citruses, were one of the fashionable plants of the day.

on access to the results of his pioneering journeys in the Ottoman Empire and the scientific results the Flora contained. His estate sponsored what would be one of the world's rarest and most magnificent Floras and at the same time ensured that its use was restricted to a privileged elite.

The botanic garden

The origins of botanic gardens stretch back to the foundation of the scientific study of plants in the sixth century BC, Greek-speaking Ionian cities. Collections of living plants are known from the Lyceum, in Athens, as well as Babylon, ancient China, India and Egypt. However, it was in southern Europe, with the rise of medical schools and humanism in the sixteenth century, that our current views of botanic gardens became established. Initially, botanic gardens were a means of surgeons having access to, and control over, the sources of their medicines. By 1545, there were gardens at Padua, Florence and Pisa, and by 1621 at Leiden, Leipzig, Montpellier, Heidelberg and Oxford. The surgeons of Louis XIII were responsible for the formation of the *Jardin des Plantes* in Paris in 1635, and the Physic Garden in Edinburgh (later the Royal Botanic Garden Edinburgh) was established in 1690. In some cases gardens, for example in Padua, were surrounded by workshops manufacturing medicines. In other cases, the links with medicine were less obvious, for example in Oxford.

Oxford Physic Garden (later Oxford Botanic Garden) was established in 1621 and has the accolade of being the oldest botanic garden in Britain. However,

planting did not start until the arrival of the Garden's first Keeper, Jacob Bobart the Elder, in 1641. By 1648 the published catalogue for the Garden shows that it contained over 1,400 types of plant. At the same time, Jacob Bobart the Elder was creating a collection of dried plants and training the next Keeper, his son Jacob Bobart the Younger (1641–1719). In 1675, the artist David Loggan (1635–1692) included an engraving of the Oxford Botanic Garden in his *Oxonia Illustrata*. The four fenced quadrants in Loggan's engraving appear to correspond to the four regions of the known world: Europe, Africa, Asia and the Americas. In Evans's words in *Vertumnus* (1713): 'Exotick Plants, which finely Bred / In softer Soils, Thy Succour need; / Whose Birth far distant Countries claim, / Sent here in Honour to Thy Name.'

Exotic plant cultivation

The initial focus on medicinal plants in the Oxford garden quickly gave way to a broader interest in the cultivation of unusual forms of known species, new species that were being introduced from an expanding empire and the investigation of botanical problems of the day. The trickle of North American plants that passed through the hands of the John Tradescants (Elder and Younger) in the seventeenth century increased dramatically in the eighteenth century, through the activities of collectors such as Peter Collinson and John Bartram.

Furthermore, private gardeners, of whatever class, were increasing their influence. In the early eighteenth century, one of the most prominent was Mary Somerset, Duchess of Beaufort (?1630–1714) at Badminton; others included James Sherard (1666–1737) at Eltham and

FIGURE 16   The view of the Botanic Garden from the Superintendent's house,
in Lansdown Guilding's *Account of the Botanic Garden in the Island of St. Vincent* (1825).

Charles DuBois (1656–1740) at Mitcham. Later, the efforts of gardeners such as John Blackburne (1690–1786), near Warrington, were admired and a source of horticultural inspiration.

Interest in plants was found in all levels of society, although it was in the higher echelons where the fads and fashions of the day took root. In 1759, Princess Augusta (1719–1772) was persuaded to set aside 9 acres of land at her house at Kew for exotic plant cultivation. This garden eventually became the Royal Botanic Gardens Kew and was at the centre of a web of colonial gardens furthering the interests of the burgeoning British Empire. Many plants cannot be moved between dramatically different growing conditions without first allowing them to adjust to the different conditions; this is the process of acclimation. Acclimation is similar to hardening-off, which is used by gardeners when seedlings raised in the glasshouse are transferred outdoors. It was the Dutch who first saw the opportunities for gardens of acclimatising plants at the crossroads of global navigation. The Dutch East India Company established a garden in the South African Cape, which was an important stopping point for ships sailing between Holland and the Far East.

The economic role of plants

Through access to secure plant resources Britain, along with other imperial powers, thought she could ensure her population would benefit from wealth, health and happiness. The economic role of plants, especially control over their supply, was emphasised about fifteen years after the foundation of Kew by the most significant English botanist of the eighteenth century, Joseph Banks.[24] Banks made his name through participation in Captain James Cook's (1728–1779) first triumphant circumnavigation of the globe between 1768 and 1771. Banks's haul of dried botanical specimens was enormous and he eventually described over a thousand new species and at least a hundred new genera from this journey. This journey did much to stimulate English scientific society's interest in global plant diversity.

Banks was convinced that it was important to send professional plant collectors around the globe to secure plants for the British Empire; a model that would be replicated by other European powers, particularly the French. St Vincent Botanic Garden, established in 1765, and, unlike such gardens in the mother country, was conceived as a nursery for economically important plants to be distributed throughout the West Indies. General Robert Melville (1723–1809), Governor of the southern British Caribees, gave 6 acres of land for the garden and appointed the military surgeon George Young (1732–?1810) as its first superintendent. Young achieved much in his thirteen-year stewardship, despite little support for the fledgling garden from London, and the indifference of Melville's immediate successors. In 1778 the British lost St Vincent to the French, but reclaimed it again in 1784. However, the garden had decayed, parts had been given over to agriculture and there were legal wrangles over land ownership. In 1785, Alexander Anderson (?1748–1811) was appointed as superintendent with the full support of Banks, Melville and the British government. By the end of his tenure in 1811, Anderson presided over a garden that was the pride of the British Empire. Eventually, using gardens similar to the one in St Vincent dotted around the world, Kew would move economically important plants from their native habitats (often outside of the British Empire) to areas of British influence: for example, tea from China to India, rubber from Brazil to Malaysia, and quinine from the Andes to India, as related in Chapters 4 and 5.

Cook's expedition, and Banks's role in it, raised public interest in the exotic. However, Banks had returned principally with dried herbarium specimens. The British public, plus wealthy potential patrons, wanted material they could grow in their gardens. Banks's professional plant collectors could remain abroad for years and send living material back to England. Banks identified South Africa as the best place to start his programme and Francis Masson (1741–1805), a resourceful botanist and excellent gardener, as his first plant collector. Masson set out with Cook on his second voyage (1772–75) and arrived in Cape Town in October 1772. By the time of his isolated death in Canada, Masson had introduced over a thousand new plants to the gardeners of England.

Botanic and private gardens are expensive to maintain and botanical enthusiasm is difficult to sustain when funds start to dry up. In the early eighteenth century, George Clifford's (1685–1760) garden Hartekamp at Heemstede in the northern Netherlands was one of the most celebrated in Europe, and was crucial to Linnaeus's development as a botanist. When John Sibthorp visited at the end of century, he observed that the 'magnificent Garden of Cliffords … is now no more the Paradise he [Linnaeus] described it when I saw it some Years since it was neglected & gone to decay of the more curious Plants, except two Tulip Trees of an immense Size, which an ancient Gardener

told me where there in the Time of Linnaeus none now remain.'[25] As for Oxford, the study of botany was in the doldrums and the University was losing interest in the Botanic Garden, which was John Sibthorp's responsibility. In the early 1790s, Sibthorp acknowledged Kew as 'certainly yᵉ. first in Europe'; as for the Oxford garden, he wryly observed that 'we render it as rich & useful as the Nature of our Circumstances & Support will admit'. However, he rather tetchily asserted that

> Academic Gardens tho' greatly inferior in Magnificence & Splendour to those supported by Royal Expenditure may be considered as the more useful Schools of Botany. – not under the Restrictions of royal or private Collections, they are at all Times open to the Public, & their Object is to inform as well as amuse.[26]

The wave of late-eighteenth-century national botanical interest had passed over Oxford and its garden, leaving little or no trace.

The herbarium

Herbaria are collections of flattened, dried plants that have been at the centre of our understanding of plants since the mid-sixteenth century. Traditionally, such collections have been referred to as *Horti Sicci* or 'winter gardens' and are treated as libraries of dried plants. One of the oldest herbaria in the world and probably the oldest in Britain was made by the Capuchin monk Gregorio da Reggio (d. ?1618). Da Reggio had gained his experience, and botanical reputation, as a physician and in the field, rather than in gardens or libraries. The herbarium was given to William Sherard by the Italian professor of botany and director of the Botanic

Garden Giuseppe Monti (1682–1760) in Bologna, with the expectation that he would receive the second volume of Hans Sloane's *Natural History of Jamaica* (1725). However, Sherard died before he could give Monti the book, and Sherard's brother refused to do so. After the early death of John Sibthorp, the da Reggio herbarium lay apparently abandoned and forgotten in outbuildings in the Oxford Botanic Garden until the late nineteenth century: 'some important discoveries were made, including the unearthing from a pile of material in the coke-house, the Herbarium of Gregory of Reggio of 1606'.[27]

Today, herbaria are often seen as old-fashioned, as the efforts of 'a sort of learned men, who are wholly employed in gathering together the refuse of nature'.[28] Yet they provide the link between a plant's identity and the evidence of its occurrence at a particular point in time and place and are crucial to contemporary debates about plant extinction, climate change and species evolution. Professor Charles Daubeny (1795–1867), one of the most dynamic professors of the natural sciences that Oxford University boasted during the nineteenth century, was clear about the importance and role of herbaria. Speaking when the University formally accepted the Fielding Bequest in 1853, he stated, 'a Collection of living and dried plants should always go together',[29] and went on to emphasise the duality of the living and the dead plant for scientific investigation. The living plant provides the initial enthusiasm for botany and the means to understand details of plant structure. The dead plant advances study through access to species impossible to grow and ensures they are always available. John Ray (1627–1705), the most famous English

naturalist of the seventeenth century, had herbarium specimens at his disposal for cataloguing all the plants he knew in his *Historia Plantarum*, but he felt keenly the lack of a botanic garden when it came to linking the structures he saw on the specimen with the appearance of the plant in life.[30] Ray's great rival, Robert Morison (1620–1683), Professor of Botany in Oxford, had ready access to a garden. The link between the living and the dead plant was also made by nurserymen. Thus, in 1691, Darby of Hoxton was using a herbarium as a sales catalogue:

> He has a folio paper book in which he has pasted the leaves and flowers of almost all manner of plants, which make a pretty show, and are more instructive than any cuts in herbals.[31]

Pressing plants

It is unknown how the technological innovation of pressing plants was conceived. It has been speculated that the technique might have been suggested when flowers being used by limners for manuscript illumination were accidentally caught between sheets of vellum or parchment. Whatever the inspiration, the first person to make a herbarium is accepted as Luca Ghini (*c.* 1490–1556), Professor of Botany at the University of Bologna. Modern herbarium specimens are mounted on single sheets of card. In contrast, many pre-eighteenth-century herbaria were often bound like books. The earliest evidence of a book herbarium is a reference to the herbarium of John Falconer (d. 1560), a pupil of Ghini, by William Turner (1508–1568) in 1551: 'I never sawe it [*Glaux maritima*] in England savinge onelye in Master Falkonner's boke and that had he brought

34

FIGURE 17 The da Reggio herbarium, *Herbarium Diversarum Naturalium Gregorio a Reggio*, was made in 1606 from specimens collected around Bologna, and comprises approximately 300 dried specimens bound in the form of a book. All the specimens are named using pre-Linnaean phrase names and, unusually for the period, the labels give detailed information about the plants.

out of Italy except my memory do fayle me'.[32] However, it was not until paper became fairly cheap in the late seventeenth century that herbaria became a common scientific tool and a desirable object for the curious in Britain.

Preparing herbarium specimens

The eighteenth-century botanical titan Linnaeus identified best practice for the preparation, labelling and organisation of herbarium specimens; this differs very little from that used today. Fresh plants, with fruits and/or flowers, are spread out between papers and dried quickly in a press, which keeps the specimens flat. Once dried, specimens are mounted on separate sheets of paper together with their labels. The mounted specimens are placed in lightweight paper folders, species from the same genus are placed in heavier folders, and all the specimens are arranged into a suitable filing system where the specimens can be readily retrieved. This apparently simple technology will produce specimens that, if protected from dust, fungi and insects, last indefinitely. However, herbaria must be actively curated if they are to remain of scientific value rather than drift into mediocrity or become mere historical curiosities.

Oxford University is rich is pre-1800 herbaria, which must have appealed to the desire of the Oxford-based pharmacist–botanist George Druce (1850–1932) to place the work of others in broad historical contexts, when he took over responsibility for the University's collections in the late nineteenth century. Druce sketches a vivid tableau of the state of the herbaria, which he was to transform over the rest of his life:

> When ... I first saw these volumes [Du Bois Herbarium] ... they were placed on the top shelf in what was little more than a loft above the lecture room at the Botanic Garden. There were no facilities for warming, and the place was damp.... The immense mass of the Morisonian (Bobartian), Dillenian, and Sherardian collections were in loose unarranged sheets, often unmounted. Even the Fielding Herbarium was mostly unnamed and roughly sorted into the different families.[33]

When Henry Danvers gave the University of Oxford £5,000 to establish a botanic garden in 1621, he provided the garden with its mission statement until the present day: 'the glorification of God and for the furtherance of learning'. Danvers clearly saw the function of the Garden as bringing together the vegetable products of creation and increasing our understanding of them. However, the first Keeper of the Garden also saw the importance of the herbarium, the library and botanical exploration for botanical research.

A scientific approach to the study of plants was starting to take hold in the early sixteenth century. However, more fanciful approaches to the study of plants were also significant parts of botanical thought. Thus Danvers equated the Garden with the creation of a Paradise and the mitigation of the consequences of the Fall, whilst others believed they could tell what human ailments a plant might cure by looking at what it resembled. The scientific merged with the fanciful, and in some cases the fanciful persists to the present day.

CHAPTER 3

Botanical mysticism, mythology and monsters

Naked like Truth, as Truth without disguise
Was Gardner made to Gods own Paradize

RI, in Stephens & Brown,
Catalogus horti botanici Oxoniensis, 1658

PARADISES that evoke sylvan or pastoral idylls pre-date myths of a biblical Eden. As early as 4000 BC Sumerians wrote of a fabulous land, Dilmun, where man was never ill and lived peacefully with other animals; in the Epic of Gilgamesh, two millennia later, Babylonians looked back to a land of plenty. However, it is the echoes from the story of the garden in Genesis, and Man's expulsion from its confines, that have reverberated through centuries of western cultures and the societies these cultures have touched. Myths of paradise are powerful, constantly receding dreams; as one moves back through the centuries, the illusion disappears further back into antiquity. Virgil (70–19 BC), in his *Bucolics*, saw a lost paradise in a Greek pastoral idyll, Arcadia, whilst, in his *Georgics*, Italy was portrayed as perfect: 'here spring is perpetual, and summer extends to months other than her own; twice a year the cows calve, twice a year the trees serve us fruit …

no ravening tigers or savage brood of lion; no aconite deceives the wretch who picks it'.[34]

Gardens as paradise

Eden, the garden in Genesis, is an earthly paradise in which food for perpetually healthy humans was readily available; illness only became part of human experience following the expulsion of Adam and Eve from its confines. The word 'paradise' has its origin in the Old Persian word *pairidaeze*, meaning a 'park or pleasure garden', which in turn is derived from *daeza*, or 'wall', and *pairi*, meaning 'around'. Paradise was therefore an enclosed space, somehow separate from the rest of the world. The known was separated from the unknown, the domesticated from the wild, and the cultivated from the uncultivated. Eden is a familiar, stereotypical image of a luxuriant landscape or garden, rich in unfamiliar

FIGURE 18 Christopher Switzer's whimsical title page to Parkinson's *Paradisi in Sole Paradisus Terrestris* (1629) is in contrast to the empiricism of the book. Adam hugs what is often interpreted as an apple tree, whilst Eve grabs at a strawberry plant. A stream flows through the garden; in the background there is a forest and in the foreground a meadow. The forest includes fig, apple, mulberry and medlar trees, as well as a date palm, grapes and roses. The meadow includes tulips, a pineapple, colchicum, lilies, an *Opuntia*-type cactus, pinks, a cyclamen, a strawberry and a Scythian lamb.

species, and separate from the day-to-day experience of the observer.

The title page of John Parkinson's *Paradisi in Sole Paradisus Terrestris* (1629), a landmark in English horticultural literature, presents a familiar vision of a garden as paradise. The title, a pun on Parkinson's name, may be literally translated as 'Park-in-sun's earthly paradise'. Parkinson considered the *Paradisi* to represent all the plants of the pleasure garden, and dedicated it to Henrietta Maria (1609–1669), the wife of Charles I (1600–1649). The frontispiece, a woodcut, was made by the German artist Christopher Switzer (*fl.* 1593–1611) and is in whimsical contrast to the evidence-based contents of the book. Two winds are represented in the upper corners and in the lower corners two vases are filled with a variety of flowers that were widely planted in seventeenth-century England. In the centre, a Lilliputian Adam and Eve are shown in the Garden of Eden, overseen by the Tetragrammaton (יהוה), the Hebraic name of God. Yet despite Parkinson's broad vision he warns the reader against hubris: 'for whoever tries to compare Art with Nature and gardens with Eden measures the stride of the elephant by the stride of the mite and the flight of the eagle by that of the gnat'.

Finding Eden

Innumerable human lives have been spent, and acres of paper consumed, debating the niceties of the Edenic myth, such as the earthly location of the garden. Those that treated it as literal argued that Eden had either been destroyed by or survived the Flood. If Eden had been damaged by the Flood but survived, then it was to be found far away from the civilised world, cut off by

seas or mountains, well above sea level, perhaps even in the southern hemisphere or in the polar regions. Furthermore, Eden was to be found where day and night were of similar length, the climate was neither too hot nor too cold, and plants grew all year round. When Columbus first came upon the coast of Venezuela (Paria) in August 1498 he confided to his journal that he believed the new continent was the biblical Eden. All the signs were there: the land was fertile, the people fine and even the animals talked. Furthermore, Columbus had encountered no hot weather; he had found strange new fruits; the Amerindians wore golden ornaments; and immense quantities of fresh water flowed into the Gulf of Paria from the Orinoco. Columbus was also convinced that the earth at this point was breast-shaped and he had sailed uphill to discover Eden set on the world's nipple.

Columbus's claims to have found Eden in the Americas were treated with scepticism by some of his contemporaries. However, many sixteenth-century Western European explorers appear to have expected to find Eden in the tropics during their voyages. The discovery of passion flowers confirmed in some minds that Eden was indeed to be found in the New World, since they thought the biblical associations of the plant were clear. The early Latin name, *Flos passionis*, and the plant's English common name reflect complex religious iconography, strongly associated with the biblical teaching of South American Catholic missionaries. At its simplest the flower corona represents the Crown of Thorns; the styles the three nails of the Crucifixion; the anthers the five wounds; the petals and sepals the ten Apostles who stayed with Christ; the palmate leaves the hands of Christ's persecutors; and the tendrils the scourge. These ideas grew up around the flower following the translation of Nicolás Monardes's *Historia medicinal* by Carolus Clusius (1526–1609), in 1574, and were adopted by Linnaeus when he named the passion flower genus *Passiflora*.

Despite the presence of the passion flower, there were worrying signs that Paradise was not to be found in the Americas. Strange new plants and animals were being discovered that were not to be found in the Bible or the texts of the Ancients: maize, potato, chocolate, pineapple, llama, turkey and toucan. Furthermore, the Amerindians lacked an alphabet and engaged in practices, such as cannibalism, that early modern theologians could hardly conceive as occurring in an earthly Paradise.

Creating Eden

If one could not wait for the discovery of Eden, perhaps one could create it. If the elements of Eden had been scattered, the discovery of the Americas once more allowed these elements to be brought together in one place. The early modern botanic gardens were in the hands of the academic princes of Europe, just as other gardens were the dominions of temporal and spiritual princes, and it has been argued that the establishment of early modern botanic gardens was an attempt at re-creating Eden under man's dominion. Given the intolerance and tetchiness of the Church, however, it hardly seems likely.

The establishment of botanic gardens was accompanied by the development of scientific rationalism and an increase in the importance of direct observation rather than reliance on precedent; reliance on authority was more difficult to eradicate. Alfred Russel Wallace, with his characteristic attention to empirical evidence, gently demolished religious and artistic speculations about an anthropocentric botanical world:

> Poets and moralists, judging from our English trees and fruits, have thought that small fruits always grew on lofty trees, so that their fall should be harmless to man, while the large ones trailed on the ground. Two of the largest and heaviest fruits known, however, the Brazil-nut fruit (*Bertholletia*) and durion, grow on lofty forest-trees, from which they fall as soon as they are ripe, and often wound or kill the native inhabitants. From this we may learn two things: first, not to draw general conclusions from a very partial view of nature, and secondly, that trees and fruits, no less than the varied productions of the animal kingdom, do not appear to be organized with exclusive reference to the use and convenience of man.[35]

By the end of the nineteenth century, Wallace's observations, along with those of Charles Darwin, would provide a scientific explanation for plant and animal diversity and a realisation that life was about change; stasis eventually leads to extinction. Yet romantic, anthropocentric notions persist, to a greater or lesser extent.

Doctrine of Signatures

The winding road of botanical discovery is replete with crossroads and T-junctions leading to new avenues of knowledge. However, there are cul-de-sacs of misconception, ambition, hubris and superstition, especially when plants are apparently associated with

FIGURE 19 The diverse genus *Passiflora*
is a horticultural prize. Its approximately
five hundred species, with their primarily
neotropical distributions, were unknown
until the exploration of the New World,
especially South America. However, a
few, such as the one illustrated here,
are found in the Old World. *Murucuja
baueri*, named in honour of Ferdinand
Bauer, is a synonym of *Passiflora aurantia*.
John Lindley published this lithograph
in his *Collectanea Botanica* (1821) based
on a drawing made by Bauer when he
was on his Australian adventures in the
early nineteenth century. Maracujá, the
common name still used in Brazil, is the
Tupi-Guarani name for the passionflower
fruit, meaning 'fruit that is served'; a
reference to the fruit's tough rind which
resembles a bowl and the edible pulp that
surrounds the seeds.

Murucuja Baueri.

human health. Two of the most famous such cul-de-sacs were the dalliances with the Doctrine of Signatures and astrological botany found in some of the more curious and popular sixteenth- and seventeenth-century English herbals. The Doctrine of Signatures states that the form of a plant indicates the ailment against which it can be used, whilst adherents of astrological botany believed plants were influenced by the stars and the planets. However, such beliefs were restricted to neither the English nor to the sixteenth and seventeenth centuries; these beliefs are ancient and are found in many cultures. There is a myth that, in the fifth century AD, Bodhidharma, the first patriarch of Zen, cut off his eyelids and threw them away to stop himself falling asleep. A bush with leaves in the form of eyelids grew and an infusion of the leaves could alleviate drowsiness. In Europe, the Doctrine was constructed within a framework dominated by the idea of a 'chain of being', that all life was for Man's benefit and that plants were merely 'green animals'. However, some folklorists have argued that the Doctrine of Signatures has been overplayed by recorders of plant knowledge who were literate, and that the Doctrine was merely a mnemonic device for the unlettered to remember the properties of useful plants. In the late seventeenth century, the astrological botanist Robert Turner (active 1640–64), summed up the Doctrine of Signatures as a divine game of hide and seek, with the assertion that 'God hath imprinted upon the Plants, Herbs, and Flowers, as it were in Hieroglyphicks, the very signature of their Vertues.'[36]

The controversial Swiss physician Philippus Theophrastus Bombastus von Hohenheim (1493–1541),

better known as Paracelsus, was an early promoter of the Doctrine of Signatures. However, it was the Italian physicist and mathematician Giambattista Porta (c. 1535–1615) and the English herbalist William Cole (?1626–1662) who presented the Doctrine in its most expansive and readily ridiculed form.

Giambattista della Porta developed his views in the many editions of *Phytognomonica* published from the late sixteenth to the mid-seventeenth centuries; perennial plants lengthened life and annuals reduced it, plants with yellow sap cured jaundice, and plants with jointed roots or fruits were cures for scorpion stings. Porta's fertile imagination for divining the relationships between human physiognomy and plant characteristics was wide-ranging and subtle. In one woodcut, a human jaw and teeth are surrounded by species with assorted similarities to human teeth. Other woodcuts show bristly-leaved plants associated with oxen and dogs, and animal testicles are shown with a range of orchid species. A unicorn even makes an appearance.

William Cole, in *Adam in Eden* (1657), carried the Doctrine of Signatures to further fantastical extremes. Cole believed that:

Wall-nuts have the perfect Signature of the Head: The outer husk or green Covering, represent the *Pericranium*, or outward skin of the skull, whereon the hair groweth, and therefore salt made of those husks or barks, are exceeding good for wounds in the head. The inner wooddy shell hath the Signature of the Skull, and the little yellow skin, or Peel, that covereth the Kernell of the hard *Meninga* and *Pia Mater*, which are the thin scarfes that envelope the brain. The Kernel hath the very figure of the Brain, and therefore it is very profitable for the Brain, and resists poysons; For if the Kernel be bruised, and moystned with

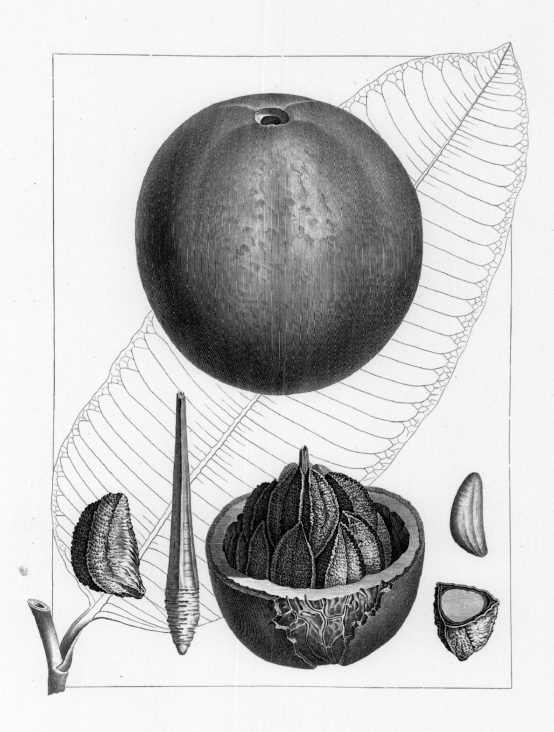

FIGURE 20 Aimé Bonpland gave the brazil nut its scientific name, *Bertholettia excelsa*, in honour of the French chemist Claude Louis Berthollet and the enormous size of the tree. Bonpland and Alexander Humboldt had collected specimens on their South American odyssey. A life-sized engraving of the magnificent, cannon-ball-sized, woody fruit was published in 1805 in their *Plantae Aequinoctiales* (1805–18) based on a painting by the French artist Pierre-Jean-François Turpin.

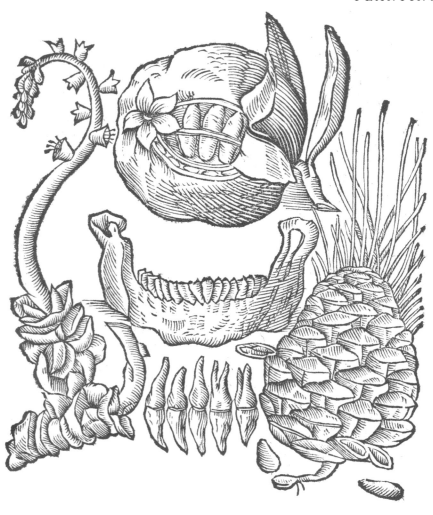

FIGURE 21 Giambattista della Porta's *Phytognomonica* (1650) reproduces a woodcut of a human jaw and teeth surrounded by species with assorted similarities to human teeth. The parasitic flowering plant *Lathraea squamaria*, commonly known today as toothwort, is shown with its tooth-like scales at the bottom of the stem. The seeds and scales of the pine cone reminded Porta of teeth. Rows of pulp-covered pomegranate seeds, arranged in a broken fruit, appear as teeth in a jaw.

the quintessence of Wine, and laid upon the Crown of the Head, it comforts the brain and head mightily.[37]

However, the location of the signature was in the eye of the beholder. The signature of a man's 'triple regions' might be found in the triple leaves of strawberries (is this perhaps why Eve is making a grab for a strawberry in the frontispiece to Parkinson's *Paradisi in Sole*?) or the paired tubers of the male orchid. Cole was aware God had omitted to sign a large proportion of plants; this he thought was on purpose so that Man would be encouraged to use his own skill and ingenuity to discover their medicinal properties. The most famous sixteenth-century English herbalist John Gerard (1545–?1611) was proud of his skills in having discovered the 'properties and privie marks' of thousands of plants.[38]

The Doctrine of Signatures was resisted by mainstream botanical thought. Rembert Dodoens (1517–1585), the best sixteenth-century herbalist, dismissed it as having no reputable ancient authority and, being so changeable and uncertain, 'as far as science or learning is concerned, it seems absolutely unworthy of acceptance'.[39] At the end of the seventeenth century, the Doctrine was rejected by the great Cambridgeshire naturalist John Ray. Half a century earlier, the apothecary John Parkinson had been of a similar view, having discarded the philosophical and mystical in favour of the experimental. However, he did allow the quack and leading London-based exponent of the Doctrine, Simon Baskerville (?1574–1641), to write a dedication in his *Theatrum Botanicum* (1640). Ironically, just over a decade later, Parkinson's work was dismissed, with seventeenth-century directness, by the colourful apothecary and astrological botanist Nicholas Culpeper (1616–1654):

> Neither Gerrard or Parkinson … ever gave one wise reason for what they wrote, and so did nothing else but train up young Novices in Physick in the School of Tradition, and teach them just as a Parrot is taught to speak; an Author saith so, therefore 'tis true; and if al that Authors say be true, why do they contradict one another? But in mine, if you view it with the eye of Reason you shall see a Reason for everything that is written.[40]

Astrological botany

In astrological botany, not only are the lives of men and their diseases governed by the movements of the planets and stars, but plants are merely pawns in a celestial game played for the benefit of Man. The belief that plants were influenced by the movement of the stars and planets was advocated by numerous vociferous personalities in sixteenth- and seventeenth-century Europe. The most notorious were Paracelsus, Porta and Culpeper. Culpeper, perhaps the most famous of this trio, wrote at great length trying to justify the associations that he was drawing. However, it was Porta who illustrated the astrological links with plants. In one woodcut, the crescent moon (with its human face) is associated with species that have moon-shaped fruits or leaves. In another woodcut, the roundish leaves of cyclamen and the spherical, clustered fruits of cuckoo pint (*Arum maculatum*) were associated with the full moon in Porta's mind.

Culpeper was notorious as a botanical astrologer, and as a thorn in the flesh of mid-seventeenth-century orthodox physicians, whom he described as 'a company

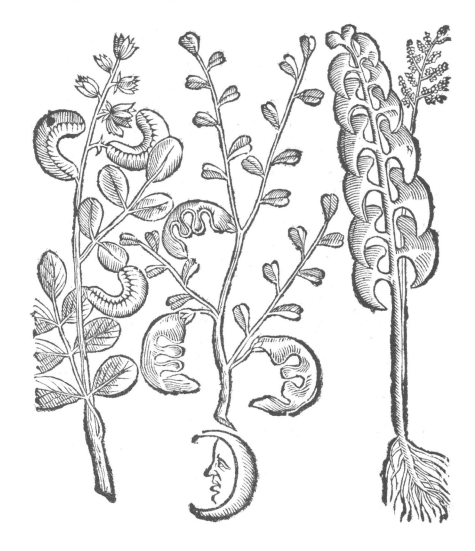

FIGURE 22   The woodcut from Giambattista della Porta's *Phytognomonica* (1650) shows a species of senna, together with the legume horse vetch (*Hippocrepis*), with its divided moon-shaped fruits, and the fern *Botrychium lunaria* (commonly known as moonwort), represented by a leaf divided into exaggerated moon-shaped leaflets. All of these species were supposedly influenced by the moon.

of proud, insulting, domineering Doctors, whose wits were born above five hundred years before themselves'.[41] Culpeper considered himself both to have been guided by reason and to have surpassed all of his predecessors, who were 'as ful of nonsense and contradictions as an Egg is ful of meat'.[42] However, despite being guided by 'reason', Culpeper's arguments for the astrological influences on particular plants and disease were, at best, fanciful.

> Wormwood is an Herb of *Mars*, … I prove it thus; What delights in Martial Martial places, is a Martial Herb; but Wormwood delights in [Martial] places (for about Forges and Iron Works you may gather a Cart load of it) *Ergo* it is a Martial Herb.[43]

Wormwood is of use for the eyes since

> The Eyes are under the Luminaries; the right Eye of a Man, and the left Eye of a Woman, the *Sun* claims Dominion over: The left Eye of a Man, and the right Eye of a Woman, are the priviledg of the *Moon*, Wormwood an Herb of *Mars* cures both; what belongs to the *Sun* by Sympathy, because he is exalted in his House; but what belong to the *Moon* by Antipathy, because he hath his Fal in hers.[44]

Many of Culpeper's contemporaries were not convinced. Cole, regardless of his belief in the Doctrine of Signatures, was dismissive of the astrologers, and used a subtle theological argument that since plants were created on the third day and planets on the fourth in the Genesis Creation myth, astrological botany was ridiculous since cause cannot follow effect. Cole's anger was reserved especially for Culpeper since 'he understood not those Plants he trod upon',[45] and furthermore,

> Master *Culpeper* (a man now dead, and therefore I shall speak of him as modestly as I can, for were he alive I should be more plain with him) was a great Stickler; And he, forsooth, judgeth all men unfit to be Physitians, who are not Artists in Astrology, as if he and some other Figure-flingers his companions, had been the onley Physitians in England, whereas for ought I can gather, either by his Books, or learne from the report of others, he was a man very ignorant in the forme of Simples.[46]

Despite such criticisms, Culpeper's work was very popular and his books went into many editions. Indeed, Culpeper's work remains in print.

Like the myriad forms seen in clouds on a summer's day, believers in the Doctrine of Signatures and astrological botany could let their imaginations roam. Freed from the constraints of science, reason or principle, all that remained was imagination, authority and faith in the 'practicioner'. The residues of such beliefs are still found in folklore. Today, more insidiously, such beliefs proliferate and mutate in fringe 'medical' practices. Thus, stavesacre (*Delphinium staphysagria*), the seeds of which have been widely used in Europe to control pests since the late eighteenth century, is described in homeopathic literature as having

> to struggle through rock in order to grow and unfold. Likewise, the human personality in need of the remedy Staphysagria [stavesacre] feels angered and suppressed, as if having to break or cut through rock in order to live freely.[47]

Astrology is as ridiculous when applied to botany as it is when applied to the affairs of Man. The only star that influences terrestrial plant life is the sun and that largely through photosynthesis. Cole expressed the potential harm of such astrological pseudoscience when presented as fact:

> I goe not about to deceive them [country people] with a few empty Notions, as Mr Culpeper hath lately done tell them many Nonsensicall stories of I know not what.[48]

Botanical curiosities

What botanist could have predicted that in 1818 the members of Thomas Stamford Raffles's (1781–1826) expedition to Sumatra would discover a parasitic plant, *Rafflesia arnoldii*, with neither leaves nor visible stems, but with a flower nearly one metre in diameter, weighing nearly ten kilograms?[49] Raffles clearly thought that he would not be believed:

> had I been alone, and had there been no witnesses, I should I think have been fearful of mentioning the dimensions of this flower ['a full yard across'], so much does it exceed every flower I have ever seen or heard of.[50]

Given the surprises the natural world has to offer, the botanist must expect the unexpected. However, with fragmentary information, some interpreters of early botanical discoveries constructed chimeras. Explorers often came across objects they could not explain, and their reports were often misunderstood, misinterpreted or deliberately fabricated. Fantastic organisms are replete in mediaeval bestiaries, and range from mermaids through Cyclopes to manticores; and herbals from the same period are not immune to such fancies.

FIGURE 23
Rafflesia arnoldii is the world's largest flower and was first described by Robert Brown in *Transactions of the Linnean Society* (1822). Joseph Arnold (1782–1818), after whom Robert Brown named the plant, was another botanist who 'fell a sacrifice to his exertions' when collecting plants.

232.

Atropa Mandragora

FIGURE 24   The presumed anthropoid form of the medicinally important mandrake root influenced the development of an extensive mythology over many thousands of years. One such myth concerns the belief that as the plant is uprooted it screams, and kills any that hear it. Hence the recommendation that dogs be used to harvest the plant. Furthermore, it was believed that plants had either male or female roots. Even the critical botanical eye of Ferdinand Bauer was not immune to the whimsy of myths, as shown in this copper engraving from Volume 3 of Sibthorp and Smith's *Flora Graeca* (1819).

Belief in some of these fantastic organisms was linked to the Greek idea of the 'chain of being'. This idea argued there was no clear division between plants and animals; everything could be placed into a chain that formed a continuous link between earth (rocks) and heaven (angels). Thus, rocks and plants were linked through the sponge, whilst the Scythian lamb (Borametz, Vegetable lamb or Lamb of Tartary) was the link between plants and animals. Scythian lambs were believed to inhabit the remoter regions of Asia, and had the roots and stems of a young tree which supported the body of a lamb. Once the Scythian lamb had eaten all the plants within its reach it would die and propagate itself by seed. Guillaume de Saluste in his poem *La Semaine* (1578) represents the Scythian lamb as one of the organisms that astonished Adam as he wandered through the Garden of Eden; an allusion represented on the title page of John Parkinson's *Paradisi in Sole*.

Curiosity is not only found in fantastical plants but in the properties applied to real plants. Mandrake (*Mandragora officinarum*), a Mediterranean and western Asian member of the potato family, is perhaps the most famous real plant around which stories have been woven. The source of the mythology is the anthropoid root, whilst its chemical constituents have been used in medicines, poisons and magic potions. It has been used for thousands of years and rejoices in many common names, in many languages: for example, Satan's apple, fool's apple, Satan's testicles and dragon doll. Mandrake was reputed to shriek when 'torn out of the earth, that living mortals, hearing them, run mad'.[51] Incantations with swords and circles were believed to protect the

collector, but the most common means of harvesting was to have a dog:

> he who would take up a plant thereof must tie a dog therunto to pull it up, which will give a great shreeke at the digging up; otherwise if a man should do it, he should surely die in a short space after.[52]

Indeed, early mandrake illustrations usually show the root with a dead dog attached. Mandrake roots with a strong human form were considered so powerful that judicial whittling could increase a root's market value dramatically, and fake mandrake roots are commonly found in sixteenth-century collections of curiosities. Mandrake extracts have been used as narcotics, aphrodisiacs, hypnotics, hallucinogens and poisons. Dose makes the difference between a plant's ability to cure or to kill. At low doses mandrake is an effective anaesthetic; as the dose increases it induces delirium, and at high doses death. Mandrake wine, an anaesthetic, was often given to those condemned to burn at the stake and, ironically, as an important component of witches' ointments. Parkinson condemns the superstitions surrounding mandrake root, in *Theatrum Botanicum* (1640):

> Mandrakes and Womandrakes, as they are foolishly so called, which have been exposed to publike view both in ours and other lands and countries, are utterly deceitfull being the work of cunning knaves onely to get mony by their forgery.[53]

The origins of plant myths are often difficult to discern. The German explorer and polymath Engelbert Kaempfer (1651–1716), after extensive searches, '*ad risum et nauseam*', through Central Asia and Persia, believed

Scythian lambs to be nothing more than aborted sheep foetuses. However, other explanations of the Scythian lamb have also been put forward, including the carved rhizome of the fern known today as *Cybotium borametz*, misunderstandings of the cotton plant in fruit, and confusion with the fibres that hold a species of Mediterranean mollusc to rocks.

A natural response to plant diversity is awe at both the numbers of species and the variety of forms. This leads on to using and trying to explain diversity; that is, the tension between the application (applied science) and the explanation (pure science) of knowledge. Early explanations of diversity were based around theology and mysticism, although scientific explanations soon became the focus of attention during the seventeenth and eighteenth centuries. However, even in the early nineteenth century there was a prevalent view that

'He [God] had fixed certain boundaries to human knowledge, beyond which mortal ken cannot pass.'[54] Clearly, the walls of the intellectual *hortus conclusus* which Man inhabits are plastic and their limits remain undiscovered. By the end of the century, Charles Darwin had published his *On the Origin of Species* (1859), whilst the monk Gregor Mendel had laid the foundations of genetics. Together, with the discovery of the behaviour of chromosomes and the structure of DNA, these advances stimulated research that would finally produce a rational explanation for the diversity of life on earth and explode the dogma of Special Creation. Gardens were more than mere philosophical or theological playgrounds; they were places that provided access to material for serious scientific investigations of how plants functioned and evolved, as well as sources of food and medicine.

CHAPTER 4

Utilitarian plants

———

Wonderful little, when all is said,
Wonderful little our fathers knew.
Half their remedies cured you dead —
Most of their teaching was quite untrue

'Our Fathers of Old', Rudyard Kipling, 1897

PEOPLE have their strongest associations with plants that they use as food or medicine. It is no surprise therefore that the first early modern botanic gardens were concerned with practical aspects of plant study, such as medicine and agriculture. Since before the time of Christ, investigation of plants and their conservation has been justified with the explicitly anthropocentric objectives of the desire to feed people and improve their health. The Egyptian *Ebers Papyrus* (*c.* 1550 BC) refers to knowledge of medicinal plants that dates to at least 3000 BC, whilst for the first 1,500 years of the Christian era European investigations of plants were driven by the writings of the duumvirate Dioscorides ('the father of botanical pharmacology') and Theophrastus ('the father of botany').

Investigations of plants has been approached from two, often diametrically opposed, viewpoints: the philosophical and the applied. In Western culture, the philosophical approach had its origin in Greece. The collection of facts about plants was relegated to studies such as medicine. However, 'practical' is often thought of as disparaging: 'a vague and foolish word with which, from the days of Plato to our own, men have sought to conceal from themselves and from others their destitution of anything in the nature of general ideas'.[55] The chemist Robert Boyle (1627–1691) had divided alchemists into practical 'laborants' and the theoretician 'adepti', and considered the former mainly charlatans whilst the latter were serious-minded; a derogatory distinction between knowledge gained through experience and experience gained through knowledge.

Plants for physic

In European medicine there was a division between the physician, who diagnosed the malady, and

The grete herball

Whiche gyueth parfyt knolwlege and vnder standyng of all maner of herbes & theyr gracyous vertues whiche god hath ozdeyned for our prosperous welfare and helth, for they hele & cure all maner of dyseases and sekenesses that fall oz mysfoztune to all maner of creatures of god created practysed by many expert and wyse maysters (as Auicenna & other. &c. Also it gyueth parfyte vnderstandynge of the booke lately pzynted by me (Peter treueris) named the noble experiēce of vertuous handwarke of surgery.

John Pennington

FIGURE 25   Title page from *The Grete Herball* (1537). This book, first printed by Peter Treveris in 1526, was an English translation of the French *Le Grand Herbier* and influenced by the German *Ortus Sanitatis* (1491) and incorporated woodcuts that had first appeared in the German *Herbarius zu Teutsch* (1485). The amalgamation of images from earlier works was characteristic of many of the early herbals.

apothecaries, who supplied plant-based medicines directly to the patient. Physicians recognised that careful investigation was important if plants were to be used effectively in medicines; mistaken identifications could be fatal. However, it was the business of the maligned herbalists and druggists to collect, prepare and sell plant material for medicines; a craft often protected by superstitions and mysteries. The rigmarole of swords, dogs and magic circles that surrounded mandrake harvesting had even been ridiculed by Theophrastus. The advocate of the Doctrine of Signatures, William Cole, complained that physicians left the herb gathering to apothecaries, who relied 'commonly upon the words of the silly Hearb-women, who many times bring them Quid for Quo, then which nothing can be more sad'.[56] Similar concerns had been expressed by Pliny in AD 70:

> But little by little experience, the most efficient teacher of all things, and in particular of medicine, degenerated into words and mere talk. For it was more pleasant to sit in a lecture-room engaged in listening, than to go out into the wilds and search for the various plants at their proper season of the year.[57]

By 1889, the Oxford-based pharmacist–botanist George Druce was grumbling that

> our medical friends, … have almost excised botany from their scientific training. I am afraid their fierce and frantic zeal to add a new hypnotic, or some new organic compound with wonderful temperature reducing power, to our groaning shelves will prevent them giving much attention to this the more humble and less showy handmaid of therapeutics.[58]

Herbals

The Grete Herball (1526), an English translation of the French *Le Grand Herbier* (pre-1526), was the most reputable of all the early English herbals and emphasised the utilitarian importance of plants, their God-given role in relieving man's illnesses, and the revelation of the divine in nature.

> O ye worthy reders or practicyens to whome this noble volume is preset I beseche yow take intellygence and beholde ye workes and operacyons of almyghty god which hath endewed his symple creature mankynde with the graces of ye holy goost to have parfyte knowlege and understandynge of the vertue of all maner of herbes and trees in this booke comprehendyd.[59]

Sixteenth- and seventeenth-century remedies such as bloodletting appear brutal, which makes people appear much tougher than today. *The Grete Herball* took the same view, albeit it some five centuries ago:

> in olde tyme it ['Whyte elebore', *Veratrum album*] was commely used in medycyns as we use squamony [*Convolvulus scammonia*]. For the body of man was stronger than it is now, and myght better endure the vyolence of elebore, for man is weyker at this time of nature.[60]

The Grete Herball also makes liberal use of Christian, Roman and Greek mythology. Those bitten by a mad dog are exhorted to appeal to the Virgin Mary, 'as sone as ye be byten go to the chyrche, and make thy offrynge to our lady, and pray here to helpe and heale'.[61] Yet the medicinal virtues of wormwood (*Artemisia*) are attributed to the Roman goddess Diana. One of the most noticeable features of the herbal is the exposure of methods of 'faking' drugs, for the protection of the

public, 'to eschew ye frawde of them that selleth it', and concern for access to medical information, 'enformynge how man may be holpen with grene herbes of the gardyn and wedys of ye feldys as well as by costly receptes of the potycarys prepayred'.[62]

A botanic garden provided the opportunity to train physicians to recognise the plants that they were prescribing and eliminate the waves of charlatans and snake-oil peddlers. In the early seventeenth century, the apothecary John Parkinson (1567–1650) published two tomes, *Paradisi in Sole* (1629) and *Theatrum Botanicum* (1640), to emphasise the importance of practical knowledge of plants to physicians and apothecaries. However, these two works, which are based on Parkinson's practical experience of plants, are relatively poorly known compared to John Gerard's fabled and, sometimes, fabulous *The Herball or general historie of plantes* (1597).

John Gerard (1545–1611/12) was a wealthy barber–surgeon and a recognised botanical authority of his time. He also owned a well-stocked garden in Holborn that was visited by many of the botanical notables of the day, including Parkinson and the physician and botanist Matthias de l'Obel (1538–1616). When it was published, the well-illustrated *Herball* got an enthusiastic reception by a public with an appetite for information about plants, especially their medicinal uses. However, this

FIGURE 26 John's Gerard's *Herball* (1597), despite its imperfections, is one of the most popular books about plants that has ever been published. The elaborate title page is notable since it includes an image of Gerard holding a potato flower. This is the earliest published illustration of the potato, which had been brought to Spain from the Americas in about 1570.

54

masked the fact that the book was little more than a plagiarized translation of a book by the Flemish scholar Rembert Dodoens (1517–1585). Gerard had not only taken Dodoens's text and translated it; he embellished it with assertions and fantasies of his own creation, and destroyed its objectivity. For example, he relates how he observed a goose barnacle giving birth to a goose, so propagating a myth that had persisted in Europe since the twelfth century. The published text is replete with errors, and one can only imagine what the text must have been like when Matthias de l'Obel was asked to correct the worst excesses before publication. The title page of the 1597 *Herball* is a splendid mixture of allegorical figures and images of the important garden plants of the day. In 1633, a second edition of the *Herball* was published. This had been completely revised by the apothecary Thomas Johnson (1600–1644); many of Gerard's errors were corrected and hundreds of new illustrations and descriptions were added.

Gerard's success showed there was demand for books about plants, and that if fame were the objective then facts should never be allowed to get in the way of a good story. In early-seventeenth-century Europe, Peruvian bark was in great demand as a cure for malaria. The sale of a 'secret' recipe to Louis XIV (1638–1715) in 1679 made the Cambridge quack Richard Talbor (1642–81) very wealthy. Talbor's secret was that he had bought up all the best Peruvian bark in England and served the ground powder in wine. Talbor had realised that, to be effective, Peruvian bark had to be from the best sources and that alcohol was effective at dissolving the active ingredients. However, as the eighteenth and nineteenth centuries progressed, growing all the medicinal plants used by physicians in British gardens became impossible.

Native and introduced plants have historically always been used side by side, although their relative importance has often varied according to the fashions of the day. In the herbals of the fifteenth and sixteenth centuries there is constant reference to the idea that plants native to a country provide the means to overcome the diseases of that country. The promoters of the Doctrine of Signatures, Paracelsus and Porta, disparaged the use of introduced plants as a source of medicine for this reason, and in 1664 Robert Turner states 'for what Climate soever is subject to any particular Disease, in the same Place there grows a Cure'.[63] This belief survived through the nineteenth century to the present day. 'Nature has, in this country, as well as in all others, provided, in the herbs of its own growth, the remedies for the several diseases to which it is most subject';[64] witness the widespread belief that nettles and docks are found together *because* the leaves of the latter relieve the stings of the former.

Alternatively, exotic plants were given high status, for example the seventeenth-century use of lignum vitae wood for syphilis. The use of introduced plants as medicines is not a recent phenomenon. The Ebers Papyrus describes some 150 medicinal plants, including some introduced to Egypt; for example, frankincense and aloes. The Assyrian herbal of King Asshur-bani-pal (r. 699–626 BC) includes names of some 200 species, including introductions such as rice from Southeast Asia, *Commiphora* from Arabia and turmeric from India.

Plants vary morphologically and chemically across their ranges and from season to season. These differences may be due to the plant's genetic make-up or its interaction with the environment. Thus, plants from different areas may look similar but produce very different medicinal effects when grown in the same locality. Historically, pharmacists have expended much effort in obtaining plant material from specific regions of the world, in order to ensure that drugs were of a consistent and reliable quality. Growing plants in a garden ensures a year-round supply of specific medicinal plants, albeit at the risk of poor yields of the medicinally active compounds.

In Western cultures, the use of medicinal plants is usually investigated through examination of manuscript and printed sources dating back to ancient authorities. Irrespective of the difficulties of correlating names in such documents with modern names, the process is potentially flawed since it is biased; it largely ignores the knowledge of the peasant. The knowledge in such sources is that of the literate, yet much traditional knowledge is likely to have been held by peoples with an oral tradition; these people are likely to have known nothing of the Ancients and cared even less. Furthermore, other important voices with knowledge about plants are not found in such sources due to race, creed or sex. Such 'unrecorded' knowledge about medicinal plants is likely to be easily lost or only recorded piecemeal and out of context.

The dash for quinine

Traditionally, quinine, one of the most valuable medicines in Western Europe, was extracted from the Peruvian bark tree, until it was artificially synthesised in 1945. Industrially manufactured quinine is responsible for the memorable bitterness of a gin and tonic. The myth of quinine's discovery is a familiar one. In 1638, Dona Francisca Henriques de Ribera (d. 1639), Condesa de Chinchón, was dying from malaria in Peru. In desperation a Jesuit priest suggested that her husband, the Viceroy, might try a bark extract he had used successfully, although whether the indigenous people knew the bark as a febrifuge is disputed. The bark was effective, the Condesa recovered, and, following her return to Spain, the story of her salvation became widespread. The European dash for Peruvian bark had started.

Peruvian bark is derived from the genus *Cinchona*, a member of the coffee family, and was named by Linnaeus in honour of the Condesa. For over a century, little was known about the Peruvian bark tree, and there was dispute over its efficacy in treating malaria and prejudice about its application. The genus *Cinchona* contains twenty-three species, which are mainly distributed in the Andes, although during the nineteenth century there was no consensus over what these species should be called, especially for those producing quinine. Barks from different parts of the distributional range of *Cinchona* have different amounts of the compounds effective against malaria and the high price of the bark led to almost any bitter bark being called Peruvian bark. In the seventeenth century, prejudice against Peruvian bark was based on its association with Jesuits and the general prejudice against Catholics, especially in Britain and northern Europe. Indeed, legend has it that Oliver Cromwell (1599–1658), Lord Protector during the Commonwealth, refused the bark as a cure for his (ultimately fatal) malaria, because it was a 'Popish remedy'.

5364

FIGURE 27 In 1863 Joseph Hooker published a lithograph of *Cinchona officinalis* in *Curtis's Botanical Magazine*. The genus *Cinchona*, the source of quinine, was one of the prizes of empire acquired from the New World. However, Hooker omitted to mention the work of his elder brother William, in 1839, which had poured scorn on many of the legends surrounding the discovery of quinine as a medicinal plant and the concern that it was threatened with extinction in the Andes.

Until the mid-nineteenth century, raw Peruvian bark came from diverse sources in the New World. However, the British and Dutch needed control over Peruvian bark supply since malaria was a major disease in their colonies. These powers therefore funded major programmes to collect, often illegally, seed for cultivation in their respective colonies. The British justified the introduction of the Peruvian bark tree to India in order to conserve the South American resource and intervene in the apparently destructive way bark was harvested; mature trees were felled to collect the bark. However, in 1839, William Dawson Hooker (1816–1840), the eldest son of the director of Kew, wrote a thesis in which he made clear that coppicing was the most appropriate method for maintaining productivity and promoting growth of *Cinchona*. Hooker's research was apparently overlooked by his father when Kew promoted the scheme of introducing Peruvian bark to British India. There were other indicators that the Peruvian bark tree was not on the verge of extinction; for example, the Andean Republics exported nearly 900,000 kilogrammes of bark in 1860. However, such evidence was perhaps politically inconvenient and therefore ignored.

Numerous mountebanks, adventurers and botanists went to South America, either independently or sponsored by European powers, to bring material to Europe for cultivation. In 1853, the Dutch botanist Justus Charles Hasskarl (1811–1894) arrived on the Peruvian–Bolivian border, disguised as a German businessman, searching for *Cinchona* and illegally procured plants and seeds of *C. calisaya*; the plants died but the seeds were transferred to Java. The seed grew poorly and contained little of the compounds active against malaria, either because good-quality seed had been swapped for lesser-quality seed or because Hasskarl had collected the wrong species. In contrast, *C. calisaya* collected by the botanist Hugh Algernon Weddell (1819–1877) from Bolivia in 1851 contained about twelve times more active compounds than Hasskarl's collection. In Java, nearly 1 million plants were raised from Hasskarl's seeds and only 7,000 plants were raised from Weddell's seeds; this very expensive mistake was only realised after the plants had grown.

In 1860, the English Amazonian explorer Richard Spruce collected seed and plants of *C. pubescens* from Ecuador, at the behest of the civil servant and explorer Clements Markham (1830–1916), after securing rights to collect the seed from local landowners. This material was dispatched to Kew and in 1861 463 healthy plants reached India for establishment in plantations. Once problems associated with climatic conditions and diseases were overcome, these trees became the source of Indian quinine until the early twentieth century. Establishment of the plantations in India was not easy since the wrong seed was planted, the climatic and soil conditions were wrong and plant diseases were rife. Furthermore, there were political and personality clashes among the main protagonists involved with the introduction. The Indian plantations gradually fell into ruin, as manufacturers preferred to import Peruvian bark from Java because of its very high content of active compounds.

The Javanese trees came from an English businessman, Charles Ledger (1818–1906), who in 1865 illegally collected a 40 lb bag of *C. calisaya* seeds from Bolivia; *Cinchona* export was a government monopoly.

Ledger had used the local knowledge of the indigenous Bolivian Manuel Incra Mamani, who was beaten to death in 1877, apparently for his part in Ledger's export of Peruvian bark seed. Ledger offered the seed to the British, who turned it down; they had trees growing in India. The Dutch grudgingly took 1 lb of the seed and grew it in Java, where they found that the trees contained up to thirty-two times more antimalarial compounds than Hasskarl's seeds. These plantations were the basis of the Dutch quinine monopoly until 1939, when Japanese occupation broke the quinine supply. In the post-war years, synthetic antimalarials became important for the prevention and cure of malaria, and the commercial value of Peruvian bark diminished.

The efforts of the British, after Spruce's successful expedition, to collect Peruvian bark seeds in Ecuador were not encumbered by the knowledge that material was being illegally collected. In November 1861, the botanist and gardener Robert Cross (1834–1911) wrote to the Secretary of State for India stating:

> it was stated to me that the Government of Ecuador has passed an edict prohibiting the exportation of either seeds or plants of the quina tree, under the penalty of 100 dollars for every plant, and for every drachm of seed. However, after consulting with Mr Mocatta [The British vice-consul], I undertook to go to Loxa and make a collection of seeds of the C. Condaminea [*C. officinalis*].[65]

Peruvian bark cultivation raises three issues common to growing plants outside of their native ranges. First, European growers may not know how to cultivate the plant. Second, correct identification and understanding of a plant's basic biology are crucial. Third, variation within the species may be important for the plant's cultivation and for the efficacy of its products.

Plants for food

Humans have transformed natural landscapes to accommodate food production. Forests have been razed to the ground, marshes and fenland drained, savannahs and prairies ploughed, and hills and mountains terraced. The crops planted in these cultivated landscapes evolved in at least eight different regions of the world or 'agricultural Edens'. The greatest diversity of cereals such as wheat and barley is to be found in the Near East; the maximum diversity of chili, runner beans and maize is found in Mesoamerica, of potatoes in the Andes and aubergines in India.

European and Asian civilisations would be impossible without food plants such as wheat, dates, barley and rice. The movement of these 'old' staple crops from their agricultural Edens, and the knowledge of their cultivation, pre-date the establishment of even the most ancient botanic gardens. In other cases, 'new' worldwide staple crops – for example, maize and potatoes – have only become part of European and Asian agricultural systems in the last five hundred years. Many 'new' and 'old' food plants were nursed into wider cultivation in gardens, where there was the opportunity to experiment with new variants, in order to improve quality, productivity and general acceptance.

Vegetables

Cabbages have fed Europeans for hundreds, if not thousands, of years, but originated in the eastern

Mediterranean and Asia Minor. As cabbages were moved out of the Mediterranean, different people selected different features and diverse forms were generated. In 1648, Jacob Bobart the Elder was growing in the Oxford Botanic Garden many of the cultivated cabbages known to Gerard and Parkinson: 'White Cabbage Colewort', 'Coleflower', 'Savoy Cabbage', 'Common Colewort' and 'Parsly Colewort', together with 'Wild Colewort' and 'Sea Colewort'. By 1658, 'Red Cabbage' had been added to the horticultural menu, and in the 1660s the unusual forms 'Childing Colewort' and 'Narrow Childing Colewort', with small leaves sprouting from the leaf surface, were being cultivated. These diverse cabbage forms are all derived from the wild cabbage (*Brassica oleracea*) through artificial selection of particular features. In the kales (*B. oleracea* var. *acephala*) and headed cabbages (*B. oleracea* var. *capitata*) variation in stem length between leaves produces plants that have either loosely or tightly packed heads. The cauliflowers and broccolis (*B. oleracea* var. *botrytis*) have thickened, undeveloped flowers and flower stalks, whilst kohlrabi (*B. oleracea* var. *caulo-rapa*) has a grossly enlarged stem, and brussels sprouts (*B. oleracea* var. *gemmifera*) have greatly expanded buds. In 1860, just one year after Darwin published *On the Origin of Species*, researchers at Cirencester Agricultural College used simple selection experiments to breed broccoli, and other cabbage-like forms, from wild cabbages found on the English coast.

Kales are the most ancient of the cultivated cabbage forms. Until the middle of the eighteenth century, cabbages generally, and kales particularly, were known in England under their Anglo-Saxon name 'colewort'. However, kales are not well suited to the cool conditions of northern Europe, where cold-tolerant headed cabbages were selected. There is no mention of headed cabbages by classical authors and only ambiguous references to them in the mediaeval European literature. However, by 1536, Jean Ruel (1479–1537) gives an unmistakable description of a white, headed cabbage; red cabbage appeared thirty-five years later. The western migration of headed cabbage from Europe started in 1541, with its introduction to Canada by the French navigator Jacques Cartier (1491–1557), and by 1669 it was growing in the English colonies of the United States.

In England, sprouting broccoli, which was familiar to Pliny, was not grown until the early eighteenth century. Today, the calabrese type, with its large, green, tasteless, cauliflower-like heads, is more commonly found. The cauliflower (coleflower) is an ancient cultivated form. Spanish cauliflower cultivars from the twelfth century were described as Syrian introductions, and their cultivation was described by sixteenth-century travellers in Turkey and Egypt. In sixteenth-century England, cauliflowers were rare and called Cyprus coleworts, emphasising the eastern Mediterranean source of the original seeds. However, by the early seventeenth century, cauliflowers were common in London markets.

In contrast, kohlrabi and brussels sprouts are types of cabbage that have been developed much more recently than other forms. Kohlrabi was selected in late-fifteenth-century northern Europe. The first descriptions of kohlrabi were made by the Italian botanist Pier Andrea Matthiolus (1501–1577) in 1554, and by the end of the sixteenth century it was known from the Iberian Peninsula in the west, Libya in the south and

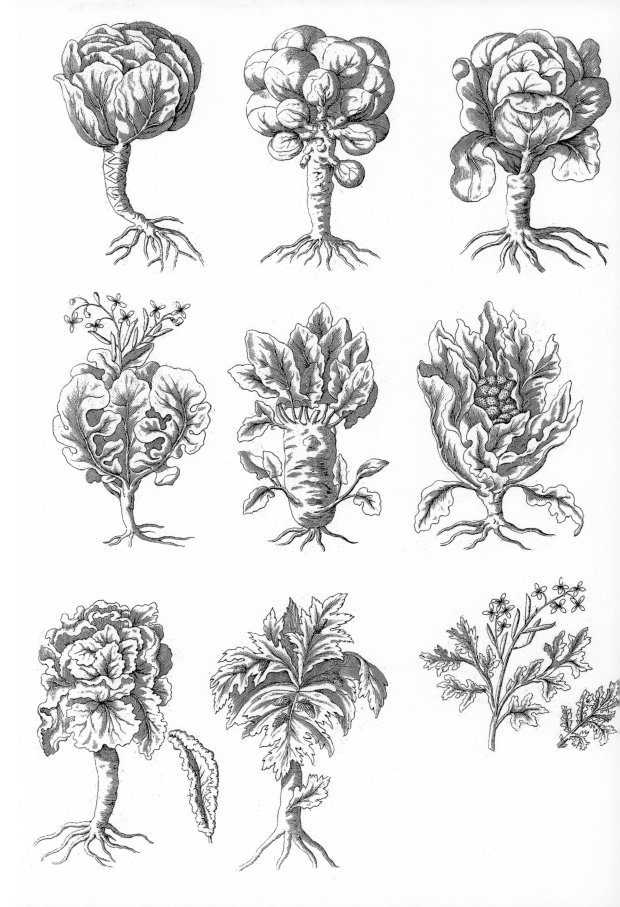

FIGURE 28 Robert Morison conceived his *Historia Plantarum Universalis Oxoniensis* (1680–99) as a systematic catalogue of plants arranged according to Morison's own classification system. The *Historia* is remarkable for the magnificent plates, engraved by some of the most significant engravers of the day and funded by subscriptions from aristocratic families. Many of the species in the plates are also to be found in Morison's personal herbarium. In the plate reproduced here, the diversity of cabbages found in seventeenth-century gardens is shown. The original copper plates were discovered being used as lift counterweights in the Bodleian Library in Oxford University, and are now conserved as part of the library collection.

across the eastern Mediterranean. However, kohlrabi was not grown extensively in England until the late nineteenth century. Brussels sprouts, despite being so common today, were not described until 1587, and in the seventeenth century English botanists described them as something heard of but never seen.

Apples and pears

Food plants bear the signature of man's interest in them through the vast numbers of different named types found in particular crops. Before the twentieth century there were thousands of apple varieties in Britain and hundreds of varieties of pears. The ability to grow the right food plant brings great economic or social advantages to the grower. Just as war stimulates technological development, so competition among generations of gardeners, farmers and breeders has produced tremendous changes in food plants. By the start of the nineteenth century, fruit culture had made huge advances, and those who had created the innumerable varieties wanted the fact recorded, using the latest high-quality coloured engravings or lithographs that were being produced across northern Europe. The nineteenth-century weakness for the publication of lavish volumes of plant illustrations, which went far beyond the pockets of those who would use them for practical or scientific purposes, reached its zenith with the Pomonae. Pomology, the study of fruit culture, is derived from the word 'Pomona', which had first been used in the seventeenth century by John Evelyn – a man who had little truck with publishing for the masses – for fruit culture. In 1844, the horticulturalist John Claudius Loudon (1783–1843) noted that the sumptuousness of

many fruit books ensured they were 'publishing for the few'. Robert Hogg (1818–1897), a fanatical pomologist, acerbically stated 'the Pomonas are all of such a class, as from their great cost to be regarded more as works of art, than of general utility'.[66] Despite this, he co-authored the *Herefordshire Pomona* (1876), a fabulous example of the art.

Gooseberries

The variations and changes in cultivated plants, compared to their wild forms, were described in detail by Charles Darwin in *The variation of animals and plants under domestication* (1868), whilst Alphonse de Candolle (1806–1893) catalogued the origins of domesticated plants in *Origin of cultivated plants* (1884). A dramatic example that attracted Darwin's attention was the increase in the size of gooseberry fruits that had been achieved by gardeners from the north of England, especially Lancashire, during the late eighteenth and early nineteenth centuries. Domesticated gooseberries are derived from wild *Ribes uva-crispa*, which is native to northern Europe. Gooseberries had been grown in Britain since the Middle Ages. However, it was in the nineteenth century, when hundreds of named varieties were available, that the wealth of variation the species contained was revealed. Cultivated gooseberry cultivars vary in features such as habit, leaf type, thorniness, flowering and fruiting date, and fruit shape and colour. A wild gooseberry fruit weighs about 8 g (about ⅓ oz). By 1786, fruit weights had doubled; thirty years later, the largest cultivated gooseberry fruits were weighing in at about 40 g (about 1½ oz) each, and by 1852 they were reaching 58 g (about 2 oz). In just over 75 years,

FIGURE 29 Robert Hogg's *Herefordshire Pomona* (1876) is one of the most fabulous examples of a form of botanical publication that took the illustration of plants to a new level of magnificence and cost. Such volumes were not for the practical gardener; they were for the libraries of the very wealthy.

individual cultivated gooseberry fruits were being harvested that were over seven times the weight of wild gooseberry fruits. Darwin describes

> this gradual, and on the whole steady increase of weight from the latter part of the last century to the year 1852, ... due to improved methods of cultivation, for extreme care is now taken; the branches and roots are trained, composts are made, the soil is mulched, and only a few berries are left on each bush; but the increase no doubt is in main part due to the continued selection of seedlings which have been found to be more and more capable of yielding such extraordinary fruit.[67]

In modern language, a plant's appearance is a combination of nature and nurture; to get the best from a plant, the best nature must be nurtured. Gardeners excel at nurturing plants, even if the nature of the plants they try to grow is less than ideal.

The daily caffeine fix

The foundation of the Rio de Janeiro Botanic Garden, in 1808, was explicitly to further the economic advantage of Brazil. In a directive, published in 1811, this role was made clear:

> [the Board is] directing also a botanical garden for the culture of exotic plants ... promoting the culture of nutmeg, camphor, clove, cinnamon, pepper and cochineal cacti; gaining the necessary experience to know the best way to grow and spread them and lead to the greatest degree of perfection possible in the planting of plantations of quality wood, such as peroba, tapinhoans, cinnamon, vinháticoa, teak, etc. and, finally, directing and promoting the creation of good pastures for the sustenance of the cattle ranch and all articles concerning efficient agriculture.[68]

In 1822, the English diarist Maria Graham (1785–1842), who was living in Rio, observed that

> This garden was destined by the King for the cultivation of the oriental spices and fruits, and above all, of the tea plant, which he obtained, together with several families accustomed to its culture, from China. Nothing can be more thriving than the whole of the plants. The cinnamon, camphor, nutmeg, and clove, grow as well as in their native soil. The bread-fruit produces its fruit in perfection, and such of the oriental fruits as have been brought here ripen as well as in India. I particularly remarked the jumbo malacca, from India, and the longona (*Euphoria Longona*), a dark kind of lechee from China. I was disappointed to find no collection of the indigenous plants. However, so much has been done as to give reasonable hopes of farther improvement, when the political state of the country shall be quiet enough to permit attention to these things.[69]

However, in 1836 the young botanist George Gardner, who had just arrived in Rio from Britain, steeped in the ideas of British imperial botany, saw the Botanic Garden differently and observed that 'with the exception of a few East Indian trees and shrubs, and a few herbaceous European plants, there is little to entitle it to that name. Of the immense number of beautiful plants indigenous to the country, I saw few.'[70] Gardner had come to the Americas with a view of botanic gardens moulded by mature European institutions such as Kew and the University of Glasgow. Several years later, Gardner was more appreciative of Brazilian efforts to cultivate exotic plants, when he commented on a botanic garden near Ouro Preto, one of the colonial gold-mining towns in the interior of Brazil:

> principally intended for the propagation of useful exotic plants, to be given gratis to those who may apply for them.

64

I found the plants principally cultivated here, to be the Tea plant, Cinnamon, the Jaca, Breadfruit Mango, &c. Several acres are devoted to the cultivation of tea, of which a considerable quantity is manufactured yearly, and sold in the city at about the same price as that which is imported from China.[71]

Despite its cultural importance, especially to the British, tea, and the caffeine it contains, can hardly be described as a necessity of life. Until the arrival of chocolate, c. 1502, Europeans survived without caffeine. By 1650 the first coffee house in England had been established in Oxford and coffee houses soon mushroomed in English cities, becoming associated with the socio-political and intellectual revolutions of the seventeenth and eighteenth centuries. Caffeine, the active chemical in coffee, became a national addiction. Coffee was supplemented by chocolate and tea.

Humans use all the main caffeine-producing plant genera. Tea (*Camellia sinensis*), coffee (*Coffea arabica* and *C. robusta*) and chocolate (*Theobroma cacao*) are immediately familiar. The least familiar caffeine sources are the southern South American maté, made from the leaves of a species of holly (*Ilex paraguariensis*), cola nuts (*Cola sp.*), from the seeds of West African trees, and guaraná (*Paullinia cupana*), made from the seeds of a Brazilian liana. With the exception of tea, all these plants are tropical or subtropical, and naturally distributed outside of areas that have historically been under British control.

Coffee

The coffee genus comprises some one hundred species, distributed through tropical Africa to the Mascarines.

However, only three species, *Coffea arabica*, *C. robusta* and *C. liberica*, are commercially important. *Coffea arabica* is naturally distributed in the mountains of south-west Ethiopia. The legend of the discovery of the peculiar properties of coffee is a familiar one of giddy sheep being observed after eating the coffee shrub's berries. By AD 1000, coffee was being cultivated by Arabs on the Red Sea coast. In 1718, the Cambridge Professor of Botany and horticultural enthusiast Richard Bradley (c. 1688–1732) was enthusing about the Dutch and their success in growing coffee in Holland and her colonies:

> In the *Amsterdam Garden*, which is so famous for curious *Plants*, I have seen some of these Trees near eighteen Foot high, so full of *Berries*, that several Pound Weight of Fruit was gather'd off of two Trees only. The *Hollanders* first got Plants from *Arabia*, which they afterwards planted about *Batavia*, and having increas'd them there, they supply'd the *Garden* at *Amsterdam* with them, and have now raised so many from Seeds that ripen'd in *Holland*, that they have sent over several Trees to their Settlement at *Surinam* in the *West-Indies*, in order to cultivate them in that Country, where they will undoubtedly turn to good Account.[72]

Bradley was convinced that the propagation of coffee 'in the *South* Parts of *Carolina* … would be well worth our Trial, if that Country remains in our Hands'.[73] Coffee never became a significant crop for the early North American colonists, and the Thirteen Colonies themselves were lost to Britain by the end of the eighteenth century. Bradley's thoughts on economic self-sufficiency were reflected in the actions of Carolus Linnaeus and the Swedish government in the eighteenth century, when methods for the cultivation of all economic plants in the borders of Sweden were promoted; this policy failed.

FIGURE 30 Mark Catesby was one of the great plant collectors of the early eighteenth century. Through the patronage of a cartel of wealthy gentlemen Catesby collected plants through the southern United States of America and the Bahamas. In addition to herbarium specimens and seeds, Catesby also made watercolours of these plants. Catesby published the watercolours in his *Natural History of Carolina, Georgia, Florida and the Bahama Islands* (1754). Catesby's engraving of his own watercolour of cocoa is shown here.

Chocolate

Theobroma, 'food of the gods', the source of chocolate, is a genus of about twenty neotropical tree species. In the Americas, only *T. cacao* has been extensively cultivated. This cultivation was ancient even before Columbus encountered the seeds on his fourth voyage. In August 1502, off the Bay Islands of Honduras, Columbus captured a huge Mayan trading canoe and among the treasures he took were cocoa beans. This was Columbus's one and only encounter with a plant which, within a century and a half, would be causing a sensation across Europe. As the Spanish conquistadors conquered Mexico, they became familiar with the importance of cocoa beans to the Aztecs, as both a currency and a drink. However, it fell to the Italian Girolamo Benzoni (b. c. 1519), in his *La Historia del Mundo Novo* (1575), to be the first European to describe cocoa and chocolate as a drink: 'it seemed more a drink for pigs, than a drink for humanity … the taste is somewhat bitter, it satisfies and refreshes the body, but does not inebriate'.[74] The Spanish had been 'given' a plant that had benefited from two millennia of Mayan horticultural skills. However, wider cocoa cultivation needed to await the development of the European chocolate market and a source of cheap labour – slaves.

There are three main types of cocoa. The high-quality, low-yielding *criollo* type comes from Central America, whilst the Amazon basin has spawned the high-yielding, hardy and vigorous *forastero* type. The *trinitario* type, a hybrid that was developed when both the *criollo* and *forastero* types were introduced to Trinidad, combines the characteristics of the two parents. In the 1820s, the Portuguese transported *forastero*

seedlings from Brazil to the island of São Tomé off West Africa, and then on to the West African mainland. Further movements involved the British taking plants to Sri Lanka and the Dutch taking plants to Java. Eventually West African *forastero* cocoa trees dominated cocoa production; hardiness won over taste.

Tea

The gardener is familiar with the tea genus as camellias. Commercial tea was known for thousands of years only in the Chinese medical literature, and until the mid-nineteenth century China was the only commercial source of tea in Western Europe. Human use of tea has created a complex taxonomy that recognises specific features of the tea plant selected for during cultivation. Thus tea varieties are sometimes recognised as separate species. Processing differences produce black and green tea, which led Linnaeus to the erroneous conclusion that there were two species. Difficulties over supply from China meant that there were strong economic imperatives for the British to grow tea outside of its presumed native range. However, the native distribution of tea is controversial. In the nineteenth century, the British introduced tea from China to India, and discovered tea growing in Assam. Experimental introductions had been tried earlier; tea was introduced to Java from China in 1690 but it was not commercially viable until seed was introduced from Japan in 1824. Indeed, tea cultivation in India was apparently uneconomic until the Assam types were discovered and introduced to cultivation in 1878, via the Calcutta Botanic Garden.

The British were not the only European colonial power interested in the cultivation of tea. The Botanic

Garden in Rio de Janeiro, at the base of Corcovado, was founded by Dom João VI (1767–1826), ruler of Brazil. Portugal, the colonial power, thought Brazil would be a good alternative to China as a source of tea. In 1814, tea plants and 300 Chinese workers with knowledge of tea cultivation arrived in Rio. The plantation was a great success, and in 1817 6,000 plants were producing tea commercially. The German travelling artist Johann Moritz Rugendas (1802–1858) first visited Brazil in 1824; together with the French artist Jean-Baptiste Debret (1768–1848), he moulded Europeans' images of early-nineteenth-century Brazil. Initially, Rugendas was the artist on Georg Heinrich von Langsdorff's (1774–1852) expedition to Brazil, but severe personal differences between the two men soon meant they went their separate ways. The Scottish botanist and tea-drinker George Gardner observed that the product 'in appearance is scarcely to be distinguished from that of Chinese manufacture, but the flavour is inferior, having more of an herby taste'.[75] The quality of the tea produced by the plantation was clearly not high enough for the British market, the largest international tea consumer of the day, and eventually it was abandoned.

The great riches discovered by adventurers and explorers in new lands were not the immediately gratifying gewgaws and artefacts of gold and gemstones; they were the plants and knowledge that have ultimately fed, healed, built and enslaved human societies. Today, a country's animal and plant resources are seen to be as important as its mineral and cultural resources. Any garden is a tapestry of botanical histories. Some plants are native, some have been introduced, and others have evolved in the garden. Some plants are medicinal, some are food, some are educational, some require conservation, and some are merely pretty. However, for a plant to be in the garden, the technology of horticulture and the science of botany must work together. Each plant needs to have been successfully transported to the garden and be able to grow, survive and be propagated.

FIGURE 31 *Chinese tea plantation in the Rio de Janeiro Botanic Garden.* Rugendas's lithograph of a Chinese tea plantation in Rio Botanic Garden, published in *Voyage pittoresque dans le Brésil* (1835), presents an idyll set against the improbably located Corcovado and Pão de Açúcar hills. Slaves are at work on a seed bed, being directed by a Chinese worker, whilst another Chinese worker waters the ground. More slaves work in the background. Under the shade of a breadfruit tree and a parasol, a white gentleman appears to be directing activities through a translator and Chinese intermediary.

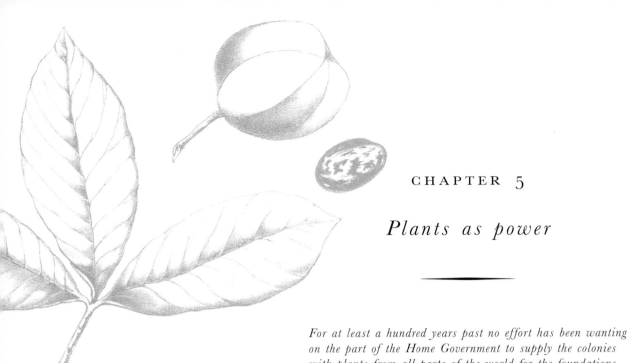

CHAPTER 5

Plants as power

For at least a hundred years past no effort has been wanting on the part of the Home Government to supply the colonies with plants from all parts of the world for the foundations of new cultures.[76]

Daniel Morris, *Report on the Economic Resources of the West Indies*, 1898

THE stereotypical British breakfast of tea, toast and marmalade bears a botanical footprint of multiple botanical adventures. By the end of the seventeenth century, tea was becoming a fashionable drink in England. However, all tea was imported from the south of Imperial China, and no European knew anything about the plant, how it was grown or even how the final product was prepared. Ultimately, tea transformed English society, was a driver of the Industrial Revolution in the early nineteenth century, maintained the opium trade with China and became a new crop for colonial India. Milk and butter are likely to be produced from cattle raised on pastures improved by the inclusion of introduced grasses and legumes. Sugar can be made from either beet (*Beta vulgaris* ssp. *vulgaris*) or cane (*Saccharum officinarum*). Since antiquity, northern European *B. vulgaris* has been known to contain sugar but it was Franz Karl Achard (1753–1821) who started to

select high-sugar-content beets from the White Silesian fodder beet in 1784, which led to today's familiar sugar beet. In contrast, sugar cane was introduced from Southeast Asia across the tropics, and the sweet tooth of the British was at least partially responsible for that 'execrable sum of all villainies', the slave trade. Bread wheat originated in southwest Asia thousands of years ago and passed around the globe though many different empires, including those of Rome, Greece, Persia, Spain, France, Britain and China. Marmalade, based on oranges and sugar, is an English modification of a Portuguese preserve, originally based on the quince (*Cydonia oblonga*), a species introduced to southern Europe from the Caucusus and Kurdistan. Oranges (*Citrus sinensis*), native to China, and citrus fruit were the subjects of some of the earliest plant collection expeditions. In Japan there is a monument to Tajimamori, who went to China at the command of the eleventh Japanese emperor, Suinin (29 BC–AD 70), to search for the 'ever shining citrus', believed to be an elixir of immortality, in AD 61. Oranges were soon to be important crops in the Mediterranean, and scattered into the Americas by Iberian empires. As a young man, Bernal Díaz (1492–?1580) marched across Mexico with Hernán Cortés (1485–1547) and was involved in the subsequent conquest of Mexico in 1519. At the age of seventy-six, he described his role in these events and in an expedition he made to the Yucatan Peninsula from Cuba, led by Juan de Grijalva (c. 1489–1527), in 1518. Díaz claimed to have

> sowed these [orange] pips, which I had brought from Cuba, for it is rumoured that we were returning to settle. The trees came up well, for when the *papas* saw that they were different plants from any they knew, they protected them and watered them and kept them free from weeds. All the oranges in the province are descendants of these trees.[77]

Furthermore, citrus eventually enabled British sailors to survive the nutritional rigours of long sea voyages.

Theatrum Botanicum

The multifarious origins of plants of commerce and cultivation are vividly revealed on the title page of John Parkinson's *Theatrum Botanicum* (1640). The subtitle, *An universall and compleate Herball*, emphasised Parkinson's view that the *Theatrum* contained all of the plants known from the four continents, the division of which is clearly displayed on the title page. This title page reveals much about seventeenth-century English perceptions of society and the limitations of botanical knowledge. For example, maize is associated with Asia, taking up Jean

Ruel's claim from 1536 that maize was of Turkish origin. Many of the familiar plants portrayed with Europe also had their origins in Asia – for example, oranges, apples and tulips. The plant sketches are copied from many different sources, and some show that the original artists had not studied the plants they were portraying – for example, the banana, pineapple and millet.

Botanical trade and adventure

Any British garden bears similar hallmarks of botanical trade and adventure, networks of information exchange and horticultural skill. In late winter, the distinctive and heavily scented flowers of Chinese viburnums and North American witch hazel attract both the eye and the nose. Spring reveals the muted colours of European hellebores and a kaleidoscope of Mediterranean crocuses and Middle Eastern and Central Asian tulips, whilst the patchwork of apple, cherry and pear blossom discloses plants that have travelled in tortuous manner from their native homes. Summer brings with it a riot of colour contributed from all the continents: European myrtles, Asian buddleia, African marigolds, North American sunflowers, South American petunias and Australian leptospermums.

Europe's empires

In the fifteenth century, England's concept of the world was narrower than other European powers, especially Portugal and Spain. Major exploratory expeditions had set out from the Iberian Peninsula in the late fifteenth and early sixteenth centuries. For the Portuguese, Bartolomeu Dias sailed down the west coast of Africa to the Cape of Good Hope (1486–88) and Vasco da Gama rounded the Cape to reach the west coast of India (1497–99). For the Spanish, Christopher Columbus discovered the New World and explored the Caribbean (1492–93; 1498–1500; 1502–04); Amerigo Vespucci, who lent his name to two continents, explored the north-east coast of South America (1499–1500); and Fernão de Magalhães (Magellan), together with Juan Sebastian del Cano (1476–1526), were the first to circumnavigate the earth (1519–22). Pope Alexander VI, via the Treaty of Tordesillas (1494), divided South America between the Spanish and Portuguese. In the early sixteenth century, although England's old enemy France, and Holland, began to assert their ambitions in the New World, the supremacy of the Iberian empires appeared unassailable.

The only significant expeditions of empire by the English before the sixteenth century were those of Italian Giovanni Cabato (John Cabot) to Newfoundland (1497–98). However, power waxes and wanes, and by the late sixteenth century Holland and England were taking exploration and exploitation of foreign natural resources seriously. The English made expeditions in search of north-west (Martin Frobisher, 1576–78) and north-east (Hugh Willoughby and Richard Chancellor, 1553) routes to India. Francis Drake (1577–80) and Thomas Cavendish (1586–88) circumnavigated the world, whilst John Hawkins established a slave trade between Africa and the Caribbean (1562–68).

By the end of the seventeenth century, England's imperial ambitions were coalescing; they would reach their zenith in the nineteenth century, when the British Empire encircled the globe. However, in 1690 England's outposts were much more modest. The greatest concentration of English interest was in the New World. In North America, Hudson Bay was surrounded by lands controlled by the eponymous Company and the English had colonised a fringe of the east coast, from the Carolinas in the south to Newfoundland in the north. England's other New World interests were to be found in the Caribbean (Bahamas, Bermuda, Jamaica, St Kitts and Nevis, Antigua, Montserrat and Barbados) and Belize. In the New World, the English were directly confronted by the empires of France, Holland and Spain.

In other parts of the globe, England's colonies were much more scattered, although she continued to be confronted by European colonial powers. In Africa, Fort James (Upper Guinea) and, further south, the Gold Coast forts were the points of departure for ignoble cargoes of wretchedness that were to be enslaved to English colonial interests in the New World. In Asia, colonies in the Indian subcontinent were to be found in Surat, Mumbai, Tellicherry, Madras and Calcutta, with the furthest extent of the nascent empire in Bencoolen (Sumatra). The most isolated part of the growing empire was a volcanic peak, St Helena, in the Atlantic ocean. This island was to become the final prison of Napoleon, who dared to challenge British imperial interests at the start of the nineteenth century.

Evoking an ancient image of evil, an Italian satirical chromolithograph, *Allegoria sull' impero Inglese* (1878), was published that caricatured the influence of the nineteenth-century British Empire as a snake wrapped firmly around the globe. However, European empires were in decline, and today the British dependent territories Bermuda, Montserrat and St Helena are the

FIGURE 32   The title page of John Parkinson's *Theatrum Botanicum* (1640) clearly shows the position of continents in relation to the divine. The Tetragrammaton (יהוה) is flanked on the right by Europe and the left by Asia, below which are representations of Adam and Solomon. At the bottom, Africa and the New World flank a portrait of an ageing Parkinson. Crowned and armed with sword and cornucopia, Europe is sumptuously dressed and conveyed in an elaborate carriage drawn by a pair of horses; she is surrounded by fourteen species, which include pear, orange, lemon, pomegranate, pine, pink, peach, tulip, strawberry, wheat, apple and grape. An elegantly dressed Asia is carried by a rhinoceros and armed with a spear; she is surrounded by the mythical Scythian lamb and ten real species, which include banana, coconut, clove, cotton, nutmeg, black pepper, lily, maize, a proliferating daisy and iris. In contrast, an unarmed Africa and the New World, armed with bow and arrow, are all but naked, being carried by a zebra and llama, respectively. The New World is surrounded by sunflower, passion flower, pineapple, cassava, opuntia and a barrel cactus. Africa is surrounded by six species, which includes date palm, dragon tree, millet and African marigold.

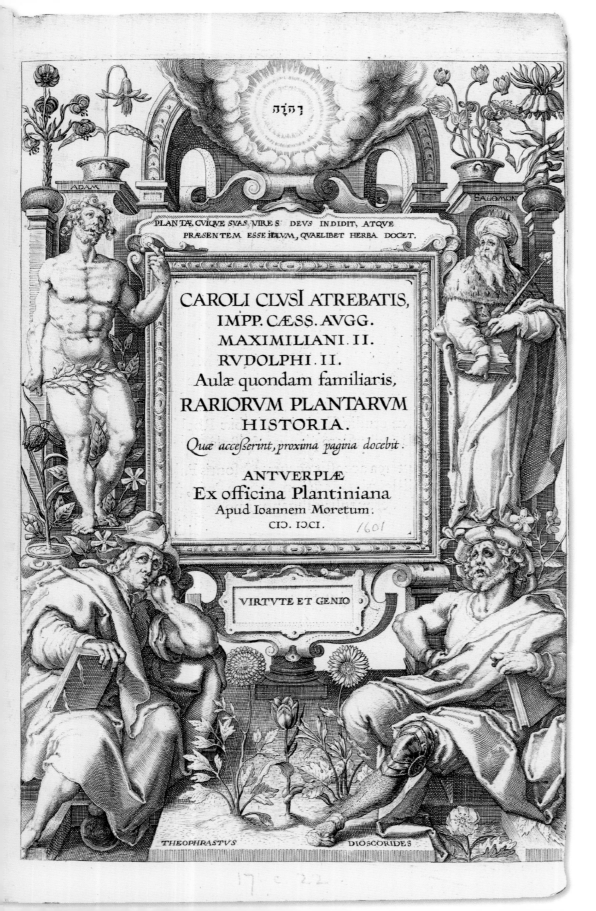

PLANTÆ CVIQVE SVAS VIRES DEVS INDIDIT, ATQVE
PRÆSENTEM ESSE IDEM, QVÆLIBET HERBA DOCET.

CAROLI CLVSI ATREBATIS,
IMPP. CÆSS. AVGG.
MAXIMILIANI. II.
RVDOLPHI. II.
Aulæ quondam familiaris,
RARIORVM PLANTARVM
HISTORIA.
Quæ accesserint, proxima pagina docebit.

ANTVERPIÆ
Ex officina Plantiniana
Apud Ioannem Moretum.
CIƆ. IƆCI.

1601

VIRTVTE ET GENIO

FIGURE 33   The title page to Carolus
Clusius's *Rariorum Plantarum Historia*
(1601) combines plants and real
and mythical figures in a powerful
allegorical interpretation of the transfer
of knowledge. The divine botanical
knowledge of Adam and Solomon is
implied to have passed to Theophrastus
and Dioscorides. Plants are arranged
in pots or as isolated specimens, in the
style familiar in Leiden. Above Adam is
a potted martagon lily and dog's-tooth
violet, whilst above Solomon there is a
potted cyclamen and crown imperial.
At Adam's feet are lesser periwinkle and
fritillary. Between Theophrastus and
Dioscorides are isolated specimens of
tulip and dahlias. Overarching this entire
allegory is the Tetragrammaton (יהוה).

rump of England's late-seventeenth-century overseas interests.

Transporting plants

The tantalizing catalogue of the natural world revealed in a herbarium delights the imagination. The usefulness of these specimens relies on the collector's skills at preparing them so they are a credit to her efforts, often under arduous conditions, rather than embarrassments more appropriate for the compost heap. In the late nineteenth century, the botanist William Harvey made the case for timely preparation of specimens:

> no time must unnecessarily be lost in preparing the more delicate Algae for drying ... if left for a few hours ... will completely decompose and become worthless.[78]

Once preserved, if kept dry and free of pests, and barring Acts of God, herbarium specimens are easily transported and stored.

Herbarium specimens are botanically exciting corpses, which are unlikely to satisfy a general public that wants to grow plants for commercial, medicinal, horticultural or agricultural purposes. People want to be surrounded by living, not dead, plants. Some of the most popular bulbs of European gardens were introduced by the Flemish botanist Carolus Clusius 1526–1609), the most significant botanist of the late sixteenth century. He was instrumental in the movement of tulips from the Ottoman Empire, through the Holy Roman Empire to Protestant Holland, where they arrived in 1571.

Clusius, in a long botanical career, was familiar with studying plants in the field, in the herbarium and in the garden. He had worked in many parts of Europe,

including for Emperor Maximilian II (1527–1576) in Vienna, and ended his career at the botanic gardens in Leiden, the Netherlands. *Rariorum plantarum historia* (1601) is Clusius's most famous work and illustrates Clusius's plants from Spain and Hungary and rare plants from other parts of the world. The most significant of these was the Jacobean lily (*Sprekelia formosissima*) from Central America. Clusius states: 'I have only one plant ... sent by the learned doctor Simon D. Tovar, Spanish physician, which flowered in June 1594.' He was seventy-five years old when it was published and in a reflective mood, enthusing about the delight of studying plants from different regions and bringing them into cultivation. The allegorical title page shows plants that would become popular in gardens.

In 1763, the draper and horticulturalist Peter Collinson could take pride in his garden at Mill Hill and

> stand with wonder and amazement when I view the inconceivable variety of flowers, shrubs, and trees, now in our gardens, and what there were forty years ago; in that time what quantites from all North America have annually been collected by my means and procuring, and from some years past a great variety of seeds are brought from China, and many fine plants raised; ... and from Siberia many curious shrubs and flowers, very few gardens, if any, excel mine at Mill Hill, for the rare exotics which are my delight.[79]

In March 1694,[80] Bobart the Younger had visited the celebrated gardens of the Duchess of Badminton, 'who daly makes appeare the transcendent wealth of the Vegetable Kingdome', and was keen for her to purchase some of his plants: 'I send now a packet of such seeds as to me seem hopefull' and 'I send allsoe Madam a note of such good plants as I do not remember to have seen in yr Graces plantations.' Safe transport of the growing plants was a major concern for Bobart, who deftly pushed the responsibility on to the Duchess:

> The Plants herein mention'd, both in pots and wthout pots, may safely be handled, transplanted and carryed, about a fortnight hence; and if it may be consist wth yr Grace's pleasure to use any of them, it appears to me, the best way to send a man and horse of yr owne choosing, rather than commit them to the carelessness of a publick Carrier.

Three hundred years later, transport routes may be more rapid, carriers may be similar, but the safe transport of living plants remains a problem. Consider how much packing and care is needed to transport safely a newly purchased plant from the garden centre.

Transporting seeds

Seeds are the easiest means to transport living flowering plants. They are packages of potential that allow plants to be transported naturally vast distances and to survive for tens, if not hundreds, of years. Most seeds are difficult to damage, are naturally resistant to desiccation, will remain dormant until stimulated to germinate, and are conveniently sized for transport. There are numerous, often apocryphal, stories of seeds being germinated from ancient grave deposits. Most of these prove to be little more than hoaxes or contamination; some are more thoroughly authenticated. In 2006, there was short-lived public interest in the seedlings that had germinated from three seeds discovered in the British National Archive. The seeds had been collected by a Dutch merchant, Jan Teerlink, during a trip to the Cape of Good Hope in 1803, and, for seeds, had been stored

FIGURE 34 (*right*) *Magnolia grandiflora* was introduced to the United Kingdom by Mark Catesby in 1734, and illustrated in his *Natural History of Carolina, Georgia, Florida and the Bahama Islands* (1754). The plant was a sensation in early-eighteenth-century Britain. Through careful manipulation of growing conditions gardeners were able to propagate this slow-growing plant successfully.

FIGURE 35 (*overleaf*) The breadfruit (*Artocarpus incisa*) is shown here in a lithograph by Walter Fitch and published in *Curtis's Botanical Magazine* (1828). This highly versatile fruit was originally a species from the South Pacific. The spread of breadfruit from the Pacific to the Caribbean in the eighteenth century has become highly romanticized through its association with the mutiny on the *Bounty* and the fate of Captain Bligh. Today breadfruit is found throughout the tropics.

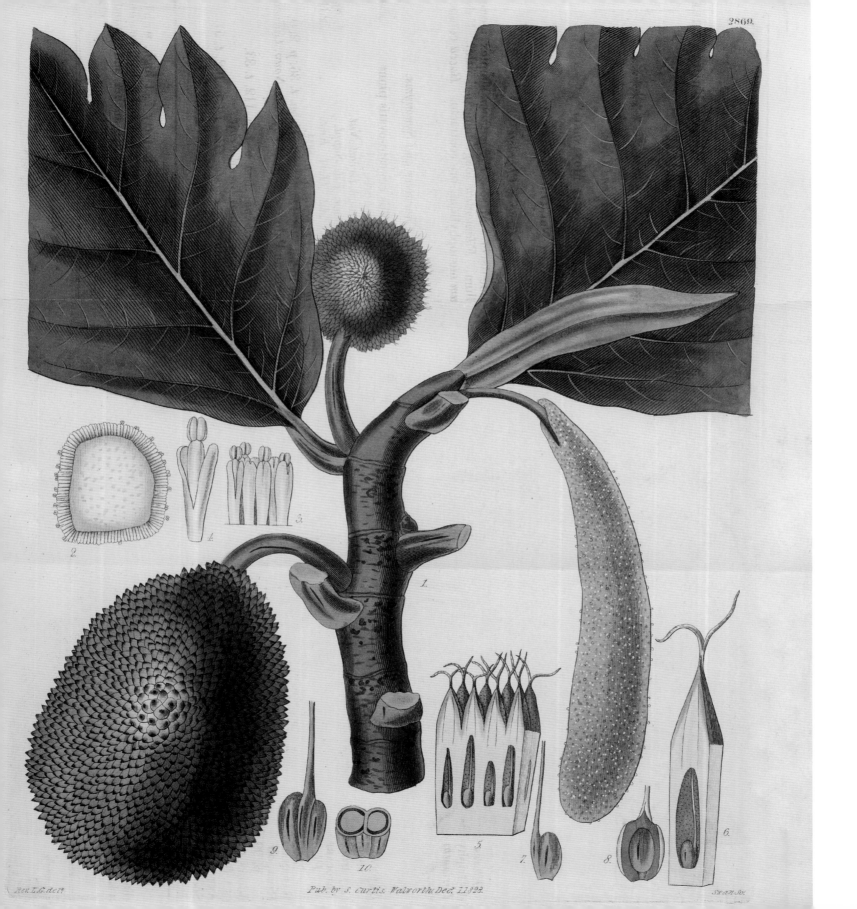

Pub. by S. Curtis. Walworth. Dec.r 1.1828.

under less than ideal conditions. More dramatically still, a group of researchers were able to germinate a seed of the sacred lotus from a Chinese lakebed; the seed was carbon-dated at 1,288 years old. The ability of seeds to survive long-term storage has become a major strand of global plant conservation strategies, whether it is the Millennium Seedbank at Wakehurst Place or the vast Global Seed Vault, 120 metres inside a mountain, under the ice of Svalbard. Such vast collections had their intellectual origins in the economically important seed collections created by the Soviet geneticist Nicolai Vavilov (1887–1943), and, depending on one's viewpoint, may be considered as sepulchres, arks or temples of plant conservation. However, the fact that many seeds remained dormant, and therefore could be stored and germinated when needed, had been known to farmers for thousands of years.

Based on eleven years' collecting experience in North America in the early eighteenth century, Mark Catesby could provide authoritative advice about the practicalities of seed collection and transport from the Thirteen Colonies. In the case of the magnificent *Magnolia grandiflora*, Catesby states:

> procuring the seeds of this tree in good condition, the success depends in a great measure on their being kept in such a degree of heat and moisture as is requisite to preserve them in their long passage; for if they are put up too dry, their juices will remain inactive and make no effort towards vegetation; if they are kept too warm and moist, they will sprout in the box and perish; and too much moisture and cold rots them.[81]

Catesby goes on to give specific instructions about when to harvest the seeds from the trees: 'the seeds manifest their beginning to ripen by bursting forth from the little cells wherein they are contained'. His instructions for packing the seeds for the voyage back to England were equally precise:

> prepare a square box of the size of a bushel or less, at the bottom of which put a layer of light earth two inches deep, spread thereon a single layer of seeds, then again a layer of earth, and so dispose your seeds and earth alternately, stratum super stratum, until the box be full; then nail down the lid and let it be placed between decks.

Based on his experience Catesby even provided advice on successful germination and establishment of these magnolias in the English climate.

Seeds are not the answer to all plant transportation problems. Some seeds simply are not dormant. The seeds of the *Dipterocarpaceae*, a family of important Southeast Asian timber trees, survive for only a few days. Fruit tree varieties, if they are to breed true, must be transported as either potted plants or graft material. Similarly, the majority of colour and form variants that are so familiar in garden plants cannot be transported as seed. When nineteenth century gardeners tried to germinate tropical orchid seeds they were often frustrated with failure. They did not know that the minute seeds of orchids, which are little more than an embryo surrounded by a seed coat, need specific fungal associations if they are to establish successfully. Even if seeds are dormant, elaborate conditions were, and are, often used to break dormancy. Plants of the world's savannahs may need fire or smoke to break seed dormancy, whilst some seeds need to pass through animals. Finally, time, patience and luck are needed for successful seed germination. Bobart's 'hopefull' seeds were from 'partly East Indies, Partly West Indies, and perhaps some out of our Garden; perhaps where nothing is wanting some may be raised, and our Nation enriched therwith'.[82] Whereas a handful of seeds can be dropped in the pocket, growing plants have to be seriously looked after in the hostile environment of a ship at sea.

Transporting plants

Joseph Banks, characteristically, had forthright views on fitting out vessels for botanical exploration; views which eventually meant he refused to go on Cook's second expedition. Banks was one of the architects of the 1787 expedition to collect breadfruit in the South Pacific and transport them to the West Indies. He was adamant that,

> as the sole object of Government in Chartering this Vessel [the *Bounty*] in our Service at a very considerable expense is to furnish the West Indian Islands with the Bread-fruit & other valuable productions of the East, the Master & Crew of her must not think it a grievance to give up the best part of her accommodation for that purpose.[83]

William Bligh (1754–1817) discovered this meant the quarters he might have expected as the Master of the *Bounty* had been converted to accommodate 629 potted breadfruit plants. This expedition was a famous failure. However, in 1791, with his experience of the earlier expedition, Bligh sailed from England for the South Seas to complete his mission. This time he was successful and in 1793 he delivered 544 plants to the Botanic Garden in St Vincent, 620 to Jamaica and 12 to the governor of St Helena. As Banks implied, the costs and risks of moving growing plants long distances, in terms of lives and money, were high and affordable only to Governments or the very wealthy. With some sense of irony, William Hooker, in 1828, reported on a living breadfruit in Glasgow: 'both imported and kept alive in our shores with great difficulty: so that we dare not expect to see it ever flourishing in Europe'.[84]

Glazed growing cases

In 1823, Nathaniel Bagshaw Ward (1791–1868), an amateur naturalist and general practitioner from the East End of London, made the necessary transportation breakthrough: the Wardian Case, a closed, glazed box that protects growing plants from unfavourable conditions. Before the Wardian Case, approximately 99 per cent of plants imported to the UK from China were lost; after the Wardian Case was introduced losses were reduced to 14 per cent and it is said that Hooker imported six times as many exotics into Kew in fifteen years as had been sent in the previous century. This simple technology was soon adopted worldwide and, combined with the development of high-speed transport routes such as tea clippers and steam ships, was the standard means by which growing plants were moved around the world until after the Second World War. Wardian Cases helped the British move tea from China to India, rubber from Brazil to Sri Lanka, and quinine from South America to India. Ward saw a role for his cases in 'their application to the relief of the *physical* and *moral* wants of densely crowded populations in the large cities' and they become part of Victorian and Edwardian households as the terrarium.[85] With Ward's cases, the many as well as the few could afford a glimpse of the tropics.

Plants for power

Plants had been deliberately moved by people long before 1500. As the extent of the world opened to European empires, their governments considered the provision of exotic luxuries to satisfy the tastes and pretensions of their gods and secular populace to be important. Similar ideas drove deliberate plant movements in the Ancient World. In 1495 BC the Egyptian pharaoh Hatshepsut (c. 1508–1458 BC) sent a trading expedition to the land of Punt (probably along the coast of the Horn of Africa). The deeds of the expedition Hatshepsut funded were sufficiently notable to be recorded in friezes in the Temple of Deir el-Bahari, south-east of the Valley of the Kings in Egypt. This was the earliest recorded government-funded plant collection expedition, and appears to have yielded great riches for a 'handful of trade beads'. Botanically, the focus of this expedition appears to have been *Boswellia sacra*, the source of frankincense, which was planted in the Temple of Amun. Importantly, if these trees survived being planted in the Temple the valuable resins could be extracted, a supply could be guaranteed and the need for costly future collecting expeditions circumvented. Hatshepsut provided the scheme for all future exploitation of valuable plant resources: ensure there is a supply of the resource where it can be readily controlled.

Hatshepsut was not alone in the Ancient World in linking plants with power. In his Great Temple at Karnak, Hatshepsut's stepson, Pharaoh Thutmosis III (c. 1450 BC), had a botanical frieze carved to illustrate his victorious Syrian campaign. The Assyrian king Sargon (d. 705 BC) created parks specifically to grow introduced plants. Following the Roman conquest of Britain, trees such as figs and apples were introduced to bring 'variety, charm, colour and usefulness'.[86] The movement of cultivated apples by the Romans was merely the latest episode in a complex story involving diverse cultures from Assyria, China, Central Asia and Greece.

Following the Crusades, Middle Eastern plants such as quince (*Cydonia oblonga*) and soapwort (*Saponaria officinalis*) were introduced to European monastic gardens. During the same period, the economic and medicinal value of products such as pepper (*Piper nigrum* and *P. longum*), cinnamon (*Cinnamomum verum*) and nutmeg (*Myristica fragrans*) meant that there were great economic stimuli to introduce these plants outside of their native ranges. Eventually, with the establishment and expansion of botanic gardens in the seventeenth and eighteenth centuries, the institutional structures for deliberate plant introduction changed.

Resource exploitation was an important imperial activity; colonies produced raw materials the imperial power needed. It is tempting to assume that this was done by trial and error. However, a system of plant movement across empires was critical to colonial resource exploitation. Crop introduction was not ad hoc but based on communication, cooperation and exchanges among botanists. Central to this system were: the search for new crops; the exchange of information, plants and seeds across the empire; and testing new plants in different environmental conditions. By the eighteenth century, the Spanish monarchy had recognised the economic importance of introduced plants and engaged Hipólito Ruiz (1754–1816) and José

FIGURE 36   Edouard Naville's work *The Temple of Deir El Bahari* (1898–1908) reproduces the friezes that tell the story of the expedition that Hatshepsut ordered to the land of Punt in 1495 BC. Carefully potted trees are shown being carried between poles by four bearers onto a boat. The care with which these trees are treated is a reflection of their value, as is the planting of these trees in the temple of Amun, which is depicted in a later scene from the frieze.

Pavón (1754–1840) to explore Peru. Indeed, Spain had been one of the first European countries to benefit economically from the steady flow of exotic plants from the New World. Other European colonial powers acknowledged the strategic importance of plant resources for food and medicines and established networks of gardens across the tropics.

West Indies

Between 1762 and 1766, the *Transactions* of the Society of Arts offered rewards to anyone who 'should cultivate a spot in the West Indies in which plants, useful in medicine and profitable articles of commerce might be propagated and where a nursery of the valuable products of Asia and the distant parts might be formed for the benefit of His Majesty'.[87] Fewer than twenty years after the Royal Botanic Garden Kew (1759) was established, the first botanic gardens in the British West Indies were formed in St Vincent (1765) and Jamaica (1774). Plants meant commerce, commerce meant profit, and profit meant power.

The St Vincent garden started well. Spices from the French West Indian islands were introduced in 1787, and transferred to Santo Domingo (cloves) and Jamaica (cinnamon). St Vincent even played a part in the (in)famous story of Captain Bligh and the breadfruit. In 1792, the St Vincent garden was enriched with botanical booty (mainly mango and cinnamon) taken from a French man-of-war. However, the fate of individual gardens was subservient to the greater good of the empire.

By 1823, London had become exasperated by the management and increasing costs of the St Vincent Botanic Garden; therefore it was transferred, lock, stock and barrel, to Trinidad. The Trinidad Botanic Gardens had been established five years earlier on an abandoned sugar estate close to the capital Port-of-Spain, and was the new jewel in the botanical crown of the British West Indies. Almost overnight, Trinidad benefited from nearly sixty years of plant acquisitions by the St Vincent Botanic Garden, and made good use of them.

In Trinidad, the living and herbarium collections were integrated and became a powerful partnership. Plants were introduced from all over the tropics for testing in field trials and, importantly, local plants were collected and studied. By the end of the century, the Trinidad Botanic Gardens were playing a central role in the agricultural economy of the island and the British West Indies more generally. In the late nineteenth century the West Indian cane sugar industry had suffered from the development of European beet sugar. The Trinidad Botanic Gardens were instrumental in identifying and distributing sugar cane strains that produced high yields in Trinidad and, importantly, were disease resistant.

The 1897 Norman Commission, although dismissive of the Trinidad Botanic Gardens' role in ornamental plant supply, emphasised the importance of the Gardens for the empire, the region and the island:

> The Botanical Department in Trinidad … should devote itself to the introduction and experimental cultivation of economic plants, and to attempts to secure improved varieties of such plants, and especially of sugar cane. It should comprise a branch for the teaching of tropical agriculture, and should form a centre from which teachers would be sent to give practical lessons in the cultivation of tropical

plants and the selection of suitable locations for growing them. ... In the mean time the Botanical Department in Trinidad should encourage the introduction and growth of the better descriptions of fruit, and give instructions as to the best means of cultivation and of packing fruit for export.[88]

Trinidad was not alone. During the eighteenth and nineteenth centuries botanic gardens had played key roles in the transfer of tung oil, ipecacuanha, coffee, rubber and tea from their native ranges to areas under European control. In Britain, the increasing importance of horticulture saw the establishment of the Royal Horticultural Society in 1804 and the creation of a new market for plant introductions. However, by the beginning of the twentieth century, the economic role of botanic gardens was waning and they were never to enjoy the same economic power again. Rather, they were to become important centres for plant conservation, recreation and education; the modern equivalents of Danvers's 1621 mission statement ('glorification of God and for the furtherance of learning') for the Oxford Botanic Garden.

Rubber

The rubber plant (*Ficus elastica*) is a familiar rubber-producing houseplant. Yet confined in our living rooms and offices, these plants are pale imitations of the 40 metre behemoths that grow in the forests of their native India and Southeast Asia. Rubbers are naturally produced by many different, unrelated plants. However, it was not until the last half of the nineteenth century that they became more than novelty products derived from plants. Rubbers became vital commodities of

the industrial age, especially for waterproof clothing, machinery washers and belts, and, importantly, pneumatic tyres for bicycles and the emerging motor car. Rubber is the most obvious gift of nineteenth-century botany and forestry to the industries of the twentieth century. However, in the killing fields of commerce in Amazonia and the Belgian Congo, this gift cost millions of lives.[89] One set of tyres for a Model T Ford cost four Congolese lives, or one thirteenth of an Amazonian life.

In 1869, James Collins, curator of the Museum of the Pharmaceutical Society, wrote an article on rubber that changed the British imperial view of this raw material. He identified the best source of rubber as the elusive Brazilian Pará rubber (*Hevea brasiliensis*). The rubbers the British had been using were of lower quality or had different properties, for example from the genus *Landolphia* from Congo, and gutta percha and jelutong from Asia. Collins made clear that he thought Pará rubber could be grown in plantation in the Southeast Asian parts of the British Empire. Clement Markham, who was knighted for masterminding the introduction of cinchona to India, noticed Collins's report and became directly involved in the introduction of rubber trees from Brazil to Southeast Asia. The plant had been identified and a course of action suggested. The problem for the powers in the imperial homeland was that they had no seeds and few ideas of where the tree was distributed, what it looked like, how the seeds could be harvested or grown and how rubber could be harvested or processed.

There had been previous attempts to introduce Pará rubber to territories of the British Empire but these had failed; even the great Amazonian explorer Richard Spruce had not acquired viable seed. Into this gap came a book, *Rough Notes of a Journey through the Wilderness from Trinidad to Para, Brazil, by Way of the Great Cataracts of the Orinoco, Atabagao, and Rio Negro* (1872), by a roguish adventurer and would-be plantation owner Henry Wickham (1846–1928), which contained Wickham's sketch of Pará rubber and a description of how it was tapped. Joseph Dalton Hooker (1817–1911), director of Kew, who had been bombarded by letters from Wickham in Amazonia, spotted the sketch and decided, through Markham, to procure seeds of Pará rubber from Wickham. The seeds were to be grown at Kew and seedlings shipped to the Southeast Asian colonies. Markham also sent Robert Cross to Amazonia to obtain seeds; if Cross met Wickham then he was to take over the whole operation (Cross and Wickham crossed paths at Liverpool, without even meeting).

Wickham was a complex character, a restless opportunist who was in the right place at the right time. He was never entirely trusted by Hooker, who thought him an arrogant, amateur outsider – traits the patrician Hooker greatly disliked. Wickham arrived at Hooker's house at Kew in the early hours of 14 June 1876 with a sample of the 70,000 Pará rubber seeds that he had just brought to Liverpool from the River Tapajos, Brazil. The next day, all 70,000 seeds were planted at Kew in a special greenhouse; by 7 July, 2,700 of the seeds had germinated and been potted on. In August 1876, 1,919 seedlings were sent to Sri Lanka in thirty-eight Wardian Cases in the care of the Kew gardener William Chapman and 1,700 seedlings arrived safely at the

FIGURE 37　In 1872, Henry Wickham published his rough sketch of the Pará rubber tree in *Rough Notes of a Journey through the Wilderness from Trinidad to Para, Brazil, by Way of the Great Cataracts of the Orinoco, Atabagao, and Rio Negro*. Together with the description of how rubber trees were tapped, Wickham became an instant authority on this Pará rubber. Pará rubber would become one of the most important industrial non-timber tree species of the late nineteenth and twentieth centuries for Europe and the United States of America.

85

Heneratgoda Gardens in Columbo on 16 September (by 1880, only 30 were alive). Fifty seedlings were also sent to Singapore but these died in harbour. In September 1876, a further 100 seedlings were sent to Sri Lanka from Kew.

Robert Cross returned to Kew on 21 November 1876 with 1,080 less-than-healthy seedlings from the margins of the River Amazon; fewer than 30 survived, and from these 100 plants were propagated and sent to Sri Lanka. On 11 June 1877, 22 seedlings were sent from Sri Lanka to Singapore. Henry Ridley (1855–1956), director of the Singapore Botanic Gardens, claimed that 75 per cent of the rubber trees grown in Malaysia had been propagated from these seedlings. One of the controversies surrounding rubber is whether these plants were propagated from Sri Lankan material that had been supplied by Wickham or by Cross; there remains no definitive answer. However, Wickham maintained that much of the early Southeast Asian planting had been inappropriate:

> A very general error seems to obtain that swampy or wet land is the fitting locality. This seems to have arisen from the 'explorers' of a few weeks naturally in going up rivers in boats would observe a group of these trees scattered along the margins. Whereas the true forests of the 'Para' Indian rubber lies back in the high lands.[90]

For over a century, the means by which Wickham obtained the seeds from Brazil, the exact place of collection, the dubious legality of Wickham's collection, and Kew's role in dispersing the seed have been debated. Wickham's involvement in the rubber story is often considered a tangible example of where the artfulness of biopiracy can lead. It is upon details that

reputations are lost and maintained; upon patronage and influence that honours are bestowed. Henry Wickham, the upstart and outsider, who was sidelined by the botanical establishment, eventually gained the favour and recognition that produced a knighthood and a comfortable retirement. In contrast, James Collins, the herald of Southeast Asian Pará rubber plantations, and Robert Cross, the establishment toiler, were sidelined and derided. The British Empire treated its servants little differently to the ways in which it treated its colonies and those countries from which it took economically valuable seeds. Once the growing conditions for rubber were correctly established, the Southeast Asian colonial plantations destroyed the Brazilian rubber economy.

Accidental movements

As well as moving plants deliberately, humans move plants accidentally. Generally, accidental plant movement is an unforeseen consequence of other activities, such as man's animals (for example, *Senecio inaequidens* from South Africa to Europe in wool in the nineteenth century) or his means of transport (for example, plantain from Europe to North America by ship in the early 1600s). As a classic 'camp follower', hemp (*Cannabis sativa*) has been widely spread from its region of nativity in temperate Asia. Unlike the majority of flowering plants, hemp has separate male and female plants. *Cannabis sativa* has been used for three main purposes: as a fibre (ssp. *sativa*), as a narcotic resin (ssp. *indica*) and as an oil seed. Hemp provided the rope to hang and haul, whilst hempen cloth was ideal for

FIGURE 38   The perceptions that people have of species may change over time. When Ludovicus Reichenbach published *Icones Florae Germanicae et Helveticae* (1838–39), many of the pheasant's eyes (*Adonis*) were considered to be serious agricultural weeds. Today, with the changes in agriculture over the past fifty years these same species are now rare and are considered to be in need of protection.

sail-making since it resists long exposure to sunlight and salt water. Resin from hemp flowers was the source of tetrahydrocannabinol and the cannabis culture. Different cultures have cultivated and selected hemp plants for different purposes; for example, those interested in the narcotic effects have tended to live close to the equator, where the plants are adapted to long days, and to favour female plants. In contrast, for fibre production, male plants have tended to be selected in northerly latitudes that are adapted to short days.

Such 'camp followers' used to be dismissed as beneath the dignified concerns of serious botanists. However, by the mid-nineteenth century, botanists were moving away from merely recording plant distributions to trying to understand them; 'camp followers' became interesting as they might give clues as to how plants establish themselves naturally. Furthermore, as transport became easier and quicker more plants were being accidentally moved. The Mexican plant known commonly as gallant soldier (*Galinsoga parviflora*) accidentally escaped from the Royal Botanic Gardens Kew in about 1860 and has since become a familiar feature of the southern English flora.

In the late nineteenth century, accidental plant introductions were recorded growing around wool-processing factories in Scotland, England and France. Similarly, warfare moves plant species; for example, during the Franco-Prussian war (1870–71) a 'siege flora' of grasses and legumes from southern France and Algeria developed around Paris. The majority of such introductions survive for only a few years before they die out; some become familiar parts of a flora with no major ecological effects; others cause severe ecological damage, and become notorious weeds.

Leaping the garden wall

Britain has about 1,800 native wild flowering plant species. However, at the dawn of the twentieth century, this figure was dwarfed by the thousands of hardy exotic species that are grown outdoors in British gardens, and the thousands more grown under glass or as houseplants. Controlled and corralled within a garden's boundaries, exotic plants present few ecological problems. Some exotic garden plants will succeed and become widely grown, others will remain the playthings of connoisseurs, and others will fail to arouse any interest. However, some will exceed beyond all expectations and become serious weeds.

In the mid-seventeenth century, the familiar purple-flowered ivy-leaved toadflax (*Cymbalaria muralis*), whose 'trailing branches … variously interwoven form a thick and beautiful kind of tapestry on old walls',[91] was a plant to be treasured in the garden. First recorded by John Parkinson in 1640 from Hatfield, this Italian introduction was a novelty. By the nineteenth century, ivy-leaved toadflax had escaped the confines of the garden and expanded its range across Britain, having found a home and habitat that suited it. The story of the Oxford ragwort (*Senecio squalidus*) is similar. It was introduced to Oxford Botanic Garden at the start of the eighteenth century, from the slopes of Mount Etna in Sicily, via a complex route that included the Duchess of Beaufort's gardens at Badminton. Oxford ragwort remained confined to the Oxford garden and the walls of the city until the early nineteenth century. Prelate dispersal, by clergymen trained in Oxford wanting a souvenir of Oxford in their new parishes, became an important element in the early history of the spread of Oxford ragwort in Britain. For example, some time before 1830 the Reverend William Bree deliberately introduced Oxford ragwort from Oxford to Allesley, in Warwickshire. Both ivy-leaved toadflax and Oxford ragwort spread had relatively benign effects on the British flora.

The same cannot be said for other garden plants that have become widespread; once an exotic plant has 'jumped the garden wall' it can have profound effects and is often very difficult to control. Three of the worst weeds in Britain today were also garden plants that have leapt the garden wall. However, reactions to these plants vary dramatically. The Victorian gardeners who introduced rhododendrons were attracted by their garish flowers, and, despite its causing significant ecological damage each year, it is very difficult to convince people that *Rhododendron ponticum* ought to be exterminated. Equally dramatic is the statuesque giant hogweed, with its 6 metre stems and inflorescences 50 cm in diameter. The south-west Asian giant hogweed (*Heracleum mantegazzianum*) found favour for adding structure to the Victorian garden. Yet when it became established on riverbanks and waste places outside of gardens from the late nineteenth century, another of its features became obvious: it causes severe photosensitive responses in people. The other serious weed of this Victorian triumvirate is Japanese knotweed (*Fallopia japonica*), a species which has now spread over much of the UK following the flurry of interest it aroused in the mid-nineteenth century.

The benign name *Rhododendron*, literally 'rose tree', was taken by Linnaeus from the classical Greek for

oleander because of the apparent similarities between *R. ponticum* and oleander leaves. The genus, with approximately 850 species, is distributed through the northern hemisphere, Southeast Asia and Australasia. *Rhododendron ponticum* was discovered by Joseph Tournefort, whose classification scheme Linnaeus had learnt as a student, on his pioneering expedition to the Levant between 1700 and 1702. Rhododendrons have been cultivated in Britain since the late eighteenth century. *Rhododendron ponticum* is thought to have been introduced to Britain in 1763 from the Iberian Peninsula, although subsequent introductions occurred from the Black Sea region. By the late nineteenth century, *R. ponticum* was commonplace in Victorian shrubberies, along with many of its North American and Himalayan cousins, with which it has hybridised.

Rhododendron cultivation became an obsession with some mid-nineteenth century English gardeners, as the immense diversity of the Asian species was revealed and fashionable shrubberies had to be filled. The Himalayas and the northern regions of the Indian subcontinent are centres of global plant diversity, and more than two-thirds of known *Rhododendron* species have been recorded from the area. Furthermore, the climate of these high-altitude regions means many plants are suitable for cultivation in British gardens.

Until the late twentieth century, botanists and gardeners had few qualms about collecting whatever came within their grasp; plants were available for all to exploit, wherever they happened to be growing. Attitudes had changed very little since the early eighteenth century, when Mark Catesby stated:

their [trees] plenty may afford opportunities of discovering
their uses and virtues; which in an infant country, little
inclined to improvements, and depending on its mother
country for all kinds of utensils, cannot be expected. By
the concurrent endeavours of the philosopher and artisan,
I question not but many of them will be found useful
to purposes, of which at present we have not the least
conception.[92]

The average garden is full of the global rewards
of historical smash-and-grab raids. Some species, for
example, Himalayan rhododendrons, or complex species
crosses, for example, Russell lupines, proved to be
great money-spinners. The majority, of course, did not.
Furthermore, the fruitless shipment of vast numbers
of tropical orchids back to European gardens, in the
nineteenth century, may have affected detrimentally
natural orchid populations.

FIGURE 39   On the title page of Joseph Dalton Hooker's *Illustrations of Himalayan Plants* (1855), the accomplished lithographer Walter Fitch managed to incorporate six rhododendrons (*R. campanulatum, R. dalhousiae, R. fulgens, R. griffithianum, R. hodgsoni, R. thomsonii*), which were based on paintings by Mughal artists. John Ferguson Cathcart employed Indian artists to illustrate the plants of the Darjeeling area. Following Cathcart's death, Hooker made a selection of the more than a thousand paintings in Cathcart's collection for inclusion in *Illustrations of Himalayan Plants*. The plants were those that combined 'scientific interest with remarkable beauty in form or colour, or some other qualification that would render them eminently worthy of cultivation in England'. Other plants shown in the title page which became popular garden plants include the yellow-flowered *Mecanopsis nepaulensis* and *M. villosa*, the blue-flowered *M. simplicifolia* and the pink-flowered tree *Magnolia campbellii*.

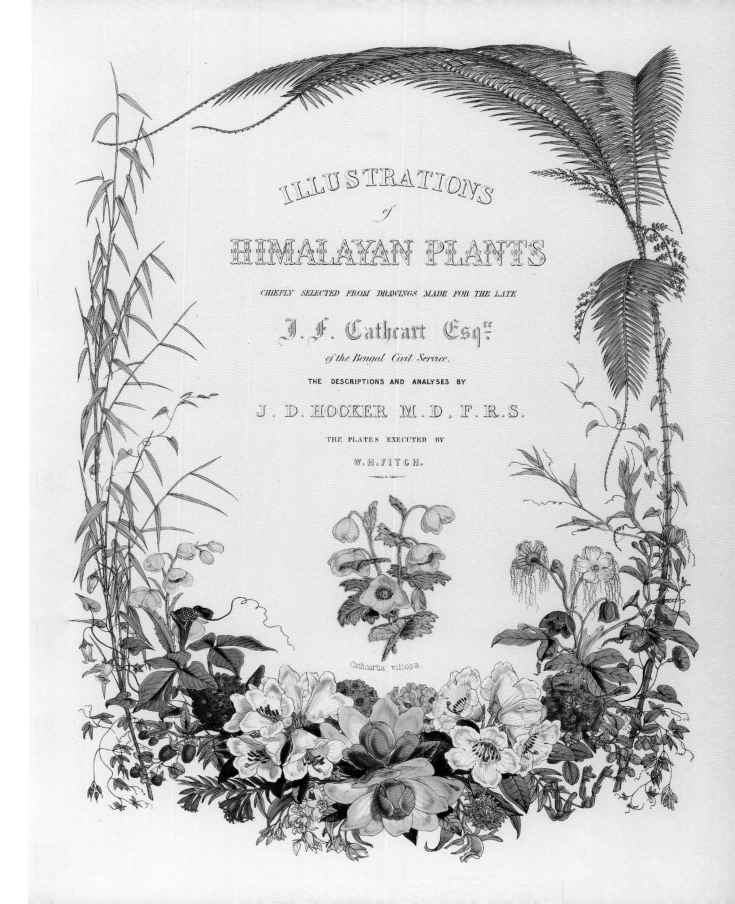

ILLUSTRATIONS

of

HIMALAYAN PLANTS

CHIEFLY SELECTED FROM DRAWINGS MADE FOR THE LATE

J. F. Cathcart Esq.re

of the Bengal Civil Service.

THE DESCRIPTIONS AND ANALYSES BY

J. D. HOOKER M.D. F.R.S.

THE PLATES EXECUTED BY

W. H. FITCH.

Cathcartia villosa.

CHAPTER 6

Acclimatising plants

THOU, *next to Him, art truly Great;*
On Earth his Mighty Delegate:
The Vegetable World to guide,
And o'er all BOTANY *preside*

Abel Evans, *Vertumnus*, 1713

HUMAN CARGOES transported from Britain to Australia, from Portugal to Africa and, as slaves, from Africa to the New World had to be tough to survive the rigours of ocean travel and incarceration under sail. Those who survived such voyages were faced with completely alien environments in which to live. Seasons were reversed, day length and climate unfamiliar, perhaps more extreme than that faced at home. New and terrifying diseases and cultures, together with new and unusual foods, were encountered. Dislocation from any previous life was complete. Behaviours had to change; people either acclimatised or they died. Plants that were introduced to European gardens and colonies made similar journeys and experienced similar environmental stresses; to survive they had to 'make the best of it'. However, unlike human cargoes, they were often cosseted and helped to acclimatise to their new conditions.

On the west coast of northern Europe there is little sun, with cool summers, high rainfall and short growing seasons. However, we are beguiled by wanting to grow unusual plants from around the globe. Northern European gardeners rose to the challenge. In the mid-eighteenth century, Mark Catesby was eloquent on the problems of growing North American plants in England.

This whole ... continent ... produces few plants but what will stand the rigour of our winters in England; for it is remarkable, that notwithstanding the most southern part of the English colonies on the continent of America are twenty degrees more south than England, the cold is there no less severe than it is in England itself; and consequently their plants are so much the better adapted to the air of our more northern situation: and indeed, experience has sufficiently proved how well the English soil and climate agree with these plants; for though they are not equally hardy, and some (when small) require a little protection, yet there are other kinds which brave our winters as stoutly as if they were our own productions.[93]

Despite the general view that the British climate is miserable, cold and wet, the Gulf Stream means we are able to grow botanical treasures outside that would otherwise be impossible at such high latitudes. *Magnolia grandiflora*, with its glossy green leaves and huge white flowers shaped like cupped hands, is one of Catesby's most dramatic introductions that acclimatised to the British climate. However, coaxing exotic plants to grow under artificial conditions was a luxury for the few, since it demanded both the time and the money to experiment with growing conditions.

> Many kinds of American plants ... have been procured and raised from thence; which, though hitherto principally in the possession of the opulent and curious, they, it is to be hoped, will for the benefit of their country be excited to encourage their propagation and increase ... as well for the benefit of our woods, as for ornaments to our gardens.[94]

If Catesby started the craze for North American plants, and through his collaboration with commercial nurserymen promoted the cultivation of these species, it was the relationship between Peter Collinson and John Bartram in the mid-eighteenth century that solidified the British gardener's enjoyment of North American plants. For new plants to flourish, they had to be successfully transported, but getting a seed or growing plant to European shores or her colonies was not enough. The seed needed to germinate, thrive and survive if it was to be of use to those who wanted to exploit it. It is no surprise, therefore, that the exotics easiest to grow on British soils were capable of thriving with little help from their new masters.

Many familiar plants are easily grown survivors that are difficult to kill, for example mother-in-law's tongue (*Sansevieria trifasciata*), native to Nigeria and Congo, which was imported in the early nineteenth century. Highly adaptable plants, capable of growing rapidly in a wide range of conditions and surviving long-distance travel, often become a region's weeds. The Virginian spiderwort (*Tradescantia virginiana*) caused a sensation when it was first introduced from North America by John Tradescant the Younger in the early sixteenth century. The rare may become the commonplace, and this American import is now a weed over much of its introduced range. However, many introduced species are much more difficult to grow, and require all the ingenuity and experience of generations of gardeners. Between 1501 and 1900 the climate in northern Europe changed, with periods of severe winters and late spring frosts, which created additional challenges for those wishing to grow exotic species.

Methods had to be found to coax plants through the difficult months. The practical tips for growing southern European plants given by Roman authors, such as Cato (234–149 BC), Varo and, most importantly, Columella (AD 4–70) were understood. Other plants could be moved indoors through the winter, but orangeries were luxuries of the wealthy few and inappropriate for many tropical species. Just as war spurs technological development, so competition and one-upmanship among gardeners to be the first to grow rare exotics increased the diversity of plants grown in gardens. Huge efforts were often made to keep plants alive, which would make little sense other than for a person to be able to claim it could be done, and they had done it.

Temperature and the invention of the greenhouse

I conceive the little Regard for *Exotick Plants* is chiefly owing to the Difficulties which Gentlemen have met with in preserving them in the Winter, so I have endeavour'd to lay down such Rules for their Management, as may render the Manner of their Culture, easy and familiar to every lover of those Rarities; and when I consider how much the Beauty and Advantage of the *Orangery* is owing to the good Condition of the *Conservatory*, I am the less surprised to meet every Day with valuable Collections of Trees half poisoned with Charcoal, or pinch'd to Death with the Frosts; and all this is owing to the ill Contrivance of our *English* Green-Houses.[95]

In the early eighteenth century, the Cambridge professor of botany Richard Bradley was concerned that impatient gentlemen – or, more likely, their gardeners – were unsuccessful in growing exotic plants and that their greenhouses were letting them down.

The *Green-Houses*, as they are commonly built, serve more for Ornament than Use; their Situation to receive the *South Sun*, is the only thing that seems to be regarded towards the Health of the *Plants* they are to Shelter; It is rare to find one among them that will keep a *Plant* well in the *Winter*, either by reason of their Situation in moist Places, their want of *Glasses* enough in the Front, the Disproportion of the Room within them; and sometimes where it happens that a *Green-House* had been well consider'd in these Points, all is confounded by the *Flues* under it, which convey the Heat from the *Stoves*.[96]

Bradley engaged the young Italian architect Alessandro Galilei (1691–1736) to design 'a Green House as might be agreeable to the Rules of Architecture, and at the same time be rightly adapted to the Welfare of Foreign Plants'.

Bradley's concept of a grand greenhouse was aimed at the very wealthy but was meagre compared to what was to come. Fashionable people had engaged in the competitive cultivation of trophy plants outdoors for centuries, but the stage was now set for this horticultural arms race to move indoors. The great temples to exotic horticulture, the glasshouses of the nineteenth century, were not sudden innovations; they evolved from seventeenth-century stovehouses via the fruit wall and the orangery.

Walls as protection for the growth of fruit trees and grapevines were an ancient horticultural device to create a warm microclimate for fruit ripening. The arrangement of plants on the south-facing walls, which might be purpose-built or on appropriate buildings, was based on the degree of sun and warmth needed for fruit maturation. Walls provided protection against the north wind, and the sun's warmth was retained in the masonry. In sixteenth-century England, fruit trees and vines were an enthusiasm of the wealthy and there was a steady flow of new plants from the Continent. In 1665, in his *Flora, seu, de florum cultura, or, a complete florilege, furnished with all requisites belonging to a florist*, John Rea listed choice fruits that included varieties of apple, pears, quinces, cherries, plums, peaches, apricots, nectarines and a hundred types of vine, only nine of which were suitable for the English climate.

Orangeries developed because citrus trees grown in seventeenth-century Europe needed to be protected during the winter months; the trees were not expected to flower or fruit. In the words of John Rae:

The Orenge-tree considered as it groweth with us, may more fitly be placed among the Greens then with the

FIGURE 40   The Victoria water lily is one of the most sensational plants introduced in Europe during the nineteenth century. Joseph Paxton managed to germinate seeds of the plant and get them to flower. Paxton created a fashion for water lilies and changed the way in which glasshouses were designed. This lithograph was published in *Curtis's Botanical Magazine* (1847), two years before Paxton managed to get the water lily to flower. Illustrations of the Victoria water lily were first published in John Lindley's *Notice of Victoria Regia* (1837), after drawings made in the wild by the South American explorer Robert Schomburgk.

Fruits; for all that the benefit it affordeth us, consisteth in the beauty of the evergreen leaves, and sweet-smelling flowers, the fruit in our cold Countrey never coming to maturity.[97]

Citrus trees were generally moved into rather mean, small-windowed, poorly heated buildings, which would eventually become the more elaborate constructions of the eighteenth century. The Dutch were the great developers of orangery technology, and the horticultural books they wrote became essential to French, German and English citrus enthusiasts. The major Dutch developments were the use of glass to increase the amount of light in the orangery and the improvement of heating technology. The adoption of these developments meant that by the end of the seventeenth century, English estates could boast that thousands of fruits were being produced in their orangeries. However, in terms of lavishness, few could compete with the orangery at Versailles under Louis XIV. Bringing plants indoors for the winter might be the best way to protect expensive exotics, but cheaper methods had been tried and tested, including sheds, pits, cloth covers, straw matting and bell jars.

Manipulation of the indoor environment was hit and miss, but it was appreciated that light, air and temperature were important. While the manipulation of day length in greenhouses would have to await the arrival of the electric lights from the mid-1900s, greenhouses could be artificially heated in the seventeenth century. Greenhouses were directly heated through open fireplaces, raised hearths, pans of burning charcoal and iron stoves. These methods were crude and heat distribution was unequal and largely uncontrolled,

the air was dried, and smoke and soot polluted the atmosphere. The breakthrough came when the direct heat source was removed and atmospheres became cleaner and heat more evenly distributed. In 1684, a new building was erected at Chelsea Physic Garden to house exotic plants. John Evelyn was an early visitor:

> I went to Lond: next day to see Mr. Wat[t]s, keeper of the Apothecaries Garden of simples at Chelsey: where there is a collection of innumerable rarities of that sort: particularly, besides many rare annuals the Tree bearing the Jesuits bark, …: & what was very ingenious the subterranean heate, conveyed by a stove under the Conservatory, which was all Vaulted with brick; so as he leaves the doores & windowes open in the hard[e]st frosts, secluding onely the snow.[98]

Plants could be grown rather than merely made to survive. Subterranean heat was not perfect and greenhouse development continued; Evelyn made his contribution and was one of the first to use the recently invented thermometer in practical gardening. Greenhouses became essential equipment for the serious horticulturalist interested in exotic, and not so exotic, plants. In 1691, John Gibson found greenhouses in twenty-two of the twenty-eight English gardens that he visited. However, he damned Evelyn's own greenhouse with faint praise: 'pretty little greenhouse, with an indifferent stock in it'.[99] Greenhouses could also be immensely productive, although at great financial cost, and also at the cost of the rest of the garden. In the glasshouse of Beddington Gardens, the Duke of Norfolk's aged gardener could claim to have 'gathered … at least ten thousand oranges last year [1690]', although the rest of the garden was 'all out of order'.[100] Through the eighteenth century an increasing proportion of wealthy Europeans were either living or working in the tropical colonies. As they returned home, the rich and the hopeful could venture the possibility of growing the tropical plants with which they had become familiar.

Glasshouses fit for the giant Amazonian water lily

Over a century later, in 1828, the young Joseph Paxton (1803–1865) started work at Chatsworth House, as gardener to William George Spencer Cavendish (1790–1858), sixth Duke of Devonshire. Almost immediately, Paxton began to experiment with improvements on the greenhouse designs of Bradley and others. Paxton's experiments with new ways of constructing glasshouses culminated in Chatsworth's conservatory or great stove (1836–41), a vast glass building measuring approximately 70 metres by 37.5 metres by 20 metres high. Such an enormous, and expensive, glasshouse had never before been built. Yet the vastness of the design, and the evident costs of its maintenance, enhanced the Duke's horticultural reputation. Furthermore, when, in 1849, Paxton won the race to raise the giant Amazonian water lily (*Victoria amazonica*), the Duke's horticultural reputation was assured. To achieve this feat, Paxton needed a glasshouse with a water tank 9 metres in diameter, and a heating system that would ensure water temperature was maintained between 30°C and 32°C.

In 1849, the Amazonian explorer Richard Spruce had seen the Amazonian water lily, near Santarem, Brazil and told his reader that it is 'called in Portuguese the Forno or Oven … from the resemblance of its enormous leaves to the circular oven used for baking

farinha'.[101] The mere size of the floating leaves (2.4 metres) is impressive, but the complex system of supports on the underside of the leaf also demands attention, as does the flower some 40 cm in diameter and its strong, aromatic scent. Numerous Amazonian explorers had seen the water lily since the Bohemian botanist Thomas Haenke had first seen it in 1801. In 1837, the plant was named *Victoria regia* by John Lindley, in honour of the recently crowned Queen Victoria (1819–1901). However, nomenclatural rules mean the plant's correct scientific name is *V. amazonica*.

Paxton had persuaded his friend Sir William Hooker, Director of Kew, to give him a seedling of the plant, which Kew had been trying to grow since seeds had been sent back to Britain from British Guiana by the German explorer Robert Schomburgk (1804–1865). When Paxton showed the water lily to the public the showman in him arranged for his daughter to appear in a fairy costume standing on one of its leaves. This dramatic demonstration was recorded in doggerel by the playwright and journalist Douglas William Jerrold (1803–1857):

> On unbent leaf, in fairy guise
> Reflected in the water,
> Beloved, admired by heart and eyes,
> Stands Annie, Paxton's daughter.[102]

In 1850, the architect in Paxton designed a simple rectangular glasshouse specifically for the water lily based on the extraordinary ribbing of the leaves, a design that was the basis of the Crystal Palace at the Great Exhibition of 1851. However, not all of Paxton's horticultural efforts were rewarded. In 1837,

FIGURE 41 The frontispiece of Linnaeus's *Hortus Cliffortianus* (1737) is an elaborate allegory. A crowned and triumphant Europe, enthroned below a garlanded bust of Clifford, receives homage from three continents. From Asia, a woman offers a coffee plant; from Africa, a woman offers an aloe; and from the New World, a befeathered man offers *Hernandia nymphaeifolia*. On the left stands a flowering and fruiting banana; the first to set fruit in Europe and grown in Clifford's greenhouse. Apollo, with the features of the young Linnaeus, stands over a slain dragon, whilst in the foreground two plump cherubs, portrayed near a brazier, hold the technology of horticulture: a spade and a thermometer. Spread in front of Europe is a plan of Clifford's garden and propped against a potted *Cliffortia*, the genus Linnaeus named in honour of Clifford, is a pair of dividers. The whole scene is set against a background of a topiaried hedge and glasshouse, surrounding a tamed and controlled landscape.

his apprentice John Gibson (1815–1875) returned from Calcutta with the coveted Burmese temple tree, *Amherstia nobilis*. Despite his efforts, Paxton failed to get this remarkable tree to flower.

Patronage for botanists

Greenhouses remained the province of very wealthy individuals and large institutions. For a botanist to have access to a greenhouse, patronage was necessary. As Linnaeus wrote in the early eighteenth century:

> botany is indeed very difficult, especially in regard to exotic plants; yes, but it is also very costly, since the earth does not produce everything everywhere, since those innumerable families of plants are scattered all over the world. To hurry forth to the far-off Indies, to enter the New World, to strike ones head against the limits of the world, to view the sun, where it never sets, this is not for the life of a single Botanist, or for his purse; and his resources will fail at the undertaking. The Botanist requires world wide commerce, libraries of practically all books published about plants, gardens, greenhouses, hothouses, and gardeners.[103]

Linnaeus found patronage from numerous powerful men during his career. One of his earliest patrons was the financier George Clifford (1685–1760) at his garden, and its greenhouses, at de Hartecamp in Holland. Linnaeus wrote *Hortus Cliffortianus* (1737) in nine months, and described Clifford's collection, including many new species. *Hortus Cliffortianus* was a collaboration between Linnaeus and the finest botanical artist of the age, Georg Dionysius Ehret (1710–7170). The banana in the frontispiece to *Hortus Cliffortianus* required the humidity and heat of the greenhouse to thrive.

Other plants, such as Sturt's pea (*Swainsonia formosa*), require dry, hot conditions. Sturt's pea, with its

dramatic scarlet and black flowers, was one of the first plants ever collected by a European in Australia. The privateer William Dampier made a small collection of plants from Shark Bay, Western Australia, in August 1699, which included a specimen of the pea. Sturt's pea was first illustrated in Dampier's 'best-selling' travel book *A Voyage to New Holland* (1703), based on his specimen now housed in Oxford University Herbaria. Despite having numerous names in Aboriginal cultures, it was not until the 1850s that this plant acquired its common name Sturt's pea, in honour of Charles Sturt (1795–1869), who led an expedition to Central Australia (1844–45). Sturt's Pea is widely distributed across the southern part of Australia from the east to the west coasts, and shows tremendous colour and form variation in natural populations, meaning that it has been frequently collected and described under different names. Most recently, it has been suggested that Sturt's pea be moved into its own genus, *Willdampia*, named in its piratical discoverer's honour. As might be expected, the dramatic flowers have attracted the attention of gardeners. Despite, or because of, Sturt's pea being difficult to grow, it was flowering in Britain as early as 1858, in the greenhouses of Messrs Veitch & Sons in London.[104]

FIGURE 42 (*overleaf*) Sturt's pea (*Swainsonia formosa*), with its scarlet and black flowers, was one of the first plants ever collected by a European in Australia. William Dampier collected it in Western Australia in 1699, and illustrated the plant in 1703. The dramatic flowers have attracted the attention of gardeners, despite Sturt's pea being difficult to grow. The specimen illustrated here, in *Curtis's Botanical Magazine* (1858), was brought to flowering in the greenhouses of Messrs Veitch & Sons, London, in March 1858.

Manure: the magic of muck

Cultivating plants is not for the fastidious; growing the exotic and the mundane is about the magic of muck. Varro (116–27 BC), writing on Roman agriculture, reported that Cassius Dionysius of Utica ranked pigeon dung as the best manure, followed by human excrement and then goat, sheep and ass dung. However, in Varro's experience the best manure was from thrushes and blackbirds, 'as it is not only good from the land, but is excellent food both for cattle and swine'.[105] Plants in Oxford Botanic Garden have flourished for centuries on academic ordure. The contents of the bladders, bowels and kitchens of Oxford's Town and Gown transformed the soil of the fledgling garden enclosed within Danvers's wall. Between 1621 and 1626, 'ye Universitie Scavenger' delivered '4000 loads of mucke & dunge' and the slow, dynamic change of the garden's soil began.[106]

Botanic gardens were not alone in their reliance on such resources of essential plant nutrients. The woodcut on the title page of Jean Ruel's *De natura stirpium libri tres* (1536) reveals an early-sixteenth-century pleasure garden and arbour, set near an agricultural landscape, which must have relied on the careful control of manure. Jean Ruel was the physician to Francis I of France (1494–1547), the patron of *De natura stirpium*, and a noted translator of Dioscorides. Besides the title page of *De natura stirpium*, the book is notable for attempting to provide a systematic, descriptive morphology of plants, together with an extensive consideration of the technical vocabulary used by botanists of the period.

In *Floraes Paradise, Beautified and Adorned with Sundry Sorts of Delicate Fruites and Flowers* (1608), Sir Hugh Platt recommended that shredded cats and dogs or a paste of ox blood and pigeon droppings be applied to the roots of ailing fruit trees as a pick-me-up. The market gardens that fed London in the eighteenth and nineteenth centuries were themselves fed with a rich confection of metropolitan ordure. In 1800, Erasmus Darwin (1731–1802) stated:

> all kinds of animal and vegetable substances ... as the flesh, fat, skin, and bones, of animals; with their secretions of bile, saliva, mucus; and their excretions of urine, and ordure; and also the fruit, meal, oil, leaves, wood, of vegetables, when properly decomposed on or beneath the soil, supply the most nutritive food to plants.[107]

In the nineteenth century, vast quantities of animal bones were being imported from the slaughter houses of Europe for the manufacture of bonemeal. More disturbingly, the German chemist Justus Liebig (1803–1873) ranted that to fertilise the soil of England's 'green and pleasant land', Britain was

> robbing all other countries of the condition of their fertility. Already in her eagerness for bones she turned up the battle-fields of Leipsic, of Waterloo, and of the Crimea; already from the catacombs of Sicily she has carried away the skeletons of many successive generations ... removes from the shores of other countries the manurial equivalent of 3 millions and a half of men whom she takes from us the means of supporting and squanders down her sewers to the seas. Like a vampire, she hangs upon the neck of Europe – nay the entire world.[108]

As the Anglo-German polymath Samuel Hartlib (1600–1662) wrote about a Kentish woman, a little knowledge of how plants grow might be suspicious:

who saveth in a paile, all the droppings of the houses, I mean the urine, and when the paile is full, spinckleth it on her Meadow, which causeth the grasse at first to look yellow, but after a little time, it growes wonderfully, that many of her neighbours wondered at it, and were like to accuse of her of witch-craft.[109]

Others were more concerned over the actual sources of plant nutrients. The agriculturalist Jethro Tull (1674–1741), had his concerns over the use of animal and human waste:

Tis a Wonder how delicate Palates can dispense with eating their Own and their Beast's Ordure, but a little more putrefy'd and evaporated; together with all sorts of Filth and Nastiness, a Tincture of which those Roots must unavoidably receive that grow amongst it.[110]

It was understood that plants cannot survive on just water, fresh air and light. By the end of the nineteenth century it was known that they also needed nutrients such as nitrogen, phosphorus and potassium. Nitrogen and phosphorus are needed to build proteins and potassium for growth. Different soils have different physical and chemical components and support different types of plants; even in the same garden a particular species may grow well in one spot but not in another. However, all of the care that a gardener devotes to growing a plant is in vain if the soil is inappropriate; few gardeners would attempt to grow acid-loving rhododendrons in calcareous soils.

Fertile soils

Soils are highly complex, and are often overlooked until they disappear or are no longer fertile. Virgil, in the *Georgics*, commended 'the genius of soils, the strength of each, its hue, its native power for bearing'.[111] Good fertile soil, which, like paradise, is more likely to be found on one's neighbour's land than on one's own, is the combination of minerals, organic matter, air, water and microbes. A good soil should hold sufficient moisture, allow easy root penetration, hold and slowly release all of the nutrients that a plant needs, have a suitable pH and organic matter content, and have the organisms needed to break down and release the nutrients. The importance of soil fertility was recognised by the ancient writers such as the Greek Theophrastus and the Romans Columella, Varro and Cato. The most famous natural addition of nutrients to soil is the periodic flooding of the Nile, which fed plants upon which the Ancient Egyptian civilisation was constructed. The rich manure added to the fledgling botanic garden in Oxford by Bobart the Elder contained the nutrients the growing plants needed and the humus to stop these nutrients being leached into the nearby River Isis.

Nitrogen comprises about four-fifths of the air but plants cannot use it directly. They must take it up from the soil in the form of nitrates, which in turn are produced by bacteria, especially those found in the root nodules of legumes. This is the so-called nitrogen cycle, and is one of the numerous sequences through which atoms have been recycled through 3.8 billion years of life on earth. Carbon atoms exhaled by Theophrastus, phosphorus atoms from skeletons on the battlefield of Waterloo, and nitrogen atoms excreted by monarchs may be part of the plants sitting on your windowsills. Cato and Columella described the role of legumes, such as clover and lupines, in maintaining soil fertility.[112] In the early seventeenth century, John Parkinson was one of the first gardeners to study seriously, and record, the effect of different manures on plant growth. The agricultural revolution of eighteenth-century Britain would investigate in detail the effectiveness of manures. During the eighteenth and nineteenth centuries, there was a cottage industry of publications by gardeners describing their own nostrums for manure preparation. Practical experience showed gardeners and farmers how to manipulate manures to affect plant growth; the scientific understanding of these effects had to await the scientific revolutions of the mid-nineteenth century.

Discovering guano

Until the discovery of South American guano in the early nineteenth century and the Haber–Bosch process in the twentieth century, nitrogen and phosphorus had been at a premium in soils. Guano, the accumulated droppings of South American seabirds, proved to be a rich source of plant nutrients and profit in nineteenth-century Britain. The guano trade between Peru and Britain started in 1820 and reached its peak in 1858, when approximately 300,000 tons was being imported annually. The trade was a virtual monopoly of Antony Gibbs & Sons and the family became extremely wealthy. There was profit to be made in the poet William Cowper's (1731–1800) 'stercoraceous heap';[113] the neo-Gothic pile Tyntesfield, near Bristol, Keble College Chapel in Oxford and Gibbs's baronetcy were all funded from the profits of the bird dropping trade. Indeed, the financial rewards from fertilisers were so great that Chile, Peru and Bolivia fought the War of the Pacific (1879–83) over the control of the nitrate-producing regions.

Just as humans had evolved in an environment where sugars were limited, so most plants had evolved in environments where nutrients were limited. Sugar cane and slavery gave Europeans access to a continuous sugar supply; bird droppings and nitrates gave them access to industrial quantities of useful nitrogen and phosphorus. However, like the sweetness of sugar, fertilisers can be addictive.

Propagating plants

Acquisitive botanists and gardeners want to have what their rivals have acquired and be surrounded by their own novelties. Other, less mercenary, motivations may include the wish to ensure that desirable plants are not lost. If the evidence of a plant's cultivation is not to be confined to books or herbaria, botanical insurance is needed to ensure living plants survive. If plants are not propagated, they will not survive. Many cultivated plants are killed by disease; others are killed by lack of interest and changing fashions. Gardening books of the seventeenth and eighteenth centuries are filled with descriptions of plants that have not survived in cultivation. The thousands of hyacinth cultivars developed by obsessive members of florists' societies have been whittled down to a few hundred today. This is not a new phenomenon. A plant known to Pliny the Elder as *silphium* (a member of the carrot family) had a high social and economic value to the Romans. Indeed, it was so important to the Cyrenians that it featured on their coins. Yet silphium is thought to be the earliest recorded example of a plant driven to extinction by humans, despite being widely cultivated. The decline

or three feet, generally several from one root, with small, alternate, divaricated branches. The leaves are oval, somewhat toothed towards the apex, and placed alternate. The flowers are produced in spikes terminating the stalks; they are sessile, and each furnished with a bractea or floral leaf, which is ovate, rough externally, longer than the empalement and sitting close at their base; they are produced early in the spring and being thick set, make a beautiful appearance with their long, snowy white stamina. The fruit or seed-vessel very much resembles that of the Hamamalis or Witch Hazel, but is much small-

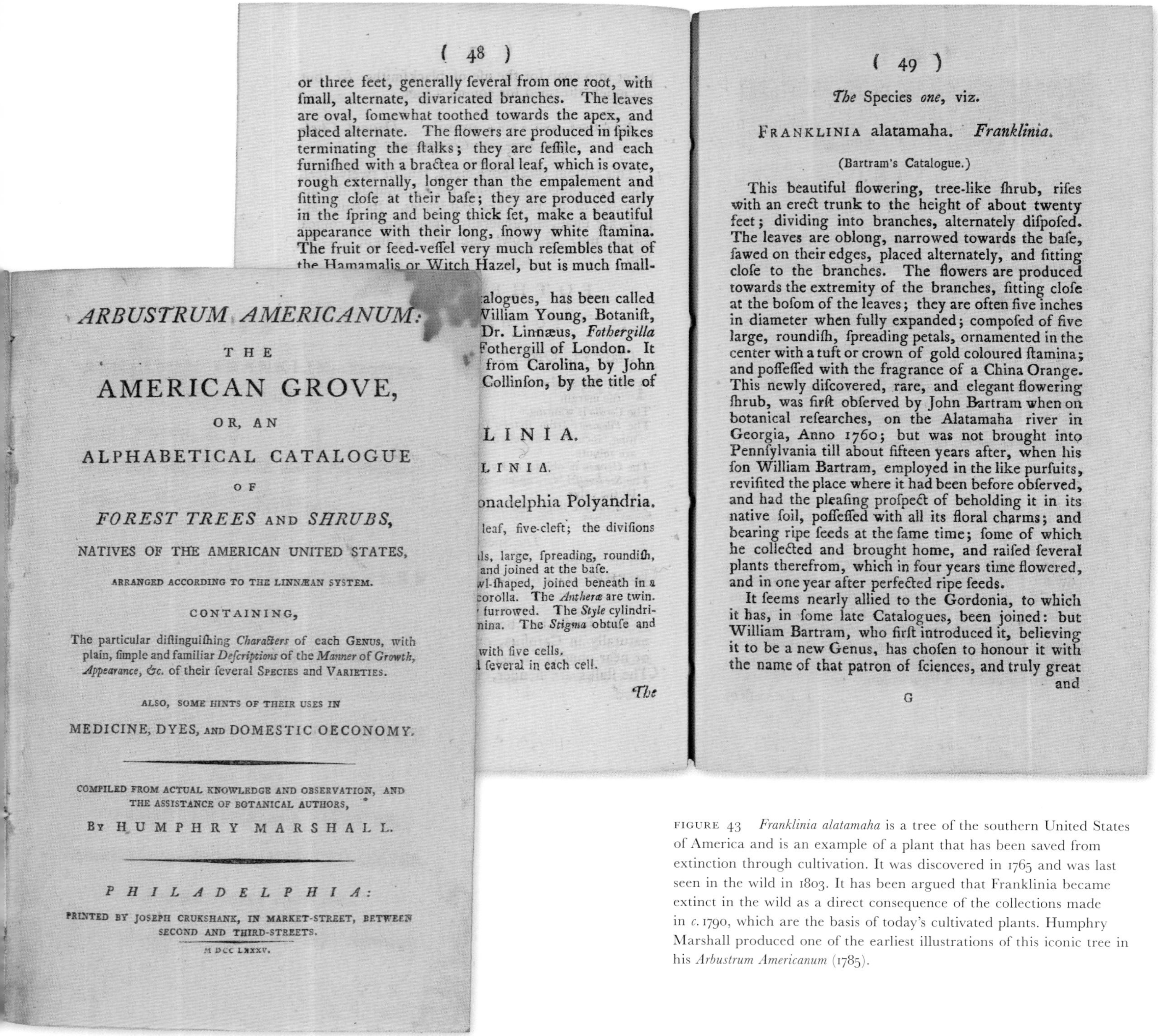

... alogues, has been called
... William Young, Botanist,
... Dr. Linnæus, *Fothergilla*
... Fothergill of London. It
... from Carolina, by John
... Collinson, by the title of

... L I N I A.

... L I N I A.

... onadelphia Polyandria.

... leaf, five-cleft; the divisions

... ls, large, spreading, roundish,
... and joined at the base.
... wl-shaped, joined beneath in a
... corolla. The *Antheræ* are twin.
... furrowed. The *Style* cylindri-
... mina. The *Stigma* obtuse and

... with five cells.
... several in each cell.

The

ARBUSTRUM AMERICANUM:

THE
AMERICAN GROVE,

OR, AN

ALPHABETICAL CATALOGUE

OF

FOREST TREES AND SHRUBS,

NATIVES OF THE AMERICAN UNITED STATES,

ARRANGED ACCORDING TO THE LINNÆAN SYSTEM.

CONTAINING,

The particular distinguishing *Characters* of each GENUS, with plain, simple and familiar *Descriptions* of the *Manner of Growth, Appearance, &c.* of their several SPECIES and VARIETIES.

ALSO, SOME HINTS OF THEIR USES IN

MEDICINE, DYES, AND DOMESTIC OECONOMY.

COMPILED FROM ACTUAL KNOWLEDGE AND OBSERVATION, AND THE ASSISTANCE OF BOTANICAL AUTHORS,

BY HUMPHRY MARSHALL.

PHILADELPHIA:

PRINTED BY JOSEPH CRUKSHANK, IN MARKET-STREET, BETWEEN SECOND AND THIRD-STREETS.
M DCC LXXXV.

49

The Species one, viz.

FRANKLINIA alatamaha. *Franklinia.*

(Bartram's Catalogue.)

This beautiful flowering, tree-like shrub, rises with an erect trunk to the height of about twenty feet; dividing into branches, alternately disposed. The leaves are oblong, narrowed towards the base, sawed on their edges, placed alternately, and sitting close to the branches. The flowers are produced towards the extremity of the branches, sitting close at the bosom of the leaves; they are often five inches in diameter when fully expanded; composed of five large, roundish, spreading petals, ornamented in the center with a tuft or crown of gold coloured stamina; and possessed with the fragrance of a China Orange. This newly discovered, rare, and elegant flowering shrub, was first observed by John Bartram when on botanical researches, on the Alatamaha river in Georgia, Anno 1760; but was not brought into Pennsylvania till about fifteen years after, when his son William Bartram, employed in the like pursuits, revisited the place where it had been before observed, and had the pleasing prospect of beholding it in its native soil, possessed with all its floral charms; and bearing ripe seeds at the same time; some of which he collected and brought home, and raised several plants therefrom, which in four years time flowered, and in one year after perfected ripe seeds.

It seems nearly allied to the Gordonia, to which it has, in some late Catalogues, been joined: but William Bartram, who first introduced it, believing it to be a new Genus, has chosen to honour it with the name of that patron of sciences, and truly great

and

G

FIGURE 43 *Franklinia alatamaha* is a tree of the southern United States of America and is an example of a plant that has been saved from extinction through cultivation. It was discovered in 1765 and was last seen in the wild in 1803. It has been argued that Franklinia became extinct in the wild as a direct consequence of the collections made in *c.* 1790, which are the basis of today's cultivated plants. Humphry Marshall produced one of the earliest illustrations of this iconic tree in his *Arbustrum Americanum* (1785).

of silphium is a familiar story of over-exploitation and habitat destruction.

Other species, which are extinct in the wild, have survived through assiduous propagation in cultivation. The white-flowered Franklinia tree (*Franklinia alatamaha*), a native of the American state of Georgia, was first noted in the wild by the naturalist John Bartram and his son in October 1765. The tree was last seen in the wild in 1803. Serendipitously, in about 1790, a nurseryman, Moses Marshall (1758–1813), brought some plants into cultivation and propagated them; today, this plant is only known in cultivation. If a plant is to become widespread in cultivation it must be propagated quickly, easily and cheaply. Traditionally, gardeners have two basic approaches to multiplying the numbers of a plant: sexual propagation using seed or clonal propagation using some form of cutting.

Propagating from seed

Seeds, as mobile, self-contained packets of potential delight, tolerate desiccation and germinate in response to environmental conditions. As we have seen, they are the obvious means by which plants may be moved from their natural homes into gardens. Furthermore, if plants produce abundant, fertile seed in cultivation then seeds can be readily dispersed. In the late seventeenth century, Jacob Bobart the Younger, at the Oxford Botanic Garden, appears to have been one of the first garden directors to produce formalised lists of seeds that he made available for purchase or exchange. Jacob Bobart the Younger even placed an advert for 'good new St Foyn Seed' in the *London Gazette* on 5 February 1690. However, Bobart's entrepreneurial activities may have detracted from the upkeep of the garden, as numerous visitors compared the Oxford garden unfavourably to its European rivals. The distribution of seed from botanic gardens, for personal, institutional or scientific profit, was revolutionary, although was commonplace among naturalists of seventeenth-century Europe. Furthermore, seed exchange had been practised for millennia within and among communities as activities associated with the annual cycles of food production. Yet seeds do not live forever; they lose viability over time. Seed viability is species-dependent, and may be a matter of weeks to tens of years. Until the development of seed storage facilities in the twentieth century that could ensure cold and dry conditions, seeds needed to be grown regularly to maintain supplies. Mark Catesby was well aware of problems of seed viability:

> as those who … have it in their power to procure large quantities of seeds and plants from America, may be at a loss what instructions to send their correspondents abroad, I have been particular in giving an account where the several kinds of plants are to be found that are uncommon, and in directing how they are to be collected, packed up, and secured, so as to preserve them in good condition during their passage; which are matters of the utmost consequence, though less known even than their culture.[114]

Dormancy

Dormancy is a natural survival characteristic of most seeds and may take numerous forms. Once the seed starts to germinate, there is no going back. A seedling must cope with whatever conditions surround it; otherwise it will die. Today, dormancy is thought about in terms of physical characteristics, such as thick seed coats, which are barriers to water getting into the seed. In other species the embryo may be immature when the seeds are harvested and additional time is needed to complete maturation. In other cases, embryo development may be inhibited by chemical factors. The gardener and botanist may need to coax seeds out of dormancy.

Without knowing much about the precise basis of seed dormancy, gardeners had discovered subtle ways of overcoming it. In some cases merely storing seed was sufficient, in others it was necessary to damage physically the seed through scarification, and in others it was necessary to chill the seed. More elaborate techniques, such as exposure to smoke, were needed for plants naturally found in fire-prone areas, such as the Mediterranean and savannahs.

Orchids

The drama and exoticism of orchid flowers attract the horticulturalist. However, orchids can be a particular challenge to propagate from seeds. The minute seeds have no dormancy and specific fungal associations must be established rapidly if seedlings are to survive. John Lindley, the premier British orchid specialist of the nineteenth century, was frustrated that 'nothing certain is known of the germination of Orchidaceae'.[115] Orchids also attract academic and artistic minds. Franz Bauer (1758–1840) was at least as talented an artist as his brother Ferdinand Bauer. For most of his career, Franz worked for Joseph Banks at Kew, and in contrast to his brother looked at the botanical world through a magnifying glass. Bauer's detailed illustrations of orchid flowers are characterised by detailed attention to the relationship of floral parts. His published work forms 'but a small part of the invaluable materials illustrating Vegetable Anatomy and Physiology, to the execution of which Mr Bauer's long and active life has been devoted'.[116]

Clonal propagation

Clonal propagation relies on any living plant cell being able to regenerate into any other plant cell, a condition called totipotency. Anyone who has broken a leaf or a stem from a desired plant, pushed it into soil and seen a new plant regenerate is familiar with the process. Totipotency has been the basis of plant theft and propagation technologies for millennia, although how it works is something of a mystery. Trial and error by generations of gardeners has meant that much horticultural wisdom and mythology has developed around which parts of a plant are most appropriate for propagation in which species. North American sumacs, Asian *Chaenomeles* and South American passionflowers are propagated by root cuttings. American potatoes and Jerusalem artichokes are propagated as tubers, Mediterranean mint and Chinese rhubarb are propagated by rhizomes, and numerous familiar spring flowers, such as Central Asian crocuses, tulips and lilies, are propagated as corms, or swollen underground stems, and bulbs. Simply splitting large plants or snapping off runners and offsets are effective means of propagating North American asters and strawberries, and South American pineapples. Other methods of clonal propagation rely on a plant's ability to produce roots or new shoots if it is damaged. North American magnolias, the Indian rubber tree or Himalayan rhododendrons are readily propagated by layering, and many fruit trees are propagated by stooling, a process whereby a tree is cut down to ground level and new

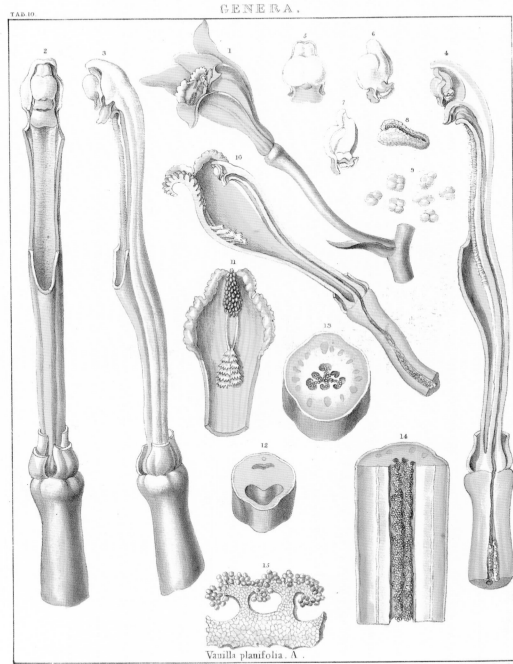

Vanilla planifolia . A .

FIGURE 44 Franz Bauer's *Illustrations of orchidaceous plants* (1830–36) reveals his affinity with orchids and his command of drawing the intricate and detailed anatomies of plants as revealed by the microscope. The cured seed pods of the Mesoamerican orchid *Vanilla planifolia* are the commercial source of vanilla. *Vanilla planifolia* is a climber that can be over 20 metres in height, yet in the wild, the plants flower infrequently and seedlings are rarely found. Sexual reproduction in the wild is therefore rare, so commercial plantations are established from cuttings.

FIGURE 45 Plants with variegated leaves
have been popular garden plants. Many
of the plants, which are the result of
mutations that disrupt the production of
the green pigment chlorophyll, have been
selected from the normal green plant
found in the wild. Varieties with leaves
that have spots or stripes of yellow or
white are frequently found, and these are
reflected in the names gardeners give to
the cultivars. One of the most familiar
variegated plants is the South African
Pelargonium (the gardener's geranium),
some of which are shown here from an
illustration in Shirley Hibberd's *New and
rare beautiful-leaved plants* (1870).

shoots are produced. However, stem or leaf cuttings are familiar to most people. Begonias, African violets, gloxinias and pelargoniums have all found their way into the houses and hearts of European flower-lovers through such cuttings. In the early nineteenth century, the plant collector Francis Masson was credited by the founder of the Linnean Society, James Smith, with filling 'every garret and cottage window'[117] in Yorkshire and Norfolk with geraniums (*Pelargonium*). However, Masson would not have been able to do this without the collaboration and practical knowledge of the nurserymen who were propagating the new botanical discoveries of the eighteenth century, and making them available to a public thirsty for botanical novelty.

Tulipomania

The late-spring-flowering tulips are propagated as bulbs. In the early 1630s a famous speculative bubble, 'tulipomania', expanded in Holland as propagation did not keep up with demand. During tulipomania, staggeringly high prices were paid for individual bulbs; a single bulb of one of the rarest and most prized, 'Semper August', was sold for up to twice the price of an Amsterdam house. Through a series of complex inter-crossings and selections, the almond-shaped flowers familiar to the Ottoman sultans were transformed into the florists' tulips with which we are familiar. By the late eighteenth century, as more cultivars were developed and effectively propagated, prices had dropped dramatically; 730 named tulips in one catalogue ranged in price from a few pence to several shillings per bulb. The irony of tulipomania is that the varieties which commanded the highest prices were infected with a virus that led to the breaking of petal colour and, eventually, weakening of the bulb. Today, the virus is all but eliminated from cultivated tulips through the concerted efforts of generations of tulip growers.

Grafting

Even without knowing the function of a seed, and how they were formed, practical gardeners knew that some plants could not be propagated for seed. Trying to regenerate particular apple, pear or grape cultivars from seed was a waste of time. Since these plants produce seed by crossing, each seed is likely to produce a plant that is very different to its parents. A vegetative propagation technique, grafting, was needed that produced plants which were identical to the parent plant. Grafting was in use in ancient Mesopotamia, and recorded in cuneiform text. Virgil, in the *Georgics*, states: 'the rough arbutus is grafted with a walnut shoot, and barren planes have oft borne hardy apple boughs; the beech has grown white with the chestnut's snowy bloom, the ash with the pear's; and swine have crunched acorns beneath the elm',[118] giving the impression that anything will graft on to anything else. Varro was clear that this was not the case: 'you cannot, for instance, graft a pear on an oak, even though you can on an apple'.[119] The importance of grafting as a propagation technology can be seen in the numbers and volumes of named cultivars that were being imported into Britain from Europe in the sixteenth century by gardeners such as the John Tradescants.

Graft hybrids

As might be expected, experiments with grafting also produced oddities, so-called graft hybrids. The earliest recorded graft hybrid was the bizzarria orange raised by a gardener in Florence in 1644 and described by the director of the Pisa Botanic Garden, Pietro Nati (1624–1715), in *Florentina Phytologica Observatio De Malo Limonia Citrata-Aurantia Florentinae Vulgo La Bizzarria* (1674). A sour orange (*Citrus* x *aurantium*) was grafted onto a citron (*Citrus medica*) stock. The resulting tree produced fruits, flowers and leaves identical with the citron and bitter orange, plus fruit that had sectors characteristic of citron and orange. A better-known example of a graft hybrid is the widely cultivated curiosity tree, Adam's laburnum (+*Laburnocytisus adamii*). So far as we know, this tree has only been produced once, in a Monsieur Adam's nursery near Paris in 1825. In this case, purple-flowered broom (*Cytius purpureus*) was grafted onto yellow-flowered laburnum (*Laburnum anagyroides*) to produce a chimaera with yellow laburnum flowers, purple broom flowers and dingy reddish flowers that combined features of both the broom and the laburnum.

The sinuous terracing of mountainside in the Andes, China and Southeast Asia are some of the great engineering feats of man over the last two millennia. These community achievements were made by generations of farmers so that soil and nutrients were trapped and their crops could grow productively. In Europe, people had practised the less spectacular three-field system for generations before the direct application of emerging knowledge about plant growth produced the agricultural revolution in eighteenth-century Britain. Man the great plant manipulator was beginning to understand how plants worked, and a scientific approach to plant husbandry was starting to inform the 'instinctive' approach of the gardener.

FIGURE 46 The bizzarria orange, illustrated here from Risso et al.'s *Histoire naturelle des orangers* (1818), is the earliest recorded graft hybrid. The bizzarria orange, with its fruit combining the citron and the orange, is a product of grafting sour orange onto a citron stock.

CHAPTER 7

Understanding plants

———

He was their Lord and could command a view
As of their faces, so their natures too

RI, in Stephens & Brown,
Catalogus horti botanici Oxoniensis, 1658

PLANTS are the raw materials of the gardener, just as pigments are the raw materials of a painter. A painter may know little about the sources, histories, chemistries and physics of her pigments. A gardener may never ask from where her particular plants originate or exactly how they work. Foreign travel and trade increased the number and range of pigments in the palettes of European artists, and the range of plants in European gardens. Pliny the Elder had complained about the increasing popularity of foreign pigments over traditional Roman pigments: 'when purple finds its way even on the party-walls and when India contributes the mud of her rivers and the gore of her snakes and elephants, there is no such thing as high-class painting'.[120] However, Titian (*c.* 1485–1576) took advantage of the variety of pigments imported through Venetian ports to create his works. Traditionalist gardeners may complain about foreign garden plants

but these same plants are commonplace in European gardens.

By the mid-eighteenth century, artists' palettes were being expanded by chemists who were starting to understand the chemical basis of pigmentation. It was no longer necessary to search for ever more bizarre natural pigments to find preferred colours; they could be synthesised. At the same time, plant breeders were expanding the palette of familiar garden plants available to the gardener, just as foreign travel had done a century earlier. By the end of the nineteenth century, chemists were providing whole spectra of colours based on manipulations of simple chemical compounds and botanists were starting to glimpse the possibilities of manipulating plants based on an understanding of inheritance. Some of the chemists' pigments were highly labile or toxic and found no favour among artists; similarly many of the botanists' efforts were prone to

112

disease and died out. However, in both chemistry and botany, principles were being understood that meant that chemical synthesis and plant breeding could be put on a scientific footing rather than the hit-and-miss approach of earlier centuries.

As plant breeders came to understand genetics, they produced particular forms, just as chemists produced particular colours when they understood colour chemistry. The palette available to a gardener in the form of cultivated plants is the product of sweat, toil, manure, chemistry, death and genetics. It is the job of an individual gardener to arrange plants in a pleasing manner. It is the job of the botanist to answer questions about plants such as: What is it? Where and how does it grow? How does it vary? How did it evolve? Can it be made 'better'?

Classification and naming

As knowledge of the world increased, it was no longer practical for flowering plants to be divided into the three groups of trees, shrubs and herbs, as Theophrastus had done. Humans name and minutely classify their activities, beliefs and attitudes, and these activities are extended to their interactions with, and the objects in, the natural world. Indeed, one of Adam's first challenges in Eden, according to Genesis, was to name 'cattle, … fowl of the air and every beast of the field'. Communication about the natural world depends on giving objects names, which is helped by ordering the names into classification systems. Names, the key to communicating information, are a means by which knowledge is communicated between peoples and generations, whilst classifications provide a means

of ordering and retrieving information. To be most effective, names should refer unambiguously to one object, whilst a classification scheme should be simple to use, have high information content and readily allow new objects to be added to it. From the Egyptian and Assyrian, through the Chinese and Indian to the Greek understanding of plants, the generation and application of names has been crucial. The development of a universal classification system, associated with consistently applied names, was an important early goal of the scientific study of plants, and required the integration of knowledge derived from botanical exploration, the library, garden and herbarium.

Andrea Cesalpino's classification of plants

The establishment of medical schools in southern Europe and the increasing popularity of private gardens in the sixteenth century raised two major questions: what were the best features to distinguish plant species, and what were the best ways to group the enormous diversity of plants being discovered? Numerous publications sought to address these issues, but *De Plantis Libri* (1583) by the Italian botanist Andrea Cesalpinio (1519–1603) was one of the important milestones. Cesalpinio's system was only one of numerous systems, the so-called pre-Linnaean classifications, proposed between the sixteenth and early eighteenth centuries. Most of these classification systems emphasise the importance of specific plant parts or organs.

Robert Morison's classification of plants

This was the case for the Scotsman Robert Morison's plant classification system. Morison was severely wounded as he fought the Royalist cause during the English Civil War in the mid-seventeenth century. Following his escape to France he distinguished himself as a botanist, eventually becoming intendant of the Duke of Orleans's gardens at Blois. It was during this period that Morison started to develop his own system of plant classification, which was based on fruit characteristics. On his return to England, following the restoration of Charles II (1630–1685), he was appointed King's Physician; in 1669 he was made Professor of Botany at the University of Oxford. Morison's reputation rests on the *Historia Plantarum Universalis Oxoniensis (Pars 2)*, published in 1680. This work was supposed to be a catalogue of all of the plants known to Morison, arranged according to his classification scheme (the *Sciagraphia*), but he only lived to see *Pars 2* published. *Pars 3* was eventually published by Jacob Bobart in 1699 and *Pars 1* remains incomplete.

During Morison's lifetime, his classification scheme enhanced his reputation. However, his arrogance at refusing to recognise the debt he owed to others, particularly Cesalpinio, has severely tarnished the view posterity has of him. Furthermore, he had a very difficult relationship with that other great English botanist of the period, John Ray. Linnaeus was particularly forthright in his opinion of Morison and his classification system:

> Caesalpinus appears great to me, inasmuch as he was the father of systematic botanists. Morison was vain … yet he cannot be sufficiently praised for having revived system, which was half expiring. If you look over Tournefort's genera, you will readily admit how much he owes to Morison, full as much as the latter was indebted to Caesalpinus.… All that is good in Morison is taken from Caesalpinus.[121]

Whatever Morison's character flaws may have been, another book he published is generally considered the first monograph on a plant family, *Plantarum Umbelliferarum Distributio Nova* (1672). This work also contains the first published, formal key for the identification of species.

Linnaeus's classification of plants

By the end of the nineteenth century, classification systems would start to be based around a universal idea: plants should be grouped together based on evolutionary principles. However, the big idea of the mid-eighteenth century was Linnaeus's classification of plants based on sex.

In 1729, Linnaeus wrote an influential thesis, *Praeludia Sponsaliarum Plantarum*, in which he synthesised information about plant sex, then a controversial subject. He went further, produced a plant classification system based on plant sex, and became a botanical celebrity. Linnaeus's reputation and celebrity were based on two achievements: the replacement of complex phrase names (polynomials) for plants with a simple two-word name (binomial) – that is, a genus followed by a species name; and a classification system. Linnaeus was not the first to use binomial names and he was not the first to produce a plant classification system. However, he was the first to use binomials consistently and produced a classification system that was simple to use:

> The Animal, the Vegetable & the Fossil Kingdoms marched in a new but regular Order into his System and

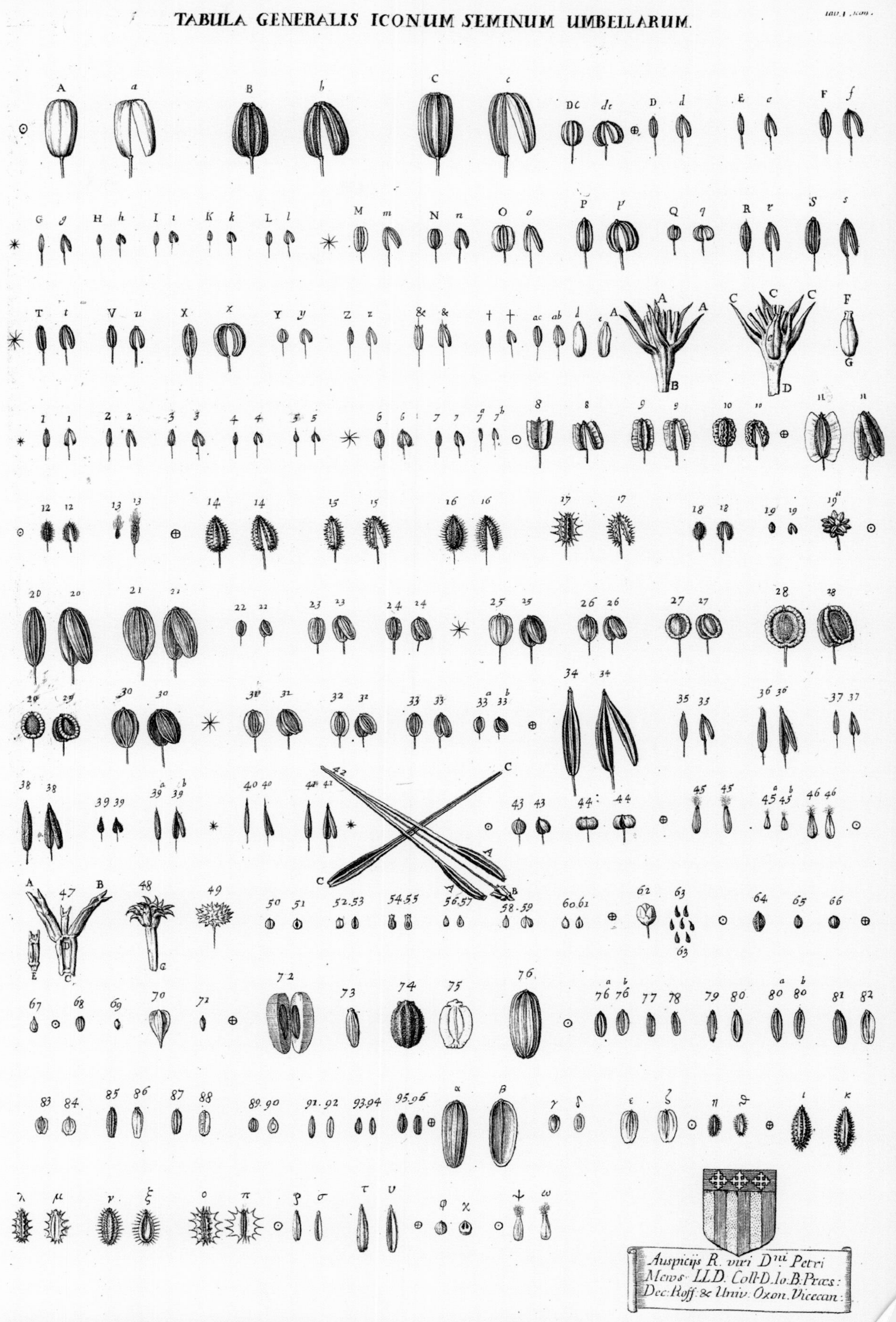

FIGURE 47 Robert Morison's *Plantarum Umbelliferarum Distributio Nova* (1672) has the distinction of containing the first published formal key for identifying a group of plants. The copper engraving shows the details of the distinctive fruits of members of the carrot family and is dedicated to Peter Mews, vice-chancellor of the University of Oxford from 1669 until 1673.

he [Linnaeus] supported it by Laws so well contrived & devised that the Appearance of a new Plant or a new Animal occasioned neither Confusion nor Disorder. The One or the Other readily found its Place. The Number of Links were increased but the Chain was not disturbed.[122]

Linnaeus had imposed a hierarchy on the natural world; each organism had its rightful place in the grand scheme of life. Linnaeus argued that since the anthers and stigma were closer to a plant's 'sexual essence' than structures such as flowers or fruits, concentration on these characteristics should produce the 'best' classification. Linnaeus classified plants into twenty-four classes based primarily on the arrangement and number of male (stamens) and female (pistils) parts. Thus, the class *Monandria* had one stamen, class *Diandria* had two stamens, class *Hexandria* had six stamens, whilst class *Tetradynamia* had six stamens (four long and two short). Linnaeus's overall botanical philosophy was laid out in *Philosophia Botanica* (1751). This book was deliberately printed at a price students could afford, and therefore enjoyed wide circulation; the Latin he used was direct and earthy and his botanical instructions clear. The language used to explain his plant classification system was no less direct. Thus, the Class *Hexandria* was described as 'one wife in a marriage with six husbands'.

Such explicit language caused a wave of moral apoplexy among some botanists, clergy and other members of society. Notoriously, Johann Siegesbeck (1686–1755), Demonstrator of the Botanical Garden, St Petersburg, was concerned that 'such loathsome harlotry' and 'so licentious a method' was being taught to students, whilst Samuel Goodenough (1743–1827), Bishop of Carlisle, stated that 'nothing could equal the gross

prurience of Linnaeus's mind' and that 'Linnean botany is enough to shock female modesty'. Yet Linnaeus's system was to enjoy very wide currency, especially in England, among both men and women interested in plants. More thoughtful, and ultimately devastating, intellectual rather than moral arguments were to be mounted against Linnaeus's system, especially by French botanists in the Jardin du Roi, Paris. The intellectual *coup de grâce* would not be delivered to Linnaeus's system until the early nineteenth century. Had it not been for Linnaeus's promotion of the consistent application of binomial names, he may well have drifted into obscurity – the fate of so many botanists who produced novel, and often lauded, classification systems in their times.

Linnaeus's binomial naming system was not enough. Poor application of names creates a lexicographical Babel. Rules were needed that could be used by all, so the application of names could be judged. Furthermore, names needed to be associated with physical specimens and so the concept of the type specimen was born. All plant names should have an associated type specimen: the herbarium specimen used by the author of a name, when the name was first described. By the end of the nineteenth century, the apparently tedious rules of botanical nomenclature were being codified as two documents, the *International Code of Botanical Nomenclature* and its sister publication the *International Code of Nomenclature for Cultivated Plants*, both of which are regularly updated. The aim of the two codes is to ensure that all plant names refer unambiguously to one species or variety.

Plant names may appear to be a rather academic concern. However, consider the case of scurvy, a disease that almost crippled the supremacy of the British Navy

FIGURE 48 The genus *Nicotiana* is familiar as the source of tobacco. However, members of the genus have been widely grown in Europe as garden flowers since the seventeenth century. The illustration shown here is from Jane Loudon's *The ladies' companion to the flower garden* (1840). Loudon was an important promoter of the science of botany for the beginner in the nineteenth century, and presented botany in a palatable manner; something she argued was difficult for many of her male colleagues.

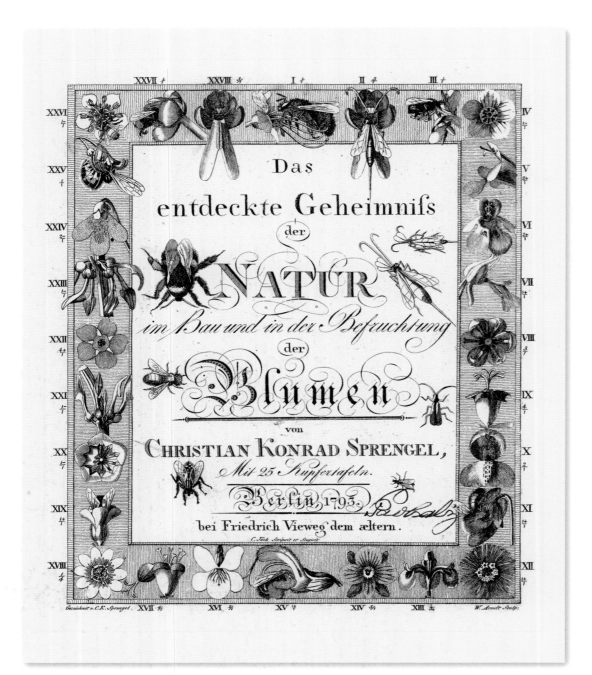

FIGURE 49   The title page of Christian Sprengel's *Das entdeckte Geheimnis der Natur im Bau und in der Befruchtung der Blumen* (1793) shows numerous flowers and their pollinators, e.g. the horse chestnut (*Aesculus hippocastanum*) with a bumblebee, the orchid *Ophrys ouata* with a pollinating solitary wasp, and figwort (*Scrophularia nodosa*) with a pollinating wasp. A carving of the title page is included on a monument to Sprengel in the Berlin Botanical Gardens.

in the eighteenth and nineteenth centuries and resulted in the deaths of thousands of sailors. Scurvy is caused by a deficiency of vitamin C, which is prevalent in diets that are deficient in fresh fruit and vegetables. By the end of the eighteenth century, lemon (*Citrus* x *limon*) juice had been identified as an excellent means of preventing scurvy. However, confusion over the names of citrus fruits and, to some extent political expediencies, saw limes (*C. aurantiifolia*) being used by the British Navy. However, limes, with only about a quarter of the vitamin C content of lemons, were effectively useless for preventing scurvy; thousands of British sailors died unnecessarily because of this taxonomic error.

Sex and hybridisation

Sex outrages, embarrasses and titillates, yet it is central to understanding biology. Today, the idea that plants sexually reproduce is taken for granted, but in the eighteenth century the idea was sufficiently modern to be outrageous. In previous centuries, through religious doctrine, it had been suggested that plants were asexual entities and therefore had not shared the fate of animals following the Fall of Man. There were, however, exceptions to the 'asexual rule'. The date palm, which has been cultivated since at least 4000 BC, was one. Sexual differentiation in the date palm had been understood since at least 2300 BC, since artificial pollination was practised by the ancient Babylonians as a standard management technique. However, plants that engaged in sex, like animals, were considered odd.

The first significant experimental work on understanding plant sex was made by Rudolf Jakob Camerer (1665–1721), Professor of Natural Philosophy at the University of Tübingen, when he published *De sexu plantarum epistola* (1694). Camerer demonstrated experimentally the occurrence of sex in plants. At about the same time, the English scientists Nehemiah Grew (1641–1712) and Sir Thomas Millington (1628–1704) proposed that stamens served as males in seed formation, and, in 1717, the French botanist Sebastien Vaillant (1669–1722) wrote a highly influential paper on plant sexuality. Ideas of plant sex were accepted by the great English botanist John Ray, and, in 1704, a posthumous paper was published by the English diplomat Samuel Morland (1625–1695) that unravelled some of the ways in which the process of plant sex worked.

Between 1761 and 1766, Joseph Gottlieb Kölreuter (1733–1806), Professor of Natural History at the University of Karlsruhe, published a series of seminal papers on the results from his experiments on crossing within and between plant species, especially members of the tobacco genus *Nicotiana*. Kölreuter showed that individuals of the same species commonly crossed, and that fertile hybrids were produced when different species were crossed. However, the significance of these experiments was largely overlooked by the scientific establishment. Just before he died, the German physician and plant hybridiser Carl Friedrich von Gärtner (1772–1850) summarised attitudes to Kölreuter's work:

> hybridisation in its scientific significance was so little thought of, and at the most regarded merely as a proof of the sexuality of plants, that the many important suggestions and actual data which this diligent and exact observer recorded in various treatises have found but little

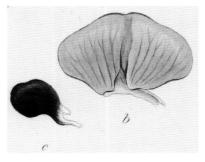

Pisum arvense

FIGURE 50 The garden pea was been a staple of European agriculture for thousands of years and many different types have been selected. The variation within the garden pea made this plant an ideal model plant for the breeding studies of Andrew Knight and Gregor Mendel, which ultimately led to our understanding of the genetic basis of inheritance. This copper engraving, based on a watercolour by Ferdinand Bauer, is from Volume 7 of Sibthorp and Smith's *Flora Graeca* (1832).

FIGURE 51   James Sowerby's *English Botany* (1790–1813) is a defining publication about British plants. Not only did it illustrate all British plants as high-quality colour images; *English Botany* also established Sowerby and his family as the pre-eminent printers of natural history illustrations of the early nineteenth century. Sowerby not only illustrated wild type plants; he also illustrated mutants such as this peloric form of yellow toadflax published in 1797.

acceptance in plant physiological papers up to the most recent time. On the other hand, even in respect of the sexuality of plants, they were attacked to such a degree that their genuineness was doubted and strenuously contradicted, or else they were regarded as a sort of inoculation phenomenon belonging to gardening.[123]

The third member of the Germanic trio who changed our view of plant sex was the botanist and classicist Christian Konrad Sprengel (1750–1816). Sprengel is intimately associated with our understanding of plant pollination and the interactions between flowers and their insect visitors. Sprengel was one of the founders of pollination ecology, together with Kölreuter. Sprengel's most famous publication was *Das entdeckte Geheimnis der Natur im Bau und in der Befruchtung der Blumen* (The newly-revealed secret of nature in the structure and fertilisation of flowers) (1793). However, this book, and most of Sprengel's work, was ignored during his lifetime. It was not until the publication of Charles Darwin's *On the various contrivances by which British and foreign orchids are fertilised by insects, and on the good effects of intercrossing* (1862) that the study of pollination gained scientific respectability, and the pioneering nature of Sprengel's work was understood.

In Britain, practical horticulturalists were starting to make crosses within and between plant species to improve crops or garden plants. Gardens, nurseries and orchards provided an ideal location to put into practice ideas of plant improvement; they were, and are, a plant hybridiser's paradise. However, these plant improvers were often working in isolation from each other and the wider scientific community. Prominent among the early plant improvers was the English

fruit and vegetable breeder Thomas Andrew Knight (1759–1838), whose primary interests were soft and top fruit, especially apples and pears. Working at the start of the nineteenth century, he was pragmatic enough to realise that if he wanted quick results he needed a plant with a short lifecycle; the plant he chose was the annual garden pea. Through hybridisations between different types of garden pea, Knight made considerable progress in showing how variation was inherited from one generation to the next. However, unlike a Moravian monk who chose to cross peas later in the same century, Knight did not count the different offspring that resulted from the crosses. Knight appeared to be more interested in the products of the hybridisation rather than determining the rules of inheritance that Gregor Mendel eventually uncovered. Knight made significant general observations, including that:

> new varieties of every species of fruit will generally be better obtained by introducing the farina (pollen) of one variety of fruit into the blossom of another, than by propagating from one single kind.[124]

At the start of the eighteenth century, the nurseryman Thomas Fairchild (1667–1729) had transferred the pollen of a sweet william onto the pistil of a carnation and produced plants that became known as Fairchild's mules. Fairchild's results had little impact beyond curiosity value; their significance was ignored, just like the more comprehensive hybridisation experiments conducted by Kölreuter and Sprengel. The results of hybridisation experiments, and the possibility that hybrids occurred naturally, led people to start questioning, at least implicitly, the assumption that species numbers had been fixed at the Creation. 'Fairchild's mule', a dramatic, if largely forgotten, horticultural event, and the activities of florists' societies were presaging, albeit 'through a glass darkly', the science of genetics that would come to dominate biology in the latter half of the twentieth century.

Understanding variation

Mutant plants appear naturally in the garden and the wild. Some attract people's attention and are likely to be propagated and cultivated; others are merely recorded as curiosities; most go unrecorded. However, there is a particular breed of botanist who wishes to name every minute morphological variant as separate species.[125] Highly variable plant groups – for example, carnations and pinks, auriculas and oriental hyacinths – attracted the attention of such botanists, and the florists' societies of early-seventeenth-century Europe flourished. Natural variation was being used to select artificially particular forms of plants.[126] Yet Linnaeus derided the florists' activities:

> these men cultivate a science peculiar to themselves, the mysteries of which are known only to the adepts; nor can such knowledge be worth the attention of the botanist; wherefore let no sound botanist ever enter into their societies.[127]

Others, such as the early-nineteenth-century physician Robert Thornton, admired how the florists transformed the wild ancestors of garden flowers: 'in its [carnation] wild state it … attracts no notice from its beauty, … Art accomplishes all the rest'.[128]

In 1742, one of Linnaeus's students brought him an unusual variant of the yellow toadflax (*Linaria vulgare*), which had been collected near Uppsala. Rather than

the flowers having one spur and one plane of symmetry, the flowers had five spurs and five planes of symmetry. Linnaeus grew seeds from this unusual type and showed that more of the same were produced. He decided that the plant was a new species, which he called *Peloria*, and that it was derived from yellow toadflax. However, the French botanist Michel Adanson (1727–1806) found that *Peloria* plants and the seed supplied to him, in Paris, by Linnaeus produced a mixture of plants with normal and peloric flowers. Adanson concluded that *Peloria* was merely a monstrosity, not a new species.

Botanical monstrosities

'Botanical monstrosities' had been part of botanic gardens since they were founded. Indeed, they were seen by some as a means to discover the 'mind of God'. Besides colour variants, the most commonly seen 'aberrations of nature' were double flowers. In the 1648 catalogue to the Oxford Botanic Garden, Bobart the Elder recorded nine types of anemone, of which five had double flowers. The mid-Victorian gardener Maxwell Tylden Masters (1833–1907) wrote a seminal work on the subject of monstrosities, *Vegetable teratology* (1869), which described 'the principal deviations from the usual construction of plants'.

The debate over variants such as *Peloria* questioned the church's dogma of the fixity of species, and Linnaeus was having his doubts:

> the flowers of some species are impregnated by the farina [pollen] of different genera, and species, inasmuch that hybridous or mongrel plants are frequently produced, which if not admitted as new species, are at least permanent varieties.[129]

By the end of the eighteenth century, the evidence being built against the belief that species were divinely fixed and immutable was becoming overwhelming. It would only be a matter of time before the dogma was finally rejected. In 1800, the French naturalist and evolutionary theorist Jean-Baptiste Lamarck (1744–1829) proposed a coherent theory of evolution based around two main themes. First, a force drove organisms from simple to complex forms; second, another force adapted organisms to their local environments and differentiated them from each other. These ideas became known as the theory of acquired characteristics. Despite the popularity of Lamarck's general ideas, as always, the devil was in the detail. There were many cases where the theory of acquired characteristics could not explain natural variation.

Darwinian evolution

In *On the Origin of Species* (1859), Charles Darwin amassed evidence from nature and animal and plant breeders to show the variability of species, why the variation was important, and how species could evolve. When he received a copy of *On the Origin of Species* from Darwin, the natural theologian and author Charles Kingsley (1819–75) was of the view that, rather than species being fixed by a deity at creation, a divine bump-start got the evolutionary charabanc moving:

> All I have seen of it *awes* me; both with the heap of facts, & the prestige of your name, & also with the clear intuition, that if you be right, I must give up much that I have believed & written.... From two common superstitions, at least, I shall be free, while judging of your book. 1) I have long since, from watching the crossing of domesticated animals & plants, learnt to disbelieve the dogma of the permanence of species. 2) I have gradually learnt to see that it is just as noble a conception of Deity, to believe that he created primal forms capable of self development into all forms needful pro tempore & pro loco, as to believe that He required a fresh act of intervention to supply the lacunas wh he himself had made. I question whether the former be not the loftier thought.[130]

Others were not so open-minded, and a century of debate followed before the mechanism of evolution proposed by Darwin was accepted by the rational majority. The scientific significance of the florists' activities, so derided by Linnaeus, and that of plant and animal breeders, was becoming clear. They were selecting particular parts of natural species' variability, mimicking what occurred in natural populations.

Mendel's genetic breakthrough

Despite the beauty of Darwin's theory, he failed to resolve the means by which genetic information was passed from one generation to the next. It was the monk Gregor Mendel, and his quantitative approach to experiments on garden peas at a monastery in Brno, that provided a solution to this problem. Mendel's experiments showed that if a wrinkly seeded pea was crossed with a round-seeded one, then all round-seeded peas were produced. However, if this pea was then crossed with itself, it would produce three round-seeded peas for every wrinkly-seeded pea. These results were repeated for traits that ranged from stem length to seed coat colour. In the language of today, Mendel showed that each inherited trait is governed by a gene. Each individual has two sets of genes. One gene is inherited from each parent and transmitted unchanged from one generation to the next. The traits of each generation are produced by reshuffling gene combinations of the previous generation. Gene forms (alleles) can be dominant or recessive. An individual that inherits two dominant alleles or a single dominant allele for a trait displays the dominant trait. To display a recessive trait, an individual must inherit two recessive alleles for that trait. However, this work was overlooked, and, despite having a copy of Mendel's 1866 paper that reported these results, Darwin failed to grasp the significance of Mendel's discovery for his own ideas. This insight would come at the start of the twentieth century, as the new science of genetics was born.

Darwinian evolution has become the unifying principle of biology: a rational process that could be invoked to explain plant and animal diversity. The vista Darwin and Mendel had opened to understanding the diversity of life on earth is based on: variation in natural populations; the inheritance of genetic information from one generation to the next; and the selection of genetic types, through time, that are adapted to particular environments. The understanding of selection (both natural and artificial), together with genetics, meant that humans had the opportunity to manipulate plants towards particular forms, whether it

was shorter wheat, peas that were suitable for machine harvest, or plants that were resistant to particular diseases. Man, the great manipulator, was no longer working with his eyes closed; rather, he was able to see through a distorted lens the genetic bases of characters that had been manipulated by his ancestors. The garden was one arena where these evolutionary battles had been fought out blindly for generations; they would now be fought with an understanding of the underlying mechanisms.

Human relationships with plants, understanding plant diversity and cultivation, and how plants work, have not stopped. Between 1501 and 1900 the basic pattern of plant diversity was mapped and some of the details defined. The last century saw a move away from the description of diversity, and a dividend placed on knowing how plants worked and how they can be manipulated scientifically. As human populations continue to grow and the planet's climate changes, it is likely a premium will be placed on maximising the exploitation of economically important plants, understanding how plants respond to different climate-change scenarios, and protecting, conserving and understanding those fragments of vegetation that survived the twentieth century.

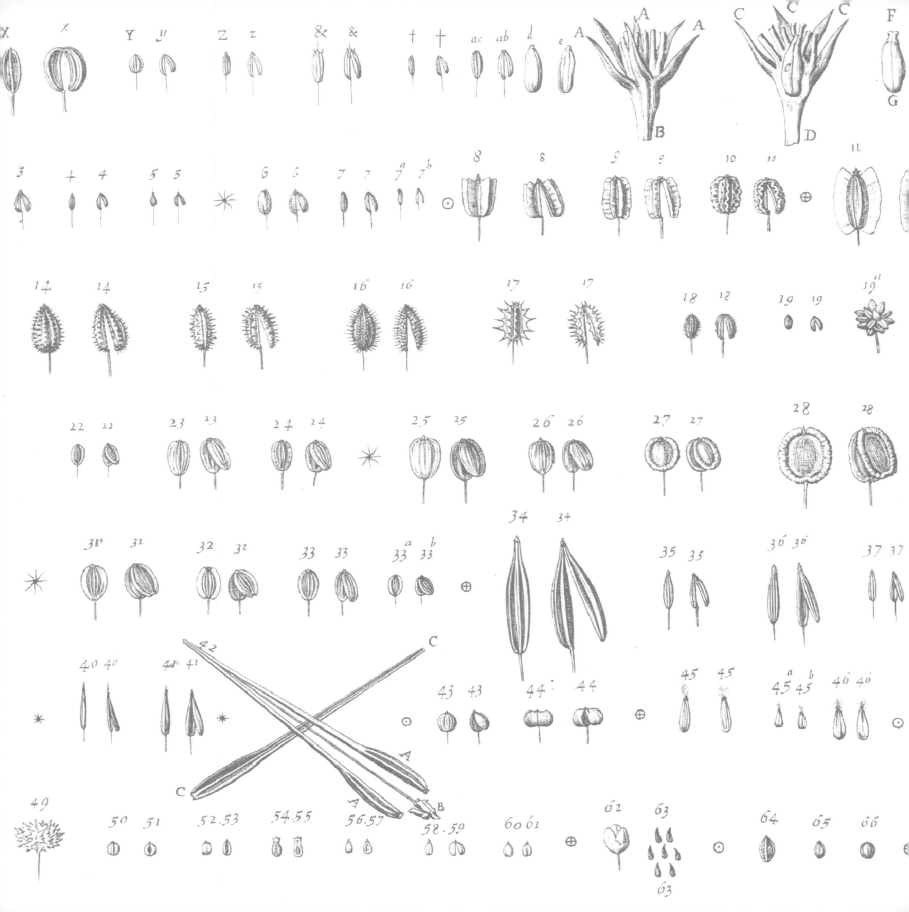

Notes

1. In this book, 'Oxford Botanic Garden' will be used, irrespective of period.
2. Gerard (1633, p. 754).
3. Wallace (1869, pp. 85–6).
4. Harvey (1858, p. vi).
5. Papenfuss (1976).
6. Harvey (1858, p. i).
7. Harvey (1858, p. vi).
8. Catesby (1767, Preface).
9. Whitehead (1979).
10. Wilson (1995, p. lii).
11. Parkinson (1640, p. 1064).
12. Parkinson (1629, p. 339).
13. Fontenelle (1708); author's translation.
14. Lecture notes by Professor John Sibthorp (MS Sherard 219, f.45r, Plant Sciences Library, University of Oxford).
15. Harris (2007, p. 72).
16. Gardner(1846, p. vii).
17. Bates (1989, pp. 248–9).
18. von Humboldt (1995, p. 8).
19. Turrill (1938, p. 197).
20. Harvey (1858, pp. v–vi).
21. Anonymous (1804, p. 883).
22. Lindley (1821, additional page at front of volume; dated London Oct. 31, 1821).
23. Botany lectures delivered by John Sibthorp between 1788 and 1793 (MS Sherard 219, f.14r; Plant Sciences Library, University of Oxford).
24. Banks et al. (1994) and Desmond (1998).
25. Botany lectures delivered by John Sibthorp between 1788 and 1793 (MS Sherard 219, f.43r; Plant Sciences Library, University of Oxford).
26. Botany lectures delivered by John Sibthorp between 1788 and 1793 (MS Sherard 219, f.24r; Plant Sciences Library, University of Oxford).
27. Druce (1928, p. 465).
28. Anonymous (1710).
29. Daubeny (1853, p. 4).
30. Raven (1950, p. 259).
31. Hamilton (1796, p. 192).
32. Turner (1586, p. 12).
33. Druce (1928, p. 465).
34. Fairclough (1916, 149–54).
35. Wallace (1869, pp. 86–7).

36. Turner (1687, To the Reader).

37. Coles (1657, p. 3).

38. Jackson (1881, p. 7).

39. Dodoens (1583) cited in Arber (1986, p. 255).

40. Culpeper (1656, To the Reader).

41. Culpeper (1649, p. Aiv).

42. Culpeper (1656, To the Reader).

43. Culpeper (1656, p. 375).

44. Culpeper (1656, p. 377).

45. Coles (1656, 'To the most exquisite lover of plants, Elias Ashmole Esq').

46. Coles (1656, pp. 76–7).

47. Richardson-Boedler (1999, p. 172)

48. Coles (1656, 'To the most exquisite lover of plants, Elias Ashmole Esq').

49. Brown (1822) and Nais (2001).

50. Letter from T.S. Raffles to Joseph Banks, dated 13th August 1818, transcribed in Brown (1822, pp. 202–3).

51. William Shakespeare, *Romeo and Juliet*, Act IV, Scene III.

52. Gerard (1633, p. 351).

53. Parkinson (1640, p. 343).

54. Bishop Butler in Walker (1833, p. viii).

55. Singer (1927, p. 1).

56. Coles (1656, p. 4).

57. Jones (2001, p. 273).

58. Druce (1890, p. 538).

59. Treveris (1526, Introduction).

60. Treveris (1526, p. ca clvii).

61. Treveris (1526, p. ca clvii).

62. Treveris (1526, p. ca clvii).

63. Turner (1664, Preface).

64. Green (1824, p. 38).

65. Robert Cross to Secretary of State for India, dated 9 November 1861 in PBB (1852–1863).

66. Cited by Juniper and Mabberley (2006, p. 148).

67. Darwin (1868, p. 378).

68. Quoted in Nepomuceno (2008, p. 26; author's translation).

69. Graham (1824, entry for 21 December 1821).

70. Gardner (1846, p. 34).

71. Gardner (1846, p. 512).

72. Bradley (1718, p. 234).

73. Bradley (1718, p. 235).

74. Cited in Coe and Coe (1996, p. 109).

75. Gardner (1846, p. 35).

76. Morris (1898, Preface).

77. Díaz (1963, p. 42).

78. Harvey (1858, Advertisement).

79. Dillwyn (1843, Preface, p. vii).

80. Letter from Jacob Bobart the Younger to Mary Somerset, Duchess of Badminton, dated 28th March 1694 [British Library; Sloane MS 3343 f.f.37r-37v].

81. Catesby (1767, pp. 1-2).

82. Letter from Jacob Bobart the Younger to Mary Somerset, Duchess of Badminton, dated 28th March 1694 [British Library; Sloane MS 3343 ff.37r-37v].

83. Cited by Alexander (2004, p. 49).

84. Hooker (1828).

85. Ward (1852, p. 87) and Allen (1984).

86. Lemmon (1968, p. 2).

87. Guilding (1825, p. 5).

88. Norman (1897, p. 369).

89. In Amazonia, 4,000,000 kg rubber cost 30,000 lives (1 life ≈ 130 kg) and in Congo, 75,000,000 kg rubber cost 15,000,000 lives (1 life ≈ 5 kg). Figures are derived from Loadman (2005, Chapters 7 and 8).

90. Letter from Wickham to Thistleton-Dyer, dated 4 September 1901, cited in Jackson (2008, p. 270).

91. Walker (1833, p. 177).

92. Catesby (1767, Preface).

93. Catesby (1767, Preface).

94. Catesby (1767, Preface).

95. Bradley (1718, pp. 113–16).

96. Bradley (1718, p. 198).

97. Rea (1676, p. 16).

98. De Beer (2006, entry for 6 August 1685).

99. Hamilton (1796, p. 188).

100. Hamilton (1796, p. 182).

101. Spruce (1908, p. 75).

102. *Illustrated London News*, 17 November 1849.

103. Linnaeus (1737, *Dedicatio*).

104. Hooker (1858).

105. Hooper (1934, XXXVIII).

106. Günther (1912, p. 2).
107. Darwin (1800, pp. 230–31).
108. Lamer (1957, p. 37).
109. Hartlib (1651, 47).
110. Tull (1743, p. 18).
111. Fairclough (1916, pp. 177–8).
112. Hooper (1934).
113. 'The Stable yields a stercoraceous heap, / Impregnated with quick fermenting salts' in Cowper (1830, p. 80).
114. Catesby (1767, Preface).
115. Bauer (1830–1838, p. xiv).
116. Bauer (1830–1838, p. xiv).
117. Smith (1819).
118. Fairclough (1916, pp. 69–73).
119. Hooper (1934, I: XL).
120. Rackham (2003, Book 35, 50).
121. Smith (1821, vol. 2, p. 281).
122. Botany lectures delivered by John Sibthorp between 1788 and 1793 (MS Sherard 219, f.39, Plant Sciences Library, University of Oxford).
123. von Gärtner (1849) quoted from a translation in Roberts (1929, p. 78).
124. Knight (1823, p. 378).
125. Allen (1986).
126. Duthie (1988).
127. Cited in the entry for carnations by Thornton (1807).
128. Cited in the entry for carnations by Thornton (1807).
129. Bremer (1759) cited by Briggs and Walters (1997, p. 14).
130. Letter from Charles Kingsley to Charles Darwin, dated 18 November 1859 (Darwin Correspondence project, www.darwin-project.ac.uk/home).

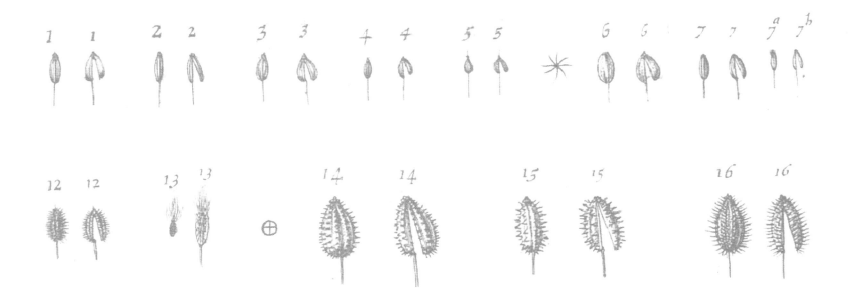

Further reading

———

References from many diverse sources were used in the writing of this book. Many are referred to in the text, either by name or as sources of quotations. Other useful general sources of additional information are described below for each chapter.

Chapter 1   Introductions to human relationships with plants are to be found in Hobhouse (1999), Murphy (2007) and Harlan (1992). Morton (1981) provides a useful history of botany between 1501 and 1900. Allen (1969) discusses the Victorian and Edwardian fern craze.

Chapter 2   Crosby (2003) and Dunmire (2004) describe the exchange of plants between the Old and New Worlds. Pavord (2005) gives an introduction of the history of plant names and classification systems. Cook (2007) discusses the impact of new scientific discoveries on commerce in seventeenth century Holland. Arber (1986) remains the classic account of the printed Herbal, whilst Collins (2000) makes a specialised study of medieval manuscripts. Bushnell (2003) provides a fascinating discussion of at whom books in the seventeenth and eighteenth centuries may have been aimed, together with Allen (1984). Brockway (1979) looks at botanic gardens, especially Kew, in relation to imperial expansion. Findlen (1994) discusses Italian botanic gardens specifically. The history of the botanic garden in St Vincent is presented by Howards (1997) and Guilding (1825). Allen and Walker (1995) is a modern history of the Oxford Botanic Garden. Clokie (1964) discusses the history of

the Oxford University herbaria, whilst Marner (2006) discusses the da Reggio herbarium in particular. Honigsbaum (2001) and Jackson (2008) are semi-popular accounts of the stories of quinine and rubber. Potter (2007) discusses the life of the Tradescants, whilst Carter (1988) and Preston and Preston (2005) look at the lives of Joseph Banks and William Dampier, respectively. The North American plant collectors Peter Collinson and John and William Bartram are discussed by Slaughter (1996) and Wulf (2008). Frick and Stearns (1961) discuss the life and work of Mark Catesby, whilst Parkinson (2007) writes about the life of John Parkinson. Harris (2007) considers the work of John Sibthorp and Ferdinand Bauer, and the publication of the *Flora Graeca*. Wilson (2000) is a biography of Alfred Russel Wallace. Henig (2000) describes the life and work of Gregor Mendel. Raven (1950) gives a comprehensive account of the life and work of John Ray.

Chapter 3   Prest (1981) discusses in detail the notion that botanic gardens are imitations of Paradise. Morison (1978) describes the voyages of Columbus to the New World. Ogilvie (2006) describes the intellectual environment surrounding investigations of natural history in Renaissance Europe. Griggs (1996) describes the Doctorine of Signatures, Hatfield (2005) argues that the Doctorine has been misunderstood by academic writers on the subject. Nais (2001) describes *Rafflesia*. Lee (1887) and Thompson (1934) provide detailed accounts of the folklore surrounding the Scythian lamb and mandrake, respectively. Appleby (1997) gives a modern interpretation of the Scythian lamb story.

Chapter 4   Ebbell (1937) describes the *Ebers Papyrus*. Schiebinger (2004, 2005) describes the effects of bioprospecting by European naturalists on tropical colonies. Holloway (1991) is an invaluable history of pharmaceutical medicine in Britain. Allen and Hatfield (2004) is a history of folk medicine in Britain and Ireland. Honigsbaum (2001) is the best popular account of the complex history of *Cinchona* and its cultivation. Markham (1880) gives a fascinating account of the issues associated with the introduction of quinine, as they were perceived by one of the main architects of the introduction of *Cinchona* into British India. Spruce (1908) provides an exceptional account of the difficulties of collecting *Cinchona* seed in Ecuador. Brockway (1979) has an excellent chapter on the role of the Royal Botanic Garden Kew in the introduction of *Cinchona* to British India. Camp (1949) investigates the distribution of quinine alkaloid across the genus's geographical range. Hodgkin (1995) and Hedrick (1919) give brief introductions to the history and domestication of cabbages. A history of the apple is presented by Juniper and Mabberley (2006). Purseglove (1968), Weinberg and Bealer (2002), Coe and Coe (1996) and Moxham (2004) provide details on the biology, history and consumption of various caffeine-producing plants. Koerner (1999) discusses the Swedish policy of cameralism under Linnaeus. Nepomuceno (2008) gives a history of the Rio Botanic garden (in Portuguese).

Chapter 5   Thoday (2007) provides a valuable introduction to the history and science of plant cultivation. Juma (1989) gives a useful introduction some of the issues involved in moving seeds, whilst Harvie (2002) gives history of scurvy. Pavord (1998) and Dash (1999) provide histories of the tulip. Egmond et al. (2007) provides context for the importance of Carolus Clusius. Baskin and Baskin (2000) is the standard text on seed biology, whilst Daws et al. (2007) reports on the seeds discovered in the British National Archives, and Shen-Miller et al. (1995) is an account of sacred lotus seed longevity. Alexander (2004) is one of numerous accounts of the voyage of the *Bounty*. Ward (1852) and van Schoenermarck (1974) describe Wardian cases and their importance for the movement of plants. Tyldesley (1998) gives an account of the life and legacy of Hatshepsut. Dahlgren (1940) and Ruiz (1998) are accounts of the expeditions of Ruiz and Pavon. Grove (1995) gives an account of botanic gardens in the Caribbean, with a focus on St. Vincent. Mylechreest (1984) considers the contribution of Andrew Knight. French (1987) was the source of information regarding rubber content in Model T Ford Tyres, whilst accounts of rubber are given by Loadman (2005) and Jackson (2008). A critical view of the role of European

countries in the Brazil rubber economy is provided by Dean (1987). Salisbury (1964) remains a population introduction to weeds and alien plants. Harris (2002) gives a detailed history of the introduction of Oxford ragwort to Britain, whilst Abbott (1992) considers some of the evolutionary consequences. Brown (2004) gives a rhododendron enthusiast's account of the genus. Cross (1975) specifically discusses *Rhododendron ponticum*, whilst Milne and Abbott (2000) investigate its origin and evolution in the UK. Tiley et al. (1996) discusses the ecology of giant hogweed in Britain, whilst Bailey and Conolly (2000) discuss Japanese knotweed.

Chapter 6   Britz (1974) is an account of the early development of the greenhouse. Spary (2000) discusses the development in gardening technology made in the Jardin d'Roi in Paris. Slocum (2005) discusses waterlily cultivation. Colquhoun (2003) is an account of the life and work of Joseph Paxton. Symon and Jusaitis (2007) is an account of Sturt's pea, whilst George (1999) makes a case for changing the scientific name of the pea to commemorate William Dampier. Mather and Hart (1956) is a fascinating account of manure and Leigh (2004) looks at the importance of nitrogen. Duthie (1988) is an account of the activities of the florist societies. Parejko (2003) describes the extinction of silphium in ancient times, whilst Del Tredici (2005) describes the background to the cultivation on *Franklinia*. Weiss (1930) and Grant (1975) discuss graft-hybrids.

Chapter 7   For an entertaining and informative discussion of the history of chemistry and colour, see Ball (2008). A semi-popular account of the history of pre-Linnaean classification systems is given by Pavord (2005); a more detailed account is provided by Morton (1981, Chapters 3, 7 and 8). For details on the life of Robert Morison, see Boulger (1909) and Vines (1913). See Stevens (1994) for an account of alternative approaches to Linnaean classification in the eighteenth century. Spencer et al. (2007) is a modern introduction to the intricacies of botanical nomenclatural codes. Bernasconi and Taiz (2002) give an account of Vaillant's seminal 1717 lecture on the structure and function of flowers. Roberts (1929) and Zirkle (1935) are fascinating histories of hybridisation before the work of Mendel. Leapman (2000) discusses the life and work of Thomas Fairchild. Linnaeus's account of peloria can be found in Rudberg (1744). Fairbanks and Rytting (2001) give an account of the controversies that surround the work on Mendel, whilst an English translation of Mendel's paper may be found in Druery and Bateson (1901).

References

Abbott, R.J. (1992) Plant invasions, interspecific hybridisation and the evolution of new plant taxa. *Trends in Ecology & Evolution* 7: 401–5.

Alexander, C. (2004) *The Bounty. The true story of the mutiny on the Bounty.* London: Harper Perennial.

Allen, D.E., & Hatfield, G. (2004) *Medicinal plants in folk traditions. An ethnobotany of Britain and Ireland.* Portland: Timber Press.

Allen, D.E. (1969) *The Victorian fern craze.* London: Hutchinson.

Allen, D.E. (1984) *The naturalist in Britain. A social history.* Princeton: Princeton University Press.

Allen, D.E. (1986) *The botanists. A history of the Botanical Society of the British Isles through a hundred and fifty years.* Winchester: St Paul's Bibliographies.

Allen, L., & Walker, T. (1995) *The University of Oxford Botanic Garden.* Oxford: University of Oxford Botanic Garden.

Anonymous (1710) From my own apartment, August 25. *The Tatler* 216: 150.

Anonymous (1804) A Description of the Genus Pinus. By Aylmer Bourke Lambert, Esq. F.R.S. Vice President of the Linnaean Society. *Annual review, and history of literature* 2 (1803): 882–8.

Appleby, J.H. (1997) The Royal Society and the Tartar Lamb. *Notes and Records of the Royal Society of London* 51: 23–34.

Arber, A. (1986) *Herbals.* Cambridge: Cambridge University Press.

Bailey, J.P., & Conolly, A.P. (2000) Prize-winners to pariahs – A history of Japanese Knotweed s.l. (Polygonaceae) in the British Isles. *Watsonia* 23: 93–110.

Ball, P. (2008) *Bright earth. The invention of colour.* London: Vintage Books.

Banks, R.E.R., Elliot, B., Hawkes, J.G., King-Hele, D., & Lucas, G.L. (1994) *Sir Joseph Banks. A global perspective.* Kew: The Royal Botanic Gardens.

Baskin, C.C., & Baskin, JM. (2000) *Seeds: ecology, biogeography, and evolution of dormancy and germination.* San Diego: Academic Press.

Bates, HW. (1989) *The naturalist on the river Amazons.* London: Penguin Books.

Bauer, F. (1830–1838) *Illustrations of orchidaceous plants.* London: James Ridgway & Sons.

Bernasconi, P., & Taiz, L. (2002) Sebastian Vaillant's 1717 lecture on the structure and function of flowers. *Huntia* 11: 97–128.

Boulger, G.S. (1909) *Morison, Robert.* In Lee, S., ed., *Dictionary of national biography*, pp. 958–60. London: Smith, Elder & Co.

Bradley, R. (1718) *New improvements of planting and gardening, both philosophical and practical; explaining the motion of the sapp and generation of plants.* London: W. Mears.

Bremer, P. (1759) *Somnus plantarum.* In Linnaeus, C., ed., *Amoenitates academicae*, pp. 333–350. Holmiae: Laurentii Salvii.

Briggs, D., & Walters, S.M. (1997) *Plant variation and evolution*. Cambridge: Cambridge University Press.

Britz, B.S. (1974) Environmental provisions for plants in seventeenth-century northern Europe. *Journal of the Society of Architectural Historians* 33: 133–44.

Brockway, L.H. (1979) *Science and colonial expansion. The role of the British Royal Botanic Gardens*. New Haven: Yale University Press.

Brown, J. (2004) *Tales of the rose tree. Ravishing rhododendrons and their travels around the world*. London: HarperCollins.

Brown, R. (1822) An account of a new genus of plants, named *Rafflesia*. *The Transactions of the Linnean Society of London* 13: 201–34, t.215–222.

Bushnell, R. (2003) *Green desire. Imagining Early Modern English gardens*. Ithaca: Cornell University Press.

Camp, W.H. (1949) Cinchona at high altitudes in Ecuador. *Brittonia* 6: 394–430.

Carter, H.B. (1988) *Sir Joseph Banks, 1743–1820*. London: British Museum (Natural History).

Catesby, M. (1767) *Hortus Europae Americanus: or, a collection of 85 curious trees and shrubs, the produce of North America; adapted to the climates and soils of Great-Britain, Ireland, and most Parts of Europe, &c. together with their blossoms, fruits and seeds; observations on thier culture, growth, constitution and virtues with directions how to collect, pack up, and secure them in their passage*. London: J. Millan.

Clokie, H.N. (1964) *An account of the Herbaria of the Department of Botany in the University of Oxford*. Oxford: Oxford University Press.

Coe, S.D., & Coe, M.D. (1996) *The true history of chocolate*. London: Thames & Hudson.

Coles, W. (1656) *The art of simpling. An introduction to the knowledge and gathering of plants*. London: Nath. Brook.

Coles, W. (1657) *Adam in Eden; or, Natures Paradise. The history of plants, fruits, herbs and flowers*. London: J. Streater.

Collins, M. (2000) *Medieval herbals. The illustrative traditions*. London: British Library and University of Toronto.

Colquhoun, K. (2003) *A thing in disguise. The visionary life of Joseph Paxton*. London: HarperPerennial.

Cook, H.J. (2007) *Matters of exchange. Commerce, medicine, and science in the Dutch Golden Age*. New Haven: Yale University Press.

Cowper, W. (1830) *The poetical works of William Cowper*. Volume II. London: William Pickering.

Crosby, A.W. (2003) *The Columbian exchange. Biological and cultural consequences of 1492 Connecticut*. Westport: Praeger.

Cross, J.R. (1975) Biological flora of the British Isles: *Rhododendron ponticum* L. *Journal of Ecology* 63: 345–64.

Culpeper, N. (1649) *A Physicall Directory of a translation of the London dispensatory*. London: Peter Cole.

Culpeper, N. (1656) *The English Physitian enlarged*. London: Peter Cole.

Dahlgren, B.E. (1940) *Travels of Ruiz, Pavon and Dombey in Peru and Chile (1777–1788)*. Chicago: Field Museum of Natural History.

Darwin, C.R. (1868) *The variation of animals and plants under domestication*. London: John Murray.

Darwin, E. (1800) *Phytologia; or the Philosophy of agriculture and gardening with the theory of draining morasses and with an improved construction of the drill plough*. Dublin: P. Byrne.

Dash, M. (1999) *Tulipomania. The story of the world's most coveted flower and the extraordinary passions it aroused*. London: Indigo.

Daubeny C. (1853) *Oxford Botanic Garden; or a popular guide to the Botanic Garden of Oxford*. Oxford: privately published.

Daws, M.I., Davies, J., Vaes, E., van Gelder, R., & Pritchard, H.W. (2007) Two-hundred-year seed survival of *Leucospermum* and two other woody species from the Cape Floristic region, South Africa. *Seed Science Research* 17: 73–9.

de Beer, E.S., ed. (2006) *The diary of John Evelyn*. London: Everyman's Library.

Dean, W. (1987) *Brazil and the struggle for rubber. A study in environmental history*. Cambridge: Cambridge University Press.

Del Tredici, P. (2005) Against all odds. Growing *Franklinia* in Boston. *Arnoldia* 63: 2–7.

Desmond, R. (1998) *Kew. The history of the Royal Botanic Gardens*. London: The Harvill Press.

Díaz, B. (1963) *The conquest of New Spain*. London: Penguin Books.

Dillwyn, L.W. (1843) *Hortus Collinsonianus. An account of the plants cultivated by the late Peter Collinson, Esq., F.R.S.* Swansea: W.C. Murray and D. Rees.

Dodoens, R. 1583. *Stirpium historiae pemptades sex. sive libri xxx*. Antverpiae: Christophori Plantini.

Druce, G.C. (1890) History of botany. – (Herbaria) [cont.]. *The Pharmaceutical Journal and Transactions* 20: 536–9.

Druce, G.C. (1928) British plants contained in the Du Bois Herbarium at Oxford. *B.E.C. Report for 1927* 1927: 463–93.

Druery, C.T., & Bateson, W. (1901) Experiments in plant hybridization. *Journal of the Royal Horticultural Society* 26: 1–32.

Dunmire, W.M. (2004) *Gardens of New Spain. How Mediterranean plants and foods changed America*. Austin: University of Texas Press.

Duthie, R. (1988) *Florists' flowers and societies*. Princes Risborough: Shire Press.

Ebbell, B. (1937) *The Papyrus Ebers. The greatest Egyptian medical document.* London: Oxford University Press.

Egmond, F., Hoftijzer P., & Visser, R.P.W. (2007) *Carolus Clusius. Towards a cultural history of a Renaissance naturalist.* Amsterdam: Koninklijke Nederlandse Akademie van Wetenschappen.

Fairbanks, D.J., & Rytting B. (2001) Mendelian controversies: a botanical and historical review. *American Journal of Botany* 88: 737–52.

Fairclough, H.R. (1916) *Virgil. Eclogues, Georgics, Aeneid I–VI.* Cambridge: Harvard University Press.

Findlen, P. (1994) *Possessing nature. Museums, collecting, and scientific culture in early modern Italy.* Berkeley: University of California Press.

Fontenelle, B.B. (1708) Eloge de M. de Tournefort. *Histoire de l'Académie royale des sciences* 3484: 143–54.

French, M.J. (1987) The emergence of a US multinational enterprise: the Goodyear Tire and Rubber Company, 1910–1939. *Economic History Review* 1: 64–79.

Frick, G.F, & Stearns R.P. (1961) *Mark Catesy: the colonial Audubon.* Urbana: University of Illinois Press.

Gardner, G. (1846) *Travels in the interior of Brazil, principally through the Northern Provinces and the gold and diamond districts, during the years 1836–1841.* London: Reeve Brothers.

George, A.S. (1999) *Willdampia*, a new generic name for the Sturt pea. *The Western Australian Naturalist* 22: 191–3.

Gerard, J. (1633) *The Herball or General Historie of Plantes. Gathered by John Gerarde of London Master in Chirurgerie Very much enlarged and amended by Thomas Johnson Citizen and Apothecarye.* London: Adam Islip, Joice Newton & Richard Whitakers.

Graham, M. (1824) *Journal of a voyage to Brazil, and residence there, during part of the years 1821, 1822, 1823.* London: Longman, Hurst, Rees, Orme, Brown, & Green.

Grant, V. (1975) *Genetics of flowering plants.* New York: Columbia University Press.

Green, T. (1824) *The Universal herbal; or, Botanical, medical, and agricultural dictionary.* London: Caxton Press.

Griggs, B. (1996) *Green pharmacy. The history and evolution of Western herbal medicine.* Rochester, Vermont: Healing Arts Press.

Grove, R.H. (1995) *Green imperialism. Colonial expansion, tropical island Edens and the origins of environmentalism, 1660–1860.* Cambridge: Cambridge University Press.

Guilding, L. (1825) *An account of the botanic garden in the island of St. Vincent, from its first establishment to the present time.* Glasgow: Richard Griffin & Co.

Günther, RT. (1912) *Oxford gardens based upon Daubeny's popular guide to the Physick Garden of Oxford: with notes on the gardens of the colleges and on the University park.* Oxford: Parker & Son.

Hamilton, W. (1796) A short account of several gardens near London, with remarks on some particulars wherein they excel, or are deficient, upon a view of them in December 1691. Communicated to the Society by the Reverend Dr. Hamilton, Vice President, from an original Manuscript in his possession. *Archaeologia* 12: 181–92.

Harlan, J.R. (1992) *Crops and man.* Madison: American Society of Agronomy.

Harris, S.A. (2002) Introduction of Oxford ragwort, *Senecio squalidus* L. (Asteraceae), to the United Kingdom. *Watsonia* 24: 31–43.

Harris, S.A. (2007) *The magnificent Flora Graeca. How the Mediterranean came to the English Garden.* Oxford: Bodleian Library.

Hartlib, S. (1651) *Samuel Hartlib his Legacie: or an Enlargement of the Discourse of Husbandry used in Brabant and Flaunders; wherein are bequeathed to the Common-Wealth of England more outlandish and domestick experiments and secrets in reference to universal husbandry.* London: H. Hills.

Harvey, W.H. (1858) *Phycologia Australica; or, a history of Australian seaweeds; comprising coloured figures and descriptions of the more characteristic marine algae of New South Wales, Victoria, Tasmania, South Australia, and Western Australia, and a synopsis of all known Australian algae.* London: Lovel Reeve & Co.

Harvie, D.I. (2002) *Limeys. The conquest of scurvy.* Stroud: Sutton.

Hatfield, G. (2005) *Memory, wisdom and healing.* Stroud: Sutton.

Hedrick, U.P. (1919) *Sturtevant's notes on edible plants.* Albany: J.B. Lyon.

Henig, R.M. (2000) *A monk and two peas. The story of Gregor Mendel and the discovery of genetics.* London: Phoenix.

Hobhouse, H. (1999) *Seeds of change.* London: Papermac.

Hodgkin, T. (1995) Cabbages, kales, etc. In Smartt, J., & Simmonds, N.W., eds, *Evolution of crop plants*, pp. 76–82. Harlow: Longman.

Holloway, S.W.F. (1991) *Royal Pharmaceutical Society of Great Britain 1841–1991. A political and social history.* London: Pharmaceutical Press.

Honigsbaum, M. (2001) *The fever trail. The hunt for the cure for malaria.* London: Macmillan.

Hooker W.D. (1828) *Artocarpus Incisa.* Bread Fruit Tree. *Curtis's Botanical Magazine* 55: t. 2869–2870.

Hooker, W.D. (1858) *Clianthus Dampieri. Curtis's Botanical Magazine* 84: t. 5051.

Hooper, W.D. (1934) *Cato and Varro on agriculture.* Cambridge: Harvard University Press.

Howards, R.A. (1997) The St. Vincent botanic garden – the early years. *Arnoldia* 1997–98: 12–21.

Jackson, B.D. (1881) A draft of a letter by John Gerard. *Cambridge Antiquarian Communications* 4: 1876–80.

Jackson, J. (2008) *The thief at the end of the world. Rubber, power, and the seeds of empire.* London: Duckworth.

Jones, W.H.S. (2001) *Pliny. Natural history. Books 24–27.* London: Harvard University Press.

Juma, C. (1989) *The gene hunters. Biotechnology and the scramble for seeds.* Princeton: Princeton University Press.

Juniper, B.E., & Mabberley, D.J. (2006) *The story of the apple.* Portland: Timber Press.

Knight, T.A. (1823) Some remarks on the supposed influence of the pollen, in cross-breeding, upon the color of the seed-coats of plants, and the qualities of their fruits. *Transactions of the Horticultural Society* 5: 377–80.

Koerner, L. (1999) *Linnaeus. Nature and nation.* Cambridge: Harvard University Press.

Lamer, M. (1957) *The world fertilizer economy.* Stanford: Stanford University Press.

Leapman, M. (2000) *The ingenious Mr Fairchild. The forgotten father of the flower garden.* New York: St. Martin's Press.

Lee, H. (1887) *The vegetable lamb of Tartary. A curious fable of the cotton plant.* London: Sampson Low, Marston, Searle & Rivington.

Leigh, G.J. (2004) *The world's greatest fix. A history of nitrogen and agriculture.* Oxford: Oxford University Press.

Lemmon, K. (1968) *The golden age of plant hunters.* London: Phoenix House.

Lindley, J. (1821) *Collectanea Botanica: or, figures and botanical illustrations of rare and curious exotic plants.* London: Richard & Arthur Taylor.

Linnaeus, C. (1737) *Hortus Cliffortianus. Plantas exhibens quas in hortis vivis quam siccis, Hartecampi in Hollandia.* Amstelaedami.

Loadman, J. (2005) *Tears of the tree. The story of rubber – a modern marvel.* Oxford: Oxford University Press.

Markham, C.R. (1880) *Peruvian bark. A popular account of the introduction of Chinchona cultivation into British India 1860–1880.* London: J. Murray.

Marner, S.K. (2006) 400 years old! [A book herbarium from Italy]. *Oxford Plant Systematics* 13: 9–10.

Mather, E., & Hart, J.F. (1956) The geography of manure. *Land Economics* 32: 25–38.

Milne, R.I., & Abbott, R.J. (2000) Origin and evolution of invasive naturalized material of *Rhododendron ponticum* L. in the British Isles. *Molecular Ecology* 9: 541–56.

Morison, S.E. (1978) *The great explorers. The European discovery of America.* New York: Oxford University Press.

Morris, D. (1898) Report on the economic resources of the West Indies. *Bulletin of Miscellaneous Information*, Additional Series II.

Morton, A.G. (1981) *History of botanical science. An account of the development of botany from ancient times to the present day.* London: Academic Press.

Moxham, R. (2004) *Tea. Addiction, exploitation and Empire.* London: Robinson.

Murphy, D.J. (2007) *People, plants and genes. The story of crops and humanity.* Oxford: Oxford University Press.

Mylechreest, M. (1984) Thomas Andrew Knight and the founding of the Royal Horticultural Society. *Garden History* 12: 132–7.

Nais, J. (2001) *Rafflesia of the world.* Kota Kinabalu: Sabah Parks Publications.

Nepomuceno, R. (2008) *O jardim de D. João.* Rio de Janeiro: Casa da Palavra.

Norman, H.W., Grey, E., & Barbour, D. (1897) West India Royal Commission. *Bulletin of Miscellaneous Information* 131: 339–402.

Ogilvie, B.W. (2006) *The science of describing. Natural history in Renaissance Europe.* Chicago and London: University of Chicago Press.

Papenfuss, G.F. (1976) Landmarks in Pacific North American marine phycology. In Abbott, I.A., & Hollenberg, G.J., eds, *Marine algae of California*, pp. 21–46. Stanford: Stanford University Press.

Parejko, K. (2003) Pliny the Elder's Silphium: first recorded species extinction. *Conservation Biology* 17: 925–7.

Parkinson, A. (2007) *Nature's alchemist. John Parkinson, herbalist to Charles I.* London: Frances Lincoln.

Parkinson, J. (1629) *Paradisi in Sole. Paradisus Terrestris or A Garden of all Sorts of pleasure, flowers which our English ayre will permitt to be noursed up: with A Kitchen garden of all manner of herbes, rootes, & fruites, for meate or sause used with us and An Orchard of all sorte of fruitbearing Trees and Shrubbes fit for Our land together With the right ordering planting & preserving of them and their uses & vertues.* London.

Parkinson, J. (1640) *Theatrum Botanicum. The Theater of Plantes or An Universall and Complete Herball.* London: Thomas Cotes.

Pavord, A. (1998) *The tulip.* London: Bloomsbury.

Pavord, A. (2005) *The naming of names. The search for order in the world of plants.* London: Bloomsbury.

PBB (1852–63) *Parliamentary Blue Book, Cinchona. 1852–1863.* London: Stationery Office.

Potter, J. (2007) *Strange blooms. The curious lives and adventures of the John Tradescants.* London: Atlantic Books.

Prest, J. (1981) *The Garden of Eden. The botanic garden and the re-creation of Paradise*. New Haven and London: Yale University Press.

Preston, D., & Preston, M. (2005) *A pirate of exquisite mind. The life of William Dampier: explorer, naturalist and buccaneer*. London: Corgi.

Purseglove, J.W. (1968) *Tropical crops. Dicotyledons 2*. London: Longmans.

Rackham, H. (2003) *Pliny. Natural history. Books 33–35*. London: Harvard University Press.

Raven, C.E. (1950) *John Ray. Naturalist*. Cambridge: Cambridge University Press.

Rea, J. (1676) *Flora, Ceres, Pomona*. London: Printed by T.N. for George Marriott.

Richardson-Boedler, C. (1999) The Doctrine of Signatures: a historical, philosophical and scientific view (I). *British Homeopathic Journal* 88: 172–7.

Roberts, H.F. (1929) *Plant hybridization before Mendel*. Princeton: Princeton University Press.

Rudberg, D. (1749) Peloria. In Linnaeus, C., ed., *Amoenitates academicae* Volume 1, pp. 280–98. Lugduni Batavorum: Cornelium Haak.

Ruiz, H. (1998) *The journals of Hipólito Ruiz. Spanish botanist in Peru and Chile 1777–1778*. Portland: Timber Press.

Salisbury, E. (1964) *Weeds and aliens*. London: Collins.

Schiebinger, L. (2004) *Plants and empire. Colonial bioprospecting in the Atlantic world*. London: Harvard University Press.

Schiebinger, L. (2005) *Prospecting for drugs: European naturalists in the West Indies*. In Schiebinger, L., & Swan, C., eds, *Colonial botany. Science, commerce and politics in the early modern world*, pp. 119–33. Philadelphia: University of Pennsylvania Press.

Shen-Miller, J., Mudgett, M.B., Schopf, J.W., Clarke, S., & Berger R. (1995) Exceptional seed longevity and robust growth: ancient sacred lotus from China. *American Journal of Botany* 82: 1367–80.

Singer, C. (1927) The herbal in antiquity and its transmission to later ages. *Journal of Hellenic Studies* 47: 1–52.

Slaughter, T.P. (1996) *The natures of John and William Bartram*. New York: Alfred A. Knopf.

Slocum, P.D. (2005) *Waterlilies and lotuses. Species, cultivars and new hybrids*. Portland: Timber Press.

Smith, J.E. (1819) Francis Masson. In Rees, A., ed., *Rees's New Cyclopaedia*, vol. 22(2). London: Longman, Hurst, Rees, Orme, & Brown.

Smith, J.E. (1821) *A selection of the correspondence of Linnaeus, and other naturalists, from the original manuscripts*. London: Longman, Hurst, Rees, Orme, & Brown.

Spary, E.C. (2000) *Utopia's garden. French natural history from Old Regime to Revolution*. Chicago and London: University of Chicago Press.

Spencer, R., Cross, R., & Lumley, P. (2007) *Plant names. A guide to botanical nomenclature*. Collinwood: CSIRO Publishing.

Spruce, R. (1908) *Notes of a botanist on the Amazon & Andes: being records of travel on the Amazon and its tributaries as also to the cataracts of the Orinoco during the years 1849–1864, 1817–1893*. London: Macmillan.

Stevens, P.F. (1994) *The development of biological systematics. Antoine-Laurent de Jussieu, nature, and the natural system*. New York: Columbia University Press.

Symon, D., & Jusaitis, M. (2007) *Sturt pea. A most splendid plant*. Adelaide: Board of the Botanic Gardens and State Herbarium.

Thoday, P. (2007) *Two blades of grass. The story of cultivation*. Corsham: Thoday Associates.

Thompson, C.J.S. (1934) *The mystic mandrake*. London: Rider & Co.

Thornton, R.J. (1807) *New illustration of the sexual system of Carolus von Linnaeus: and the temple of Flora, or garden of nature*. London: published for author.

Tiley, G.E.D., Dodd, F.S., & Wade, P.M. (1996) *Heracleum mantegazzianum* Sommier & Levier. *Journal of Ecology* 84: 297–319.

Treveris, P. (1526) *The grete herball*. London.

Tull, J. (1743) *The horse-hoing husbandry; compleat in four parts: or, an essay on the principles of tillage and vegetation*. London: A. Millar.

Turner, R. (1664) ΒΟΤΑΝΟΛΟΓΙΑ. *The Brittish Physician: or, the nature and vertues of English Plants*. London: Printed by R. Wood for Nath. Brook.

Turner, R. (1687) ΒΟΤΑΝΟΛΟΓΙΑ. *The British Physician: or, the nature and vertues of English Plants*. London: Obadiah Blagrave.

Turner, W. (1586) *The seconde part of William Turners Herball wherein are conteyned the names of herbes in Greke, Latine, Duche, Frenche and in the Apothecaries Latin and somtyne in Italiane, with the vertues of the same herbes with diverse confutationes of no smalle errours that men of no small learning have committed in the intreating of herbes of late yeares*. London: Arnold Birchaman.

Turrill, W.B. (1938) A contribution to the botany of Athos Peninsula. *Bulletin of Miscellaneous Information* 1937: 197–273.

Tyldesley, J. (1998) *Hatchepsut. The female pharaoh*. London: Penguin Books.

van Schoenermarck, H. (1974) Nathaniel Bagshaw Ward: how a sphinx moth altered the ecology of the earth. *Garden Journal* 24: 148–54.

Vines, S.H. (1913) Robert Morison (1620–1683) and John Ray (1627–1705). In Oliver, F.W., ed., *Makers of British botany. A collection of* biographies by living botanists, pp. 8–43. Cambridge: Cambridge University Press.

von Gärtner, C.F. (1849) *Versuche und Beobachtungen über die Bastarderzeugung in Pflanzenreich, mit Hinweisung auf die ähnlichen Erscheinungen im Thierreiche*. Stuttgart.

von Humboldt, A. (1995). *Personal narrative of a journey to the Equinoctial regions of the New Continent*. London: Penguin Books.

Walker, R. (1833) *The Flora of Oxfordshire, and its contiguous counties*. Oxford: Henry Slatter.

Wallace, A.R. (1869) *The Malay Archipelago. The land of the Orang-Utan, and the Bird of Paradise*. Oxford: Oxford University Press.

Ward, N.B. (1852) *On the growth of plants in closely glazed cases*. London: John von Voorst.

Weinberg, B.A., & Bealer, B.K. (2002) *The world of caffeine. The science and culture of the world's most popular drug*. London: Routledge.

Weiss, F.E. (1930) The problem of graft hybrids and chimaeras. *Biological Reviews* 5: 231–71.

Whitehead, P.J.P. (1979) The biography of Georg Marcgraf (1610–1643/4) by his brother Christian, translated by James Petiver. *Journal of the Society for the Bibliography of Natural History* 9: 301–14.

Wilson, J. (1995) Introduction. In von Humboldt, A., ed., *Personal narrative of a journey to the Equinoctial regions of the New Continent*, pp. xxxv–lxxii. London: Penguin Books.

Wilson, J.G. (2000) *The forgotten naturalist. In search of Alfred Russel Wallace*. Kew, Victoria: Australian Scholarly Publishing.

Wulf, A. (2008) *The brother gardeners. Botany, empire and the birth of an obsession*. London: William Heinemann.

Zirkle, C. (1935) *The beginnings of plant hybridisation*. Philadelphia: University of Pennsylvania Press.

Picture credits

Index

COOKING
FOR SPECIAL DIETS

KATHERINE POLENZ

Photography by Jennifer May

THE
CULINARY
INSTITUTE
OF AMERICA®

THE WORLD'S PREMIER
CULINARY COLLEGE

WILEY

THE CULINARY INSTITUTE OF AMERICA

President	Dr. Tim Ryan '77, CMC, AAC
Provost	Mark Erickson '77, CMC
Director of Publishing	Nathalie Fischer
Senior Editorial Project Manager	Margaret Wheeler '00
Editorial Assistants	Erin Jeanne McDowell '08 Laura Monroe '12

Library of Congress Cataloging-in-Publication Data:

Polenz, Katherine.
  Cooking for special diets / Katherine Polenz.
      pages   cm
  "The Culinary Institute of America."
  Includes index.
  ISBN 978-1-118-13775-8 (cloth)
  1. Diet therapy.   2. Diet in disease.   3. Cooking for the sick.   I. Culinary Institute of America.   II. Title.
  RM216.P675 2014
  641.5'631--dc23
                        2013046025

Printed in the United States of America

10 9 8 7 6 5 4 3 2 1

Cover Design: Wendy Lai

Interior Design: Maureen Eide

CONTENTS

RECIPE CONTENTS

CHAPTER 6   Salads   142

CHAPTER 7   Entrées   174

CHAPTER 8   Side Dishes   232

CHAPTER 9   Desserts and Breads   260

CHAPTER 10   Pantry Items   298

PREFACE

Balanced eating habits are important to any lifestyle, but for an increasing number of people, maintaining these habits is a difficult thing to achieve. More and more people suffer from food allergies, food intolerances, or one of an array of health problems that prevent them from being able to eat certain foods. These health issues can range from allergies to wheat to lactose intolerance to diabetes to heart or cholesterol problems. For others, such as vegans or vegetarians, not including certain foods in their diets is a choice. But strict adherence to dietary restrictions does not have to mean restricting flavor or variety. *Cooking for Special Diets* offers hundreds of recipes that will appeal not only to customers with specific dietary needs but also to those who are looking to make healthier choices every day.

The statistics regarding the current health trends in the United States can be frightening. For those living with various health conditions, learning how to manage them can be daunting. Professional chefs, cooks, and managers are asked daily to make modifications in their food preparations and service in order to accommodate the needs of their clientele. Because of this, chefs are being called upon to expand their understanding of general nutrition as well as the basics of recipe modification for specialized diets. Knowledge of nutrition, diet, and diet-related health concerns is critical for today's general population. But for those of us who cook professionally, this knowledge is invaluable. Every day we serve customers who are experiencing myriad of health concerns, such as being overweight, or having diabetes or food allergies, just to name a few.

Sometimes these health concerns are singular, but often they are compound issues because so many health issues are interconnected. Therefore, it is not unusual to serve a customer that may be seeking out a meal that is both heart-healthy and diabetes-friendly, or low-fat and gluten-free. Acquiring basic nutritional knowledge and understanding of ingredients will help professional chefs and cooks design, create, plan, and execute delicious menu offerings that are both appealing to the senses and healthful. *Cooking for Special Diets* compiles the information that professional chefs need to serve their customers with special dietary needs into an easy-to-navigate format. The book is useful not only to professional chefs but also to instructors who are teaching future chefs.

The dietary concerns of our customers can present challenges that force us to re-evaluate how we combine and prepare foods. The heavy use of butter, salt, dairy, processed foods, white sugar, white flour, and animal fats must make way for the use of healthy fats such as grapeseed or olive oil, or the use of vegetable- and fruit-based sauces, dairy alternatives such as rice or almond milk, as well as a greater use of whole, unprocessed foods with minimal additives. Applying the creativity of a chef's mind, learning how to use and manipulate familiar ingredients, along with expanding our repertoire and use of "alternative" ingredients will produce winning results. *Cooking for Special Diets* approaches recipe formulation from a holistic standpoint rather than focusing on specific calorie restrictions. The recipes focus on portion control and using high-fat and high-sugar ingredients sparingly. They offer the customer the option of eating healthfully without feeling like they are "on a diet."

There is much talk about the health and well-being of our food supply and the impact that may have on our own well-being. The age old saying "you are what you eat" has proven to be correct. As processed foods, convenience foods, and increased consumption of salt, sugar, and animal fats has become a way of life so have diseases of the heart, brain, liver, blood, and digestive tract. Obesity has increased to near-epidemic proportions among children and adults alike. What we eat, how much of it we eat, and the quality of what we eat plays out in our physical and emotional health. Thus, questions such as how and where is our food grown; if sustainable farming practices were used; if the meat was naturally and humanely raised and slaughtered; if growth hormones and antibiotics were used; if the grains, fruits and vegetables were non-GMO; and if the storage, milling, and processing of nuts and grains were free from cross contamination are all valid questions and concerns.

Structure of the Book

This book identifies at least eight of the most common diet-related health concerns currently plaguing the U.S. population: heart disease, hypertension, obesity, diabetes, celiac disease, inflammation, food allergies, and high cholesterol. It shows you ways to understand the dietary needs of people living with those health issues. The strategy and recipes included herein demonstrates how to tastefully modify recipes and menu offerings to accommodate these dietary needs.

Chapter 1 explains the key current health concerns including heart disease, hypertension, high cholesterol, cancer, and the underlying prevalence of inflammation in these diseases. The chapter also discusses food allergies and the health challenges that can be specific to professional chefs.

Chapter 2 focuses on the variety of aspects of creating a healthy meal. It gives the reader details about portion size, focusing on healthy cooking techniques, identifying nutrient requirements, and providing information on how to customize existing recipes for the different diets.

Chapter 3 gives specific details about the ingredients that should be used to create healthy dishes including superfoods and power foods for certain diets. The types of ingredients run the gamut from produce to fats and oils to dairy alternatives. The detailed tables for each ingredient category offer the reader information specific to the types of diets discussed in the book. There are also a number of substitution tables that inform the reader which ingredients can be used to tailor recipes for specific diets.

Chapters 4 to 10 offer recipes for every meal part from appetizers to desserts and breads. Each recipe has a calorie count and portion size so that the professional chef can not only have that information handy for their customers but also use the information to create balanced plates. These recipes will inspire professional chefs, instructors, and students alike to try new ingredients and flavor combinations in a way that will improve their customers' overall health.

Supplemental Materials

Cooking for Special Diets offers an **Instructor's Manual** including a **Test Bank** to help instructors who are designing courses based around healthy menu items. The **Test Bank** has been specifically formatted for **Respondus,** an easy-to-use software program for creating and managing exams.

A password-protected Wiley Instructor **Book Companion website** (www.wiley.com/college/CIA) provides access to the online **Instructor's Manual** and the text-specific teaching resources. The PowerPoint lecture slides are also available on the website for download.

Icon Key

The recipes in each chapter have annotations after the recipe titles that indicate which diet for which the recipe is appropriate.

C indicates a recipe that can be served to someone with celiac disease.

V indicates recipes for vegetarians.

D is for recipes that are appropriate for a diabetes-friendly diet.

H is for recipes that are suitable for customers with heart disease

ACKNOWLEDGMENTS

I would like to offer a heart-healthy thank you to Nathalie Fischer and the publishing department of The Culinary Institute of America for the opportunity to author *Cooking for Special Diets*. The conceptualization of this book would not have been possible without the encouragement and guidance of Maggie Wheeler, my senior editorial project manager extraordinaire. When my thoughts got all tangled up in agave and gluten and my vision became a little murky, Maggie was quick to take on the role of a dynamic antioxidant that effectively swept away the plaque that was blocking my progress and brilliantly brought focus and clarity to this project. Maggie, the words *thank you* barely skim the surface of my gratitude for your direction, support, and professionalism!

This is the second time I have been blessed with, and blessed by, the editorial assistance of Erin McDowell. Erin dutifully researched background material that added a healthy dose of dietary fiber to the text of this book. She tweaked my grammar and kept track of the moving parts to help assure that nothing was forgotten. Thank you, Erin, for falling in love with dark leafy greens and succulent blueberries!

A special thank-you to Shelly Malgee and Michelle Dykes who also worked as research assistants, combing volumes of nutritional information so that this project would have access to the freshest, most organic sources of data.

In order to test, prepare, and photograph the ingredients and recipes found in this book, it took a small army of dedicated students. Casey Platt, Helen Morganto, Neal Murikami, Christopher Kelly, Shannon Aubin, Brian Griffin, Karin Ou Yang, Malika Khanna, Sa Rang Park, Giovanni Ray, and Victoria Micharski worked tirelessly chopping, measuring, weighing, organizing, and cooking delicious, photo-ready food. Thank you for sharing your enthusiasm, excitement, and energy. I could not have done this without you!

As an educator, I am surrounded, day in and day out, by colleagues and students, who think, breathe, and live food! It is through countless discussions with my colleagues and students that I continue to learn and grow. I would especially like to thank Rick Coppedge, Tom Kief, Henry Rapp, Bill Phillips, Corky Clark, John Kowalski, Greg Zifchak, Rich Vergilli, Hubert Martini, Elizabeth Briggs, Shuliang Cheng, and Brendan Walsh for their thoughtful sharing of information and expertise. Numerous students, staff, and faculty members who live daily with health conditions that are food-related have also graced my life's learning. It is by way of preparing food for them that I have learned the most about how to modify recipes to meet specific dietary needs.

Every chef needs a hungry, willing audience. I offer deepest gratitude to my family members, daughter Kristina, son-in-law Ryan, grandson Alex (the most enthusiastic eater I know), and my sweetheart Al, as well as friends, Mary and Stephen, Ed and Keith, Roberta and Reagan, and Linda who, know it or not, were the audience of tasters for many of my creations. Their honesty and feedback proved invaluable in the development and refinement of these recipes.

My dear friend Belinda Mulpeter served as therapist and typist in times of need, especially when I was shoulder-deep in deadlines and tastings. And, as if that were not enough, our brainstorming sessions offered up several delicious recipe adaptations.

Special thanks to nutritionist and colleague Jennifer Stack for reviewing all of the nutritional analyses found in this book. Jennifer's attention to detail in this project is invaluable. The food, it's all about the food.

Brad Matthews, Anthony DiBenedetto, James Creighton, Chance Coluccio, and Ralph Chianese did a stunning job acquiring the foods for recipe testing and our photo shoots. The entire storeroom staff graciously filled every requisition with picture-perfect produce, grains, legumes, and proteins. You guys are the best! Thank you.

Jennifer May, you see food in a way like no other! Thank you for helping make heart-healthy, diabetic-friendly, gluten-free, low-sugar, low-fat, anti-inflammatory food look so beautiful and appealing. You were a joy to work with, as was your assistant, Kazio Sosnowski.

In joyous gratitude for Wesley, my second-born grandchild.

KMP

ABOUT THE AUTHOR

Katherine Polenz is a professor of culinary arts at The Culinary Institute of America. Chef Polenz currently teaches Cuisines of the Americas in the college's degree programs. In her more than two decades at the CIA, Chef Polenz has taught various culinary arts courses to students pursuing associate and bachelor's degrees. Through the CIA's Continuing Education Department, she has also taught cooking courses in Mexico and Brazil. She owns The Pampered Palate, an off-premises catering operation specializing in nutritional food and special diet preparation. Chef Polenz serves on the Board of Directors of Women Chefs and Restaurateurs. She is also a member of the American Culinary Federation and the Mid-Hudson Culinary Association, for which she served for seven years as a vice president and committee chair.

Founded in 1946, **The Culinary Institute of America** is an independent, not-for-profit college offering associate and bachelor's degrees with majors in culinary arts, baking and pastry arts, and culinary science, as well as certificate programs in culinary arts and wine and beverage studies. As the world's premier culinary college, the CIA provides thought leadership in the areas of health and wellness, sustainability, and world cuisines and cultures through research and conferences. The CIA has a network of 45,000 alumni that includes industry leaders such as Grant Achatz, Anthony Bourdain, Roy Choi, Cat Cora, Dan Coudreaut, Steve Ells, Johnny Iuzzini, Charlie Palmer, and Roy Yamaguchi. The CIA also offers courses for professionals and enthusiasts, as well as consulting services in support of innovation for the foodservice and hospitality industry. The college has campuses in Hyde Park, NY; St. Helena, CA; San Antonio, TX; and Singapore.

CHAPTER ONE

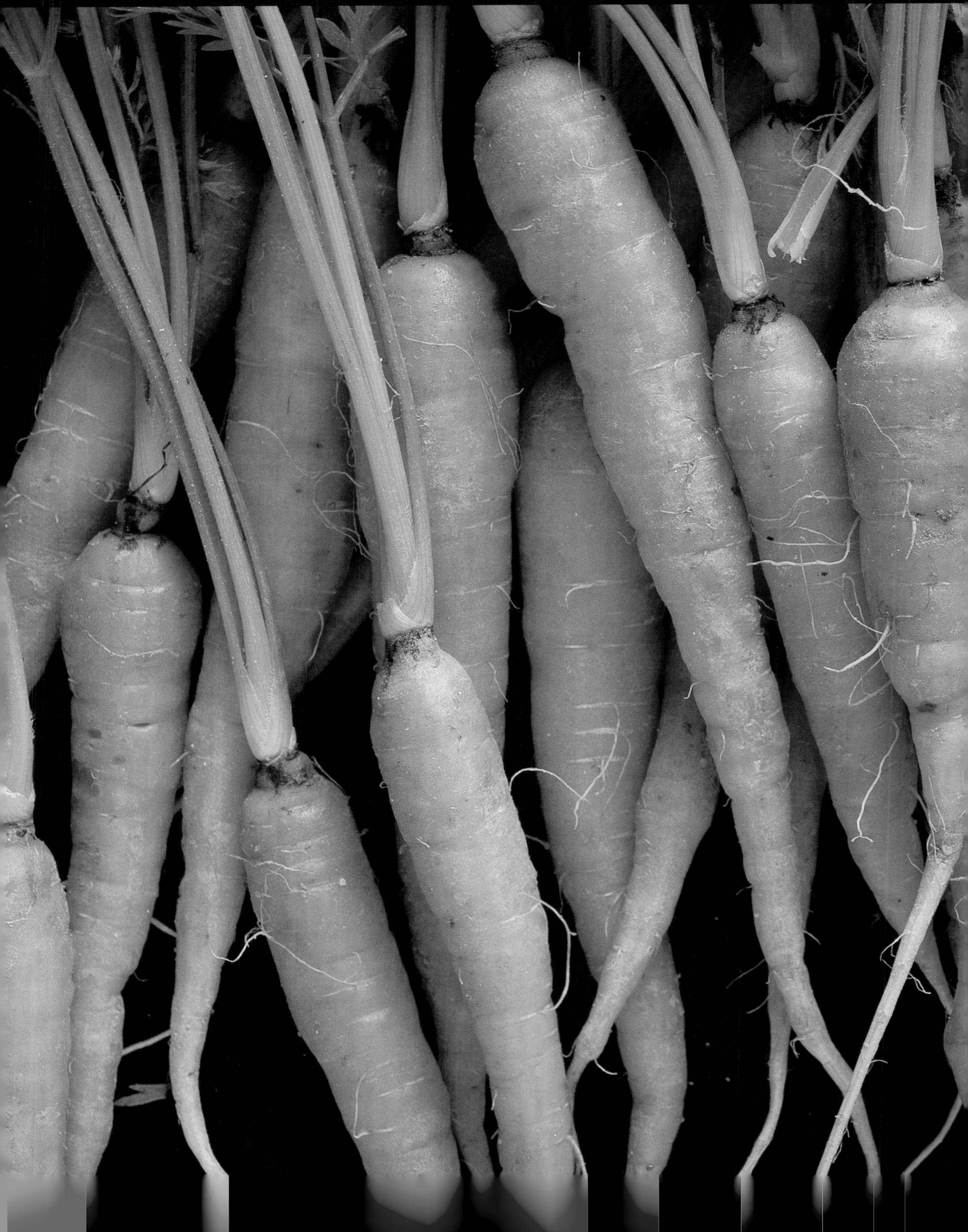

Many of the health concerns you will read about in this chapter are not new to us, nor are the facts that these concerns are also diet related. In fact, in the United States the top three health concerns, heart disease, diabetes, and obesity, have been in the news with increasing regularity for decades. The health and diet concerns that will be discussed throughout this book are heart disease, hypertension, high cholesterol, diabetes, obesity, celiac disease, food allergies and sensitivities, vegetarianism, and last, but certainly not least, inflammation, one of the underlying contributors to many health conditions.

Current health conditions and concerns will be defined in this chapter. As research findings become available, we realize why the need to understand the relationship between diet and disease is becoming more important for all sectors of the general population. Chefs are also often personally affected by these health concerns. Given the demands of the profession, it is no surprise that numbers of chefs fall victim to these diseases. The culprits: cooking, sampling and tasting countless foods, working long hours, not getting enough exercise or downtime to rest and rejuvenate, and persistent stress. Taking care of ourselves is one very important reason to expand our knowledge and practice of a healthy diet. For those working in the food-service and hospitality industries, attaining and applying clear understanding of the diet–disease connection is critical if we are to serve our clientele with respect for their need to eat food that is properly and safely prepared.

Common Health Concerns

Today the world's population suffers from a number of health challenges. Some of these challenges are hereditary, some environmental, some influenced by lifestyle and habits, and still others are a combination of all of these factors. While these issues and illnesses are wide and varied, they can be affected by the types of food the individual consumes or simply alter a person's nutritional needs altogether. The types of health concerns that exist today are as unique as the individuals who experience them. It is important that the professional chef is as educated as possible on the issues at hand and is prepared to meet the needs of clients who may have special health concerns.

The concerns that impact diets may be broken into three major categories: medical conditions and diseases, food-related disorders, and diet-based choices due to personal and/or religious reasons. On the surface, medical conditions may be simple to understand, but can often present complex challenges for the chef, as the needs of the affected customer can vary greatly. Some of the most prevalent health conditions that commonly affect an individual's diet include the following:

HEART DISEASE—An illness diagnosed primarily due to high cholesterol, which causes plaque or other debris to develop on the inner walls of the arteries. When this affects the heart

The Glycemic Index

The glycemic index is a form of measurement that quantifies the glycemic value of foods that are predominantly composed of carbohydrates. Foods are ranked on the glycemic index according to the negative impact they have on blood sugar levels. Foods are ranked on the following scale:

- **Low:** a value of 55 or lower
- **Medium:** a value of 56 to 69
- **High:** a value of 70 or higher

Generally, foods with higher levels of refined carbohydrates will rank higher on the glycemic index. For example, white flours (all-purpose, bread, cake, etc.) are high, while stone-ground 100 percent wheat flour is medium on the scale. Foods with low glycemic values include fresh vegetables, whole grains (such as steel-cut oats or barley), legumes (such as pinto beans or lentils), dark chocolate, unsweetened dairy products, and nuts. The glycemic index does not rate proteins or fats, but if these foods are consumed along with a carbohydrate, they can affect the overall glycemic impact of that food.

directly, it narrows the passageway to the heart and can cause an obstruction of blood flow. Individuals diagnosed with heart disease are encouraged to eat heart-healthy foods and focus on lowering their cholesterol.

HYPERTENSION—Also known as high blood pressure, this disease can result from many contributors, including obesity, unhealthy diet, and/or an inactive lifestyle. In addition to other problems caused by hypertension, it also puts people at higher risk of being diagnosed with heart disease. Individuals diagnosed with hypertension are encouraged to reduce sodium in their diet, eat a balanced diet, and reduce their intake of alcohol.

HIGH CHOLESTEROL—A primary contributor to heart disease, high cholesterol causes fatty deposits to develop in the blood cells, reducing the amount of oxygen-rich cells in the bloodstream. This can affect the heart (as mentioned regarding heart disease) or reduce blood flow, increasing the probability of a stroke. Individuals diagnosed with high cholesterol are encouraged to eat a balanced diet, increase their activity level, and are sometimes prescribed medication as part of treatment.

CANCER—Encompassing an array of diseases that can affect many parts of the body, cancer defines illnesses where abnormal cells divide without control and invade other tissues in the body through the blood and lymph systems. During cancer treatment, patients can lose their appetite or feel nauseous, making it difficult to consume the proper amounts of food recommended for their health. In addition, cancer can affect the way an individual's body processes food, and oftentimes the full amounts of nutrients present in a food source are not fully absorbed. Individuals diagnosed with cancer are encouraged to monitor their food intake to ensure they are eating enough and to eat a healthy, balanced diet, especially focusing on consuming the correct levels of vitamins, minerals, proteins, and carbohydrates.

DIABETES—Encompassing several disorders, diabetes causes the blood glucose (or blood sugar) levels to elevate. This elevation is caused by the pancreas, which produces the body's insulin. A diabetic's pancreas is unable to supply the proper levels of insulin that the body needs. In some cases, the supply is low. In others, the body resists its own insulin production. Sometimes, it is a combination of the two. Depending on the type of diabetes, individuals are encouraged to closely monitor their diet by reducing saturated and trans fats, cholesterol, and sodium. Diabetics are encouraged to focus on consuming healthy carbohydrates (such as fruit, whole grains, legumes, etc.), foods high in fiber, and foods containing monounsaturated and polyunsaturated fats.

OBESITY—Obesity occurs when an individual has an excessive amount of body fat. This can lead to an array of health problems, including diabetes, hypertension, and heart disease. Unlike many of the health concerns listed here, obesity is in most cases preventable and able to be resolved entirely through an active lifestyle and the consumption of a healthy, balanced diet.

Body Mass Index (BMI)

The body mass index is commonly used by physicians to determine if an individual is at a healthy weight, is overweight, or is obese. BMI is calculated using the height and weight of the individual, and uses the following scale:

- **Underweight:** 18.5 and under
- **Healthy weight:** 18.5 to 24.9
- **Overweight:** 25 to 29.9
- **Obese:** 30 or higher

BMI is a useful form of measurement in determining obesity, but it is not always entirely accurate because it does not take into consideration the ratio of lean muscle to fat on the individual. Because lean muscle weighs more than fat, a muscular person could be categorized as overweight because BMI is calculated on height and weight alone.

For a more effective determination, physicians will often use a bioelectrical impedance device to determine an individual's lean muscle to fat ratio. The combination of the results from this device along with the information obtained from the BMI calculation can be a more accurate determination of a person's health.

Food Allergies

In addition to these illnesses, numerous individuals are faced with food-related disorders such as food allergies or food sensitivity/intolerance. These health concerns have varying degrees of intensity and can produce an array of effects in the body. It is imperative that chefs understand the distinction between these issues, as well as the severity of the reactions that can occur, so that they can avoid potentially hazardous issues and still successfully serve their customers.

Food allergies are one of the most common ailments that customers bring into a restaurant. An individual with a food allergy cannot consume that food, or the immune system will respond inappropriately, causing an intense inflammatory reaction in the body. Allergies vary from person to person, but the following allergies are among the most common and/or severe:

- Peanuts

- Tree nuts (including almonds, Brazil nuts, cashews, chestnuts, hazelnuts, macadamia nuts, coconut, pecans, pine nuts, pistachios, and walnuts)

- Eggs

- Dairy products

- Shellfish

- Fish

- Wheat

- Soy

- Tomatoes

- Chocolate

Food allergies can create a host of symptoms, including swelling of the throat, mouth, or eyes, hives, itching, digestive discomfort, diarrhea, vomiting, and/or cold sweats. Oftentimes these allergies can induce anaphylactic shock, and can even be life-threatening. Having a food allergy can increase the likelihood of being or becoming allergic to other foods as well. A person with an allergy to fish and shellfish carries a 50 to 75 percent risk of being allergic to other fish and shellfish. A person who is allergic to one type of tree nut, such as a walnut, has just under a 40 percent chance of being allergic to other types of tree nuts.

A sensitivity, or intolerance, to a type of food is often mistaken for an allergy because they can have similar symptoms. However, an intolerance does not engage or affect the immune system. Instead, the body is often incapable of processing the food in question, which leads to any number of symptoms or health problems. Essentially, because an individual has a food intolerance does not mean that reactions resulting from it are less severe than an allergic reaction. Individuals with a food intolerance can experience violently uncomfortable symptoms from consuming even a small amount of the food that they are sensitive to. There are many kinds of intolerances, including carbohydrate intolerance (which can prevent the afflicted individual from losing weight) and alcohol intolerance (in which the body cannot break down alcohol). Two of the most common food intolerances are:

LACTOSE INTOLERANCE—An individual who is lactose intolerant cannot fully digest lactose, or the milk sugar present in dairy products. This is due to a deficiency of lactase, an enzyme produced by the lining of the small intestine. Symptoms are not always severe, but can be extremely uncomfortable, and include nausea, diarrhea, stomach cramps, etc. Individuals diagnosed with lactose intolerance are encouraged to reduce or eliminate dairy products from their diet to avoid symptoms.

CELIAC SPRUE DISEASE—Also known as CD, individuals with celiac sprue disease are affected by the consumption of gluten, a protein found in wheat, rye, and barley. The body attacks the villi, small projections that line the small intestine. CD can lead to a host of uncomfortable symptoms, including abdominal pain, gas, diarrhea, weight loss, and bone pain. In addition, if left untreated, the body can lose enough of the villi to create other health problems. The villi allow the body to properly absorb the nutrients in food, and without them, an individual is more likely to be malnourished, or develop anemia or osteoporosis. Individuals diagnosed with CD are encouraged to eliminate gluten from their diets completely, which can alleviate all of the symptoms.

| ESTIMATED FOOD ALLERGY RATES IN NORTH AMERICA FOR THE MOST COMMON ALLERGENS FOR BOTH CHILDREN AND ADULTS | | | | | | | | | |
| AGE GROUP | PERCENTAGE OF THE POPULATION | | | | | | | | |
	ALL ALLERGENS	MILK	EGG	PEANUT	TREE NUTS	FISH	SHELLFISH[a]	WHEAT	SOY
Children	6.0	2.5	1.3	0.8	0.2	0.1	0.0	UNK[b]	0.2
Adults	3.7	0.3	0.2	0.6	0.5	0.4	2.0	UNK[b]	UNK[b]

[a]Shellfish includes both crustaceans and mollusks. [b]UNK = unknown.

SOURCES: Cordle, 2004; Sampson, 1997; Sampson, 2004; Sampson, 2005; Sicherer et al., 2003; Sicherer et al., 2004. http://www.fda.gov/downloads/Food/IngredientsPackagingLabeling/UCM192048.pdf

In addition to coping with the aforementioned health problems with which an individual may have been diagnosed or which cannot be controlled, some people may opt to eliminate or restrict certain foods from their diet. These choices may be made to help regulate wellness or perhaps with respect to religious or personal beliefs. These types of dietary concerns include (but are not limited to) many types of vegetarianism, keeping kosher, a raw food diet, or the Ital diet of the Rastafari.

In the food-service and hospitality industry, one of the primary charges is to meet the needs or demands of your clientele. As a chef or food-service professional, it is important to have a working knowledge of the most common diet-related health issues as well as some of the dietary solutions. Acquiring basic knowledge and understanding of these nutritional needs is key to being able to manipulate menu items to accommodate special diets. This can be challenging, particularly when it comes to the specifics of dietary restrictions and choices. The following chapters will go into further detail as to how to address these concerns from a cook's standpoint, resulting in delicious, healthy, intriguing menu items that will satisfy a diverse audience.

Health Challenges for Chefs

In addition to the concerns of your customer base, there are also a number of concerns for the kitchen staff themselves. Some of the greatest personal health challenges for any chef come as the result of daily, sometimes even hourly, food tasting. Chefs often don't experience the feeling of hunger because they taste and sample all day long, often consuming many more calories than are found in an extravagant meal. Yet at the end of the day or evening of work, chefs have been known to say they are famished and haven't eaten a thing all day! Sampling foods all day long, on the go, doesn't satisfy in the same way that sitting down and quietly eating a meal does. To help fight the battle of the bulge and ever-rising cholesterol and blood sugar levels caused by overindulging and stress, many contemporary chefs have established creative ways to get control.

Take smaller tastes and samplings. Focus on the purpose of the tasting—when the goal is achieved, move on.

Practice mindful eating. Take a break once a day to eat a small nutritious meal, rich in whole grains, fruits, and vegetables. Eat slowly and savor each bite.

Learn a few simple stress-relieving techniques such as stretching or deep, slow breathing.

Stay active. Take a brisk walk or jog each day, ride a bicycle to work, or take yoga classes.

Take up a relaxing hobby such as playing a musical instrument or fly-fishing.

When designing and preparing recipes within a nutritional mind-set, one must always be cognizant of portion control. The "free-hand" skill that a chef develops over time for seasoning with salt or utilizing fats must be reined in or even abandoned and the dedicated use of an accurate scale and measuring devices must take its place. Precise measure coupled with skillful preparation methodology is the focus of nutritional cooking.

One must become aware of the importance of each of the nutrient categories that are evaluated in a nutritional analysis. What are nutrients, vitamins and minerals, phytonutrients, macro- and micronutrients? What is dietary fiber? Where does it come from and why it is so important to the human diet? These questions will be answered. The parameters for specific health-related diets are provided. Employment of proper portion size and controls will play a major role in providing healthy options for restaurant customers. And of course, identifying cooking methods or techniques that are best suited for healthy, nutritional food preparation will be critical. Methods such as grilling, poaching, steaming, roasting, and sous vide are among the best choices. One more piece to the puzzle is ingredient substitution. Information regarding ingredient substitution and easy-to-use charts are provided to assist you in learning how to modify current menu offerings in order to accommodate special dietary requests (see chart on page 58).

Nutritional Cooking

For the purposes of most restaurant chefs, nutritional cooking can be defined as the preparation of food guided by nutritional and dietary recommendations and portion-size control. To execute properly, a chef must use sound cooking techniques and maintain respect for the integrity of the ingredients being used. When creating menu items with health and nutrition in mind, it is safe to say that keeping things simple and unencumbered is a good thing. Choosing fresh ingredients that are locally grown or raised in a sustainable manner will help ensure that you are using the most wholesome, environmentally clean, and healthful ingredients possible. Quality ingredients are key to nutritional food preparation. Combined with skilled cooking techniques, these ingredients will be transformed into nutritious and beneficial meals for your clientele. There are many factors that contribute to the concept of nutritional cooking. The core guidelines chefs should consider when developing dishes include the following:

Emphasize Accurate Portion Size

Learn what a standard serving or portion size is for all foods (see the chart on page 343 for USDA recommendations). Build menu items that provide nutritionally sound portion sizes (see photos at right). Understanding and serving standard nutritional portion sizes will provide your guests with healthful choices and might benefit your bottom line. While there can be additional restrictions if a customer has a specific health concern, a good basic guideline is to divide a plate in half. One half should be composed of fruits and vegetables. The other half should be composed of a portion of lean protein and a healthy starch, such as whole grains.

Scooping this frozen yogurt ahead of time maintains the proper portion size and also helps it to freeze properly.

Equip your staff with the appropriate serving tools—this spoon is the correct size to ensure that the customer is receiving the proper portion.

Many items in a kitchen can be used to help designate portion sizes and keep them consistent. Here, grain pilaf is portioned evenly using a ramekin.

Typical restaurant portion: steak with mushroom sauce, baked potato with sour cream and chives, and broccoli rabe.

USDA recommended portion: steak with mushroom sauce, baked potato with sour cream and chives, and broccoli rabe.

Portion with healthy alterations made: filet mignon steaks with black trumpet mushroom coulis, grilled sweet potatoes, and broccoli rabe.

Typical restaurant portion: poached salmon with hollandaise, rice, and squash noodles.

USDA recommended portion: poached salmon with hollandaise, rice, and squash noodles.

Portion with healthy alterations made: poached salmon with yellow pepper coulis, brown rice, and squash noodles.

Typical restaurant portion: pasta carbonara.

USDA recommended portion: pasta carbonara with steamed vegetables.

Portion with healthy alterations made: multigrain pasta with vegetables and ricotta.

Focus on Cooking Techniques That Are Naturally Healthy

This concept can include a variety of techniques. Cook foods as close to the time of service as possible to minimize nutrient loss, and cook foods quickly in as little water or oil as possible to maximize nutrient retention. Serve a variety of foods, including whole grains, unprocessed fruits and vegetables, and legumes—this will introduce additional flavors and textures without compromising nutritional value. A strong emphasis on the use of these ingredients is seen in traditional cuisines from around the world. They are rich in complex carbohydrates and provide an array of vitamins, minerals, and fiber, which play an important part in a flavorful, balanced diet.

Ingredient-compatible cooking methods should be chosen carefully. Whenever possible, choose methods that introduce a minimal addition of fats and oils. Grilling, roasting, poaching, and steaming are perfect choices. Serving certain foods raw is another way to highlight their flavor while maintaining their full nutritional value.

Use Healthy Levels of Various Ingredients

While this applies to the knowledge and balance of many vitamins and minerals in food, it is especially important that chefs minimize the use of salt. Controlling sodium consumption is a primary factor in reducing or resolving a variety of health issues. There are a variety of herbs and seasonings that can be used to create flavorful dishes that are lower in sodium. Fresh herbs, seaweed, dried mushrooms, wine, vinegar, citrus juices, and low-sodium soy sauces all enhance the flavor of a dish without adding excessive sodium. Additionally, sodium-dense ingredients such as capers, olives, or hard grating cheeses can be used in lieu of salt, giving the dish salty flavors without introducing additional salt. Avoid the use of processed foods, which may have excessive levels of sodium and other preservatives. For more information on other nutrients, see page 12.

Small, medium, and large apples

4-oz, 8-oz, and 12-oz cuts of pork

2-oz, 6-oz, and 9-oz portions of pasta

Identify the Correct Requirements for a Meal

Limit the use of foods dense in calories, cholesterol, and saturated fats (commonly eggs, cream, butter, cheeses), as well as refined sugars. Chefs should also avoid excessive use or reliance on calorie-laden prepared products such as rich sauces, pastries, or desserts. Select mono-unsaturated cooking fats and oils whenever possible (see page 27 for more information). Skillful cooks know that fats carry flavor, but they also know how to maximize the natural flavor value of foods without falling back on the use of calorie-dense fats. For instance, using only a teaspoon or so of an herb, spice, or fruit- or vegetable-infused grape-seed or olive oil can add tremendous flavor impact to a plate without a huge calorie commitment. A chef cannot make healthy choices for the consumer, but chefs can provide healthy options from which their customers can choose.

The portion sizes of carbohydrates and proteins have increased excessively over the years (see portion comparison photos at left). It would be prudent for chefs to familiarize themselves with the recommended portion sizes for various types of protein and carbohydrates, especially because whole grains can be served in larger, more satisfying portions than many other carbohydrate sources, which are primarily composed of empty calories.

Identify Parameters for General Health Concerns

Chefs should strive to select foods that achieve the nutritional goals and guidelines for a variety of health concerns. Understand the foods being utilized—how they are best cooked, what portion size to serve, and what nutritional benefits the foods possess. As a general rule of thumb, the closer a food is to its natural state, the higher its nutritional value. Locally grown fruits and vegetables are typically harvested close to full ripeness, travel less distance, and spend less time en route before arriving to the customer. Therefore, this type of produce generally retains maximum nutritional value. Whole grains (grains with the nutrient-dense germ and bran intact) are an excellent source of antioxidants, vitamins, magnesium, iron, and fiber. Processed, refined, and/or quick-cooking grain varieties have lost much of their nutrient content by way of the processing. It is also important for chefs to be aware of the foods that are welcomed into the diet of an individual with a specific health issue. With a basic knowledge of ingredients coupled with knowledge regarding an array of common health issues, a chef can begin to create dishes designed to accommodate any customer, including making substitutions that are both healthy and flavorful.

Identifying Nutrients and Understanding Daily Intake Requirements

With an understanding of the basic key concepts of nutritional cooking, a chef can begin to delve deeper into the specific guidelines provided by the USDA. These requirements are crucial to understanding how to cook nutritionally and/or for a customer with a specific health concern.

Calories

A calorie is defined as the amount of energy needed to raise the temperature of 1 gram of water by 1°C. Nutritionally, this unit is measured as the body obtains energy after digesting food. Different nutrients have different caloric values, and in general, a healthy diet is dictated by keeping an individual's calorie intake under a certain amount.

Fat

Fats are composed of linked chains made up of fatty acids and can come from animal sources (butter, lard, etc.), plant sources (oils made from nuts, vegetables, etc.), or through a process called hydrogenation, where liquid oils are made into a solid fat (such as shortening or margarine). Fats are broken into four main categories: saturated, monounsaturated, polyunsaturated, and trans fats. One gram of fat contains 9 calories.

Monounsaturated Fats

Monounsaturated fats are most commonly found in plant-based fats and are known to raise levels of high-density lipoprotein (HDL) in the blood. HDL, also known as "good cholesterol," is associated with reduced health risks for circulatory diseases, such as heart disease. Some foods that are high in monounsaturated fats include olive oil, some nut oils, avocados, pumpkin seeds, Brazil nuts, and cashews.

Polyunsaturated Fats

Polyunsaturated fats are also associated with reduced health risks, including a reduced rate of heart disease and reduced risk of type 2 diabetes. Polyunsaturated fats are generally found in fats that are liquid at room temperature. Corn oil, safflower oil, sunflower oil, and soybean oil all contain polyunsaturated fats. These fats can also be found in foods high in omega-3 and omega-6 fatty acids (such as sardines, salmon, or flaxseeds).

Saturated Fats

Saturated fats can cause elevated levels of low-density lipoprotein (LDL) in the blood. High levels of LDL can lead to an increased risk of circulatory diseases and put an individual at risk for high cholesterol. They can also cause levels of HDL to increase, which, in some cases, can slightly balance the increase of LDL in the bloodstream. Saturated fats can be found in butter, lard, and other animal fats as well as in tropical oils such as coconut and palm oil.

Trans Fats

Trans fats are uncommon in nature, but are found in hydrogenated fats such as shortening or margarine. They cause levels of LDL to increase and levels of HDL to decrease, creating a generally negative ratio that can lead to a range of health problems. Unlike other fats, they can also be carcinogenic.

Carbohydrates

Nutritionally, carbohydrates can be one of two things—complex carbohydrates (such as starch) and simple carbohydrates (such as sugar). One gram of carbohydrate contains 4 calories. Carbohydrates are a major source of food energy for humans, but are not an essential nutrient; therefore, diets high in carbohydrates can lead to obesity and a wide range of health problems. Dietary guidelines recommend that only 45 to 65 percent of daily food energy should be sourced from carbohydrates, and that less than 10 percent should be sourced from simple carbohydrates. An emphasis should be put on whole grains whenever possible (see page 43).

Protein

Proteins are composed of chains of amino acids and are a major source of food energy. In addition to providing energy, proteins are necessary for human growth. Protein is needed to form blood cells, and is essential for building body tissue (including hair, skin, and muscle). It is recommended that a sedentary individual consume 0.8 gram of protein per kilogram of body weight daily. A more active individual may need a higher intake of protein to compensate for activity level. One gram of protein contains 4 calories. Proteins can derive from both animal and plant sources, including meat, dairy products, fish, eggs, whole grains, legumes, soy products, nuts, and seeds.

Sodium

The suggested daily intake of sodium is 1,500 milligrams to a maximum of 2,500 milligrams (or 1 teaspoon of salt). On average, Americans consume between 2,300 and 4,700 milligrams of sodium each day. A diet high in sodium puts individuals at risk for hypertension as well as inflammatory diseases. Once an individual has been diagnosed with one of these diseases, the level of recommended daily sodium intake decreases to below 1,500 milligrams. Chefs must be aware of the importance of reducing sodium when considering health concerns and find ways to boost flavor without relying excessively on salt. In addition, chefs should remember that sodium is naturally present in many common ingredients, and that these must be considered when creating a lower-sodium dish. In general, the human palate is less likely to detect the natural salt in foods (such as capers, olives, or Parmesan cheese), so it is important to balance these items and consider the overall sodium content in foods.

Fiber

Dietary fiber is the indigestible portion of plant foods and is composed of two parts: soluble fiber and insoluble fiber. Soluble fiber is water soluble. Foods that contain soluble fiber slow down digestion, which makes you feel full sooner and stay full longer. Slower digestion can lower blood cholesterol levels and have a positive impact on insulin sensitivity. Soluble fiber is found in the following foods: oats, apples, oranges, pears, strawberries, lentils, and nuts.

Insoluble fiber is not water soluble. Foods that contain insoluble fiber add bulk to a diet because they do not break down as quickly, which also makes you feel full sooner and stay full longer. Unlike soluble fiber, foods that contain insoluble fiber are not digested and therefore speed up the passage of food through the digestive system; this can often have a laxative effect. Insoluble fiber is found in whole grains and most vegetables.

Vitamins and Minerals

Vitamins and minerals do not supply calories, and are generally required in smaller quantities than energy-providing nutrients. Recommended Daily Values (DVs) have been established for many of the vitamins and minerals known to be important to good health. DVs are the amounts listed on Nutrition Facts labels of packaged food, and they are based on the standard 2,000-calorie diet. They are not necessarily the amount that a person needs to prevent disease or to enjoy or maintain health. The Dietary Reference Intake (DRI) for a food is based on age and gender, and gives the amount each subgroup requires.

The DV for calcium, for example, is 1,000 milligrams. If a Nutrition Facts label says that 1 cup of yogurt supplies 35 percent of the DV for calcium, that food contains 350 milligrams. Not everyone needs only 1,000 milligrams of this mineral, though. Adolescents and young adults should get at least 1,300 milligrams, and people over fifty need at least 1,200. For them, that cup of yogurt supplies only 27 percent or 29 percent of the DV of calcium.

Water-Soluble Vitamins

Water-soluble vitamins dissolve in water and are easily transported throughout the body in the bloodstream. These vitamins include the B-complex vitamins (thiamin, riboflavin, niacin, folacin, biotin, pantothenic acid, B_6, and B_{12}) and vitamin C. B-complex vitamins are found in grains, legumes, vegetables, meats, and fortified cereals. They perform many functions; thiamin, riboflavin, niacin, and B_6 are used in metabolizing nutrients. B_{12}, which is found only in animal foods, is used to synthesize amino acids and is important in the formation of blood. Folacin, also called folate (when it occurs naturally in foods), and folic acid (when it is synthetic) are used in blood formation and amino acid metabolism.

Deficiencies of the B-complex vitamins can range from reduced stamina and insomnia to nervous system damage, liver damage, ulcers, and death. Insufficient folacin is the most common vitamin deficiency and has been linked to birth defects such as spina bifida.

Vitamin C is found in fruits and vegetables. Although oranges are practically synonymous with vitamin C, they are not the richest source; guava, strawberries, broccoli, and red bell peppers supply more per serving. Vitamin C performs hundreds of functions in the body. It increases the body's absorption of iron and is imperative to the growth and maintenance of body tissues. Vitamin C is used to produce collagen, a protein substance that helps hold tissues together, like muscles to bone or teeth to gums. Vitamin C also boosts the immune system and has antioxidant properties that protect cells from damage caused by oxygen. It may also protect against heart disease and cancer.

A small amount of water-soluble vitamins can be stored briefly in lean tissue such as muscles and organs, but the body's supplies must be replenished daily. Toxic levels of these vitamins are possible but unlikely because any excess is excreted from the body. Water-soluble vitamins can be affected by ordinary food-handling techniques and cooking methods. B vitamins are somewhat more stable than vitamin C, but both can be lost through the following:

- Exposure to air (removing peels, cutting foods, or storing food uncovered)

- Heat (cooking or storing at room temperature)

- Exposure to water (rinsing cut foods before they are cooked, cooking foods in water, holding foods in water)

- Time (as foods age, they lose moisture and, along with the moisture, vitamins)

To retain water-soluble vitamins, observe the following recommendations:

- Keep cooking times to a minimum.

- Cook foods in as little water as possible, or choose a dry-heat technique like roasting.

- Prepare foods as close to their time of service as possible.

- Purchase foods in reasonable amounts to avoid prolonged storage.

Fat-Soluble Vitamins

Vitamins A, D, E, and K are fat-soluble—they are stored in fat tissues and, once ingested, cannot be easily flushed from the body. In the proper amounts, fat-soluble vitamins are basic to health, but exceeding the DVs for these vitamins can cause them to build up in the body, making it easy for toxic levels to accumulate. Once toxic levels are reached, a variety of dangerous and even fatal conditions may develop. These vary by vitamin, but kidney stones, nerve damage, and abnormal bone growth are just a few.

Fat-soluble vitamins are far more stable than water-soluble ones. They cannot be destroyed by contact with air or water, and are less affected by heat than are water-soluble vitamins. Some fat-soluble vitamins increase in bioavailablity when they are heated. Carotenoids such as lycopene in tomatoes and beta-carotene in carrots are more available to the body after cooking. Cooking breaks down cell walls and concentrates these nutrients.

The type of vitamin A present in animal foods is called retinol. Vitamin A itself is not found in plant foods, but beta-carotene, a phytochemical that the body uses to produce vitamin A, is found in orange and deep yellow vegetables, such as squash, sweet potatoes, and carrots, as well as in dark green leafy vegetables (the orange pigment is hidden by the chlorophyll) like kale, collards, and spinach. Beta-carotene cannot be quickly converted to vitamin A, so it is difficult for toxic levels to be reached. Excess beta-carotene levels may, however, cause a person to appear jaundiced because the pigment is stored in fat layers just beneath the skin.

Vitamin D is responsible for proper bone formation. It works in concert with calcium and phosphorus and helps the body use these minerals. Vitamin D is present in foods such salmon, sardines, shrimp, cod, eggs and egg yolks, as well as in fortified milk and cereals. The skin, when exposed to sunlight, produces vitamin D from cholesterol. Ten to fifteen minutes per day is often enough. People with limited exposure to sunlight may need to get the amounts they need through fortified foods or supplements. The body's ability to manufacture vitamin D declines with age, so people over age sixty should consider supplementation. Recent studies show that our diets are deficient in this vitamin. Debate is under way concerning how much we should consume on a daily basis. Some experts have suggested more than doubling the current DV.

Vitamin E, like vitamin C, is an antioxidant that protects the body from oxygen damage and may have cancer-fighting potential. It is found in a variety of foods, especially whole grains and nuts. It is usually not difficult to obtain adequate vitamin E with a healthy and varied diet, but followers of extremely low-fat diets may be deficient.

Vitamin K is associated with proper formation of blood clots and makes a protein that is necessary for strong bones. Although vitamin K is produced by bacteria found in the intestines, a person who eats a varied diet obtains about half of the DV from food, particularly dark green leafy vegetables. Those who take anticoagulants should avoid foods high in vitamin K because it can interfere with the action of these drugs.

Macrominerals

Calcium, phosphorus, magnesium, sodium, and potassium are called macrominerals because they are required in relatively large amounts. Of these, calcium is the most abundant mineral in the body.

Ninety-nine percent of the calcium needed by the body is used in the development of bones and teeth; the remaining 1 percent is used to regulate blood pressure and to aid in muscle contractions, transmit nerve impulses, and clot the blood. A deficiency in calcium may cause stunted growth and a loss of bone density. Because the body requires so much calcium, excess calcium in the body is rare unless supplements are taken. Good sources of calcium include dairy products such as milk and yogurt, leafy greens such as collards and turnip greens, and canned fish with bones. Many foods are now fortified with calcium, including orange juice and cereal.

Phosphorus is used by the body in conjunction with calcium to maintain bone and tooth structure; it is also integral to releasing energy from food for the body to use. Deficiencies in this mineral are rare, but may result in weakness, decreased heart function, and neurological problems. Phosphorus is present in animal protein, nuts, cereals, and legumes.

Magnesium is used for bone and tooth structure, muscle contraction, nerve transmission, and bowel function. Too little magnesium can cause possible growth failure, behavioral disturbances, tremors, weakness, and seizures. The typical diet in the United States tends to be deficient in magnesium. Good sources include green vegetables, nuts, legumes, and whole grains.

Sodium and potassium are known as electrolytes. These are essential to regulating bodily functions, helping to maintain the balance of fluid in the body, and they are involved in nerve and muscle functions. Both are plentiful in food, so dietary deficiencies are uncommon. Adequate potassium has been linked to lower blood pressure levels and reduced risk of stroke and heart disease. Bananas have a reputation for being a rich source of potassium, but in fact they have almost half the amount of a baked potato. Avocados, white beans, yogurt, dark leafy greens like spinach, kale, and collard greens, and tomato and orange juices are also good sources.

Microminerals

Fluoride, iodine, and iron are known as trace minerals or microminerals because they are needed in minute amounts. Fluoride helps prevent tooth decay and may play a role in preventing osteoporosis. Many community water supplies contain added fluoride. This mineral is also present in saltwater fish, shellfish, and tea.

Iodine is essential for the normal functioning of the thyroid gland, and it helps to regulate energy metabolism, cellular oxidation, and growth. Iodine is found most abundantly in saltwater fish and some dairy products; its content in fruits and vegetables depends on the soil they are grown in. A deficiency of iodine results in goiter, or enlargement of the thyroid gland. Since the early 1900s, when goiter was common in the midwestern United States, iodine was added to table salt (iodized salt) to eliminate this deficiency.

Iron is a component of hemoglobin, the part of the red blood cells that carries oxygen from the lungs to the cells. About 75 percent of the body's iron is found in the blood. The remaining iron functions as a component of myoglobin, the oxygen-supplying molecule found in muscles, as part of certain enzymes involved in cellular energy metabolism. Iron deficiencies are a worldwide health problem, particularly for women of childbearing age, and cause a form of anemia in which blood cells lack sufficient hemoglobin. Someone who is anemic may appear pale and feel weak; they will also have an impaired immune system. The best food sources of iron are liver and red meat, but it is also found in whole grains, legumes, green leafy vegetables, dried fruit, and egg yolks.

How to Read and Interpret Food Labels

Nutrition labels contain specific information about food products. Labeling can appear on packaged goods or on menus, or the information may appear in advertisements. The content is created by the food manufacturer or restaurant, but any claims or promises used may be mandated by law.

A Brief History of Food Labeling in the United States

Since 1906, the U.S. government has developed legislation to inform consumers about the safety and quality of foods by requiring information on food labels. In 1969, the White House Conference on Food, Nutrition, and Health recommended that a system be developed to deliver nutrition information to consumers. For nearly two decades, nutrition labeling was largely voluntary and minimally regulated unless a food contained added nutrients or included a claim about its

nutrient content or usefulness in the daily diet. Because information was inconsistent, it was difficult for consumers to make accurate comparisons.

Until fairly recently, there were no rules governing what qualified as "light" or "healthy," and the terms were used indiscriminately. The term "light," for example, might only have meant a slight reduction in calories, fat, or sodium. Sometimes, those reductions were nothing more than a manipulation of the serving size recorded on the label.

In 1990, Congress enacted the Nutrition Labeling and Education Act (NLEA), which required that standardized nutrition information be included on packaged food labels. Terms like "fat-free," "low-sodium," "light," and "healthy" were clearly defined to ensure that nutrition and health claims were used responsibly and consistently by food producers. Today, to qualify for a nutrition claim, specific standards must be met.

Industry Terms

When determining the menu and how different products are incorporated into it, it is worth discussing the meaning of some terms used when talking about where and how the product is grown. There is much debate on the exact meaning of some of these terms, but this should provide a general overview of the terms.

Seasonality

"Seasonality" is simply a term meaning to buy what is growing best at that time of year. Seasonal produce charts that identify seasonal items by region are helpful when researching this, but weather is the wild card in determining what is in season. If the weather remains cold and wet well into spring, the season will start late; likewise if there is a hard frost early in the fall, the summer growing season will end early. The calendar will give you a guide to when something might be expected but it cannot make that product grow.

Interaction between the chef and grower or vendor is important as seasons change. Purchasing according to season will give you the best product at the best price; it's a great way to buy. However, adhering to this philosophy may also limit your choices and require more flexibility in planning your menu. Supporting your local grower and lessening your carbon footprint are reasons to limit purchases to local and regional products and indicate that you also employ seasonal purchasing practices. The limit on how "local" or "regional" are defined is a question that can only be determined by you, but is worth some discussion. How rigid are you willing to be, as a chef or buyer, when making these choices? Can chefs in the northern parts of America opt to not purchase citrus, bananas, and coffee? Possibly, but it's more than likely that customer demand will dictate purchasing to some extent. Other chefs may believe that to please their customers they will purchase whatever is available at a reasonable cost from anywhere it is grown in the world and not operate at all with a local or regional agenda. These are decisions that can only be made based on the operation's needs.

Sustainability

Growing product in a way that does not deplete the environment or that is not harmful to people and animals in addition to ensuring that the land will continue to support both the growth of product and the farmer in the future is seen as being sustainable. Simply put, this means to satisfy the needs of people now without any risk to the people and environment later on. These practices include making sure that the soil is neither depleted by erosion nor depleted of nutrients with excessive use of chemical additives such as phosphates. Another issue of sustainability includes the management of water to guarantee that the produce grown can survive on the amount of water that is renewably available and that the water is not contaminated by animal waste or chemical runoff.

The wages and living conditions of the farm workers, the distance the produce is shipped to market, and other factors are also argued to be part of the sustainability equation. Defining whether, what, and how much artificial or chemical means of fertilization to use is also part of the sustainable debate. The Slow Food movement is a grass-roots effort to promote the sustainability of our food system. They are advocating that the food we eat be good both for our bodies and the ecosystem in which the produce is grown and economically fair to those who grow it. The idea is simply that the food we raise and eat should be good for the planet and those eating it. The process should be economically fair to both grower and consumer and this will supply food that simply tastes better.

Organic

Organic produce refers to plants that are cultivated without the use of any artificial or chemical herbicides, pesticides, or fertilizers. Instead, organic farmers rely on renewable and natural means to grow their product without damage to the soil or water. This is the fastest-growing segment in agriculture and its popularity is attracting the interest and involvement of the large players in both agribusiness and retail vending. Large corporate influence in this segment of the industry may serve to diminish the standards that have been used for produce to be certified organic.

Alternatively, many small farms that are growing their produce properly in a sustainable and organic fashion opt not to be certified organic due to the time and expense of the certification process. This drives home the point that the best way to be absolutely sure that your produce is grown in a manner that meets your standards is to learn about your source and, if possible, know and visit the grower. Labels and certifications are an indication that the produce meets the standards that you are expecting, but nothing beats knowing your source whenever this is possible.

Heirloom

Heirloom produce is grown from original native seeds, not hybridized variations that are developed to grow faster, extend the shelf life, or grow in a broader season. Some growers insist that heirloom seeds must have been introduced from up to a century ago to be truly heirloom; others feel anything that is unique in look and flavor when it is introduced can be considered an heirloom. This produce is not as pretty or uniform in appearance and is much more fragile and difficult to package and ship. Therefore heirloom varieties represent just a small portion of the produce market; heirloom tomatoes comprise the largest segment of that. What these fruits and vegetables do offer is a much richer and more fully developed flavor. Heirloom varieties are most commonly found at farm stands and from specialty vendors. They command a higher price due to their quality, high perishability, and lower yield. The flavor and unique colors can make them well worth it, however. In addition to tomatoes, other heirloom produce items include: potatoes such as Purple Peruvians, apples such as the Golden Russet, and some varieties of melons, eggplant, cherries, peaches, and asparagus. Many of these, however, are rarely found in the commercial market.

Wild and Foraged

There is another category of produce on the market that could certainly be characterized as heirloom because no one has introduced these items as seeds into the market. These are fresh produce items that are found or harvested in natural environments and are not cultivated. The items classified as wild or foraged only grow in their own season when the weather and growing conditions are correct. These circumstances bring uniqueness in appearance and flavor to the produce that is only available when nature permits. These traits and the need for specially trained foragers to go out into the wild and find them cause this product to drive a steep price, but those who crave their woodsy, grassy, or funky goodness find them well worth the price they bear.

When purchasing wild produce items, *especially mushrooms*, it is critical that they be purchased from a very knowledgeable and experienced source, as some wild items can be confused with similar-looking plants that are poisonous. Also, many foraged items may cause allergic reactions unless cooked thoroughly. Items foraged alongside highways or near industrial sites may be contaminated and therefore dangerous for consumption. Having a trustworthy source is critical when buying wild, foraged items.

Financial Considerations

The choices made when selecting, buying, and receiving produce have a direct impact on an operation's bottom line. This impact is felt in several ways both before and after the produce arrives in the receiving area or kitchen. As discussed earlier, seasonality is a key factor. Purchasing product well out of season can drive up the food cost to more than 100 percent higher than optimal seasonal pricing. Purchasing an item just as it comes into season will almost guarantee that it will be much higher in price than waiting just a few days or weeks until the markets have ample inventory. Some items, like berries, when purchased out of season, may need to be cooked or augmented in some way to improve their palatability, and will still command a premium price. Freezing delicious and affordably priced berries in season and then using the frozen berries in the winter months will yield a better-tasting product for a lesser cost. Otherwise, consider leaving berries off the menu in the winter and utilizing those items when they are in season and a better value.

Proper turnover of inventory is also a factor affecting the bottom line. Produce held too long in storage will not maintain its nutritional value. Even if the product appears in reasonable condition upon receipt, it will not retain its vibrant appearance or its bright flavor over time. Also, many produce items will dehydrate as they sit on the shelf under refrigeration. This is detrimental to both their flavor and texture. Water loss is the equivalent of pounds of produce purchased and never served or sold. Inventory levels need to be determined by factoring the rate at which the product is sold and the frequency of available deliveries. Purchase only what is needed to meet demand from one delivery to the next. Being overly cautious to ensure that product is always in inventory, or stocking to fill all available kitchen space, will cost you both in dollars and customer satisfaction over the long run. Diligence in monitoring inventory levels and adjusting par stocks is also important.

Proper utilization is also a key factor in maximizing yield and improving the value of your produce purchases. Utilizing all usable vegetable trim in soups or stocks, finding a use for all edible, but often wasted, parts such as papaya seeds and fennel fronds, and utilizing the same item in several menu applications to ensure rapid turnover are all ways to further a product's value. You can also improve the bottom line by puréeing and freezing excess product for soups, or purchasing product in season, at a lower price, and freezing, pickling, or canning it for later use.

Working with Recipes

Adapting recipes for customers with special dietary requirements may seem like an arduous task, but there are some basic guidelines that can be used. Starting with recipes that follow general nutrition guidelines will make the job much easier. There are areas of overlap in all of the health concerns, so if a recipe can address these areas as well, the foundation will be easy to build upon. In addition to the ingredients used in the recipe, the plating style can alter the guest's perception of the dish so that it doesn't seem inferior to the original recipe (see photos below). The following example recipes will illustrate and explain these ideas.

A basic plating style

Use a long plate to draw attention to the various ingredients without using large quantities.

Use height to make the plate appear very full while showcasing the components.

New England Clam Chowder

Makes 2 quarts/1.89 L

~~3 dozen fresh littleneck clams~~ — *REPLACE WITH SEAWEED-INFUSED VEGETABLE STOCK*

~~32 fl oz/960 mL water~~

2 oz/57 g ~~bacon~~, minced — *REPLACE WITH SMOKED TEMPEH AND GRAPESEED OIL*

4 oz/113 g onion, diced

3 tbsp/30 g all-purpose flour

1 bay leaf

½ tsp/1 g thyme leaves, chopped

1 lb/454 g potatoes, peeled and diced

20 fl oz/600 mL ~~heavy cream~~ — *REPLACE WITH ALMOND OR RICE MILK*

4 fl oz/120 mL dry sherry, or as needed

½ tsp/2 g kosher salt

Pinch freshly ground black pepper

½ tsp/3 mL Tabasco sauce, or as needed

½ tsp/3 mL Worcestershire sauce

1 oz/28 g flat-leaf parsley chiffonade

2 oz/57 g oyster crackers, for garnish

REPLACE CLAM MEAT WITH CHOPPED SEAWEED, CORN, AND ZUCCHINI

MAKE SEAWEED STOCK

1. Scrub the clams, and place the clams and water in a deep 2-gal/7.57-L pot. Cover the pot and bring the clams to a simmer. Gently simmer until the shells open. Remove the clams from the pot, separate meat from shells, reserve the meat, and discard the shells. Coarsely chop the clam meat. Strain the cooking liquid through a coffee filter and reserve the liquid. The yield should be approximately 32 to 36 fl oz/ 946 mL to 1.06 L.

SAUTE TEMPEH THEN ADD ONION AND GARLIC

2. Heat a 4-qt/3.84-L soup pot over medium heat, add the minced ~~bacon~~ *TEMPEH*, and cook slowly until the fat is rendered and the ~~bacon~~ *TEMPEH* is lightly crisp, about 8 minutes.

3. Add the onion and cook, stirring occasionally, until the onion is translucent, 5 to 7 minutes. Add the flour and cook over low heat, stirring with a wooden spoon, for 2 to 3 minutes.

4. Whisk in 1 quart of the reserved cooking ~~liquid from the clams~~ *SEAWEED STOCK*, bring to a simmer, and cook for 5 minutes, stirring occasionally. The liquid should be the consistency of heavy cream. If it is too thick, add more cooking liquid to adjust the consistency. Add the bay leaf and thyme.

5. Add the potatoes and simmer until tender, about 15 minutes. *ADD ZUCCHINI AND CORN*

6. Meanwhile, place the chopped ~~clams~~ *SEAWEED* and ~~cream~~ *ALMOND MILK* in a saucepan and simmer together until the clams are cooked, 5 to 8 minutes.

7. When the potatoes are tender, add the ~~clams and cream~~ *SEAWEED AND ALMOND MILK* to the soup. Simmer for 1 to 2 minutes.

8. Stir in the sherry. Season with salt, pepper, Tabasco, and Worcestershire sauce, and add the parsley. Serve in bowls with the crackers on the side.

New England Vegetable Chowder

Makes 10 portions

1 oz/28 g grapeseed oil

2 oz/57 g minced smoked tempeh

32 fl oz/960 mL Vegetable Stock (page 106)

2 oz/56 g dried seaweed (such as dulse or kombu), roughly chopped

4 oz/113 g diced onion

¼ oz/7 g minced garlic

3 tbsp/30 g all-purpose flour

1 bay leaf

½ tsp/1 g chopped thyme leaves

12 oz/340 g peeled and diced potatoes

4 oz/113 g fresh corn kernels

4 oz/113 g medium-dice zucchini

20 fl oz/600 mL almond milk or rice milk

4 fl oz/120 mL dry sherry, or as needed

½ tsp/1 g kosher salt, or as needed

Pinch freshly ground black pepper, or as needed

½ tsp/3 mL Tabasco sauce, or as needed

½ tsp/3 mL Worcestershire sauce, or as needed

1 oz/28 g flat-leaf parsley chiffonade

2 oz/57 g oyster crackers, as needed for garnish

1. Heat a 4-qt soup pot over medium heat, add the oil and minced tempeh, and cook slowly until the tempeh is lightly crisp, about 8 minutes. In a separate pot, heat the vegetable stock to a gentle simmer, add the seaweed, and steep the seaweed until tender and rehydrated. Strain the seaweed from the broth, reserving both.

2. Add the onion and garlic, and cook, stirring occasionally, until the onion is translucent, 5 to 7 minutes.

3. Add the flour and cook over low heat, stirring with a wooden spoon, for 2 to 3 minutes.

4. Whisk in the vegetable stock, bring to a simmer, and cook for 5 minutes, stirring occasionally. The liquid should be the consistency of heavy cream. If it is too thick, add more vegetable stock to adjust the consistency. Add the bay leaf and thyme.

5. Add the potatoes and simmer until nearly tender, about 10 minutes. Add the corn and zucchini and cook for an additional 5 minutes.

6. Meanwhile, place the chopped seaweed and almond milk in a saucepan and simmer together until hot.

7. When the potatoes are tender, add the seaweed and almond milk to the soup. Simmer for 1 to 2 minutes.

8. Stir in the sherry. Season with salt, pepper, Tabasco, and Worcestershire sauce, and add the parsley. Serve in bowls with the crackers on the side.

Pan-Fried Chicken Cutlets with Remoulade Sauce

Makes 10 portions

REMOULADE SAUCE

3 cups/720 mL mayonnaise

2 oz/57 g chopped capers

2 oz/57 g chopped cornichons

3 tbsp/45 mL chopped chives

1½ tbsp/22.5 mL chopped chervil

1½ tbsp/22.5 mL chopped tarragon

1 tbsp/15 mL Dijon mustard

1 tsp/5 mL anchovy paste

Salt, as needed

Freshly ground black pepper, as needed

Worcestershire sauce, as needed

Tabasco sauce, as needed

REPLACE WITH FLAVORFUL DIP PRIOR TO DREDGING

NOTE

The remoulade makes enough for 20 portions.

FRIED CHICKEN BREAST

5 lb/2.27 kg boneless, skinless chicken breasts

Salt, as needed

Freshly ground black pepper, as needed

2 lb/907 g all-purpose flour

12 eggs

1 cup/240 mL milk

1 lb/454 g Japanese bread crumbs

2 qt/1.92 L vegetable oil, for pan frying

REPLACE STANDARD BREADING PROCEDURE AS FOLLOWS...

NO FLOUR

NO EGG WASH

USE BUTTERMILK WITH ALMOND BUTTER, ONION, GARLIC, LEMON JUICE, AND SEASONINGS

REPLACE BREAD CRUMBS WITH GROUND FLAXSEED AND ALMOND AND HERBS

1. Combine all ingredients; mix together well. *FOR THE SAUCE*

2. Hold the sauce under refrigeration. Adjust the seasoning just before serving if necessary.

3. Trim the chicken breasts of any surface fat skin. Lightly pound each portion to an even thickness.

4. Blot the meat dry and season with salt and pepper. Bread each portions by dipping them in flour and shaking off the excess, dipping into egg wash, transferring to the bread crumbs, and pressing the crumbs evenly over the surface. Transfer to the sheet pan. Continue breading as needed. If the bread crumbs starts to clump together due to the

   MARINATE
   THE ... *IN THE SEASONED BUTTERMILK MARINADE. MARINATE FOR 30+ MINUTES.*
   DREDGE THE MARINATED PORTIONS IN SEASONED FLAX AND ALMOND MIXTURE
   COATING
   FLAX-ALMOND MIXTURE

MARINADE   GROUND FLAX AND ALMONDS   COATING

   egg wash, sieve the crumbs to remove clumps. (Breading may be done in advance; hold refrigerated, uncovered, for no more than 3 to 4 hours for best quality).

5. In a sauteuse, heat oil to a depth of about ¼ inch over moderate heat until the oil is hot. Add the breaded breasts to the hot oil. Pan fry on the first side for 5 to 6 minutes, or until golden brown and the cutlets release easily from the pan. Turn the breasts once and finish cooking on the second side, 5 to 6 minutes.

6. Remove the fried portions from the oil and drain briefly on absorbent paper toweling. Serve immediately.

DON'T PAN FRY
INSTEAD USE NONSTICK SHEET PAN, SPRAY PAN AND CHICKEN WITH OLIVE OIL

BAKE IN 350°F/176°C OVEN TILL COOKED THROUGH

Almond-Flax Crusted Chicken

Makes 10 portions

2 oz/57 g onion

¼ oz/7 g garlic cloves, roasted and puréed

1½ fl oz/45 mL olive oil

3 lb 2 oz/1.42 kg boneless, skinless chicken breasts

1½ oz/43 g almond butter

½ fl oz/15 mL lemon juice

4 fl oz/120 mL nonfat buttermilk

1 tsp/2 g sea salt

Pinch cayenne

Pinch paprika

1½ oz/42 g golden flaxseed, coarsely ground

4 oz/113 g almonds, toasted and finely ground

2 tbsp/6 g chopped flat-leaf parsley

1 tbsp/3 g chopped thyme

1 lemon, cut into 10 wedges, seeded

1. Preheat the oven to 350°F/176°C.
2. Wrap the onion, garlic, and ½ fl oz/15 mL olive oil in aluminum foil and roast in the oven until aromatic and tender, 20 to 25 minutes.
3. Rinse the chicken, and pat dry with paper towels. Lightly pound the chicken with a mallet to even out the thickness.
4. Place the onion, garlic, remaining olive oil, almond butter, lemon juice, buttermilk, salt, cayenne, and paprika into a blender and purée until smooth.
5. Place the purée in a resealable bag and add the chicken breasts. Seal the bag and massage the bag to make sure the purée coats the breasts thoroughly. Allow the breasts to marinate for 30 minutes.
6. Combine the flax, almonds, parsley, and thyme in a shallow pan and stir to mix evenly.
7. Remove the marinated chicken breasts, and dip each breast in the almond-flax mixture to coat.
8. Place the coated breasts on a nonstick sheet pan that has been lightly sprayed with olive oil cooking spray and bake until cooked through, about 15 minutes.
9. Serve immediately. Garnish with a wedge of fresh lemon.

How do we make the paradigm shift from quantity = value to quality (not quantity) = value? Much of the time it's about the ingredients: not just the quantity of the ingredient being prepared, but specifically the qualities of the ingredient and the manner in which it is being prepared. Purchasing ingredients that are optimally fresh, grown or raised with integrity and not chemicals, and then prepared with utmost care will undoubtedly provide your clientele deliciously beautiful and nutrient-rich meals.

Establishing a pantry or arsenal of essential ingredients will be invaluable. Research has demonstrated that there are key nutrients that are critical for human development and maintenance of a healthy body. This chapter will provide lists of ingredients that are believed to be of most value when it comes to providing those key nutrients and particularly in combating certain health conditions. Also provided is a list of the foods that should be used in moderation or, in some cases, not at all.

Healthful Ingredients

Becoming adventurous with "alternative" ingredients will open up new avenues of creativity. The use of sea vegetables is merely one example of this concept. When added to a broth or marinade, sea vegetables such as kombu or arame deliver a savory or umami quality and reduce the need for added salt (see photo below). These dried seaweeds can also be ground to a powder and used in spice blends or dry rubs.

Learn to use common ingredients in atypical ways to provide added nutrient value or limit fats or wheat gluten. Using nuts as an emulsifier, vegetable purées as thickeners, and pure starch to dust a piece of chicken or to create a slurry instead of flour and fat-based roux are a few ways that food preparations can be cleaned up.

When creating menus with specific nutritional needs in mind, it is necessary to keep a number of special ingredients and basic prepa-

From left to right, top to bottom: nori, gim, red nori, wakame, and kombu.

Inflammation

According to recent research, inflammation in the body is believed to be one of the underlying culprits behind many of our current health challenges such as heart disease, diabetes, and hypertension. Consuming a diet that is high in anti-inflammatory foods and low in inflammatory foods will help support reduction of inflammation in the body. It's interesting that many of the foods that are considered to be antioxidant foods also appear on the list of anti-inflammatory foods.

ANTI-INFLAMMATORY	INFLAMMATORY
Kelp, arame, kombu	Sugar
Turmeric, cinnamon, rosemary	Oils such as soy, corn, cottonseed
Ginger, thyme, basil, chile peppers	Trans fats
Garlic, curry powder	Dairy
Wild salmon	Feedlot-raised meats
Green tea, white tea, oolong tea	Red meat and all processed meats
Asian mushrooms such as shiitake	Alcohol
Papaya	Refined grains
Blueberries, berries in general	Artificial food additives
Extra-virgin olive oil	Nightshades such as tomato, potato, broccoli, and eggplant
Sweet potato (yam)	
Dark chocolate (70% cocao or higher)	
Red wine	
Fish and seafood	
Whole soy foods	
Pasta (especially bean thread noodles, whole wheat, buckwheat, etc.)	
Beans and legumes	

rations at the ready that easily facilitate recipe modification. Although most menu items for those with nutritional concerns can be made with the same ingredients used to make items on a regular menu, having a diverse pantry is key to successful nutritional adaptations.

Some commonly useful ingredients include: dried seaweed, sugar alternatives (such as agave syrup), salt alternatives (such as larger flaked sea salts), special flours (such as garbanzo or buckwheat), dried mushrooms, and versatile thickeners (such as potato or tapioca starch). In addition, making specialized, commonly used ingredients from scratch (such as stocks or broths) can be invaluable. These items lend themselves to fixing many of the health concerns that a specific recipe may pose as well as providing powerful flavor bases and boosters for a variety of recipes.

This chapter includes several charts and lists to assist in building a pantry of versatile specialty ingredients. An important thing to remember is that processed foods or convenience products should be avoided. These items can contain dyes, artificial flavorings, and chemical additives as well as traces of many of the most common allergens. Choosing foods that are sustainably, locally, or organi-cally grown is ideal from a nutritional perspective. It also creates the added benefit of familiarizing yourself and your staff with where food is being sourced, leading to a higher level of awareness of the nutrition received from the food and how best to prepare it. Foods sourced from nearby will have better flavor, texture, and color as they have not been stored for lengthy periods of time prior to arriving at your restaurant. Likewise, using fresh products rather than commercially frozen or canned will provide a better source of nutrients and often flavor for your customers.

Fats and Oils

Fats and oils are known for adding rich flavor, silky mouthfeel and texture, and a pleasing aroma to dishes. Fat performs a multitude of chemical functions such as tenderizing, leavening, aiding in moisture retention, and creating flaky/crumbly textures. Fats and oils act as insulators for food, transfer heat to food, prevent sticking, emulsify or thicken sauces, and create crisp textures when used for frying. While similar in many ways, fats are defined as solid at room temperature,

From left to right, top to bottom: Coconut fat, pepper oil, peanut oil, almond oil, hazelnut oil, walnut oil, tomato-infused oil, sesame oil, canola oil, corn oil, vegetable oil, sunflower oil, extra-virgin olive oil, Kalamata olive oil.

while oils are liquid. The smoke point of a fat or oil determines its appropriate use in cooking.

It is important for chefs to remember that fats should generally be limited when cooking for most types of special dietary concerns. Substitutions can be made, but simply reducing the amount used in a given recipe is often the best way to achieve the correct result without sacrificing too much texture or flavor.

CHEF'S NOTE

Fruit purées and/or yogurt can be used as fat replacers in many baking recipes. They simulate a texture similar to butter and provide moisture to baked goods. Fruit purées will, however, increase the product's sugar content. Adding yogurt will increase the acidity and protein in the finished product.

TYPE	DESCRIPTION	COMMON CULINARY USES
BUTTER, WHOLE	Solid fat churned from milk; a minimum of 80% milk fat, 20% water and milk solids. Quality based on flavor, body, texture, color, and salt content. Grades: AA (finest), A, B, C	Cooking, baking. In pastry, sauces, compound butters (Smoke point 350°F/177°C)
BUTTER, CLARIFIED/DRAWN/GHEE	Purified butterfat. Unsalted butter with milk solids removed. Longer shelf life than butter. High smoke point	In roux, warm butter sauces, Indian cooking, savory dishes (Smoke point 485°F/252°C)
CANOLA/RAPESEED	Light. Extracted from rapeseeds; similar to safflower oil. Golden colored. Low in saturated fat. Neutral flavor. Fairly high to very high smoke point	Cooking. In salad dressings (Smoke point 400°F/204°C)
COCONUT	Heavy. Extracted from dried coconut meat. Nearly colorless. Neutral flavor when deodorized. High in saturated fat. High smoke point	In commercial packaged goods, blended oils, shortenings (Smoke point 350°F/177°C)
CORN	Refined oil. Medium yellow color. Odorless; mild flavor. High smoke point	Deep-frying. In commercial salad dressings, margarine (Smoke point 450°F/232°C)
GRAPESEED	Light. Pale color. Neutral flavor. High smoke point	Sautéing, frying. In salad dressings (Smoke point 485°F/252°C)
MARGARINE	Commonly used as a butter substitute. Pale yellow. Similar fat content as butter without the same texture or flavor. Some margarines are lower in saturated fat, although they can contain trans fats.	Cooking, baking, pastry (Smoke point 302°F/150°C)
OLIVE	Varies in viscosity. Pale yellow to deep green (depending on type of olive and processing). Quality based on acidity level, the finest being extra-virgin. Two distinct classes: virgin and blended. The flavor of olive oil varies greatly depending on region; can range from mild to herbaceous to grassy to peppery. Low to high smoke point	Common to Mediterranean cuisines. Low- to high-heat cooking, depending on type of processing. In marinades, salad dressings (Smoke point 375°–465°F/ 191°–241°C)
OIL SPRAYS	Light vegetable oils. Blended. Packaged in pump or aerosol sprays. Varieties include vegetable, olive oil, and butter-flavored oil	Light coating for pans and griddles
PEANUT	Light. Refined. Clear to pale yellow. Subtle scent/flavor; less refined varieties have stronger scent/flavor. High smoke point	Deep-frying, stir-frying. In commercial salad dressings, margarine, shortening (Smoke point 450°F/232°C)
SESAME	Two types: One is light and mild with nutty flavor, the other is dark with stronger flavor and aroma. Extracted from sesame seeds. Low to moderate smoke point, depending on type	Frying, sautéing. In salad dressings, flavor additive (Smoke point 350°–410°/177°–210°C)
SOYBEAN	Heavy. Light yellow. Pronounced flavor and aroma. High smoke point	Common to Chinese cuisine. Stir-frying. In commercial margarine, shortening (Smoke point 450°F/232°C)
SUNFLOWER	Light. Extracted from sunflower seeds. Pale yellow. Subtle flavor. Low in saturated fat. Medium-low smoke point	All-purpose cooking. In salad dressings (Smoke point 440°F/227°C)
VEGETABLE	Light refined blended vegetable oils. Mild flavor and aroma. High smoke point	All-purpose cooking, deep-frying, baking (Smoke point varies)
WALNUT	Light. Unrefined. Pale to medium yellow. Delicate nutty flavor and aroma. Highly perishable; refrigerate to prevent rancidity	Flavor additive in salad dressings, meat dishes, pasta, desserts. Best used uncooked (Smoke point 320°F/160°C)

Starches and Thickeners

Starch is a carbohydrate, a polysaccharide molecule made up of chains of multiple simple sugar molecules. Starch is the stored energy source in plants, and tends to come in two forms: root- or tuberous-based starches and those that come from seeds such as rice, oats, or wheat. In cooking and baking, starches absorb moisture, increase the viscosity of a mixture, and act as stabilizers. There are two primary forms of starch: amylose and amylopectin. Amylose starches are found most abundantly in seeds. They are excellent thickeners, but can maintain a cloudy appearance when cooked. Amylopectin starches come from root or tuberous sources. It is not as strong of a thickener as amylase and tends to have a gooier texture, but it stays clear when cooked.

Starch Profile of Common Starchy Foods

STARCH	% AMYLOSE	% AMYLOPECTIN
DENT CORN	25	75
WAXY CORN	<1	>99
TAPIOCA	17	8
POTATO	20	80
HIGH-AMYLOSE CORN	55–70 or more	45–30 or less
WHEAT	25	75
RICE	19	81

Use a large pan—more surface area allows for quicker reducing.

Stock halfway reduced.

TYPE	DESCRIPTION	COMMON CULINARY USES
ALBUMEN POWDER	Powdered eggs whites add protein to cooking and baking recipes.	Stabilizer, leavener
ARROWROOT STARCH	A strong thickener that can be more expensive than other starches. It has a more neutral flavor and works better than cornstarch in frozen products. It is sometimes used in gluten-free baking.	Thickener, stabilizer
CORNSTARCH	Stays clear when used as a thickener, but can have a somewhat springy texture and a noticeable flavor.	Thickener, stabilizer
GUAR GUM	A naturally occurring gum made from guar beans.	Binder in flour blends, stabilizer
POTATO STARCH	Less detectible flavor than cornstarch. Has a clear consistency and a slightly more subtle thickening effect.	Thickener, stabilizer
TAPIOCA STARCH	Also called tapioca flour, this starch is a derived from the South American manioc plant, also known as cassava. Clear when cooked, but can be gooey.	Thickener, stabilizer
WHEY POWDER	Made from whey, a liquid by-product of cheese making. Whey adds protein and additional nutrition in cooking and baking recipes.	Stabilizer
XANTHAM GUM	Made in a laboratory from sugars fermented with a certain strain of bacteria. More expensive than guar gum.	Binder in flour blends, stabilizer

(continued on page 31)

Stock fully reduced.

Stock thickened with arrowroot (left), stock thickened with cornstarch (center), and reduced stock (right).

From top to bottom, left to right: Pastry flour, all-purpose flour, cake flour, whole wheat flour, garbanzo bean flour, barley flour, rice flour, semolina flour, oat flour, corn flour, graham flour, cornstarch, arrowroot starch, potato starch, tapioca starch, rye flour, buckwheat flour, spelt flour.

TYPE	DESCRIPTION	COMMON CULINARY USES
BEAN FLOURS	Bean flours may be made from any legume. Some of the most widely used in gluten-free baking include navy, pinto, garbanzo, and garbanzo-fava bean blends. Bean flours are made by grinding up whole dry beans into a fine powder. Some of these flours can cause flatulence, so look for a brand that is precooked to avoid or reduce this problem. To keep bean flour fresh, store it in the refrigerator or freezer.	Thickener, baked goods
BUCKWHEAT FLOUR	Buckwheat itself is gluten-free and is not related to wheat—it is in the same botanical family as rhubarb. Buckwheat is not considered a grain even though it is often used like one. Look carefully at the label when shopping for buckwheat flour or mixes: Sometimes it is blended with wheat flour.	Baked goods, general cooking
CORNMEAL/CORN FLOUR	Cornmeal is coarsely ground from whole dried corn and is available in yellow, white, and blue varieties. Corn flour is a more finely ground than cornmeal and has a lighter texture and detectable corn taste. Store these products in the freezer to prevent mold.	Baked goods, general cooking
GRAIN FLOURS	Many whole grains can be ground into nutritious flours. Commonly available are barley flour, oat flour, rye flour, spelt flour, quinoa flour, and teff flour.	Baked goods, general cooking, thickener
NUT FLOURS	Can be made from any nut, but most commonly from almonds, chestnuts, pecans, pistachios, and walnuts. They contain a high proportion of fat to protein and carbohydrate. Depending on the grind, it can have a mealy texture.	Baked goods, general cooking
RICE FLOUR	Available in white and brown varieties. Brown rice contains the bran and therefore is higher in fiber. Both types of rice flour can be gritty or grainy when used on their own. Brown rice flour can become rancid because of its bran content, so it should be refrigerated or frozen for long-term storage.	Thickener, baked goods
SOY FLOUR	Made from soybeans, high in protein, and can have a strong flavor. Defatted soy flour is less prone to rancidity. Should be stored in the refrigerator or freezer.	Thickener, baked goods
WHEAT FLOUR	Contains both protein and starch. The starch in wheat flour gelatinizes at a lower temperature range than cornstarch. When thickening a product with wheat flour, the gluten proteins can lump together easily. These proteins also tend to have a clouding effect on thickened sauces such as gravy. Whole wheat flours are made from the entire wheat kernel and have better nutritional value.	Thickener, baked goods, pasta

Sweeteners

Sugar is extracted from plant sources and refined into the desired form. Most varieties of syrup are derived from plants as well. The flavor intensity of sweeteners typically corresponds with the color—the darker the sugar or syrup, the more concentrated the flavor. This is especially important when considering various health concerns, as less of a more intense sweetener can be used while still imparting the desired flavor. One way to reduce calories is by reducing, removing, or replacing sugar in a recipe. Sugar serves many purposes: It provides bulk, acts as a liquefier, keeps items moist, and plays a role in caramelization. No sugar substitute can perform all of these functions.

TYPE	DESCRIPTION	COMMON CULINARY USES
AGAVE SYRUP	Comes from the sap of a succulent plant, the same substance from which tequila is made. The sap contains a high level of the polysaccharide inulin, and when exposed to enzymes, the inulin is broken apart into units of fructose. Since agave syrup is high in fructose, it is touted as having a low glycemic index, which is useful for diabetics. But like all sweeteners with high amounts of fructose, should be used sparingly to avoid gastric discomfort and health problems related to consuming too much fructose. The syrup is thin, much like the consistency of maple syrup.	Table use, baking, sauces, marinades, salad dressings, general cooking
ARTIFICIAL SWEETENERS	Sugar substitutes. Nonnutritive values. Varieties include (but not limited to): aspartame, acesulfame-K, saccharin, stevia, and sucralose.	Table use. Not recommended for all baking and cooking uses
BROWN	Refined, granulated sugar with some impurities remaining or molasses added. Somewhat moist. Two variations: light and dark; dark brown has more intense (molasses) flavor.	In baked goods, pastry, sauces, savory dishes
CONFECTIONERS'/POWDERED/10X	Pure refined sugar. White. Fine powder. Minimal amount of cornstarch added to prevent clumping.	In baked goods, pastry, icings, confections. As decorative garnish
CORN	Liquefied sugar created by processing cornstarch. Three varieties: light (clarified to remove color), dark (color added, caramel flavor), and high-fructose. Less sweet than granulated sugar; the darker the syrup, the more intense the flavor. Inhibits crystallization.	In baked goods, pastry, confections, spreads
GRANULATED/WHITE	Pure refined cane or beet sugar. White. Generally small granules; available in various sizes: coarse (crystal/decorating), superfine, cubes, tablets.	In baked goods, pastry, sauces, savory dishes
HONEY	Thick, sweet liquid produced by bees from flower nectar. Pale yellow to dark brown. Flavor intensifies as color deepens. Countless varieties. Named according to specific flower. Available in comb, chunk-style, liquid, whipped.	In baked goods, pastry, savory dishes, beverages, spreads
MAPLE	Maple sap boiled until near evaporation. Pale tan. Fine powder. Much sweeter than granulated sugar. Also available in syrup form.	In baked goods and savory dishes. As sweet additive to cereals, yogurt, coffee, tea
MOLASSES	Liquid by-product of sugar refining. Three varieties: light (first boil), dark (second boil), and blackstrap (third boil, darkest and thickest). Flavor and aroma intensifies as color deepens.	Accompaniment to pancakes, waffles, and French toast. In baked goods, pastry, savory dishes
PILONCILLO	Unrefined, hard compressed sugar from Mexico. Medium to dark brown. Cone shaped; ¾-ounce to 9-ounce cones. Two varieties: *blanco* (lighter) and *oscuro* (darker).	Substitute for dark brown sugar. In savory dishes
JAGGERY/PALM	Unrefined; from palm tree sap or sugarcane. Dark. Coarse grains. Available in several forms; two most popular: soft/spreadable and solid.	Popular in Indian cuisine. As spread for breads. In baked goods, confections
RAW	Purified sugarcane residue. Several varieties: Demerara (white sugar crystals with added molasses; coarse grains), Barbados/muscovado (moist, dark, fine-texture grains), turbinado (steam-cleaned, light brown, coarse grains).	Coarse grains are best suited for decorating and as a sweet additive. Fine-textured grains used as substitute for light brown sugar
RICE SYRUP	Has a thicker consistency than agave syrup. It is processed from rice starch, in much the same way as corn syrup, but is less refined. It can be a suitable replacement for honey in vegan recipes.	
SUGARCANE	Source of sugar; member of the grass family. Made edible by boiling. Available in stalks. Less sweet than granulated sugar.	As snack, garnish

From left to right, top to bottom: Molasses, honey, maltitol syrup, agave syrup, turbinado sugar, granulated maltitol, powdered maltitol, brown maltitol, granulated sugar, powdered sugar, Splenda™.

Dairy and Dairy Alternatives

Dairy products are key ingredients in most kitchens. They should be stored carefully and used quickly to ensure freshness. Canned, evaporated, skimmed milk and aseptically packaged 8-ounce boxes of whole milk can be stored without refrigeration until they are opened. Since whole milk is used in small amounts in some of the recipes, it is easier to have these individual servings on hand rather than purchasing a pint or quart of whole milk when a recipe only calls for a half cup. Canned, evaporated, skimmed milk can be used in some of the recipes in place of cream but you may also want to keep some aseptically package individual creamers in the pantry for the few situations where you need just a tablespoon or two of real cream.

FORM	DESCRIPTION	COMMON CULINARY USES
NONFAT OR SKIM MILK	Contains less than 0.25% milk fat	As a beverage. To enrich dishes. In baked goods, desserts
REDUCED-FAT MILK	Contains 1% or 2% milk fat, labeled accordingly	As a beverage. To enrich dishes. In baked goods, desserts
WHOLE MILK	Contains 3.5% milk fat	In béchamel sauce. As a beverage. To enrich dishes. In baked goods, desserts
HALF-AND-HALF	Contains 10.5% milk fat	As table or coffee cream. To enrich soups and sauces. In baked goods, desserts
LIGHT CREAM	Contains 18% milk fat	As table or coffee cream. To enrich soups and sauces. In baked goods, desserts
POWDERED OR DRY MILK	Milk from which water is completely removed; made from either whole or skim milk and labeled accordingly	In baked goods, charcuterie, and drink mixes
EVAPORATED MILK	Milk that has been heated in a vacuum to remove 60% of its water; may be made from whole or skim milk and is labeled accordingly	To enrich custards and sauces. In baked goods and desserts
YOGURT	Lightly fermented with a bacterial strain or cultured; contains less than 0.25% to 3.5% milk fat, labeled accordingly	With fruit. In soups, sauces, baked goods, desserts
SOUR CREAM	Treated with lactic acid culture; contains 18% milk fat	To enrich soups and sauces. In baked goods, desserts
SOY MILK	Made from soybeans that have been soaked in water, ground, and strained. Contains approximately as much fat as 2% cow's milk	As a vegan and dairy-free substitute for cow's milk, As beverage. To enrich dishes. In baked goods, desserts
NUT MILK	Made from nuts that have been soaked in water, ground, and strained. Almond, cashew, and coconut are common nut milks	As a vegan and dairy-free substitute for cow's milk, As beverage. To enrich dishes. In baked goods, desserts
GRAIN MILK	Made from grains that have been soaked in water, ground, and strained. Rice and barley are common grain milks	As a vegan and dairy-free substitute for cow's milk, As beverage. To enrich dishes. In baked goods, desserts

Eggs

Eggs are incredibly versatile and are a naturally good source of protein. Eggs are available in varying sizes (small, medium, large, and extra-large), colors (brown, white, and even pastel shades), and grades (AA is the top grade). It is very important to cook eggs correctly, regardless of the technique being used, because when eggs are overcooked, they coagulate excessively, forcing water out and making them dry and unappealing.

Try to use the freshest eggs available. You can determine this by finding the date of harvest stamped on the carton. Eggs generally can remain fresh for up to two weeks. As they age, the white becomes thinner and more alkaline. The yolk sac also thins and may rupture the fat-containing yolk into the white.

Egg Grading

Eggs are graded according to quality and appearance—*not* freshness.

USDA GRADE	DESCRIPTION
AA	Firmest whites
A	Fairly firm whites
B	One or more defect; these whites tend not to foam well

From left to right, top to bottom: Ener-G egg replacer, Iowa egg replacer, medium, large, and extra-large eggs, whole Egg Beaters, white Egg Beaters.

FORM	DESCRIPTION	COMMON CULINARY USES
EGG WHITES	Available fresh, frozen, and pasteurized. Gums, acids, or whipping agents may be added to pasteurized or frozen egg whites. Whips to 7 times volume.	General cooking, baked goods
EGG YOLKS	Available fresh or frozen. Frozen usually has added sugar to help lower the freezing point. Whips to 6 times volume.	General cooking, baked goods, sauces
WHOLE EGGS	Available fresh, liquid, or frozen. Citric acid may be added to liquid or frozen eggs to preserve freshness. Whips to 4 times volume.	General cooking, baked goods, sauces

Egg Substitutes

Egg substitutes may be entirely egg-free or may be produced from egg whites, with dairy or vegetable products substituted for the yolks. Before deciding how to replace the eggs in a recipe, you must consider what role the egg plays. As mentioned earlier, eggs contribute stability to baked goods, along with flavor and leavening power.

The egg white consists of 90 percent water, along with two major proteins: ovalbumin and albumen. The yolk contains fat: both cholesterol and lecithin, a natural phospholipid that serves as an emulsifying agent.

FORM	DESCRIPTION	COMMON CULINARY USES
ENER-G EGG REPLACER	Provides leavening that may be lost when eggs are replaced. When mixed with water, Ener-G powder resembles egg whites. The product does not taste like eggs, does not have a creamy consistency or egg-like appearance, and does not emulsify. Ener-G egg replacer is gluten-free and dairy-free; another powdered egg replacer, Iowa egg replacer, is not gluten-free.	Leavening
FLAXSEEDS	A good binding agent when ground and mixed with water. Regular flaxseeds can give a baked product a gray cast, so look for golden flaxseeds when using these as an egg replacer.	Binding agent, body/texture
SILKEN TOFU	Adds body to a product and is a good replacer in custards. Choose a tofu with a mild taste.	Body/texture, custards, baked goods
VERSAWHIP	An enzymatically treated soy powder that can be combined with water and whipped to make a foam to replace egg whites or gelatin.	Body/texture, leavening

Proteins

The category of proteins is broad and encompasses many types of foods—most notably meat, fish, poultry, and vegetable-sourced protein such as tempeh, soy (including tofu), seitan (or vital wheat gluten), and TVP (texturized vegetable protein). Beans are also a source of protein (for more information, see page 40).

Kosher Meats

Kosher meats are specially slaughtered, bled, and fabricated in order to comply with religious dietary laws. In this country, only beef and veal forequarters, poultry, and some game are customarily used for kosher preparations. Kosher meats are butchered from animals slaughtered by a *shohet*, or by a specially trained rabbi. The animal must be killed with a single stroke of a knife, then fully bled. All the veins and arteries must be removed from the meat. This process would essentially mutilate the flesh of loins and legs of beef and veal; therefore, these are generally not sold as kosher.

FORM	DESCRIPTION	COMMON CULINARY USES
BEEF	A significant source of protein, beef is available in a variety of cuts. The older the bovine, the tougher the meat. The same can be said for the cuts—the more exercised, the tougher the meat. For most individuals with health concerns, lean cuts of beef should be used and portion sizes should be monitored to avoid excess servings.	Grilling, braising, stewing, sautéing, roasting, stir-frying
FISH	The skeletal structure of fish is a useful means of separating finfish into smaller groupings. The three basic types of finfish are flat, round, and nonbony. Fish may also be categorized by their activity level: low, medium, or high. The more a fish swims, the darker its flesh will be. Darker-fleshed fish have a higher oil content and, therefore, a stronger flavor. Fatty fish such as these are powerful sources of nutrients and healthy protein for individuals with dietary issues.	Sautéing, grilling, poaching, soup, steaming, roasting
GAME	Free-roaming and domesticated wild animals fall under the category of game. A variety of game meats have become increasingly popular due in part to customer awareness of their lower fat and cholesterol content. Depending upon the area of the country, several types of furred game are available. Game meats are categorized into two segments: large and small. Venison is the most popular large game, characterized by lean meat that is free from intramuscular fat. Similarly lean cuts are buffalo and wild boar. The most popular small game is rabbit.	Sautéing, grilling, roasting, braising, stewing
LAMB	Lamb is the tender meat produced by young, domesticated sheep. Its texture is a direct result of what it consumes and the age at which it is slaughtered. The milk-fed varieties of lamb are inclined to yield the most delicate meat. Once a lamb begins to eat grass, the flesh loses some of its tenderness. As with other varieties of meat, lamb becomes tougher as it ages. Because of its strong flavor, lamb is a meat that is often easier to use in smaller quantities and portions when cooking for individuals with dietary restrictions.	Roasting, grilling, sautéing, braising, stewing
PORK	Pork, the meat of domesticated pigs, is among the most popular meat sold in the United States. Typically high in fat, pigs have been specifically bred over many generations to produce leaner cuts of meat. Because many cuts have such a high fat content, pork products should be used in limited quantities or lean cuts should be used when cooking for individuals with health concerns.	Grilling, roasting, braising, stewing, sautéing, smoking, stir-frying
POULTRY	Poultry refers to any domesticated bird used for human consumption. The subtle and familiar flavor of chicken lends itself well to a number of different cooking methods. Considered very nutritious, poultry entrées are among the most popular on most menus and are versatile for chefs cooking for customers with restricted diets.	Grilling, roasting, braising, stewing, sautéing, stir-frying, poaching, soup
SEITAN	Also known as vital wheat gluten, seitan is gluten flour that has been made into a dough and then simmered, resulting in a meaty texture. Easily flavored. High in protein.	Grilling, roasting, sautéing
TEMPEH	Made from cooked and slightly fermented soybeans and formed into a patty, with additional grain sometimes added. Low in fat, high in protein, with a meaty texture. Easily flavored.	Grilling, sautéing, stir-frying
TOFU	Made from soybeans, water, and a coagulant, or curdling agent. It is high in protein and calcium and well known for its ability to absorb new flavors through spices and marinades. Available in silken, soft, firm, and dried varieties (see page 39).	Sautéing, grilling, stir-frying, stewing
TVP	High-fiber, high-protein meat substitute made from soy flour and available in a variety of flavored and unflavored varieties, as well as different sizes, from large chunks to small flakes.	May be reconstituted and, based on the texture chosen, may be stewed, braised, or formed into patties and fried or sautéed

From left to right, top to bottom: Firm tofu, smoked tofu, vital wheat gluten, TVP, silken tofu, seitan, tempeh.

Varieties of Tofu

The many different varieties of tofu, along with its readiness to absorb flavor, make it one of the most versatile proteins. Besides varying by type, different brands of tofu will vary slightly in flavor and texture as well.

TYPE	TEXTURE	FLAVOR	APPLICATION
JAPANESE-STYLE Usually packed in aseptic boxes			
SILKEN	Purées and mashes easily. Does not hold shape well when diced or sliced.	Overall, bland; readily takes on the flavor of other ingredients and seasonings	Best suited for smooth preparations such as smoothies, sauces, soups, custards, salad dressings, baked goods such as cheesecake
SOFT	Like soft custard	Bland	Smoothies
MEDIUM	Like medium-firm custard	Bland	Soft fillings and purée soups
FIRM	Like firm custard	Bland	Soft fillings and purée soups
EXTRA-FIRM	Like extra-firm or dense custard	Bland	Cheesecake
SOME FLAVORED VARIETIES AVAILABLE		Flavored varieties include smoked, curry, hot and spicy, and five-spice	
CHINESE-STYLE Generally packed in water in clamshell containers or sold loose; found in the produce or refrigerator section			
REGULAR	Texture is generally drier than the silken varieties and more dense. When cut, these types hold their form, especially if pressed first.	Generally bland, readily takes on the flavor of other ingredients and seasonings	Generally best used to stir-fry, pan fry, roast, bake, grill, deep-fry, and as soup garnish. Crumbled, diced, or sliced. Breaded, battered; coated in seeds, nuts, spices, and spice rubs
SOFT	If crumbled, like ricotta cheese	Bland	Fillings, dessert
MEDIUM	If crumbled, like scrambled eggs	Bland	Fillings, garnish
FIRM	If crumbled, like egg salad	Bland	Very good to sauté, grill, or pan fry. Can be marinated or dry-rubbed
EXTRA-FIRM	If crumbled, mock chicken salad	Bland	Very good to sauté, grill, or pan fry. Can be marinated or dry-rubbed
SOME FLAVORED VARIETIES AVAILABLE		Flavored varieties include smoked, five-spice, Italian seasoning, teriyaki, Cajun seasoning, mock turkey, and mock bacon	Very good to sauté, grill, or pan fry; soups and stews

Marinating Alternative Proteins

Tempeh, seitan, and tofu all respond very well to marinating. Because their textures are similar to meat, they are able to absorb the flavors of a marinade. Marinades can be as simple as flavored oils, vegetable or fruit juices, or a mixture of spices, or you can use any basic marinade. Refer to specific recipes for instructions, but marinate the protein in a shallow dish. Turn it occasionally as it marinates for best results.

Beans and Other Legumes

Beans and other legumes are considered superfoods, with nutritional benefits that are helpful to people with many types of health concerns or dietary restrictions. Paired with vegetables, beans and legumes can be considered a complete meal and healthy source of protein. The photos below exemplify plates of foods that provide complete proteins, either through the combination of grains and legumes or the inclusion of protein such as eggs and poultry.

Beans are available dried and canned. Canned beans have been fully cooked and can be used immediately, but dried beans must be soaked and cooked until tender before they are eaten. Sort dried beans by spreading them into a single layer and removing any stones and other debris and any moldy beans. Rinse the beans with cold water to remove any dust. Put the beans in a container and cover them with cold water. Remove any that float to the surface; they are too dry to be eaten. After soaking, drain the beans and cook them. This technique works for legumes as well. Beans, peas, and lentils are in the plant family known as legumes. Beans are typically kidney or oval in shape and other legumes, such as peas and lentils, are round or elliptical in shape. Soaking beans and legumes will soften their skins, allowing them to hydrate slightly; this makes for faster and more even cooking.

Steamed brown rice, stewed black beans, and sautéed broccoli rabe.

Grilled smoked tofu with sautéed kale and quinoa pilaf.

Grilled chicken and poached egg over salad greens.

From left to right, top to bottom: Black-eyed peas, pinto beans, white navy beans, chickpeas, cannellini beans, red kidney beans, flageolet beans, cranberry beans, red lentils, brown lentils, beluga lentils, green lentils, daal.

Dried Legumes

NAME(S)	DESCRIPTION	COMMON CULINARY USES
BEANS		
ADZUKI	Small. Reddish-brown. Available whole or powdered. Sweet flavor	Popular in Japanese cuisine. Used in confections as a sweet paste or sugar-coated. In savory dishes
BLACK/TURTLE	Large. Black exterior, light creamy interior. Sweet flavor	In soups, stews, salsas, salads, side dishes
CANARY	Slightly smaller than pinto beans. Canary yellow. Sweet and nutty flavor	Popular in Peruvian dishes, specifically stews
CANNELLINI/ITALIAN KIDNEY	Medium; kidney-shaped. White. Nutty flavor	Minestrone soup, salads, stews, side dishes
CRANBERRY/BORLOTTI	Small; round. Light tan with maroon markings. Nutty flavor	In soups, stews, salads, side dishes
FAVA/BROAD	Large, flat oval. Tan. Herbaceous flavor with a firm texture	Popular in Mediterranean and Middle Eastern cuisines. In falafel, soups, stews, salads, side dishes
FLAGEOLETS	Small; kidney-shaped. Pale green to creamy white. Delicate flavor	Served with lamb. Braised and puréed as a side dish
GARBANZO/CHICKPEAS	Medium; acorn-shaped. Beige. Nutty flavor	Popular in many ethnic dishes. In couscous, hummus, soups, stews, salads, side dishes
GREAT NORTHERN	Large; slightly rounded. White. Mildly delicate flavor	In soups, stews, casseroles side dishes
KIDNEY	Medium; kidney-shaped. Pink to maroon. Full-bodied flavor	In chili con carne, refried beans, beans and rice, soups, stews, casseroles, side dishes
LENTILS	Small; round. Brown; varieties include French (gray-green exterior with pale yellow interior), red, yellow, split white. Peppery flavor	Served whole or puréed as an accompaniment. In soups, stews, salads, side dishes
LIMA/BUTTER	Medium; slightly flat kidney shape. White to pale green. Buttery flavor	In succotash, soups, stews, salads, side dishes
MUNG	Small; round. Green. Tender texture and slightly sweet flavor	Sprouted for bean sprouts. Ground into flour to make cellophane noodles and bean threads
NAVY/YANKEE	Small; round. White. Mild flavor	In baked beans, chili, soups, salads
PINTO/RED MEXICAN	Medium; tubular. Beige with brown streaks	In chili, refried beans, stews, soups
RICE	Heirloom bean. Very small, plump, capsule-shaped; resembles rice grains. Mild, slightly bitter flavor	As substitute for rice. In soups, stews, casseroles, side dishes
SOYBEANS	Small; pea- to cherry-shaped; dried version is mature bean. Red, yellow, green, brown, black. Bland flavor	In soups, stews, casseroles, side dishes
HEIRLOOM (CALYPSO, TONGUES OF FIRE, JACOB'S CATTLE, MADEIRA, AND OTHERS)	Range tremendously in size and color; many have stripes or speckles	In soups, stews, casseroles, side dishes, salads
PEAS		
BLACK-EYED	Small; kidney-shaped. Beige with black "eye." Earthy flavor	In Hoppin' John, soups, side dishes
PIGEON/GANDULES	Small; nearly round. Beige with orange spotting. Sweet flavor similar to lima beans	Popular in African, Caribbean, and Indian dishes
SPLIT	Small; round. Green or yellow. Earthy flavor	In split pea soup, salads, side dishes

Grains and Meals

This broad category extends from whole grains such as rice and barley to grain preparations such as cornmeal and farina. They are important sources of nutrition, especially whole grains—which contain fiber, protein, and other nutrients.

NAME	DESCRIPTION	COMMON CULINARY USES
BUCKWHEAT	Whole or milled into flour. Light brown. Mildly nutty flavor	As hot cereal. In pilaf. Flour is used for pancakes, blinis, baked goods.
KASHA	Hulled, crushed kernels (buckwheat groats), roasted. Reddish-brown. Chewy texture. Toasty, nutty flavor	In pilafs, salads, savory pancakes
MILLET	Whole or milled into flour. Bland flavor	As hot cereal. In pilaf. Flour is used for puddings, flatbreads, cakes.
SORGHUM	Commonly boiled down to a thick syrup	In porridge, flatbreads, beer, syrup, molasses
RYE	Whole, cracked, or milled into flour. Ranges from light to dark brown. Dense. Pumpernickel flour is very dark, coarsely ground rye.	In pilafs, salads. Flour is used for baked goods
TEFF	Whole; extremely tiny. Light to reddish-brown. Sweet, chestnut-like flavor	In soups, casseroles. As thickening agent
AMARANTH	Whole or milled into flour. Color ranges from white to tan, gold, or pink. Sweet flavor	As hot and cold cereal. In pilaf, salads, soups
SPELT	Whole or milled into flour. Moderately nutty flavor	In pilafs, salads. Flour is used for baked goods.
JOB'S TEARS	Whole; small, white. Slightly chewy texture. Grass-like flavor	In pilafs, salads
QUINOA	Whole or milled into flour. Very tiny circles. Off-white, red, or black. Mild flavor	In pilafs, salads, puddings, soups, as an addition to polenta
BARLEY	Hulled and pearl (hull and bran removed). Varieties: grits, flour. Tan to white. Nutty flavor	In pilafs, salads, soups. Used to make whiskey and beer
OAT GROATS	Hulled, usually crushed grain, especially oats, but can be wheat, buckwheat kasha	As hot cereal. In salads, stuffing, or mixed with other cereals
ROLLED/OLD-FASHIONED OATS	Groats, steamed and flattened. Very pale brown, almost white. Round, flake-like. Tender. Also available as "quick-cooking" and "instant"	As hot cereal (oatmeal). In granola, baked goods
STEEL-CUT IRISH/SCOTCH OATS	Groats, cut into pieces. Brown, chewy	As hot cereal. In baked goods
OAT BRAN	Outer covering of the oat	As hot and cold cereal. In baked goods
HOMINY	Dried corn kernels, soaked in lye to remove the hull and germ. Available canned or dried	In succotash, casseroles, soups, stews, side dishes. In Mexican posole
GRITS	Ground hominy. Available in fine, medium, and coarse grinds	As hot cereal. In baked goods, side dishes. Popular in the southern United States
MASA	Dried corn kernels, cooked and soaked in limewater, then ground into dough. Pale yellow. Moist. Variation: masa harina, dried and ground to a fine flour. Must be reconstituted to make a dough	Used to make tortillas, tamales, and other Mexican dishes. Masa harina is often used in baked goods or as a coating for pan frying or deep-frying.
CORNMEAL	Dried corn kernels, ground to fine, medium, or coarse texture. White, yellow, or blue. Variations: corn flour (finely ground); polenta (coarsely ground)	As hot cereal. In baked goods. To coat items for sautéing or pan frying

Continued on page 45

From left to right, top to bottom: **Amaranth, millet, kasha, basmati rice, wild rice, Arborio rice, Forbidden Rice, jasmine rice, purple rice, farro, barley flour, barley malt, bulgur, quinoa, barley.**

NAME	DESCRIPTION	COMMON CULINARY USES
BROWN RICE	Whole grain, with the inedible husk removed. Light brown. Chewy texture. Nutty flavor. Available as short, medium, or long grain	In pilaf, salads
WHITE/POLISHED RICE	Husk, bran, and germ removed. White. Mild flavor. Available as short, medium, or long grain	In pilaf, salads. Short grain used to make rice pudding
CONVERTED/ PARBOILED RICE	Unhulled grain soaked and steamed before the husk, bran, and germ are removed. Very light brown color. Fluffy, separate grains when cooked	In pilaf, salads
BASMATI RICE	Extra-long grain. Fine, delicate texture. Aromatic, nutty flavor. Aged to reduce moisture content. Available as brown or white rice. Popcorn rice is a variety of basmati.	In pilaf, salads
JASMINE RICE	Aromatic, delicate flavor. Long grain. White	In pilaf, steamed, rice pudding
ARBORIO/ITALIAN RICE	Very short, very fat grain. Off-white. High starch content; creamy when cooked. Varieties include Carnaroli, Piedmontese, and Vialone Nano	In risotto, pudding
CALASPARRA RICE	Very short, very fat grain. Off-white. High starch content; creamy when cooked	In paella
WILD RICE	Marsh grass, unrelated to regular rice. Long, thin grain. Dark brown. Chewy texture. Nutty flavor	In salads, stuffing, pancakes, forcemeats. Often combined with brown rice
STICKY/PEARL/ GLUTINOUS/SUSHI RICE	Round, short grain. Very starchy; sticky when cooked. Sweet, mild flavor	In sushi, desserts, and other culinary uses
HEIRLOOM RICES	Varieties include Bhutanese Red, Forbidden Black, and Kalijira rice. Length and color vary	In salads, stuffing. Often combined with brown rice
WHEAT BERRIES/ WHOLE WHEAT KERNELS	Unrefined or minimally processed whole wheat kernels. Light brown to reddish brown. Somewhat chewy. Nutty flavor	As hot cereal. In pilaf, salads, breads
CRACKED WHEAT	Coarsely crushed, minimally processed wheat kernels. Light brown to reddish brown. Somewhat chewy. Nutty flavor	As hot cereal. In pilaf, salads, breads
BULGUR	Steamed, dried, and crushed fine, medium, or coarse wheat. Light brown. Tender. Mild flavor	As hot cereal. In pilaf, salads (tabbouleh)
WHEAT BRAN	Separated outer covering of wheat kernel. Brown flakes. Mildly nutty flavor	As hot and cold cereal. In baked goods (bran muffins)
WHEAT GERM	Separated embryo of wheat kernel. Small, brown, pellet-like. Strong nutty flavor. Available toasted and raw	As hot and cold cereal. In baked goods
FARINA	Polished, medium-grind wheat. White, flour-like. Very mild flavor	As hot cereal

Seeds and Nuts

Nuts are the fruits of various trees, with the exception of peanuts, which grow underground in the root system of a leguminous plant. Since they are part of the most common types of food allergens, it is important to store and use nuts properly when cooking for individuals with dietary restrictions.

NAME	DESCRIPTION	COMMON CULINARY USES
NUTS		
ALMOND	Teardrop-shaped. Pale tan, woody shell. Sweet flavor. Available whole in shell; also shelled, blanched, slivered, sliced, split, chopped, ground (meal and flour)	Eaten out of hand. Used to produce almond paste, almond butter, and almond oil. Used raw or toasted in baked goods, confections, granola, curry dishes
BRAZIL	Large, triangular nut. Dark brown, hard shell. White, rich nut	Eaten out of hand. Used raw or toasted in baked goods
CASHEW	Kidney-shaped. Tan nut. Buttery, slightly sweet flavor. Only sold hulled (its skin contains inflammatory oils similar to those in poison ivy)	Eaten out of hand. Used to produce cashew butter. Used raw or toasted in baked goods, confections
CHESTNUT	Fairly large, round to teardrop-shaped. Hard, glossy, dark brown shell; brown internal skin. Off-white nut. Sweet flavor. Available whole in shell; shelled canned in water or syrup, frozen, dried, or puréed	Used cooked in sweet and savory dishes. Roasted, boiled, puréed
HAZELNUT/FILBERT	Small, nearly round. Smooth, hard shell. Rich, sweet, delicate flavor. Available whole in shell; also shelled, whole, blanched, or chopped	Eaten out of hand. Used raw or toasted in sweet or savory dishes, baked goods, salads, cereals
MACADAMIA	Nearly round; extremely hard shell. Golden yellow nut. Rich, slightly sweet, buttery. Available shelled only	Eaten out of hand. Used raw or toasted in baked goods, confections
PEANUT	Tan, pod-like shell; papery brown skin. Off-white nut. Distinctive, sweet flavor. Available whole in shell; also shelled, skinned	Eaten out of hand. Used to produce peanut butter and peanut oil. Used raw or toasted in sweet or savory dishes, baked goods, confections, salads
PECAN	Smooth, hard, thin, oval shell. Two-lobed, brown-skinned nut; cream-colored interior. Rich, buttery flavor. Available whole in shell; also shelled halved or chopped	Eaten out of hand. Used raw or toasted in sweet or savory dishes, baked goods, pie, confections, salads
PINE/PIGNOLI	Small, elongated kernel, about ½ inch long. Light tan. Buttery, mild flavor	Used raw or toasted in sweet and savory dishes, baked goods, salads, pesto
PISTACHIO	Tan shell opens slightly when nut is mature; shells sometimes dyed red. Green nut. Subtle, sweet flavor. Available whole in shell, roasted, usually salted; also shelled, chopped	Eaten out of hand. Used raw or toasted in sweet and savory dishes
WALNUT	Thick or thin light brown shell. Brown-skinned nuts grow in gnarled segments; tender, oily. Mild flavor. Available whole in shell; also shelled, halved, chopped, or pickled	Eaten out of hand. Used to produce walnut oil. Used raw or toasted in sweet or savory dishes. In baked goods, confections, salads
SEEDS		
POPPY	Very tiny, round blue-black seeds. Crunchy texture. Rich, slightly musty flavor. Available whole or ground	As filling and topping for baked goods. In salad dressings. Popular in cuisines of central Europe and the Middle East
PUMPKIN	Small, flat soft oval. Cream-colored hulls. Greenish brown, oily interior. Delicate flavor. Available whole or hulled, usually salted	Used raw or toasted in sweet or savory dishes, baked goods. Popular in Mexican cuisine
FLAX	Tiny, oval seeds. Golden or dark brown. Mildly nutty. Must be cooked before eating	Used to produce linseed oil. In baked goods, hot and cold cereal
SESAME	Tiny, flat, oval seeds. Black, red, or tan. Crunchy. Sweet, nutty flavor	Used to produce oil and tahini (paste). Used raw or toasted in sweet and savory dishes, baked goods, confections, as garnish
SUNFLOWER	Small, somewhat flat, teardrop-shaped seeds. Woody black and white shell. Light tan seed. Mild flavor. Available whole in shell or shelled, usually salted	Used to make sunflower oil. Used raw or toasted in baked goods, salads

Herbs, Spices, and Spice Blends

Herbs and spices are some of the most important ingredients for any chef, but especially a chef who is cooking for customers with dietary restrictions or health concerns. Herbs and spices are the best way to boost flavor in a dish without upping the caloric content or adding excessive salt. Fresh herbs should be stored carefully, and do not have a long shelf life. Dried herbs will last longer, but should not be stored any longer than six months. Whole spices will keep longer than ground spices, which is important to remember, especially as you consider crafting your own spice blends.

VARIETY	DESCRIPTION	COMMON CULINARY USES
HERBS		
BASIL	Small to large delicate oval, pointed leaves. Green or purple. Pungent, licorice-like flavor. Varieties include opal, lemon, and Thai basil. Also available dried	Flavoring for sauces, dressings, infused oils, and vinegars. Pesto sauce. Popular in Mediterranean and Thai cuisine
BAY LEAF/LAUREL LEAF	Smooth, oval green leaves. Aromatic. Most commonly available dried	Flavoring for soups, stews, stocks, sauces, grain dishes. Remove before serving
CHERVIL	Small, curly green leaves; delicate texture. Anise flavor. Also available dried	Garnish. Component of fines herbes
CHIVES	Long, thin bright green cylindrical leaves. Mild onion flavor	Flavoring for salads and cream cheese. As garnish. Component of fines herbes
CILANTRO	Similar shape to flat-leaf parsley, but frillier; lighter green; delicate. Fresh, clean flavor. Leaves can be found in dried form; dried seeds are known as coriander	Flavoring for salsa and uncooked sauces
CURRY LEAVES	Small to medium pointed oval; dark green. Mild, aromatic, slightly bitter flavor	Stir-fries, curry
DILL	Long feather-like green leaves. Distinct flavor. Also available dried	Flavoring for salads, sauces, stews, braises
LEMONGRASS	Long blades with rough surface; pale yellow green; lemon flavor	Flavoring for soups, stocks, stir-fries, steamed preparations
MARJORAM	Small, oval pale green leaves. Mild flavor similar to oregano. Commonly available dried	Flavoring for lamb and vegetable dishes
MINT	Pointed, textured pale green to bright green leaves; color, size, strength depend on variety. Includes peppermint, spearmint, chocolate mint	Flavoring for sweet dishes, sauces, and beverages. Garnish for desserts. Mint jelly is an accompaniment to lamb
OREGANO	Small, oval pale green leaves. Pungent flavor. Mexican and Mediterranean varieties are available. Commonly available dried	Flavoring for tomato-based dishes. On pizza
PARSLEY	Curly or flat bright green leaves; pointed, scalloped edges. Clean tasting. Flat-leaf parsley is also known as Italian parsley. Commonly available dried	Flavoring for sauces, stocks, soups, dressings. As garnish. Component of fines herbes; in bouquet garni and sachet d'épices
ROSEMARY	Pine needle–shaped grayish, deep green leaves; woody stem. Strong pine aroma and flavor. Commonly available dried	Flavoring for grilled foods (especially lamb) and marinades. Popular in Mediterranean cuisine. Branch-like stems can be used as skewers
SAGE	Thin, oval, velvety grayish green leaves. Musty flavor. Varieties include pineapple sage. Commonly available dried, both crumbled and ground	Flavoring for stuffing, sausage, stews
SAVORY	Oblong dark green leaves. Soft, fuzzy texture. Commonly available dried	Flavoring for pâtés, stuffing. Component of poultry seasoning
TARRAGON	Thin, pointed dark green leaves. Delicate texture. Anise flavor. Commonly available dried	Flavoring for béarnaise sauce. Component of fines herbes
THYME	Very small deep green leaves; woody stem. Varieties include garden thyme, lemon thyme, wild thyme. Commonly available dried	Flavoring for soups, stocks, sauces, stews, braises, roasted items. Component of bouquet garni and sachet d'épices

Continued on page 48

VARIETY	DESCRIPTION	COMMON CULINARY USES
SPICES		
ALLSPICE	Dried, unripened, pea-size berry of the small evergreen pimiento tree. Dark reddish-brown. Tastes like cinnamon, nutmeg, and cloves. Available whole or ground	In braises, forcemeats, fish, desserts
ANNATTO	Dried, small achiote seeds. Deep red. Nearly flavorless; imparts yellowish orange color to foods. Available whole	Popular in Latin American and Caribbean cooking. In stews, soups, sauces
ANARDANA	Dried pomegranate seeds. Muted, deep red. Sour flavor. Available whole or ground	Popular in Indian cuisine as souring agent
ANISE SEED	Dried ripe fruit; member of the parsley family. Light brown. Similar flavor to fennel seeds; sweet, spicy, licorice taste and aroma	Popular in Southeast Asian and Mediterranean cooking. In savory dishes, desserts, baked goods, liqueur
CARAWAY	Dried fruit of the aromatic caraway plant, member of the parsley family. Small striped crescent-shaped seeds. Distinct flavor similar to, but sweeter than, anise seed	Popular in Austrian, German, and Hungarian cuisines. In rye bread, pork, cabbage, soups, stews, some cheeses, baked goods, liqueur (kümmel)
CARDAMOM	Dried, unripened fruit; member of the ginger family. Small round seed in green, black, or bleached white pod. Strong aroma; sweet, spicy flavor. Available as whole pod, seeds, or ground	In curries, baked goods, pickles
CAYENNE	Dried, ripened fruit pod; member of the nightshade family. Bright red. Hot; spicy. Available fresh or dried, whole or ground	In sauces, soups, meat, fish, poultry
CELERY	Dried seed of a wild celery (lovage). Strong vegetal flavor. Available whole or ground	In salads, coleslaw, salad dressings, soups, stews, tomatoes, baked goods
CINNAMON	Dried inner bark of a tropical tree. Reddish brown. Available in sticks or ground	In baked goods, curries, dessert sauces, beverages, stews
CLOVES	Dried, unopened flower of the tropical evergreen clove tree. Reddish brown, spike shaped. Sweet, pungent aroma and flavor. Available whole or ground	In stocks, sauces, braises, marinades, curries, pickles, desserts, baked goods
CORIANDER	Dried, ripe fruit of the cilantro plant. Small, round, tannish brown seeds. Unique citrus-like flavor. Available whole	Popular in Asian, Indian, and Middle Eastern cuisines. In curries, ground forcemeats, pickles, baked goods
CUMIN	Dried fruit of a plant in the parsley family. Small, crescent-shaped seeds; three colors: amber, black, white. Nutty flavor. Available whole or ground	Popular in Indian, Mexican, and Middle Eastern cuisines. In curries, chili
DILL	Dried fruit of a plant in the parsley family. Small tan seeds. Available whole	Popular in northern and Eastern European cuisines. In pickles, sauerkraut, cheeses, breads, salad dressings
EPAZOTE	Medium green leaves. Distinctive flavor and aroma. Available dried or fresh	Popular in Mexican and Caribbean cuisines. In chili, beans, soups, stews
FENNEL	Dried, ripe fruit of a plant in the parsley family. Small oval seeds, light greenish brown. Sweet licorice flavor and aroma. Available whole or ground	Popular seasoning blends of Mediterranean, Italian, Chinese, and Scandinavian cuisines. In sausages, fish, shellfish, tomatoes, baked goods, marinades, liqueurs
FENUGREEK	Seed pods from an annual herb. Small, flat, rectangular seeds; yellowish brown. Bitter taste and pungent, hay-like, maple-like aroma. Available whole or ground	Popular in Indian cuisine. In curries, meat, marinades, poultry, chutneys, spice blends, teas
FILÉ POWDER	Dried leaves of the sassafras tree. Woodsy flavor, similar to root beer. Available ground	Popular in Creole cuisine. In gumbo as a thickener
GINGER	Plant from tropical and subtropical regions. Tan, knobby, fibrous rhizome. Sweet, peppery flavor; spicy aroma. Available fresh, candied, pickled, or ground	Popular in Asian and Indian cuisines. In curries, braises, baked goods

VARIETY	DESCRIPTION	COMMON CULINARY USES
HORSERADISH	Large, white root. Member of the mustard family. Sharp, intense flavor; pungent aroma. Available dried or fresh	In sauces, condiments, egg salad, potatoes, beets
JUNIPER BERRIES	Small, round dried berry of the juniper bush. Dark blue. Slightly bitter; must crush to release flavor	In marinades, braises, meats/game, sauerkraut, gin, liqueurs, teas
MACE	Membrane covering of the nutmeg seed. Bright red when fresh; yellowish orange when dry. Strong nutmeg taste and aroma. Available whole or ground	In forcemeats, pork, fish, spinach and other vegetables, pickles, desserts, baked goods
MUSTARD	Seeds from plants within the cabbage family. Three types: traditional white/yellow (smaller; less pungent flavor), brown, and black (larger; pungent, hot flavor). Available whole or powdered	In pickles, meats, sauces, cheese, eggs, prepared mustard
NUTMEG	Large seed of a fruit that grows on the tropical evergreen *Myristica fragrans*. Small egg shape; dark brown. Sweet, spicy flavor and aroma. Available whole or ground	In sauces, soups, veal, chicken, aspics, vegetables, desserts, baked goods, eggnog
PAPRIKA	Dried, ground pods of sweet red peppers. Many varieties. Superior from Hungary; colors range from orange-red to deep red. Mild to intense flavor and aroma. Available ground; also Spanish (smoked, sweet, and hot)	In braises, stews, goulashes, sauces, garnishes
SAFFRON	Dried stigmas of flowers of *Crocus sativus*. Thread-like; yellow-orange. One ounce requires 14,000 stigmas; expensive due to labor-intensive harvesting process. Available as threads or powdered. The threads are superior in quality and assure authenticity	Essential in paella, bouillabaisse, risotto Milanese. In poultry, seafood, rice pilafs, sauces, soups, baked goods
STAR ANISE	Dried 8- to 12-pointed pod from Chinese evergreen, member of the magnolia family. Star shape; dark brown. Intense licorice flavor and aroma. Available whole or ground	Popular in Asian dishes. Used sparingly in pork, duck, baked goods, teas, liqueurs
TURMERIC	Dried root of a tropical plant related to ginger. Shape similar to ginger; bright yellow. Intense spicy flavor. Available powdered	Popular in Indian and Middle Eastern cuisines. In curries, sauces, mustard, pickles, rice
SPICE BLENDS		
CHILI POWDER	Blend of ground spices with dried chiles as the base. Can include cumin, cloves, coriander, garlic, and oregano. Degree of spiciness changes with variety of chile	Popular in Southwestern and Mexican cuisines. In chili, chili con carne, soups, stews, sauces
CHINESE FIVE-SPICE	Blend of ground spices; equal parts Szechwan peppercorns, star anise, cinnamon, cloves, and fennel. Pungent flavor and aroma	Popular in Chinese cuisine. In meats, fish, vegetables, marinades, sauces
CURRY POWDER	Blend of ground spices. Can include cardamom, chiles, cinnamon, cloves, coriander, cumin, fennel seed, fenugreek, mace, nutmeg, red and black pepper, poppy and sesame seeds, saffron, tamarind, turmeric. Degree of spiciness and color change with variety	Popular in Indian cuisine. In meats, seafood, vegetables, sauces, rice, soups
GARAM MASALA	Blend of dry-roasted spices; many variations. Can include black pepper, cardamom, cinnamon, cloves, coriander, cumin, dried chiles, fennel, mace, nutmeg. Warm flavor and aroma. Whole or ground	Popular in Indian cuisine. In fish, lamb, pork, poultry, cauliflower, potatoes
QUATRE ÉPICES	French term meaning "four spices"; refers to a variety of ground spice mixtures. Can include pepper, allspice, ginger, cinnamon, cloves, nutmeg	In stews, soups, vegetables, pâtés, terrines

Infused Oils and Vinegars

Infusing flavorful liquids, such as oils and vinegars, boosts their overall flavor—making them powerful additions to any dish without affecting the nutritional content in a negative way. To make your own infused oils and vinegars, use any of the following methods:

1. Heat the oil or vinegar very gently over low heat. The flavoring ingredients, such as citrus zest or garlic, may be added to the oil or vinegar as it warms. Let the oil or vinegar steep off the heat with the flavoring ingredients until cool, then pour into storage bottles or containers.

2. Heat the oil or vinegar without any added flavorings, then pour it over the flavoring ingredients and cool. Pour the infused oil or vinegar into storage containers.

3. Purée raw, blanched, or fully cooked vegetables, herbs, or fruits. Bring the purée to a simmer and reduce it, if necessary, to concentrate the flavors. Add the purée to the oil or vinegar and transfer to a storage container. Leave the oil or vinegar as is and use it like a purée, or strain it to remove the fibers and pulp.

4. Combine room-temperature oils or vinegars with ground spices and transfer them to a storage container. Let the mixture sit until the spices have settled in the bottom of the container and the vinegar or oil is clear.

5. Refrigerate the flavored oil or vinegar to rest for at least 3 hours and up to 36 hours. The time will vary according to the intensity of the flavoring ingredients and the intended use. Taste the oil or vinegar occasionally and, if necessary, strain or decant it into a clean bottle.

6. Strain the vinegar or oil for a clearer final product, or leave the aromatics in for a more intense flavor. Add fresh aromatics after the oil or vinegar has steeped for several days to give an even more intense flavor, if desired.

Blend the herbs with the oil to combine.

Strain the mixture in a cheesecloth-lined chinois.

The finished infusion will be brightly colored with no visible chunks or pieces.

CHEF'S NOTE

Fresh or raw ingredients added to an oil or vinegar increase the risk of foodborne illness. Keep scratch-made versions refrigerated. Use within a few days for the best flavor and color.

Fruits and Vegetables

Fruits are the ovaries that surround or contain the seeds of plants. Naturally sweet, fruits are an excellent source of vitamins, minerals, and other beneficial nutrients. Vegetables are the roots, tubers, stems, leaves, stalks, seeds, pods, and flower heads of plants that can be eaten. Chock-full of healthy nutrition, vegetables are a crucial part of any healthy diet.

Juicing fruits and vegetables is a great way to incorporate intense color and flavor into a variety of dishes.

VARIETY	DESCRIPTION	COMMON CULINARY USES
APPLES	Red, yellow, or green skinned with white flesh. Tart and sweet, but low in calories. High in fiber, making them a filling snack or addition to a meal	Sauces, jams/jellies, eaten out of hand, baked goods, general cooking
BERRIES	Berries are highly perishable and should be stored carefully. Available fresh or frozen, berries are excellent source of antioxidants	Eaten out of hand, sauces, baked goods, to flavor vinegars, relishes/ jams/jellies, syrups, liquors
CABBAGES	The cabbage family (or *Brassica*) includes an array of vegetables including heading cabbage as well as leafier items such as bok choy. These vegetables are incredibly healthy as well as versatile. They also have a long shelf life	Soups, stewing, braising, roasting, baking, sautéing, stir- frying
CITRUS FRUITS	Citrus fruits have segmented, juicy flesh. Available fresh or juiced. High source of vitamin C and other vitamins and minerals	Eaten out of hand, sauces, juices, baked goods, general cooking
CUCUMBERS	Delicate in flavor and incredibly versatile in cooking. Cucumbers are hydrating, good for reducing blood pressure, low in calories, and excellent source of nutrition for those with diabetes, joint pain, or obesity	Raw, salads, pickles, general cooking
EGGPLANTS	Quick cooking with mild flavor and meaty texture, eggplant is a common ingredient in many cuisines. Reduces risk of cancer and supports weight loss	Stewing, roasting, baking, sautéing, stir-frying
GRAPES	Member of the berry family, but contain many varieties of their own. High in antioxidants and known to reduce risk for stroke and heart attack	Eaten out of hand, sauces, juices, salads, pickled, general cooking

(continued on page 52)

VARIETY	DESCRIPTION	COMMON CULINARY USES
LEAFY GREENS	From head lettuce to cooking greens, this category is full of some of the healthiest superfoods. High in fiber, low in carbohydrates. The darker varieties contain the most health benefits	Raw, salads, sautéing, stir-frying, grilling, baking, general cooking
MELONS	Members of the gourd family with flavorful flesh. High source of vitamins A and C as well as potassium	Eaten out of hand, chilled soups, sauces, baked goods, raw
MUSHROOMS	A fungus that is available in thousands of varieties. Some are cultivated, but many are wild and uncultivable. Their meaty flavor and texture makes them an excellent addition to an array of dishes. They have anti-inflammatory benefits and are cancer preventers	Raw, sautéing, stir-frying, grilling, roasting
ONIONS	Members of the lily family, onions are available in two varieties: dried and green (fresh). Onions are excellent for cardiovascular help and are known to prevent cancer	Raw, sautéing, grilling, stir-frying, roasting, braising, stewing, soups, sauces, general cooking
PEARS	Red, green, or yellow skin with white flesh. High in fiber as well as many vitamins and minerals	Eaten out of hand, roasting, sauces, chilled soups, salads, baked goods, poaching
PEPPERS	There are two primary types of peppers: sweet peppers and chiles. Most peppers contain a large number of phytochemicals as well as a number of vitamins	Raw, sautéing, grilling, stir-frying, roasting, soups, sauces, braising, general cooking
POD AND SEED VEGETABLES	This group includes fresh legumes (peas, beans, and sprouts) as well as corn and okra. All varieties are best eaten young, when they are at their most sweet and tender. Many in this family contain heart-healthy folic acid as well as vitamins and protein	Raw, sautéing, stir-frying, soups
ROOT VEGETABLES	Roots serve as a food-storage area for plants; therefore, they are rich in sugars, starches, vitamins, and minerals. Roots move nutrients and moisture to the tops of the plant. Some are directly attached to stems and/or greens, which are edible. Root vegetables contain many vitamins and minerals and are high in potassium, phosphorus, and magnesium. They are also made up of primarily complex carbohydrates, which are ideal for individuals with dietary concerns	Roasting, raw, sautéing, stir-frying, braising, stewing, soups, general cooking
SHOOTS AND STALKS	This family consists of plants that produce shoots and stalks used as vegetables, including artichokes, asparagus, celery, fennel, and fiddleheads. These vegetables are high in fiber and antioxidants and many are excellent for cancer prevention and cholesterol reduction	Raw, sautéing, stir-frying, steaming, roasting
SQUASH	Available in both hard- and soft-skinned varieties, squash is full of vitamins, minerals, and fiber and supports a healthy immune system as well as heart health	Raw, roasting, stewing, soups, grilling, baking, sautéing
STONE FRUITS	Fruits that have a large central pit (stone) in the center, such as cherries, peaches, and plums. High in fiber and versatile in cooking	Eaten out of hand, roasting, grilling, chilled soups, salads, baked goods, jams/jellies
TOMATOES	Grown in hundreds of varieties, varying in color from green to yellow to red to purple. High in vitamins A, C, and K as well as potassium. Prevents cancer, regulates blood sugar, and promotes healthy cholesterol levels	Raw, roasting, soups, salads, sauces, stewing
TROPICAL FRUITS	Including a variety of otherwise uncategorized fruits, these flavorful fruits are versatile and have varying health benefits. Category includes pineapples, bananas, papayas, mangoes, kiwi, avocados, coconut, guavas, figs, etc.	General cooking and baking
TUBERS AND RHIZOMES	Includes the many varieties of potatoes as well as Jerusalem artichokes and jícama. They are vegetables that are connected to a root system by an underground stem. These vegetables are nutrient dense for the amount of calories they contain, but are high in carbohydrates. Good source of vitamin B_6, potassium, fiber, iron, and copper	Roasting, baking, sautéing, salads, soups

Ingredients for Special Diets

The following sections will detail ingredient information specific to each of the special diets. When we compare various food lists of the best foods to consume for healthful support of diabetes, heart disease, hypertension, and weight loss, the lists are nearly the same. Below you will find the top contenders for best or most healthy foods to eat for each of the special diets. The question marks indicate foods that may not be suitable for people with food allergies and specific cancers. An X implies an acceptable choice for specific diets.

	HEART DISEASE	HYPERTENSION	HIGH CHOLESTEROL	DIABETES	CELIAC SPRUE DISEASE	FOOD ALLERGY	CANCER	OBESITY
Whole Grains	X	X	X	X	No wheat, rye, oats, or barley	?	X	X
Nuts	X	X	X	X	X	?	X	Limited
Plant Oils	X	X	X	X	X	?	X	Limited
Dairy	Limited, low-fat, and fat-free only	Limited, no aged cheeses	Limited, low-fat, and fat-free only	Low glycemic only	X	?	?	Limited, low fat
Fresh Vegetables	X	X	X	Low glycemic only	X	Most	X	X
Fresh Fruits	X	X	X	Low glycemic only	X	Most	X	Low glycemic only
Animal Fats	Restricted quantities, none	Restricted quantities, none	Restricted quantities, none	Restricted quantities, none	X	Most	?	
Fish	X	X	X	Low-cholesterol varieties and wild-caught fatty fishes	X	Most	X	X
Shellfish	Low-cholesterol varieties	X	Low-cholesterol varieties	X	X	?	X	Low-cholesterol varieties
Legumes	X	X	X	Low glycemic only	X	X	X	X
Beef/Veal	Lean only	Lean only	Lean only	Lean only	X	X	?	Lean only
Chicken/Poultry	Lean only	Lean only	Lean only	Lean only	X	?	?	Lean only
Lamb	Lean only	Lean only	Lean only	Lean only	X	X	?	Lean only
Game Meat/Offal	Lean only	X	X	Lean only	X	X	X	Lean only
Added Sodium					X	X	?	
Added Sweeteners				Low glycemic only	X	X	?	Low glycemic only
Eggs	Egg whites only	Egg whites only	Egg whites only	Egg whites only		?	?	Limited
Soy	Whole bean preferred, moderate to limited use	Whole bean preferred, moderate to limited use	Whole bean preferred, moderate to limited use	Whole bean preferred, moderate to limited use		?	?	Limited

Superfoods

The following foods are healthy sources of energy that will keep your body full and running. Apples are packed with vitamins and minerals, as well as flavonoids and polyphenols (two powerful antioxidants). Bananas are a great source of potassium, which helps boost energy levels by maintaining normal blood pressure and heart rhythms. Red peppers provide an abundance of vitamins A and C, which are both powerful antioxidants, and lycopene, which has been associated with lowering cancer risks. Food that is high in sugar can deplete our B vitamin reserves, but one to two ounces of dark chocolate as an occasional treat or dessert boosts energy. Use nondairy, organic dark chocolate, which often contains the highest percentage of antioxidants compared to other types of chocolate. Pumpkin seeds are a lighter alternative to nuts and satisfy crunchy cravings, delivering magnesium, iron, calcium, vitamin K, and protein. Celery is easy to digest and chock-full of fiber and vitamins B and C; it also helps to balance potassium and sodium levels while reducing inflammation in the body.

Leafy greens are abundant in chlorophyll and a wide range of vitamins and minerals, making them one of the easiest ways to get a quick energy burst.

Berries in general, and blueberries in particular, are known to promote brain function and boost energy levels, and are an excellent pre-test snack for children or a delicious treat when you need to focus on a big project. Avocados are packed full of fiber and healthy fats; they can also help lower cholesterol. Quinoa is a complete protein, which means it contains all of the essential amino acids our bodies need. It is also one of the most nutritious and filling grains. Mushrooms are loaded with the potent disease-fighting antioxidant called ergothioneine and are a good source of potassium, which may cut the risk of high blood pressure and stroke. Sweet potato is packed with beta-carotene, vitamins A, C, E, and fiber. Grapes (and red wine) contain the chemical resveratrol, which is a very potent antioxidant that can prevent cell damage before it begins. Tomatoes contain lycopene, which has been shown to prevent breast, lung, and prostate cancer.

Ten Foods to Eliminate from Your Diet

1. All charred food, which create *heterocyclic aromatic amines*, known carcinogens.

2. Well-done red meat. Medium or rare is better, little or no red meat is best.

3. Sugar, both white and brown, which is simply white sugar with molasses added. If you crave sweets, eat fruit, or use a little stevia to sweeten your foods.

4. Heavily salted, smoked, and pickled foods, which lead to higher rates of stomach cancer.

5. Sodas/soft drinks, which pose health risks, both for what they contain—sugar and various additives—and for what they replace in the diet—beverages and foods that provide vitamins, minerals, and other nutrients.

6. French fries, chips, and snack foods that contain trans fats. These are among the worst offenders.

7. Food and drink additives such as aspartame. All artificial sweeteners are on the no list.

8. Excess alcohol.

9. Baked goods, for the acrylamide.

10. Farmed fish, which contains higher levels of toxins such as PCBs. Wild-caught fish is always labeled, so if it doesn't say wild caught it should be assumed that it is farmed.

Cancer-Fighting Foods

Although customers might not often ask for a dish that is suitable for someone with cancer, the following foods have the additional dietary advantage of being able to fight off cancer. These foods appear on several of the other lists to use when cooking for special diets.

1. Cruciferous vegetables such as broccoli, cauliflower, cabbage, Brussels sprouts, bok choy, and kale contain many anticancer substances such as isothiocyanates.

2. Globe artichokes have very high levels of salvestrols.

3. Dark greens, such as spinach and kale, and other dark-colored veggies, such as beets and red cabbage, contain fiber, folate, and a wide range of cancer-fighting carotenoids.

4. Grapes and red wine are excellent sources of cancer-fighting resveratrol.

5. Legumes, such as beans, peas, and lentils, contain saponins and protease inhibitors.

6. Berries, and especially blueberries, include ellagic acid and anthocyanosides.

7. Flaxseed is best if ground and consumed when fresh; it has the essential fatty acid alpha-linolenic acid, lignans, and other "good fats."

8. Garlic, onions, green onions, leeks, and chives contain many anticancer substances including allicin.

9. Green tea is a potent antioxidant and known for its anti-cancer catechins.

10. Tomatoes are well-known for containing the flavonoid lycopene.

Heart-Healthy Foods

There are several identifiable nutrients in heart-healthy foods:

- Phytoestrogens are substances in plants (like flaxseed) that have a weak estrogen-like action in the body. Studies suggest that flaxseed lowers the risk of blood clots, stroke, and cardiac arrhythmias. It may also help lower total and LDL "bad" cholesterol and triglycerides, and even blood pressure.

- Phytosterols are plant sterols that chemically resemble cholesterol—and seem to reduce blood cholesterol. All nuts and seeds, including wheat germ, have phytosterols.

- Carotenoids are heart-protective antioxidants in many colorful fruits and veggies. Alpha-carotene, beta-carotene, lutein, and lycopene are carotenoids.

- Polyphenols are another set of antioxidants that protect blood vessels, lower blood pressure, and reduce LDL "bad" choles-

terol. Flavonoid polyphenols include catechins, flavonones, flavonols, isoflavones, resveratrol, and anthocyanins. Nonflavonoid polyphenols include ellagic acid (found in all types of berries).

- Omega-3 fatty acids (found in fatty fish like salmon) and alpha-linolenic fatty acids (found in plant foods like walnuts) help boost the immune system, reduce blood clots, and protect against heart attacks. They also increase HDL levels, lower triglyceride levels, protect arteries from plaque buildup, are anti-inflammatories, and lower blood pressure.

- B-complex vitamins, such as vitamin B_{12} (folate) and vitamin B_6, protect against blood clots and atherosclerosis, or hardening of the arteries. Niacin (vitamin B_3) helps increase HDL "good" cholesterol.

- Vitamins C and E are antioxidants that protect cells from free radical damage. Magnesium, potassium, and calcium help lower blood pressure. Fiber-rich foods help lower cholesterol levels.

Heart-Healthy Foods and Their Nutrients

FOOD	SUPPLIES
VEGETABLES	
ASPARAGUS	B_6, folate, fiber
BELL PEPPERS	B_1, B_2, B_6, folate, C, fiber
BOK CHOY	B_6, C, K, calcium, fiber
BROCCOLI	B_6, C, E, K, folate, fiber
CARROTS	A, C, fiber, carotenoids
ALLIUM FAMILY: GARLIC, ONIONS, LEEKS	Phytochemicals, fiber
LEAFY GREENS	A, B_2, B_6, C, E, folate, calcium, copper, magnesium, potassium, zinc, fiber
POTATOES	B_6, C, potassium, magnesium, fiber
SWEET POTATOES	A, C, E, copper, fiber
TOMATOES	A, C, E, potassium, fiber
ACORN OR BUTTERNUT SQUASH	A, B_1, B_6, C, folate, calcium, copper, magnesium, potassium, fiber
PROTEINS	
TUNA: CANNED IN WATER OR FRESH	B_{12}, D, protein, niacin, selenium, omega-3 fatty acids
SALMON: FRESH OR CANNED PINK	B_6, B_{12}, D, phosphorus, potassium, selenium
NATURAL PEANUT BUTTER	E, protein, fiber, niacin, magnesium, phosphorus
FRUITS	
APPLES	C, fiber, flavonoids
APRICOTS	A, C, E, K, fiber
BANANAS	B_6, C, magnesium, potassium, fiber
BERRIES	B_6, C, magnesium, potassium, fiber
CANTALOUPE	A, B_6, C, folate, potassium, fiber
CITRUS	A, B_6, C, folate, potassium, fiber
KIWI	C, E, magnesium, potassium, fiber

Continued on page 56

FOOD	SUPPLIES
PAPAYA	A, C, E, folate, calcium, magnesium, potassium
PEACHES	Potassium
SOY FOODS	
SOY MILK AND SOY CHEESE	B_1, B_{12}, D, protein, niacin, folate, calcium, copper, iron, magnesium, manganese, potassium, zinc
SOY NUTS	Folate, magnesium, manganese, protein, phytoestrogens
TOFU AND TEMPEH	B_1, protein, niacin, folate, calcium, copper, iron, magnesium, manganese, potassium, zinc
GRAINS	
BARLEY	A, B_2, protein, fiber, niacin, copper, iron, magnesium, manganese, selenium, zinc
BROWN RICE	B_1, B_6, fiber, niacin, magnesium, manganese, selenium, zinc
BULGUR	Fiber, niacin, manganese, selenium, magnesium
FLAXSEED	Fiber, iron, omega-3 fatty acids
OATMEAL	Soluble fiber, magnesium, manganese, potassium, zinc
WHEAT GERM	B_1, E, niacin, folate, magnesium, manganese, potassium, zinc
LEGUMES	
BLACK BEANS	B_1, protein, folate, copper, iron, magnesium, manganese, potassium, zinc
BLACK-EYED PEAS	B_1, B_6, niacin, folate, copper, iron, magnesium, manganese, potassium, zinc
KIDNEY BEANS	B_1, niacin, folate, iron, magnesium, manganese, potassium, zinc, omega-3 fatty acids
LENTILS	B_1, B_6, protein, fiber, niacin, folate, iron, magnesium, manganese, potassium, zinc

Power Foods for a Diabetes-Friendly Diet

The following foods are highly recommended to incorporate into a dish meant for a person with diabetes.

- Asparagus is high in fiber, B vitamin, folate, vitamin C, and the antioxidant glutathione, which may help boost the immune system and promote lung health by protecting against viruses. The cardiovascular benefits of folate and other B vitamins have been studied in relation to homocysteine, an amino acid in the blood that has been linked to a higher risk of coronary heart disease. The American Heart Association recommends including foods containing folate and other B vitamins in the diet to help lower homocysteine levels.

- Blueberries are high in fiber, vitamins, and flavonoids that provide antioxidant protection, such as boosting the immune system and fighting inflammation. Flavonoids may also help decrease the LDL oxidation process that can lead to arterial plaque.

- Red grapefruit decreases LDL and triglycerides and is high in vitamin C.

- Dried beans are high in fiber, protein, vitamins, and minerals.

- Broccoli is high in fiber, nonstarchy, very high in vitamin C, and high in beta-carotene for the production of vitamin A.

- Carrots contain vitamin A and flavonoids, and may reduce insulin resistance.

- Fish, particularly omega-3 rich fatty fish such as wild-caught salmon, trout, tuna, sardines, catfish, mackerel, and herring, lower triglycerides, and reduce blood pressure, inflammation, and the risk of blood clots.

- Flaxseed, which is high in omega-3 fatty acids, lowers triglycerides, inflammation, and the risk of heart disease. It is also high in soluble and insoluble fiber and is a good source of lignans, which provide the antioxidant phytoestrogen.

- Cranberries are high in vitamin C and numerous phytonutrients including anthocyanins, which guard against cancer and cardiovascular disease.

- Apples contain both soluble and insoluble fiber; soluble fiber helps slow digestion, which in turn helps regulate cholesterol and stabilizes blood glucose levels.

- Melons of all types are beneficial, but especially watermelon, which is rich in vitamins C, B$_6$, and the antioxidant lycopene, which may help guard against cancer. Honeydew and cantaloupe are both rich in potassium, which can help maintain or lower blood pressure.

- Unsalted nuts are rich in protein, vitamin E, fiber, and flavonoids as well as plant sterols, which are known to lower cholesterol. Walnuts, almonds, macadamia nuts, pecans, and hazelnuts are just a few examples of nuts that can help lower LDL levels, which make them heart healthy as well.

- The soluble fiber in oats can help lower cholesterol, improve blood pressure, and stabilize blood glucose by slowing digestion. Oats are a good source of antioxidants and also provide vitamin E, B vitamins, magnesium, and potassium, which may help lower blood pressure.

- Red onions are very high in antioxidant properties followed by yellow onions, then white, and are an excellent source of fiber, potassium, and folate. Their high flavonoid content also puts them on the map for cancer and cardiovascular research and other chronic diseases such as asthma. Quercetin, one of the flavonoids, may also help lower the risk of these chronic diseases.

- Raspberries are high in fiber due to their seeds, and also vitamin C. Vitamin C is beneficial for bone and skin health as well as cancer and heart disease prevention.

- Spinach is rich in many vitamins, but especially vitamins B$_2$ and B$_6$, folate, copper, magnesium, potassium, zinc, and calcium, as well as being a good source of fiber. Spinach is rich in beta-carotene, which helps protect the body's cells from free radicals that contribute to chronic illness and aging.

- Soy, in whole bean form, such as baby green soybeans called edamame, are highest in protein. Other products include soy milk or cheese, tofu, and soy nuts. Soy is a good source of niacin, folate, zinc, potassium, iron, and alpha-linolenic acid (ALA), a fatty acid that can be converted into omega-3 fatty acids, known to help lower cholesterol.

- Tomatoes are an excellent source of vitamin C, potassium, and lycopene, which is a powerful antioxidant most readily absorbed when cooked or processed such as in canned tomato juice or cooked tomatoes. Lycopene-rich foods help protect against certain cancers such as prostate as well as improve cardiovascular and anti-inflammatory protection.

Low-Carbohydrate Vegetables

Clearly, if portions of the starchy side dishes are to remain modest you need to fill your plate with low-carbohydrate vegetables that you enjoy to keep the meal filling. Following is a list of fifteen vegetables that are low in carbohydrates and are highly suited for a diabetes-friendly diet. They are on the must-try and keep-on-hand list not only because they are low in carbohydrates, but because of their flexibility in recipes (mushrooms, celery, cucumbers), ability to hold well (cabbage, cauliflower, radishes, fennel), or they are packed with phytonutrients and antioxidants (arugula, broccoli rabe, bell peppers, kale)—and they taste great.

VEGETABLE	PORTION SIZE	CARBOHYDRATE AMOUNT
ARUGULA	½ cup	½ g
BELL PEPPER, GREEN	½ cup sliced	2 g
BELL PEPPER, RED	½ cup sliced	3 g
BELL PEPPER, YELLOW	½ cup sliced	3 g
BROCCOLI RABE	½ cup cooked	3 g
CUCUMBER	½ cup sliced	1.5 g
CAULIFLOWER	½ cup cooked	2.5 g
CABBAGE, GREEN OR SAVOY	½ cup cooked	4 g
	½ cup raw shredded	2 g
CELERY	2 medium stalks	2.5 g
FENNEL BULB	½ cup raw sliced	3 g
KALE	½ cup cooked	4 g
MUSHROOMS	½ cup cooked	2 g
RADISHES	½ cup	2 g
SPINACH	½ cup cooked	3.5 g
SUGAR SNAP PEAS	½ cup raw	2 g

CHART OF COMMON SUBSTITUTIONS

This chart will outline the substitutions that can be made in order to tailor a recipe for a specific diet.

FOOD ITEM	HEART-HEALTHY SUBSTITUTION	DIABETIC SUBSTITUTION	NUT ALLERGY SUBSTITUTION	GLUTEN-FREE SUBSTITUTION	LOW-FAT SUBSTITUTIONS	LACTOSE INTOLERANCE SUBSTITUTIONS
HIGH-FAT NUTS SUCH AS PEANUTS, MACADAMIA, HAZELNUTS, WALNUTS	Almonds, pistachios	Almonds, pistachios	Soy nuts if processed in a nut free environment or omit altogether		Almonds, pistachios, or omit altogether	
SOY SAUCE	Low-sodium soy sauce, low-sodium tamari	Low-sodium soy sauce, low-sodium tamari		Gluten-free tamari sauce		
WHEAT FLOUR FOR BAKING OR DUSTING FOODS TO BE COOKED	Whole wheat flour, other whole-grain flours such as brown rice flour, amaranth, teff, quinoa, corn flour, oat flour, rye flour, spelt flour			Brown rice flour, amaranth flour, quinoa flour, almond flour, chickpea flour, coconut flour, corn flour, teff flour. Rye, oats, barley, and all wheat relatives must be avoided.		
WHEAT FLOUR USED AS A THICKENER SUCH AS ROUX	Make a slurry using arrowroot, cornstarch, potato starch, rice starch, tapioca starch	Make a slurry using arrowroot, cornstarch, potato starch, rice starch, tapioca starch		Arrowroot, cornstarch, potato starch, rice starch, tapioca starch	Arrowroot, cornstarch, potato starch, rice starch, tapioca starch	Make roux with canola oil, or use slurry of arrowroot, cornstarch, potato starch, rice starch, tapioca starch
HEAVY CREAM	Full-fat coconut milk	Reduce quantity, omit, or replace with skim milk or nonfat milk substitutes such as fat-free rice milk			Omit or replace with skim milk or nonfat milk substitutes such as fat-free rice milk	Full-fat coconut milk, rice milk, soy milk, almond milk
MILK, WHOLE OR PARTIALLY FATTED	Almond milk, soy milk, coconut milk	Reduce quantity, omit, or replace with skim milk or nonfat milk substitutes such as fat-free rice milk			Omit or replace with skim milk or nonfat milk substitutes such as fat-free rice milk	Almond milk, soy milk, coconut milk, rice milk
BUTTER	Extra-virgin olive oil, grapeseed oil, canola oil, nut or seed oils, avocado oil. For baking, substitute fruit purée such as applesauce or prune purée for butter or oil.	Extra-virgin olive oil, grapeseed oil, canola oil, nut or seed oils, avocado oil. For baking, substitute fruit purée such as applesauce or prune purée for butter or oil.	Avoid all nut or seed oils. Use high-quality, extra-virgin olive oil, avocado oil, grapeseed oil, soy oil.		Reduce quantity, substitute with extra-virgin olive oil, grapeseed oil, canola oil, coconut oil, avocado oil, nut or seed oils, or omit altogether	Extra-virgin olive oil, grapeseed oil, canola oil, coconut oil, avocado oil, nut or seed oils
SUGARS: BROWN SUGAR, HONEY, MAPLE SYRUP	Omit or replace with small quantity of agave syrup	Omit or replace with small quantity of agave syrup or a sugar substitute such as stevia				

FOOD ITEM	HEART-HEALTHY SUBSTITUTION	DIABETIC SUBSTITUTION	NUT ALLERGY SUBSTITUTION	GLUTEN-FREE SUBSTITUTION	LOW-FAT SUBSTITUTIONS	LACTOSE INTOLERANCE SUBSTITUTIONS
FATTY MEATS	Small quantities of lean meats such as white meat chicken, turkey, venison, bison, lean cuts of meat, or fatty fishes, or omit altogether and choose a vegetarian replacement such as tempeh or seitan	Small quantities of lean meats such as white meat chicken, turkey, venison, bison, lean cuts of meat, or fatty fishes, or omit altogether and choose a vegetarian replacement such as tempeh or seitan			Small quantities of lean meats such as white meat chicken, turkey, venison, bison, lean cuts of meat, or fatty fishes or omit altogether and choose a vegetarian replacement such as tempeh or seitan	
WHITE RICE: ALL VARIETIES INCLUDING CARNAROLI OR ARBORIO	Brown rice or any unpolished whole-grain rice or grain variety	Brown rice or any unpolished whole-grain rice or grain variety	Brown rice or any unpolished whole-grain rice or grain variety	Brown rice or any unpolished whole-grain rice or grain variety	Brown rice	Brown rice or any unpolished whole-grain rice or grain variety
POTATOES: ALL VARIETIES	Small quantities only or replace with sweet potatoes or yams	Small quantities only or replace with sweet potatoes or yams	Small quantities only or replace with sweet potatoes or yams	Small quantities only or replace with sweet potatoes or yams	Small quantities only or replace with sweet potatoes or yams	Small quantities only or replace with sweet potatoes or yams
BUTTER-BASED OR FATTY SAUCES	Vegetable or fruit-based purée sauces such as a roasted red pepper coulis	Vegetable purée sauces using low-glycemic vegetables such as a roasted red pepper coulis	Vegetable or fruit-based purée sauces such as a roasted red pepper coulis	Vegetable or fruit-based purée sauces such as a roasted red pepper coulis	Vegetable or fruit-based purée sauces such as a roasted red pepper coulis	Vegetable or fruit-based purée sauces such as a roasted red pepper coulis
GRAVY- OR STOCK-BASED ROUX-THICKENED SAUCES	Use fully defatted stocks or broths; fortify with vegetable and lean meat scraps, herbs and spices, reduce to a syrupy consistency, or reduce by 50% and thicken with a pure starch slurry	Use fully defatted stocks or broths; fortify with vegetable and lean meat scraps, herbs and spices, reduce to a syrupy consistency, or reduce by 50% and thicken with a pure starch slurry	Use fully defatted stocks or broths; fortify with vegetable and lean meat scraps, herbs and spices, reduce to a syrupy consistency, or reduce by 50% and thicken with a pure starch slurry	Use fully defatted stocks or broths; fortify with vegetable and lean meat scraps, herbs and spices, reduce to a syrupy consistency, or reduce by 50% and thicken with a pure starch slurry	Use fully defatted stocks or broths; fortify with vegetable and lean meat scraps, herbs and spices, reduce to a syrupy consistency, or reduce by 50% and thicken with a pure starch slurry	Use fully defatted stocks or broths, fortify with vegetable and lean meat scraps, herbs and spices, reduce to a syrupy consistency or reduce by 50% and thicken with a pure starch slurry
SALT	Reduce or omit all added salt. Choose low-sodium vegetables, seafoods, and meats. Use seaweed for added salt and savory flavors. Use reductions of vinegars, wines, stocks, and broths to fortify flavors. Use infusions of herbs and spices	Reduce or omit all added salt. Choose low-sodium vegetables and meats. Use seaweed for added salt and savory flavors. Use reductions of vinegars, wines, stocks, and broths to fortify flavors. Use infusions of herbs and spices	Use reductions of vinegars, wines, stocks, and broths to fortify flavors. Use infusions of herbs and spices. Use seaweed for added salt and savory flavors	Use reductions of vinegars, wines, stocks, and broths to fortify flavors. Use infusions of herbs and spices. Use seaweed for added salt and savory flavors	Use reductions of vinegars, wines, stocks, and broths to fortify flavors. Use infusions of herbs and spices. Use seaweed for added salt and savory flavors	Use reductions of vinegars, wines, stocks, and broths to fortify flavors. Use infusions of herbs and spices. Use seaweed for added salt and savory flavors

CHEF'S NOTES

Heavy cream substitutes can be foamed or frothed, but will not whip in the same manner as heavy cream.

Whenever possible, replace a fatty animal protein with a lean one. Remember to include plenty of fishes rich in omega-3 oils from cold-water fish such as salmon, sardines, herring, mackerel, black cod, and bluefish.

Whenever possible, use dark leafy greens and whole grains.

Avoid the use of white sugar, processed foods, artificial sweeteners, and artificial flavorings.

CHAPTER FOUR

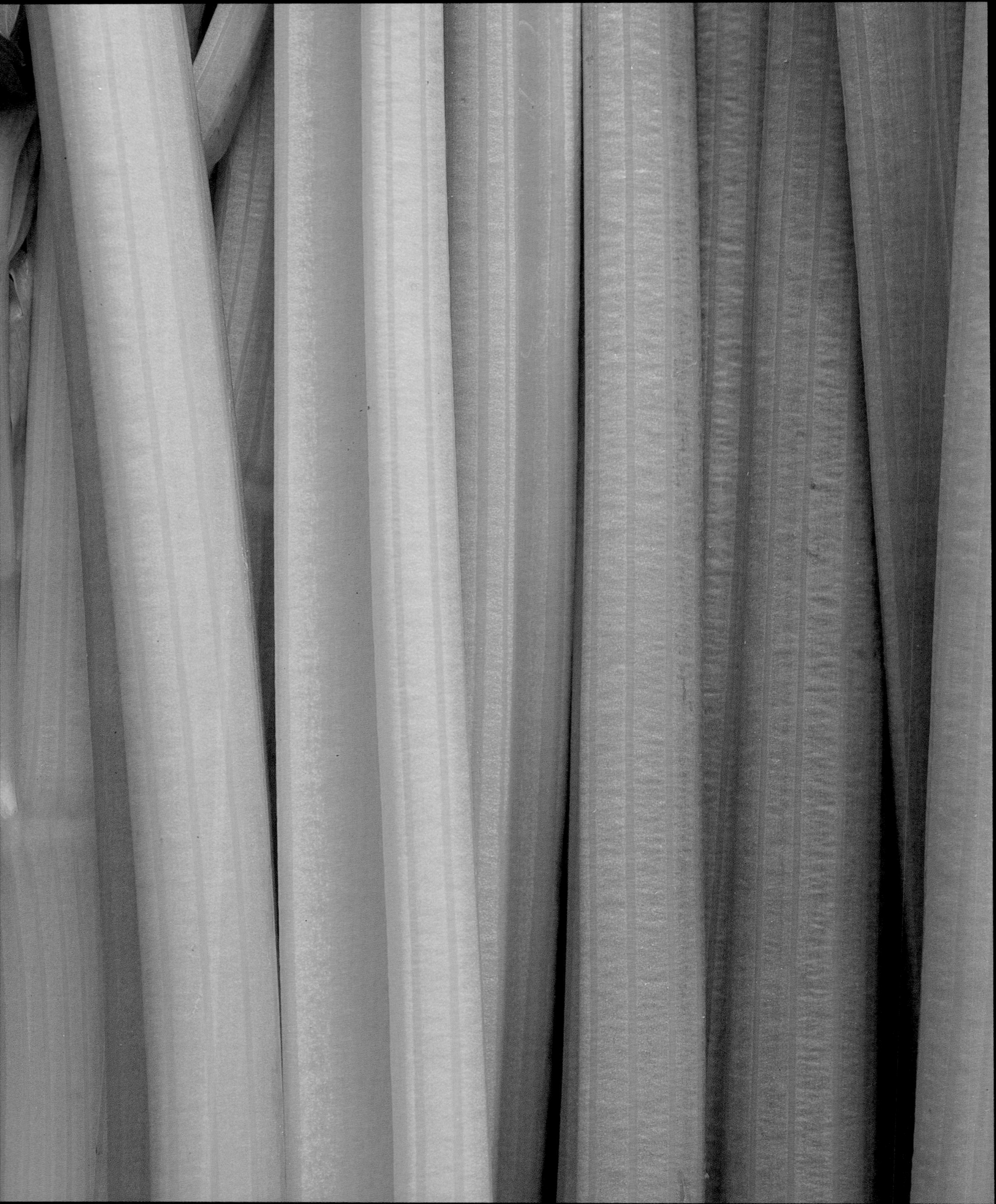

The intent of appetizers is to whet the appetite. These inspired savory bites should be exciting to the palate, but not necessarily satiating to the appetite. Adept applications of intensely flavored foods, colorful and unusual vegetables, or foods that are exotic in reputation not only provide interest, but also imply value.

This menu category is a great place to play with flavors, colors, and textures. Using carefully measured amounts of protein supported by whole grains or greens and flavorful garnishes such as a shaving of rich cheese, a drizzle of aromatic oil like truffle or basil oil, or the use of a perfectly balanced compote or jam can be a great way to begin the dining experience. And for the customer who wishes to dine on a variety of "small plates" rather than a main course, appetizers can offer a diverse and intensely satisfying meal. Be mindful of the fact that people initially eat with their eyes and nose, so creating and serving appetizers that are visually striking as well as scintillating to the olfactory sense can be a truly irresistible combination.

Not every appetizer should be meat-, fish-, or poultry-centric. In fact, a vegetable or fruit preparation teamed up with a whole grain or nuts is not only a healthy option, but can also be quite cost-effective. Try using a small amount of intensely flavored protein or cheese as the garnish to a vegetable or grain appetizer. Remember, bold or concentrated flavors used in small amounts will command attention.

Creaminess is one of the texture sensations we associate with decadent, rich, fatty foods and flavors. Quite often, proteins may be accompanied by a creamy, rich, or fatty sauce. As an alternative, try making a perfectly smooth purée of cauliflower finished with a small amount of extra-virgin olive oil, avocado purée, nut oil, or fat-free Greek-style yogurt, or use a brilliantly colored and intensely flavored infused oil instead of the traditional butter or fat-based emulsion sauces—the results are delectable.

Carpaccio of Beef with Fresh Artichokes and Tomato Salad C H

....

Makes 10 portions

12 oz/340 g trimmed beef tenderloin

1 lb 12 oz/794 g cooked artichoke hearts, quartered

10 oz/284 g peeled, seeded, small-dice plum tomatoes

1¾ oz/50 g minced shallots

½ oz/14 g chopped basil

5 fl oz/150 mL Reduced Oil Dressing (page 333)

7 oz/199 g mixed salad greens

Cracked black peppercorns, as needed

5 fl oz/150 mL Anchovy-Caper Dressing (page 317)

1. Chill the beef thoroughly so that it is firm enough to slice easily. Slice it very thinly on a meat slicer or with a sharp slicing knife. Lay the slices out on parchment paper as they come off the blade. Do not stack them on top of one another. Cover and refrigerate.

2. In a large bowl, toss the artichokes, tomatoes, shallots, and basil to combine. Add the balsamic vinaigrette and toss to coat evenly. Remove the solid ingredients with a slotted spoon and allow the excess vinaigrette to drain back into the bowl. Reserve the vinaigrette to dress the greens.

3. To serve, toss ¾ oz/21 g of the salad greens with 1 tbsp/15 mL of the reserved balsamic vinaigrette to coat the leaves lightly. Arrange the dressed greens on a chilled plate and top with 3½ oz/100 g of the artichoke-tomato mixture. Place 1¼ oz/35 g of the sliced beef on the plate and season with a generous amount of cracked black pepper. Spoon 1 tbsp/15 mL of the anchovy-caper dressing on the plate near the beef and serve immediately.

Nutritional Information per Serving (¾ oz/20 g salad, 2 tbsp/30 mL dressing, 3½ oz/100 g vegetables, and 1¼ oz/34 g beef):

231 calories, 13 g fat, 4 g saturated fat, 27 mg cholesterol, 261 mg sodium, 15 g total carbohydrates, 5 g fiber, 4 g sugar, 12 g protein

Grilled Kibbe Kebobs D H

Makes 10 portions

4 oz/113 g fine bulgur

1 lb/454 g 90% lean ground turkey

6½ oz/184 g diced onions

2 oz/57 g seeded and minced jalapeño

1 tbsp/15 mL yogurt

2 tbsp/30 mL olive oil

1 tbsp/3 g chopped flat-leaf parsley

2 tbsp/6 g chopped cilantro

1 tbsp/3 g chopped mint

2 tsp/4 g ground cumin

1 tsp/2 g ground allspice

¼ tsp/0.5 g ground cinnamon

½ tsp/1 g freshly ground black pepper

¼ tsp/0.5 g cayenne

GLAZE

1 tbsp/15 mL molasses

1 tbsp/15 mL reduced-sodium soy sauce

1 tbsp/15 mL olive oil

1. Preheat a gas grill to medium-high heat.

2. Thoroughly rinse the bulgur and soak it in warm water for 10 minutes. Drain in a strainer for 20 minutes. Squeeze any excess moisture from the bulgur.

3. Combine the bulgur with the turkey, onions, jalapeño, yogurt, oil, parsley, cilantro, mint, cumin, allspice, cinnamon, black pepper, and cayenne in a food processor. Pulse to fully incorporate.

4. Mold 3-oz/85-g portions of the meat mixture onto 8-in/ 20-cm bamboo skewers that have been soaked in water for 1 hour.

5. Whisk together the ingredients for the glaze. Brush the meat mixture with the glaze just before grilling.

6. To serve, grill 1 skewer for about 3 minutes on each side. Serve on a heated plate.

Nutritional Information per Serving (3 oz/85 g):

168 calories, 8 g fat, 6 g saturated fat, 103 mg cholesterol, 103 mg sodium, 36 g total carbohydrates, 3 g fiber, 2 g sugar, 10 g protein

---

Rare Lamb Loin with Z'hug and Grilled Pappadums

Rare Lamb Loin with Z'hug and Grilled Pappadums C D H

Makes 10 portions

1¾ oz/50 g minced garlic

1 fl oz/30 mL lemon juice

½ oz/14 g whole-grain mustard

2 oz/57 g olive oil

1 tsp/3 g sea salt

¼ tsp/.5 g finely ground black pepper

2 lb 8 oz/1.13 kg lamb loin, boneless, trimmed lean

10 oz/284 g packaged pappadum wafers with cumin seeds

15 oz/425 g Z'hug (page 320)

1. Combine the garlic, lemon juice, mustard, oil, sea salt, and pepper to make a marinade.

2. Add the trimmed lamb loin and roll the loin to fully coat with the marinade. Allow the lamb to marinate for at least 1 hour.

3. Preheat a gas grill to high heat.

4. Grill the lamb loin to an internal temperature of 125°F/52°C. Transfer to a pan with a rack and rest in a warm area for 5 minutes.

5. Meanwhile, quickly grill 2 pappadum wafers per portion, just until lightly charred and the surfaces develop bubbles.

6. To serve, lay 1 pappadum wafer on a plate. Slice 4 oz/113 g of the rare lamb loin and place it on the pappadum. Garnish the plate with 1½ oz/43 g of the z'hug and an additional pappadum wafer.

CHEF'S NOTE

This meal beautifully complements the Indian-Style Lentil and Cauliflower Biryani on page 231.

Nutritional Information per Serving (4 oz/113 g lamb, 2 pappadums, 1½ oz/43 g z'hug):

209 calories, 13 g fat, 4 g saturated fat, 74 mg cholesterol, 295 mg sodium, 2 g total carbohydrates, 0 g fiber, 1 g sugar, 20 g protein

---

Crab Rolls C D H

Makes 10 portions

1 fl oz/30 mL canola oil

¾ oz/21 g minced garlic

¾ oz/21 g minced lemongrass

3½ oz/99 g sliced green onions

1 lb/454 g 90% lean ground turkey

8½ oz/241 g red bell peppers, seeded and cut into strips ⅛ in/3 mm thick

3 oz/85 g green cabbage

4 oz/113 g bean sprouts

4 fl oz/120 mL Thai chili paste (*nam prik pao*)

½ oz/14 g roughly chopped Thai basil

½ oz/14 g roughly chopped cilantro leaves

1 tbsp/15 mL tamarind pulp

1 tsp/3 g raw sugar

8 oz/227 g Jonah crabmeat, gently squeezed dry

10 rice paper spring roll wrappers

1. In a large pan, heat the oil over medium heat. Add the garlic, lemongrass, and green onions and cook until fragrant, about 1 minute.

2. Add the ground turkey, bell peppers, and cabbage and cook until the meat is brown and the vegetables are tender, 12 to 15 minutes. Transfer to a large bowl and cool completely.

3. When the mixture is cool, add the bean sprouts, Thai chili paste, Thai basil, cilantro, tamarind pulp, sugar, and crabmeat and mix to combine.

4. Moisten the rice paper wrappers in cool water, and transfer to a plastic wrap–lined countertop or a bamboo sushi mat.

5. Scoop 4 oz/113 g of the filling onto the lower half of the wrapper. Fold the bottom edge over the filling, and fold each side inward. Continue to roll up the filling, rolling away from you. The filling should be tightly enclosed. Serve immediately.

Nutritional Information per Serving (1 roll):

143 calories, 7 g fat, 1 g saturated fat, 50 mg cholesterol, 130 mg sodium, 7 g total carbohydrates, 2 g fiber, 2 g sugar, 14 g protein

Asparagus with Lump Crabmeat and Sherry Vinaigrette C D H

Makes 10 portions

> 1 lb 4 oz/567 g peeled and trimmed asparagus, green or white, or combined
>
> 10 fl oz/300 mL Vinaigrette-Style Dressing (page 333; see Chef's Note)
>
> 10 oz/284 g lump crabmeat
>
> 10 oz/284 g julienned tomato
>
> 3½ tbsp/10 g chopped chives

1. Bring a large pot of salted water to a boil. Add the asparagus and cook until tender-crisp, 4 to 6 minutes. Remove from the pot, and shock in ice water. Drain and transfer to a large bowl.

2. Toss the asparagus with the vinaigrette and marinate for at least 1 hour.

3. To serve, arrange 2 oz/57 g of the asparagus on a plate and top with 1 oz/28 g of the crabmeat, 1 oz/28 g of the julienned tomato, and 1 tsp/1 g of the chives. Serve immediately.

CHEF'S NOTE

Use sherry vinegar in the preparation of the dressing.

Nutritional Information per Serving (2 oz/57 g asparagus, 1 oz/28 g crabmeat, 1 oz/28 g tomatoes, 1 tsp/1 g chives):

175 calories, 14 g fat, 0 g saturated fat, 30 mg cholesterol, 150 mg sodium, 3 g total carbohydrates, 1 g fiber, 1 g sugar, 7 g protein

---

Tuna Carpaccio with Shiitake and Red Onion Salad H

Makes 10 portions

15 oz/425 g trimmed, skinless tuna fillet

2 tbsp/30 mL sake

SHIITAKE AND RED ONION SALAD

7 oz/199 g julienned shiitake mushrooms, cooked

3½ oz/99 g julienned carrot, blanched

3½ oz/99 g julienned red onion

2 oz/57 g julienned bok choy

4 fl oz/120 mL rice wine vinegar

2 tbsp/30 mL reduced-sodium soy sauce

WASABI SAUCE

2 tbsp/30 mL reduced-sodium soy sauce

2 fl oz/60 mL plain nonfat yogurt

2 tsp/4 g wasabi powder

¾ oz/21 g cucumber, very fine julienne

¾ oz/21 g daikon, very fine julienne

1 oz/28 g carrot, very fine julienne

1. Place the tuna in the freezer until it is partially frozen. Slice the tuna very thinly. Arrange the tuna slices on parchment paper and sprinkle with the sake. Cover and refrigerate for at least 10 minutes.

2. To prepare the salad, combine the shiitakes, carrot, onion, bok choy, vinegar, and soy sauce in a large bowl. Refrigerate for at least 20 minutes.

3. Combine the wasabi sauce ingredients and mix until smooth.

4. For each portion: Arrange 1½ oz/43 g of the tuna and 2 oz/57 g of the salad on a chilled plate. Serve immediately with 1½ tsp/7.5 mL of the wasabi sauce. Garnish with a very fine julienne of cucumber, daikon, and carrots.

CHEF'S NOTE

Change the soy sauce to tamari to make celiac-friendly.

> **Nutritional Information per Serving (1½ oz/43 g tuna, 2 oz/57 g salad, 1½ tsp/7.5 mL wasabi sauce, ¼ oz/7 g vegetable garnish):**
>
> 85 calories, .5 g fat, 0 g saturated fat, 20 mg cholesterol, 190 mg sodium, 6 g total carbohydrates, 1 g fiber, 2 g sugar, 11 g protein

Tuna Seviche C H

Makes 10 portions

BASIC SEVICHE MARINADE

4 fl oz/60 mL lime juice

4 fl oz/60 mL lemon juice

4 fl oz/60 mL orange juice

2 fl oz/30 mL extra-virgin olive oil

½ oz/14 g Dijon mustard

1 tsp/5 mL Worcestershire sauce

2 tsp/10 mL Tabasco sauce

2 tsp/6 g sugar

1 ½ tsp/8 mL tamari sauce

Kosher salt

Pinch freshly ground black pepper, or as needed

1 lb 9 oz/709 g tuna loin or belly, cut into medium dice

SEVICHE GARNISH

1 oz/28 g cilantro chiffonade

1 oz/28 g flat-leaf parsley chiffonade

1 lb 4 oz/567 g peeled, seeded, small-dice plum tomatoes

4 oz/113 g small-dice green bell pepper

8 oz/227 g minced red onion

1. To make the marinade, combine the lime, lemon, and orange juices, oil, mustard, Worcestershire sauce, sugar, and tamari. Mix well. Season with salt and pepper. Add the diced tuna to the marinade and toss to thoroughly combine. Refrigerate for up to 3 hours.

2. Just before serving, add the cilantro, parsley, tomatoes, bell pepper, and onion, and toss well to coat.

> **Nutritional Information per Serving (5¾ oz/163 g):**
>
> 160 calories, 7 g fat, 1 g saturated fat, 34 mg cholesterol, 122 mg sodium, 10 g total carbohydrates, 2 g fiber, 4 g sugar, 17 g protein

Seared Tuna Loin Cakes D H

Makes 10 portions

1¼ oz/35 g Thai sweet chili sauce

½ oz/14 g toasted sesame seeds

½ fl oz/15 mL sesame oil

¾ fl oz/22 mL soy sauce

5 oz/142 g chopped water chestnuts

1 oz/28 g minced pickled ginger

Pinch freshly ground black pepper

1 lb 4 oz/567 g small-dice tuna loin scraps

1 oz/28 g chopped chives

1. In a large bowl, combine the Thai chili sauce, sesame seeds, sesame oil, soy sauce, water chestnuts, pickled ginger, and pepper. Mix well and reserve. This seasoning mixture can be made in advance and used when needed.

2. Two hours before service, add the tuna and chives to the chili sauce mixture and toss well to combine. Form into 3-oz/85-g cakes and reserve, covered, until ready to cook.

3. To cook the cakes, heat a nonstick pan over high heat and spray lightly with oil. Add the cakes and sear for approximately 1 minute on each side. Serve immediately.

CHEF'S NOTES

These cakes are delicious when served with Miso-Shiitake Sauce (page 314) (1 fl oz/30 mL per portion).

Change the soy sauce to tamari to make celiac-friendly.

> **Nutritional Information per Serving (3 oz/85 g):**
>
> 125 calories, 5 g fat, 1 g saturated fat, 20 mg cholesterol, 288 mg sodium, 6 g total carbohydrates, 1 g fiber, 2 g sugar, 14 g protein

Tuna Tiradito C H

Makes 10 portions

SEVICHE

4 fl oz/120 mL lime juice

2 fl oz/60 mL lemon juice

2 fl oz/60 mL orange juice

3 tbsp/45 mL extra-virgin olive oil

1 tsp/5 g Dijon mustard

¼ tsp/1 mL Worcestershire sauce

2 tsp/10 mL sriracha, or as needed

½ tsp/3 mL agave syrup, or as needed

½ tsp/1.5 g kosher salt

¼ tsp/.5 g freshly ground black pepper

1 lb 4 oz/567 g tuna loin, sliced ⅛ in/3 mm thick

GARNISH

3 tbsp/9 g cilantro chiffonade

2 tbsp/6 g flat-leaf parsley chiffonade

5 plum tomatoes, peeled, seeded, and cut into small dice

1 serrano, minced

2¾ oz/80 g minced white onion

1. In a large bowl, whisk together the lime juice, lemon juice, orange juice, oil, mustard, Worcestershire sauce, sriracha, and agave syrup to combine. Season with the salt and pepper.

2. Add the tuna and toss well to coat with the marinade (see Chef's Note). Transfer 2 oz/57 g of the marinated tuna mixture to a plate, and garnish with cilantro, parsley, tomatoes, serrano, and onion. Serve immediately.

CHEF'S NOTE

The tuna will hold, refrigerated, in the marinade for up to 3 hours. Alternatively, the tuna can be brushed with the marinade just before serving so that portions can be made to order.

Nutritional Information per Serving (2 oz/57 g):

129 calories, 6 g fat, .5 g saturated fat, 0 mg cholesterol, 36 mg sodium, 7 g total carbohydrates, 1 g fiber, 3 g sugar, 14 g protein

Tuna Tartare C H

Makes 10 portions

TUNA TARTARE

1 lb 8 oz/680 g minced grade 1 tuna

¾ oz/21 g small-dice red onion

1½ oz/43 g chopped chives

1½ oz/43 g capers

2 tbsp/30 mL extra-virgin olive oil

½ tsp/1.5 g kosher salt

Pinch freshly ground black pepper

AVOCADO MOUSSE

3 gelatin sheets, bloomed in cold water

1 fl oz/30 mL lemon juice

1½ fl oz/45 mL pasteurized egg yolks

12 fl oz/360 mL olive oil

1½ avocados, pitted, peeled, and chopped

4 fl oz/120 mL heavy cream, whipped to soft peaks

1 tsp/3 g kosher salt, or as needed

Pinch freshly ground black pepper, or as needed

Pinch cayenne

TOMATO SOUP

2 lb/907 kg seeded and chopped beefsteak tomatoes

2 fl oz/60 mL extra-virgin olive oil

2 fl oz/60 mL sherry vinegar

¼ tsp/1.25 mL xanthan gum

½ tsp/2 kosher salt, or as needed

¼ tsp/.25 g freshly ground black pepper, or as needed

GARNISH

2 tbsp/30 mL chive oil (see Chef's Note page 331)

2 tbsp/28 g caviar, or as needed

½ oz/14 g chives, or as needed

1. To make the tuna tartare, combine the tuna, onion, chives, capers, and extra-virgin olive oil in a stainless-steel bowl and season with the salt and black pepper.

2. To make the avocado mousse, squeeze any excess water from the gelatin sheets, place them in a bowl, and add the lemon juice. Heat the gelatin to 110°F/43°C over a water bath, and then allow it to cool to 80°F/27°C.

3. Combine the gelatin and the egg yolks in a food processor and pulse to blend. While processing, add the oil in a slow, steady stream to emulsify the mixture. Add the avocados and continue puréeing until smooth. Transfer the avocado mixture to a bowl and gently fold in the whipped cream. Season the mixture with the salt, black pepper, and cayenne. Chill over an ice bath.

4. To make the tomato soup, place the tomatoes and extra-virgin olive oil in a food processor and purée until smooth. Add the vinegar and process until combined. Add the xanthan gum and process for about 5 minutes, or until the mixture begins to thicken. Strain through chinois and season with the salt and black pepper. Hold in the refrigerator until ready to serve.

5. To assemble, place a 3-in/7.5-cm ring mold on a plate. Fill the mold three-quarters full with 2¾ oz/78 g of the tuna tartare. Pipe 2½ oz/71 g of the avocado mousse on top of the tuna to finish filling the mold. Using an offset spatula, smooth out the surface of the mousse. Spoon 2 fl oz/60 mL of the tomato soup around the mold. Drizzle the soup with drops of the chive oil (¾ tsp/3.75 mL). Remove the ring mold and garnish the mousse with caviar and chives. Repeat until all the remaining tuna and mousse are plated.

> **Nutritional Information per Serving (2¾ oz/79 g tuna tartare, 2½ oz/70 g avocado mousse, 2 fl oz/60 mL tomato soup):**
>
> 601 calories, 55 g fat, 10 g saturated fat, 61 mg cholesterol, 732 mg sodium, 8 g total carbohydrates, 3 g fiber, 3 g sugar, 19 g protein

Salmon Cakes with Green Goddess Dressing

Makes 10 portions

GREEN GODDESS DRESSING

6 fl oz/180 mL low-fat mayonnaise

2 fl oz/60 mL low-fat sour cream

1 oz/28 g chopped anchovies

½ oz/14 g chopped chives

½ oz/14 g chopped flat-leaf parsley

½ oz/14 g drained and chopped capers

1 tbsp/3 g finely grated lemon zest

1 tsp/3 g kosher salt

Pinch freshly ground black pepper

SALMON CAKES

8 oz/227 g salmon, cut into ¼-in/6-mm dice

8 oz/227 g finely chopped salmon

4 oz/113 g shrimp, cut into ¼-in/6-mm dice

2 oz/57 g egg whites, beaten

2 oz/57 g blanched red pepper, seeded and finely diced

1 oz/28 g finely chopped green onions

½ oz/14 g finely grated lemon zest

1 tsp/7 g seeded and minced jalapeño

1 tbsp/15 mL mayonnaise

¾ tsp/2 g kosher salt

¼ tsp/.5 g freshly ground black pepper

2 oz/57 g panko bread crumbs

6 oz/170 g panko bread crumbs, seasoned with salt and pepper, for dredging

4 fl oz/120 mL extra-virgin olive oil

1. To make the dressing, combine all the ingredients for the dressing except for the lemon zest, salt, and pepper in a food processor and pulse for about 10 seconds to combine. Season as needed with the lemon zest, salt, and pepper. Store the dressing, covered, in the refrigerator for up to 3 days.

2. To make the salmon cakes, combine all the ingredients for the salmon mixture in a medium bowl. It should just hold together and not be too dense and heavy. Add more bread crumbs or mayonnaise if needed.

3. Divide the mixture and pat into cakes no thicker than 1 in/2.5 cm (5 oz/142 g) each. The salmon cakes may be prepared in advance to this point. Store them, uncovered, in the refrigerator for up to 4 hours.

4. Dredge the salmon cakes in the remaining seasoned bread crumbs. In a large sauté pan over moderate heat, add enough oil to just cover the bottom of the pan. Add the cakes and sauté until golden brown, about 4 minutes per side. Serve immediately with 2 tbsp/30 mL of the Green Goddess Dressing.

Nutritional Information per Serving (one 5-oz/142-g cake and 2 tbsp/30 mL dressing):

268 calories, 9 g fat, 6 g saturated fat, 67 mg cholesterol, 133 mg sodium, 16 g total carbohydrates, 4 g fiber, 1 g sugar, 29 g protein

---

Lobster Wrapped in Rice Paper
with Asian Salad C D H

Makes 10 portions

ASIAN SALAD

1 tsp/5 mL peanut oil

3 oz/85 g julienned shiitake mushrooms

1½ tbsp/23 mL reduced-sodium soy sauce

4 oz/113 g julienned carrots

6 oz/170 g bean sprouts

6 oz/170 g julienned snow peas

6 oz/170 g julienned daikon

2 oz/57 g chopped pickled ginger

2 oz/57 g thinly sliced green onions

5 oz/142 g mixed salad greens

10 fl oz/300 mL Lemon-Parsley Vinaigrette (page 318)

LOBSTER

5 (1-lb/454-g) lobsters

3 gal/11.52 L water

½ oz/14 g butter

4 oz/113 g julienned leek

1½ fl oz/45 mL brandy

2 tsp/6 g kosher salt

½ tsp/1 g freshly ground black pepper

20 rice paper sheets (8 in/20 cm)

2 tbsp/30 mL peanut oil

1. To make the Asian salad, heat the peanut oil in a large sauté pan over high heat. Add the shiitake mushrooms and sweat them until tender. Add the soy sauce and reduce all the liquid. Chill completely. Combine the mushrooms with the carrots, bean sprouts, snow peas, daikon, ginger, green onions, and salad greens. Toss with the vinaigrette.

2. Place the lobsters into a large pot, and add enough cool water to cover the lobsters. Cover the pot and bring the lobsters to a full boil over high heat. Immediately remove the lobsters from the boiling water and shock in ice water and drain. Remove all the meat from the tails, claws, and knuckles and cut into medium dice.

3. Heat the butter in a large sauté pan over medium heat. Add the leek and sweat until tender. Add the lobster meat, brandy, salt, and pepper. Continue to cook for 5 minutes more, or until the lobster is cooked.

4. Remove the solids from the pan, and reduce any excess liquid to a syrup. Add the reduced liquid to the lobster meat and chill thoroughly.

5. Soften the rice paper sheets in warm water for a few minutes; drain. Place 1½ oz/43 g of the lobster mixture onto the lower half of the wrapper. Fold the bottom edge over the filling, and fold each side inward. Continue to roll up the filling, rolling away from you. The filling should be tightly enclosed.

6. Heat the oil in a large skillet over high heat. Add the lobster rolls and sauté until golden brown on two sides.

7. Mound 2½ oz/70 g of the Asian salad in the middle of a plate. Arrange 2 rolls over the greens. Dress the salad with 1 fl oz/30 mL of the vinaigrette.

CHEF'S NOTE

Change the soy sauce to tamari to make celiac-friendly.

Nutritional Information per Serving (1½ oz/43 g lobster, 2½ oz/70 g Asian salad, 1 fl oz/30 mL vinaigrette):

302 calories, 11 g fat, g saturated fat, 45 mg cholesterol, 728 mg sodium, 30 g total carbohydrates, 2 g fiber, 5 g sugar, 17 g protein

Mediterranean-Style Seafood Terrine [C] [D] [H]

Makes one 2-lb/907-g terrine; 16 portions

5 fl oz/150 mL heavy cream

½ tsp/1 g saffron threads

1 lb 2 oz/510 g sea scallops, muscle tabs removed, quartered

½ tsp/1.5 g kosher salt

2 large egg whites

¼ tsp/.5 g freshly ground black pepper

1 lb/454 g peeled and deveined shrimp, diced

1 tbsp/3 g chopped flat-leaf parsley

2 tsp/2 g chopped basil

1. Bring the cream to a simmer in a small saucepan over medium-low heat. Add the saffron, remove from the heat, and allow to steep for 30 minutes. Chill thoroughly.

2. Place half the scallops and the salt into a chilled food processor bowl. Purée to form a smooth paste, scraping down the sides of the bowl as necessary. Combine the chilled saffron cream, egg whites, and pepper. Add the mixture to the puréed scallops in thirds, pulsing the processor to incorporate. Transfer the forcemeat to a metal bowl placed over an ice bath.

3. Poach a small amount of the forcemeat in simmering water to test for consistency and seasoning. Make any necessary adjustments.

4. Pat the remaining scallops and the shrimp dry with paper towels. Fold the scallops, shrimp, parsley, and basil into the forcemeat.

5. Lightly oil the inside of a 2-lb/907-g terrine mold, or spray with cooking spray. Line with plastic wrap, leaving a 2-in/5-cm overhang, and pack with the forcemeat. Fold the overhang over the forcemeat and cover. Place in a 170°F/75°C water bath and bake in the oven at 325°F/165°C to an internal temperature of 145°F/62°C.

6. Cool the terrine to 120°F/49°C and cover with a piece of aluminum foil–wrapped cardboard, cut to fit the inside of the mold. Press with a brick or other heavy object and refrigerate for 8 to 10 hours.

7. Slice into sixteen ¼-in/6-mm slices and serve.

Nutritional Information per Serving (1 slice):

148 calories, 7 g fat, 4 g saturated fat, 106 mg cholesterol, 260 mg sodium, 2 g total carbohydrates, 0 g fiber, 0 g sugar, 19 g protein

---

Seared Scallops with Beet Vinaigrette C D H

Makes 10 portions

BEET VINAIGRETTE

8 oz/227 g beets

2½ fl oz/75 mL apple cider vinegar

3 tbsp/45 mL extra-virgin olive oil

2 tsp/2 g chopped dill

1 tsp/3 g kosher salt

¼ tsp/.5 g freshly ground black pepper

2 lb 4 oz/1.02 kg sea scallops, muscle tabs removed

5 oz/142 g mixed greens

3 oz/85 g julienned carrot

3 oz/85 g julienned daikon

1. Prepare the beet vinaigrette by simmering the beets in acidulated water until tender (see Chef's Note). Drain, and when cool enough to handle, peel and chop the beets. Place the beets and vinegar in a blender and purée until smooth. Whisk in the oil, and season with the dill, salt, and pepper.

2. For each portion, dry approximately 3½ oz/100 g of the scallops with paper towels and dry sear in a seasoned sauté pan over high heat until browned on both sides and just cooked through. Arrange ½ oz/14 g of the greens and 1 tbsp/15 mL each of the julienned carrot and daikon on a room temperature plate. Drizzle or spoon 2 tbsp/30 mL of the beet vinaigrette as desired, place the seared scallops on top of the vinaigrette and serve.

CHEF'S NOTE

For a more intense color and flavor, use a juice machine to juice the raw beets. Combine the juice and vinegar, whisk in the oil, and season with dill, salt, and pepper.

Nutritional Information per Serving (3½ oz/99 g scallops, ½ oz/14 g salad, 1 fl oz/30 mL dressing):

150 calories, 5 g fat, .5 g saturated fat, 35 mg cholesterol, 230 mg sodium, 7 g total carbohydrates, 1 g fiber, 2 g sugar, 18 g protein

Seared Scallops with Avocado, Grapefruit, and Citrus Vinaigrette C D H

Makes 12 portions

Seviche Plate C D H

Makes 15 portions

1 qt/960 mL salted water

3 green onions, chopped

1 lb/454 g sea scallops, cut in half (to create disk-shaped slices)

1 lb/454 g shrimp, peeled, deveined, halved lengthwise

1 lb/454 g squid, tubes and tentacles

50 small clams

50 mussels

BASIC SEVICHE MARINADE

4 fl oz/120 mL lime juice

4 fl oz/120 mL lemon juice

4 fl oz/120 mL orange juice

2 fl oz/60 mL extra-virgin olive oil

2 tsp/10 g Dijon mustard

1 tsp/5 mL Worcestershire sauce

2 tsp/10 mL Tabasco sauce

1 tsp/3 g sugar

1 tsp/3 g kosher salt, or as needed

½ tsp/1 g freshly ground black pepper, or as needed

SEVICHE GARNISH

3 tbsp/3 g chopped cilantro

2 tbsp/2 g chopped flat-leaf parsley

6 plum tomatoes, peeled, seeded, and minced

1 small green bell pepper, seeded and minced

8 oz/227 g minced onion

1. Combine the salted water with the green onions in a large saucepan and bring to a boil. Drop the scallop halves into the boiling cooking liquid for 20 seconds. Remove and cool. Add the shrimp to the same boiling cooking liquid and cook for 20 seconds. Remove and cool.

2. Slice the squid into ⅛-in/3 mm rings, and split the tentacles. Drop into the same boiling cooking liquid for 20 seconds. Remove and cool.

3. Using the remaining cooking liquid, steam open the clams and mussels in a small rondeau over medium heat. Allow the shellfish to cool, then remove the shells.

4. To make the basic seviche marinade, combine the lime, lemon, and orange juices, oil, mustard, Worcestershire sauce, Tabasco, and sugar. Adjust the seasoning with salt and black pepper. Add the seafood to the marinade, toss to coat well, and refrigerate for 2 hours.

5. Before serving, add the cilantro, parsley, tomatoes, bell pepper, and onion and mix well to combine. If necessary, adjust the seasoning with salt and black pepper.

> **Nutritional Information per Serving (5 oz/142 g):**
>
> 378 calories, 18 g fat, 2 g saturated fat, 60 mg cholesterol, 160 mg sodium, 15 g total carbohydrates, 3 g fiber, 5 g sugar, 21 g protein

Almond Milk–Poached Shrimp with Forbidden Rice C D H

Makes 10 portions

FORBIDDEN RICE

1 tbsp/15 mL grapeseed oil

1 oz/28 g minced shallot

9¾ oz/277 g Forbidden Rice

16 fl oz/480 mL water

6 fl oz/180 mL unsweetened coconut milk

1 tsp/3 g kosher salt

SAUCE

1 oz/28 g ginger, peeled and thinly sliced

1 dried Thai bird chile

12 fl oz/360 mL unsweetened coconut milk

2 tbsp/30 mL lime juice

1 tsp/5 mL agave syrup

POACHED SHRIMP

1 qt/960 mL unsweetened almond milk

One 3-in/7.5-cm piece lemongrass, split lengthwise

Three 1-in/2.5-cm pieces orange peel

1 star anise

Pinch kosher salt

30 shrimp (21–25 count), peeled and deveined

GARNISH

3½ oz/99 g green onions, sliced thinly on the bias

3 tbsp/10 g sesame seeds, toasted

1½ oz/43 g shredded fresh coconut

1. To make the rice, heat the oil in a medium pot over medium heat. Add the shallot and sweat until aromatic, 1 to 2 minutes. Add the rice and stir to combine.

2. Add the water, coconut milk, and salt and bring to a boil. Cover the pot, reduce the heat to medium-low, and simmer until the rice is tender and has absorbed all of the liquid, 25 to 30 minutes. Keep warm.

3. To make the sauce, bring the ginger, chile, and coconut milk to a simmer in a small pot over medium-low heat. Remove the pot from the heat, cover, and steep until aromatic, 15 to 20 minutes.

4. Remove the ginger and chile with a slotted spoon and return the pot to the heat. Bring the liquid to a simmer over medium heat and simmer until reduced by about half.

5. Stir in the lime juice and agave syrup and continue to reduce to a syrupy consistency. Keep warm.

6. To poach the shrimp, bring the almond milk, lemongrass, orange peel, anise, and salt to a simmer in a pot over medium heat. Remove the pot from the heat, cover, and steep until aromatic, 15 to 20 minutes.

7. Remove the lemongrass, orange peel, and anise from the pot with a slotted spoon and return the pot to the heat. Bring the infused liquid to 165°F/74°C.

8. Working in batches, add the shrimp to the liquid and poach until they are pink and cooked through, 3 to 5 minutes. Remove from the liquid and keep warm. Repeat with remaining shrimp.

9. To serve, place a 2½-in/6.35-cm ring mold onto a plate. Pack 3½ oz/97 g of the prepared rice into the mold. Top the rice with ⅓ oz/10 g of the green onions, and top with 3 shrimp. Drizzle 2 tbsp/30 mL of the sauce around the cake and garnish with 1 tsp/1 g of the sesame seeds and 2 tbsp/4 g of the coconut.

> **Nutritional Information per Serving (3½ oz/97 g rice, ⅓ oz/10 g green onions, 3 shrimp, 2 tbsp/30 mL syrup, 1 tsp/1 g sesame seeds, 2 tbsp/4 g coconut):**
>
> 230 calories, 18 g fat, 13 g saturated fat, 30 mg cholesterol, 350 mg sodium, 12 g total carbohydrates, 3 g fiber, 5 g sugar, 6 g protein

Chili-Roasted Peanuts with Dried Cherries

Makes 1 lb/454 g roasted nuts

2 tbsp/28 g butter

1 lb/454 g raw peanuts

1 tbsp/6 g chili powder

2 tsp/6 g ground cumin

2 tsp/6 g ground white pepper

1 tbsp/10 g kosher salt

½ tsp/1 g dried oregano

½ tsp/1 g cayenne

8 oz/227 g dried cherries (or raisins)

1. In a small saucepan over medium heat, melt the butter. Add the peanuts and toss to coat.
2. Spread out the peanuts on a large baking sheet and toast in the oven at 325°F/163°C until fragrant, about 10 minutes.
3. Transfer the peanuts to a large bowl and toss with the chili powder, cumin, white pepper, salt, oregano, and cayenne. Mix in the cherries.
4. Cool completely before serving. The finished peanuts will keep in an airtight container for up to 2 weeks.

CHEF'S NOTE

Be aware of nut allergies with this recipe.

Nutritional Information per Serving (1 oz/28 g):

220 calories, 15 g fat, 2 g saturated fat, 2 mg cholesterol, 377 mg sodium, 16 g total carbohydrates, 4 g fiber, 10 g sugar, 8 g protein

---

Grilled Artichokes with Hazelnut Romesco Sauce

Makes 10 portions

2 qt/1.89 L water

2 bay leaves

1 lemon, halved

½ tsp/2 g kosher salt

½ tsp/1 g freshly ground black pepper

10 artichokes

6 fl oz/180 mL extra-virgin olive oil

3 garlic cloves, sliced

20 fl oz/600 mL Hazelnut Romesco Sauce (page 318)

1. Pour the water into a large stockpot and add the bay leaves and 1 lemon half. Season with the salt and pepper and bring to a simmer over medium-low heat.
2. Trim the stems of each artichoke and peel them to expose the tender flesh. Remove the outer petals to expose the soft, light green petals toward the center. Slice 1 in/2.5 cm off the top of each artichoke.
3. Add the artichokes to the simmering water. Cover the pot and simmer over medium-low heat until tender, about 20 minutes. Remove the artichokes from the water and allow to cool.
4. Quarter each artichoke and remove the hairy choke from the center of each. Place the artichoke quarters in a resealable plastic bag. Add the oil, garlic, and the juice of the remaining lemon half. Let marinate in the refrigerator for at least 30 minutes, or for up to 4 hours.
5. Preheat a gas grill to medium heat.
6. Remove the artichokes from the marinade and grill, uncovered, over direct heat, turning often, until golden, about 10 minutes.
7. Serve the artichoke quarters on individual plates with 2 fl oz/60 ml of the hazelnut romesco sauce drizzled over the top.

Nutritional Information per Serving (1 artichoke, 2 fl oz/60 mL romesco sauce):

334 calories, 28 g fat, 4 g saturated fat, 0 mg cholesterol, 243 mg sodium, 20 g total carbohydrates, 9 g fiber, 6 g sugar, 6 g protein

---

Maitake Mushroom, Leek, and Brie Turnovers D V H

Makes 12 portions

1 tbsp/15 mL extra-virgin olive oil

6 oz/170 g coarsely chopped maitake mushrooms

3 oz/85 g sliced leeks

1 tsp/3 g minced garlic

2 tbsp/30 mL Madeira

½ tsp/2 g kosher salt

¼ tsp/.5 g freshly ground black pepper

1 lb 8 oz/680 g Blitz Puff Pastry (page 272)

Egg Wash (page 264)

3 oz/85 g Brie

1. Line a half sheet pan with parchment paper.

2. Heat the oil in a sauté pan over medium-high heat until it shimmers. Add the mushrooms to the pan and sauté until lightly caramelized, 2 to 3 minutes. Add the leeks to the pan and reduce the heat to medium. Sauté the leeks until they are light golden brown, 3 to 4 minutes. Add the garlic and cook for 1 minute.

3. Deglaze the pan with the Madeira and reduce until nearly dry, about 1 minute. Season the mixture with the salt and pepper. Cool the mixture to room temperature.

4. Roll the dough into a rectangle 12 by 16 in/30 by 40 cm. Cut the dough into twelve 4-in/10-cm squares. Place the squares on the prepared baking sheet and let chill in the refrigerator until firm, about 10 minutes.

5. Brush each square lightly with egg wash. Place 1 tbsp/15 mL of the mushroom filling in the center of each square. Top the filling with 1½ teaspoons/7 g of the Brie. Fold one corner of the dough over the filling and line it up with the opposite corner of the dough. Press the edges firmly together to seal the filling inside the puff pastry dough. Chill the turnovers for about 10 minutes before baking. Brush the turnovers lightly with egg wash. Cut a small opening in the center of each turnover to allow steam to vent.

6. Bake the turnovers in the oven at 425°F/218°C until golden brown, 20 to 25 minutes. Serve immediately.

Nutritional Information per Serving (3 oz/85 g):

435 calories, 30 g fat, 5 g saturated fat, 9 mg cholesterol, 324 mg sodium, 36 g total carbohydrates, 1 g fiber, 1 g sugar, 7 g protein

Vietnamese Five-Spice Pâté C D V H

Makes 10 portions

2 lb 8 oz/1.13 kg pork shoulder, cubed

1¾ oz/51 g minced lemongrass

½ oz/14 g peeled and minced ginger

¼ oz/7 g minced garlic

1½ tsp/5 g sugar

1½ tsp/3 g freshly ground black pepper

1½ tsp/3 g five-spice powder

1 fl oz/30 mL kecap manis (sweet soy sauce)

1 fl oz/30 mL tamarind pulp

1 tbsp/15 mL oyster sauce

1 tbsp/10 g kosher salt

1. In a large bowl, toss the pork with the lemongrass, ginger, garlic, sugar, black pepper, five-spice powder, soy sauce, tamarind, oyster sauce, and salt.

2. Grind the mixture in a meat grinder through a ¼-in/6-mm die. Repeat the process through the same die a second time.

3. Pack the seasoned ground meat into 1-lb/454-g loaf pans or pâté molds.

4. Bake the pâtés in the oven at 325°F/152°C until they reach an internal temperature of 165°F/74°C.

5. Cool completely, then unmold from the pans, wrap tightly in plastic wrap, and store, refrigerated, until ready to serve.

CHEF'S NOTE

For a leaner pâté, 2½ lbs/1.13 kg lean turkey meat can be substituted for half of the pork.

Nutritional Information per Serving (4 oz/113 g):

171 calories, 7 g fat, 2 g saturated fat, 70 mg cholesterol, 305 mg sodium, 2 g total carbohydrates, 0 g fiber, 2 g sugar, 24 g protein

---

Summer Rolls D V H

Makes 10 portions

SEASONED RICE

11 oz/311 g cooked brown rice

4 fl oz/120 mL unsweetened coconut milk

1 tbsp/15 mL soy sauce

Red pepper flakes, as needed

SUMMER ROLLS

10 rice paper sheets (8 in/ 20 cm)

5 oz/142 g peeled, julienned, and blanched carrots

2½ oz/71 g julienned and blanched red bell pepper

2½ oz/71 g julienned and blanched snow peas

5 oz/142 g julienned celery

2½ oz/71 g rice noodles, soaked

1 oz/28 g mint leaves (20 each)

1 oz/28 g basil leaves (20 each)

1. In a medium bowl, mix the rice, coconut milk, soy sauce, and red pepper flakes to combine. Reserve.
2. Working one at a time, soak the rice paper sheets in hot water, then transfer to a clean, damp towel on a flat surface.
3. Place 1½ oz/43 g of the rice mixture inside of the rice paper sheet. Flatten gently.
4. Place ½ oz/14 g of the carrots, ¼ oz/7 g of the bell pepper, ¼ oz/7 g of the snow peas, and ½ oz/14 g of the celery on top of the rice, aligning the julienned vegetables with the top edge of the rice paper sheet. Top with ½ oz/14 g of the soaked rice noodles. Place 2 mint leaves and 2 basil leaves on top.
5. Fold the bottom edge of the rice paper sheet up to cover the base of the julienned vegetables. Roll the left side of the rice paper sheet toward the center to form a tight bundle. Roll the right side toward the center to finish the roll.

CHEF'S NOTE

Change the soy sauce to tamari to make this recipe celiac-friendly.

Nutritional Information per Serving (1 roll):

70 calories, 3 g fat, 2 g saturated fat, 0 mg cholesterol, 25 mg sodium, 11 g total carbohydrates, 2 g fiber, 2 g sugar, 2 g protein

Vietnamese Summer Rolls C D V H

Makes 14 portions

DIPPING SAUCE

2 oz/57 g sugar

2 fl oz/60 mL fish sauce (*nam pla*)

1½ fl oz/45 mL lemon juice

1½ fl oz/45 mL rice wine vinegar

1 fl oz/15 mL water

2 tsp/7 g minced garlic

2 tsp/10 mL Thai chili sauce (*nahm prik pao*)

FILLING

6 oz/170 g rice noodles

8 oz/227 g shrimp (26–30 count)

6 oz/170 g finely julienned carrots

½ tsp/1.5 g kosher salt

4 oz/113 g iceberg lettuce chiffonade

1½ tsp/1 g sugar

2 fl oz/60 mL lemon juice

1 oz/28 g sugar

8 fl oz/240 mL warm water

14 rice paper wrappers (8 in/20 cm)

½ oz/14 g cilantro leaves

1. Whisk together the ingredients for the dipping sauce and refrigerate.

2. Cook the rice noodles in boiling water. Shock the noodles in cold water and drain.

3. Blanch the shrimp in boiling water until cooked, about 3 minutes. Shock, peel, and clean the shrimp. Slice the shrimp in half lengthwise.

4. Toss the carrots with the salt and marinate for 10 minutes. Rinse thoroughly and blot any excess moisture from the carrots. Combine the noodles, carrots, lettuce, sugar, and lemon juice.

5. To assemble the summer rolls: Combine the sugar and warm water in a large bowl. Moisten 1 wrapper in the sugar water and place on a clean, damp towel on a flat surface. Place 2½ oz/70 g of the noodle mixture, 2 shrimp halves, and a few cilantro leaves in the center of each wrapper. Fold in each end of the wrapper and roll to completely encase the filling. Refrigerate until needed.

6. To serve, serve 1 cold summer roll with approximately 1 tbsp/15 mL of the dipping sauce.

> **Nutritional Information per Serving (1 roll, 1 tbsp/15 mL sauce):**
>
> 119 calories, 4 g fat, 0 g saturated fat, 15 mg cholesterol, 494 mg sodium, 17 g total carbohydrates, 1 g fiber, 8 g sugar, 5 g protein

Stuffed Cherry Tomatoes with Minted Barley-Cucumber Salad D V H

Makes 10 portions

10½ oz/298 g pearl barley

6 oz/170 g minced tomato

5 oz/142 g minced cucumber

1¾ oz/50 g chopped flat-leaf parsley

6 tbsp/19 g chopped mint

3 tbsp/12 g finely sliced green onions, white portion only

2 tbsp/30 mL extra-virgin olive oil

1 tbsp/15 mL lemon juice

1 tsp/3 g kosher salt, or as needed

½ tsp/1 g freshly ground black pepper, or as needed

50 cherry tomatoes

1. Soak the barley in enough cold water to cover for 30 minutes; drain well.

2. Bring the barley and enough water to cover to a boil in a large pot over high heat. Reduce the heat and simmer until tender, about 40 minutes. Strain through a sieve, transfer to a bowl of ice water, and let cool for 1 minute. Set the sieve over a bowl and drain the barley.

3. Combine the barley, tomato, cucumber, parsley, mint, and green onions in a large bowl. Stir in the oil, lemon juice, salt, and pepper.

4. Cut the core from each cherry tomato and make two cuts into the tomato to open it out like a flower. Stuff each cherry tomato with some of the salad, and serve on a chilled platter or individual chilled salad plates.

Nutritional Information per Serving (5 tomatoes):

153 calories, 3 g fat, 0 g saturated fat, 0 mg cholesterol, 203 mg sodium, 28 g total carbohydrates, 6 g fiber, 3 g sugar, 4 g protein

---

Turkey Satay with Peanut Sauce C D H

Makes 10 portions

TURKEY SATAY

3 oz/85 g minced lemongrass

¾ oz/21 g peeled and minced ginger

6 oz/170 g minced garlic

2 tbsp/30 mL Thai chili paste (*nahm prik pao*)

¼ cup/24 g curry powder

3 oz/85 g palm sugar

8 fl oz/240 mL fish sauce (*nam pla*)

2 lb 8 oz/1.2 kg turkey breast, cut into pieces 4 in/10.16 cm long and ⅛ in/3 mm thick

PEANUT SAUCE

2 tbsp/30 mL roasted peanut butter

1 oz/28 g minced garlic

16 fl oz/480 mL unsweetened coconut milk

1 tbsp/15 mL tamarind pulp

2 tbsp/30 mL sambal

2½ fl oz/75 mL kecap manis (sweet soy sauce)

1 tbsp/6 g finely minced kaffir lime leaves

1. Preheat a gas grill to high heat.
2. To make the satay, combine the lemongrass, ginger, garlic, chili paste, curry powder, sugar, fish sauce, and turkey in a large bowl.
3. Thread the turkey onto bamboo skewers that have been soaked in water for at least 1 hour and transfer to the marinade. Marinate, refrigerated, for 8 to 10 minutes.
4. Remove the skewers from the marinade and shake to remove excess.
5. Grill the skewers, turning occasionally, until the turkey is thoroughly cooked, 4 to 6 minutes. Keep warm.
6. To make the peanut sauce, combine the peanut butter, garlic, coconut milk, tamarind, sambal, kecap manis, and kaffir lime leaves. Serve the skewers, warm, with the peanut sauce.

Nutritional Information per Serving (2½ oz/71 g, 2½ oz/71 g sauce):

337 calories, 19 g fat, 11 g saturated fat, 73 mg cholesterol, 231 mg sodium, 11 g total carbohydrates, 2 g fiber, 2 g sugar, 3 g protein

Smoked Duck with Red Lentil Salad and Golden Beets C D H

Makes 10 portions

DUCK

1 lb/454 g boneless duck breast

½ oz/14 g kosher salt

1 tbsp/6 g cracked black peppercorns

2 oz/57 g finely grated orange zest

2 oz/57 g chopped basil

MARINATED BEETS

1 lb/454 g baby golden beets, trimmed

4 fl oz/120 mL balsamic vinegar

1 oz/28 g chopped basil, chives, thyme, and parsley

½ oz/14 g whole-grain mustard

4 fl oz/120 mL extra-virgin olive oil

8 oz/227 g sliced Maui or other sweet onion

1 lb/454 g Red Lentil Salad (page 163)

1. Place the duck breast in a medium bowl. Rub the duck with the salt, pepper, orange zest, and basil. Cover tightly with plastic wrap and refrigerate for about 8 hours.

2. Cold smoke the duck breast for 1½ to 2 hours.

3. Sear the duck breast in a seasoned skillet over moderate heat, transfer to the oven, and roast at 275°F/135°C to an internal temperature of 165°F/74°C. Remove from the oven, transfer to a wire rack, cool, cover, and refrigerate.

4. Cook the beets in simmering acidulated water until tender. Shock the beets, remove their skins, and quarter.

5. Make a vinaigrette by combining the vinegar, herbs, and mustard in a bowl. Gradually whisk in the oil in a slow, steady stream, or use an immersion blender. Toss the beets and onion with the vinaigrette.

6. To serve, arrange about 1¼ oz/35 g of the thinly sliced duck breast on a plate. Serve with 1½ oz/45 g of the red lentil salad and 1½ oz/45 g of the beets.

Nutritional Information per Serving (1¼ oz/35 g duck, 1½ oz/45 g lentil salad, 1½ oz/45 g beets):

550 calories, 26 g fat, 3 g saturated fat, 35 mg cholesterol, 620 mg sodium, 52 g total carbohydrates, 12 g fiber, 8 g sugar, 29 g protein

BBQ Tempeh Kebobs C D V H

Makes 10 portions

10 oz/284 g cooked tempeh, cut into ¾-in/1.9-cm cubes

16 fl oz/480 mL BBQ Sauce (page 317)

5 oz/142 g red bell pepper, seeded and cut into 1-in/2.5-cm squares

10 oz/284 g portobello mushrooms, cut into 1-in/2.5-cm squares

5 oz/142 g blanched and peeled red pearl onions

10 oz/284 g blanched and halved Brussels sprouts

5 oz/142 g sweet potatoes, cut into ¾-in/1.9-cm cubes, blanched

1. In a medium bowl, combine the tempeh with 4 fl oz/ 118 mL of the BBQ sauce and marinate for 30 minutes.

2. Preheat a gas grill to high heat.

3. Thread the ingredients onto metal skewers or bamboo skewers that have been soaked in water for 1 hour, alternating the ingredients. Each kebob should include 1 oz/28 g of the tempeh, ½ oz/14 g of the bell pepper, 1 oz/28 g of the portobello mushrooms, ½ oz/14 g of the red pearl onions, 1 oz/28 g of the Brussels sprouts, and ½ oz/14 g of the sweet potatoes.

4. Spray each kebob lightly with olive oil cooking spray. Grill the kebobs until lightly charred, brushing with additional BBQ sauce as they cook. Cook until the vegetables are tender-crisp, 8 to 10 minutes. Brush with sauce once more before plating.

Nutritional Information per Serving (1 kebob):

90 calories, 4 g fat, 1 g saturated fat, 0 mg cholesterol, 100 mg sodium, 11 g total carbohydrates, 2 g fiber, 3 g sugar, 7 g protein

---

Sesame Tempeh Sticks with Apricot Dipping Sauce D V H

Makes 10 portions

FILLING

1 oz/28 g toasted sesame seeds

10½ oz/298 g cooked tempeh

1 oz/28 g chopped green onions

½ fl oz/15 mL sesame oil

½ fl oz/15 mL soy sauce

1½ tsp/4 g cornstarch

2 tsp/7 g peeled and minced ginger

1 tsp/3.5 g minced garlic

2½ oz/71 g phyllo dough (6 sheets approximately 12 in by 16 in/30 by 40 cm)

2 oz/57 g grapeseed oil

2 fl oz/60 mL Egg Wash, or as needed (page 264)

2 tbsp/15 g sesame seeds, toasted

Pinch kosher salt

APRICOT DIPPING SAUCE

4 fl oz/120 mL apricot preserves, no sugar added, all fruit

1 fl oz/30 mL lime juice

½ fl oz/15 mL water

1 tsp/5 g Dijon mustard

½ tsp/1 g peeled and minced ginger

1. Line a sheet pan with parchment paper.
2. In a blender or food processor, blend the sesame seeds, tempeh, green onions, sesame oil, soy sauce, cornstarch, ginger, and garlic until the mixture forms a coarse paste.
3. Cover the phyllo dough with plastic wrap and then a dampened kitchen towel. Remove only 1 sheet of phyllo at a time as you work, to prevent the phyllo from drying out.
4. Brush 1 sheet of phyllo dough generously with grapeseed oil. Stack another sheet on top and brush with oil again. Repeat with 1 last piece of phyllo.
5. Cut the stack of phyllo in half lengthwise, and then arrange one half with a long side nearest you.
6. With dampened fingers, shape about 3 tbsp/45 mL of the filling mixture into a narrow rope along the edge nearest

you, then roll up the paste tightly in the phyllo to form a long, thin roll.

7. Repeat with the other half of the phyllo stack, and then repeat the whole process with the remaining 3 sheets of phyllo dough.
8. Lightly brush the top of the sticks with egg wash, and sprinkle with the sesame seeds and kosher salt.
9. Using a sharp knife, cut each roll into 5 sticks and place, seam side down, onto the prepared sheet pan. Bake in the oven at 350°F/175°C until the phyllo is golden brown, 12 to 15 minutes. Cool slightly.
10. In a small bowl, combine the ingredients for the dipping sauce. Serve the sticks warm with the dipping sauce.

CHEF'S NOTE

Change the soy sauce to tamari to make celiac-friendly.

Nutritional Information per Serving (2 oz/57 g sticks, and ½ fl oz/15 mL dipping sauce):

174 calories, 13 g fat, 2 g saturated fat, 0 mg cholesterol, 137 mg sodium, 12 g total carbohydrates, 1 g fiber, 2 g sugar, 7 g protein

Stocks and broths are the foundation upon which fine sauces are built, delicious soups are created, and cooking methods are enhanced. This chapter features stocks and broths that go beyond the norm, and will serve as inspiration for recipe modifications and new creations. Making not only delicious vegetable stock but also broths that are very specific in nature such as mushroom broth, or roasted garlic broth lead the way to the creation of healthful soups and sauces.

Soup nurtures the soul. Soup fuels the body. Adding a diverse selection of soups to the menu is a thoughtful way to offer nutritionally rich options for the consumer with dietary restrictions while satisfying the desires of those without. For instance, it's easy to offer a vegetarian or even vegan soup such as Black Bean and Poblano Soup (page 110) that will be appealing to a broad audience. Likewise it is also possible to craft a soup such as Tortilla Soup (page 134) or Vegetable Chili (page 127), that is rich tasting and enticing while still being nutritionally sound and perhaps fits the dietary needs of someone with celiac disease or diabetes.

Soups can also play a variety of roles. A cup of perfectly clear rich consommé or hearty broth soup makes a perfect little starter for a multicourse meal while a more filling soup such as a bean soup or vegetable purée soup makes a great lunch entrée or late-night supper. Some soups can even double as a sauce, poaching liquid, or braising liquid.

And, as mentioned earlier, selecting a few "small plates" is an approach that some choose in order to meet the needs of a restrictive diet without overindulging. Because soups typically include a variety of vegetables, modest amounts of fat and protein, and can easily include whole grains or legumes, they offer a perfect fit for the "small plates" model.

Chicken Stock CDH

Makes 1 gal/3.84 L stock

8 lb/3.62 kg chicken bones, cut into 3-in/8-cm lengths

6 qt/5.75 L cold water

MIREPOIX

8 oz/227 g roughly cut onions

4 oz/113 g roughly cut carrots

4 oz/113 g roughly cut celery

1 Sachet d'Épices (page 340)

1. Rinse the bones with cold water.
2. In a large stockpot over high heat, combine the bones with the cold water. Simmer slowly for 5 hours, uncovered, skimming the surface when necessary. Add the mirepoix and sachet and simmer until flavorful, about 1 hour more. Strain through a fine-mesh sieve or a sieve lined with several layers of cheesecloth into a storage container and cool to 45°F/6°C in a cold water bath. Store in a sealed, labeled container in the refrigerator for up to 7 days, or freeze for up to 3 months.

Nutritional Information per Serving (3 fl oz/90 mL):

56 calories, 2 g fat, 0 g saturated fat, 7 mg cholesterol, 201 mg sodium, 4 g total carbohydrates, 0 g fiber, 2 g sugar, 4 g protein

---

Mushroom Broth

CDVH

Makes 1 gal/3.84 L broth

4 garlic cloves, crushed

2 lb/907 g Spanish onions, cut into eighths

12 oz/340 g carrots, very coarsely chopped

4 celery stalks, very coarsely chopped

2 tbsp/30 mL vegetable oil

1 bay leaf

6 black peppercorns

2 sprigs thyme

¼ bunch flat-leaf parsley stems

1 lb/454 g sliced mushrooms

2 ½ oz/71 g mushroom stems

2 oz/57 g dried mushrooms

1 gal/3.84 L water

1. In a roasting pan, toss the garlic, onions, carrots, and celery with the oil. Spread them out in a single layer and roast in the oven at 350°F/175°C until the vegetables are wilted but not brown, 10 to 15 minutes.
2. Transfer the vegetables to a large pot. Add the bay leaf, peppercorns, thyme, parsley, mushrooms, and water and bring to a boil over high heat. Lower the heat to medium and simmer for 1 hour, skimming often.
3. Strain through a fine-mesh sieve or a sieve lined with several layers of cheesecloth into a storage container and cool to 45°F/6°C in a cold water bath. Store in a sealed, labeled container in the refrigerator for up to 5 days, or freeze for up to 3 months.

Nutritional Information per Serving (8 fl oz/240 mL):

45 calories, .5 g fat, 0 g saturated fat, 0 mg cholesterol, 23 mg sodium, 5 g total carbohydrates, 1 g fiber, 1 g sugar, 1 g protein

---

Vegetable Stock C D V H

Makes 1 gal/3.84 L stock

2 tsp/10 mL olive oil

½ oz/14 g chopped garlic

1 oz/28 g chopped shallots

7 oz/200 g roughly cut carrots

6 oz/170 g wild mushrooms

5 oz/142 g button mushrooms

6 oz/170 g roughly cut celery

3½ oz/99 g roughly cut fennel

3 oz/85 g roughly cut leeks

7 qt/6.72 L cold water

8 fl oz/240 mL dry vermouth

1 Bouquet Garni (see below)

1 tbsp/6 g juniper berries

1 tsp/2 g crushed black peppercorns

2 bay leaves

1. Heat the oil in a large stockpot over medium heat. Add the garlic and shallots and sauté until the shallots are translucent. Add the remaining vegetables and sweat, covered, for 5 minutes.

2. Add all the remaining ingredients and bring to a boil. Reduce the heat and simmer slowly for about 45 minutes, uncovered, skimming the surface when necessary.

3. Strain through a fine-mesh sieve or a sieve lined with several layers of cheesecloth into a storage container and cool to 45°F/6°C in a cold water bath. Store in a sealed, labeled container in the refrigerator for up to 5 days, or freeze for up to 3 months.

CHEF'S NOTE

A variety of vegetables may be used, including parsnips, celeriac, onions, green onions, and green beans. Beets and leafy green vegetables will discolor the stock. Starchy vegetables such as squash, potatoes, and yams will slightly thicken the stock and give it a cloudy appearance.

BOUQUET GARNI

A bouquet garni is a bundle of fresh herbs and aromatic vegetables tied up with a string. The standard combination includes 3 or 4 parsley stems, a sprig of thyme, a bay leaf, a piece of carrot or celery, and 2 or 3 black peppercorns, enclosed inside a piece of leek.

Nutritional Information per Serving (8 fl oz/240 mL):

25 calories, .5 g fat, 0 g saturated fat, 0 mg cholesterol, 25 mg sodium, 4 g total carbohydrates, 0 g fiber, 1 g sugar, 1 g protein

---

Rabbit Stock C D H

Makes 1 gal/3.84 L stock

8 lb/3.62 kg rabbit bones

MIREPOIX

8 oz/227 g roughly cut onions

4 oz/113 g roughly cut carrots

4 oz/113 g roughly cut celery

2 fl oz/60 mL canola oil

6 qt/5.75 L cold water

1 Sachet d'Épices (page 340)

1. Rinse the bones with cold water. Drain thoroughly.
2. Toss the bones and mirepoix vegetables with the canola oil on a sheet pan and roast in the oven at 400°F/205°C until golden brown.
3. In a large stockpot over medium heat, combine the roasted bones and vegetables with the cold water and bring to a boil. Reduce the heat and simmer slowly for 4 hours, uncovered, skimming the surface when necessary. Add the sachet and simmer 1 to 2 hours more, until flavorful.
4. Strain through a fine-mesh sieve or a sieve lined with several layers of cheesecloth into a storage container and cool to 45°F/6°C in a cold water bath. Store in a sealed, labeled container in the refrigerator for up to 7 days, or freeze for up to 3 months.

> **Nutritional Information per Serving (8 fl oz/240 mL):**
>
> 40 calories, 4 g fat, 0 g saturated fat, 0 mg cholesterol, 12 mg sodium, 2 g total carbohydrates, .5 g fiber, 1 g sugar, 0 g protein

Shrimp Stock C D H

Makes 1 gal/3.84 L stock

2 fl oz/60 mL canola oil

2 lb/907 g shrimp shells

1 lb/454 g mirepoix

4 fl oz/120 mL tomato paste

16 fl oz/480 mL white wine

5 qt/4.73 L water

4 bay leaves

5 sprigs thyme

1 tbsp/3 g black peppercorns

1. In a large stockpot, heat the oil over high heat until smoking, then add the shrimp shells. Cook the shrimp shells for 4 to 5 minutes, until they turn dark red.
2. Add the mirepoix and tomato paste and cook 2 to 3 minutes more.
3. Deglaze the pot with the white wine and add the water.
4. Bring to a simmer, add the bay leaves, thyme, and peppercorns, and simmer for 1 hour.
5. Strain through a fine-mesh sieve or a sieve lined with several layers of cheesecloth into a storage container and cool to 45°F/6°C in a cold water bath. Store in a sealed, labeled container in the refrigerator for up to 7 days, or freeze up to 3 months.

> **Nutritional Information per Serving (8 fl oz/240 mL):**
>
> 121 calories, 6 g fat, 1 g saturated fat, 2 mg cholesterol, 261 mg sodium, 13 g total carbohydrates, 2 g fiber, 2 g sugar, 2 g protein

Basic Consommé

Makes 10 portions

CLARIFICATION MIXTURE

1 *oignon brûlé*

1 lb 8 oz/680 g ground lean chicken meat

4 oz/113 g sliced onions

2 oz/57 g sliced celery

2 oz/57 g sliced carrots

6 oz/170 g tomato concassé

4 large egg whites, lightly beaten

1 Sachet d'Épices (page 340)

2½ qt/2.4 L Chicken Stock (page 105), cold

1. Combine the clarification mixture in a stockpot. Add the Sachet d'Épices cold stock to the mixture and blend well. Slowly bring the stock to a simmer, stirring frequently until the clarification begins to form a mass, or raft. Once the raft forms, break a small hole in the raft to help you monitor the cooking speed. Baste the raft occasionally with the stock. Simmer gently until the consommé is clear and flavorful, about 45 minutes.

2. Drain the consommé through a cheesecloth-lined sieve. Do not disturb the raft if possible. Degrease the consommé by skimming the surface with food-quality paper, or cool and remove the solidified fat layer.

CHEF'S NOTES

The smaller the vegetables are cut, the more flavor they release into the stock. The vegetables may be ground with the meat.

This recipe is not appropriate for anyone with an egg allergy.

Nutritional Information per Serving (6 fl oz/180 mL):

200 calories, 8 g fat, 2 g saturated fat, 52 mg cholesterol, 413 mg sodium, 12 g total carbohydrates, 1 g fiber, 6 g sugar, 19 g protein

---

Black Bean Soup

Makes 10 portions

2 tbsp/30 mL olive oil

4 oz/113 g diced onion

2 tbsp/16 g minced garlic

½ tsp/1 g ground cumin

1 lemon, thickly sliced

1 oz/28 g chopped sun-dried tomatoes

1 tsp/3 g seeded and minced jalapeño

1 tsp/2 g dried oregano

½ tsp/2 g kosher salt, or as needed

3 lb/1.36 kg cooked black beans

2 qt/1.92 L Vegetable Stock (page 106)

2 tbsp/30 mL sherry vinegar

1. In a large pot, heat the oil over medium heat. Add the onions and sweat until translucent, 3 to 4 minutes. Add the garlic and cook until fragrant, about 1 minute more. Add the cumin and continue to cook until fragrant, about 1 minute.

2. Add the lemon slices, sun-dried tomatoes, jalapeño, oregano, salt, beans, and vegetable stock. Bring the mixture to a simmer over medium heat. Simmer until a good flavor develops, 15 to 20 minutes.

3. Remove and discard the lemon slices. Using a handheld blender, food processor, or blender, partially purée 24 fl oz/720 mL of the soup; it should be thick and chunky. Return it to the pot, bring back to a simmer, and cook for 10 minutes more.

4. Stir in the sherry vinegar to finish the soup.

Nutritional Information per Serving (6 fl oz/180 mL):

246 calories, 4 g fat, 1 g saturated fat, 0 mg cholesterol, 424 mg sodium, 42 g total carbohydrates, 12 g fiber, 3 g sugar, 12 g protein

---

Hlelem C D V H

Makes 10 portions

2 tbsp/30 mL olive oil

4 tsp/12 g minced garlic

1 oz/28 g celery, diced

1½ oz/43 g onions, minced

5 oz/142 g canned lima beans, drained, juices reserved

5 oz/142 g canned chickpeas, drained, juices reserved

1 qt/960 mL Vegetable Stock (page 106)

3 fl oz/90 mL tomato paste

9 oz/255 g Swiss chard leaves, stems removed and cut into 1-in/2.5-cm pieces, leaves shredded

3¾ oz/106 g capellini, broken into bite-size pieces

1½ tsp/7 mL red curry paste

1 tsp/3 g kosher salt

½ tsp/1 g freshly ground black pepper

½ oz/14 g chopped flat-leaf parsley

1. Heat the oil in a soup pot over medium heat. Add the garlic, celery, and onion. Cook, stirring occasionally, until the onion is translucent, 5 to 7 minutes.

2. Combine 4 fl oz/118 mL of the reserved lima bean liquid with 4 fl oz/120 mL of the reserved chickpea liquid. Add the stock, reserved bean liquids, and the tomato paste to the pot. Mix together until well blended, and simmer for 10 minutes.

3. Approximately 10 minutes before serving, add the lima beans and chickpeas, Swiss chard, and pasta. Simmer until the pasta and chard stems are tender, about 10 minutes.

4. Add the red curry paste and stir until blended. Season with the salt and pepper. Garnish with the parsley.

Nutritional Information per Serving (6 fl oz/180 mL):

152 calories, 5 g fat, 1 g saturated fat, 3 mg cholesterol, 406 mg sodium, 21 g total carbohydrates, 3 g fiber, 4 g sugar, 7 g protein

Mushroom-Barley Soup

C D H

Makes 10 portions

1 tbsp/15 mL vegetable oil

8 oz/227 g finely diced onions

4 oz/113 g finely diced carrots

2 oz/57 g finely diced celery stalk

3 oz/85 g finely diced parsnips (optional)

10 oz/284 g sliced white mushrooms

2 qt/1.92 L Chicken Stock (page 105)

6 oz/170 g pearl barley

½ tsp/2 g kosher salt

½ tsp/1 g freshly ground black pepper

1 tbsp/3 g chopped flat-leaf parsley

2 tbsp/30 mL dry sherry or sherry wine vinegar (optional)

1. Heat the oil in a soup pot over medium heat. Add the onions and cook, stirring frequently, until golden brown, about 10 minutes.

2. Add the carrots, celery, parsnips, if using, and mushrooms. Stir well to combine with the onion. Cover and cook over low heat for 3 to 4 minutes.

3. Remove the cover and add the stock and barley. Bring to a simmer and cook until the barley is tender, about 30 minutes.

4. Season with the salt and pepper. Stir in the parsley. Stir in the sherry, if using, just before serving. Serve in heated bowls.

CHEF'S NOTE

Substitute vegetable stock for the chicken stock to make celiac-friendly.

Nutritional Information per Serving (6 fl oz/180 mL):

112 calories, 4 g fat, 1 g saturated fat, 6 mg cholesterol, 407 mg sodium, 13 g total carbohydrates, 1 g fiber, 6 g sugar, 6 g protein

Black Bean and Poblano Soup C D V H

Makes 10 portions

1 fl oz/30 mL olive oil

6 oz/170 g small-dice onions

2 oz/57 g small-dice celery

3 garlic cloves, minced

6 oz/170 g poblano chiles, roasted, peeled, and cut into small dice

½ oz/14 g chili powder

Pinch ground cloves

1½ tsp/3 g ground cumin

1½ tsp/3 g paprika

½ tsp/1 g red pepper flakes

1 lb/454 g dried black beans, soaked

2½ qt/2.4 L Vegetable Stock (page 106)

1 tsp/3 g kosher salt

10 tsp/10 g cilantro leaves

1. In a large stockpot, heat the oil over medium heat. Add the onions and celery and sweat until the onions are translucent and the vegetables begin to soften, 4 to 5 minutes.

2. Add the garlic and cook until fragrant, about 1 minute more. Stir in the poblano chiles, chili powder, cloves, cumin, paprika, and red pepper flakes. Continue to cook, stirring occasionally, until the spices are fragrant, about 2 minutes.

3. Add the soaked beans and the vegetable stock, stirring well to combine, and bring the mixture to a simmer over medium-low heat. Cover and simmer until the beans are soft and the soup has developed a good flavor, 1 to 1½ hours. Season with the salt.

4. If desired, purée the soup to a smooth consistency. Garnish the finished, portioned soup with about 1 tsp/1 g of the cilantro just before serving.

Nutritional Information per Serving (6 fl oz/180 mL):

216 calories, 4 g fat, 0 g saturated fat, 0 mg cholesterol, 684 mg sodium, 37 g total carbohydrates, 8 g fiber, 2 g sugar, 10 g protein

Carrot Consommé with Lemongrass, Ginger, Spicy Asian Grilled Shrimp, and Bean Threads C D H

Makes 10 portions

2 qt/1.92 L carrot juice

5 large egg whites

1 lb/454 g julienned carrots

½ lemongrass stalk

1 tbsp/6 g peeled and minced ginger

5 kaffir lime leaves, chopped

1 tsp/3 g kosher salt

½ tsp/2 g freshly ground white pepper

GARNISH

8½ oz/240 g bean thread noodles, cooked and shocked

3 oz/85 g carrot curls

1 lb 4 oz/567 g Spicy Asian Grilled Shrimp (page 199), halved

2 tbsp/6 g Thai basil chiffonade

2 tbsp/6 g mint chiffonade

3 tbsp/9 g chopped cilantro

1 tbsp/6 g white sesame seeds

1 tbsp/6 g black sesame seeds

1. In a large pot, mix the carrot juice, egg whites, carrots, lemongrass, ginger, and lime leaves to combine.

2. Bring the mixture to a simmer over medium-low heat, stirring frequently until a raft forms. Break a small hole in the raft to help monitor the cooking speed. Baste the raft occasionally with the carrot juice. Simmer until the soup is clear, about 20 minutes.

3. Strain the consommé through a cheesecloth-lined fine-mesh sieve. Season with the salt and white pepper.

4. To serve, place ¾ oz/21 g of the noodles into an individual soup bowl, topped with ⅓ oz/8 g of the carrot curls and 2 oz/57 g of the shrimp. Ladle 6 fl oz/180 mL of the hot consommé into the bowl and garnish with ½ tsp/1 g of each herb and ¼ tsp/1 g of the sesame seeds.

CHEF'S NOTES

Strips of lime zest may be substituted for the lime leaves, and sweet basil for the Thai basil. Rice sticks or capellini may be used instead of the bean threads.

If made without the shrimp, this recipe is vegetarian-friendly.

Nutritional Information per Serving (6 fl oz/180 mL, 2 oz/57 g grilled shrimp, ¾ oz/ 21 g noodles):

152 calories, 1 g fat, 1 g saturated fat, 26 mg cholesterol, 177 mg sodium, 31 g total carbohydrates, 1 g fiber, 0 g sugar, 4 g protein

Corn Velvet Soup with Crabmeat D H

Makes 10 portions

7 oz/199 g fresh corn kernels (about 2 ears corn)

1 oz/28 g butter

4½ oz/128 g green onions, split lengthwise and thinly sliced

4½ oz/128 g diced onions

1½ oz/43 g peeled and minced ginger

½ oz/14 g seeded and minced jalapeños

2 sprigs thyme

2 qt/1.92 L Chicken Stock (page 105)

12 fl oz/360 mL evaporated skim milk

2 fl oz/60 mL reduced-sodium soy sauce

½ tsp/2 g kosher salt

Freshly ground black pepper, as needed

6 oz/170 g lump crabmeat

10 tsp/50 mL Red Pepper Coulis (page 342)

1. Cut the corn kernels from the cob; scrape the milk from the corn cobs and reserve.

2. In a large soup pot over low heat, melt the butter. Add the green onions, onions, ginger, and jalapeños and sweat until tender, 1 to 2 minutes.

3. Add the corn kernels and sweat for 2 minutes. Add the thyme and stock and bring the soup to a simmer. Simmer until the vegetables are tender, about 10 minutes.

4. Using a food processor, blender, or immersion blender, purée the soup until smooth. Stir in the evaporated skim milk and the soy sauce. Season with the salt and pepper.

5. If the soup is too thick, adjust the consistency with more stock. The soup is ready to serve now, or it may be cooled and stored until ready to serve.

6. To serve, ladle 6 fl oz/180 mL of the soup into an individual bowl and garnish with ⅔ oz/17 g of the crabmeat and 1 tsp/5 mL of the red pepper coulis just before serving.

CHEF'S NOTE

Substitute tamari for the soy sauce to make celiac-friendly.

Nutritional Information per Serving (6 fl oz/180 mL, ⅔ oz/17 g crabmeat, 1 tsp/5 mL pepper coulis):

122 calories, 5 g fat, 1 g saturated fat, 22 mg cholesterol, 392 mg sodium, 14 g total carbohydrates, 2 g fiber, 7 g sugar, 9 g protein

Curried Apple-Squash Soup C D H

Makes 10 portions

1 oz/28 g minced garlic

9½ oz/269 g diced celery

11 oz/312 g diced onions

5½ oz/156 g diced leeks

3 qt/2.88 L Chicken Stock (page 105)

2 tbsp/12 g curry powder

½ tsp/1 g freshly grated nutmeg

1 tbsp/6 g ground cinnamon

2 lbs 4 oz/1.02 kg chopped butternut squash

1 lb 6 oz/624 g diced apples

½ tsp/1 g kosher salt

12 fl oz/360 mL buttermilk

½ oz/14 g chopped chives

1. In a large pot over medium heat, sweat the garlic, celery, onions, and leeks in a small amount of the stock until the onions are translucent, 4 to 5 minutes.

2. Add the remaining stock, curry, nutmeg, and cinnamon and bring to a boil. Add the squash and simmer until tender, about 8 minutes. Add 1 lb/454 g apples and continue to simmer until all the ingredients are tender, about 5 minutes more.

3. Purée the soup using a food mill or immersion blender. Season with salt and stir in the buttermilk.

4. Chill the soup for at least 4 and up to 24 hours before serving. To serve, ladle 6 fl oz/180 mL of the cold soup into a chilled bowl or cup. Garnish each portion with ⅔ oz/19 g of the remaining apples and 1 tsp/1 g of the chives.

CHEF'S NOTE

Substitute vegetable stock for the chicken stock to make vegetarian-friendly.

Nutritional Information per Serving (6 fl oz/180 mL soup, ⅔ oz/19 g apples, 1 tsp/1 g chives):

138 calories, 4 g fat, 4 g saturated fat, 5 mg cholesterol, 519 mg sodium, 27 g total carbohydrates, 1 g fiber, 2 g sugar, 4 g protein

Ham Bone and Collard Greens Soup C D H

Makes 10 portions

1 smoked ham hock

3 qt/2.88 L Chicken Stock (page 105)

1 lb 4 oz/567 g collard greens

1 tbsp/15 mL vegetable oil

2 oz/57 g minced salt pork

7 oz/199 g minced onion

1¾ oz/50 g minced celery

2¼ oz/64 g all-purpose flour

SACHET

5 black peppercorns

4 sprigs flat-leaf parsley

1 sprig thyme

4 fl oz/120 mL heavy cream

1 tbsp/15 mL malt vinegar, or as needed

Tabasco sauce, as needed

1. Place the ham hock and stock in a pot large enough to accommodate both. Bring to a simmer over medium heat and cook, partially covered, for 1½ hours. Remove the ham hock from the stock and allow both the hock and the stock to cool slightly.

2. Bring a large pot of salted water to a boil. Cut the tough ribs and stems away from the collard greens and discard. Plunge the greens into the boiling water and cook for 10 minutes. Drain and cool slightly. Chop the greens coarsely and set aside.

3. Heat the oil in a soup pot over medium heat. Add the salt pork and cook until crisp, 3 to 5 minutes. Add the onion and celery and cook, stirring occasionally, until tender, about 5 minutes.

4. Add the flour and cook, stirring frequently, for 5 minutes. Gradually add the stock, whisking constantly to work out any lumps of flour, and bring to a simmer. Add the collard greens, ham hock, and sachet and simmer for 1 hour.

5. Remove and discard the sachet. Remove the ham hock and cool slightly. Trim away the skin and fat and discard. Dice the lean meat and return it to the soup.

6. Add the cream and season as needed with the vinegar and Tabasco. Serve in heated bowls.

Nutritional Information per Serving (6 fl oz/180 mL):

192 calories, 14 g fat, 5 g saturated fat, 26 mg cholesterol, 298 mg sodium, 15 g total carbohydrates, 2 g fiber, 2 g sugar, 11 g protein

Louisiana Chicken and Shrimp Gumbo D H

Makes 10 portions

2½ oz/71 g bread flour

1 oz/28 g diced andouille sausage

2½ oz/71 g chopped chicken

2½ oz/71 g diced green bell peppers

2½ oz/71 g diced celery

2 tbsp/11 g seeded and diced jalapeños

1 oz/28 g thinly sliced green onions

1 tsp/3 g minced garlic

1½ qt/1.41 L Chicken Stock (page 105)

2½ oz/71 g brown rice

1¼ tsp/2 g filé powder

1 tsp/1 g chopped oregano

1 bay leaf

1 tsp/2 g dried thyme

1 tsp/1 g chopped basil

1 tsp/2 g freshly ground black pepper

½ tsp/1 g onion powder

1 tsp/3 g kosher salt

7½ oz/213 g okra

3½ oz/99 g tomato concassé

1¾ oz/50 g chopped shrimp

1. Toast the flour in the oven at 325°F/165°C until it turns dark brown.

2. Render the sausage in a large soup pot over medium-high heat. Add the chicken and sauté until browned. Add the bell peppers, celery, jalapeños, green onions, and garlic and sauté until aromatic. Add the stock and bring to a boil. Add the rice, filé powder, oregano, bay leaf, thyme, basil, black pepper, onion powder, and salt and simmer until the rice is almost cooked, about 30 minutes. Add the okra and tomato concassé.

3. Place the browned flour in a large bowl. Slowly whisk some of the soup liquid into the flour until smooth. Add the mixture to the pot and simmer until thickened, about 10 minutes. Add the shrimp and simmer until cooked through, about 5 minutes. Remove and discard the bay leaf.

4. The soup is ready to serve now, or it may be properly cooled and stored. To serve, ladle 6 oz/180 mL of the hot soup into a heated bowl.

Nutritional Information per Serving (6 fl oz/180 mL):

140 calories, 3 g fat, 1 g saturated fat, 20 mg cholesterol, 440 mg sodium, 18 g total carbohydrates, 1 g fiber, 2 g sugar, 9 g protein

---

Fire-Roasted Gazpacho `D` `V` `H`

Makes 10 portions

2 lb/907 g plum tomatoes

42 fl oz/1.26 L fresh tomato juice

1 tbsp/4 g toasted ground cumin seeds

1 tsp/1 g toasted chili powder

7½ oz/212 g small-dice cucumbers

7½ oz/212 g corn kernels, fresh or frozen

5 oz/142 g small-dice green bell peppers

3 fl oz/90 mL lime juice

½ oz/14 g minced cilantro

1 fl oz/30 mL low-sodium soy sauce

½ oz/14 g minced basil

2½ tsp/3 g toasted ground cumin

1 tsp/1 g toasted chili powder

¼ oz/7 g minced garlic

¼ oz/7 g seeded and minced serrano or jalapeño

1 tsp/5 mL Tabasco sauce

½ tsp/3.5 g sea salt

¼ tsp/.5 g freshly ground black pepper

½ oz/14 g flat-leaf parsley leaves, cut into chiffonade

1. Grill or char the whole plum tomatoes until the skins are blistered and blackened, 10 to 15 minutes. Roughly chop.

2. Place the tomatoes and juice in blender and blend until smooth.

3. Combine all the remaining ingredients except for the parsley in a large bowl.

4. Add the tomato juice and tomato purée to the bowl and mix well.

5. Allow the gazpacho to chill for several hours before serving.

6. Serve chilled, garnished with the parsley chiffonade.

CHEF'S NOTE

Substitute tamari for the soy sauce to make celiac-friendly.

Nutritional Information per Serving (6 fl oz/180 mL):

76 calories, 1 g fat, 0 g saturated fat, 0 mg cholesterol, 214 mg sodium, 16 g total carbohydrates, 3 g fiber, 8 g sugar, 3 g protein

Manhattan Clam Chowder CDH

Makes 10 portions

1 tbsp/15 mL canola oil

2 leeks, diced

1 onion, diced

1 carrot, diced

1 celery stalk, diced

1 red bell pepper, seeds and ribs removed, diced

2 garlic cloves, minced

2 canned plum tomatoes, coarsely chopped

2 white or yellow potatoes, peeled and diced

24 fl oz/720 mL clam juice

8 fl oz/240 mL tomato juice

1 bay leaf

Pinch dried thyme leaves

3 dozen chowder clams, shucked, chopped, and juices reserved

1 tsp/3 g kosher salt, or as needed

½ tsp/1 g freshly ground black pepper, or as needed

Tabasco sauce, as needed

1. Heat the oil in a large soup pot over medium-high heat. Add the leeks, onion, carrot, celery, bell pepper, and garlic. Cover the pot and cook over medium-low heat, stirring occasionally, until the vegetables are soft and translucent, 8 to 10 minutes.

2. Add the tomatoes, potatoes, clam juice, tomato juice, bay leaf, and thyme. Bring to a simmer and cook until the potatoes are tender, about 15 minutes.

3. Add the clams with their juices and simmer until the clams are cooked, 1 to 2 minutes more. Using a shallow, flat spoon, remove any surface fat and discard. Remove and discard the bay leaf. Season with the salt, black pepper, and Tabasco.

Nutritional Information per Serving (9 fl oz/270 mL):

90 calories, 2 g fat, 0 g saturated fat, 20 mg cholesterol, 460 mg sodium, 11 g total carbohydrates, 2 g fiber, 4 g sugar, 9 g protein

Summer-Style Lentil Soup C D V H

Makes 10 portions

1 oz/28 g olive oil

3 oz/85 g diced onions

¼ oz/7 g minced garlic

2½ oz/71 g diced leeks

2 oz/57 g sliced carrots

1¾ oz/50 g sliced celery

1 oz/28 g tomato paste

2 qt/1.92 L Vegetable Stock (pages 106)

10 oz/284 g French lentils

1 Sachet d'Épices (page 340)

3 strips lemon peel

1 tbsp/15 mL white wine

1 tbsp/15 mL sherry vinegar

1 tsp/3 g kosher salt

¼ tsp/.5 g freshly ground black pepper

1 tbsp/3 g chopped chives

1 tbsp/3 g chopped flat-leaf parsley

1. Heat the oil in a soup pot over medium heat. Add the onions and garlic and sweat until translucent.

2. Add the leeks, carrots, and celery, cover, and sweat until the vegetables are tender. Add the tomato paste and sauté until browned. Add the stock, lentils, sachet, and lemon peel strips and simmer until the lentils are tender, about 20 minutes.

3. Remove and discard the sachet and lemon peel strips. Add the wine, vinegar, salt, and pepper. The soup is ready to serve now, or it may be properly cooled and stored.

4. Heat the soup (by batch or by portion) just before serving. Garnish each portion of soup with chives and parsley.

Nutritional Information per Serving (6 fl oz/180 mL):

160 calories, 3 g fat, 0 g saturated fat, 0 mg cholesterol, 560 mg sodium, 24 g total carbohydrates, 4 g fiber, 6 g sugar, 4 g protein

---

Mussel Soup C D H

Makes 10 portions

4 fl oz/120 mL white wine

4 oz/113 g minced onions

1 bay leaf

2 thyme sprigs (optional)

8 fl oz/240 mL water, or as needed

3 lb/1.36 kg mussels, beards removed, scrubbed well under cold running water

2 tbsp/30 mL g olive oil

6 oz/170 g finely diced leeks, white and light green parts only

3 oz/85 finely diced celery stalk

½ oz/14 g minced garlic

1 lb/454 g plum tomatoes, drained, seeded, and chopped, juices reserved

1 oz/28 g basil chiffonade

1 tsp/3 g kosher salt, or as needed

Pinch freshly ground black pepper, or as needed

½ tsp/1 g finely grated lemon zest

1 oz/28 g chopped flat-leaf parsley

1. In a pot large enough to accommodate the mussels, combine the wine, 2 oz/57 g of the onion, bay leaf, thyme sprigs, if using, and enough of the water to raise the liquid level to about 1 in/2.5 cm. Bring to a boil over high heat. Add the mussels, cover, and steam until the mussels open, about 5 minutes. Using a slotted spoon, transfer the mussels to a bowl and allow them to cool slightly. Discard any mussels that do not open.

2. Remove the mussels from their shells and reserve the mussel meat. Discard the shells. Strain the cooking liquid, including the liquid released by shucked mussels, through a coffee filter and set aside.

3. Heat the oil in a soup pot over medium heat and add the remaining onion, leek, celery, and garlic. Cover the pot, reduce the heat to medium-low, and cook until the vegetables are translucent, 5 to 7 minutes.

4. Combine the mussel cooking liquid with the reserved tomato juice. Add enough water to bring the amount of liquid to 1 qt/960 mL. Add this mixture along with the tomatoes to the soup pot. Bring to a simmer and cook, partially covered, for 10 to 12 minutes.

5. Add the mussels and half of the basil to the soup pot and cover the pot. Simmer until the mussels are heated through, about 2 minutes.

6. Season with the salt, pepper, and lemon zest. Garnish with the remaining basil and parsley chiffonade.

Nutritional Information per Serving (6 fl oz/180 mL):

153 calories, 5 g fat, 1 g saturated fat, 28 mg cholesterol, 422 mg sodium, 11 g total carbohydrates, 2 g fiber, 3 g sugar, 13 g protein

---

New England Vegetable Chowder

Makes 10 portions

1 oz/28 g grapeseed oil

2 oz/57 g minced smoked tempeh

32 fl oz/960 mL Vegetable Stock (page 106)

2 oz/57 g dried seaweed such as dulse or kombu, roughly chopped

4 oz/113 g diced onions

¼ oz/7 g minced garlic

3 tbsp/30 g all-purpose flour

1 bay leaf

½ tsp/1 g chopped thyme leaves

12 oz/340 g peeled and diced potatoes

4 oz/113 g fresh corn kernels

4 oz/113 g medium-dice zucchini

20 fl oz/600 mL almond milk or rice milk

4 fl oz/120 mL dry sherry, or as needed

½ tsp/1 g kosher salt, or as needed

Pinch freshly ground black pepper, or as needed

½ tsp/3 mL Tabasco sauce, or as needed

½ tsp/3 mL Worcestershire sauce, or as needed

1 oz/28 g flat-leaf parsley chiffonade

2 oz/57 g oyster crackers, or as needed for garnish

1. Place a 4-qt soup pot over medium heat, add the oil and minced tempeh, and cook slowly until the tempeh is lightly crisped, about 8 minutes.

2. In a separate pot, bring the vegetable stock to a gentle simmer. Add the seaweed and steep until tender and rehydrated. Strain the seaweed from the stock; reserve both.

3. Add the onions and garlic to the soup pot and cook, stirring occasionally, until the onion is translucent, 5 to 7 minutes.

4. Add the flour and cook over low heat, stirring with a wooden spoon, for 2 to 3 minutes.

5. Whisk in the reserved vegetable-seaweed stock, bring to a simmer, and cook for 5 minutes, stirring occasionally. The liquid should be the consistency of heavy cream. If it is too thick, add more stock to adjust the consistency. Add the bay leaf and thyme.

6. Add the potatoes and simmer until nearly tender, about 10 minutes. Add the corn and zucchini and cook for 5 minutes more.

7. Meanwhile, place the chopped seaweed and almond milk in a saucepan over low heat and simmer together until hot.

8. When the potatoes are tender, add the seaweed and almond milk to the soup. Simmer for 1 to 2 minutes.

9. Stir in the sherry. Season with the salt, pepper, Tabasco, Worcestershire sauce, and parsley. Serve in bowls with the crackers on the side.

Nutritional Information per Serving (6 fl oz/180 mL):

164 calories, 5 g fat, 1 g saturated fat, 0 mg cholesterol, 461 mg sodium, 27 g total carbohydrates, 3 g fiber, 4 g sugar, 4 g protein

Vegetable Chili C D V H

Makes 10 portions

4 oz/113 g medium-dice sun-dried tomatoes

2 dried Anaheim chiles, toasted, seeded, and cut into medium dice

12 fl oz/360 mL tomato purée

24 fl oz/720 mL Vegetable Stock (page 106)

2 oz/57 g coarsely chopped cilantro

1 fl oz/30 mL honey

1½ fl oz/45 mL red wine vinegar

1 tsp /3 g ground cumin

1 tsp/3 g chili powder

½ oz/14 g minced garlic

1 fl oz/30 mL grapeseed oil

12 oz/340 g small-dice onions

8 oz/227 g cooked black beans

8 oz/227 g cooked pinto beans

8 oz/227 g cooked hominy

1 tsp/3 g kosher salt

¼ tsp/.5 g freshly ground black pepper

½ oz/14 g cilantro chiffonade

1. In a large soup pot, combine the sun-dried tomatoes, chiles, tomato purée, stock, cilantro, honey, vinegar, cumin, chili powder, and garlic. Bring to a simmer over medium heat and cook until a good flavor develops, about 45 minutes.

2. Let the mixture cool slightly and then purée in a food processor or blender until smooth. Set aside.

3. In a large soup pot, heat the oil over medium heat. Add the onions and sauté until transparent, 4 to 5 minutes. Add the black beans, pinto beans, and hominy. Stir in the puréed tomato mixture, and bring the chili to a simmer. Season with the salt and pepper.

4. Serve immediately, garnished with cilantro chiffonade.

Nutritional Information per Serving (6 fl oz/180 mL):

234 calories, 4 g fat, 0 g saturated fat, 0 mg cholesterol, 421 mg sodium, 40 g total carbohydrates, 9 g fiber, 15 g sugar, 10 g protein

---

Potage au Pistou (Vegetable Soup with Garlic and Basil) D V H

Makes 10 portions

PISTOU

2 oz/57 g chopped basil leaves

2 oz/57 g grated Parmesan cheese

2 tbsp/10 g toasted pine nuts

2 garlic cloves, chopped

2½ fl oz/75 mL olive oil

SOUP

6 oz/170 g dried navy beans, soaked overnight in 24 fl oz/720 mL of water

1 qt/960 mL water

2 tbsp/30 mL olive oil

6 oz/170 g diced carrots

8 oz/227 g diced leeks, white and light green parts only

6 oz/170 g diced onions

2½ qt/2.36 L Vegetable Stock (page 106), heated

Pinch saffron threads (optional)

6 oz/170 g green beans, cut into 1-in/2.5-cm length

6 oz/170 g peeled and diced yellow or white potatoes

5 oz/142 g medium-dice zucchini

2 oz/57 g vermicelli or capellini, broken into 2-in/5-cm lengths

4 oz/113 g tomatoes, peeled, seeded, and diced

1 tsp/3 g kosher salt, or as needed

Pinch freshly ground black pepper, or as needed

1. To make the pistou, purée the basil, Parmesan, pine nuts, and garlic to a fine paste in a food processor or blender.

2. With the machine running, add the oil in a thin stream. Scrape down the sides of the bowl or blender jar as necessary. Purée until the oil is completely incorporated.

3. To make the soup, drain the beans and place in a large saucepan. Add the water and bring to a simmer over medium heat. Cook until tender, about 1 hour, adding more water, if necessary, to keep the beans covered.

4. Heat the oil in a soup pot over medium heat. Add the carrots, leeks, and onion. Cook until the onion is translucent, about 10 minutes. Add the stock and the saffron, if using. Bring to a simmer, and cook for 10 minutes.

5. Add the green beans, potato, zucchini, and vermicelli. Continue to simmer for 8 to 10 minutes, or until all the vegetables and the pasta are just tender to the bite.

6. Drain the beans of their cooking liquid and add them to the soup along with the tomatoes. Season as needed with the salt and pepper and continue to simmer for 1 minute more.

7. Add the pistou, as desired, just before serving. Serve in heated bowls.

CHEF'S NOTE

Use gluten-free pasta to make this recipe celiac-friendly.

Nutritional Information per Serving (6 fl oz/180 mL, ¼ fl oz/7.5 mL pistou):

230 calories, 13 g fat, 3 g saturated fat, 5 mg cholesterol, 930 mg sodium, 21 g total carbohydrates, 4 g fiber, 4 g sugar, 9 g protein

Potage Solferino C D H

Makes 10 portions

1 oz/28 g unsalted butter

2 oz/57 g bacon, minced

4 oz/113 sliced carrots

4 oz/113 g diced celery

8 oz/227 g sliced leeks, white and green parts only

12 oz/340 g diced onions

8 oz/227 g peeled and diced yellow turnips

1 lb/454 g shredded cabbage

1 qt/960 mL Chicken Stock or Vegetable Stock (page 105 or 106)

1 lb/454 g peeled and diced yellow or white potatoes

2 oz/57 g finely diced carrot

3 oz/85 g sliced green beans

4 oz/113 g peeled, seeded, and chopped tomatoes

1 tbsp/3 g chopped flat-leaf parsley

1 tsp/3 g kosher salt

Pinch freshly ground black pepper

SACHET

1 bay leaf

1 tsp/1 g chopped oregano

4 to 5 black peppercorns

1 garlic clove

1 tsp/1 g chopped marjoram

1. Melt the butter in a soup pot over medium heat. Add the bacon and cook until the bacon is crisp and brown, 6 to 7 minutes.

2. Add the carrots, celery, leeks, onions, turnips, and cabbage; stir to coat evenly. Cover and sweat until the onion is tender and translucent, 4 to 5 minutes.

3. Add the stock, potatoes, and sachet and bring to a simmer and cook until the vegetables are tender, 25 to 30 minutes.

4. Meanwhile, boil or steam the diced carrot and sliced green beans separately until just tender. Set aside to cool.

5. Remove the sachet and discard. Strain the soup through a sieve; reserve the liquid. Purée the solids and return them to the pot. Add enough of the reserved liquid to achieve a thick consistency.

6. Add the diced carrot, green beans, tomato, and parsley. Season with the salt and pepper. Simmer the soup until heated through, about 5 minutes. Serve in heated bowls.

Nutritional Information per Serving (6 fl oz/180 mL):

140 calories, 5 g fat, 2 g saturated fat, 10 mg cholesterol, 570 mg sodium, 21 g total carbohydrates, 4 g fiber, 6 g sugar, 5 g protein

---

Purée of Split Pea Soup C D H

Makes 10 portions

2 oz/57 g minced bacon

8 oz/227 g diced onions

4 oz/113 g diced carrots

4 oz/113 g diced celery

2 oz/57 g diced leeks, white and light green parts only

2 qt/1.92 L Chicken Stock (page 105)

8 oz/227 g peeled and diced yellow or white potatoes

8 oz/227 g green or yellow split peas, or lentils

1 smoked ham hock

SACHET

1 bay leaf

1 clove

1 garlic clove

4 to 5 black peppercorns

Pinch freshly ground black pepper, or as needed

1. Cook the bacon in a soup pot over medium-high heat until crisped and browned. Remove the bacon with a slotted spoon, transfer to paper towels to drain, and set aside. Pour off all but 3 tbsp/45 mL of the bacon fat in the pot.

2. Add the onion, carrot, celery, and leek to the pot and stir to evenly coat with the reserved fat. Cover the pot and sweat the vegetables over medium-low heat, stirring occasionally, until the onion is tender and translucent, 6 to 8 minutes. Do not brown the vegetables.

3. Add the stock, potatoes, split peas, and ham hock. Bring to a simmer and cook over medium heat, 20 minutes, stirring occasionally. Add the sachet and simmer until the split peas are soft, about 30 minutes, skimming away any scum that rises to the surface during cooking.

4. Remove the sachet from the pot and discard. Remove the ham hock and set aside to cool. When cool enough to handle, cut the hock meat off the bone and dice it.

5. Strain the soup through a sieve; reserve the liquid. Purée the solids and return them to the pot. Add enough of the reserved liquid to achieve a thick consistency. Blend well. Stir in the hock meat and bacon. Season the finished soup with pepper. Serve in heated bowls.

> **Nutritional Information per Serving (6 fl oz/180 mL):**
>
> 208 calories, 5 g fat, 2 g saturated fat, 10 mg cholesterol, 393 mg sodium, 29 g total carbohydrates, 7 g fiber, 7 g sugar, 10 g protein

Tomato and Escarole Soup [C] [D] [V] [H]

Makes 10 portions

3 tbsp/45 mL extra-virgin olive oil

6 oz/170 g large-dice onions

2 tbsp/20 g minced shallots

2 tsp/6 g minced garlic

3 lb/1.36 kg coarsely chopped escarole, stemmed

20 fl oz/600 mL Vegetable Stock (page 106)

1 lb/454 g chopped tomatoes, peeled and seeded

6 fl oz/180 mL Pomodoro Sauce (page 336)

1 tsp/3 g kosher salt, or as needed

Pinch freshly ground black pepper, or as needed

1. Heat the oil in a soup pot over medium-high heat. Add the onions, shallots, and garlic and stir to coat with the oil. Sauté, stirring frequently, until the onions are softened and translucent, about 5 minutes.

2. Add the escarole and cook, stirring frequently, until it wilts, about 5 minutes.

3. Add the stock, chopped tomatoes, and tomato sauce and bring the soup to a boil, skimming the surface to remove any foam. Reduce the heat to low and simmer until the escarole is very tender and all of the ingredients are very hot, about 10 minutes.

4. Season with the salt and pepper. Serve in heated bowls or cups.

Nutritional Information per Serving (6 fl oz/180 mL):

87 calories, 5 g fat, 1 g saturated fat, 0 mg cholesterol, 512 mg sodium, 10 g total carbohydrates, 5 g fiber, 4 g sugar, 3 g protein

---

Tortilla Soup C D H

Makes 10 portions

6 corn tortillas

2 tsp/10 mL vegetable oil

8 oz/227 g finely grated or puréed onions

½ oz/14 g minced garlic

1 tbsp/9 g mild chili powder

1½ tsp/3 g ground cumin

8 oz/227 g tomato purée

1 tbsp/3 g chopped cilantro leaves

2 qt/1.92 L Chicken Stock (page 105)

1 bay leaf

1 lb 4 oz/567 g shredded cooked chicken breast

2½ oz/71 g grated Chihuahua cheese

10 oz/284 g diced avocado

1. Cut the tortillas into matchsticks. Place them in an even layer on a sheet pan and toast them in the oven at 300°F/148°C for about 15 minutes. Or, toast the strips by sautéing them in a dry skillet over medium heat, tossing frequently. Reserve about 1½ oz/43 g of the strips for a garnish. Crush the remainder in a food processor or blender.

2. Heat the oil in a soup pot over medium heat. Add the onion and garlic and cook, stirring frequently, until they release a sweet aroma, 5 to 6 minutes. Add chili powder and cumin and continue to cook for 1 minute more to allow the aromas to develop. Add the tomato purée and continue to cook for another 3 minutes. Add the cilantro, and cook for 2 minutes more.

3. Add the stock, crushed tortillas, and bay leaf and bring the soup to a simmer, stirring well. Continue to simmer for 25 to 30 minutes. Remove and discard the bay leaf.

4. Using an immersion blender, purée the soup, then strain the soup through a sieve, and serve immediately in heated bowls, garnished with 2 oz/57 g of the shredded chicken, ¼ oz/7 g of the Chihuahua, 1 tbsp/4 g of the reserved tortilla strips, and 1 oz/28 g of the diced avocado.

Nutritional Information per Serving (6 fl oz/180 mL soup, 2 oz/57 g chicken, ¼ oz/7 g cheese, 1 tbsp/4 g tortilla strips, and 1 oz/28 g avocado):

211 calories, 10 g fat, 2 g saturated fat, 38 mg cholesterol, 731 mg sodium, 18 g total carbohydrates, 5 g fiber, 3 g sugar, 17 g protein

---

Udon Noodle Pot D H

Makes 10 portions

DASHI

3 qt/2.88 L cold water

Two 3-inch/7.5-cm pieces dried kombu seaweed

4 oz/113 g bonito flakes

1 lb 2 oz/851 g fresh udon noodles

2 tbsp/30 mL peanut or canola oil

2¾ qt/2.60 L dashi

30 littleneck clams

1 lb 4 oz/567 g boneless, skinless chicken thighs, cut into bite-size pieces

1 lb 4 oz/567 g small shrimp (31–36 count), peeled and deveined

10 oz/284 g sliced shiitake mushroom caps

7½ oz/213 g finely shredded napa cabbage

7½ oz/213 g finely shredded spinach

5 oz/142 g thinly sliced carrots

2½ oz/71g snow peas, trimmed

2½ fl oz/75 mL soy sauce

1 tbsp/15 mL mirin

4 green onions, thinly sliced on the bias

1. To make the dashi, combine the water, kombu, and bonito flakes in a large saucepan. Bring the water to a simmer over medium-high heat. Continue to simmer until the broth is very flavorful, 20 to 25 minutes. Strain the dashi and use as directed, or it can be stored in a clean, covered container in the refrigerator for up to 1 week.

2. Bring a large pot of salted water to a boil. Cook the noodles until just tender, 2 to 3 minutes. Drain the noodles and rinse under cold water. Drain the noodles again, toss with the oil, and reserve.

3. Bring the dashi to a simmer in a soup pot over medium heat. Add the clams, chicken, shrimp, and mushrooms to the pot and ladle the simmering dashi over the top. Cover and cook until the clams have opened and the chicken is cooked through, 10 to 12 minutes. Discard any clams that do not open. Transfer the clams, chicken, shrimp, and mushrooms to a bowl and keep warm.

4. Add the cabbage, spinach, carrots, and snow peas to the pot and simmer until all of the vegetables are cooked through and very hot, about 10 minutes. Return the noodles to the pot and simmer until they are very hot, 3 to 4 minutes. Add the soy sauce and mirin and continue to simmer until the soup is very flavorful, 2 to 3 minutes.

5. Serve the clams, chicken, shrimp, and mushrooms over the noodles and vegetables and ladle the broth over the top. Garnish with the green onions.

CHEF'S NOTE

Substitute tamari for the soy sauce to make this recipe celiac-friendly.

Nutritional Information per Serving (4 oz/112 g noodles, 6 fl oz/180 mL dashi, 3 clams, 2 oz/56 g chicken breast, 2 oz/56 g shrimp, 3½ oz/82 g vegetable mixture):

216 calories, 4 g fat, 1 g saturated fat, 13 mg cholesterol, 479 mg sodium, 11 g total carbohydrates, 2 g fiber, 3 g sugar, 33 g protein

Asparagus-Edamame Bisque C D V H

Makes 10 portions

1 oz/28 g olive oil

8 oz/227 g thinly sliced leeks

2 oz/57 g minced shallots

½ oz/14 g minced garlic

1½ qt/1.4 L Vegetable Stock (page 106)

7 oz/199 Carolina rice

1 lb/454 g shelled edamame beans

1 lb/454 g asparagus stems, cut into 1-in/2.5-cm slices (see Chef's Note)

1 tsp/3 g kosher salt

¼ tsp/.25 g freshly ground black pepper

4 fl oz/120 mL heavy cream

½ oz/14 g chopped chives, or as needed

Reserved asparagus tips, for garnish (optional; see Chef's Note)

1. In a large soup pot, heat the oil over medium heat. Add the leeks, shallots, and garlic and cook until tender, about 5 minutes.

2. Add the stock, rice, and edamame and bring the soup to a boil. Reduce the heat and simmer the soup until the rice begins to get tender, about 15 minutes.

3. Add the asparagus, salt, and pepper and bring the soup to a boil. Reduce the heat to a simmer, place the lid on the pot, and cook until the vegetables are tender, 10 to 12 minutes.

4. Purée the soup in a food processor or blender until smooth. Strain the soup through a fine-mesh sieve, and discard any solids. Return the soup to the pot, stir in the cream, and heat through well. Serve garnished with chives and asparagus tips.

CHEF'S NOTE

Reserve the tips when trimming the asparagus stems.

VARIATION

Zucchini and Butter Bean Bisque

Replace the leeks with onions, the edamame with butter beans (or lima beans), and the asparagus stems with 1 lb/453 g zucchini. Garnish the soup with finely chopped roasted red peppers.

Nutritional Information per Serving (6 fl oz/180 mL):

218 calories, 10 g fat, 3 g saturated fat, 15 mg cholesterol, 14 mg sodium, 26 g total carbohydrates, 4 g fiber, 3 g sugar, 8 g protein

---

Purée of Beet and Carrot Soup

Makes 10 portions

1 lb/454 g beets

1½ oz/43 g olive oil, or as needed

1 tsp/1 g kosher salt, plus more as needed

13½ oz/385 g peeled and chopped carrots

4 oz/113 g chopped onions

4 oz/113 g chopped leeks

¼ oz/7 g garlic

40 fl oz/1.2 L Vegetable Stock (page 106)

2 sprigs thyme

¼ tsp/1 g freshly ground black pepper, or as needed

2 oz/57 g feta cheese, crumbled

½ oz/14 g cilantro chiffonade

1. To roast the beets, rub the beets with ½ oz/14 g of the oil and season with a sprinkling of salt, and wrap in aluminum foil. roast in the oven at 300° F/146°C until tender, 45 minutes to 1 hour.

2. Meanwhile, heat the remaining 1 oz/28 g oil in a large pot over medium heat. Add the carrots and cook until soft and lightly browned, about 10 minutes.

3. Add the onions and leeks and sweat until translucent, 3 to 5 minutes more. Add the garlic and cook until aromatic, about 1 minute.

4. Add the vegetable stock and thyme and bring the soup to a boil. Reduce the heat to low and simmer the soup until a good flavor develops, about 20 minutes. Remove the thyme.

5. Peel and roughly chop the beets and mix them into the soup. Transfer the mixture to a blender and purée the soup until it is smooth.

6. Return the soup to the pot, and stir over medium heat until reheated. Season with the salt and pepper. Serve garnished with the crumbled feta and a sprinkling of cilantro.

CHEF'S NOTE

This soup may be thinned with additional stock and used as a sauce. It is a beautiful accompaniment to seared scallops or poached or steamed fish or chicken.

Nutritional Information per Serving (6 fl oz/180 mL):

109 calories, 6 g fat, 2 g saturated fat, 5 mg cholesterol, 485 mg sodium, 13 g total carbohydrates, 3 g fiber, 7 g sugar, 2 g protein

What an amazing variety of flavors and textures can be offered up in the name of salad. Salads are hot, warm, or cold, soft, tender, or crisp. A salad may include a variety of textures such as tender roasted beets, juicy blueberries, crisply toasted nuts, crunchy and succulent lettuces, bristly bitter greens, crisp apples or grapes, chewy dried fruits, or some type of protein. The combinations are endless.

Salads can be eaten as a starter for a multicourse meal, as a palate cleanser between courses, and in some traditions, the salad is eaten following the entrée as a digestive, yet for some a salad can be an entire meal. In its most simple form a salad can be a type of lettuce or selection of lettuces with a dressing and a sampling of garnishes, usually vegetables and possibly nuts or seeds. A salad can also be a collection of marinated or dressed vegetables, or grains such as barley or farro.

The salads showcased in this chapter find their roots in the cultures of many. Flavor profiles from all over—Asia, the Middle East, India, Europe, Africa, America, Mexico, the Caribbean, and Latin America—are included here. In fact, you will find that the flavor profiles of these faraway places are the very flavors that seem to invigorate our senses and bring profound joy to our palates!

When designing salads for your clientele, remember to keep the portions of greens generous; flavors of dressings and garnishes should be big, bold, and intense. Garnishes or supporting ingredients should include lots and lots of vegetables, and whole grains. Stay away from processed foods.

Daikon Salad C D V H

Makes 10 portions

1 lb/454 g peeled and julienned daikon

1 European cucumber, peeled, seeded, and julienned

1 carrot, peeled and julienned

½ tsp/2 g sea salt or kosher salt

2 fl oz/60 mL rice vinegar

2 tbsp/20 g sugar

1 tsp/2 g Korean red pepper powder (*kochukaru*)

1. In a colander, toss the daikon, cucumber, and carrot with the salt and set aside to drain until the daikon is pliable, about 45 minutes. Squeeze firmly to remove any excess water and transfer to another bowl.

2. Add the remaining ingredients and mix well to combine. Cover the salad and refrigerate until well chilled.

3. If necessary, adjust the seasoning just before serving.

Nutritional Information per Serving (2 oz/57 g):

35 calories, 0 g fat, 0 g saturated fat, 0 mg cholesterol, 2 mg sodium, 2 g total carbohydrates, 1 g fiber, 0 g sugar, 0 g protein

---

Asian Chicken Salad

Makes 10 portions

2 lb 8 oz/1.14 kg boneless, skinless chicken breast

½ oz/14 g kosher salt, or as needed

½ tsp/1 g freshly ground black pepper, or as needed

3 oz/85 g julienned red bell peppers

3 oz/85 g julienned green bell peppers

3 oz/85 g julienned yellow bell peppers

4 oz/113 g julienned carrots

4 oz/113 g sliced Asian celery (*heung kun*)

½ cup/120 mL black bean sauce

1 lb 14 oz/851 g Asian mixed baby greens

3 oz/85 g sliced green onions

1 oz/28 g fried bean thread noodles

1½ oz/43 g toasted chopped peanuts

1. Season the chicken with the salt and black pepper and cook on a preheated griddle or flat top until evenly browned, 12 to 15 minutes.

2. Transfer the chicken to a cutting board and cut into medium dice. Transfer to a large bowl, and add the bell peppers, carrots, and celery.

3. Add the black bean sauce and toss well to coat. Cover the bowl and refrigerate until well chilled.

4. To serve, place 3 oz/85 g of the mixed greens in a salad bowl and top with 6 oz/170 g of the prepared chicken salad. Garnish with ⅓ oz/8 g of the green onions, 1 tsp/2 g of the noodles, and 1 tbsp/4 g of the peanuts.

Nutritional Information per Serving (3 oz/84 g greens, 6 oz/170 g chicken salad, ⅓ oz/8 g green onions, 1 tsp/2 g noodles, 1 tbsp/4 g peanuts):

180 calories, 8 g fat, 1 g saturated fat, 65 mg cholesterol, 690 mg sodium, 7 g total carbohydrates, 1 g fiber, 2 g sugar, 26 g protein

---

Minted Barley-Cucumber Salad D V H

··

Makes 10 portions

8 oz/227 g pearl barley

8 oz/227 g quartered cherry tomatoes

2 oz/57 g diced cucumbers

1 oz/28 g chopped flat-leaf parsley

2 tbsp/6 g chopped mint

1 tbsp/6 g thinly sliced green onions

2 tbsp/30 mL extra-virgin olive oil

2 tsp/10 mL lemon juice

1 tsp/3 g kosher salt, or as needed

¼ tsp/.5 g freshly ground black pepper

1. Soak the barley in enough cold water to cover for 30 minutes, then drain well.

2. Bring the barley and enough water to cover by 2 inches to a boil in a saucepot over high heat. Reduce the heat to low and simmer until tender, about 40 minutes. Strain the cooked barley through a sieve and rinse under cold running water to cool the barley and remove surface starch. Allow the barley to drain thoroughly.

3. Combine the barley, quartered tomatoes, cucumber, parsley, mint, and green onions in a large bowl. Stir in the oil, lemon juice, salt, and pepper. Cover the bowl and refrigerate until well chilled. Store the salad in the refrigerator.

Nutritional Information per Serving (3 oz/84 g):

110 calories, 3 g fat, 0 g saturated fat, 0 mg cholesterol, 241 mg sodium, 19 g total carbohydrates, 4 g fiber, 1 g sugar, 2 g protein

---

Cara Cara Orange Salad with Dates and Feta

 C D V H

··

Makes 10 portions

5 Cara Cara oranges

1 lb/454 g Boston lettuce leaves

10 pitted Medjool dates, julienned

1 oz/28 g mint chiffonade

5 oz/142 g feta cheese, cut into small dice

1. Using a sharp knife, peel the oranges, removing the skin and white pith. Cut the oranges crosswise into round slices ⅛ in/3 mm thick.

2. Separate and wash the Boston lettuce leaves. Pat dry with paper towels.

3. To serve, lay 1½ oz/43 g lettuce leaves on a serving plate. Arrange the slices from half an orange on top of the lettuce. Garnish with the dates, a pinch of the mint leaves, and ½ oz/14 g of the cheese.

Nutritional Information per Serving (4½ oz/128 g):

103 calories, 3 g fat, 2 g saturated fat, 12 mg cholesterol, 161 mg sodium, 16 g total carbohydrates, 3 g fiber, 13 g sugar, 3 g protein

---

Cucumber, Tomato, and Feta Salad C D V H

Makes 10 portions

1 lb 8 oz/680 g sliced and quartered cucumbers

1 lb 2 oz/510 g diced tomatoes

8 oz/227 g thinly sliced red onions

8 oz/227 g crumbled feta cheese

4 fl oz/120 mL red wine vinegar

2 tbsp/6 g chopped oregano

1 tsp/3 g kosher salt

1 tsp/2 g freshly ground black pepper

8 fl oz/240 mL extra-virgin olive oil

1. In a large bowl, toss the cucumbers, tomatoes, onions, and cheese to combine.
2. In a medium bowl, combine the vinegar, oregano, salt, and pepper. Stream in all of the oil while whisking constantly.
3. Toss the salad ingredients with the dressing and serve.

Nutritional Information per Serving (7 oz/199g):

281 calories, 27 g fat, 7 g saturated fat, 20 mg cholesterol, 450 mg sodium, 6 g total carbohydrates, 6 g fiber, 4 g sugar, 4 g protein

---

Chayote Salad with Oranges C D V H

Makes 10 portions

3 chayotes, peeled and thinly sliced

5 cups/1.2 L peeled and thinly sliced jícama

5 cups/1.2 L thinly sliced carrots

5 oranges, peeled and cut into suprêmes, juices reserved

2 bunches green onions, thinly sliced

⅓ cup/75 mL extra-virgin olive oil

⅓ cup/75 mL lime juice

2 tsp/4 g sugar

¾ tsp/2 g kosher salt

½ tsp/1 g freshly ground black pepper

5 tbsp/15 g chopped cilantro

5 tbsp/15 g chopped mint

1. Mix the chayote, jícama, carrot, orange sections, and green onions to combine.
2. In a small bowl, whisk together the oil, lime juice, sugar, salt, pepper, and reserved orange juice. Drizzle the dressing over the vegetables.
3. Add the cilantro and mint, and toss to combine.

Nutritional Information per Serving (9½ oz/269 g):

130 calories, 7 g fat, 1 g saturated fat, 0 mg cholesterol, 120 mg sodium, 17 g total carbohydrates, 6 g fiber, 5 g sugar, 2 g protein

---

Chayote Salad with Oranges

Chinese Long Bean Salad with Tangerines and Sherry-Mustard Vinaigrette C D V H

Makes 10 portions

SALAD

1 lb/454 g Chinese long beans (see Chef's Note)

8 tangerines, peeled and cut into suprêmes, juices reserved

6 oz/170 g sliced Vidalia onions

6 oz/170 g toasted sunflower seeds

1 tsp/3 g kosher salt

½ tsp/1 g freshly ground black pepper

VINAIGRETTE

2 tsp/4 g cornstarch

2 tsp/10 mL water

8 fl oz/240 mL Vegetable Stock (page 106)

6 tbsp/90 mL olive oil

¼ cup/60 mL sherry vinegar

¼ cup/60 mL tangerine juice

1 oz/28 g Dijon mustard

1 oz/28 g light brown sugar

4 tsp/14 g minced shallots

2 tsp/12 g minced garlic

1 tsp/3 g kosher salt

1 tsp/2 g freshly ground black pepper

1. Trim the beans, cut into 1½-in/4-cm lengths, and cook in boiling water until barely tender. Drain and cool.

2. Combine the beans, tangerine segments, onion, and sunflower seeds in a large bowl. Season with the salt and pepper.

3. To make the vinaigrette, in a small bowl, combine the cornstarch with the water to form a slurry. In a saucepan, bring the stock to a boil over medium heat. Stir in the slurry and cook until the stock has thickened, about 2 minutes. Cool to room temperature. Combine the remaining ingredients in a small bowl, then whisk into the thickened stock.

4. Toss the bean mixture with the vinaigrette. The salad is ready to serve at room temperature, or it may be chilled for up to 24 hours before serving.

CHEF'S NOTE

Chinese long beans are also known as yard-long beans, though they are seldom left to grow to this length. They are part of the same plant family as the black-eyed pea. Green beans may be substituted if Chinese long beans are unavailable.

Nutritional Information per Serving (5 oz/142 g):

155 calories, 10 g fat, 1 g saturated fat, 0 mg cholesterol, 331 mg sodium, 13 g total carbohydrates, 3 g fiber, 2 g sugar, 2 g protein

Farro Salad

Makes 10 portions

VINAIGRETTE

4 fl oz/120 mL lemon juice

12 mint sprigs

4 fl oz/120 mL red wine vinegar

½ oz/12 g chopped mint

¼ tsp/.5 g sugar, or as needed

10 fl oz/300 mL extra-virgin olive oil

Kosher salt, as needed

½ tsp/1 g freshly ground black pepper, or as needed

4 beefsteak tomatoes, seeded and chopped

7 oz/199 g diced seeded cucumbers

6 oz/170 g diced celery or fennel

6 oz/170 g diced red or yellow bell peppers

4 oz/113 g diced red onions

1 oz/28 g chopped basil or mint

1 oz/28 g chopped flat-leaf parsley

FARRO SALAD

6 cups/1.44 L water, lightly salted

1 lb/454 g farro, soaked in cold water for 1 hour

1. In a saucepan, bring the water to a boil over high heat. Add the farro and stir once or twice to separate the grains. Reduce the heat to medium and simmer, covered, until the farro doubles in volume and is tender to the bite, 25 to 30 minutes. Drain the farro, transfer it to a salad bowl, and allow it to cool to room temperature. Set aside.

2. To make the vinaigrette, combine the lemon juice and mint sprigs in a small pan and bring to a boil over high heat. Immediately remove the pan from the heat, cover, and let the mint infuse the lemon juice until flavorful, about 10 minutes.

3. Remove and discard the mint sprigs. Whisk in the vinegar, chopped mint, and sugar. Add the oil in a slow, steady stream, whisking constantly, until the dressing is blended and slightly thickened. Season with salt and black pepper.

4. Add the tomatoes, cucumbers, celery, bell peppers, red onion, basil, and parsley to the farro in the bowl. Pour the dressing over the salad ingredients and fold the salad together until it is evenly dressed. Serve on chilled plates.

> **Nutritional Information per Serving (8 oz/227 g):**
>
> 327 calories, 29 g fat, 4 g saturated fat, 0 mg cholesterol, 16 mg sodium, 21 g total carbohydrates, 4 g fiber, 4 g sugar, 3 g protein

Grilled Garlic Shrimp and Radish Salad

Makes 10 portions

2 lb/907 g peeled and deveined shrimp (21–25 count) (about 40), shells reserved

½ oz/14 g minced garlic

Juice of 2 limes

VINAIGRETTE

1 tbsp/15 mL olive oil

8 oz/227 g reserved shrimp shells

½ oz/14 g minced garlic

¾ oz/21 g diced shallots

2 oz/57 g tomato paste

2 fl oz/60 mL brandy

14 fl oz/420 mL Chicken Stock (page 105)

2 tsp/4 g arrowroot

3 tbsp/45 mL apple cider vinegar

3 tbsp/45 mL rice vinegar

1 oz/28 g tahini

2 tbsp/30 mL reduced-sodium soy sauce

2 tbsp/14 g seeded and minced jalapeños

1 tbsp/15 mL sesame oil

1 tbsp/15 mL peanut oil

RADISH SALAD

5½ oz/156 g finely julienned daikon

5½ oz/156 g finely julienned red radishes

5½ oz/156 g finely julienned carrots

5½ oz/156 g finely julienned celery

5 oz/142 g soba noodles

2 oz/56 g cilantro leaves

¼ tsp/1 g black sesame seeds

¼ tsp/1 g white sesame seeds

1. Toss the shrimp with the garlic and lime juice. Thread 4 shrimp (approximately 2 oz/57 g total) onto a bamboo skewer. Repeat with the remaining shrimp and refrigerate until needed.

2. To make the vinaigrette, heat the oil in a medium saucepan. Add the shrimp shells and sauté until opaque. Add the garlic and shallots and sweat until the shallots are translucent. Add the tomato paste and sauté until rust colored. Deglaze the pan with the brandy and allow the liquid to reduce until almost dry. Add the stock and simmer until reduced by half. Strain through a fine-mesh sieve. If necessary, add water or reduce further to yield about 6 fl oz/180 mL. Return to a clean pan and bring to a boil.

3. Combine the arrowroot with enough water to form a slurry. Stir the slurry into the boiling stock. Remove the stock from the heat, add the vinegars, and cool the vinaigrette completely. Stir in the tahini, soy sauce, and jalapeños. Whisk in the oils.

4. Combine the daikon, radishes, carrots, and celery and toss with 2¾ fl oz/80 mL of the vinaigrette.

5. Cook the noodles in boiling water until tender to the bite. Drain and cool. Gently toss the noodles with 6 fl oz/180 mL of the vinaigrette.

6. For each portion, grill a shrimp skewer until the shrimp are cooked, 3 minutes on each side. On a room-temperature plate, arrange a bed of approximately 2 oz/57 g of the radish salad and place 1 oz/28 g of the noodles on top of the salad. Remove the shrimp from the skewer, if desired, and arrange over the radish salad. Garnish with cilantro leaves and a pinch each of black and white sesame seeds. Drizzle the plate with 1 tbsp/15 mL of the remaining vinaigrette and serve.

Nutritional Information per Serving (7½ oz/213 g):

270 calories, 2 g fat, 2 g saturated fat, 98 mg cholesterol, 320 mg sodium, 5 g total carbohydrates, 2 g fiber, 2 g sugar, 24 g protein

Cracked Wheat and Tomato Salad D V H

Makes 10 portions

12 oz/340 g cracked wheat

2 lb/907 g peeled, seeded, medium-dice tomatoes

8 oz/227 g medium-dice red onions

3 oz/85 g medium-dice fresh mozzarella cheese

3 tbsp/45 mL red wine vinegar

7 fl oz/210 mL extra-virgin olive oil

2 tbsp/6 g chopped oregano

½ oz/14 g chopped basil

2 tsp/4 g red pepper flakes

1 tsp/3 g kosher salt

¼ tsp/.5 g freshly ground black pepper

1½ oz/43 g finely grated Parmesan cheese (optional)

1. Place the cracked wheat in a medium pot, cover with salted water, and simmer until tender, 30 to 35 minutes. Remove from the heat and drain, pressing to release any excess moisture. Let cool to room temperature.

2. Toss the tomatoes, onion, and mozzarella in a large bowl to combine.

3. Whisk together the vinegar, oil, oregano, basil, and red pepper flakes in a small bowl. Season with the salt and black pepper. Add to the tomato mixture and toss to coat. Add the wheat and toss well.

4. Serve at room temperature, or chill until needed for service. Garnish with grated cheese, if desired.

Nutritional Information per Serving (6 oz/170 g):

360 calories, 23 g fat, 5 g saturated fat, 10 mg cholesterol, 310 mg sodium, 32 g total carbohydrates, 10 g fiber, 12 g sugar, 3 g protein

Hue Chicken Salad (Ga Bop) C D H

Makes 10 portions

4 oz/113 g thinly sliced onion

3 lb/1.36 kg shredded cooked chicken

1 oz/28 g rau ram leaves, torn

1 oz/28 g mint leaves, torn

1 oz/28 g minced cilantro

4 Thai bird chiles, thinly sliced

2 fl oz/60 mL lime juice

2 tbsp/30 mL peanut oil

2 tbsp/30 mL fish sauce

2 tbsp/30 mL Vietnamese sambal

4 tsp/8 g sugar, or as needed

½ tsp/1.5 g kosher salt, or as needed

¼ tsp/.5 g freshly ground black pepper, or as needed

10 banana leaves, cut into large triangles

10 Boston lettuce leaves

1 lb 9 oz/708 g steamed jasmine rice

1 cup/240 mL crispy fried shallots (page 198)

2 red Fresno chiles, sliced paper thin

1. Combine the onion slices with enough cold water to cover and refrigerate for at least 30 minutes and up to 2 hours.

2. Combine the chicken, rau ram, mint, cilantro, and Thai bird chiles in a large bowl. Drain the onion slices and add them to the chicken. Add the lime juice, peanut oil, fish sauce, and sambal to the salad and toss gently until combined. Season as needed with the sugar, salt, and pepper.

3. Arrange the banana leaves and Boston lettuce on chilled plates. Top with the salad and serve with steamed rice, crispy shallots, and Fresno chile.

Nutritional Information per Serving (9 oz/255 g):

386 calories, 10 g fat, 2 g saturated fat, 115 mg cholesterol, 512 mg sodium, 25 g total carbohydrates, 1 g fiber, 2 g sugar, 45 g protein

Hue Chicken Salad (Ga Bop)

Kale, Cashew, and Cranberry Pasta Salad

Kale, Cashew, and Cranberry Pasta Salad

Makes 10 portions

12 oz/340 g whole wheat pasta

2 fl oz/60 mL olive oil

6 oz/170 g small-dice red onions

1 tsp/2 g finely grated lemon zest

4 tsp/20 mL balsamic vinegar

1 tsp/3 g kosher salt, or as needed

½ tsp/1 g freshly ground black pepper

2 oz/57 g dried cranberries

4 oz/113 g salted roasted cashews, chopped

1 lb 2 oz/510 g kale leaves, stems removed and cut into 1-in-/2.5-cm pieces

4 fl oz/120 mL dry white wine

1. Cook the pasta in boiling lightly salted water until it is al dente. The cooking time will vary depending on the shape of the pasta. Drain the pasta and spread it out on a sheet pan to cool to room temperature.

2. Heat the oil in a sauté pan over medium heat. Add the onions and cook until soft, about 10 minutes. Add the cooked drained pasta and toss with the lemon zest, vinegar, salt, pepper, cranberries, and cashews.

3. Steam the kale over medium heat, covered, in the white wine until wilted and the wine has almost evaporated. Cool and toss with the pasta.

Nutritional Information per Serving (3 oz/85 g):

196 calories, 3 g fat, 0 g saturated fat, 4 mg cholesterol, 26 mg sodium, 12 g total carbohydrates, 8 g fiber, 3 g sugar, 6 g protein

---

Mediterranean Salad

Makes 10 portions

1½ oz/43 g minced anchovy fillets

10 fl oz/300 mL Vinaigrette-Style Dressing (page 333)

10 oz/284 g artichoke hearts, cooked and quartered

10 oz/284 g peas

5 oz/142 g julienned carrot

2 oz/57 g pitted Picholine olives

2 oz/57 g pitted Niçoise olives

3½ oz/99 g grated Asiago cheese

2 oz/57 g chopped flat-leaf parsley, plus more for sprinkling

1 lb/454 g baby mixed greens

1. Stir the anchovies into the vinaigrette in a bowl. Add the artichokes, peas, carrots, olives, cheese, and parsley. Toss to coat evenly.

2. To serve, place a bed of 1½ oz/43 g of the mixed greens in the center of a chilled plate. Top with 1½ oz/43 g of the artichoke salad, using a slotted spoon to lift the salad so the dressing can drain away. Garnish with a sprinkling of parsley.

CHEF'S NOTE

Omit the anchovy to make vegetarian-friendly.

Nutritional Information per Serving (6 oz/170 g):

264 calories, 20 g fat, 6 g saturated fat, 13 mg cholesterol, 653 mg sodium, 13 g total carbohydrates, 5 g fiber, 5 g sugar, 9 g protein

---

Thai Seafood Salad C D H

Makes 10 portions

DRESSING

2 tsp/10 mL Thai chili paste (*nam prik pao*)

2 fl oz/60 mL fish sauce (*nam pla*)

2 fl oz/60 mL lime juice

1 tbsp/6 g sugar

2 Thai bird chiles, minced

½ oz/14 g lemongrass, very finely minced

2½ oz/71 g shallots, halved lengthwise and cut into ⅛-in/3-mm slices

SALAD

1 qt/960 mL water

2 oz/57 g lemongrass, halved lengthwise and cut into ½-in/1.25-cm sections

½ oz/14 g cilantro stems

1 lb/ 454 g shrimp (21–25 count), peeled, deveined, split lengthwise

1 lb/454 g squid, cleaned and cut into ¼-in/6-mm rings

4 red Fresno chiles, seeded and julienned

4¼ oz/120 g red bell peppers, seeded and julienned

1 oz/28 g cilantro, coarsely chopped

1¾ oz/50 g mint leaves, coarsely chopped

2½ oz/71 g toasted coconut, or as needed

1. To make the dressing, whisk the Thai chile paste, fish sauce, lime juice, sugar, minced Thai chile, and lemongrass in a medium bowl to combine. Stir in the shallots.

2. Combine the water, lemongrass and cilantro stems in a pot fitted with a steaming basket and lid, and bring the liquid to a gentle simmer. Steam the shrimp and squid separately over the simmering liquid. Remove from the steamer and allow to cool briefly.

3. Add the steamed seafood to the dressing and toss well to combine. Cool slightly, then add the Fresno and bell peppers, tossing to combine.

4. To serve, scoop 3¼ oz/92 g of the seafood salad onto a plate and garnish with 1 tbsp/3 g of the cilantro, 2 tbsp/6 g of the mint, and ¼ oz/7 g of the coconut. Serve immediately.

Nutritional Information per Serving (3¼ oz/92 g):

268 calories, 6 g fat, 2 g saturated fat, 28 mg cholesterol, 587 mg sodium, 6 g total carbohydrates, 2 g fiber, 1 g sugar, 15 g protein

Fruit Salad C D V H

Makes 10 portions

SYRUP

5 fl oz/150 mL orange blossom water (see Chef's Note)

1 oz/28 g sugar

SALAD

Zest of 1 orange, julienned

7 oz/199 g medium-dice cantaloupe

6 oz/170 g medium-dice honeydew melon

6 oz/170 g medium-dice kiwi

5 oz/142 g fresh strawberries, quartered

5 oz/142 g fresh blueberries

5 fl oz/150 mL nonfat yogurt, drained

½ oz/14 g spearmint chiffonade

1. To make the syrup, combine the orange blossom water and the sugar in a small saucepan. Heat, stirring occasionally, until the sugar has completely dissolved. Set aside until needed.

2. Place the julienned zest in a small saucepan and cover with cold water. Bring the water to a boil. Drain and repeat the blanching process twice, beginning with cold water each time. Reserve the blanched zest until needed.

3. Combine all the fruits in a large bowl. Refrigerate until needed.

4. For each portion, place 2½ oz/71 g of the fruit salad in a glass or serving dish. Top with 1 tbsp/15 mL of the syrup and about 1 tbsp/15 mL of the drained yogurt. Garnish with the blanched orange zest and the spearmint chiffonade.

CHEF'S NOTE

Orange blossom water is generally available from health food stores and wholesalers.

> **Nutritional Information per Serving (2½ oz/71 g salad, 1 tbsp/15 mL syrup, 1 tsp/5 mL yogurt):**
>
> 64 calories, 0 g fat, 0 g saturated fat, 1 mg cholesterol, 27 mg sodium, 15 g total carbohydrates, 2 g fiber, 11 g sugar, 2 g protein

Radish Salad with Pears and Blueberries C D V H

Makes 10 portions

1 lb 14 oz/851 g very thinly sliced small radishes

1 lb 8 oz/680 g peeled, small-dice pears

2 fl oz/60 mL champagne vinegar

2 tbsp/30 mL olive oil

1 tsp/3 g honey

½ tsp/2 g kosher salt

Pinch freshly ground black pepper

10 tbsp/150 mL plain Greek-style yogurt

20 Boston lettuce leaves

10 oz/284 g fresh blueberries

1. Combine the sliced radishes and diced pears in a large bowl. Add the vinegar, oil, honey, salt, and pepper. Stir gently until well combined. Cover and marinate at room temperature for 15 minutes.

2. Put the yogurt into a squirt bottle.

3. To plate the salad, arrange 2 leaves of Boston lettuce on a plate, top with 5⅓ oz/153 g of the marinated radishes and pears, sprinkle with 1 oz/28 g of the blueberries. Decorate with 1 tbsp/15 mL of the yogurt.

> **Nutritional Information per Serving (7 oz/199 g):**
>
> 100 calories, 3 g fat, 0 g saturated fat, 0 mg cholesterol, 130 mg sodium, 19 g total carbohydrates, 5 g fiber, 12 g sugar, 2 g protein

Radish Salad with Pears and Blueberries

Red Lentil Salad

Red Lentil Salad C D V H

Makes 10 portions

3 oz/85 g diced red bell peppers

2 tsp/4 g seeded and minced jalapeños

4 oz/113 g diced red onions

4 tbsp/36 g minced garlic

2 fl oz/60 mL olive oil

1 lb 8 oz/680 g red lentils, cooked briefly and cooled

3 oz/85 g tomato concassé

3 oz/85 g orange suprêmes, diced

2 fl oz/60 mL extra-virgin olive oil

2 fl oz/60 mL white balsamic vinegar

4 tbsp/12 g basil chiffonade

1. In a large sauté pan over medium heat, sweat the bell pepper, jalapeño, onion, and garlic in the olive oil until the onion is translucent. Set aside to cool.

2. When cool, combine with the remaining ingredients and refrigerate the salad for at least 4 hours and up to 24 hours before serving.

> **Nutritional Information per Serving (4 oz/113 g):**
>
> 370 calories, 13.5 g fat, 1.5 g saturated fat, 0 mg cholesterol, 10 mg sodium, 46 g total carbohydrates, 11 g fiber, 4 g sugar, 19 g protein

Korean Spinach Salad (Namul) C D V H

Makes 10 portions

2 lb 8 oz/1.13 kg baby spinach, stems removed

½ oz/14 g kosher salt

DRESSING

2 fl oz/60 mL sesame oil

¼ oz/7 g minced garlic

4 oz/113 g toasted sesame seeds

½ oz/14 g sugar

1½ fl oz/45 mL tamari

1. Blanch the spinach in lightly salted water just until wilted, then shock in cold ice water. Drain the spinach and squeeze out excess water.

2. To make the dressing, heat the sesame oil in a sauté pan over low heat and add the garlic. Gently cook until the garlic softens. Remove the pan from the heat.

3. Combine the garlic, sesame seeds, sugar, and tamari in a bowl. Add the spinach and toss to coat well.

> **Nutritional Information per Serving (4 oz/113 g spinach, 1¼ fl oz/45 mL dressing):**
>
> 170 calories, 8 g fat, 1 g saturated fat, 0 mg cholesterol, 80 mg sodium, 17 g total carbohydrates, 7 g fiber, 4 g sugar, 5 g protein

Tunisian Chickpea Salad C D V H

Makes 10 portions

CHICKPEAS

9 oz/255 g chickpeas

3 oz/85 g onion, cut into ½-in/1.25-cm slices

2 bay leaves

2 garlic cloves

1 tsp/3 g sea salt

HARISSA VINAIGRETTE

1 oz/28 g dried ancho or nora chiles, rinsed, toasted, stemmed, seeded, and ground

2 tsp/4 g ground coriander

1 tsp/2 g ground caraway

½ tsp/1 g cayenne

1 tsp/3 g salt

½ oz/14 g minced garlic

1½ fl oz/45 mL extra-virgin olive oil

½ fl oz/15 mL warm water, or as needed

3 fl oz/90 mL lemon juice

8 fl oz/240 mL olive oil

1 lb/454 g red bell peppers, fire roasted, cut into large dice

2 oz/57 g capers, salt packed, rinsed

2 oz/57 g green or Moroccan black olives, pitted and sliced

4 large eggs, hard boiled, yolks and whites roughly chopped separately, for garnish

1½ oz/43 g cilantro, chopped (optional)

1. Soak the chickpeas overnight in enough water to cover by 4 to 5 in/10 to 13 cm.

2. Drain and rinse the chickpeas and place in a medium saucepan. Add fresh cold water to cover by 1 in/2.5 cm. Place the onion, bay leaves, and garlic in cheesecloth to make a sachet. Add to the chickpeas and bring the mixture to a boil. Cover, reduce the heat to low, and simmer until the chickpeas are tender, about 2 hours, adding water as needed to keep the chickpeas covered at all times. Drain the chickpeas and discard the sachet. Season with the sea salt.

3. To make the vinaigrette, combine the chiles, coriander, caraway, cayenne, salt, garlic, and extra-virgin olive oil in the jar of a blender and purée until the mixture is a paste. Thin the paste with a bit of warm water, and whisk in the lemon juice and olive oil. If using a blender, stream in the oil and blend until fully emulsified.

4. Add the bell peppers and capers to the chickpeas and toss with 4 fl oz/120 mL of the vinaigrette. Garnish the salad with the olives, eggs, and cilantro. Serve warm or at room temperature.

Nutritional Information per Serving (5 oz/142 g):

245 calories, 17 g fat, 1 g saturated fat, 55 mg cholesterol, 365 mg sodium, 13 g total carbohydrates, 8 g fiber, 5 g sugar, 6 g protein

Roasted Beet "Tartare" with Maytag Blue Cheese C D V H

Makes 10 portions

TARTARE

1 lb 8 oz/680 g beets

½ fl oz/15 mL extra-virgin olive oil

¼ tsp/1 g kosher salt

DRESSING

1 fl oz/30 mL sherry vinegar

1½ fl oz/45 mL extra-virgin olive oil

¼ oz/7 g minced garlic

½ oz/14 g minced capers

¼ oz/7 g honey

SALAD

2½ oz/70 g pea shoots

2½ oz/70 g Maytag Blue cheese

1 oz/28 g shallots, diced

¼ oz/7 g chopped chives

1. To make the tartare, wash and dry the beets well and rub them with the oil. Season with a sprinkling of the salt. Place them on a baking sheet and roast in the oven at 375°F/190°C until fork-tender, 45 minutes to 1 hour.

2. Allow the beets to cool. Peel off the outer skin, and finely dice the beets. Place the beets into a medium bowl.

3. To make the dressing, in a small bowl, whisk the vinegar, oil, garlic, capers, and honey to combine. Pour the dressing over the beets and toss to coat. Taste the mixture, and add more vinegar or honey, if necessary, to obtain a tart, sweet flavor.

4. Portion ¼ oz/7 g of the pea shoots onto a small plate. Using a small ring mold, portion 2 oz/56 g of the tartare next to or on top of the shoots. Garnish with ¼ oz/7 g of the cheese, the minced shallots, and the chives. Serve immediately.

CHEF'S NOTE

This tartare is delicious served with crostini.

Nutritional Information per Serving (¼ oz/7 g pea shoots, 2 oz/56 g beet tartar, ¼ oz/7 g blue cheese):

110 calories, 6 g fat, 1 g saturated fat, 0 mg cholesterol, 180 mg sodium, 13 g total carbohydrates, 2 g fiber, 6 g sugar, 2 g protein

Red Salad C D V H

Makes 15 portions

8 fl oz/240 mL white balsamic vinegar

½ fl oz/15 mL light agave syrup

1 lb/454 g cooked and peeled red beets

8 oz/227 g red grapes

4 oz/113 g thinly sliced red onions

4 fl oz/120 mL extra-virgin olive oil

¼ oz/7 g opal basil chiffonade

½ tsp/1.5 g kosher salt

Pinch freshly ground black pepper

8 oz/227 g fresh blueberries

7 oz/199 g fresh goat cheese, crumbled (optional)

1. Combine the balsamic vinegar and agave syrup in a small saucepan and simmer over low heat to yield 4 fl oz/120 mL of reduced syrup. Remove from the heat and cool to room temperature.

2. Cut the beets into medium dice. Cut the red grapes in half lengthwise. Thinly slice the red onions.

3. In a small bowl, combine the vinegar-agave reduction with the oil. Add the opal basil, salt, and pepper. Set the dressing aside.

4. In a large bowl, combine the cut beets, grapes, blueberries, and red onion. Dress the salad and toss to thoroughly combine. Serve 3 oz/85 g of the salad per portion, topped with ½ oz/14 g of the crumbled goat cheese, if desired.

Nutritional Information per Serving (3 oz/85 g):

149 calories, 11 g fat, 4 g saturated fat, 12 mg cholesterol, 197 mg sodium, 10 g total carbohydrates, 0 g fiber, 7 g sugar, 4 g protein

Thai Beef and Cucumber Salad ⊞C⊞ ⊞D⊞ ⊞H⊞

Makes 10 portions

DRESSING

2 oz/57 g cilantro stems, ground

2 tbsp/20 g palm sugar

2 fl oz/60 mL lime juice

2 fl oz/60 mL fish sauce (*nam pla*)

STEAK SALAD

1 lb 8 oz/680 g flank steak

½ tsp/1.5 g kosher salt, or as needed

¼ tsp/.5 g freshly ground black pepper, or as needed

10½ oz/300 g European cucumber

8 oz/227 g red onion, sliced paper thin, rinsed

8½ oz/240 g finely julienned red bell pepper

1½ oz/43 g finely julienned red Fresno chiles

1¾ oz/50 g finely chopped mint leaves

3½ oz/99 g finely chopped cilantro leaves

1. To make the dressing, combine the cilantro stems, sugar, lime juice, and fish sauce in a food processor or blender and purée until smooth. Reserve.

2. Season the steak with the salt and black pepper and cook over a hot grill until medium rare. Let rest, then slice into pieces ¼ in/6 mm thick.

3. Transfer the steak to a medium bowl and toss with half of the dressing.

4. In another medium bowl, toss the cucumber, onion, bell pepper, chile, mint, and cilantro to combine.

5. To serve, place 3 oz/85 g of the vegetable mixture onto a plate and top with 3 slices of the beef. Drizzle an additional 1½ tsp/7 mL of the dressing on top. Serve immediately.

Nutritional Information per Serving (3 oz/85 g vegetables, 2 oz/57 g beef, 1½ tsp/7 mL dressing):

151 calories, 5 g fat, 2 g saturated fat, 30 mg cholesterol, 620 mg sodium, 6 g total carbohydrates, 2 g fiber, 4 g sugar, 21 g protein

Xato Salad from Catalonia

Makes 10 portions

SALAD

15 oz/425 g frisée lettuce

10 oz/284 g quartered artichoke hearts

5 oz/142 g pitted olives

8 oz/227 g grape tomatoes

8 oz/227 g peeled and seeded European cucumbers, cut on the bias

SHERRY VINAIGRETTE

5 fl oz/150 mL sherry vinegar

½ tsp/1.5 g xanthan gum

½ oz/14 g minced shallots

⅛ oz/3 g minced garlic

¼ tsp/1 g red pepper flakes

½ tsp/2.5 mL agave syrup

2 fl oz/60 mL pure olive oil

3 fl oz/90 mL canola oil

2½ oz/71 g roasted red pepper brunoise

¼ oz/7 g chopped basil

⅛ oz/3 g chopped oregano

⅛ oz/3 g chopped flat-leaf parsley

½ tsp/1.5 g kosher salt

Pinch freshly ground black pepper

1. To make the vinaigrette, whisk the vinegar, xanthan gum, shallots, garlic, red pepper flakes, and agave syrup in a small bowl to combine.

2. Whisk in the oils gradually to emulsify the dressing.

3. Add the bell pepper brunoise, herbs, and salt and pepper.

4. For each portion, toss together 1½ oz/43 g of the frisée, 1 oz/28 g of the artichokes, ½ oz/14 g of the olives, ¾ oz/ 21 g of the grape tomatoes, ¾ oz/21 g of the cucumber, and 2 oz/60 mL of the dressing, and adjust the seasoning with salt and black pepper.

> **Nutritional Information per Serving (1½ oz/43 g, frisée, 1 oz/28 g artichoke, ½ oz/14 g olives, ¾ oz/21 g grape tomatoes, ¾ oz/21 g cucumber 2 fl oz/60 mL dressing):**
>
> 204 calories, 18 g fat, 2 g saturated fat, 0 mg cholesterol, 452 mg sodium, 8 g total carbohydrates, 2 g fiber, 1 g sugar, 2 g protein

Putting together a thoughtful, conscientiously prepared meal for a patron with specific dietary needs can present interesting challenges. This chapter provides main-course recipes that can be partnered with a variety of side dishes, to create meals that meet those needs. You will notice that the portion sizes are smaller than what are typically offered in a restaurant setting. These smaller, accurate serving sizes are accomplished not only by scaling the portions back but also by changing the cut of the proteins being used. For instance, the standard portion size for a boneless sirloin strip steak is typically a minimum of 10 to 12 ounces per entrée portion (more than double the size of a recommended serving of beef protein) because to cut the steak any smaller would render a steak that is too thin, being nearly impossible to regulate the doneness. An alternate choice might be to use two 2-ounce medallions or one 4-ounce medallion of beef taken from the narrower section of the beef tenderloin. Chicken breasts will be skinless, boneless breasts that are cut into cutlets or paillards. Because fish is typically much leaner and lower in cholesterol than meats, fish portions may vary from a portion size of 4 ounces upward to a 6-ounce portion. In addition to the protein portions being consistently smaller, you will also notice the use of stock reductions or vegetable purées as the foundation for sauces in place of using traditional base sauces such as demi-glace or velouté. Furthermore, the sauces in this book are not commonly finished with cream or butter.

One of the principles of balanced healthy eating is using an abundance of vegetables, legumes such as lentils or beans, and whole grains such as brown rice or farro. In vegetarian cooking, meat, fish, and poultry proteins are replaced by legumes coupled with grains. And, the use of a wide variety of dark green and colorful vegetables is always in order no matter what diet you are cooking for.

In some ethnic cuisines, meat, fish, and poultry proteins are not typically the focal point of a preparation, but are actually used more as a flavoring agent or garnish for a dish that is based on vegetables, legumes, and grains. This is a very healthful approach! Use the examples set forth in this chapter to guide you as you learn to modify your own recipes for specific dietary requests.

Penne Pomodoro with Ricotta and Basil D V H

Makes 10 portions

2 lbs 8 oz/1.14 kg dried multigrain or whole wheat penne pasta

1 lb 4 oz/567 g ricotta impastata

10 oz/284 g shredded low-fat mozzarella cheese

2½ oz/71 g shredded Parmesan cheese

2½ oz/71 g basil chiffonade

2 lbs 8 oz/1.14 kg baby spinach, stems removed

1 tbsp/10 g kosher salt

1½ tsp/3 g freshly ground black pepper, or as needed

3 qt/2.8 L Pomodoro Sauce (page 336)

1½ oz/43 g chopped flat-leaf parsley, or as needed, for garnish

1. Cook the pasta in a large pot of salted boiling water until al dente, 6 to 8 minutes. Drain and transfer to sheet pans to cool.

2. In a large bowl, mix the ricotta, 5 oz/142 g of the mozzarella, 1¼ oz/35 g of the Parmesan, the basil, and spinach to combine. Season with salt and pepper.

3. Toss the cooled pasta with the ricotta mixture and the pomodoro sauce to combine.

4. Divide the mixture into 10 equal portions, and place each portion into a 12-oz/340-g oval gratin dish. Top each with ½ oz/14g of the remaining mozzarella and ¼ oz/7 g of the remaining Parmesan.

5. Place the gratin dish on a sizzle platter or half sheet pan and bake in the oven at 350°F/176°C until the cheese has melted, the sauce is bubbly, and the dish has reached an internal temperature of 145°F/63°C, 15 to 20 minutes. Garnish with chopped parsley and serve.

CHEF'S NOTE

Use gluten-free pasta to make celiac-friendly.

> **Nutritional Information per Serving (10 oz/280 g):**
>
> 646 calories, 18 g fat, 8 g saturated fat, 41 mg cholesterol, 643 mg sodium, 88 g total carbohydrates, 21 g fiber, 5 g sugar, 38 g protein

Bahn Mi

Makes 10 portions

VIETNAMESE CARROT AND DAIKON PICKLES

2 lb/907 g peeled and julienned carrots

2 lb/907 g peeled and julienned daikon

2 tsp/6 g kosher salt

7½ oz/213 g granulated sugar

20 fl oz/600 mL white vinegar

16 fl oz/480 mL warm water

VIETNAMESE FIVE-SPICE PÂTÉ

2 lb 8 oz/1.13 kg cubed pork shoulder

1¾ oz/50 g minced lemongrass

½ oz/14 g peeled and minced ginger

¼ oz/7 g minced garlic

1½ tsp/5 g granulated sugar

1½ tsp/3 g freshly ground black pepper

1½ tsp/3 g five-spice powder

1 fl oz/30 mL kecap manis (sweet soy sauce)

1 fl oz/30 mL tamarind pulp

1 tbsp/15 mL oyster sauce

1 tbsp/10 g kosher salt

BAHN MI SAUCE

4 fl oz/120 mL lime juice

2 tsp/10 mL tamari

1 tsp/5 mL fish sauce (*nam pla*)

¼ oz/7 g minced garlic

2 oz/57 g palm sugar

2½ fl oz/75 mL water

½ tsp/2 mL sesame oil

1 fl oz/30 mL canola oil

10 mini Vietnamese baguettes

5 oz/142 g shredded napa cabbage

1 oz/28 g cilantro leaves

5 oz/142 g seedless cucumbers, sliced on the bias ⅛ in/3 mm thick

1 oz/28 g Thai basil chiffonade

1. To make the pickles, sterilize five 1-pint jars, lids, and bands by submerging clean jars, bands, and lids in boiling water for 1 minute. Remove from the water and place upside down on a cooling rack until ready to fill.

2. Toss the carrots and daikon together in a large bowl. Sprinkle with the salt and 4 tsp/17 g of the granulated sugar, and toss until the vegetables are well coated.

3. Let the vegetables sit, tossing them occasionally, until they begin to soften, about 3 minutes. When the vegetables can be bent in half without breaking, they are ready to brine.

4. Transfer the vegetables to a colander, rinse with cool water, and drain well.

5. In a medium pot over low heat, mix the remaining granulated sugar, vinegar, and warm water to combine. Heat the mixture until the sugar dissolves.

6. Pack the carrots and daikon tightly into the sterile jars. Pour the warm brine over the vegetables to cover, leaving ½ in/6 mm of headspace at the top of the jar.

7. Seal the jars and refrigerate the pickles for a minimum of 24 hours before serving. Their flavor will continue to improve over time.

8. To make the pâté, toss the pork with the lemongrass, ginger, garlic, granulated sugar, black pepper, five-spice powder, soy sauce, tamarind, oyster sauce, and salt in a

Continued on page 178

large bowl. Grind the mixture in a meat grinder through a ¼-in/6-mm die. Repeat the process through the same die a second time.

9. Pack the seasoned ground meat into a 3-lb/1.36-kg loaf pan or pâté mold. Bake the pâté in the oven at 325°F/152°C until it reaches an internal temperature of 165°F/74°C.

10. Cool completely, then unmold from the pan, wrap tightly in plastic wrap, and store, refrigerated until ready to serve.

11. To make the sauce, combine the lime juice, tamari, fish sauce, garlic, palm sugar, and water in a small bowl. Slowly whisk in the sesame oil and canola oil. Store in the refrigerator until needed.

12. To assemble the sandwiches, slice the baguettes in half, leaving the side seam intact.

13. Slice the pâté into 20 slices, weighing about ¾ oz/21 g each.

14. On each baguette, layer 2 slices (1½ oz/42 g each) of the pâté topped with ½ oz/14 g of the shredded cabbage, ½ oz/14 g of the carrot and daikon pickles, 2.8 g of the cilantro leaves, ½ oz/14 g of the sliced cucumber, and 2 g of the Thai basil.

15. Drizzle each sandwich with 1 fl oz/30 mL of the bahn mi sauce. Serve immediately.

CHEF'S NOTES

To lower the glycemic impact of the pickles, 7½ oz/213 g of the sugar can be replaced with 4 oz/112 g agave syrup. The pickles will keep for up to 4 weeks, refrigerated.

For a leaner pâté, 2 lb 8 oz/1.13 kg lean turkey meat can be substituted for half of the pork.

Nutritional Information per Serving (1 sandwich):

287 calories, 10 g fat, 2 g saturated fat, 70 mg cholesterol, 872 mg sodium, 32 g total carbohydrates, 0 g fiber, 7 g sugar, 25 g protein

Bibimbap

Makes 10 portions

5 fl oz/150 mL Korean soy sauce (*ganjang*) (see Chef's Note)

5 tsp/10 g sugar

2½ oz/71 g minced green onions

3 tbsp/42 g minced garlic

6 tsp/12 g peeled and minced ginger

6 tsp/12 g toasted sesame seeds

3 tbsp/45 mL dark sesame oil

½ tsp/1 g freshly ground black pepper

2 lb/907 g beef skirt steak, cut into ¼-in/6-mm strips

2 fl oz/60 mL peanut oil

1 lb 9 oz/709 g steamed medium-grain rice

10 oz/284 g iceberg lettuce chiffonade

10 oz/284 g grated or julienned red radish

10 oz/284 g grated or julienned daikon

10 oz/284 g grated or julienned carrot

10 oz/284 g grated or julienned seedless cucumber

10 shiso leaves, cut into chiffonade

10 large eggs, fried

5 tbsp/75 mL Korean red pepper paste (*gochujang*), or more as needed

1. In a medium bowl, combine the soy sauce and sugar. Add the green onions, garlic, ginger, and sesame seeds. Add the sesame oil and pepper. Add the skirt steak and toss until evenly coated. Cover, refrigerate, and let the steak marinate for at least 1 and up to 8 hours.

2. Heat 2 tbsp/15 mL of the peanut oil in a wok over high heat. Add half the beef strips and stir-fry until the beef is cooked, about 4 minutes. Transfer to a bowl and keep warm. Repeat with the remaining oil and beef.

3. Fill a bowl with 2½ oz/51 g of the rice. Top the rice with 1 oz/28 g of the lettuce. In a large bowl, toss together the red radish, daikon, carrot, cucumber, and shiso leaves. Place 4 oz/113 g of the vegetable mixture on top of the lettuce.

4. Top with 3 oz/85 g of the warm steak and a fried egg. Serve with 1½ tsp/7.50 mL red pepper paste.

CHEF'S NOTES

Shiso leaves, sometimes known as *perilla*, come from an herb related to both basil and mint. In fact, it is similar in flavor to those herbs, although most would agree that shiso leaves have a more complex flavor than either herb. Green shiso leaves are typically used in salads, stir-fries, or tempura. Red shiso leaves are used to flavor and color Japan's famous pickled plums, umeboshi. If you can't find shiso leaves, you can use either basil or mint, or both.

You may also use regular soy sauce, or tamari for a gluten-free option, instead of the Korean soy sauce.

Nutritional Information per Serving (2½ oz/51 g rice, 5 oz/142 g vegetables, 3 oz/85 steak, 1 egg):

315 calories, 11 g fat, 4 g saturated fat, 56 mg cholesterol, 748 mg sodium, 29 g total carbohydrates, 3 g fiber, 6 g sugar, 18 g protein

Huevos con Barbacoa ⬛C⬜D⬛H

Makes 10 portions

12 fl oz/360 mL beer (such as lager)

4 fl oz/120 mL tequila

8 oz/227 g thinly sliced white onions

1 oz/28 g seeded and minced jalapeños

6½ oz/186 g chopped plum tomatoes

12 fl oz/360 mL beef stock

4 fl oz/120 mL lime juice

2 bay leaves

2 tbsp/12 g dried Mexican oregano

2 dried chipotle, toasted, seeded, and minced

1 tsp/2 g epazote

½ tsp/2 g kosher salt

Pinch freshly ground black pepper

2 lb 8 oz/1.13 kg beef cheeks

14 oz/397 g Creamed Pinto Beans (page 250), warm

10 tostada shells, warm

3 tbsp/9 g minced cilantro

2 tbsp/6 g minced flat-leaf parsley

2 oz/57 g lettuce chiffonade

10 large eggs

10 fl oz/295 mL Salsa de Arbol (page 322)

1. In a large, shallow container, mix the beer, tequila, onion, jalapeño, tomatoes, stock, lime juice, bay leaves, oregano, chipotle, epazote, salt, and black pepper to combine.

2. Add the beef cheeks and toss well to coat in the marinade. Cover and marinate, refrigerated, for 8 to 12 hours.

3. Transfer the meat and the marinade to a large rondeau, and bring the liquid to a simmer over medium heat. Cover the pot and transfer to the oven and roast at 300°F/148°C until the meat is fork-tender, 6 to 8 hours. Remove the meat from the pot, shred, and reserve. Remove and discard the bay leaves.

4. Bring the braising liquid to a simmer over medium heat. Simmer until the mixture reduces to a syrupy consistency. Toss the shredded meat with the reduced liquid.

5. To serve, spread 2 oz/57 g of the pinto beans onto the tostada shells and top with 2 oz/57 of the shredded meat mixture. Top with 1 tsp/1 g of the cilantro, ½ tsp/.5 g of the parsley, and 2 tbsp/6 g of the lettuce chiffonade.

6. Spray a small nonstick sauté pan lightly with cooking spray. Add an egg and sauté until over easy, 2 to 3 minutes. Place the egg on top of the assembled tostada. Finish with 1 tbsp/15 mL of the salsa.

Nutritional Information per Serving (1 tostada, 2 oz/57 g beans, 2 oz/57 g meat, 1 egg, and 1 tbsp/14 g salsa):

425 calories, 14 g fat, 3 g saturated fat, 288 mg cholesterol, 683 mg sodium, 36 g total carbohydrates, 8 g fiber, 7 g sugar, 30 g protein

---

Poblano Rellenos C D V H

Makes 10 portions

10 poblano chiles

VEGETABLE ESCABÈCHE

4 oz/113 g small-dice yellow squash

4 oz/113 g small-dice zucchini

3 oz/85 g small-dice carrots, blanched

4 oz/113 g small-dice plum tomatoes

4 oz/113 g small-dice tomatillos

6 oz/170 g small-dice red onions

3 oz/85 g minced canned chipotle in adobo sauce

2 oz/57 g chopped cilantro

1 fl oz/30 mL extra-virgin olive oil

1 fl oz/30 mL rice vinegar

1 tsp/1 g kosher salt

GUACAMOLE

3 ripe Hass avocados

4 oz/113 g minced white onions

3 oz/85 g small-dice plum tomatoes

¼ oz/7 g chopped cilantro

1 fl oz/30 mL lime juice

¼ oz/7 g seeded and minced serranos

1 tsp/3 g kosher salt

TOMATO SAUCE

2 lb/907 g tomatoes, cored and quartered

½ oz/14 g garlic cloves

8 oz/227 g onion, quartered

16 fl oz/480 mL water

1½ tsp/7 mL extra-virgin olive oil

One 2-in/5-cm cinnamon stick

¼ oz/7 g epazote

1 tsp/3 g kosher salt

POBLANO FILLING

32 fl oz/960 mL water

6 oz/170 g black beans, soaked

1 fl oz/30 mL extra-virgin olive oil

4 oz/113 g small-dice onions

½ oz/14 g thinly sliced garlic cloves

1½ oz/43 g chopped chipotle in adobo sauce

2 oz/57 g minced sun-dried tomatoes

10 oz/284 g cooked amaranth

½ tsp/1 g ground cumin

½ tsp/1 g ground coriander

2 oz/57 g chopped cilantro

1½ tsp/2 g dried Mexican oregano

1 tsp/3 g kosher salt

1 oz/28 g bunch cilantro

5 fl oz/150 mL nonfat Greek-style yogurt

Continued on page 186

1. To prepare the poblano chiles, blister the chiles using a blowtorch. Once the skin is blistered, let the chiles steam in a bowl covered with plastic wrap until they are cool enough to handle; set aside. Remove the skin, carefully cut a seam in one side of each chile and remove the seeds, leaving the peppers in one whole piece.

2. To make the escabèche, combine all the ingredients and mix well; adjust the seasoning as needed. Reserve, covered, in the refrigerator until needed.

3. To make the guacamole, split the avocados, discard the pit, score the flesh with a knife, and scoop out the flesh.

4. Combine the avocados with the remaining ingredients and mix well. Reserve, covered, in the refrigerator until needed. Try to make this as close to service as possible.

5. To make the tomato sauce, heat a large cast-iron skillet over high heat. Place the tomatoes, garlic, and onions into the skillet and dry roast until their surfaces are deeply browned. Place the roasted vegetables in a large saucepan and add water to cover. Simmer over medium heat until the tomatoes are completely cooked and most of the water has been absorbed, about 15 minutes. Blend with an immersion blender and pass through a fine-mesh strainer.

6. Heat the oil in a saucepan over high heat, add the tomato sauce, cinnamon stick, and epazote, reduce the heat to medium, and simmer for 10 minutes, or to a medium (nappé) consistency.

7. Discard the cinnamon stick and season with salt. Reserve warm until needed.

8. To make the poblano filling, bring the water and beans to a boil in a medium sauce pot over high heat. Reduce to a simmer and cook until tender, about 1 hour 10 minutes.

9. In a small sauté pan, heat the oil over medium heat, add the onions and garlic, and sweat until translucent, about 3 minutes. Add to the beans. During the last 10 minutes of cooking, add the chipotles and the tomatoes and season as needed. The beans should be thick with most of the liquid absorbed; be mindful and stir periodically to avoid scorching.

10. Combine the beans, amaranth, cumin, coriander, cilantro, oregano, and salt. Stuff the prepared poblano chiles with the filling and top with the tomato sauce.

11. Pluck the cilantro leaves and store in cold water. Thin the yogurt with a small amount of water and place in a squirt bottle.

12. At service time, reheat the stuffed chiles in the oven at 350°F/176°C for 15 to 20 minutes until heated through and tender. Spoon 3 oz/85 g of the tomato sauce on the plate and place a stuffed chile on a bed of 3 oz/85 g of the vegetable escabeche near the tomato sauce. Top the chile with ½ oz/14 g of the yogurt and 5 to 6 cilantro leaves and serve with 3 oz/85 g of the guacamole.

Nutritional Information per Serving (1 pepper, 3 oz/84 g escabèche, 3 oz/84 g tomato sauce, 5 oz/14 g yogurt, and 3 oz/84 g guacamole):

388 calories, 17 g fat, 3 g saturated fat, 0 mg cholesterol, 932 mg sodium, 52 g total carbohydrates, 15 g fiber, 15 g sugar, 12 g protein

Pork Paprikash D H

Makes 10 portions

2 lb 8 oz/1.13 kg cubed pork loin

4 oz/113 g all-purpose flour

1 fl oz/30 mL extra-virgin olive oil

11½ oz/325 g chopped onions

½ oz/14 g chopped garlic

⅛ oz/ 4 g cayenne

⅓ oz/10 g Hungarian paprika

1 lb 8 oz/680 g Chicken Stock (page 105)

2 bay leaves

Salt and freshly ground black pepper

4¼ oz/121 g low-fat sour cream

¾ oz/21 g chopped flat-leaf parsley

1. Dredge the pork lightly in the flour. In a large, heavy pot, heat the oil over medium heat. Add the pork cubes and brown quickly. Remove the pork from the pan and reserve.

2. Add the onions, garlic, and cayenne to the pan and sauté until the onions are lightly browned.

3. Add the paprika, then add the stock and bay leaves and season with salt and pepper. Simmer until reduced by about half and the pork is fully cooked. Skim any excess fat. Remove and discard the bay leaves.

4. Whisk in the sour cream and simmer for 5 minutes. Adjust the seasoning with salt and additional paprika, if desired. Finish with the chopped parsley.

Nutritional Information per Serving (5⅔ oz/160 g):

391 calories, 27 g fat, 7 g saturated fat, 101 mg cholesterol, 199 mg sodium, 15 g total carbohydrates, 1 g fiber, 3 g sugar, 32 g protein

---

Sautéed Grouper with Mango Chutney and Grilled Bananas C H

Makes 10 portions

MANGO CHUTNEY

2 lb 8 oz/1.13 kg diced fresh mangoes

7 oz/199 g brown sugar

6 oz/170 g diced onions

5 oz/142 g raisins

1 oz/28 g walnuts

½ oz/14 g minced garlic

1 fl oz/30 ml apple cider vinegar

Zest and juice of 1 lemon

½ oz/14 g peeled and minced ginger

½ oz/14 g seeded and minced jalapeños

½ tsp/2.5 ml ground mace

¼ tsp/1.25 ml ground cloves

GRILLED BANANAS

5 firm-ripe small bananas (about 4 oz/113 g each), cut into ½-in/1.25-cm slices

Few drops lemon juice

1½ oz/43 g granulated sugar

2 lb 4 oz/1.02 kg grouper fillets, trimmed

2 tbsp/30 ml olive oil

1. To make the chutney, combine all the ingredients in a saucepan and simmer over low heat until reduced and thickened, about 30 minutes. Cool the chutney. If necessary, adjust the seasoning with additional lemon juice.

2. To make the grilled bananas, sprinkle the bananas evenly with the lemon juice and granulated sugar. Grill them on a hot grill or broil until marked and heated through, about 1 minute per side.

3. Trim the grouper and divide it into 3 portions, weighing ½ oz/100 g each.

4. Heat the oil in a sauté pan over medium heat. Working in batches to avoid overcrowding, sauté the grouper until lightly browned and cooked through.

5. Serve each grouper portion with 1⅔ oz/45 g of the chutney and 2⅓ oz/68 g of the grilled bananas.

Nutritional Information per Serving (3½ oz/99 g grouper, 1⅔ oz/45 g chutney, and 2⅓ oz/68 g grilled bananas):

230 calories, 4 g fat, 1.5 g saturated fat, 55 mg cholesterol, 110 mg sodium, 30 g total carbohydrates, 3 g fiber, 1 g sugar, 21 g protein

---

Tenderloin of Beef
with Mild Ancho Chile Sauce
and Pepper Jack Polenta C D H

Makes 10 portions

2 lb 4 oz/1.02 kg beef tenderloin, trimmed

2 lb/907 g prepared Polenta (page 236), cooled

3½ oz/99 g pepper Jack cheese (10 slices)

1 lb 8 oz/680 g zucchini, cut into "leaves" (see Chef's Note)

16 fl oz/480 mL Ancho Chile Sauce (page 314)

1. Cut the beef into 10 medallions, weighing about 3½ oz/ 99 g each. To maintain an even shape and thickness, tie butcher's twine around the circumference of each medallion. Refrigerate until needed.

2. Slice the polenta into 10 pieces, weighing about 3 oz/85 g each. Top the polenta pieces with a slice of cheese and broil until the cheese has melted.

3. Pan steam the zucchini until tender and keep hot.

4. For each portion: Dry sauté a beef medallion in a small cast-iron skillet or sauté pan over high heat to the desired doneness. Remove the meat from the skillet and keep warm in a low oven. Deglaze the skillet with 3 tbsp/45 mL of the sauce.

5. Serve the beef with the sauce, 1 slice of polenta, and 2½ oz/75 g of the zucchini.

CHEF'S NOTE

Cut the skin of the zucchini away from the flesh in ⅓-in/1-cm slices. Use a paring knife to cut the skin into leaf shapes.

Nutritional Information per Serving (3½ oz/99 g beef, 3 oz/85 g polenta, 3 tbsp/45 mL sauce, 2½ oz/75 g zucchini):

535 calories, 7 g fat, 1 g saturated fat, 85 mg cholesterol, 379 mg sodium, 9 g total carbohydrates, 2 g fiber, 3 g sugar, 32 g protein

Bocadillo from Catalonia

Makes 10 portions

1 lb 4 oz/567 g tuna canned in extra-virgin olive oil

10 Herbed Sandwich Rolls (page 263)

5 fl oz/150 mL Hazelnut Romesco Sauce (page 318)

1 lb 4 oz/567 g grilled zucchini slices, about ¼ in/6 mm thick (20 slices)

10 oz/284 g grilled eggplant slices, about ¼ in/6 mm thick (10 slices)

10 oz/284 g grilled red onion slices, about ¼ in/6 mm thick (10 slices)

1 lb 4 oz/567 g quartered roasted red peppers

5 hard-boiled large eggs, sliced

1. Crumble the tuna and drain it in a colander to remove excess oil.

2. To assemble the sandwiches, split the rolls and spread 1 tbsp/15 mL of the romesco sauce on each half. Place the roll bottoms on a tray.

3. Top each roll bottom with 2 slices of zucchini, 1 slice of eggplant, 1 slice of grilled onion, and a roasted pepper quarter. Top with 4 slices of egg and 2 oz/57 g of the crumbled tuna.

4. Place the tops of the rolls on top of the tuna. The sandwiches may be wrapped in deli paper at this point and reserved for service.

CHEF'S NOTE

Sandwiches are best made 1 to 2 hours before serving. Serve with Xato Salad from Catalonia (page 172).

Nutritional Information per Serving (1 sandwich):

760 calories, 29 g fat, 4 g saturated fat, 127 mg cholesterol, 577 mg sodium, 84 g total carbohydrates, 6 g fiber, 6 g sugar, 32 g protein

---

Eggplant Parcels D V H

Makes 10 portions

2 lb/907 kg eggplant, thinly sliced lengthwise (30 slices)

2 fl oz/60 mL olive oil

1 tsp/3 g kosher salt

½ tsp/1 g finely ground black pepper

12 oz/340 g pinto beans, cooked

2 lb 8 oz/1.13 kg Mixed Grain Pilaf (page 242)

2 tsp/2 g ground cumin

¼ tsp/.25 g cayenne, or more as needed

2 oz/57 g grated Monterey Jack cheese

3 oz/85 g grated pepper Jack cheese

2 oz/57 g seeded and minced jalapeños

2 oz/57 g minced sun-dried tomatoes

1 oz/28 g cilantro chiffonade

½ tsp/1 g kosher salt

¼ tsp/.5 g freshly ground black pepper

Red Chile Salsa (page 332), for serving

1. Brush the eggplant lightly with oil and season with the salt and pepper. Heat a large sauté pan over medium heat. Add the eggplant slices and cook until the eggplant is golden and tender, 3 to 5 minutes per side. Transfer the eggplant to a sheet pan.

2. In a large bowl, combine the beans, grain pilaf, cumin, cayenne, cheeses, jalapeño, tomatoes, and cilantro. Season with the salt and black pepper.

3. Spoon 2½ fl oz/75 mL of the filling onto each slice of eggplant, and roll the eggplant up to encase the filling. Place the parcels, seam side down, on a sheet pan (if desired, toothpicks can be used to keep the parcels closed).

4. Bake the parcels in the oven at 350°F/176°C until they are lightly browned and cooked through, 10 to 12 minutes. Serve the parcels with Red Chile Salsa.

Nutritional Information per Serving (9 oz/252 g):

533 calories, 13 g fat, 3 g saturated fat, 14 mg cholesterol, 541 mg sodium, 81 g total carbohydrates, 14 g fiber, 10 g sugar, 20 g protein

---

Sea Bass with Tomato and Serrano Chile

Makes 10 portions

3 lb 2 oz/1.42 kg sea bass fillet, cut into 5-oz/142-g portions

1½ tsp/4 g kosher salt

½ fl oz/15 mL lemon juice

1½ fl oz/45 mL extra-virgin olive oil

1½ oz/43 g thinly sliced garlic

1 oz/28 g seeded and thinly sliced serranos

2½ fl oz/75 mL dry white wine

2 lb/907 g plum tomato concassé

2 oz/57 g chopped flat-leaf parsley

1. Pat the fish dry. Season lightly with some of the salt and sprinkle with a few drops of lemon juice.

2. Place a sauté pan over high heat and add just enough of the oil to lubricate the pan. Heat the oil over medium heat. Place the bass portions, presentation side down, in the sauté pan.

3. Sear the fish on each side just long enough to form a golden brown crust, 1 to 2 minutes per side. Remove from the heat; the fish should be rare to medium rare. Hold the cooked portions on a rack set over a sheet pan and allow to rest in a 180°F/82°C oven while you make the sauce.

4. Add the remaining oil to the pan and heat until it shimmers. Add the garlic and sauté until aromatic. Add the sliced serranos and sauté until the garlic is a light golden color. Deglaze the pan with the wine.

5. Add the tomato concassé and toss to heat through. Add half of the parsley, and adjust the seasoning with the remaining salt as needed.

6. Plate the cooked fish and immediately top with 1¾ oz/51 g of the sauce. Garnish with the remaining parsley.

> **Nutritional Information per Serving (5 oz/142 g sea bass, 1¾ oz/49 g sauce):**
>
> 210 calories, 7 g fat, 2 g saturated fat, 60 mg cholesterol, 390 mg sodium, 6 g total carbohydrates, 1 g fiber, 3 g sugar, 27 g protein

Mujadra C D V H

Makes 10 portions

1 qt/960 mL water

6¾ oz/194 g chickpeas

2¼ fl oz/67.5 mL extra-virgin olive oil

7 oz/198 g small-dice onions

1 garlic clove, chopped

2¼ oz/63 g peeled and finely chopped ginger

¼ oz/7 g tomato paste

¼ tsp/.5 g ground allspice

Pinch chili powder

5 oz/142 g lentils, washed

1 qt/960 mL Vegetable Stock (page 106), simmering

3½ oz/99 g medium-grain brown rice

¼ oz/7 g kosher salt

CRISPY FRIED SHALLOTS

24 fl oz/720 mL canola oil, room temperature

2 oz/57 g shallots, sliced

5 pitas, split in half

5 fl oz/150 mL plain Greek-style yogurt

½ oz/14 g chopped dill

1. In a medium sauce pot over high heat, bring the water and chickpeas to a boil. Reduce to a simmer and cook, covered, until tender, 1 hour and 45 minutes. Drain and reserve.

2. In a small sauce pot, heat 1 fl oz/30 mL of the oil over medium heat. Add the onions and caramelize over low heat until a deep golden brown color is reached, about 30 minutes. Add the garlic and cook for 1 minute. Add the ginger, tomato paste, allspice, and chili powder and stir well.

3. Add the lentils and stir until fully coated with the oil. Add 16 fl oz/480 mL of simmering stock and bring to a boil, reduce the heat to a simmer, and cook, covered, until tender, about 20 minutes. Drain and reserve.

4. In a separate small saucepan, bring the remaining stock to a boil. Add the brown rice, reduce to a simmer, and cook, covered, for 30 minutes, or until tender. Drain and combine with the lentil mixture, and season with half the salt. Hold warm until ready to serve.

5. For the crispy fried shallots, in a small saucepan over medium to high heat, combine the oil and the sliced shallots and heat to 250°F/121°C. The shallots are done cooking when they are crispy and a golden brown color, about 10 minutes. Remove the shallots with a slotted spoon or spider and reserve on paper towels. Reserve the pan with the oil.

6. When the chickpeas are cooked, drain and dry. Using the same oil as for the shallots, over medium heat, fry the chickpeas in batches until the skin blooms, 2 to 3 minutes. Drain on a paper towel and reserve. Season lightly with the remaining salt.

7. Very lightly brush the remaining extra-virgin olive oil onto each pita and season. Heat in the oven at 200°F/93°C until warm, about 10 minutes.

8. To serve, place 3 oz/85 g of the filling into each pita half. Garnish each pita with fried chickpeas, fried shallots, and yogurt. Sprinkle with the dill.

CHEF'S NOTE

As an alternative, the rice, lentil, and chickpea components may be puréed or ground together after cooking and formed into 3-oz/85-g patties. Refrigerate the patties to allow them to set up. For service, dust the patties in chickpea flour and cook in a lightly oiled nonstick pan. Serve in a warmed whole wheat pita half topped with the yogurt and dill.

Nutritional Information per Serving (5 oz/142 g):

386 calories, 10 g fat, 1 g saturated fat, 0 mg cholesterol, 624 mg sodium, 59 g total carbohydrates, 12 g fiber, 7 g sugar, 13 g protein

Seared Salmon with Fiery Fruit Salsa C D H

Makes 10 portions

SALSA

10 oz/284 g peeled, pitted, small-dice mangoes

4 oz/113 g peeled, seeded, small-dice papayas

4 oz/113 g peeled, cored, small-dice pineapples

2 oz/57 g seeded, small-dice red bell peppers

4 oz/113 g diced red onions

1 tbsp/3 g chopped cilantro

1½ tsp/7.5 mL lime juice

1½ tsp/7.5 mL white wine vinegar

1 tsp/3 g seeded and minced jalapeños

½ tsp/2 mL extra-virgin olive oil

3 lbs 12 oz/1.7 kg salmon fillet, skinned, pin bones removed

¼ tsp/1 g kosher salt

2 tbsp/30 mL canola oil

1. Combine all the ingredients for the salsa in a medium bowl. Allow the salsa to sit at room temperature for 15 minutes before serving.

2. Cut the salmon into 6-oz/170-g portions, blot dry with paper towels, and season with the salt. Heat a sauté pan over medium-high heat. Add the canola oil to coat the bottom of the pan. Place the salmon in the pan and sauté on the first side for 1 to 2 minutes, until golden brown. Turn the salmon once and sauté on the opposite side for an equal amount of time. Do not overcrowd the salmon in the pan. If necessary, cook the salmon in batches, holding those that are cooked in a warm oven.

3. Serve the salmon with 2½ oz/70 g of the fruit salsa.

> **Nutritional Information per Serving (6 oz/170 g salmon, 2½ oz/71 g salsa):**
>
> 370 calories, 17 g fat, 2 g saturated fat, 120 mg cholesterol, 240 mg sodium, 9 g total carbohydrates, 1 g fiber, 7 g sugar, 44 g protein

Spicy Asian Grilled Shrimp C D H

Makes 10 portions

2 lb 4 oz/1.02 kg peeled and butterflied shrimp (21–25 count)

1½ tsp/3 g five-spice powder

1 tsp/5 mL Tabasco sauce

1½ tsp/4.5 g peeled and minced ginger

½ oz/14 g minced garlic

1 fl oz/30 mL rice wine vinegar

1 tsp/5 mL fish sauce (*nam pla*)

1 tsp/5 mL sesame oil

1. Combine the shrimp with the remaining ingredients and marinate, refrigerated, for at least 1 hour.

2. Grill the shrimp until thoroughly cooked, about 2 minutes on each side.

CHEF'S NOTE

This shrimp is delicious served with Forbidden Rice or coconut rice and a scallion salad.

> **Nutritional Information per Serving (3½ oz/100 g):**
>
> 100 calories, 1.5 g fat, 0 g saturated fat, 180 mg cholesterol, 300 mg sodium, 2 g total carbohydrates, 0 g fiber, 1 g sugar, 20 g protein

Whole Wheat Quesadillas with Roasted Chicken, Ancho Chile Caciotta, and Mango Salsa D H

Makes 10 portions

One 3½-lb/1.6-kg whole chicken

½ tsp/.5 g kosher salt

½ tsp/.5 g ground black pepper

20 whole wheat flour tortillas (8 in/20 cm)

8 oz/227 g green onions, split lengthwise and thinly sliced

3 oz/85 g pine nuts, toasted

10 oz/284 g grated ancho chile caciotta cheese

10 oz/284 g Mango Salsa (page 334)

1. Season the chicken with the salt and pepper and roast in the oven at 350°F/165°C to an internal temperature of 165°F/74°C. Cool, remove all the meat, and shred to yield 2¼ lb/1 kg cooked meat.

2. Cover the tortillas with a lightly dampened towel and warm in a 225°F/107°C oven until soft.

3. For each portion, place 3½ oz/100 g of the shredded chicken, some green onions, pine nuts, and 1 oz/30 g of the cheese in the center of a tortilla. Top with another tortilla and place in a heated sauté pan that has been sprayed with cooking spray and lightly brown on both sides, making certain that the cheese is melted in the middle before removing it from the heat. Cut the quesadilla into quarters and serve with 1 oz/30 g of mango salsa.

Nutritional Information per Serving (3½ oz/99 g chicken, 1 oz/28 g cheese, 1 tortilla, 1 oz/28 g salsa):

605 calories, 30 g fat, 11 g saturated fat, 95 mg cholesterol, 654 mg sodium, 51 g total carbohydrates, 9 g fiber, 6 g sugar, 43 g protein

---

Grilled Vegetable Jambalaya C D H

Makes 10 portions

JAMBALAYA BASE

2 fl oz/60 mL olive oil

1 lb/454 g diced onions

10 oz/284 g seeded and diced green bell peppers

10 oz/284 g diced celery

1 oz/28 g minced garlic

½ tsp/1 g freshly ground black pepper

½ tsp 1 g freshly ground white pepper

1 tsp/2 g cayenne

1 tbsp/6 g paprika

3 lb/1.36 kg diced tomatoes

1½ qt/1.44 L Vegetable Stock (page 106)

1 bay leaf

2 tsp/6 g kosher salt

1 tbsp/6 g dried oregano

1 tbsp/3 g chopped thyme

½ oz/14 g basil chiffonade

½ fl oz/15 mL Tabasco sauce

½ fl oz/15 mL Worcestershire sauce

RICE

1 lb /454 g long-grain brown rice

1 gal/3.84 L water

1 tsp/3 g kosher salt

GRILLED VEGETABLES

10 oz/284 g zucchini, cut on the bias into ¼-in/6-mm slices (20 slices)

10 oz/284 g yellow squash, cut on the bias into ¼-in/6-mm slices (20 slices)

10 oz/284 g red bell peppers, seeded and cut into 20 evenly sized pieces

10 oz/284 g red onion, cut into ¼-in/6-mm slices (10 slices)

1 lb 4 oz/567 g eggplant, peeled and cut into ¼-in/6-mm rounds (20 rounds)

2 fl oz/60 mL olive oil

2 oz/57 g BBQ Spice Rub (page 307)

4 oz/113 g green onions, thinly sliced on the bias, for serving

1. In a large pot, heat the oil over medium heat. Add the onions, bell pepper, celery, and garlic and stir to coat with the hot oil. Cover with a lid and sweat the vegetables until tender, about 5 minutes. Add the black pepper, white pepper, cayenne, and paprika and cook until the mixture becomes aromatic, about 10 minutes.

2. Add the tomatoes, vegetable stock, bay leaf, salt, oregano, thyme, basil, Tabasco, and Worcestershire sauce. Bring the mixture to a simmer over medium-low heat.

3. Meanwhile, boil the brown rice in the water, seasoned with the salt, until the rice is al dente, 30 to 35 minutes. Drain the rice in a colander and spread out on a sheet pan to cool.

4. Lightly brush the prepared vegetables with oil and season them with the spice rub. Grill the vegetables until they are tender.

5. To serve, remove and discard the bay leaf from the jambalaya base. Add the cooked rice to the base and heat thoroughly. Portion the jambalaya rice into large bowls, and top with the grilled vegetables and green onions.

> **Nutritional Information per Serving (12 oz/340 g):**
>
> 372 calories, 13 g fat, 2 g saturated fat, 0 mg cholesterol, 644 mg sodium, 53 g total carbohydrates, 9 g fiber, 12 g sugar, 8 g protein

Rabbit, Shrimp, and Andouille Jambalaya

Makes 10 portions

1 lb 4 oz/567 g boneless, skinless rabbit leg meat

2 oz/57 g BBQ Spice Rub, or as needed (page 307)

2 fl oz/60 mL olive oil

10 oz/284 g andouille sausage, cut on the bias into 20 slices

1 lb/454 g diced onions

12 oz/340 g seeded and diced green bell peppers

12 oz/340 g diced celery

1 oz/28 g minced garlic

½ tsp/1 g freshly ground black pepper

½ tsp/1 g freshly ground white pepper

1 tsp/2 g cayenne

1 tbsp/4 g paprika

3 lb/1.36 kg diced tomatoes

1.75 qt/1.66 L Shrimp Stock or Rabbit Stock (page 107)

1 bay leaf

2 tsp/6 g kosher salt

1 tbsp/6 g dried oregano

1 tbsp/3 g chopped thyme

½ oz/14 g basil chiffonade

½ fl oz/15 mL Tabasco sauce

½ fl oz/15 mL Worcestershire sauce

1 lb 4 oz/567 g long-grain brown rice

2 gal/7.57 L water

1 tsp/3 g kosher salt

1 lb 4 oz/567 g peeled, deveined, and butterflied shrimp (16–20 count)

1 fl oz/30 mL olive oil

4 oz/113 g green onions, thinly sliced on the bias

1. Cut the rabbit leg meat into ½-in/1.25-cm cubes and generously season with the spice rub.

2. In a large rondeau, heat the oil over medium-high heat. When the oil begins to shimmer, add the pieces of rabbit and sear to a rich brown color. Remove from the pan and reserve.

3. In the same pan, brown the andouille slices. Remove from the pan and reserve. There should be an accumulation of deep brown fond on the bottom of the rondeau.

4. To the hot rondeau, add the onions, bell pepper, celery, and garlic and stir to coat with the hot oil. Cover with a lid and sweat the vegetables for 6 to 8 minutes, until they have wilted and the fond has lifted from the bottom of the pan. Add the black pepper, white pepper, cayenne, and paprika and cook until the mixture becomes aromatic, about 10 minutes.

5. Add the tomatoes, shrimp stock, bay leaf, salt, herbs, Tabasco, and Worcestershire sauce. Bring the mixture to a simmer.

6. Return the rabbit meat to the rondeau and simmer the mixture until the rabbit meat is tender, about 30 minutes. Remove and discard the bay leaf.

7. Meanwhile, boil the brown rice in the water, seasoned with the salt, until the rice is al dente, 30 to 35 minutes. Drain the rice in a colander, and spread out the cooked rice on a sheet pan to cool.

8. Season the shrimp with a generous amount of the spice rub.

9. To plate, add the cooked rice to the jambalaya base and heat thoroughly. Sauté the seasoned shrimp in a small amount of oil. When the shrimp are nearly cooked, add the andouille sausage to reheat. Portion approximately 10 oz/284 g of the jambalaya rice and rabbit mixture into a large bowl, and top with 2 shrimp, 2 slices of andouille sausage, and sliced green onions.

> **Nutritional Information per Serving (10 oz/284 g jambalaya, 2 shrimp, 2 slices sausage):**
>
> 302 calories, 11 g fat, 3 g saturated fat, 13 mg cholesterol, 487 mg sodium, 30 g total carbohydrates, 6 g fiber, 8 g sugar, 13 g protein

Ricotta and Goat Cheese Gnocchi with Tuscan Kale Sauce [D] [V] [H]

Makes 10 portions

GNOCCHI

8 oz/227 g low-fat ricotta cheese

8 oz/227 g fresh goat cheese

2 oz/57 g grated Pecorino Romano cheese

3 large eggs

2 large egg yolks

½ tsp/1 g kosher salt

Pinch freshly grated nutmeg

5 oz/142 g all-purpose flour, or more as needed

KALE SAUCE

4 fl oz/120 mL extra-virgin olive oil

3 oz/85 g minced shallots

20 fl oz/600 mL Vegetable Stock (page 106)

2 lb/907 g lacinato kale chiffonade

1 tsp/3 g kosher salt

Pinch freshly ground black pepper, or as needed

2 oz/57 g butter

Poppy seeds, as needed, for garnish

1. To make the gnocchi, in a large bowl, combine the ricotta, goat cheese, and Pecorino Romano. Mix well to incorporate the three cheeses, and then fold in the eggs, egg yolks, salt, and nutmeg.

2. Mix in the flour until the dough is well combined and holds together well when pressed. Do not overwork the dough. Refrigerate the dough until firm, about 1 hour.

3. On a floured surface, roll out the dough into cylinders about ¼ in/6 mm thick. Cut the cylinder into dumplings about ½ in/1 cm long.

4. Cook the gnocchi in a large pot of salted boiling water until they are tender and float and rise to the surface, 2 to 4 minutes. Drain and reserve.

5. To make the sauce, in a large sauté pan, heat the oil over medium heat. Add the shallots and sauté until translucent, 2 to 3 minutes.

6. Add the vegetable stock and bring the mixture to a simmer. Add the kale and cook until the kale is tender and the liquid has reduced by three-quarters. Season with the salt and pepper. Keep warm.

7. In a large sauté pan, melt the butter over medium heat. Add the gnocchi and sauté until heated through, about 1 minute. Add the kale sauce and toss to combine. Portion the gnocchi into bowls and garnish with a sprinkling of poppy seeds.

> **Nutritional Information per Serving (4 oz/113 g gnocchi, 4 oz/113 g kale sauce):**
>
> 430 calories, 12 g fat, 2 g saturated fat, 1 mg cholesterol, 340 mg sodium, 41 g total carbohydrates, 7 g fiber, 4 g sugar, 5 g protein

Orzo with Broccoli Rabe, Tomatoes, and Poached Egg C D V H

Makes 10 portions

1 lb/454 g orzo

3 tbsp/30 g kosher salt

1 fl oz/30 mL olive oil

Finely grated zest of 2 lemons

¼ oz/7 g chopped basil

2 lb/907 g trimmed and blanched broccoli rabe

2 fl oz/60 mL extra-virgin olive oil

¼ oz/7 g thinly sliced garlic

1 lb/454 g halved cherry tomatoes

5 fl oz/150 mL lemon juice (juice of the 2 zested lemons)

Pinch freshly ground black pepper

4 fl oz/120 mL white vinegar

10 large eggs

2½ oz/71 g grated Parmesan cheese

1. Cook the orzo in 1 gallon of boiling water with 1 tbsp/10 g of the salt until tender, 5 to 7 minutes. Drain the orzo in a conical sieve and transfer to a medium bowl.

2. While the orzo is warm, toss it with the 1 fl oz/30 mL olive oil, the lemon zest, and half of the basil, and set aside.

3. Blanch the broccoli rabe in 2 gallons of boiling water with 1 tbsp/10 g of the remaining salt until it is beginning to become tender, 1 to 2 minutes. Drain and shock in ice water.

4. In a large sauté pan, heat the 2 oz/60 mL extra-virgin olive oil over medium heat. Add the garlic slices and broccoli rabe and sauté until tender, 4 to 5 minutes.

5. Stir in the tomatoes, lemon juice, and cooked orzo and continue to cook until heated through, 1 to 2 minutes. Season with pepper. Reserve warm.

6. In a 12- to 14-in/30- to 35-cm rondeau, bring about 1 gal/3.84 L of water to 185°F/85°C. Add the remaining 1 tbsp/10 g salt and the vinegar. Adjust the heat as needed to maintain the temperature, as vigorous boiling will break the eggs.

7. Crack the eggs first into a small cup or bowl, then gently slide the eggs into the poaching liquid. Work in small batches without crowding the eggs. Cook until the whites are completely set but yolks are still liquid, 3 to 4 minutes.

8. Portion the orzo–broccoli rabe mixture into bowls, and top each with a poached egg. Season with salt, pepper, the remaining basil, and the Parmesan cheese.

CHEF'S NOTE

Use gluten-free pasta to make celiac-friendly.

Nutritional Information per Serving (12 oz/340 g):

350 calories, 14 g fat, 3 g saturated fat, 200 mg cholesterol, 400 mg sodium, 44 g total carbohydrates, 5 g fiber, 7 g sugar, 17 g protein

Mediterranean Vegetable Bouillabaisse

Makes 10 portions

SOUP BASE

2 lb/907 g halved plum tomatoes

2 fl oz/60 mL olive oil

12 oz/340 g minced onions

6 oz/170 g minced carrots

1 oz/28 g minced garlic

8 oz/227 g minced celery

12 oz/340 g minced fennel

1 lb 4 oz/567 g minced mushrooms

8 fl oz/240 mL white wine

3 qt/2.88 L Vegetable Stock (page 106)

¼ oz/7 g fennel seeds

½ oz/14 g basil chiffonade

½ oz/14 g flat-leaf parsley chiffonade

1 tbsp/3 g chopped thyme

1 bay leaf

VEGETABLES

1 fl oz/30 mL olive oil, or as needed

10 oz/284 g cipollini onions

10 oz/284 g small-dice green bell peppers

10 oz/284 g small-dice fennel

10 oz/284 g mushrooms, cut into ⅛-in/3-mm slices

10 oz/284 g medium-dice zucchini

10 oz/284 g medium-dice waxy potato, boiled until tender

10 oz/284 g cup halved cherry tomatoes

1 oz/28 g minced garlic

1 tsp/3 g kosher salt

Pinch freshly ground black pepper

½ oz/14 g chopped flat-leaf parsley

½ oz/14 g basil chiffonade

1 lb 4 oz/567 g medium-dice firm tofu

2½ oz/71 g Modified Rouille (page 338)

1. To make the soup base, roast the plum tomatoes under a preheated broiler until lightly browned. Coarsely chop and reserve.

2. In a large pot, heat the oil over medium heat. Add the onions, carrots, and garlic and cook until lightly browned, 4 to 5 minutes. Add the celery, fennel, and mushrooms, and cook until softened, 5 to 6 minutes more.

3. Deglaze the pot with the wine. Reduce by half over medium heat.

4. Add the roasted plum tomatoes, stock, and the herbs and simmer over low heat until a full flavor and aroma has developed, about 1 hour.

5. To prepare the garnish vegetables, in a large sauté pan, heat the oil. Add the onions, bell peppers, and fennel and sauté until tender, 5 to 7 minutes. Add the mushrooms and zucchini and sauté until tender, 3 to 5 minutes more.

6. Add the cooked potatoes, cherry tomatoes, and garlic and sauté until fragrant and heated through, about 2 minutes more. Season with the salt and black pepper. Stir in the herbs, and reserve.

7. When the stock has finished simmering, add the sautéed vegetables and tofu. Simmer briefly to heat through, stirring to combine. Serve immediately, topping each portion with 1½ tsp/7.5 mL of the rouille.

Nutritional Information per Serving (12 fl oz/360 mL):

290 calories, 12 g fat, 2 g saturated fat, 0 mg cholesterol, 1320 mg sodium, 30 g total carbohydrates, 8 g fiber, 10 g sugar, 14 g protein

Whole Wheat Pappardelle with Butter Bean and Tomato Ragù D V H

Makes 10 portions

1 lb/454 g grape tomatoes, halved

5 fl oz/150 mL olive oil

12 oz/340 g onion, minced

½ oz/14 g garlic, minced

4 fl oz/120 mL cup Vegetable Stock (page 106)

3 oz/85 g tomato paste

1 lb/454 g butter beans, precooked

2 tbsp/6 g chopped thyme

1 tbsp/3 g chopped rosemary

¼ oz/7 g chopped basil

2 lb/907g Whole Wheat Pasta Dough (page 258), cut into pappardelle strips,1.25 in by 10 in/3 by 25 cm

3 gal/11.5 L boiling water seasoned with 1 oz/28 g kosher salt

1 tsp/3 g kosher salt

Pinch freshly ground black pepper, or as needed

4 oz/113 g ricotta salata cheese, grated

1. In a food processor or blender, process half of the tomatoes until smooth. Set aside.

2. In a large sauté pan, heat the oil over medium heat. Add the onion and cook until translucent, 4 to 5 minutes. Add the garlic and sauté until fragrant, about 1 minute more.

3. Deglaze the pan with the vegetable stock, add the tomato paste, and stir to combine. Stir in the puréed grape tomatoes and the beans. Add half of the herbs, and reduce the heat to a simmer. Simmer until the liquid has reduced to a thick, chunky sauce, 10 to 15 minutes.

4. Cook the fresh pappardelle in the seasoned boiling water until tender, 2 to 3 minutes. Drain the pasta thoroughly, reserving 6 fl oz/180 mL of the pasta water, and transfer to a sheet pan to cool to room temperature.

5. Stir the remaining tomato halves into the sauce and season with salt and pepper. Add the cooked pappardelle and enough of the reserved pasta water to create a nice sauce and toss to coat. Portion the pasta onto warm plates. Garnish with grated ricotta salata and the remaining chopped herbs.

CHEF'S NOTE

Use gluten-free pasta to make this recipe celiac-friendly.

Nutritional Information per Serving (9 oz/255 g):

310 calories, 23 g fat, 4 g saturated fat, 5 mg cholesterol, 234 mg sodium, 51 g total carbohydrates, 5 g fiber, 6 g sugar, 7 g protein

Jerked Pork Tenderloin with Roasted Ripe Plantain Mash and Blueberry-Tangerine-Jícama Slaw D H

Makes 10 portions

BASTING SAUCE

8 fl oz/240 mL low-sugar ketchup

1 fl oz/30 mL Jamaican Jerk Marinade (page 308)

½ fl oz/15 mL molasses

4 fl oz/120 mL amber beer

BLUEBERRY-TANGERINE-JÍCAMA SLAW

1 fl oz/30 mL extra-virgin olive oil

2 fl oz/60 mL lime juice

½ tsp/1 g kosher salt

Pinch freshly ground black pepper

¼ oz/7 g chopped cilantro

10 oz/284 g peeled and finely julienned jícama

4 oz/113 g small-dice pineapple

4 oz/113 g halved fresh blueberries

4 oz/113 g tangerine suprêmes

2 oz/57 g minced red onions, rinsed and drained

2 oz/57 g small-dice red bell pepper

1 oz/28 g seeded and minced serrano

1 qt/960 mL Jamaican Jerk Marinade (page 308)

2 lb 8 oz/1.13 kg pork tenderloin

1 lb 14 oz/851 g Roasted Ripe Plantain Mash (page 248)

1. To make the basting sauce, combine all ingredients and mix well. Reserve to brush on the grilled pork.

2. To make the slaw, mix together the oil, lime juice, salt, black pepper, and cilantro. Add the remaining ingredients and adjust the seasoning as needed.

3. Wearing food handler gloves, rub the jerk marinade into the pork tenderloin and let marinate refrigerated for several hours or overnight.

4. Preheat the grill to medium-high heat. Preheat the oven to 300°F/149°C.

5. To cook the pork tenderloin, remove the meat from the marinade and generously spray the meat with cooking spray.

6. Grill the meat on all sides to an internal temperature of 135°F/57°C degrees. Place the grilled pork on a rack set over a sheet pan, brush the pork loin with the basting sauce, place in the oven, and roast to an internal temperature of 155°F/68°C.

7. Slice the grilled tenderloin ½ in/1.25 cm thick on the bias. Serve 4 oz/113 g of the pork with 2½ oz/71 g of the plantain mash and 3 oz/85 g of the slaw.

> **Nutritional Information per Serving (4 oz/113 g pork, 2½ oz/70 g plantain mash, 3 oz/85 g slaw):**
>
> 179 calories, 6 g fat, 1 g saturated fat, 55 mg cholesterol, 234 mg sodium, 12 g total carbohydrates, 2 g fiber, 8 g sugar, 186 g protein

BBQ-Dusted Grouper with Grilled Mangoes and Blackberry Sauce D H

Makes 10 portions

5 medium, firm mangoes

½ oz/14 g honey

2 fl oz/60 mL lemon juice

2 lb 8 oz/1.13 kg grouper fillet, cut into 10 portions weighing 4 oz/113 g

6 oz/170 g BBQ Spice Rub (page 307)

1 lb 14 oz/851 g Mixed Grain Pilaf (page 242), hot

20 fl oz/600 mL blackberry sauce (see Chef's Note, page 328)

10 oz/284 g halved fresh blackberries

1 oz/28 g sliced chives

1. Preheat a well-seasoned cast-iron skillet or griddle over medium heat. Preheat a grill or grill pan as well.

2. Score, blanch, shock, and peel the mangoes. Cut in half and carefully remove the pit.

3. Combine the honey and lemon juice and brush the mixture on each mango half to prevent oxidation. Place the mangoes on a parchment paper–lined pan, cover the mangoes with plastic wrap, and refrigerate until needed.

4. At the time you are ready to cook the fish, season the fish portions liberally with the spice rub. Lightly spray the surface of the seasoned fish with cooking spray.

5. Place the fish, presentation side down, on the preheated skillet and cook for about 4 minutes. Turn the fish and continue cooking to an internal temperature of 135°F/57°C. Transfer the fish to a rack set over a sheet pan and place in a warm oven and allow to rest while assembling the plate.

6. Carefully place the mango halves on a lightly oiled preheated grill or grill pan. Cook the mangoes long enough to develop grill marks and to warm through. Be careful not to overcook the mango halves.

7. Portion 3 oz/85 g of the hot mixed grain pilaf onto a plate, and add 2 fl oz/60 mL of the blackberry sauce to the plate. Place the cooked fish on top of the sauce. Slice a grilled mango half and arrange on the plate along with 1 oz/28 g of the halved blackberries. Sprinkle the plate with chopped chives.

CHEF'S NOTE

This dish is also delicious made with salmon, halibut, or arctic char.

Nutritional Information per Serving (4 oz/113 g fish, 3 oz/85 g pilaf, 2 fl oz/60 blackberry sauce, 1 oz/28 g blackberries):

430 calories, 2 g fat, 0 g saturated fat, 42 mg cholesterol, 131 mg sodium, 74 g total carbohydrates, 5 g fiber, 23 g sugar, 30 g protein

Paillard of Chicken with Lavender Herbes de Provence and Purple Pommes Annas C D H

Makes 10 portions

2 lb 8 oz/1.13 kg boneless, skinless chicken breasts

1¼ oz/35 g herbes de Provence, finely ground

½ oz/14 g dried lavender flowers, lightly crushed

1 tsp/3 g kosher salt

¼ tsp/.5 g finely ground black pepper

5 fl oz/150 mL water

2½ oz/71 g minced shallots

5 fl oz/150 mL dry white wine

20 fl oz/600 mL glace de volaille (see Chef's Note)

3 fl oz/90 mL heavy cream

7 fl oz/210 mL almond milk

10 portions Purple Pommes Anna (Low-Fat Version) (page 238)

1. Portion the chicken breasts into 10 pieces weighing about 4 oz/113 g each. Gently pound the breasts between two sheets of plastic to form paillards about ¼ in/6 mm thick.

2. Combine the herbes de Provence with the crushed lavender flowers, salt, and pepper. Season the meat liberally with the seasoning blend.

3. Spray a sheet pan with a light coating of olive oil cooking spray, arrange the chicken on the pan, and spray the surface of the chicken with a light coating of the cooking spray.

4. Bake the chicken on the top rack of the oven at 375°F/191°C to an internal temperature of 160°F/71°C, 6 to 8 minutes, then transfer to a rack set over a sheet pan and allow to rest in a warm oven while making the sauce.

5. To make the sauce for each portion, add ½ fl oz/15 mL of water to a sauce pot and bring to a simmer. Add ¼ oz/7 g of the minced shallots and sweat until aromatic. Once the shallots are soft, about 2 minutes, add ½ fl oz/15 mL of white wine and reduce by half.

6. Add 2 fl oz/60 mL of the glace de volaille, 2 tsp/10 mL of the heavy cream, and ¾ fl oz/20 mL of the almond milk and continue to reduce the liquids until thick enough to coat the back of a spoon (nappé). Strain the sauce and use immediately.

7. To plate, place a portion of the pommes Anna on a serving plate, top with a paillard, and drizzle with 1½ fl oz/45 mL of the finished sauce.

CHEF'S NOTE

Glace de volaille is chicken stock that has been reduced by simmering over low heat to a syrupy consistency. One gallon of stock will yield approximately 1 cup/240 mL of glace de volaille.

Nutritional Information per Serving (4 oz/113 g chicken, 1½ fl oz/45 mL sauce):

187 calories, 7 g fat, 3 g saturated fat, 78 mg cholesterol, 357 mg sodium, 4 g total carbohydrates, 0 g fiber, 1 g sugar, 25 g protein

Ancho-Cumin Crusted Red Drum
with Sofrito Sauce and Stewed Black Beans C D H

Makes 10 portions

15 fl oz/450 mL Sofrito (page 333)

5 fl oz/150 mL unsweetened coconut milk

2 lb 8 oz/1.13 kg red drum fillet

6 oz/170 g Ancho-Cumin Crust Mix (page 306)

40 fl oz/1.2 L Stewed Black Beans (page 249)

1 lb 4 oz/567 g Summer Squash Noodles (page 259)

1. Combine the sofrito with the coconut milk and bring to a simmer just to heat thoroughly. Purée to a smooth consistency and keep the sofrito sauce hot until service.

2. Preheat a well-seasoned, cast-iron skillet or griddle over medium heat.

3. At service time, cut the fish into 10 portions, each weighing 4 oz/113 g. Coat the fish portions liberally with ancho-cumin crust mix. Lightly spray the coated fish with olive oil cooking spray.

4. Place the fish, presentation side down, on the preheated skillet and cook for approximately 4 minutes. Turn the fish and continue cooking to an internal temperature of 135°F/57°C. Transfer the fish to a rack set over a sheet pan, place in a warm oven, and allow to rest while assembling the plate.

5. Portion 4 fl oz/120 mL of the stewed black beans into a shallow bowl. Place 2 oz/57 g of the summer squash noodles in the center of the beans, place the cooked fish on top of the beans and squash, and drizzle with 1½ fl oz/45 mL of the sofrito sauce.

CHEF'S NOTE

This dish is also delicious made with salmon, tuna, halibut, or arctic char.

Nutritional Information per Serving (4 oz/113 g fish, 4 fl oz/120 mL black beans, 2 oz/57 g squash noodles, 1½ fl oz/45 mL sauce):

629 calories, 31 g fat, 6 g saturated fat, 14 mg cholesterol, 1063 mg sodium, 62 g total carbohydrates, 11 g fiber, 16 g sugar, 29 g protein

Prawns à la Plancha with Pimientos de Padrón

Makes 10 portions

PRAWNS

3 lb 12oz/1.7 kg whole prawns (2 to 3 oz/57 to 85 g each), legs and vein removed, butterflied from the underside

1¾ oz/49 g minced garlic

1 fl oz/30 mL lemon juice

1 fl oz/30 mL Amontillado sherry

2 fl oz/60 mL olive oil

1 tsp/3 g sea salt

¼ tsp/5 g finely ground black pepper

PEPPERS

10 oz/284 g whole padrón peppers

5 oz/142 g ripe, red serranos, cut in half lengthwise, seeds and ribs removed

2 oz/57 g olive oil

1 tsp/3 g sea salt

½ oz/14 g flat-leaf parsley chiffonade

1. In a large bowl, combine the garlic, lemon juice, sherry, oil, sea salt, and black pepper. Stir to fully combine.

2. Add the prepared prawns to the bowl, toss to coat the prawns, and allow the prawns to marinate for 1 hour.

3. Meanwhile, place the padrón and serrano peppers in a bowl, and toss with the oil and sea salt.

4. Preheat a cast-iron griddle to medium-high heat.

5. For each portion, place 6 oz/170 g marinated prawns onto the griddle, shell side down first, along with 1 oz/28 g of the padrón peppers and ½ oz/14 g of the serranos.

6. Cook the prawns until the shells become bright red and slightly golden and the peppers until they begin to blister, about 5 minutes.

7. Turn the prawns and peppers and continue to cook until the prawns are cooked through and opaque and the peppers are blistered and soft, about 4 minutes. Serve immediately, garnished with the parsley chiffonade.

CHEF'S NOTE

Serve the prawns and peppers with ½ cup/100 g brown rice pilaf with pistachios or Mixed Grain Pilaf (page 242).

Nutritional Information per Serving (6 oz/170 g fish, 1½ oz /43 g peppers):

318 calories, 14 g fat, 2 g saturated fat, 0 mg cholesterol, 509 mg sodium, 13 g total carbohydrates, 1 g fiber, 6 g sugar, 34 g protein

---

Lamb and Lentil Meatballs D H

....

Makes 10 portions

2 oz/57 g dried whole wheat bread crumbs

2 fl oz/60 mL fat-free milk

2 fl oz/60 mL eggs, beaten

1 tsp/3 g kosher salt

¼ tsp/.5 g freshly ground black pepper

1 lb/454 g spinach, blanched and squeezed dry

1 lb 8 oz/680 g ground lean lamb shoulder

8 oz/227 g cooked brown lentils

4 oz/113 g ground toasted almonds

2 oz/57 g minced onions

¼ oz/7 g garlic

¼ tsp/1 g finely grated orange zest

1 lemon, cut into 10 wedges

1. In a large bowl, combine the bread crumbs with the milk and allow the crumbs to absorb the milk and become moist.

2. Add the beaten eggs, salt, and pepper to the bowl and mix the ingredients to thoroughly combine. Add all of the remaining ingredients, except for the lemon wedges. Using your hands, mix the ingredients until fully combined.

3. Portion the mixture into 1-oz/28-g pieces and roll to form tightly packed balls. Place on a rack set over a sheet pan.

4. Bake in the oven at 400°F/205°C for 12 to 15 minutes, or until the meatballs reach an internal temperature of 165°F/74°C.

5. Serve immediately with the lemon wedges or cool to 41°F/4°C and store in the refrigerator for up to 3 days, and cooked to order when needed.

CHEF'S NOTE

....

The raw lamb meatballs may be frozen and stored for up to 30 days.

....

Nutritional Information per Serving (6 oz/170 g; 6 meatballs):

330 calories, 23 g fat, 8 g saturated fat, 85 mg cholesterol, 330 mg sodium, 14 g total carbohydrates, 5 g fiber, 2 g sugar, 19 g protein

Braised Lamb Shanks

 C D H

....

Makes 10 portions

10 lamb shanks, on the bone, trimmed lean

½ oz/14 g sea salt

2 tsp/4 g ground black pepper

4 oz/113 g diced onion

2 oz/57 g diced carrot

2 oz/57 g diced celery

½ oz/14 g crushed garlic

1½ oz/43 g unsalted tomato paste

8 fl oz/240 mL red wine

1 gal/3.84 L Brown Veal Stock (page 316)

1 Bouquet Garni (see Chef's Note, page 106)

1 oz/28 g potato starch

5 oz/142 g Gremolata (page 336)

1. Season the lamb shanks with salt and pepper. Place them on a roasting rack on a sheet tray. Roast the shanks in a 450°F/232°C oven until they are well browned, 20 to 30 minutes.

2. In a large rondeau, caramelize the onion, carrot, and celery over medium high heat. Add the garlic and cook until aromatic. Add the tomato paste and cook until browned, stirring frequently. Deglaze with red wine and reduce by one-half. Add the stock and bouquet garni and bring to a simmer.

3. Add the browned lamb shanks, bring the mixture to a simmer, cover, and place in a 350°F/175°C oven. Cook the lamb shanks until they are fork-tender, about 2 hours.

4. Remove the lamb from the liquid, cover, and reserve warm. Strain the braising liquid through a fine mesh sieve and bring the liquid to a simmer.

5. Combine the potato starch with enough water to make a slurry. Slowly stream the slurry into the simmering liquid and stir constantly until the liquid comes back to a simmer.

6. Degrease the braising liquid and reduce to nappé. Pass the sauce through a fine mesh strainer. Serve each shank with 3 fl oz/90 mL of the sauce and ½ oz/14 g gremolata.

Nutritional Information per Serving (1 shank and 3 fl oz/90 mL sauce):

353 calories, 14 g fat, 4 g saturated fat, 143 mg cholesterol, 837 mg sodium, 6 g total carbohydrates, 1 g fiber, 2 g sugar, 45 g protein

Slow-Roasted Leg of Lamb with White Beans

Makes 10 portions

LAMB

3 lb/1.36 kg lamb leg, boned

½ oz/14 g slivered garlic cloves

1 oz rosemary sprigs

½ fl oz/15 mL olive oil

1 tsp/3 g kosher salt

¼ tsp/.5 g freshly ground black pepper

BEANS

1 lb 8 oz/680 g dry white Great Northern beans, soaked overnight in water to cover by 2 in/5 cm

1 fl oz/30 mL olive oil

1 lb/454 g chopped onions

4 oz/113 g peeled whole carrot

½ oz/14 g finely chopped garlic

2 bay leaves

2 sprigs flat-leaf parsley

1 tsp/3 g kosher salt

½ tsp/1 g thyme

2 fl oz/60 mL extra-virgin olive oil

4 fl oz/120 mL dry white wine

1. Make some incisions in the lamb leg and insert the slivers of garlic. Roll the lamb leg and tie the leg with the rosemary sprigs placed under the twine. Rub with the olive oil and season with the salt and pepper. Sear the lamb on all sides in a roasting pan, add a roasting rack to the pan, and place the lamb on the rack.

2. Roast in the oven at 275°F/135°C for 4 hours or until the lamb registers 145°F/63°C on a thermometer. Remove the lamb from the roasting pan and let rest for about 20 minutes.

3. Meanwhile, drain the soaked beans. In a large pot or rondeau, heat the olive oil over medium heat Add the onions, carrot, and garlic and cook over low heat until the onion begins to soften, about 5 minutes.

4. Add the drained beans and enough fresh cold water to cover by 2 in/5 cm. Bring the beans to a simmer, add the bay leaves and parsley, and cover. Continue to simmer for 45 minutes.

5. Add the salt and thyme to the beans. Cover and continue to cook for 30 minutes more, or until the beans are tender but not mushy. Remove and discard the bay leaves, parsley sprigs, and carrot from the beans. Finish the beans with the extra-virgin olive oil and keep the beans hot in the oven at 225°F/107°C until needed. Or cool down with the cooking liquid and store the beans in the refrigerator.

6. Once the lamb has finished roasting and has rested, bring the beans back to a simmer and cook until slightly thickened.

7. Degrease the lamb roasting pan and deglaze it with white wine. Reduce the liquid by half, then stir the pan juices into the beans.

8. Cut the lamb into slices ¼ in/6 mm thick. Portion 6 oz/170 g of the cooked beans into a wide bowl and place 4 oz/112 g of the sliced lamb over the beans.

CHEF'S NOTE

Serve with oven-roasted tomatoes and sautéed greens such as broccoli rabe, kale, or mustard greens.

Nutritional Information per Serving (4 oz/113 g sliced lamb and 6 oz/170 g cooked bean mixture):

610 calories, 21 g fat, 6 g saturated fat, 115 mg cholesterol, 500 mg sodium, 50 g total carbohydrates, 15 g fiber, 4 g sugar, 53 g protein

Tamari-Washed Scallops with Green Peas and Lemongrass Purée [C] [D] [H]

Makes 10 portions

PURÉE

1 tbsp/15 mL canola oil

4 oz/113 g diced onions

7 oz/198 g dried split peas

4 oz/113 g minced lemongrass stalks

2 cups/480 mL water

1 lb/454 g green peas, fresh or frozen

4 fl oz/120 mL extra-virgin olive oil

1 tsp/3 g kosher salt

¼ tsp/.5 g freshly ground black pepper

2 lbs 4 oz/1.02 kg sea scallops, muscle tabs removed

2 fl oz/60 mL tamari

1. To make the purée, heat the canola oil in 2-qt/1.92-L sauce pot over medium heat. Add the onions and sweat until aromatic, 4 to 6 minutes.

2. Add the split peas, lemongrass, and water; cover and simmer gently until very tender, about 45 minutes. Reserve.

3. Cook the green peas in boiling salted water until tender and sweet. Drain and cool under cold running water. Drain thoroughly.

4. In the jar of a blender, purée the cooked ingredients until smooth.

5. With the blender running, add the extra-virgin olive oil. Season the purée with the salt and pepper.

6. Cool the purée to 41°F/4°C and store in the refrigerator for up to 3 days.

7. For each portion, dry approximately 3½ oz/100 g scallops with paper towels and dry sear in a seasoned sauté pan over high heat until brown on both sides and cooked through, basting with tamari as they cook.

8. To reheat the purée, place a portion of purée in a small nonstick pan with 1 tbsp/15 mL of water. Heat slowly, stirring constantly, without scorching or developing crumbles.

9. Place the purée into a heated bowl and top with the scallops.

CHEF'S NOTE

To use this purée as a sauce, adjust to the desired consistency while hot with water or vegetable stock.

Nutritional Information per Serving (5 oz/142 g):

320 calories, 14 g fat, 2 g saturated fat, 35 mg cholesterol, 760 mg sodium, 22 g total carbohydrates, 8 g fiber, 5 g sugar, 25 g protein

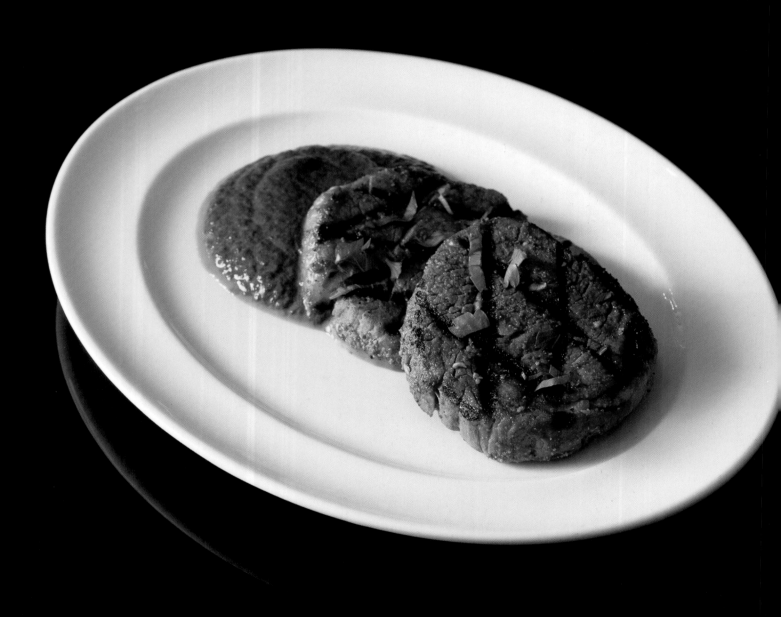

Grilled Filet of Beef with Black Trumpet Mushroom Coulis

Grilled Filet of Beef with Black Trumpet Mushroom Coulis C D H

Makes 10 portions

1 oz/28 g dried chanterelles

1½ tsp/4.5 g kosher salt

½ tsp/1.5 g black peppercorns

¼ tsp/.75 g Szechwan peppercorns

¼ tsp/.75 g garlic powder

1 lb 14 oz/850 g beef tenderloin, cut into 20 medallions (about 2 oz/57 g each)

20 fl oz/600 mL Black Trumpet Mushroom Coulis (page 341)

1. Combine the chanterelles, salt, black peppercorns, Szechwan peppercorns, and garlic powder. Grind to a fine powder in a spice grinder. Reserve.

2. Preheat a grill or cast-iron grill pan to high heat.

3. Just prior to grilling the medallions, dust the surface of the steaks with the chanterelle seasoning blend.

4. Grill the medallions to the requested doneness. Serve two 2-oz/57-g grilled medallions with 2 fl oz/60 mL of the mushroom coulis.

Nutritional Information per Serving (4 oz/113 g beef, 2 fl oz/60 mL coulis):

192 calories, 10 g fat, 5 g saturated fat, 59 mg cholesterol, 469 mg sodium, 3 g total carbohydrates, 0 g fiber, 1 g sugar, 18 g protein

---

Curry and Coconut-Marinated Chicken Breast C D H

Makes 10 portions

3 lb 2 oz/1.42 kg boneless, skinless chicken breasts, 5 oz/142 g each

½ oz/14 g minced or pressed ginger

½ oz/14 g minced or pressed garlic

1 fl oz/30 mL grapeseed oil

½ oz/14 g curry powder

1 tsp/3 g garam masala

1 tsp/3 g sea salt

¼ tsp/.5 g cayenne

4 fl oz/120 mL unsweetened coconut milk

½ oz/14 g chopped cilantro

1 oz/28 g green onions, thinly sliced on the bias

½ oz/14 g flat-leaf parsley

1. Trim the chicken breasts of any fat.

2. Combine the garlic and ginger in a bowl. Add the grapeseed oil, curry spice, garam masala, salt, cayenne, and coconut milk and whisk until well incorporated.

3. Place the chicken breasts into the bowl and toss to coat the breasts evenly with the marinade. Allow to marinate in the refrigerator for at least 1 and up to 3 hours.

4. Remove the chicken breasts from the marinade and grill over medium heat until cooked through.

5. Garnish with cilantro, green onions, and parsley.

CHEF'S NOTE

These chicken breasts are well paired with Mixed Grain Pilaf (page 242) or Indian-Style Lentil and Cauliflower Biryani (page 231).

Nutritional Information per Serving (5 oz/142 g):

340 calories, 16 g fat, 6 g saturated fat, 120 mg cholesterol, 340 mg sodium, 2 g total carbohydrates, 0 g fiber, 0 g sugar, 43 g protein

---

Almond and Flaxseed–Crusted Chicken

Makes 10 portions

2 oz/57 g onion

¼ oz/7 g garlic cloves

1½ fl oz/45 mL olive oil

3 lb 2 oz/1.42 kg boneless, skinless chicken breasts

1½ oz/43 g almond butter

½ fl oz/15 mL lemon juice

4 fl oz/120 mL fat-free buttermilk

1 tsp/2 g sea salt

Pinch cayenne

Pinch paprika

1½ oz/43 g coarsely ground golden flaxseeds

4 oz/113 g finely ground toasted almonds

2 tbsp/6 g chopped flat-leaf parsley

1 tbsp/3 g chopped thyme

1 lemon, cut into 10 wedges, seeded

1. Wrap the onion, garlic, and ½ fl oz/15 mL of the oil in aluminum foil and roast in the oven at 350°F/176°C until aromatic and tender, 20 to 25 minutes.

2. Rinse the chicken and pat dry with paper towels. Portion the chicken into 10 portions weighing about 5 oz/142 g each. Lightly pound the chicken with a mallet to even out the thickness.

3. Place the onion, garlic, remaining 1 fl oz/30 mL oil, almond butter, lemon juice, buttermilk, salt, cayenne, and paprika into a blender and purée until smooth.

4. Place the purée in a resealable plastic bag and add the chicken breasts. Seal the bag and massage the bag to make sure the purée coats the breasts thoroughly. Allow the breasts to marinate for 30 minutes.

5. Combine the ground flaxseeds, almonds, parsley, and thyme in a shallow pan and stir to mix evenly.

6. Remove the marinated chicken breasts, and dip each breast in the almond-flaxseed mixture to coat.

7. Place the coated breasts on a nonstick sheet pan that has been lightly sprayed with olive oil cooking spray. Spray the coated breasts lightly as well. Bake in the oven until cooked through, about 15 minutes.

8. Serve immediately. Garnish with a lemon wedge.

Nutritional Information per Serving (6¾ oz/191 g):

335 calories, 18 g fat, 2 g saturated fat, 85 mg cholesterol, 341 mg sodium, 6 g total carbohydrates, 4 g fiber, 2 g sugar, 34 g protein

Asparagus Risotto C D V H

Makes 10 portions

1 lb 4 oz/567 g asparagus, cut on the bias ½ in/2 cm thick

1½ qt/1.44 L Vegetable Stock (page 106)

12 fl oz/360 mL unsweetened rice milk

2 fl oz/60 mL olive oil

2 oz/57 g diced shallots

Pinch anise seed

8 oz/227 g Arborio rice

1 fl oz/30 mL lemon juice

2 fl oz/60 mL dry white wine

2 tbsp/8 g nutritional yeast

½ oz/14 g chopped tarragon leaves

½ oz/14 g minced flat-leaf parsley

1 tsp/2 g sea salt

Pinch freshly ground black pepper

1 tbsp/15 mL tamari, or as needed

1. In a large pot of boiling water, blanch the asparagus. Remove the asparagus with tongs and shock in ice water. Reserve chilled.

2. In a medium pot over medium heat, bring the stock and rice milk to a simmer.

3. In a large saucepan, heat the oil over medium-high heat. Add the shallots and cook for 3 minutes, stirring constantly. Add the anise seed and rice and continue to cook for 2 minutes, stirring constantly.

4. Reduce the heat to medium, and add the lemon juice and wine. Stir well and simmer until almost completely reduced (*sec*).

5. Gradually add the liquid in three even additions, stirring constantly and maintaining a gentle simmer. Continue to cook until each addition has been absorbed before adding the next, 5 to 7 minutes per addition.

6. When the liquid is fully incorporated and the rice is al dente, stir in the nutritional yeast, herbs, salt, pepper, tamari, and reserved asparagus. Serve immediately.

VARIATION

Roasted Squash Risotto

Replace the asparagus with 1 lb 8 oz/680 g roasted kabocha squash.

Nutritional Information per Serving (9 oz/255 g):

180 calories, 6 g fat, 1 g saturated fat, 0 mg cholesterol, 350 mg sodium, 28 g total carbohydrates, 4 g fiber, 0 g sugar, 4 g protein

Grilled Polenta with Mushroom Ragoût C D V H

Makes 10 portions

POLENTA

1 oz/28 g sun-dried tomato halves

48 fl oz/1.44 L water

1 tsp/3 g kosher salt

12 oz/340 g whole-grain polenta

MUSHROOM RAGOÛT

1 fl oz/30 mL extra-virgin olive oil

¼ oz/7 g peeled garlic cloves

1 lb 14 oz/851 g wild mushrooms such as chanterelles, morels, hen-of-the-woods, or porcini

1 tbsp/6 g chopped marjoram

2 tbsp/12 g chopped flat-leaf parsley

1 tsp/3 g sea salt

¼ tsp/7 g freshly ground black pepper

4 fl oz/120 mL Vegetable Stock (page 106)

8 oz/227 g plum tomatoes, peeled and roughly chopped

½ oz/14 g basil chiffonade

½ oz/14 g flat-leaf parsley chiffonade

1 oz/28 g shredded Parmesan cheese

1. To make the polenta: Place the sun-dried tomatoes in a bowl. Cover the tomatoes with hot water and steep for 15 minutes. Drain off the liquid and discard. Cut the tomatoes into small dice.

2. In large skillet over medium-high heat, bring the water to boil and add the salt. Reduce the heat to maintain a gentle simmer and, whisking continuously, slowly pour in the polenta. Bring to a simmer and cook stirring constantly, until the polenta has begun to thicken, about 15 minutes.

3. Add the steeped and diced sun-dried tomatoes. Continue to stir constantly until the polenta is thick and a spoon can stand straight up in it, about 45 minutes.

4. Pour the cooked polenta into ten 8-fl oz/240-mL ramekins that have been lightly coated with olive oil cooking spray. Place the filled ramekins on a sheet pan, cover with plastic wrap, and place in a refrigerator to set.

5. To make the ragoût, in a large saucepan, heat the oil over medium heat. Add the garlic and sauté until fragrant, about 2 minutes. Add the mushrooms and sauté for about 5 minutes. Add half of the marjoram and parsley. Season with salt and pepper and sauté for 4 to 5 minutes more, until the herbs become fragrant.

6. Add the vegetable stock and chopped tomatoes and simmer until the mushrooms are soft and the ragoût has started to thicken, 10 to 15 minutes. Remove from the heat and add the remaining marjoram and parsley. Serve immediately or cool to 41°F/4°C and store in the refrigerator for up to 3 days.

7. At service time, heat a grill pan or griddle to medium-high heat. Remove the polenta from the ramekins. Slice each portion into 2 evenly sized disks. Spray the disks lightly with cooking spray. Grill each polenta slice for 3 to 4 minutes per side, until heated through.

8. Place 2 grilled polenta disks in a wide bowl. Top with 4½ oz/128 g of the hot mushroom ragoût, sprinkle liberally with the basil and parsley chiffonade and shredded cheese, and serve.

> **Nutritional Information per Serving (6 oz/170 g polenta, 4½ oz/128 g mushroom ragout):**
>
> 200 calories, 6 g fat, 1.5 g saturated fat, 5 mg cholesterol, 820 mg sodium, 30 g total carbohydrates, 3 g fiber, 5 g sugar, 8 g protein

Indian-Style Lentil and Cauliflower Biryani

Makes 10 portions

36 fl oz/1.08 L Vegetable Stock (page 106)

1 lb/454 g brown basmati rice

1 qt/960 mL water

5 oz/142 g dried French green lentils

2 fl oz/60 mL grapeseed oil

8 oz/227 g small-dice yellow onions

4 oz/113 g medium-dice carrots

1 oz/28 g peeled and grated ginger

½ oz/14 g minced garlic

1½ tbsp/4 g toasted garam masala

1½ tbsp/4 g toasted ground coriander

1 tbsp/3 g dried mint

1 tbsp/3 g ground turmeric

8 fl oz/240 mL water

1 lb 4 oz/567 g small cauliflower florets

1¾ oz/50 g dried unsweetened currants or small raisins

6 oz/170 g cooked green peas

5 oz/142 g toasted slivered almonds

2½ oz/71 g toasted pistachios, roughly chopped

1 oz/28 g cilantro chiffonade

1 oz/28 g flat-leaf parsley chiffonade

1. Bring the vegetable stock to a simmer in a medium sauce pot over medium heat. Add the rice and return the liquid to a simmer. Cover the pot and lower the heat to a gentle simmer. Cook the rice until tender, about 35 minutes.

2. When the rice is cooked, fluff it with a fork, then spread it out onto a sheet pan and allow to cool.

3. In a medium sauce pot, bring the water to a boil over high heat. Add the lentils, reduce the heat to low, and simmer until tender, about 30 minutes Drain and cool.

4. In a large shallow saucepan, heat the oil over medium-high heat. Add the onion, carrot, ginger, and garlic and cook until the onion softens, about 5 minutes. Add the garam masala, coriander, mint, and turmeric and cook, stirring occasionally, about 2 minutes.

5. Stir in the water, cauliflower, and currants, and cover and simmer for 5 minutes. Stir in the peas, cooked rice, and cooked lentils, cover, and simmer until the liquid has been absorbed, about 4 minutes. Stir in the almonds, pistachios, cilantro, and parsley. Serve immediately.

CHEF'S NOTE

This dish may be prepared in stages such as having all *mise en place* prepared and preportioned: rice precooked, cooled, and portioned; and lentils precooked, cooled, and portioned in order to facilitate finishing à la minute.

Nutritional Information per Serving (4 oz/113 g cooked brown rice, 1 oz/28 g cooked lentils, 4 oz/113 g vegetables and spices, ½ oz/14 g almonds, ¼ oz/7 g pistachios, .18 oz/5 g currants):

256 calories, 3 g fat, 0 g saturated fat, 0 mg cholesterol, 304 mg sodium, 18 g total carbohydrates, 3 g fiber, 0 g sugar, 3 g protein

Side dishes fulfill a variety of roles in the world of healthful preparations. These meal accompaniments add color, taste, and texture to your finished plates. Side dishes are made up of cooked grains, vegetables, and legumes, and often may be a combination of two or all three of these. In this chapter you may notice that the side dishes have little or no animal protein or animal fat, so they are readily available for use in fulfilling vegetarian requests. In addition to being a great partner to meat-, fish-, and poultry-centric entrées, side dishes can also become a platform for an entrée. For example, whole wheat pappardelle has a fantastic grainy texture and makes a tasty starch accompaniment for Lamb and Lentil Meatballs (page 222) served with sautéed Swiss chard and roasted tomatoes. Likewise, Whole Wheat Pappardelle with Butter Bean and Tomato Ragù (page 210) makes up a complete meal.

Some side dishes can make delightful plated or passed appetizers. For instance, Roasted Eggplant Caponata is delicious served as a small bite on a petite crostini. And as an appetizer, Roasted Cremini Mushrooms with Guajillo Chiles and Garlic makes a great topping for a half-portion of grilled polenta.

The side dishes included in this chapter are just a smattering of the multitude of options that are delicious possibilities.

Beans and Greens Sauté

Makes 8 portions

2 tbsp/30 mL olive oil

2 tsp/4 g minced garlic

1 lb 4½ oz/582 g escarole, coarsely chopped

4 fl oz/120 mL Vegetable Stock (page 106)

1 tsp/3 g salt, or more as needed

½ tsp/1 g ground black pepper, or more as needed

12 oz/340 g cooked cannellini beans, drained and rinsed

1 tsp/5 mL malt vinegar

1. In a large sauté pan, heat the oil over medium-high heat. Add the garlic and sauté, stirring frequently, until tender and fragrant, about 3 minutes.

2. Add the escarole and cook, stirring and tossing to coat the greens evenly with the oil.

3. When the escarole has cooked down and is a vivid green, add the stock. Season lightly with the salt and pepper.

4. Bring the stock to a simmer, then add the beans and cook, stirring frequently, until the greens are fully wilted and the dish is very hot, 6 to 7 minutes.

5. Season as needed with the malt vinegar, salt, and pepper.

Nutritional Information per Serving (3¼ oz/90 g):

37 calories, 1 g fat, 0 g saturated fat, 0 mg cholesterol, 239 mg sodium, 5 g total carbohydrates, 4 g fiber, 1 g sugar, 1 g protein

---

Polenta

Makes 10 portions

1 qt/960 mL Chicken Stock (page 105)

6 oz/170 g whole-grain, coarse-ground yellow cornmeal

2 oz/57 g grated Parmesan cheese

¼ tsp/.5 g freshly ground white pepper

1. Heat the stock to a simmer in a medium sauce pot.

2. While whisking constantly, rain the cornmeal into the stock. Cook over low heat, stirring constantly with a wooden spoon, until the polenta pulls away from the sides of the pot, about 35 minutes.

3. Remove from the heat and stir in the cheese and pepper.

4. Brush a pan measuring 9 by 13 by 2 in/23 by 33 by 5 cm with water and pour the polenta into the pan. Cool, cover with plastic wrap, and refrigerate until firm.

5. When firm, cut the polenta into 3-oz/85-g portions. Grill or reheat the portions in the oven before serving.

CHEF'S NOTE

Substitute vegetable stock for chicken stock to make this recipe vegetarian-friendly.

Nutritional Information per Serving (4 oz/113 g):

84 calories, 2 g fat, 1 g saturated fat, 5 mg cholesterol, 86 mg sodium, 13 g total carbohydrates, 0 g fiber, 1 g sugar, 5 g protein

---

Green Beans with Frizzled Prosciutto and Gruyère C D H

Makes 10 portions

3 tbsp/45 mL lemon juice

1 tbsp/15 mL white wine vinegar

2 tbsp/30 g minced shallots

½ tsp/2 g kosher salt, or as needed

¼ tsp/.5 g freshly ground black pepper, or as needed

3½ fl oz/105 mL extra-virgin olive oil

2 lb 8 oz/1.13 kg green beans, ends trimmed

4 oz/113 g thinly sliced prosciutto

4 oz/113 g Gruyère cheese, cut into matchsticks

1. Combine the lemon juice, vinegar, shallots, salt, and pepper. Gradually whisk in 6 tbsp/90 mL of the oil. Taste and adjust the seasoning with additional salt and pepper as needed. Set the dressing aside.

2. Bring a large pot of salted water to a boil. Add the green beans and cook until bright green and just barely tender to the bite, about 3 minutes. Drain the green beans and rinse with cold water until they feel cool. Drain well.

3. Toss the greens beans and the dressing together and let them marinate at room temperature for 10 minutes.

4. Heat the remaining oil in a sauté pan over medium-high heat until it shimmers. Add the prosciutto to the hot oil and cook until it "frizzles," about 2 minutes. Add the prosciutto and the Gruyère to the beans. Season with additional salt and pepper if necessary. Serve at room temperature.

Nutritional Information per Serving (3 oz/85g):

132 calories, 14 g fat, 4 g saturated fat, 21 mg cholesterol, 578 mg sodium, 8 g total carbohydrates, 4 g fiber, 3 g sugar, 8 g protein

---

Green Beans with Frizzled Prosciutto and Gruyère

Purple Pommes Anna (Low-Fat Version)

....

Makes 10 portions

1 lb 14 oz/850 g unpeeled purple potatoes

1 tsp/3 g salt

¼ tsp/.5 g freshly ground black pepper

2 oz/57 g butter

2 fl oz/60 mL olive oil

1. Place the potatoes in a small pot, cover by 1 in/2.5 cm with water, and bring to a simmer. Gently simmer the potatoes until barely tender, 8 to 10 minutes.

2. Drain the potatoes and allow to cool slightly.

3. Peel and trim the potatoes into uniform cylindrical shapes. Using a mandoline, carefully cut the potatoes into $^1/_{16}$-in/1.5-mm slices. Place the slices in a bowl and toss with the salt and pepper to evenly season the potatoes.

4. Melt the butter and oil together.

5. Line two sheet pans with parchment paper. Trace ten 6-in/15-cm circles on the parchment paper and turn the paper over.

6. For each portion, brush each circle with ¼ tsp/1 g of the melted butter-oil blend and arrange 3 oz/84 g of the seasoned potato slices in concentric rings within the circle, starting from the center and working outward. Drizzle ¼ tsp/1 g of the butter-oil blend over the top of the arranged potatoes and around the edges. Place the pan on the top rack of the oven and bake at 400°F/205°C until the potatoes are caramelized and cooked through, about 20 minutes, pressing the potatoes occasionally to compress the slices.

7. To serve the potatoes, carefully lift the pommes Anna onto the plate they will be served on. Serve immediately while still hot and crisp.

CHEF'S NOTE

For a side dish with a lower glycemic impact, substitute purple sweet potatoes for the purple potatoes.

....

> **Nutritional Information per Serving (3 oz/85 g):**
>
> 159 calories, 10g fat, 4 g saturated fat, 12 mg cholesterol, 198 mg sodium, 15 g total carbohydrates, 1 g fiber, 6 g sugar, 2 g protein

Rainbow Swiss Chard with Roasted Walnuts

....

Makes 10 portions

2 lb/907 g Swiss chard

2 fl oz/30 mL extra-virgin olive oil

2 oz/57 g minced shallots

1 oz/28 g minced garlic

1 fl oz/30 mL Vegetable Stock (page 106)

1 tsp/3 g kosher salt

¼ tsp/.5 g freshly ground black pepper

2½ oz/71 g toasted walnuts, chopped

1. Remove the chard stems, and cut the stems into medium dice or thin slices. Cut the leaves into chiffonade.

2. Heat the oil in a large sauté pan over medium heat. Add the shallots to the pan and sweat until translucent, about 3 minutes. Add the garlic and cook until fragrant, another 2 minutes.

3. Add the chard stems to the pan, toss with the sweated vegetables, and continue to sauté for 1 minute.

4. Add the vegetable stock and bring to a strong boil. Add the chiffonade of chard leaves and season with the salt and pepper. Sauté, in batches if necessary, until just barely wilted, 3 to 5 minutes. A lid may be used to speed up the process.

5. Remove the lid, if necessary, to evaporate some of the excess liquid. Toss the walnuts with the chard and serve.

> **Nutritional Information per Serving (3½ oz/99 g):**
>
> 121 calories, 10 g fat, 1 g saturated fat, 0 mg cholesterol, 435 mg sodium, 7 g total carbohydrates, 2 g fiber, 2 g sugar, 3 g protein

Rainbow Swiss Chard with Roasted Walnuts

Whole Wheat Spätzle D V H

Makes 10 portions

4 oz/113 g large eggs

4 oz/113 g egg whites

3½ fl oz/105 mL skim milk

5 oz/142 g water

1 tsp/3 g kosher salt

½ tsp/1 g freshly ground white pepper

Pinch freshly grated nutmeg

¼ oz/7 g chopped chervil

¼ oz/7 g chopped chives

¼ oz/7g chopped flat-leaf parsley

¼ oz/7 g chopped tarragon

6 oz/170 g all-purpose flour

4 oz/113 g whole wheat flour

1 oz/28 g butter

1. Combine the whole eggs, egg whites, milk, and water in a large bowl. Season the batter with the salt, pepper, and nutmeg. In a small bowl, combine the herbs to make a fines herbes mixture. Add ½ oz/14 g of the fines herbes to the batter and stir to combine. Work in the flours by hand, and beat until smooth. Allow the mixture to rest for 1 hour.

2. Bring a large pot of salted water to a simmer. Working in batches, press the dough/batter through a spätzle maker (or perforated hotel pan) into the simmering water. When the spätzle float, remove them with a spider. Place the spätzle in a hotel pan and reserve until all the batter has been cooked.

3. Heat the butter in a large sauté pan over medium-high heat. Add the spätzle and sauté until very hot. Adjust the seasoning with salt and pepper.

4. Serve on a heated platter, garnished with the remaining fines herbes.

CHEF'S NOTE

Gluten-free flour blend may be used in this recipe with added guar gum.

> **Nutritional Information per Serving (3 oz/85 g):**
>
> 148 calories, 4 g fat, 2 g saturated fat, 54 mg cholesterol, 277 mg sodium, 22 g total carbohydrates, 2 g fiber, 1 g sugar, 6 g protein

Artichoke Caponata C D V H

Makes 10 portions

14 baby artichokes

1 oz/28 g small-dice celery

4 fl oz/120 mL extra-virgin olive oil

½ oz/14 g coarsely chopped garlic

1 oz/28 g raisins, plumped in warm water for 15 minutes

¾ tsp/2 g freshly ground black pepper

5 mint leaves, cut into chiffonade

1 fl oz/30 mL white wine vinegar

1 oz/28 g pine nuts, toasted

1 tsp/3 g kosher salt

1. Clean the artichokes and boil in acidulated water (see Chef's Note) until al dente.

2. Bring a pot of salted water to a boil. Add the celery, cook until al dente, and drain.

3. Heat the oil in a pan over medium heat. Add the garlic and cook until fragrant. Add the celery and sauté until soft. Add the artichokes, raisins, pepper, and mint and cook, stirring constantly, until the mixture is heated through.

4. Splash with the vinegar and allow it to evaporate. Sprinkle with the pine nuts, season with salt, and serve immediately, or cover and refrigerate until needed.

CHEF'S NOTE

Acidulated water is made by combining 1 gal/3.84 L water with 2 tbsp/30 mL lemon juice or vinegar.

> **Nutritional Information per Serving (3 oz/85 g):**
>
> 144 calories, 13 g fat, 2 g saturated fat, 275 mg cholesterol, 6 mg sodium, 6 g total carbohydrates, 2 g fiber, 1 g sugar, 2 g protein

Artichoke Caponata and Roasted Eggplant Caponata (page 242)

Roasted Eggplant Caponata CDVH

Makes 10 portions

8 oz/227 g peeled and small-dice eggplant

¼ oz/7 g kosher salt

4 oz/113 g small-dice red bell peppers

2 oz/57 g minced onions

½ tsp/3 g minced garlic

¾ fl oz/22.5 mL olive oil

8 oz/227 g canned plum tomatoes, cut into small dice

½ oz/14 g tomato paste

1½ tsp/3 g basil chiffonade

½ tsp/1 g minced marjoram

¼ oz/7 g balsamic vinegar

½ oz/14 g freshly grated Parmesan cheese

1. Place the diced eggplant in a large bowl, sprinkle with the salt, and toss to evenly distribute. Place the salted eggplant in a colander and allow it to drain for 20 minutes.

2. Quickly rinse the eggplant with water, then place on paper towels to absorb the excess moisture.

3. In a large bowl, combine the eggplant with the bell pepper, onion, garlic, and oil and toss to coat with the oil. Add the tomatoes and tomato paste and toss once more to thoroughly combine.

4. Place the vegetable mixture on a sheet pan and roast in the oven at 350°F/176°C for 25 to 30 minutes, until the vegetables are tender and lightly browned.

5. Remove the pan from the oven and add the basil, marjoram, and vinegar. Gently fold the ingredients together.

6. Cool to room temperature and add the cheese. Store, covered, in a glass or stainless-steel container in the refrigerator for up to 1 week. The flavor will improve if allowed to rest for 24 hours before use.

Nutritional Information per Serving (2 oz/57 g):

25 calories, 1 g fat, 0 g saturated fat, 0 mg cholesterol, 260 mg sodium, 4 g total carbohydrates, 1 g fiber, 2 g sugar, 1 g protein

---

Mixed Grain Pilaf DVH

Makes 10 portions

8 oz/227 g rye berries

8 oz/227 g wheat berries

4 oz/113 g wild rice

4 oz/113 g pearl barley

½ fl oz/15 mL olive oil

2 oz/57 g minced shallot or yellow onion

54 fl oz/1.6 L Vegetable Stock (page 106), heated

1 tsp/3 g kosher salt

¼ tsp/.5 g freshly ground black pepper

1. Rinse all the grains separately in a strainer until the water runs clear.

2. In a large pot, heat the oil over medium heat. Add the shallot and sauté until translucent.

3. Add the rye berries, wheat berries, and wild rice and coat thoroughly with the oil.

4. Add the heated vegetable stock to the grains and bring to a boil. Add the salt, cover with a tight-fitting lid, and simmer the grains gently for 30 minutes. Add the pearl barley to the pot.

5. Simmer until all of the stock has been absorbed and the grains are tender to the bite, about 1½ hours.

6. Add the pepper and fluff the grains with a fork. Serve immediately, or cool the pilaf to room temperature on a sheet pan, then store, covered, in the refrigerator for up to 3 days.

Nutritional Information per Serving (4 oz/113 g):

339 calories, 3 g fat, 0 g saturated fat, 0 mg cholesterol, 48 mg sodium, 63 g total carbohydrates, 7 g fiber, 5 g sugar, 12 g protein

---

Mixed Grain Pilaf

Panelle C D V H

Makes 10 portions

1 fl oz/30 mL olive oil

½ oz/14 g minced garlic

20 fl oz/ 600 mL warm water

6 oz/170 g chickpea flour, plus 3 oz/85 g for dusting
the fries

½ tsp/2 g kosher salt

1 oz/28 g minced herbs such as parsley, chives, rosemary,
or oregano (optional)

4 oz/113 g roughly chopped cooked chickpeas

16 fl oz/480 mL canola oil, for frying

1. In a medium sauce pot, heat the olive oil over low heat. Add the garlic and cook until softened and fragrant. Add the water and bring to a gentle simmer. Slowly sprinkle in the 6 oz/170 g of chickpea flour and the salt. Whisk to combine and work out any lumps. Bring to a boil and cook until thick, 10 to 12 minutes.

2. Add the herbs, if using, and the chopped chickpeas and stir to combine. Pour the mixture into a half hotel pan lined with plastic wrap and spread out into an even thickness. Chill for 2 or more hours in the refrigerator to firm up. Slice into French fry–size strips, and dust with the 3 oz/85 g of chickpea flour. Fry in the canola oil at 350°F/176°C degrees until golden and crisp, 5 to 7 minutes.

Nutritional Information per Serving (3 oz/85 g):

137 calories, 7 g fat, 1 g saturated fat, 0 mg cholesterol, 131 mg sodium,
14 g total carbohydrates, 3 g fiber, 2 g sugar, 5 g protein

Roasted Cremini Mushrooms with Guajillo Chiles and Garlic C D V H

Makes 10 portions

2 lb/907 g cremini mushrooms, trimmed and quartered

2 fl oz/60 mL olive oil

1 oz/28 g minced garlic

8 oz/227 g minced onions

1 oz/28 g guajillo chiles (about 5), rinsed, seeded, and cut into chiffonade

1 tsp/3 g kosher salt

Pinch freshly ground black pepper, or as needed

1. Lightly oil a sheet pan.
2. In a large bowl, toss the mushrooms, oil, garlic, onions, and guajillo chiles to combine. Season with the salt and pepper.
3. Roast in the oven at 350°F/176°C until the mushrooms are tender and fragrant, 15 to 20 minutes.

Nutritional Information per Serving (4 oz/113 g):

100 calories, 6 g fat, 1 g saturated fat, 0 mg cholesterol, 200 mg sodium, 7 g total carbohydrates, 1 g fiber, 3 g sugar, 3 g protein

---

Mushrooms with Garlic Persillade D V H

Makes 10 portions

PERSILLADE

3 oz/85 g panko bread crumbs

1 oz/28 g grated Parmesan cheese

1 oz/28 g finely chopped flat-leaf parsley

¾ oz/21 g finely minced garlic

1 fl oz/30 mL extra-virgin olive oil

½ tsp/1 g freshly ground black pepper

MUSHROOMS

1 fl oz/30 mL olive oil

2 lb/907 g cremini mushrooms, stems removed, caps reserved

2 fl oz/60 mL dry white wine

2 fl oz/60 mL Vegetable Stock (page 106)

½ oz/14 g Dijon mustard

1. In a medium bowl, combine all the ingredients for the persillade and reserve.

2. In a large sauté pan, heat the olive oil over high heat until it shimmers. Add the mushroom caps and sauté for 8 to 10 minutes, until the mushrooms have softened. Remove and reserve the mushroom caps.

3. With the heat still on high, deglaze the pan with the white wine and reduce by half. Add the vegetable stock and Dijon mustard and continue to reduce until slightly thickened.

4. Return the mushroom caps to the pan and toss to coat with the mustard glaze.

5. Arrange 3 oz/85 g of the caps, open side up, in each of 10 small oval ramekins. Top with ½ oz/14 g of the persillade mixture. Bake the mushrooms on the top shelf of the oven at 400°F/205°C oven until the persillade is golden and crisp, 7 to 10 minutes.

Nutritional Information per Serving (3½ oz/99 g):

132 calories, 7 g fat, 1 g saturated fat, 2 mg cholesterol, 111 mg sodium, 14 g total carbohydrates, 1 g fiber, 6 g sugar, 5 g protein

Roasted Ripe Plantain Mash C D V H

Makes 10 portions

10 oz/284 g peeled green plantains

2 qt/1.88 L water

1 tsp/3 g kosher salt

1 lb 4 oz/567 g peeled ripe (black) plantains

1 fl oz/30 mL melted coconut oil

2 fl oz/60 mL unsweetened coconut milk

1. Cut the green plantains into 2-in/5-cm pieces. Place them in a pot with the water. Add the salt, and bring to a boil. Cook over medium heat until the plantains are very tender, about 15 minutes. Drain and reserve.

2. Cut the black plantains into 2-in/5-cm pieces and place them on a nonstick sheet pan along with the boiled green plantains. Drizzle with the melted coconut oil and roast in the oven at 350°F/176°C until the ripe plantains are golden brown.

3. Using a large wooden pestle, mash the roasted plantains along with the coconut milk to produce a thick, smooth purée/paste. Serve warm.

Nutritional Information per Serving (4 oz/113 g):

105 calories, 44 g fat, 4 g saturated fat, 0 mg cholesterol, 212 mg sodium, 18 g total carbohydrates, 1 g fiber, 10 g sugar, 1 g protein

Callaloo with Shallots and Cremini C D V H

Makes 10 portions

4 lb/1.81 kg fresh callaloo greens, leaves and tender stems only

1½ fl oz/45 mL olive oil

2 oz/57 g minced shallots

1 oz/28 g minced garlic

1 lb/454 g thinly sliced cremini mushrooms

½ tsp/1.5 g kosher salt

¼ tsp/.5 g freshly ground black pepper

1. Stem and trim the callaloo greens and drain thoroughly.

2. In a large sauté pan or medium rondeau, heat the oil over medium heat. Add the shallots and garlic, and sweat for 3 to 4 minutes to develop the flavor, but without adding color.

3. Add the sliced mushrooms and continue to sauté over medium heat until the mushrooms become soft. Increase the heat to high, and allow the excess moisture from the mushrooms to evaporate.

4. Add the callaloo greens, salt, and pepper to the pan and toss or stir to combine all of the ingredients. Cover with a lid and cook until the greens have wilted. Serve immediately.

CHEF'S NOTE

If callaloo greens are not available, spinach or baby kale may be used.

> **Nutritional Information per Serving (3½ oz/99 g):**
>
> 57 calories, 4 g fat, 0 g saturated fat, 0 mg cholesterol, 99 mg sodium, 4 g total carbohydrates, 0 g fiber, 1 g sugar, 1 g protein

Stewed Black Beans C D H

Makes 10 portions

1 fl oz/30 mL pure olive oil

8 oz/227 g small-dice onions

½ oz/14 g minced garlic

1 lb/454 g black beans, soaked overnight

3 qt/2.88 L Chicken Stock (page 105)

2 oz/57 g finely chopped chipotles in adobo sauce

1 tsp/1 g dried Mexican oregano

2 oz/57 g small-dice sun-dried tomatoes

1 tsp/3 g kosher salt

¼ tsp/.5 g freshly ground black pepper

1. In a large sauté pan or medium rondeau, heat the oil over medium heat. Add the onions and sweat for 3 to 4 minutes to develop the flavor, but without adding color. Add the garlic and sweat for 3 minutes more.

2. Add the beans and enough stock to cover the beans by 1 in/2.5 cm and bring to a simmer. Add more stock during the cooking so that the beans remain covered with liquid. Add the salt only at the end of the cooking time.

3. After the beans are halfway cooked, add the chipotles, Mexican oregano, and the sun-dried tomatoes. Season with the salt and pepper. Reserve for service, or cool to 41°F/4°C and store in the refrigerator for up to 3 days.

> **Nutritional Information per Serving (3½ oz/99 g):**
>
> 204 calories, 3 g fat, 0 g saturated fat, 0 mg cholesterol, 312 mg sodium, 38 g total carbohydrates, 8 g fiber, 4 g sugar, 11 g protein

Creamed Pinto Beans [C] [D] [H]

Makes 10 portions

10 oz/284 g pinto beans, soaked overnight

5 oz/142 g minced white onion

2½ fl oz/75 mL nonfat milk

2 dried ancho chiles, toasted, seeded, and cut into chiffonade

½ tsp/1 g ground cumin

½ tsp/1 g dried thyme

½ tsp/1 g dried Mexican oregano

1½ tsp/7.5 mL tomato paste

1 tsp/5 mL vegetable oil

3 garlic cloves, minced

½ tsp/1.5 g kosher salt, or as needed

¼ tsp/.5 g freshly ground black pepper, or as needed

1. Transfer the soaked beans to a large stockpot with the onions. Add enough water to cover the beans by 1 in/2.5 cm and bring to a simmer over medium heat. Cover the pot and simmer until the beans are tender, about 1 hour.

2. Purée the warm beans in a food processor or with an immersion blender. Add the milk, toasted chiles, cumin, thyme, oregano, and tomato paste and mix to combine.

3. In a medium pot, heat the oil over medium heat. Add the garlic and cook until fragrant, about 1 minute. Add the beans to the pot, mix to combine, and bring to a simmer over medium heat. Cover the pot and transfer to the oven. Bake the beans in the oven at 350°F/175°C until they are thick and heated through, 45 minutes to 1 hour.

Nutritional Information per Serving (1½ oz/43 g):

112 calories, 1 g fat, 0 g saturated fat, 0 mg cholesterol, 126 mg sodium, 20 g total carbohydrates, 5 g fiber, 2 g sugar, 6 g protein

---

Cauliflower and Roasted Garlic Purée

Makes 10 portions

2 oz/57 g garlic heads

1½ fl oz/45 mL olive oil

6 oz/170 g minced Vidalia onions

4 oz/113 g peeled and quartered Yukon gold potatoes

½ tsp/1.5 g kosher salt

2 lb/907 g cored and quartered cauliflower

2 fl oz/60 mL almond milk

Pinch freshly ground black pepper

1. Wash the bulbs of garlic and split them in half across their equator. Place the split garlic on a large sheet of aluminum foil and drizzle each bulb half with ½ oz/15 mL of the oil. Seal the garlic in the foil and place in a 350°F/175°C oven. Roast for 25 to 35 minutes, until the garlic becomes very soft and golden brown. Be careful not to overbake the garlic or it will become bitter. Squeeze the roasted garlic pulp from the skins and reserve.

2. Meanwhile, in a medium pot, heat the remaining 1 fl oz/ 30 mL oil over medium heat. Add the onion and sauté until aromatic and translucent, about 5 minutes.

3. Add the potatoes and salt to the pot and enough water to just cover the potatoes. Add the cauliflower on top, cover with a lid, and bring to a boil. Simmer the vegetables over medium heat until the cauliflower and potatoes are very tender. Drain and reserve all the liquid from the potatoes and cauliflower.

4. Add the peeled roasted garlic to the cauliflower-potato mixture. Using an immersion blender or variable speed blender, purée the mixture to a very smooth paste. Add the almond milk to the purée to adjust to a piping consistency. Add the reserved cooking liquid as well if needed.

5. Keep the purée hot until service, or cool to 41°F/4°C and store in the refrigerator for up to 3 days.

CHEF'S NOTE

To use this purée as a sauce, adjust the consistency to the desired viscosity with hot vegetable stock.

Nutritional Information per Serving (4 oz/113 g):

152 calories, 9 g fat, 1 g saturated fat, 0 mg cholesterol, 257 mg sodium, 17 g total carbohydrates, 5 g fiber, 6 g sugar, 5 g protein

Sweet Potato–Apple Gratin C D V H

Makes 10 portions

1 fl oz/30 mL almond oil

1 oz/28 g thinly sliced shallots

1 tsp/2 g curry powder

¼ oz/7 g peeled and minced ginger

2 oz/57 g minced dried figs

4 fl oz/120 mL apple cider

4 fl oz/120 mL orange juice

1 lb 14 oz/850 g peeled sweet potatoes, sliced lengthwise ⅛ in/3 mm thick

8 oz/227 g peeled Honeycrisp apples, halved, cored, and sliced ⅛ in/3 mm thick

Pinch kosher salt

1. Preheat a small sauté pan over medium heat. Add the almond oil, shallots, curry powder, and ginger and sweat for 2 minutes, or until very aromatic, but with no added color.

2. Add the figs, apple cider, and orange juice and simmer for 1 minute. Remove the aromatic mixture from the heat.

3. Add the aromatic mixture to the sweet potatoes, apples, and salt and toss to evenly distribute.

4. Spray the inside of a 2-in/5-cm deep half hotel pan with cooking spray. Neatly arrange the mixture so it is level in the pan.

5. Cover the pan with aluminum foil and bake in a 350°F/176°C oven for about 30 minutes. Uncover the pan and move it to the top rack of the oven. Bake for 15 to 20 minutes more, or until the potatoes are tender and the top is lightly browned.

6. Remove the cooked gratin from the oven and allow to rest for 1 hour or more before cutting into portions.

7. Portion the gratin in half, lengthwise, then cut crosswise into 5 sections, producing 10 evenly sized portions approximately 4½ oz/128 g each. Reheat as needed to serve.

Nutritional Information per Serving (4½ oz/128 g):

136 calories, 3 g fat, 0 g saturated fat, 0 mg cholesterol, 71 mg sodium, 27 g total carbohydrates, 4 g fiber, 20 g sugar, 2 g protein

---

Roasted Cauliflower with Rice, Beans, and Mustard Vinaigrette C D V H

Makes 10 portions

ROASTED CAULIFLOWER

1 lb 14 oz/794 g cauliflower florets

3 tbsp/75 mL olive oil

½ tsp/1.5 g kosher salt

¼ tsp/.5 g freshly ground black pepper

MUSTARD VINAIGRETTE

2 fl oz/60 mL olive oil

2 fl oz/60 mL white wine vinegar

2 tbsp/28 g Dijon mustard

½ tsp/1.5 g kosher salt

¼ tsp/.5 g freshly ground black pepper

RICE AND BEANS

10 oz/284 g boiled navy beans

1 lb 4 oz/567 g boiled brown rice

3 plum tomatoes, cut into small dice

2 red bell peppers, seeded and chopped

2 celery stalks, cut into slices ¼ in/6 mm thick

1 bunch green onions, white and green parts, minced

2 tbsp/6 g chopped flat-leaf parsley

1. In a large bowl, toss the cauliflower to coat with the oil. Season with the salt and black pepper and toss again. Spread out the cauliflower in an even layer on a sheet pan. Roast the cauliflower in the oven at 425°F/218°C until tender and golden brown, 10 to 15 minutes. Remove from oven and cool to room temperature.

2. To make the vinaigrette, in a small bowl, whisk the oil, vinegar, and mustard to combine. Season with the salt and black pepper.

3. In a large bowl, combine the beans, rice, tomatoes, bell peppers, celery, green onions, and parsley. Add the roasted cauliflower and the dressing and toss to combine. Serve immediately.

Nutritional Information per Serving (7 oz/198 g):

220 calories, 10 g fat, 1.5 g saturated fat, 0 mg cholesterol, 250 mg sodium, 29 g total carbohydrates, 7 g fiber, 4 g sugar, 6 g protein

---

Brown Basmati Rice Pilaf with Toasted Pistachios

Makes 15 portions

1 lb/454 g brown basmati rice

¼ oz/7 g olive oil

1 oz/28 g minced shallots

2 cracked cardamom pods

1½ qt/1.44 L water, heated

½ tsp/1.5 g kosher salt

Pinch freshly ground black pepper

2½ oz/71 g lightly toasted and coarsely chopped pistachio nuts

1 tbsp/3 g flat-leaf parsley chiffonade

1. Rinse the rice in a strainer until the water runs clear.

2. In a large pot, heat the oil over medium heat. Add the shallots and sauté until translucent, 2 to 3 minutes.

3. Add the rice and cardamom pods and stir to coat thoroughly with the oil.

4. Add the heated water to the rice and bring to a boil. Add the salt and cover with a tight-fitting lid. Simmer the rice gently until all of the stock is absorbed and the grains are tender to the bite, about 40 minutes.

5. Add the black pepper, toasted pistachios, and parsley and gently fluff the rice with a fork to incorporate. Serve immediately, or cool the pilaf to room temperature on a sheet pan, then store, covered, in the refrigerator for up to 3 days.

> **Nutritional Information per Serving (4 ½ oz/128 g):**
>
> 265 calories, 7 g fat, 0 g saturated fat, 0 mg cholesterol, 129 mg sodium, 48 g total carbohydrates, 4 g fiber, 15 g sugar, 6 g protein

Oven-Roasted Tomatoes

Makes 10 portions

4 lb 8 oz/2.04 kg plum tomatoes

3 fl oz/90 mL extra-virgin olive oil

½ oz/14 g minced garlic

½ oz/14 g minced shallots

2 tsp/2 g basil chiffonade

2 tsp/2 g chopped oregano

1 tsp/1 g chopped thyme

Kosher salt, as needed

Freshly ground black pepper, as needed

1. Remove the stem ends from the tomatoes and cut into the desired shape (halves, quarters, wedges, or slices). Arrange in a single layer, skin side down, on a rack set over a sheet pan.

2. Combine the oil, garlic, shallots, basil, oregano, and thyme. Season with salt and pepper. Drizzle or brush this mixture over the tomatoes and turn the tomatoes carefully to coat them. Make sure that they are skin side down again before roasting.

3. Roast in the oven at 275°F/135°C until the tomatoes are dried and lightly browned, 1 to 1½ hours.

4. The tomatoes are ready to serve or use as an ingredient in another dish, or they may be cooled on the racks and stored, covered, in the refrigerator.

> **Nutritional Information per Serving (7 oz/198 g):**
>
> 120 calories, 9 g fat, 1 g saturated fat, 0 mg cholesterol, 10 mg sodium, 9 g total carbohydrates, 3 g fiber, 5 g sugar, 2 g protein

Oven-Roasted Tomatoes

Whole Wheat Pasta Dough D V H

Makes 3 lb/1.4 kg dough (about 10 portions, depending on use)

2 lb/907 g whole wheat flour

1 lb/454 g large eggs (about 8 eggs)

1 fl oz/30 mL water, or as needed

1. Place the flour into a large bowl and make a well in the center of the flour.
2. In a medium bowl, combine the eggs and water and whisk to a homogeneous mixture.
3. Pour the egg mixture into the well. Slowly stir the flour into the liquid in the well, working it in from the edges.
4. Once the liquid has been absorbed into the flour, dump the mixture onto a clean work surface and knead the dough until it is very smooth. Use additional flour as needed to ensure that the dough is not tacky to the touch. Wrap the dough in plastic wrap and allow to rest for 15 to 20 minutes.
5. Roll the dough into sheets approximately $\frac{1}{16}$ in/1.5 mm thick, 8 in/20 cm wide, and 10 in/25 cm long. Cut the dough sheets into the desired size noodles: tagliatelle, pappardelle, etc.

CHEF'S NOTE

The dough may be wrapped and stored in the refrigerator for up to 2 days or frozen for up to 4 months.

Nutritional Information per Serving (3 oz/85 g):

372 calories, 6 g fat, 1 g saturated fat, 191 mg cholesterol, 68 mg sodium, 66 g total carbohydrates, 11 g fiber, 10 g sugar, 18 g protein

---

Carrot-Ginger Purée C D V H

Makes 10 portions

½ oz/14 g butter

4 oz/113 g minced leeks, white part only

4 oz/113 g minced onions

1 tbsp/3 g minced garlic

2 lb/907 g peeled and thinly sliced carrots

1 oz/28 g peeled and minced ginger

1½ fl oz/42 g honey

2 fl oz/60 mL rice vinegar

6 fl oz/180 mL Vegetable Stock (page 106)

1 Sachet d'Épices (page 340)

Pinch kosher salt

Pinch freshly ground white pepper

1. In a large pot, heat the butter over medium heat. Add the leeks, onions, and garlic and sweat until the onions are translucent, 5 to 7 minutes.
2. Add the carrots and ginger and continue to cook for 5 minutes more without browning.
3. Add the honey and vinegar and cook for 5 minutes more.
4. Stir in the stock and the sachet and bring to a simmer. Cook over medium heat until the carrots are tender. Remove and discard the sachet. Strain the vegetables from the liquid; reserve both.
5. Place the cooked vegetables in the bowl of a food processor and blend to a smooth purée, adding the cooking liquid as needed. The purée should be thick enough to spoon or pipe onto a plate. Adjust the consistency with hot water or additional stock if purée is too thick.

CHEF'S NOTES

To use the purée as a sauce, thin the purée to nappé consistency with water or additional vegetable stock.

The honey may be substituted with 1½ fl oz/45 mL agave syrup.

Nutritional Information per Serving (3½ oz/100 g):

60 calories, 1 g fat, 0 g saturated fat, 0 mg cholesterol, 55 mg sodium, 14 g total carbohydrates, 2 g fiber, 9 g sugar, 1 g protein

---

Summer Squash Noodles

....

Makes 10 portions

8 oz/227 g seeded yellow squash, cut into long julienne

8 oz/227 g seeded zucchini squash, cut into long julienne

4 oz/113 g julienned carrots

2 oz/57 g julienned leeks, white part only

1 oz/28 g minced shallots

1 oz/28 g thinly sliced green onions

6 fl oz/180 mL Chicken Stock (page 105)

1 tsp/3 g kosher salt

¼ tsp/1 g freshly ground black pepper

1. Combine the cut squashes, carrots, leeks, shallots, and green onions and mix to distribute evenly.

2. Bring the stock to a simmer in a sauté pan over medium heat. Add the vegetables and pan steam them, tossing or stirring to coat them with the hot stock. Season with the salt and pepper.

3. Increase the heat to high and continue to pan steam until the vegetables are tender and very hot, 3 to 4 minutes more.

Nutritional Information per Serving (3 oz/85 g):

20 calories, 0 g fat, 0 g saturated fat, 0 mg cholesterol, 210 mg sodium, 4 g total carbohydrates, 1 g fiber, 2 g sugar, 1 g protein

---

Roasted Kabocha Squash with Tuscan Kale

....

Makes 10 portions

2 lb/907 g Kabocha squash

5 oz/142 g peeled and quartered shallots

1½ fl oz/45 mL balsamic vinegar

1½ fl oz/45 mL pure olive oil

1 tsp/3 g coarse sea salt

½ oz/14 g minced garlic

2 lb/907 g Tuscan or lacinato kale chiffonade

1. Peel and cut the squash in half. Remove the seeds and cut into 1-in/2.5-cm cubes.

2. In a large bowl, combine the squash with the shallots, vinegar, 1 fl oz/30 mL of the oil, and the salt. Spread it out on a sheet pan and roast in a oven at 425°F/218°F until soft, about 30 minutes. Remove from the oven and reserve.

3. Heat the remaining ½ fl oz/15 mL oil in a 12-in/25-cm sautoir over medium heat. Sauté the garlic until fragrant, about 2 minutes. Fold in the kale a little at a time until it all fits in the pot and cook until tender, 5 to 10 minutes, adding a small amount of water as needed to prevent burning. Add the roasted squash to the pan and toss to evenly distribute the squash; return to the heat until the squash is heated through. Serve immediately.

CHEF'S NOTE

....

For ease of service, the squash may be roasted in large batches, cooled, and stored in the refrigerator for up to 3 days.

....

Nutritional Information per Serving (7 oz/198 g):

130 calories, 4.5 g fat, 0.5 g saturated fat, 0 mg cholesterol, 280 mg sodium, 20 g total carbohydrates, 3 g fiber, 4 g sugar, 5 g protein

---

The earlier chapters in this book detailed the various health concerns facing the American public and the steps that professional chefs can take to address these concerns. If you understand what a customer's needs are, you are better equipped to fulfill them. The key is to fully disclose whatever you are serving your guest and not misrepresent what you are selling. Creating desserts that satisfy these various health needs may seem daunting because the foundation of dessert is sugar and fat, but it can be done. Using quality ingredients to impart maximum flavor in small bites is, once again, of paramount importance. Selecting berries and dark chocolate to use in desserts can bring additional health benefits such as antioxidant properties. Chefs can also utilize smaller portions of rich ingredients to complement an assortment of fruits or low-fat dairy items so that the portion size doesn't seem miniscule, and the customers don't overshoot their daily calorie intake. As a professional chef, you need to respond to what the market demands, and make adjustments according to what your customers want and need in their diets. Providing a selection of breads, crostini, breadsticks, or crackers that include whole-grain or multigrain varieties and gluten-free options will help satisfy a variety of dietary needs.

Serrano-Maple Lemonade C D V H

Makes 10 portions

2½ qt/2.3 L filtered water

6 fl oz/180 mL lemon juice

1½ fl oz/45 mL maple syrup

1 fl oz/30 mL agave syrup

1 oz/28 g red serrano, thinly sliced

Combine the water, lemon juice, syrups, and serrano and mix well. The lemonade may be served cold or warm.

> **Nutritional Information per Serving (9 fl oz/450 mL):**
>
> 32 calories, 0 g fat, 0 g saturated fat, 0 mg cholesterol, 0 mg sodium, 9 g total carbohydrates, 0 g fiber, 7 g sugar, 0 g protein

Extra-Virgin Olive Oil Financiers D V H

Makes 24 portions

2 oz/57 g all-purpose flour

3 oz/85 g almond flour

4 oz/113 g confectioners' sugar

¼ tsp/1 g table salt

6 fl oz/180 mL extra-virgin olive oil

2½ fl oz/75 mL egg whites (from 2 extra-large eggs)

1. Lightly spray two 12-well muffin pans with cooking spray.
2. In a large bowl, sift the flours, sugar, and salt together. Make a well in the center. Begin adding the oil in three additions, whisking continuously to combine until all of the oil has been added, to make a smooth batter.
3. In a separate bowl, whisk the egg whites to soft peaks. Gently fold the egg whites into the batter one-third at a time.
4. Portion 1 fl oz/30 mL of the batter into each well of the prepared muffin pans.
5. Bake in the oven at 350°F/176°C until the financiers are golden brown, 15 to 20 minutes. The financiers can be served warm or at room temperature.

CHEF'S NOTE

Financiers are small French cakes made with almond flour. This version is only slightly sweetened and is flavored with good-quality extra-virgin olive oil. These are perfect served with the Roasted Beet "Tartare" with Maytag Blue Cheese on page 166.

> **Nutritional Information per Serving (one 1-oz/28-g financier):**
>
> 112 calories, 9 g fat, 1 g saturated fat, 0 mg cholesterol, 31 mg sodium, 7 g total carbohydrates, 0 g fiber, 5 g sugar, 1 g protein

Herbed Sandwich Rolls D V H

Makes 30 portions

1½ oz/43 g sugar

1½ qt/1.44 L water (90° to 95°F/32° to 35°C)

1 oz/28 g instant dry yeast

3 fl oz/90 mL extra-virgin olive oil, plus more for oiling the pans and brushing the rolls

2 oz/57 g chopped herbs (such as flat-leaf parsley, oregano, thyme, etc.)

2 tbsp/21 g garlic paste (see Chef's Note, page 327)

1 tbsp/3 g red pepper flakes (optional)

2 tbsp/20 g kosher salt

5 lb 4 oz/2.38 kg bread flour

Cornmeal, for dusting

Sea salt, for sprinkling

1. Mix the sugar, water, yeast, and 1 oz/ 30 mL of the oil in the bowl of an stand mixer fitted with the dough hook until the yeast dissolves.

2. Combine the herbs, garlic paste, and red pepper flakes with the salt and add to the flour.

3. Add the flour-herb mixture to the liquids in the mixer bowl and mix until the dough pulls away from the sides of the bowl cleanly and forms a ball, 6 to 8 minutes.

4. Lightly oil the dough, place it in a bowl, and cover with plastic wrap. Allow to proof until doubled in size.

5. Punch down the dough, divide dough into 5-oz/142-g balls, and place them on sheet pans rubbed with oil, leaving a 2-in/5-cm space between them. Sprinkle the rolls with cornmeal. Cover the sheet pans with large, food-safe plastic bags tied closed with a knot. Let the rolls double in size.

6. Push the risen rolls down until they are about ½ in/1 cm thick and 5 in/12.7 cm wide. Brush the tops with oil and sprinkle with sea salt. Let sit for 4 to 5 minutes.

7. Bake the rolls at 375° to 400°F/190° to 204°C for 12 to 15 minutes, until golden brown and hollow sounding when tapped.

8. Cool and store for use as a base for any sandwich, especially for Bocadillo from Catalonia (page 192).

Nutritional Information per Serving (one 5-oz/142-g roll):

322 calories, 4 g fat, 0 g saturated fat, 0 mg cholesterol, 387 mg sodium, 60 g total carbohydrates, 2 g fiber, 2 g sugar, 10 g protein

Scones

Makes 12 portions

13 oz/369 g all-purpose flour

1 tsp/3 g kosher salt

½ oz/14 g baking powder

6 oz/170 g butter, cubed

½ fl oz/15 mL agave syrup

2 oz/60 mL egg

1 oz/30 mL egg yolk

8 fl oz/240 mL almond milk

6 oz/170 g garnish of choice (see Chef's Note)

EGG WASH

2 fl oz/60 mL egg

1 oz/30 mL egg yolk

½ fl oz/15 mL water

Pinch salt

1. Line a baking sheet with parchment paper.

2. In a large bowl, whisk the flour, salt, and baking powder together to combine.

3. Add the butter and toss to combine, then cut in the butter until the butter is distributed in small, ¼- to ½-in/3-mm to 1.25-cm pieces. Add garnish, if desired.

4. In a medium bowl, whisk the agave, whole egg, egg yolk, and almond milk together. Add the wet ingredients to the flour mixture and mix just until a dough forms.

5. Transfer the dough to a sheet pan. Cover and chill the dough until firm, 15 to 20 minutes.

6. In a small bowl, whisk together the ingredients for the egg wash. Add more water as needed to achieve a thin, brushable consistency.

7. Shape the dough into 2 equally sized disks, wrap in plastic wrap, and chill for 1 hour.

8. Cut the disks into 6 evenly sized wedges, and arrange the scones in rows on the sheet pans, leaving a 1-in/2.5-cm space on all sides. Brush the scones with the egg wash. Bake in the oven at 400°F/204°C until golden, 12 to 15 minutes.

CHEF'S NOTE

Garnishes for these scones can be varied: dried fruit (like raisins, cherries, or cranberries), fruit zest, nuts, chocolate, cheese, herbs, or even vegetables.

Nutritional Information per Serving (4 oz/113 g):

240 calories, 13 g fat, 8 g saturated fat, 70 mg cholesterol, 280 mg sodium, 26 g total carbohydrates, 0 g fiber, 2 g sugar, 4 g protein

Mango-Ginger Bars C D V H

Makes 24 portions

CRUST

13 oz/369 g gluten-free rolled oats

6 oz/170 g mango, peeled and chopped small

2 oz/57 g Sucanat

2 oz/57 g spelt flour

4 fl oz/120 mL ginger juice

4 fl oz/120 mL sunflower seed oil

2 fl oz/60 mL maple syrup

TOPPING

14 oz/396 g dates, pitted and roughly chopped

½ tsp/1 g finely grated orange zest

1⅓ fl oz/39 mL ginger juice

1⅓ fl oz/39 mL orange juice

2 fl oz/60 mL unsweetened coconut milk

½ oz/14 g ground flaxseeds

1 tbsp/5 g arrowroot

2 tbsp/10 mL water

2½ oz/70 g toasted and chopped pecans or macadamia nuts (optional)

1. Lightly oil a 9 by 9-in/22 by 22-cm baking pan.

2. To make the crust, mix the oats, mango, Sucanat, flour, ginger juice, oil, and syrup in a large bowl to combine. Let sit for 10 minutes. Spread the mixture out in the prepared baking pan and bake in the oven at 350°F/176°C for 30 minutes, or until the crust begins to brown. Remove from the oven and cool.

3. To make the topping, combine the dates, zest, juices, coconut milk, and flaxseeds in a food processor and pulse until smooth.

4. Transfer the mixture to a 3-qt/2.83-L pot and bring to a simmer over medium heat. Cook until the mixture begins to bubble around the edges, stirring frequently, 5 to 7 minutes.

5. In a small bowl, whisk together the arrowroot and water to make a slurry. Add the slurry to the topping mixture and continue to cook, stirring, until the mixture thickens, 3 to 4 minutes.

6. Pour the topping evenly over the cooled crust. Sprinkle with the nuts, if using. Cool thoroughly before slicing into 24 pieces. Serve chilled.

Nutritional Information per Serving (2 oz/57 g):

188 calories, 6 g fat, 1 g saturated fat, 0 mg cholesterol, 4 mg sodium, 33 g total carbohydrates, 4 g fiber, 16 g sugar, 4 g protein

Arepas C D V H

Makes 16 portions

1 lb 1½ oz/500 grams arepa flour (corn flour, also called Harina P.A.N. flour)

1 qt/960 mL warm water

¼ oz/7 g salt

1 pt/480 mL grapeseed oil, or as needed, for frying

1. In the bowl of a stand mixer fitted with the paddle attachment, combine the flour, water, and salt. Mix until a smooth dough forms, adding more water if needed.

2. Form the dough into 2-oz/57-g balls and, using the palm of your hand, flatten the dough into disks about ¾ in/1.9 cm thick. If the surface or edges of the disks are cracking, add more water to the dough.

3. Arepas may be cooked on a lightly oiled cast-iron griddle or skillet, or may be pan fried. If pan frying, heat about 1 in/2.5 cm of oil in a heavy-bottomed skillet. Fry the arepas until they are golden and float to the surface of the oil, 3 to 4 minutes per side. Drain on paper towels.

4. The arepas are now ready to be served, or finished with cheese or other fillings and served.

Nutritional Information per Serving (one 2-oz/57-g arepa):

238 calories, 7 g fat, 1 g saturated fat, 0 mg cholesterol, 282 mg sodium, 37 g total carbohydrates, 7 g fiber, 0 g sugar, 3 g protein

---

Cecina C D V H

Makes 10 portions

½ fl oz/45 mL olive oil

6 oz/170 g chickpea flour

12 fl oz/360 mL water, or as needed

1½ fl oz/45 mL extra-virgin olive oil

½ oz/14 g minced garlic

1 oz/28 g chopped herbs (such as sage, thyme, or rosemary)

½ tsp/2 g kosher salt

Pinch freshly ground black pepper

1. Place an 8-in/20-cm cast-iron skillet with the ½ fl oz/15 mL olive oil in a preheated 400°F/204°C oven until the oil is very hot.

2. Combine the chickpea flour, water, 1½ fl oz/45 mL extra-virgin olive oil, garlic, and herbs and mix thoroughly to create a thick batter. Pour the batter into the hot skillet; it should be ¼ to ½ in/6 to 12 mm thick. Immediately return the skillet to the hot oven. Cook until golden, 20 to 30 minutes.

3. Sprinkle the cecina with the salt and pepper, and cut into 10 wedges. Serve immediately as a snack or appetizer.

CHEF'S NOTE

Finely ground cornmeal can be used in place of part of the chickpea flour for a complete protein source and different taste.

Nutritional Information per Serving (2 oz/57 g):

116 calories, 6 g fat, 1 g saturated fat, 0 mg cholesterol, 130 mg sodium, 10 g total carbohydrates, 2 g fiber, 2 g sugar, 4 g protein

---

Socca

Makes 10 portions

12 oz/340 g chickpea flour

1 tsp/3 g kosher salt

Water, as needed (about 2 cups/480 mL or more)

3 fl oz/90 mL olive oil, or olive oil cooking spray

Freshly ground black pepper

1. In a medium bowl, mix the flour, salt, and water to make a thin crêpe-like batter and set aside for 30 minutes to 1 hour. Add more water if needed to maintain crêpe-like batter consistency.

2. Heat a nonstick skillet or griddle over high heat until hot. Pour in enough oil to coat the bottom of the pan, or, if using, spray with olive oil spray, and, when sizzling, add 1½ fl oz/45 mL of the batter and swirl. The pancake should be thin and can be as large as the pan. It should get crisp; hence all the oil. When golden brown, carefully turn over the pancake with a long spatula and brown the opposite side.

3. Add more oil to the skillet as needed, and repeat making pancakes with the remaining batter.

4. Serve the pancakes immediately with freshly ground black pepper and more salt if needed. These don't improve with age, so serve them promptly.

CHEF'S NOTE

Socca is a chickpea flour pancake or crêpe from Nice. Generally, these pancakes are fried in generous amounts of olive oil, as they tend to stick to the pan. This can be avoided by using a nonstick pan.

> **Nutritional Information per Serving (two 1½-oz/43-g pancakes):**
>
> 203 calories, 10 g fat, 1 g saturated fat, 0 mg cholesterol, 257 mg sodium, 20 g total carbohydrates, 4 g fiber, 4 g sugar, 8 g protein

Ginger-Molasses Cookies

Makes 24 cookies (12 portions)

6⅔ oz/188 g brown teff flour

1 tsp/2 g baking soda

¼ tsp/1 g sea salt

1 tsp/2 g ground cinnamon

Pinch ground cloves

½ tsp/1 g dry mustard powder

4 oz/113 g almond butter

4 fl oz/120 mL molasses

2 tsp/10 mL tamari

1 tbsp/6 g peeled and grated ginger

4 fl oz/120 mL maple syrup

1. In a large bowl, whisk the flour, baking soda, salt, cinnamon, cloves, and mustard to combine. Make a well in the center.

2. In a medium bowl, whisk together the almond butter, molasses, tamari, ginger, and maple syrup. Add to the dry ingredients and mix just to combine.

3. Line cookie sheets with parchment paper. Using a 1-oz/28-g scoop, drop the batter in mounds onto the lined sheets; there is no need to roll, flatten, or shape mounds.

4. Bake in the oven at 350°F/176°C until golden around the edges, about 12 minutes.

5. Remove from the oven and transfer to a wire rack to cool.

> **Nutritional Information per Serving (2 cookies):**
>
> 183 calories, 6 g fat, 0 g saturated fat, 0 mg cholesterol, 260 mg sodium, 30 g total carbohydrates, 1 g fiber, 14 g sugar, 3 g protein

Naan

Makes 10 portions

14 oz/396 g all-purpose flour

1 tsp/3 g sugar

1 tsp/3 g table salt

8 fl oz/240 mL warm water (100°F/38°C)

1½ tsp/4 g dry yeast

2¾ fl oz/80 mL plain yogurt

2 oz/57 g butter, melted

2 tsp/2 g kosher salt, or as needed

1. Sift the flour, sugar, and salt together in a large bowl. In a small bowl, combine the warm water and yeast and allow the yeast to bloom.

2. In the bowl of a 5- to 6-qt stand mixer fitted with the dough hook, combine the dry ingredients with the bloomed yeast and the yogurt. Mix the dough on low speed until it is completely combined.

3. Increase the mixer speed to high and continue to mix for 8 minutes. Transfer the dough to a lightly greased bowl, cover, and let rest in a warm place for 30 minutes, or until the dough has doubled in size.

4. Form the dough into 2-oz/57-g balls and allow to rest for 15 to 20 minutes.

5. On a lightly floured surface, roll the dough out into rounds about ¼ in/6 mm thick.

6. Heat a large skillet over medium heat. Working in batches, brush the naan with melted butter and sprinkle lightly with the kosher salt. Cook each naan in the skillet until golden brown and puffed on both sides, 3 to 5 minutes per side.

VARIATIONS

Garlic Naan

Mince 1 oz/28 g garlic and sprinkle on top of the naan, then press the garlic into the dough's surface and sprinkle with the salt.

Onion Naan

Dice 4 oz/113 g onion and sprinkle on top of the naan, then press the onions into the dough's surface and sprinkle with the salt.

Cilantro Naan

Roughly chop 1 oz/28 g cilantro, then press the cilantro into the dough's surface and sprinkle with the salt.

> **Nutritional Information per Serving (one 2-oz/57-g piece):**
>
> 180 calories, 4 g fat, 2 g saturated fat, 5 mg cholesterol, 630 mg sodium, 32 g total carbohydrates, 1 g fiber, 1 g sugar, 5 g protein

Hazelnut Tart Dough D V H

Makes 5 lb 8½ oz/2.65 kg dough (six 10-in/25-cm tart shells, 15½ oz/439 g each)

1 lb/454 g butter

8 fl oz/240 mL agave syrup

8 fl oz/240 mL grapeseed or hazelnut oil

1 tsp/5 mL vanilla extract

4½ oz/128 g eggs (about 2 large eggs)

14 oz/397 g whole wheat pastry flour

½ oz/14 g ground cinnamon

½ oz/14 g baking powder

2 lb/907 g lightly toasted hazelnuts, cooled and ground to a coarse meal

1. In the bowl of a stand mixer fitted with the paddle attachment, cream the butter and agave syrup on medium speed until aerated and fluffy, about 5 minutes. With the mixer running, slowly drizzle in the grapeseed oil and mix until thoroughly incorporated.

2. With the mixer running, gradually add the vanilla and eggs in three additions, scraping down the bowl after each addition.

3. Sift together the pastry flour, cinnamon, and baking powder. Add to the mixer bowl all at once and, beating on low speed, mix to fully incorporate.

4. Gradually add the ground hazelnuts and mix on low speed just until incorporated.

5. Turn the dough out onto a clean work surface and scale the dough into 15½-oz/439-g portions. Form each portion into a disk, wrap with plastic wrap, and refrigerate for at least 1 hour before rolling out the dough.

CHEF'S NOTE

This dough may be stored for 3 days in the refrigerator, or frozen for up to 3 months.

This dough is delicious made with lightly toasted pistachios, adding a small amount (¼ oz/7 g) of ground cardamom instead of the cinnamon.

Nutritional Information per Serving (1½ oz/43 g):

212 calories, 20 g fat, 5 g saturated fat, 25 mg cholesterol, 4 mg sodium, 8 g total carbohydrates, 2 g fiber, 6 g sugar, 3 g protein

Blueberry, Goat Cheese, and Tarragon Tart with Hazelnut Crust D V H

Makes 10 portions

One 15½-oz/439-g portion Hazelnut Tart Dough, for one 10-inch tart shell (page 269)

4 fl oz/120 mL almond milk

1 oz/28 g *piloncillo* (Latin American unrefined brown sugar)

¼ oz/7 g tarragon leaves

1½ fl oz/45 mL amber agave syrup

¾ oz/21 g potato starch

2 fl oz/60 mL egg

3 oz/85 g crumbled fresh goat cheese

1 lb 14 oz/851 g fresh blueberries

4 oz/113 g slivered almonds

1½ oz/43 g granulated turbinado sugar

1 oz/28 g butter, softened

1. Prepare one 10-in/25-cm hazelnut tart shell. Place pie weights into the shell and parbake the shell at 350°F/175°C for about 10 minutes, or until aromatic and just beginning to brown. Remove from the oven and allow to cool to room temperature.

2. Mix the almond milk, *piloncillo* sugar, tarragon, agave syrup, potato starch, and egg to a smooth consistency.

3. Add the crumbled goat cheese and blueberries. The mixture should be lumpy. Pour the filling into the parbaked crust.

4. Mix together the almonds, turbinado sugar, and butter and sprinkle the nut mixture over the filling. Bake at 350°F/176°C for about 30 minutes, or until golden brown and the filling is set.

5. Allow the tart to cool in the pan for about 20 minutes. Remove the ring from the tart pan. Using a very sharp knife, cut the tart into 10 even wedges. Serve the tart gently warmed for best flavor.

Nutritional Information per Serving (6 oz/170 g):

248 calories, 16 g fat, 4 g saturated fat, 31 mg cholesterol, 40 mg sodium, 23 g total carbohydrates, 4 g fiber, 16 g sugar, 8 g protein

---

Blitz Puff Pastry D V

Makes 5 lb/2.27 kg pastry

2 lb/907 g all-purpose flour

¾ oz/21 g table salt

2 lb/907 g butter, chilled, cut into 1-in/2.5-cm cubes

1 lb/454 g water, cold

1. Combine the flour and salt in the bowl of a stand mixer fitted with the dough hook. Add the butter and toss with your fingertips until the butter is coated with flour. Add the water. Mix on low speed until the dough forms a shaggy mass.

2. Place the dough on a lightly floured work surface and roll it out into a rectangle ½ in/1 cm thick and approximately 12 by 30 in/30 by 76 cm.

3. Administer a three-fold. Roll out the dough to the same dimensions as before, and administer a four-fold.

4. Repeat this process two more times for a total of 3 four-folds, refrigerating and turning the dough 90 degrees each time before rolling. After completing the final fold, wrap the dough in plastic wrap and allow it to firm under refrigeration for at least 30 minutes before using. (The dough can be held under refrigeration or frozen.)

CHEF'S NOTES

Resting the dough between folds will tend to give you better layers, yielding a product closer to traditional puff pastry.

Up to 50 percent of the all-purpose flour can be replaced with whole wheat flour.

Nutritional Information per Serving (8 oz/227 g):

980 calories, 74 g fat, 46 g saturated fat, 195 mg cholesterol, 847 mg sodium, 69 g total carbohydrates, 2 g fiber, 0 g sugar, 10 g protein

---

Buttermilk Panna Cotta C D H

Makes 10 portions

10 oz/284 g fresh blueberries

40 fl oz/1.2 L buttermilk

1 tbsp/7 g unflavored gelatin

12 fl oz/360 mL light cream

8 fl oz/240 mL agave syrup

1½ tsp/7.5 mL vanilla extract

2½ oz/71 g toasted slivered almonds

½ oz/14 g finely grated lemon zest

1. Set up 10 clean martini glasses or other serving vessels. Portion ¼ oz/7 g of the berries and place into the bottom of each glass.

2. Heat half of the buttermilk and gelatin in a bowl placed over a saucepan of simmering water, stirring constantly until the gelatin melts, about 3 minutes. Remove from the heat and set aside.

3. Whisk together the light cream and agave syrup in a heavy-bottomed, large saucepan over medium-low heat. Bring to simmer and cook, stirring often, until the sugar has dissolved, about 6 minutes.

4. Slowly whisk the gelatin mixture into the cream mixture, then whisk in the remaining buttermilk and the vanilla.

5. Pour 6 fl oz/180 mL of the mixture into each of the martini glasses, cover, and chill until set, at least 2 hours or overnight.

6. Garnish the top of each portion with ¾ oz/21 g of the remaining berries, ¼ oz/7 g of the toasted almonds, and a sprinkling of the lemon zest.

Nutritional Information per Serving (6 fl oz/180 mL):

280 calories, 12 g fat, 5 g saturated fat, 30 mg cholesterol, 150 mg sodium, 39 g total carbohydrates, 2 g fiber, 35 g sugar, 8 g protein

---

Buttermilk Panna Cotta

Fresh Peach, Fig, and Bourbon Crisp with Pecan Topping [C] [D] [V] [H]

Makes 10 portions

FILLING

4 lb/1.81 kg peaches, peeled, pitted, and cut into ¾-in/2-cm cubes (see Chef's Note)

5 fresh figs, cut into wedges

1 fl oz/30 mL agave syrup

1 tsp/5 mL vanilla extract

1½ fl oz/45 mL bourbon

3 tbsp/45 g brown rice flour

Pinch sea salt

TOPPING

12 oz/340 g pecan pieces

2 oz/57 g brown rice flour

2¾ fl oz/81 mL canola oil

2 fl oz/60 mL agave syrup

Pinch sea salt

1. Place ten 8-fl oz/240-mL ramekins on a baking sheet.

2. To make the filling, toss the peaches and figs together in a large bowl.

3. In a small bowl, mix the agave syrup, vanilla, and bourbon to combine. Add to the fruit and toss to combine. Add the flour and salt and mix to combine.

4. Portion 6¼ oz/177 g of the filling into the prepared ramekins.

5. To make the topping, place the nuts into a food processor and pulse until the mixture resembles a coarse meal. Add the flour and mix to combine.

6. Add the oil, agave syrup, and salt and process until the mixture holds together when pressed, but is still crumbly.

7. Top the fruit with 1¾ oz/50 g of the nut mixture. Cover the ramekins loosely with aluminum foil and bake in the oven at 350°F/176°C for 20 minutes. Remove the foil and bake until the peaches are soft and the top is golden and crisp, about 20 minutes more. Cool slightly; serve warm.

CHEF'S NOTE

Nectarines make a delicious substitution for peaches.

Nutritional Information per Serving (8 oz/227 g):

177 calories, 6 g fat, 2 g saturated fat, 3 mg cholesterol, 12 mg sodium, 13 g total carbohydrates, 1 g fiber, 19 g sugar, 3 g protein

Pistachio Meringues with Almond Milk Pastry Cream and Berries C D V H

....

Makes 10 portions

MERINGUES

8 oz/227 g egg whites

Pinch table salt

⅛ tsp/.5 g cream of tartar

1 lb/454 g maltitol

3 oz/85 g finely ground pistachio nuts

15 oz/425 g Almond Milk Pastry Cream (page 278)

1 lb 4 oz/567 g fresh berries

1. Place the egg whites, salt, and cream of tartar in a large stainless-steel bowl and whisk until frothy. Gradually add the maltitol and whisk to combine.

2. Place the bowl over a pot of simmering water. Whisking constantly, heat the whites to 120°F/49°C, making sure the maltitol is dissolved.

3. Pour the heated whites into the bowl of a 5-qt stand mixer fitted with the whip attachment. Whisk on high speed until the meringue is shiny and holds stiff peaks. Gently fold in half of the ground pistachios.

4. Line a sheet pan with parchment paper. Trace ten 3-in/7.5-cm circles on the paper, then turn the paper over.

5. Starting in the center of each circle, pipe the meringue in a thin even layer to fill in the circle. Pipe a decorative border around the edge of each circle. Dust the meringues with the remaining ground pistachios.

6. Bake the meringues in the oven at 200°F/90°C until hardened and dry. This may take more than a few hours depending on kitchen humidity.

7. When the meringues are finished baking, cool to room temperature and store in an airtight container at room temperature for up to 1 week.

8. When ready to serve, spread 1½ oz/43 g pastry cream on the base of one meringue shell. Dot the serving plate with a small bead of pastry cream as well to help the meringue adhere to the plate.

9. Fill the surface of the meringue with 2 oz/57 g of the fresh berries.

Nutritional Information per Serving (5½ oz/156 g):

144 calories, 6 g fat, 1 g saturated fat, 45 mg cholesterol, 72 mg sodium, 16 g total carbohydrates, 3 g fiber, 9 g sugar, 6 g protein

---

Almond Milk Pastry Cream C D V H

Makes 3 lb/1.36 kg pastry cream

1 qt/960 mL almond milk

3 fl oz/90 mL agave syrup

1 fl oz/30 mL coconut oil

Pinch kosher salt

1 oz/28 g maltitol

3 oz/85 g cornstarch

12 oz/340 g eggs (about 6 eggs), whisked

1 vanilla bean, split and scraped, seeds only

1. In a nonreactive saucepan, combine 28 fl oz/840 mL of the almond milk, the agave syrup, coconut oil, and salt. Gently bring to a simmer over medium heat.

2. In a medium bowl, combine the remaining 4 fl oz/120 mL almond milk with the maltitol and cornstarch and blend thoroughly with a whisk. Once smooth, add the eggs and vanilla seeds and whisk the mixture until completely smooth.

3. Stirring constantly, temper the egg mixture by whisking in 8 fl oz/240 mL of the simmering milk mixture.

4. Continuing to whisk constantly, streaming the tempered mixture into the simmering milk. Whisk briskly until the mixture returns to a boil and the whisk leaves visible trails in the thickened pastry cream.

5. Pour the pastry cream into a shallow nonreactive bowl. Cover with plastic wrap, pressed directly on the surface of the cream to prevent a skin from forming. Place the bowl in an ice bath to cool the cream down to 41°F/4°C, then store in the refrigerator for up to 3 days.

Nutritional Information per Serving (1½ oz/43 g):

53 calories, 2 g fat, 1 g saturated fat, 45 mg cholesterol, 34 mg sodium, 6 g total carbohydrates, 0 g fiber, 4 g sugar, 1 g protein

Common Meringue C V H

Makes 1 lb 8 oz/680 g meringue

8 oz/227 g egg whites

Pinch table salt

1 tsp/5 mL vanilla extract

1 lb/454 g sugar

1. Place the egg whites, salt, and vanilla in a bowl and whisk until frothy.

2. Gradually add the sugar while continuing to whisk, then whisk to the desired consistency.

Nutritional Information per Serving (2 oz/57 g):

157 calories, 0 g fat, 0 g saturated fat, 0 mg cholesterol, 31 mg sodium, 38 g total carbohydrates, 0 g fiber, 38 g sugar, 0 g protein

Swiss Meringue C V H

Makes 1 lb 5 oz/595 g meringue

8 oz/227 g egg whites

1 tsp/5 mL vanilla extract

1 lb/454 g sugar or maltitol

Pinch table salt

1. Place the egg whites, vanilla, sugar, and salt in the bowl of a stand mixer and stir until thoroughly combined.
2. Place the bowl over a saucepan of barely simmering water and slowly stir the mixture until it reaches between 115° and 165°F/46° and 74°C, depending on use.
3. Transfer the bowl to the mixer fitted with the whip attachment and whip on high speed until the meringue is the desired consistency.

Nutritional Information per Serving (2 oz/57 g):

157 calories, 0 g fat, 0 g saturated fat, 0 mg cholesterol, 31 mg sodium, 38 g total carbohydrates, 0 g fiber, 38 g sugar, 0 g protein

---

Italian Meringue C V H

Makes 1 lb 8 oz/680 g meringue

1 lb/454 g sugar

4 fl oz/120 mL water

8 oz/227 g egg whites

Pinch table salt

1 tsp/5 mL vanilla extract

1. Combine 12 oz/340 g of the sugar with the water in a heavy-bottomed saucepan and bring to a boil over medium-high heat, stirring to dissolve the sugar. Continue cooking, without stirring, until the mixture reaches the soft ball stage (240°F/116°C).
2. Meanwhile, place the egg whites, salt, and vanilla in the bowl of a stand mixer fitted with the whip attachment.
3. When the sugar syrup has reached approximately 230°F/110°C, whip the whites on medium speed until frothy. Gradually add the remaining 4 oz/113 g sugar and beat the meringue to soft peaks.
4. When the sugar syrup reaches 240°F/116°C, add it to the meringue in a slow, steady stream while whipping on medium speed. Whip on high speed until stiff peaks form. Continue to beat on medium speed until completely cool.

Nutritional Information per Serving (2 oz/57 g):

157 calories, 0 g fat, 0 g saturated fat, 0 mg cholesterol, 31 mg sodium, 38 g total carbohydrates, 0 g fiber, 38 g sugar, 0 g protein

---

Green Tea–Poached Pears with Pomegranate Glaze and Pistachios C D V H

Makes 10 portions

PEARS

1½ qt/1.44 L water

3 green tea bags

4 fl oz/120 mL brown rice syrup

5 Bosc or Bartlett pears, peeled, halved, and cored

1 oz/28 g lemon peel, white pith removed

1 star anise

GLAZE

12 fl oz/360 mL unsweetened pomegranate juice

8 fl oz/240 mL water

1 fl oz/30 mL lemon juice, strained

4 fl oz/120 mL maple syrup

1½ tbsp/45 mL arrowroot, dissolved in 3 tbsp/45 mL water

GARNISH

5 oz/142 g low-fat, Italian-style fresh ricotta cheese

⅛ oz/3 g minced lemon verbena leaves

2½ oz/57 g finely chopped pistachios, lightly toasted

1. To poach the pears, in a large pot, bring the water to boil. Add the tea bags and brown rice syrup and remove from the heat. Cover and let steep for 5 minutes; longer steeping will make the tea bitter.

2. Remove the tea bags, and add the pears, lemon peel, and star anise. Bring to a gentle simmer over medium heat and cook until the pears are just tender, 5 to 8 minutes depending on the ripeness of the pears.

3. Place the pears in the cooking liquid into an ice bath and cool to 41°F/4°C. Store the cooled pears in the cooking liquid in the refrigerator for up to 1 week.

4. To make the glaze, combine the pomegranate juice, water, lemon juice, and maple syrup in a medium pot and stir to combine. Cook over medium-high heat until the liquid has reduced by half; 25 fl oz/750 mL reduced to 12½ fl oz/375 mL.

5. Immediately stir in the dissolved arrowroot. Return to a simmer and cook for 1 minute, then remove the glaze from the heat and cool to 41°F/4°C. Refrigerate until ready to use.

6. To make the garnish, combine the ricotta cheese with the minced lemon verbena leaves.

7. To serve, arrange a pear half attractively on each plate, form a quenelle of the herbed ricotta, and position it on the plate. Drizzle the plate with the pomegranate glaze, and garnish with a dusting of ¼ oz/7 g of the finely chopped pistachios.

Nutritional Information per Serving (½ pear, ½ oz/14 g ricotta, ¼ oz/7 g pistachios, 1¼ fl oz/35 mL glaze):

115 calories, 4 g fat, 1 g saturated fat, 5 mg cholesterol, 10 mg sodium, 14 g total carbohydrates, 1 g fiber, 15 g sugar, 4 g protein

Seared Pineapple with Coconut Syrup and Madagascar Peppercorns C D V H

Makes 10 portions

COCONUT SYRUP

1 oz/28 g peeled and thinly sliced ginger

¼ oz/7 g dried green Madagascar peppercorns

20 fl oz/600 mL unsweetened coconut milk

1 fl oz/30 mL lime juice

1 fl oz/30 mL agave syrup

1 lb 14 oz/850 g peeled pineapple, cut into thirty 3-in/8-cm spears, about 1 oz/28 g each

1 lb 14 oz/850 g nonfat vanilla Greek-style yogurt

½ oz/14 g dried green Madagascar peppercorns, lightly crushed

1. Prepare the coconut syrup by combining the sliced ginger, whole green peppercorns, coconut milk, lime juice, and agave syrup in a small saucepan. Reduce the syrup gently over medium heat until slightly thickened and it yields 10 fl oz/300 mL of syrup after straining. Reserve at room temperature for immediate use, or refrigerate for up to 5 days.

2. Preheat a nonstick skillet over medium-high heat.

3. Lightly spray the pineapple spears with canola cooking spray. Place the spears into the skillet and sear on all sides to caramelize, 5 to 8 minutes.

4. Arrange 3 spears (3 oz/85 g) of the warm pineapple on a plate, then place two 1-oz/28-g quenelles of the vanilla yogurt onto the plate. Drizzle the pineapple with 1 fl oz/30 mL of the coconut syrup. Dust the plate with a sprinkling of the crushed green peppercorns.

Nutritional Information per Serving (5 oz/142 g):

175 calories, 13 g fat, 12 g saturated fat, 0 mg cholesterol, 38 mg sodium, 15 g total carbohydrates, 3 g fiber, 13 g sugar, 2 g protein

---

Grilled Peaches with Lemon Thyme–Infused Frozen Greek Yogurt C D V H

Makes 10 portions

5 medium, firm yellow peaches

1 fl oz/30 mL honey

2 fl oz/60 mL lemon juice

Canola oil, for the grill or grill pan

20 fl oz/600 mL Lemon Thyme–Infused Frozen Greek Yogurt (see Chef's Note)

5 oz/142 g Bing cherries, pitted, halved, sliced ⅛ in/3 mm thick

2 ½ oz/71 g lightly toasted slivered almonds

1. Score, blanch, shock, and peel the peaches. Cut them in half and carefully remove the pit.

2. In a small bowl, combine the honey and lemon juice, then brush onto each peach half to prevent oxidation. Place the peach halves onto a parchment paper–lined pan, cover with plastic wrap, and refrigerate until needed.

3. Carefully place the peach halves on a lightly oiled preheated grill or grill pan. Cook the peaches long enough to develop grill marks and to warm through. Be careful not to overcook the peaches.

4. Serve each grilled, warm peach half with 2 fl oz/60 mL of the lemon thyme–infused frozen Greek yogurt, ½ oz/14 g of the sliced Bing cherries, and ¼ oz/7 g of the toasted almonds.

CHEF'S NOTE

Prepare the Frozen Greek Yogurt as per the recipe on page 296, but delete the fruit and use the following infused syrup: In a small saucepot combine the sugar and agave syrup with ¼ oz/7 g lemon thyme sprigs and the zest of 1 lemon. Bring to a simmer and cook the syrup until the sugar melts and the syrup becomes aromatic, 2 to 3 minutes. Strain the syrup and proceed with making the frozen yogurt as per the recipe.

Nutritional Information per Serving (½ peach, ½ oz/14 g cherries, 2 fl oz/60 mL frozen yogurt, ¼ oz/7 g toasted almonds):

270 calories, 4 g fat, 0 g saturated fat, 0 mg cholesterol, 0 mg sodium, 61 g total carbohydrates, 2 g fiber, 59 g sugar, 2 g protein

Apple Charlotte D V H

Makes 10 portions

FILLING

1 oz/28 g butter

3 lb 2 oz/1.4 kg peeled, small-dice Granny Smith apples

1 vanilla bean, split and scraped

4 fl oz/120 mL lemon juice

4 fl oz/120 mL amber agave syrup

½ tsp/2 g ground cinnamon

Pinch freshly grated nutmeg

BATTER

4 fl oz/120 mL whisked egg whites

2 fl oz/60 mL whisked eggs

4 fl oz/120 mL almond milk

½ fl oz/15 mL agave syrup

2 tsp/8 g ground cinnamon

1 oz/28 g finely granulated turbinado sugar

3 oz/85 g butter, melted, for greasing ramekins

2 lb/907 g unsliced whole wheat bread

10 fl oz/300 mL nonfat vanilla Greek-style yogurt

1. To make the filling, place a sauté pan over medium heat and add the butter, diced apples, vanilla bean and pod, lemon juice, agave syrup, cinnamon, and nutmeg. Toss to coat well and cook for 20 to 25 minutes, until the apples are very tender and barely holding and all the liquid has evaporated. The apples will caramelize slightly and should be a nice, rich golden color.

2. To make the batter, in a shallow dish, combine the egg whites, whole eggs, almond milk, agave syrup, and 1¾ tsp/7 g of the cinnamon. Stir with a whisk until fully combined.

3. Combine the turbinado sugar with the remaining ¼ tsp/1 g cinnamon. Reserve the cinnamon-sugar for dusting the ramekins.

4. Brush melted butter on the inside of ten 8-fl oz/240-mL ramekins and lightly dust with the cinnamon-sugar.

5. Remove the crust from the bread, and slice the loaf lengthwise into ¼-in/6-mm-thick slices. Lay the slices flat and roll each slice with a rolling pin to flatten to a thickness of about ⅛ in/3 mm. Choose a round cutter with the same diameter as the ramekins being used.

6. Cut 20 rounds from the bread; these will be the bases and tops of the charlottes. Cut the other slices of bread into lengthwise strips that measure as tall as the height of the ramekins, about 1.25 in/3.75 cm wide. Trim the strips to line the inside circumference of the ramekins with an overlap of ⅛ in/3 mm.

7. Working with the rounds first, lightly coat them in the batter, place in the bottom of each prepared ramekin, and press to fit snugly.

8. Lightly dip the strips of bread in batter as well, and use them to line the walls of each ramekin, standing them upright around the circumference, overlapping the ends by ⅛ in/3 mm. Press the bread strips firmly against the insides of the ramekins, and press the seams to seal.

9. Fill each lined ramekin with 5 oz/142 g of the apple filling. Press the filling into place, and fold over the edges of the bread.

10. Dip the remaining 10 bread rounds into the batter and place on top of the filling and over the folded edges of the bread to completely seal the filling inside. Brush the tops with melted butter and sprinkle with the reserved cinnamon-sugar.

Continued on page 286

11. Place the filled ramekins on a sheet pan in the center of the oven and bake at 375°F/191°C for 20 to 25 minutes. If the tops begin to brown too quickly, cover loosely with aluminum foil. When done, the bread will have puffed up slightly, the edges will be brown, and the sugar on top will have caramelized.

12. Allow the ramekins to cool slightly, then run a knife around the edges and invert onto individual plates. Serve warm with a 1-fl oz/30-mL quenelle of the yogurt.

Nutritional Information per Serving (5 oz/142 g apple filling, 1 oz/28 g trimmed, rolled, and cut bread for lining the ramekins, 1½ fl oz/45 mL batter, including the ramekin preparation, 1 fl oz/30 mL yogurt):

470 calories, 17 g fat, 6 g saturated fat, 45 mg cholesterol, 390 mg sodium, 67 g total carbohydrates, 9 g fiber, 35 g sugar, 16 g protein

---

Blueberry Kanten with Creamy Cashew Topping

Makes 10 portions

KANTEN

24 fl oz/720 mL apple juice

3 tbsp/18 g agar-agar flakes

Pinch sea salt

½ fl oz/15 mL lemon juice

1 lb/454 g fresh blueberries

CREAMY CASHEW TOPPING

8 fl oz/240 mL apple juice

5 oz/142 g raw cashews, rinsed

¾ fl oz/23 mL maple syrup

5 oz/142 g fresh blueberries, halved or sliced

1. To make the kanten, bring the apple juice to a boil in a large pot over medium heat. Reduce the heat to low and stir in the agar-agar flakes, salt, and lemon juice. Continue stirring until the flakes are dissolved.

2. Add the blueberries and simmer 1 minute more. Remove the pot from the heat, and transfer the mixture to a 9 by 13-in/22 by 33-cm ovenproof glass baking dish.

3. Refrigerate until firm, about 1 hour. Remove from the refrigerator and purée with a handheld immersion blender until the texture is similar to a mousse.

4. To make the creamy cashew topping, in a small pot over medium-high heat, bring the apple juice and cashews to a simmer over medium heat. Reduce the heat to low and simmer for 5 to 7 minutes, or until the nuts are softened. Remove from the heat and cool slightly. Strain the juice from the cashews and reserve both.

5. Place the cashews and maple syrup in a variable speed blender and process for 10 to 15 seconds. With the processor running, slowly add the juice, a little at a time, until you have the reached the desired texture; you may not need all the juice.

6. To assemble the desserts, pipe or scoop 4 oz/113 g of the prepared kanten into each of 10 martini glasses. Top with 1¼ oz/35 g of the cashew cream and ½ oz/14 g of the halved blueberries.

Nutritional Information per Serving (4 oz/113 g kanten, 1¼ oz/35 g cashew cream, ½ oz/14 g blueberries):

150 calories, 5 g fat, 1 g saturated fat, 0 mg cholesterol, 0 mg sodium, 25 g total carbohydrates, 2 g fiber, 18 g sugar, 2 g protein

Brownie Fudge Cakes V H

Makes 10 portions

2½ oz/71 g macadamia nuts, finely chopped

3 oz/85 g unsweetened dark chocolate, chopped

3 oz/85 g butter

6 oz/170 g sugar

2¾ oz/73 g whole wheat cake flour

⅛ tsp/.5 g baking powder

¼ tsp/1 g kosher salt

5 fl oz/150 mL eggs, whisked (about 2 large eggs)

½ tsp/2.5 mL vanilla extract

½ fl oz/15 mL buttermilk

1. Prepare ten 4-fl oz/120-mL ramekins by coating the inside of each with canola cooking spray, then dusting the insides with ¼ oz/7 g of the chopped nuts. Place the ramekins, evenly spaced, on a sheet pan.

2. In a 3-qt/2.88-L bowl set over a saucepan of simmering water, melt the chocolate, butter, and sugar together.

3. In a small bowl, combine the flour, baking powder, and salt. Stir with a whisk to evenly distribute the ingredients.

4. In a small bowl, whisk the eggs, vanilla, and buttermilk to fully combine.

5. Once the chocolate mixture has fully melted, remove it from the heat and gently stir the egg mixture into the chocolate.

6. Gently fold the flour mixture into the chocolate mixture in three additions, making sure to fully incorporate each addition before adding the next.

7. Once the flour is fully incorporated, portion 1¾ oz/43 g of the batter into each ramekin. Bake in the oven at 325°F/163°C until the batter is set but not firm, 20 to 25 minutes. The internal temperature should register about 180°F/82°C.

8. Cool the cakes on a rack for about 30 minutes, then turn out of the ramekins and finish cooling.

Nutritional Information per Serving (2 oz/57 g):

271 calories, 17 g fat, 8 g saturated fat, 78 mg cholesterol, 90 mg sodium, 27 g total carbohydrates, 3 g fiber, 17 g sugar, 5 g protein

---

Gluten-Free Brownie Fudge Cakes [C] [V] [H]

Makes 10 portions

2½ oz/71 g macadamia nuts, finely chopped

3 oz/85 g chopped unsweetened dark chocolate

3 oz/85 g butter

6 oz/170 g sugar

2¾ oz/73 g gluten-free flour blend with guar gum

⅛ tsp/.5 g baking powder

¼ tsp/1 g kosher salt

5 fl oz/150 mL eggs, whisked (about 2 large eggs)

½ tsp/2.5 mL vanilla extract

½ fl oz/15 mL buttermilk

1. Prepare ten 4-fl oz/120-mL ramekins by coating the inside of each with canola cooking spray, then dusting the insides with ¼ oz/7 g of the chopped nuts. Place the ramekins, evenly spaced, on a sheet pan.

2. In a 3-qt/2.88-L bowl set over a saucepan of simmering water, melt the chocolate, butter, and sugar together.

3. In a small bowl, combine the flour, baking powder, and salt. Stir with a whisk to evenly distribute the ingredients.

4. In a small bowl, whisk the eggs, vanilla, and buttermilk to fully combine.

5. Once the chocolate mixture has fully melted, remove it from the heat and gently stir the egg mixture into the chocolate.

6. Gently fold the flour mixture into the chocolate mixture in three additions, making sure to fully incorporate each addition before adding the next.

7. Once the flour is fully incorporated, portion 1¾ oz/43 g of the batter into each ramekin. Bake in the oven at 325°F/163°C until the batter is set but not firm, 20 to 25 minutes. The internal temperature should register about 180°F/82°C.

8. Cool the cakes on a rack for about 30 minutes, then turn out of the ramekins and finish cooling.

CHEF'S NOTES

For reduced-fat content, replace the butter with silken tofu and the macadamia nuts with almonds or pistachios.

This recipe is not for someone with a nut allergy.

Nutritional Information per Serving (2 oz/57 g):

271 calories, 17 g fat, 8 g saturated fat, 60 mg cholesterol, 20 mg sodium, 26 g total carbohydrates, 2 g fiber, 18 g sugar, 4 g protein

Reduced-Sugar Brownie Fudge Cakes

Makes 10 portions

2½ oz/71 g finely chopped macadamia nuts

3 oz/85 g chopped unsweetened dark chocolate

2 oz/57 g butter

3 oz/85 g maltitol

1½ fl oz/45 mL agave syrup

2¾ oz/78 g whole wheat cake flour

⅛ tsp/.5 g baking powder

¼ tsp/1 g kosher salt

5 fl oz/150 mL eggs, whisked (about 2 large eggs)

1 oz/28 g silken tofu, puréed

½ tsp/2.5 mL vanilla extract

½ fl oz/15 mL buttermilk

1. Prepare ten 4-fl oz/120-mL ramekins by coating the inside of each with canola cooking spray, then dusting the insides with ¼ oz/7g of the chopped nuts. Place the ramekins, evenly spaced, on a sheet pan.

2. In a 3-qt/2.88-L bowl set over a saucepan of simmering water, melt the chocolate, butter, maltitol, and agave syrup.

3. In a small bowl, combine the flour, baking powder, and salt, and stir with a whisk to evenly distribute the ingredients.

4. In another small bowl, whisk the eggs and silken tofu purée to a homogeneous mixture. Add the vanilla and buttermilk and whisk to fully combine.

5. Once the chocolate mixture has fully melted, remove it from the heat and gently stir the egg mixture into the chocolate.

6. Gently fold the flour mixture into the chocolate mixture in three additions, making sure to fully incorporate each addition before adding the next.

7. Once the flour is fully incorporated, portion 1¾ oz/50 g of the batter into each ramekin.

8. Bake in the oven at 325°F/163°C until the batter is set but not firm, 20 to 25 minutes. The internal temperature should register about 180°F/82°C.

9. Cool the cakes on a rack for about 30 minutes, then turn out of the ramekins and finish cooling.

CHEF'S NOTE

This recipe is not for someone with a nut allergy.

Nutritional Information per Serving (2 oz/57 g):

212 calories, 15 g fat, 7 g saturated fat, 55 mg cholesterol, 70 mg sodium, 18 g total carbohydrates, 3 g fiber, 5 g sugar, 4 g protein

Sugar-Free Brownie Fudge Cakes D V H

Makes 10 portions

2½ oz/71 g finely chopped walnuts

3 oz/85 g chopped unsweetened dark chocolate

3 oz/85 g butter

6 oz/170 g maltitol

2¾ oz/73 g whole wheat cake flour

⅛ tsp/.5 g baking powder

¼ tsp/1 g kosher salt

5 fl oz/150 mL eggs, whisked (about 2 large eggs)

½ tsp/2.5 mL vanilla extract

½ fl oz/15 mL buttermilk

1. Prepare ten 4-fl oz/120-mL ramekins by coating the inside of each with canola cooking spray, then dusting the insides with ¼ oz/7 g of chopped nuts. Place the ramekins, evenly spaced, on a sheet pan.

2. In a 3-qt/2.88-L bowl set over saucepan of simmering water, melt the chocolate, butter, and maltitol.

3. In a small bowl, combine the flour, baking powder, and salt. Stir with a whisk to evenly distribute the ingredients.

4. In a small bowl, whisk the eggs, vanilla, and buttermilk to fully combine.

5. Once the chocolate mixture has fully melted, remove it from the heat and gently stir the egg mixture into the chocolate.

6. Gently fold the flour mixture into the chocolate mixture in three additions, making sure to fully incorporate each addition before adding the next.

7. Once the flour is fully incorporated, portion 1¾ oz/43 g of the batter into each ramekin. Bake in the oven at 325°F/163°C until the batter is set but not firm, 20 to 25 minutes. The internal temperature should register about 180°F/82°C.

8. Cool the cakes on a rack for about 30 minutes, then turn out of the ramekins and finish cooling.

Nutritional Information per Serving (2 oz/57 g):

230 calories, 17 g fat, 8 g saturated fat, 60 mg cholesterol, 70 mg sodium, 13 g total carbohydrates, 3 g fiber, 0 g sugar, 5 g protein

Blackberry-Peach Cobbler with Buttermilk Biscuit Topping V H

Makes 10 portions

BISCUIT TOPPING

1 oz/28 g turbinado sugar

2 tsp/7 g finely grated orange zest

4½ oz/128 g all-purpose flour

2 tsp/9 g baking powder

½ tsp/1 g kosher salt

2½ oz/71 g cold butter

2 oz/57 g fine cornmeal

4 fl oz/120 mL nonfat buttermilk

1½ fl oz/45 mL agave syrup

1 tsp/5 mL vanilla extract

FILLING

1 oz/28 g butter

1½ fl oz/45 mL agave syrup

1 tbsp/9 g cornstarch

½ tsp/1 g ground cardamom

Pinch kosher salt

2 fl oz/60 mL orange juice

2 lb/907 g peaches, peeled, halved, and cut into ½-in/1-cm-thick slices

1 lb/454 g fresh blackberries

1. To make the topping, in a small bowl, mix the turbinado sugar and orange zest to combine. Set aside.

2. In a food processor, combine the flour, baking powder, and salt. Add the butter and pulse until the butter is the size of small peas, eight to ten 1-second pulses.

3. Transfer the mixture to a medium bowl and stir in the cornmeal. Add the buttermilk, agave syrup, and vanilla and mix until the dough is evenly moistened and begins to form large, soft clumps. Do not overmix. Wrap the dough in plastic wrap and refrigerate for 25 to 30 minutes.

4. To make the filling, melt the butter in a large pan over medium heat. Add the agave syrup, cornstarch, cardamom, salt, and orange juice and bring to a boil. Reduce the heat and simmer, whisking constantly, for 2 minutes.

5. Add the peaches and cook, stirring gently, until just barely warm, about 2 minutes. Add the blackberries and gently toss to combine. Remove the pot from the heat.

6. Portion 4 oz/113 g of the fruit mixture into ten 8-fl oz/240-mL ramekins. Using a #100 scoop, drop 3 mounds of biscuit topping on top of the filling, leaving space between them. Sprinkle ⅛ oz/3 g of the turbinado sugar mixture on top of the biscuits (see Chef's Notes).

7. Bake the cobbler in the oven at 350°F/176°C until the filling is bubbling and the biscuit topping is baked through, 25 to 30 minutes. Serve warm.

CHEF'S NOTES

The flour in this recipe may be replaced with an equal amount of Wheat-Free Flour Blend (page 306) with the addition of ½ tsp/2.5 mL guar gum.

The cobblers may be assembled up through step 6, covered, and stored in the refrigerator for 1 day.

Nutritional Information per Serving (4 oz/113 g fruit filling and 1¼ oz/35 g topping):

200 calories, 6 g fat, 4 g saturated fat, 10 mg cholesterol, 210 mg sodium, 34 g total carbohydrates, 5 g fiber, 11 g sugar, 4 g protein

Plum Cobbler with Honey, Lemon, and Lavender Biscuits D V H

Makes 10 portions

TOPPING

6 oz/170 g all-purpose white whole wheat flour

1¾ tsp/8 g baking powder

¼ tsp/1 g kosher salt

3 oz/85 g cold butter, cut into large pieces

1 tsp/1 g chopped dried lavender

½ tsp/3 g finely grated lemon zest

1½ fl oz/45 mL agave syrup

3½ fl oz/105 mL heavy cream

FILLING

2 fl oz/60 mL mild-flavored honey

2 fl oz/60 mL agave syrup

1 tsp/1 g chopped dried lavender

2 lb 8 oz/1.13 kg ripe red or purple plums, halved and pitted, cut into wedges (about 12)

1 tbsp/8 g cornstarch

Pinch kosher salt

1. To make the topping, in a food processor, combine the flour, baking powder, and salt and pulse briefly to blend. Add the cold butter and pulse for 5 to 7 pulses.

2. Add the lavender and lemon zest and pulse briefly to combine.

3. Pour the agave syrup and cream over the top and pulse just until moist crumbs form, 8 to 10 pulses.

4. Turn the mixture out onto a clean work surface and gently knead until the dough comes together.

5. Lightly flour the dough and roll it into a rectangle 5 in by 10 in/12.5 cm by 25 cm.

6. Cut the rectangle in half lengthwise, and cut each half into 5 equal pieces (roughly a 2½-in/6.25-cm square) for a total of 10 pieces. Wrap in plastic and refrigerate. The dough can be made several hours in advance and stored in the refrigerator.

7. To make the filling, combine the honey, agave syrup, and lavender in a nonreactive 10-in/25-cm skillet and bring to a boil over medium-low heat.

8. In a large bowl, toss the plums with the cornstarch and salt until evenly coated. Add to the boiling honey-agave mixture and cook, stirring gently, until the plums release some juice and the sauce has thickened, about 5 minutes. Remove from the heat.

9. Divide the fruit evenly among ten individual 8-fl oz/240-mL ramekins. Place one dough piece on top of the fruit in each ramekin.

10. Bake in the oven at 350°F/176°C until the filling is bubbling and the topping is nicely browned, 30 to 40 minutes. Let set for about 10 minutes to allow the filling to settle and thicken before serving.

CHEF'S NOTES

Cobblers may be set up ahead of time and baked to order or as needed.

The plums may be replaced with nectarines or pears.

Nutritional Information per Serving (4 oz/113 g fruit filling and 1½ oz/43 g topping):

290 calories, 11 g fat, 7 g saturated fat, 35 mg cholesterol, 120 mg sodium, 48 g total carbohydrates, 4 g fiber, 28 g sugar, 3 g protein

Frozen Greek Yogurt with Fresh Berries C D V H

Makes 12 portions

4 oz/113 g fresh blackberries

4 oz/113 g fresh raspberries

4 oz/113 g fresh blueberries

4 oz/113 g sugar

3 fl oz/90 mL agave syrup

¼ tsp/1.25 mL vanilla extract

1 qt/960 mL premium plain nonfat Greek-style yogurt

1. Cut the blackberries in half. Combine the blackberries, raspberries, and blueberries in a bowl along with the sugar and agave syrup. Allow the berries to macerate for 15 minutes. For a chunky berry texture, mash the berries. For a smooth texture, purée the berries in a blender. (If you wish to prepare a seedless product, strain the purée through a fine-mesh sieve. It helps to scrape and stir the purée with a rubber spatula as it strains.) Reserve the purée.

2. In a large bowl, combine the fruit and vanilla with the yogurt. Place the mixture in the refrigerator and chill thoroughly.

3. Freeze the mixture in your ice cream maker according to the manufacturer's directions. Place in the freezer to harden. For best service texture or consistency, temper the frozen yogurt in the refrigerator for 10 to 15 minutes prior to serving.

CHEF'S NOTES

This product freezes quite hard due to its lowered sugar content.

To further reduce the glycemic load, replace all of the sugar with 4 oz/113 g maltitol.

Nutritional Information per Serving (4 fl oz/120 mL):

120 calories, 0 g fat, 0 g saturated fat, 3 mg cholesterol, 23 mg sodium, 23 g total carbohydrates, 0 g fiber, 20 g sugar, 5 g protein

Delightful Stuffed Dates C D V H

Makes 10 portions

½ oz/14 g finely grated orange zest

3 oz/85 g chopped pistachio nuts

¼ tsp/1 g ground cinnamon

5 tbsp/22 g shredded unsweetened coconut

1½ fl oz/45 mL maple syrup

½ fl oz/15 mL canola oil

20 Medjool dates (7 oz/200 g)

10 fl oz/300 mL plain, fat-free, Greek-style yogurt

¼ oz/7 g mint chiffonade

1. In small bowl, combine ¼ oz/7 g of the orange zest, pistachio nuts, cinnamon, coconut, 1 fl oz/30 mL of the maple syrup, and canola oil. Stir until evenly coated. Transfer to a parchment paper–lined baking sheet and roast in the oven at 350°F/176°C until lightly browned, 5 to 6 minutes. Remove from the oven and set aside.

2. Carefully cut a slit the length of each date. Squeeze the ends of each date toward the center to open the slit.

3. Press 1½ tsp/7.5 mL of the roasted nut mixture into each date. Press the seam together to seal shut.

4. In a small bowl, combine the yogurt with the remaining 1 tbsp/15 mL maple syrup and reserve.

5. In another small bowl, combine the remaining ¼ oz/7 g orange zest with the mint chiffonade and reserve.

6. To plate, dollop and drag 1 fl oz/30 mL of the yogurt onto a dessert plate. Position 2 stuffed dates next to the dollop. Garnish with a sprinkling of the zest-mint mixture.

Nutritional Information per Serving (2 dates):

243 calories, 7 g fat, 2 g saturated fat, 1 mg cholesterol, 13 mg sodium, 44 g total carbohydrates, 5 g fiber, 37 g sugar, 6 g protein

Warm Rice Polenta with Almonds, Walnuts, Pecans, Flaxseeds, and Cherries C D V H

Makes 10 portions

6 oz/170 g brown rice cereal

28 fl oz/840 mL unsweetened almond milk

1 tsp/2 g ground cinnamon

Pinch sea salt

3 oz/85 g toasted slivered almonds

1 tbsp/15 g ground flaxseeds

1 gal/3.84 L water

2½ fl oz/75 mL agave syrup

5 fl oz/150 mL egg whites

¼ tsp/1 g cream of tartar

1 tsp/5 mL vanilla extract

1 oz/28 g butter

10 oz/284 g halved and pitted Bing cherries

1. In a medium sauce pot, combine the brown rice cereal, almond milk, cinnamon, and salt. Place over medium heat and bring to a simmer, stirring constantly. Lower the heat to a very gentle simmer, and cook the cereal until it becomes smooth and the grains are tender, 20 to 30 minutes. Remove the rice polenta from the heat.

2. Pour the polenta into a large mixing bowl and fold in 1 oz/28 g of the toasted almonds and all of the ground flaxseed. Place a cover over the bowl to prevent a skin from forming and allow the polenta to cool down to room temperature.

3. Lightly spray ten 8-fl oz/240-mL ramekins with canola cooking spray and place on a small sheet pan. Meanwhile, bring the water to a simmer in a medium rondeau. In a large bowl, combine 2 fl oz/60 mL of the agave syrup with the egg whites and cream of tartar and whisk to combine.

4. Place the bowl containing the egg whites over the rondeau of simmering water and whisk constantly to aerate and cook the whites into a meringue. Once the whites have tripled in volume and become shiny and stiff, remove the bowl from the heat, and fold in the vanilla.

5. Using a bowl spatula, gently fold one-third of the egg white mixture into the cooled polenta. Continue to add the remaining egg whites in two more additions. Once the whites and polenta are fully combined, portion the mixture evenly into the prepared ramekins using approximately 7 fl oz/210 mL of the mixture per ramekin.

6. Cover the ramekins with plastic wrap and cool thoroughly. This mixture may be stored for up to 3 days in the refrigerator.

7. At service time, place the chilled ramekins into a hot water bath or place in the oven at 300°F/149°C to reheat to an internal temperature of 145°F/62°C.

8. Meanwhile, in a medium sauté pan over medium heat, melt the butter. Add the cherries and the remaining ½ fl oz/15 mL agave syrup and sauté very briefly just to heat through.

9. Turn out the molded rice polenta onto a dessert plate, top with 1½ oz/42 g of the sautéed cherries, and sprinkle with 1 tsp/5 g of the toasted slivered almond.

> **Nutritional Information per Serving (7 fl oz/210 mL rice polenta, 1.5 oz/42 g cherries, 1 tsp/5 g toasted almonds):**
>
> 250 calories, 8 g fat, 2 g saturated fat, 5 mg cholesterol, 85 mg sodium, 38 g total carbohydrates, 5 g fiber, 17 g sugar, 7 g protein

A well-stocked larder is one of the chef's most important tools in developing healthier and more exciting menu offerings. Pantry items, comprised here of seasonings, dressings, sauces, and condiments, are great to have on hand to add a power-packed punch of flavor to a dish without adding too many calories. These recipes can elevate a dish from the ordinary to the sublime. Although most of these foods are available commercially, they are not difficult to produce, and are always more interesting when made by hand because you can customize their flavor profile and come up with inventive ways to feature seasonal ingredients. Also, some commercial items are laden with additional sugar and salt, so making them from scratch helps the professional chef to limit the number of calories and the amount of sodium that is put on a plate.

Green Curry Paste

Makes 12 oz/340 g curry paste

½ tsp/1 g cumin seeds

1 tbsp/6 g coriander seeds

10 white peppercorns

5 oz/142 g seeded green jalapeños

4¼ oz/120 g thinly sliced shallots

½ oz/14 g thinly sliced garlic

1 oz / 28 g cilantro

¾ oz/21 g thinly sliced lemongrass

½ oz/14 g peeled and finely chopped galangal

1 tsp/2 g lime zest

8 kaffir lime leaves, roughly chopped

1 tsp/5 mL shrimp paste

1 tsp/3 g kosher salt

1. In a small sauté pan, toast the cumin and coriander seeds over medium-low heat until fragrant, 15 to 30 seconds. Transfer to a small bowl.

2. Add the peppercorns to the pan and toast until fragrant, 15 to 30 seconds. Transfer to the bowl with the other spices and let cool.

3. In a spice grinder, grind the toasted spices. Set aside.

4. In a blender or food processor, combine the jalapeños, shallots, garlic, cilantro, lemongrass, galangal, lime zest, lime leaves, shrimp paste, and salt. Process until the mixture forms a paste.

5. Transfer the mixture to a medium bowl, and stir in the ground toasted spices. Mix until well combined. This paste can be stored in a glass or stainless-steel container with a tight-fitting lid in the refrigerator for up to 1 week.

> **Nutritional Information per Serving (1 oz/28 g):**
>
> 15 calories, 0 g fat, 0 g saturated fat, 0 mg cholesterol, 160 mg sodium, 3 g total carbohydrates, 0 g fiber, 1 g sugar, 1 g protein

Left, from top to bottom: Yellow Curry Paste (page 304), Red Curry Paste (page 303), Green Curry Paste (left), and Massaman Curry Paste (page 302)

Massaman Curry Paste C D H

Makes 1 lb/454 g curry paste

1¼ oz/35 g dried red Anaheim chiles, stemmed and coarsely chopped

2 tbsp/12 g cumin seeds

1 tsp/2 g coriander seeds

1 tsp/2 g white peppercorns

1 tsp/2 g whole cloves

1 tsp/2 g ground cinnamon

1 tsp/2 g ground mace

1 tsp/2 g freshly grated nutmeg

1 tsp/2 g ground cardamom

¾ oz/21 g thinly sliced lemongrass

½ oz/14 g peeled and finely chopped galangal

8 kaffir lime leaves

2⅓ oz/68 g thinly sliced garlic

2¾ oz/78 g thinly sliced shallots

1 tsp/5 mL shrimp paste

1 tsp/3 g kosher salt

1. Place the chiles in a small bowl, cover with warm water, and soak for 20 minutes. Drain and reserve.

2. In a small sauté pan, toast the cumin, coriander, peppercorns, and cloves over medium-low heat until fragrant, 15 to 30 seconds. Transfer to a small bowl to cool.

3. In a spice grinder, grind the toasted spices. Add the cinnamon, mace, nutmeg, and cardamom.

4. In a blender or food processor, combine the chiles, lemongrass, galangal, lime leaves, garlic, shallots, shrimp paste, and salt. Process until the mixture forms a paste. If necessary, add water, 1 tbsp/15 mL at a time, to facilitate blending.

5. Transfer the mixture to a medium bowl, and stir in the ground toasted spices. Mix until well combined. This paste can be stored in a glass or stainless-steel container with a tight-fitting lid in the refrigerator for up to 1 week.

Nutritional Information per Serving (1 oz/28 g):

40 calories, 1 g fat, 0 g saturated fat, 0 mg cholesterol, 190 mg sodium, 7 g total carbohydrates, 1 g fiber, 1 g sugar, 1 g protein

Red Curry Paste C D H

Makes 12 oz/340 g curry paste

2 oz/57 g dried red chiles, such as Thai bird or cayenne, toasted, seeded, ribs removed

1 tsp/2 g cumin seeds

1 tbsp/6 g coriander seeds

½ tsp/1 g white peppercorns

½ oz/14 g thinly sliced garlic

2¾ oz/78 g thinly sliced shallots

¾ oz/21 g thinly sliced lemongrass

½ oz/14 g peeled and finely chopped galangal

1 tsp/3 g lime zest

8 kaffir lime leaves, chopped

1 tbsp/3 g finely chopped cilantro root

1 tsp/5 mL Thai shrimp paste

1 tsp/3 g kosher salt

1. Place the toasted cleaned chiles in a medium bowl, cover with hot water, and soak for 20 minutes. Drain and reserve.

2. In a small sauté pan, toast the cumin, coriander, and peppercorns over medium-low heat until fragrant, 15 to 30 seconds. Transfer to a small bowl to cool.

3. In a spice grinder, grind the toasted spices. Set aside.

4. In a blender or food processor, combine the reconstituted chiles, garlic, shallots, lemongrass, galangal, lime zest, lime leaves, cilantro, shrimp paste, and salt. Process until the mixture forms a paste. If necessary, add water, 1 tbsp/15 mL at a time, to facilitate blending.

5. Transfer the mixture to a medium bowl, and stir in the ground toasted spices. Mix until well combined. This paste can be stored in a glass or stainless-steel container with a tight-fitting lid in the refrigerator for up to 1 week.

Nutritional Information per Serving (1 oz/28 g):

10 calories, 0 g fat, 0 g saturated fat, 0 mg cholesterol, 160 mg sodium, 2 g total carbohydrates, 0 g fiber, 0 g sugar, 0 g protein

Yellow Curry Paste

Makes 7 oz/199 g curry paste

1 tsp/3 g cumin seeds

1 tbsp/6 g coriander seeds

½ tsp/2 g white peppercorns

1 oz/28 g Thai bird chiles

1 tbsp/6 g ground turmeric

½ oz/14 g sliced garlic

2¾ oz/78 g sliced shallots

½ oz/14 g peeled and finely chopped galangal

1 tbsp/3 g cilantro root

¾ oz/21 g thinly sliced lemongrass

1 tsp/3 g lime zest

8 kaffir lime leaves, chopped

1 tsp/5 mL shrimp paste

1 tsp/3 g kosher salt

1. In a small sauté pan, toast the cumin, coriander, and peppercorns over medium-low heat until fragrant, 15 to 30 seconds. Transfer to a small bowl to cool.

2. In a spice grinder, grind the toasted spices. Set aside.

3. In a blender or food processor, combine the chiles, turmeric, garlic, shallots, galangal, cilantro, lemongrass, lime zest, lime leaves, shrimp paste, and salt. Process until the mixture forms a paste. If necessary, add water, 1 tbsp/15 mL at a time, to facilitate blending.

4. Transfer the mixture to a medium bowl, and stir in the ground toasted spices. Mix until well combined. Store the paste in a sealed glass or stainless-steel container with a tight-fitting lid in the refrigerator for up to 1 week.

Nutritional Information per Serving (1 oz/28 g):

25 calories, 0 g fat, 0 g saturated fat, 0 mg cholesterol, 278 mg sodium, 5 g total carbohydrates, 1 g fiber, 1 g sugar, 1 g protein

Harissa C D V H

Makes 2 lb 8 oz/1.13 kg harissa

1 lb/454 g fresh red chiles, such as Fresno

1 oz/28 g dried habanero chile

4 oz/113 g sun-dried tomatoes

½ oz/14 g crushed garlic

¼ oz/7 g ground turmeric

½ tsp/.5 g ground coriander

½ tsp/.5 g ground cumin

½ tsp/.5 g ground caraway

½ tsp/1.5 g kosher salt

½ tsp/2.5 mL lemon juice, plus more as needed for consistency and flavor

2 fl oz/60 mL olive oil, plus more as needed for consistency and flavor

1½ tbsp/7.5 mL water, plus more as needed for consistency

1. Seed and stem the fresh chiles.

2. Toast and hydrate the dried chiles. Seed and stem them.

3. Purée everything in the blender until smooth.

4. Adjust the consistency with the lemon juice, oil, and water.

Nutritional Information per Serving (1 oz/28 g):

26 calories, 2 g fat, 0 g saturated fat, 0 mg cholesterol, 84 mg sodium, 3 g total carbohydrates, 0 g fiber, 2 g sugar, 0 g protein

Harissa

Wheat-Free Flour Blend

Makes 5 lb/2.27 kg flour blend

1 lb/454 g almond flour

1 lb/454 g brown rice flour

8 oz/227 g amaranth flour

8 oz/227 g tapioca starch

8 oz/227 g quinoa flour

8 oz/227 g corn flour

8 oz/227 g light buckwheat flour

8 oz/227 g teff flour

Mix all the flours to combine. Store in an airtight container at room temperature.

CHEF'S NOTES

This recipe is not for someone with a nut allergy.

When this flour blend is used for baking purposes, ½ tsp/2.5 mL of guar gum should be added per cup or 4 ¼ oz/120 g of the blend.

> **Nutritional Information per Serving (2 oz/57 g):**
>
> 230 calories, 8 g fat, 0 g saturated fat, 0 mg cholesterol, 10 mg sodium, 35 g total carbohydrates, 6 g fiber, 1 g sugar, 8 g protein

Ancho-Cumin Crust Mix

Makes 12½ oz/354 g crust mix

3 oz/85 g ancho chiles

1½ oz/43 g cumin seeds

1½ oz/43 g coriander seeds

½ oz/14 g black peppercorns

½ oz/14 g dried thyme leaves

½ oz/14 g dried oregano

4 oz/113 g kosher salt

½ oz/14 g dry mustard powder

¼ oz/7 g onion powder

¼ oz/7 g garlic powder

1. Remove the stems and seeds from the anchos and roughly chop the chiles.
2. Bake the anchos, cumin, coriander, and peppercorns in the oven at 300°F/149°C for 5 minutes, or until warmed and aromatic. Remove from the oven and cool thoroughly before grinding.
3. In a spice grinder, combine all the ingredients and grind to a moderately coarse texture. Store in an airtight container.

> **Nutritional Information per Serving (¼ oz/7 g):**
>
> 15 calories, 1 g fat, 0 g saturated fat, 0 mg cholesterol, 940 mg sodium, 3 g total carbohydrates, 1 g fiber, 0 g sugar, 1 g protein

BBQ Spice Rub C D V H

Makes 12 oz/340 g spice rub

8 oz/227 g kosher salt

¼ oz/7 g cayenne

¼ oz/7 g freshly ground black pepper

1 tsp/4 g freshly ground white pepper

3 oz/85 g smoked Spanish paprika (*pimentón*)

½ oz/14 g onion powder

½ oz/14 g garlic powder

1 tbsp/3 g dried thyme

1 oz/28 g maple sugar

Combine all the ingredients and mix well. Store in an airtight container.

Nutritional Information per Serving (½ oz/14 g):

19 calories, .5 g fat, 0 g saturated fat, 0 mg cholesterol, 3432 mg sodium, 4 g total carbohydrates, 1 g fiber, 1 g sugar, .5 g protein

---

Herbes de Provence

C D V H

Makes 4 oz/113 g herb blend

1¼ oz/35 g dried thyme

1¼ oz/35 g dried marjoram

1¼ oz/35 g dried savory

2½ tbsp/7.5 g dried rosemary

2½ tsp/2.5 g dried sage

2½ tsp/2.5 g dried mint

2½ tsp/2.5 g fennel seeds, lightly crushed or chopped

2½ tsp/2.5 g dried lavender flowers

Combine all the ingredients. Store any unused herb blend in an airtight container in a cool, dry place. For a bolder flavor, the herbs may be crushed fine with a mortar and pestle just before using, if desired.

CHEF'S NOTE

Crushed bay leaves are sometimes included in this blend.

Nutritional Information per Serving (1 tsp/2 g):

6 calories, 0 g fat, 0 g saturated fat, 0 mg cholesterol, 1 mg sodium, 2 g total carbohydrates, 1 g fiber, 0 g sugar, 0 g protein

---

Jamaican Jerk Marinade ⬚D⬚ ⬚V⬚ ⬚H⬚

Makes 1 qt/960 mL marinade

1 oz/28 g ground allspice

¼ oz/7 g ground cinnamon

1 tsp/2 g ground cloves

1 tbsp/6 g freshly grated nutmeg

2 oz/57 g thinly sliced green onions

1 lb/454 g diced onion

½ oz/14 g peeled and minced ginger

¼ oz/7 g chopped thyme

1 oz/28 g seeded and minced habanero chile

2 fl oz/60 mL rum, such as Myers's

4 fl oz/120 mL soy sauce

4 fl oz/120 mL vegetable oil

1. Combine all the ingredients in a blender or food processor and purée very well.
2. Store, refrigerated, until ready to use.

CHEF'S NOTES

This marinade is ideal for a number of items such as chicken, game hen, pork, shrimp, fish, or tofu. Pour the marinade into a shallow container, add the item to the container and let it marinate, refrigerated, for at least 4 hours and up to overnight; 1 to 2 hours for shrimp, fish, or tofu.

For an extra-spicy marinade, use some or all of the seeds from the habanero chile.

Substitute tamari for the soy sauce to make celiac-friendly.

Nutritional Information per Serving (1½ fl oz/45 mL):

74 calories, 6 g fat, 1 g saturated fat, 0 mg cholesterol, 231 mg sodium, 5 g total carbohydrates, 1 g fiber, 1 g sugar, 1 g protein

Ras el Hanout (Moroccan Spice Mixture) C D V H

Makes 6 oz/170 g spice mix

4 oz/113 g kosher salt

1 tsp/2 g freshly ground black pepper

1 tsp/2 g freshly ground white pepper

1½ tsp/3 g ground turmeric

2 tsp/4 g ground allspice

1 tbsp/7 g garlic powder

1 tbsp/7 g onion powder

1 tsp/2 g ground cinnamon

1 tbsp/7 g ground cumin

1 tbsp/7 g ground anise

1 tbsp/7 g ground coriander

½ tsp/1 g cayenne

½ tsp/1 g freshly grated nutmeg

Mix all of the seasonings together. Store in an airtight container.

Nutritional Information per Serving (¼ oz/7 g):

6 calories, 0 g fat, 0 g saturated fat, 0 mg cholesterol, 1891 mg sodium, 1 g total carbohydrates, 0 g fiber, 0 g sugar, 0 g protein

Seitan

Makes about 1 lb/454 g seitan

- ¾ cup/180 mL vital wheat gluten

- ⅔ cup/160 mL water

- 4½ cups/1.08 L Vegetable Stock or Mushroom Broth (page 106 or 105)

- ¼ cup/60 mL soy sauce or tamari

- 2 tbsp/30 mL dry sherry (optional)

1. Place the vital wheat gluten into a food processor or a stand mixer fitted with a dough hook. Add the water and mix until it is absorbed, about 2 minutes. The mixture will be thick, but should come together.

2. Continue to mix until it forms a smooth dough, about 1 minute more. Transfer the dough from the food processor to a bowl, cover the dough, and let it rest for 15 to 20 minutes.

3. When the dough has rested, use your hands to pull it into 2 pieces. Stretch and pull each piece until it forms a log.

4. In a large saucepan, bring the broth, soy sauce, and sherry, if using, to a simmer over medium-low heat. Place the logs in the simmering liquid and reduce the heat to low. Cover the pot and cook, turning the seitan occasionally, for 45 to 55 minutes, until it can be easily sliced with a knife.

5. Cool the seitan in the liquid until it reaches room temperature. Drain the seitan for immediate use, or store refrigerated in the cooking liquid for up to 2 days. Cooked seitan may also be frozen in the cooking liquid and stored in the freezer for up to 3 months. The cooking liquid is reusable for cooking additional seitan or as an addition to or partial replacement for broth in some recipes. Use the seitan as desired.

CHEF'S NOTE

Try adding other seasonings to the liquid you use to cook the seitan. Herbs, spices, or garlic will all help to make your seitan more flavorful.

Nutritional Information per Serving (4 oz/113 g):

239 calories, 0 g fat, 0 g saturated fat, 0 mg cholesterol, 225 mg sodium, 28 g total carbohydrates, 3 g fiber, 6 g sugar, 23 g protein

Mix the vital wheat gluten and water in a stand mixer to combine.

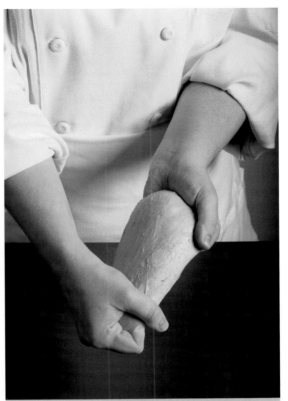

Pull the seitan to stretch it, then form it into a ball.

Cook the ball in the prepared liquid at a simmer until it is puffed and cooked through.

Tofu  C D V H

Makes 2 lb 8 oz/1.14 kg tofu

> 5¼ qt/5.04 L filtered water (see Chef's Notes)
>
> 5 lb 2 oz/2.32 kg soybeans, soaked
>
> 5 tsp/10 g nigari flakes (magnesium chloride)

1. Place 24 fl oz/720 mL of the water and the soybeans in a blender or food processor. Begin processing on low and gradually increase the speed to high, processing until the beans are fully puréed, and the mixture is milky white in color, 3 to 5 minutes.

2. Line a fine-mesh sieve with 3 layers of cheesecloth, place over a large heat-safe bowl, and set aside. In a medium, heavy-bottomed pot, bring 24 fl oz/720 mL of the water to a boil over medium-high heat. Add the soybean mixture to the boiling water and continue to cook, stirring as necessary to avoid scorching, until the mixture is heated through, 6 to 8 minutes.

3. Strain the soybean mixture in the prepared fine-mesh sieve. Allow the mixture to drain and cool to room temperature, about 20 minutes. Gather the ends of the cheesecloth and squeeze the solids to remove all traces of liquid. The recipe should yield 1.25 to 1.5 qt/1.18 to 1.41 L of soy milk. Discard the soybean purée solids.

4. In a large bowl, dissolve the nigari flakes in 3 tbsp/45 mL of the water. Set aside.

5. In a medium, heavy-bottomed pot, heat 1 qt/960 mL of the soy milk until it registers 185°F/85°C on a thermometer. Stir constantly as the milk heats to avoid scorching. When the soy milk has reached the correct temperature, slowly pour the milk into the dissolved nigari mixture and stir to incorporate. The milk will begin to coagulate and resemble wet cheese curds. Cover the bowl with plastic wrap and let stand, undisturbed, for 5 minutes.

6. Set up a tofu press by placing a perforated half hotel pan inside a second perforated half hotel pan. Line the interior hotel pan with cheesecloth. Pour the tofu into the lined pan. Take the ends of the cheesecloth and fold over the mixture. Place the second pan on top and weigh down with 5 to 10 lbs/2.27 to 4.54 kg of weight (see Chef's Notes).

7. Remove the weight, unwrap the cheesecloth, and the tofu is ready to use. If not using immediately, store the tofu in an airtight container (see Chef's Notes).

CHEF'S NOTES

Using unfiltered water can affect both the flavor and texture of the finished tofu. Use a good-quality filtered water to ensure consistency of product.

The more weight that is used as well as the length of the pressing time will affect the texture of the finished tofu. Less weight and a shorter pressing time will result in a softer product, while more weight and a longer pressing time will result in firmer tofu.

The finished tofu will keep, refrigerated, for up to 1 week.

Nutritional Information per Serving (4 oz/113 g):

80 calories, 5 g fat, 1 g saturated fat, 0 mg cholesterol, 14 mg sodium, 2 g total carbohydrates, 1 g fiber, 1 g sugar, 10 g protein

The curdled soy milk ready to be strained.

Gently ladle the curds into a cheesecloth-lined tofu press.

The finished tofu.

Miso-Shiitake Sauce

Makes 24 fl oz/720 mL sauce

18 fl oz/540 mL water

1 oz/28 g dried shiitake mushrooms

2 oz/57 g sesame seeds

1 fl oz/30 mL apple cider vinegar

½ oz/14 g miso paste

½ fl oz/15 mL tamari

½ fl oz/15 mL agave syrup

4 fl oz/120 mL sesame oil

Pinch freshly ground black pepper

1. Place the water in a small saucepan and bring to a simmer.

2. Rinse the shiitake mushrooms, remove the stems, and place the caps into the simmering water. Cover the pot, remove from the heat, and allow mushrooms to steep until rehydrated, about 15 minutes.

3. Remove the mushrooms from the liquid, blot dry with paper towels, and roughly chop.

4. Strain the steeping liquid into the jar of a blender. Add the chopped mushroom caps and all the remaining ingredients and blend until smooth. Store in the refrigerator.

CHEF'S NOTE

This sauce can be served either cold or warm.

> **Nutritional Information per Serving (1 fl oz/30 mL):**
>
> 61 calories, 6 g fat, 1 g saturated fat, 0 mg cholesterol, 65 mg sodium, 2 g total carbohydrates, 0 g fiber, 0 g sugar, 1 g protein

Ancho Chile Sauce

Makes 16 fl oz/480 mL sauce

3 oz/85 g ancho chiles

2 fl oz/60 mL boiling water

1 fl oz/30 mL olive oil

4 oz/113 g small-dice onions

1⅔ oz/47 g tomato paste

8 oz/227 g small-dice roasted red bell peppers

½ oz/14 g roasted garlic

½ oz/14 g brown sugar

½ fl oz/15 mL white wine vinegar

4 fl oz/120 mL Chicken Stock (page 105)

1 tsp/2 g ground cumin

½ tsp/1 g dried oregano

¼ tsp/.5 g ground cinnamon

Pinch cayenne

8 fl oz/240 mL Fond de Veau Lié (page 315)

1. Steep the ancho chiles in the boiling water until soft. Reserve the chiles and discard the water. Remove the stems and seeds of the chiles and chop the flesh.

2. Heat the oil in a medium saucepan. Add the onion and sauté until translucent. Add the tomato paste and cook until rust colored. Add the chiles, bell peppers, garlic, sugar, vinegar, and chicken stock and bring the sauce to a simmer. Add the cumin, oregano, cinnamon, and cayenne and simmer until flavorful and thickened, about 30 minutes.

3. Purée the sauce and combine with the fond de veau. Strain through a large-hole sieve.

> **Nutritional Information per Serving (1 fl oz/30 mL):**
>
> 174 calories, 3 g fat, 1 g saturated fat, 0 mg cholesterol, 264 mg sodium, 4 g total carbohydrates, 1 g fiber, 1 g sugar, 1 g protein

Fond de Veau Lié C D H

Makes 1½ gal/5.75 L stock

MIREPOIX

6 oz/170 g roughly cut onion

6 oz/170 g roughly cut carrots

6 oz/170 g roughly cut leeks

6 oz/170 g roughly cut celery

25 lb/11.35 kg veal bones

5 fl oz/150 mL vegetable oil

10 oz/284 g tomato paste

1½ qt/1.45 L red wine

2 garlic gloves

4 bay leaves

½ tsp/1 g dried thyme

6 gal/23 L Brown Veal Stock (page 316)

9 oz/255 g arrowroot

1. Place the mirepoix vegetables and veal bones in a roasting pan and toss with the oil. Roast in the oven at 450°F/232°C until the mirepoix is caramelized and the bones are a rich brown color, about 30 minutes. Add the tomato paste and continue to roast until brown.

2. Place the roasting pan over direct heat. Deglaze the pan by adding the wine in thirds. Allow the wine to reduce after each addition.

3. Transfer the roasted mirepoix and bones to a stockpot and combine with the garlic, herbs, and stock. Simmer until flavorful, about 6 hours, skimming the surface when necessary. Strain, pressing the solids to release all the juices.

4. Place the strained liquid in a large saucepan and reduce by half, to yield 1½ gal/5.75 L.

5. Combine the arrowroot with enough water to form a paste. Add to the saucepan, bring to a boil, and stir constantly until the stock has thickened, about 2 minutes.

Nutritional Information per Serving (2 fl oz/60 mL):

25 calories, 0 g fat, 0 g saturated fat, 0 mg cholesterol, 80 mg sodium, 3 g total carbohydrates, 0 g fiber, 1 g sugar, 1 g protein

Brown Veal Stock C D H

Makes 1 gal/3.84 L stock

2 fl oz/60 mL vegetable oil, or as needed

8 lb/3.63 kg veal bones, including knuckles and trim

6 qt/5.76 L cold water

5 oz/142 g carrots, large dice

5 oz/142 g onions, large dice

5 oz/142 g celery, large dice

6 oz/170 g tomato paste

1 Standard Sachet d'Épices (page 340)

1. Condition the roasting pan: Heat the pan with enough oil to lightly film it in a 425° to 450°F/218° to 232°C oven. (If the bones are extremely fatty, no oil is necessary. The fat will render during the roasting process and the pan will be lubricated.) Spread the bones in the pan and return to the oven. Roast the bones, stirring and turning from time to time, until they are deep brown, 30 to 45 minutes.

2. Transfer the bones to a stockpot large enough to accommodate all of the ingredients. Add 5½ qt/5.28 L of the water and bring to a simmer at 180°F/82°C.

3. Discard the excess fat from the roasting pan but reserve some for making the pináge. Return the roasting pan to the oven or place it on the range, depending on the stove space available. Caramelize the carrots and onions. When they have attained a rich brown color, add the celery and cook it until it begins to wilt and shrivel, 10 to 15 minutes. (Celery will not brown very much because of its high water content.)

4. Once the proper color of the mirepoix has been attained, add the tomato paste and continue to cook slowly until the pináge has a rich brick reddish brown color. Once the tomato paste has been cooked, remove the mixture from the pan. Add the remaining water and deglaze the fond off the bottom of the pan. Reduce the liquid to a syrupy consistency.

5. After the stock has simmered for about 5 hours, add the mirepoix mixture, reduced deglazing liquid, and the sachet.

6. Continue to simmer the stock at 180° to 185°F/82° to 85°C, skimming as necessary and tasting from time to time, until it has developed a rich flavor, noticeable body, and rich brown color, about 1 hour more.

7. Strain the stock. It may be used now (degrease by skimming, if necessary) or rapidly cooled and stored for later use.

Nutritional Information per Serving (8 fl oz/240 mL):

169 calories, 9 g fat, 2 g saturated fat, 7 mg cholesterol, 94 mg sodium, 4 g total carbohydrates, 1 g fiber, 2 g sugar, 18 g protein

Anchovy-Caper Dressing

C D H

Makes 1 qt/960 mL dressing

10 oz/284 g part-skim ricotta cheese

20 fl oz/600 mL nonfat yogurt, drained

4 fl oz/120 mL red wine vinegar

4 oz/113 g capers

2 anchovy fillets, mashed

2 oz/57 g minced shallots

½ oz/14 g minced garlic

½ oz/14 g chopped chives

½ oz/14 g chopped flat-leaf parsley

½ oz/14 g basil chiffonade

Purée the ricotta in a food processor or blender until smooth. Transfer the ricotta to a large bowl and whisk in the remaining ingredients.

Nutritional Information per Serving (1 fl oz/30 mL):

24 calories, 0 g fat, 0 g saturated fat, 5 mg cholesterol, 130 mg sodium, 3 g total carbohydrates, 0 g fiber, 1 g sugar, 2 g protein

---

BBQ Sauce C H

Makes 16 fl oz/480 mL sauce

¼ oz/7 g chili powder

¼ oz/7 g hot Hungarian paprika

¼ oz/7 g lapsang souchong tea leaves

3 fl oz/90 mL grapeseed oil

6 oz/170 g barley malt syrup or brown rice syrup

6 oz/170 g low-sugar ketchup

¾ fl oz/22 fl oz apple cider vinegar

¾ fl oz/22 fl oz Worcestershire sauce

½ oz/14 g stone-ground mustard

¼ oz/7 g finely minced basil

1 tbsp/3 g finely minced thyme

2 tsp/6 g minced garlic

½ oz/14 g peeled and minced ginger

1. In a small sauté pan, toast the chili powder and paprika until fragrant, 10 to 15 seconds. Remove from the heat and cool to room temperature.

2. Transfer to a spice grinder, and add the tea leaves. Grind the mixture to a fine powder.

3. In a medium sauce pot, combine the oil, syrup, ketchup, vinegar, Worcestershire sauce, mustard, basil, thyme, garlic, ginger, and ground spices.

4. Bring the sauce to a simmer and cook, stirring occasionally, until a good flavor develops, 10 to 15 minutes.

5. Remove the sauce from the heat, cool, and store refrigerated until ready to serve.

Nutritional Information per Serving (2 fl oz/60 mL):

190 calories, 11 g fat, 1 g saturated fat, 0 mg cholesterol, 320 mg sodium, 23 g total carbohydrates, 0 g fiber, 20 g sugar, 2 g protein

---

Lemon-Parsley Vinaigrette C D V H

··

Makes 16 fl oz/480 mL vinaigrette

6 fl oz/180 mL lemon juice

2 tbsp/30 mL balsamic vinegar

2 tbsp/6 g chopped flat-leaf parsley

1 tsp/3 g kosher salt

½ tsp/1 g freshly ground black pepper

6 fl oz/180 mL canola oil

2¾ fl oz/81 mL olive oil

1. Whisk together all the ingredients except the oils. Gradually whisk in the canola oil and olive oil until all of the oil has been added and the vinaigrette is smooth and has thickened.

2. Taste and adjust the seasoning. The vinaigrette is ready to use now, or it may be stored in a covered container in the refrigerator for up to 3 days. It may be necessary to blend the vinaigrette again before serving.

Nutritional Information per Serving (1 fl oz/30 mL):

139 calories, 15 g fat, 1 g saturated fat, 2 mg cholesterol, 120 mg sodium, 1 g total carbohydrates, 0 g fiber, 0 g sugar, 0 g protein

---

Hazelnut Romesco Sauce  C D V H

··

Makes 16 fl oz/480 mL sauce

2 dried ancho chiles, stemmed, seeded, and toasted

10½ oz/298 g chopped roasted red bell peppers

8 oz/227 g chopped skinned hazelnuts

4¾ fl oz/140 mL olive oil

2 tbsp/30 mL tomato paste

2 tbsp/30 mL red wine vinegar

1 tbsp/8 g minced garlic

1½ tsp/3 g smoked *pimentón* (Spanish paprika)

¼ tsp/.5 g cayenne

½ tsp/1.5 mL kosher salt, or as needed

1. Put the ancho chiles in a small saucepan and cover with cold water. Bring to a boil over high heat, then immediately remove the pan from the heat. Let the chiles steep for 20 minutes. Strain the chiles, reserving some of the soaking liquid to adjust the consistency of the sauce.

2. Put the roasted bell pepper, hazelnuts, oil, tomato paste, vinegar, garlic, paprika, and cayenne in a blender. Purée to a smooth consistency, adding a bit of the chile soaking liquid, if necessary, to reach a soft, sauce-like consistency (about the same consistency as mayonnaise). Place in a covered container, refrigerate, and allow to rest overnight to develop the best flavor. Adjust the seasoning with salt before serving.

Nutritional Information per Serving (1 fl oz/30 mL):

197 calories, 17 g fat, 2 g saturated fat, 0 mg cholesterol, 263 mg sodium, 8 g total carbohydrates, 2 g fiber, 1 g sugar, 3 g protein

---

Hazelnut Romesco Sauce, served with grilled vegetables

Z'hug

Makes about 1 lb/12 oz/ 794 g

1 lb/454 g jalapeños, roasted and peeled

1 oz/28 g cloves garlic

4 oz/113 g cilantro leaves

2 oz/57 g parsley

2 oz/57 g mint

1 tsp/3 g ground cardamom

1 tsp/3 g cumin seeds, toasted

4 fl oz/120 mL olive oil

1 ½ fl oz/45 mL lemon juice

½ tsp/1.5 g kosher salt

1. In a food processor or blender, pulse the jalapeños, garlic, cilantro, parsley, mint, cardamom, and cumin until finely chopped.

2. Slowly add the olive oil and purée until smooth. Season with the lemon juice and salt. Refrigerate until needed.

Nutritional Information per Serving (1 oz/28 g):

46 calories, 4 g fat, 0 g saturated fat, 0 mg cholesterol, 46 mg sodium, 2 g total carbohydrates, 1 g fiber, 0 g sugar, 0 g protein

---

Lima Bean Spread

Makes 16 fl oz/480 mL spread

2 tbsp/30 mL extra-virgin olive oil

2¾ oz/75 g minced onion

1 garlic clove, chopped

3½ oz/99 g thawed frozen lima beans

3½ oz/99 g thawed frozen peas

4 fl oz/120 mL Vegetable Stock (page 106)

½ tsp/2 g kosher salt

2 tsp/2 g chopped flat-leaf parsley

2 tsp/10 mL lemon juice

1 tsp/1 g chopped rosemary

½ tsp/1 g freshly ground black pepper

1 tbsp/5 g grated Parmesan cheese

½ tsp/2 g coarse sea salt, or as needed

1. Heat 1 tbsp/15 mL of the oil in a large sauté pan over medium heat. Add the onion and garlic and sauté until translucent, 3 to 5 minutes. Add the beans, peas, stock, and salt, reduce the heat to low, and simmer until heated through, about 5 minutes. Drain, reserving the remaining liquid.

2. While the mixture is still warm, purée it in a food processor. Slowly drizzle in the remaining 1 tbsp/15 mL oil while puréeing. Add the parsley, lemon juice, rosemary, and black pepper and continue to purée. Adjust the consistency with the reserved liquid, if needed; the spread should be thick but spreadable. Transfer to a bowl, add the cheese, and mix thoroughly.

3. Refrigerate for at least 30 minutes before serving. Garnish with sea salt, if desired.

Nutritional Information per Serving (1 fl oz/30 mL):

34 calories, 2 g fat, 0 g saturated fat, 0 mg cholesterol, 175 mg sodium, 4 g total carbohydrates, 1 g fiber, 1 g sugar, 1 g protein

---

Lima Bean Spread, served with baked vegetable chips

Pickled Ginger (Gari)

Makes 1 lb/454 g pickled ginger

1 lb/454 g ginger, peeled and very thinly sliced

2 tbsp/20 g kosher salt

16 fl oz/480 mL rice vinegar

5¼ oz/150 g sugar or 2½ oz/71 g light agave syrup

8 shiso leaves, cut into chiffonade

1. Transfer the ginger slices to a medium bowl and toss with 1 tsp/3 g of the salt. Let sit for 10 minutes. Rinse the ginger under hot water and drain well.

2. In a medium pot, bring the vinegar, sugar, remaining salt, and shiso leaves to a simmer over medium heat. Add the ginger and continue to simmer until the ginger begins to get tender, about 1 minute.

3. Remove the pot from the heat, and transfer the ginger and brine to a storage container. Allow the ginger to pickle, refrigerated, overnight before using. Pickled ginger may be sealed in a jar with a tight-fitting lid and stored in the refrigerator for up to 4 months.

Nutritional Information per Serving (1 oz/28 g):

25 calories, 0 g fat, 0 g saturated fat, 0 mg cholesterol, 290 mg sodium, 6 g total carbohydrates, 0 g fiber, 4 g sugar, 0 g protein

---

Salsa de Arbol C D V H

Makes 10 portions

4 dried arbol chiles, toasted

1 lb/454 g plum tomatoes

2¾ oz/78 g chopped white onions

2 garlic cloves, minced

1 tsp/2 g dried Mexican oregano

1 tbsp/15 mL lime juice

Pinch granulated sugar

1 tsp/3 g kosher salt

½ oz/14 g chopped cilantro

1. Place the toasted chiles in a medium bowl. In a small pot, bring approximately 4 fl oz/120 mL water to boil and pour over the chiles. Cover the bowl with plastic wrap and let the chiles soak for 15 minutes. Drain and discard the soaking liquid.

2. Preheat a grill or grill pan over high heat. Grill the tomatoes, turning occasionally, until charred on the outside, 2 to 3 minutes per side.

3. Transfer the tomatoes to a food processor. Add the chiles, onion, garlic, oregano, lime juice, sugar, and salt. Pulse the mixture until homogeneous but still chunky, 15 to 30 seconds.

4. Transfer the salsa to a storage container, cover, and let sit for 1 hour to allow the flavors to meld. Stir in the cilantro just before serving.

Nutritional Information per Serving (2 fl oz/60 mL):

15 calories, 0 g fat, 0 g saturated fat, 0 mg cholesterol, 190 mg sodium, 3 g total carbohydrates, 0 g fiber, 2 g sugar, 1 g protein

---

Salsa de Arbol and Red Chile Salsa (page 332)

Raw Beet Shred [C] [D] [V] [H]

Makes 2 lb 6 oz/1.07 kg beet shred

2 lb/907 g organic beets, thoroughly scrubbed and peeled

3 oz/85 g organic lemon juice

3 oz/85 g organic flaxseed oil

1. Finely shred or fine julienne the raw beets.
2. When ready to serve, toss the beets with the lemon juice and flaxseed oil. Serve immediately.

CHEF'S NOTES

This simple preparation should be mixed as needed, not marinated.

This is a wonderful garnish for almost any salad or entrée where beets make sense.

> **Nutritional Information per Serving (2 oz/57 g):**
>
> 60 calories, 5 g fat, 0 g saturated fat, 0 mg cholesterol, 35 mg sodium, 5 g total carbohydrates, 1 g fiber, 3 g sugar, 1 g protein

Onion Dip [C] [D] [V] [H]

Makes 1 lb 8 oz/680 g dip

2 tbsp/30 mL olive oil

8½ oz/240 g small-dice onions

½ oz/14 g minced garlic

1 tsp/3 g kosher salt

Pinch freshly ground black pepper

12 fl oz/360 mL nonfat Greek-style yogurt

6 fl oz/180 mL mayonnaise

1. Heat a sauté pan over medium heat. Add the oil and heat until it shimmers. Add the onions and season with a pinch of salt, reduce the heat to medium-low, and sauté, stirring frequently, until the onions are a deep, rich brown, 15 to 18 minutes. Add the minced garlic and continue cooking for 5 to 7 minutes more. Remove from the heat and set aside to cool.
2. Mix the remaining ingredients in a bowl, then add the cooled onions. Refrigerate for 1 hour. Stir and season with additional salt and pepper, if needed, before serving.

> **Nutritional Information per Serving (2 oz/57 g):**
>
> 199 calories, 19 g fat, 3 g saturated fat, 7 mg cholesterol, 348 mg sodium, 1 g total carbohydrates, 1 g fiber, 2 g sugar, 5 g protein

Onion Dip, Spinach Dip (page 326), and Feta Dipping Oil (page 329)

Spinach Dip C D V H

Makes 3 lb 4 oz/1.47 kg dip

> 1 lb/454 g baguette, cut on the bias into 48 slices approximately ¼ inch thick
>
> 2 lb/907 g blanched, chopped spinach, drained and squeezed dry
>
> 4 oz/113 g finely chopped artichoke hearts or bottoms
>
> 4 oz/113 g light or low-fat sour cream
>
> 4 oz/113 g nonfat Greek-style yogurt
>
> 3 oz/85 g peeled, seeded, roasted, small-dice poblano chiles
>
> 1 oz/28 g grated Parmesan cheese
>
> 2 tsp/5 g minced garlic
>
> 4 oz/113 g coarsely grated Monterey Jack cheese
>
> ½ tsp/2 g kosher salt
>
> ¼ tsp/½ g freshly ground black pepper

1. Place the sliced bread between 2 sheet pans and bake until golden brown and crisp, 12 to 15 minutes. Remove from the pans and cool down.

2. In a large bowl, mix together the spinach, artichoke, sour cream, yogurt, poblano chiles, Parmesan cheese, and garlic until thoroughly combined. Fold in the Monterey Jack cheese. Season with the salt and pepper. Portion the mixture into 2-fl oz/60-mL g ovenproof ramekins. Bake in the oven at 350°F/176°C until the mixture is very hot and bubbly, 10 to 15 minutes.

3. Reheat the toasted sliced bread and serve 3 slices with each portion of the dip.

Nutritional Information per Serving (2 oz/57 g dip, 1½ oz/43 g bread):

115 calories, 3 g fat, 2 g saturated fat, 8 mg cholesterol, 325 mg sodium, 15 g total carbohydrates, 2 g fiber, 1 g sugar, 5 g protein

Pickled Grapes C V H

Makes 2 lb/907 g pickled grapes

> 6 oz/170 g granulated sugar or 3 oz/85 g light agave syrup
>
> 6 fl oz/180 mL white wine vinegar
>
> 1 cinnamon stick
>
> ½ tsp/2 g kosher salt
>
> 12 oz/340 g seedless green grapes (about 32 grapes)
>
> 12 oz/340 g seedless black grapes (about 32 grapes)

1. Combine the sugar, vinegar, cinnamon stick, and salt in a saucepan and simmer over medium heat until the sugar has completely dissolved, about 5 minutes.

2. Pour the mixture over the grapes, and allow the grapes to cool to room temperature. Cover and refrigerate overnight. The grapes are ready to use now, or they can be stored in the refrigerator for up to 2 weeks.

Nutritional Information per Serving (1 oz/28 g):

30 calories, 0 g fat, 0 g saturated fat, 0 mg cholesterol, 20 mg sodium, 8 g total carbohydrates, 0 g fiber, 7 g sugar, 0 g protein

Tangerine-Pineapple Vinaigrette C D V H

Makes 16 fl oz/480 mL vinaigrette

4 fl oz/120 mL plus 2 tbsp/30 mL tangerine juice

2½ fl oz/75 mL pineapple juice

1 tbsp/15 mL lemon juice

1 tsp/5 mL balsamic vinegar

1 tsp/5 mL Dijon mustard

½ tsp/2 g minced garlic

1 tsp/3 g kosher salt

½ tsp/1 g freshly ground black pepper

4 fl oz/120 mL plus 2 tbsp/30 mL olive oil

2½ fl oz/75 mL macadamia nut oil

1. Whisk together all the ingredients except for the oils. Gradually whisk in the olive oil and macadamia oil until all of the oil has been added and the vinaigrette is smooth and has thickened.

2. Taste and adjust the seasoning. The vinaigrette is ready to use now, or it may be stored in a covered container in the refrigerator for up to 3 days. It may be necessary to blend the vinaigrette again before serving.

CHEF'S NOTE

This is not for someone with a nut allergy.

Nutritional Information per Serving (1 fl oz/30 mL):

83 calories, 9 g fat, 1 g saturated fat, 0 mg cholesterol, 123 mg sodium, 2 g total carbohydrates, 0 g fiber, 2 g sugar, 0 g protein

---

Aioli C D V H

Makes 1 qt/960 mL aioli

6 fl oz/180 mL pasteurized egg yolks

1½ tsp/7.50 mL white wine vinegar

1 oz/28 g garlic paste (see Chef's Note)

½ oz/14 g Dijon mustard

30 fl oz/900 mL extra-virgin olive oil

½ tsp/2 g kosher salt

1. Whisk together the egg yolks, vinegar, garlic paste, and mustard until slightly foamy.

2. Add the oil gradually in a thin stream, whisking constantly, until all the oil is incorporated and the mayonnaise is thick.

3. Season with the salt. Cover and refrigerate immediately.

CHEF'S NOTE

To make garlic paste, crush the peeled garlic cloves by pressing them under the side of the blade of a chef's knife against the surface of a cutting board, then alternately mince and press the crushed garlic to form a paste.

VARIATIONS

Rouille

Add 6 fl oz/180 mL Red Pepper Coulis (page 342) that has been reduced to 2 oz/57 g of red pepper paste.

Saffron Aioli

Bring the vinegar to a simmer and add ½ tsp/1 g saffron threads and infuse the vinegar. Cool the vinegar before continuing.

Herbed Aioli

Add up to 3 oz/85 g chopped fresh herbs.

Nutritional Information per Serving (1 fl oz/30 mL):

240 calories, 27 g fat, 4 g saturated fat, 50 mg cholesterol, 45 mg sodium, 1 g total carbohydrates, 0 g fiber, 0 g sugar, 1 g protein

---

Apple-Pepper Compote

Makes 16 fl oz/480 mL compote

1 lb 8 oz/680 g grated or brunoise of Golden Delicious apples

6 oz/170 g peeled and seeded red bell pepper, cut into brunoise

2 oz/57 g sugar (see Chef's Note)

2 fl oz/60 mL cup dry white wine (such as sauvignon blanc)

2 fl oz/60 mL apple cider

Pinch kosher salt

1. In a medium pot, combine the apples, bell pepper, sugar, white wine, and cider and simmer until most of the moisture is evaporated. The compote will look thick and the fruit will be soft.

2. Season the compote with the salt. Serve at room temperature or store until ready to serve.

CHEF'S NOTE

The sugar can be replaced with 1 fl oz/30 mL light agave syrup.

Nutritional Information per Serving (2 fl oz/60 mL):

50 calories, 0 g fat, 0 g saturated fat, 0 mg cholesterol, 5 mg sodium, 13 g total carbohydrates, 1 g fiber, 11 g sugar, 0 g protein

---

Blueberry Sauce C D V H

Makes 32 fl oz/960 mL sauce

4 fl oz/120 mL light agave syrup

6 fl oz/180 mL water

12 fl oz/360 mL balsamic vinegar

2 lb 7 oz/1.1 kg blueberries

½ oz/14 g peeled and minced ginger

½ oz/14 g grated orange zest

24 fl oz/720 mL Sauternes

1. Combine the agave syrup and water in a small sauce pot and simmer gently over medium-low heat until the syrup turns amber in color, washing down the sides of the pot frequently with a pastry brush dampened with water. Add the vinegar and reduce by one-third.

2. Add the remaining ingredients and simmer until a syrupy consistency is achieved. Strain and press through a fine-mesh sieve. Cover and refrigerate until needed.

CHEF'S NOTES

The sauce uses a gastrique, a reduction of caramelized sugar or sweetener and vinegar, which is done to achieve a rich, flavored fruit sauce that is not too sweet. It pairs well with roasted and grilled meats, poultry, and fish.

For a blackberry sauce, substitute an equal amount of blackberries for the blueberries.

Nutritional Information per Serving (1½ fl oz/45 mL):

98 calories, 0 g fat, 0 g saturated fat, 0 mg cholesterol, 5 mg sodium, 18 g total carbohydrates, 1 g fiber, 14 g sugar, 0 g protein

---

Heywood's Mustard Revisited C D V H

Makes 32 fl oz/960 mL mustard

4½ oz/128 g dry mustard powder

1 fl oz/30 mL agave syrup

2 tsp/6 g kosher salt

12 oz/340 g eggs (about 6 large eggs)

16 fl oz/480 mL malt vinegar

¼ tsp/1.25 mL Tabasco sauce

3 oz/85 g maple syrup

1. Combine the mustard, agave syrup, and salt.
2. Add the eggs and mix until smooth.
3. Whisk in the vinegar, Tabasco, and maple syrup. Cover and refrigerate for 1 to 2 hours.
4. Beat in a bowl set over a saucepan of simmering water until thick and creamy. Cover and refrigerate until cold.
5. Transfer to a clean storage container. Cover and refrigerate for up to 2 weeks.

> **Nutritional Information per Serving (½ fl oz/15 mL):**
>
> 11 calories, .5 g fat, 0 g saturated fat, 23 mg cholesterol, 48 mg sodium, 1 g total carbohydrates, 0 g fiber, 1 g sugar, 0 g protein

Feta Dipping Oil

Makes 10 portions

5 oz/142 g crumbled feta cheese

½ oz/14 g dried oregano

1½ tsp/3 g red pepper flakes

1 tbsp/6 g cracked black peppercorns

15 fl oz/450 mL pure olive oil

1. In a medium bowl, toss the feta with the oregano, red pepper flakes, and peppercorns.
2. When ready to serve, place ½ oz/25 g of the feta mixture in a 2-fl oz/120-mL ramekin, and top with 1½ fl oz/45 mL of the oil.

VARIATION

Olive Dipping Oil

Replace the feta with an equal amount of Kalamata olive paste, and replace the dried oregano with dried marjoram.

> **Nutritional Information per Serving (2 oz/57 g):**
>
> 402 calories, 45 g fat, 8 g saturated fat, 12 mg cholesterol, 158 mg sodium, 2 g total carbohydrates, 1 g fiber, 1 g sugar, 2 g protein

Herb-Infused Oil

Herb-Infused Oil

Makes 1 qt/960 mL infused oil

8 oz/227 g soft-leaf herbs (see Chef's Notes)

2 oz/57 g flat-leaf parsley

1 qt/960 mL extra-virgin olive oil (see Chef's Notes)

1. Clean the herbs, including the parsley, and pluck the leaves; discard the stems. Blanch the leaves in boiling water for 10 seconds. Remove quickly and shock in ice-cold water. Drain thoroughly.

2. Combine the blanched leaves with half of the oil and purée very finely in a blender.

3. Combine the purée with remaining oil and store, covered, in a glass or stainless-steel container in the refrigerator for 24 hours to cure.

4. After 24 hours, strain the oil through a double layer of cheesecloth, if desired. Return the strained oil to the refrigerator for storage. Use the oil within 3 to 5 days.

CHEF'S NOTES

Soft-leaf herbs include basil, tarragon, cilantro, oregano, marjoram, flat-leaf parsley, saw-leaf herb, cilantro, dill, chives, etc.

Sunflower oil can be used in place of extra-virgin olive oil.

VARIATION

Rosemary Oil

Replace the herbs with the leaves from 16 rosemary stems.

> **Nutritional Information per Serving (½ fl oz/15 mL):**
>
> 121 calories, 14 g fat, 2 g saturated fat, 0 mg cholesterol, 0 mg sodium, 0 g total carbohydrates, 0 g fiber, 0 g sugar, 0 g protein

Piperrada C D V H

Makes 1 lb/454 g piperrada

1 lb 8 oz/680 g red bell peppers

2 fl oz/60 mL extra-virgin olive oil

3 oz/85 g small-dice onions

3 garlic cloves, sliced

¾ oz/21 g finely chopped canned plum tomatoes

¼ tsp/1.25 g smoked sweet paprika (*pimentón de la Vera dulce*)

1 bay leaf

½ tsp/2 g sugar or ¼ tsp/7.5 mL agave syrup

¼ tsp/1 g kosher salt

1. Roast the bell peppers until the skins blisters. Place in a bowl, cover with plastic wrap, and allow to steam. Drain the peppers of their juices and reserve. Peel the peppers and julienne into ¼-in/3-mm strips.

2. Heat the oil in a sauté pan over medium heat. Add the onion and sauté until translucent. Add the garlic and sauté until the vegetables are fully cooked and their juices have rendered.

3. Stir in the tomatoes, paprika, roasted bell peppers with their juices, bay leaf, sugar, and salt. Bring the mixture to a boil over high heat, then immediately reduce the heat to establish a simmer. Simmer for 15 minutes, or until the desired consistency is reached. Remove and discard the bay leaf. Serve warm.

> **Nutritional Information per Serving (1 oz/28 g):**
>
> 25 calories, 2 g fat, 2 g saturated fat, 0 mg cholesterol, 18 mg sodium, 2 g total carbohydrates, 0 g fiber, 1 g sugar, 0 g protein

Tomato Oil CDVH

Makes 2 lb 8 oz/1.13 kg tomato oil

32 fl oz/960 mL extra-virgin olive oil

1 oz/28 g garlic cloves

4 oz/113 g minced onions

4 oz/113 g peeled and minced or shredded carrots

1 lb/454 g drained and seeded canned Italian plum tomatoes

1 oz/28 g basil chiffonade (optional)

1. Heat 2 oz/57 g of the oil in a sauce pot. Add the garlic, onion, and carrot and sweat until tender.

2. Chop the tomatoes and add to the sweated vegetables. Cook for about 15 minutes over medium-high heat to intensify the flavor and reduce some of the liquid.

3. Remove the tomato mixture from the heat and allow to cool to room temperature.

4. Add the basil and purée the mixture in a blender for about 30 seconds.

5. Return the purée to the pot and add the remaining oil. Bring the mixture to a simmer and cook gently over low heat for 30 to 45 minutes to infuse the flavor into the oil.

6. Remove from the heat and cool to room temperature. Store, covered, in a glass or stainless-steel container in the refrigerator to cure for 24 hours.

7. After 24 hours, strain the oil through a double layer of cheesecloth to remove the solids. Return the oil to the refrigerator. Use the oil within 3 to 5 days.

CHEF'S NOTE

Infused oil may also be flavored with peaches, plums, cherries, berries of all types, beets, or carrots. More likely than not you would eliminate or replace the garlic, onions, and carrots with shallots, and perhaps choose a different type of herb.

> **Nutritional Information per Serving (1 oz/28 g):**
>
> 201 calories, 23 g fat, 3 g saturated fat, 0 mg cholesterol, 32 mg sodium, 1.5 g total carbohydrates, 0 g fiber, 1 g sugar, 0 g protein

Red Chile Salsa CDVH

Makes 1 pt/480 mL sauce

6 oz/170 g dried red chiles, 6 each guajillo and ancho

4½ qt/4.32 L hot water, or more as needed

8 oz/227 g plum tomatoes

3 oz/85 g yellow onions

1½ oz/43 g roasted garlic cloves

¼ oz/7 g dried Mexican oregano, lightly toasted

1. Rinse, stem, seed, and toast the chiles in the oven at 350°F/176°C until aromatic, about 5 minutes.

2. Rehydrate the chiles in 3 qt/2.88 L of the hot water for about 30 minutes, or overnight. Discard the soaking liquid.

3. Roast the tomatoes and onions in the oven at 350°F/176°C for 30 to 40 minutes, or roast in a preheated cast-iron skillet.

4. Place the rehydrated chiles and the remaining 1½ qt/1.44 L hot water into the jar of a blender and pulse until smooth.

5. Add the roasted tomatoes, onions, garlic, and oregano to the blender and purée until completely smooth.

6. Pour the sauce in a sauce pot and simmer to reduce to the desired thickness or a medium coating consistency (nappé).

7. Cool to room temperature, then store in the refrigerator until needed. The salsa may be served hot or cold.

> **Nutritional Information per Serving (2 fl oz/60 mL):**
>
> 77 calories, 2 g fat, 0 g saturated fat, 0 mg cholesterol, 12 mg sodium, 14 g total carbohydrates, 5 g fiber, 1 g sugar, 3 g protein

Sofrito C D V H

Makes 1 qt/960 mL sofrito

16 fl oz/480 mL extra-virgin olive oil

4 lb/1.81 kg small-dice onions

8 large garlic cloves, minced

4 lb/1.81 kg seeded and chopped ripe tomatoes

1 tsp/1 g kosher salt, or as needed

1. Combine the oil, onion, and garlic in a heavy-bottomed pan over medium heat and cook until the vegetables are soft and a light golden color.
2. Add the tomatoes and continue to cook until the liquid from the tomatoes has completely evaporated and has taken on a jam-like consistency. Season with the salt.
3. Transfer the sofrito to a glass or stainless-steel container and cool to room temperature. Cover and store in the refrigerator for up to 1 week.

Nutritional Information per Serving (1 fl oz/30 mL):

160 calories, 14 g fat, 2 g saturated fat, 0 mg cholesterol, 65 mg sodium, 8 g total carbohydrates, 2 g fiber, 4 g sugar, 1 g protein

Balsamic Vinaigrette

 C D V H

Makes 1 qt/960 mL

16 fl oz/480 mL high-quality balsamic vinegar

16 fl oz/480 mL extra-virgin olive oil

1 tsp/3 g salt

1 oz/28 g basil chiffonade

Whisk together all of the ingredients.

Nutritional Information per Serving (½ fl oz/15 mL):

70 calories, 7 g fat, 1 g saturated fat, 0 mg cholesterol, 30 mg sodium, 1 g total carbohydrates, 0 g fiber, 1 g sugar, 0 g protein

Reduced Oil Dressing C D V H

Makes 1 qt/960 mL dressing

¼ tsp/.5 g xanthan gum

16 fl oz/480 mL water

8 fl oz/240 mL red or white wine vinegar

½ tsp/2 g kosher salt

1 oz/28 g seasonings

8 fl oz/240 mL extra-virgin olive oil

1. Combine the xanthan gum with 2 fl oz/60 mL of the water and mix to a smooth consistency. Combine with the remaining water.
2. Stir in the vinegar, and add the salt and seasonings or garnishes. Gradually whisk in the oil.

VARIATIONS

Herb Vinaigrette

Add 1 oz/28 g chopped herbs.

Orange-Cranberry Vinaigrette

Replace the water with orange juice and replace half of the red wine vinegar with cranberry juice. Garnish with a little orange zest, if desired.

Sherry Vinaigrette

Replace the red wine vinegar with sherry vinegar.

Nutritional Information per Serving (2 tbsp/30 mL):

130 calories, 14 g fat, 2 g saturated fat, 0 mg cholesterol, 60 mg sodium, 0 g total carbohydrates, 0 g fiber, 0 g sugar, 0 g protein

Mango Salsa C D V H

Makes 20 portions

- 1 lb 4 oz/567 g small-dice mangoes
- 4 oz/113 g minced red onions, rinsed and drained
- 1½ oz/43 g seeded and minced serranos
- 3 fl oz/90 mL lime juice
- 1 oz/28 g cilantro chiffonade
- 1 tsp/3 g kosher salt

Combine all of the ingredients. Store in an airtight container in the refrigerator for up to 1 day.

CHEF'S NOTE

This salsa is best if mixed at the time it is needed to keep the flavors and textures fresh.

Nutritional Information per Serving (1½ oz/43 g):

15 calories, 0 g fat, 0 g saturated fat, 0 mg cholesterol, 65 mg sodium, 4 g total carbohydrates, 0 g fiber, 3 g sugar, 0 g protein

---

Green Mango Salsa

C D V H

Makes 10 portions

- 1 lb 8 oz/680 g green mangoes (about 3 mangoes), peeled
- 2 oz/57 g peeled carrots
- 2 fl oz/60 mL lime juice
- ½ oz/14 g cilantro chiffonade
- ½ oz/14 g peeled and minced ginger
- ½ oz/14 g minced garlic
- ½ fl oz/15 mL red wine vinegar
- ½ fl oz/15 mL molasses
- ½ tsp/2 g kosher salt
- Pinch freshly ground black pepper

1. Shred the mangoes and carrots using the coarse-shred side of a box grater. Discard the hard pits. Toss the shredded mango and carrot together in a bowl.
2. Add the lime juice, cilantro, ginger, garlic, vinegar, and molasses and toss to combine. Season with the salt and pepper. Serve chilled.

CHEF'S NOTE

This salsa can also be made with green papayas.

Nutritional Information per Serving (2 oz/56 g):

35 calories, 0 g fat, 0 g saturated fat, 0 mg cholesterol, 80 mg sodium, 10 g total carbohydrates, 1 g fiber, 7 g sugar, 0 g protein

---

Chimichurri Sauce

Makes 1 qt/960 mL sauce

16 fl oz/480 mL extra-virgin olive oil

8 fl oz/240 mL sherry vinegar

1 oz/28 g minced garlic

½ oz/14 g kosher salt

1 tsp/5 mL agave syrup

1 tsp/1 g cayenne

1½ oz/43 g chopped flat-leaf parsley

1 oz/28 g chopped cilantro

½ oz/14 g minced oregano

½ oz/14 g minced cilantro or saw-leaf herb leaves

Combine the oil, vinegar, garlic, salt, agave, and cayenne and mix well. Add the herbs just before service.

CHEF'S NOTE

This sauce is the perfect accompaniment to grilled meats and fishes or as a drizzle on raw oysters.

Nutritional Information per Serving (1 fl oz/30 mL):

122 calories, 14 g fat, 2 g saturated fat, 0 mg cholesterol, 178 mg sodium, 0 g total carbohydrates, 0 g fiber, 0 g sugar, 0 g protein

---

Tomato Sauce

Makes 3 qt/ 2.88 L sauce

5 lb/2.27 kg cored and quartered tomatoes

2 oz/57 g garlic cloves

½ oz/14 g basil sprigs

1 oregano sprig

2 thyme sprigs

2 fl oz/60 mL olive oil

1 tsp/3 g kosher salt

¼ tsp/.5 g ground black pepper

1 lb/454 g onions, sliced ⅛ in/3 mm thick

2 oz/57 g celery, sliced ⅛ in/3 mm thick

4 oz/113 g carrots, ⅛ in/3 mm thick

2 fl oz/60 mL Vegetable Stock (page 106)

1. In a roasting pan, combine the tomatoes, garlic, basil, oregano sprig, thyme sprigs, oil, salt, and pepper. Mix thoroughly. Roast in a 400°F/204°C oven for 30 minutes.

2. While the tomatoes are roasting, sweat the onions, celery, and carrots in the vegetable stock until translucent.

3. Combine the roasted tomatoes and vegetables in a saucepan and cook on a low simmer for 30 minutes.

4. Pass the tomato sauce through the fine die of a food mill.

5. Cool the sauce to 41°F/4°C and store in an airtight container in the refrigerator for up to 5 days.

Nutritional Information per Serving (3 fl oz/90 mL):

40 calories, 2 g fat, 0 g saturated fat, 0 mg cholesterol, 48 mg sodium, 5 g total carbohydrates, 1 g fiber, 3 g sugar, 1 g protein

---

Pomodoro Sauce

Makes 2 quarts/1.92 L sauce

6 fl oz/180 mL extra-virgin olive oil

2 oz/57 g whole garlic cloves, peeled and crushed

4 lb/1.81 kg canned unsalted Italian plum tomatoes

1 tsp/3 g kosher salt

¼ tsp/.5 g freshly ground black pepper

½ oz/14 g basil chiffonade

¼ oz/7 g flat-leaf parsley chiffonade

1. In a saucepan, heat the olive oil over medium heat. Add the garlic and parsley and cook until garlic is golden. Remove from the heat and set aside.

2. Drain the tomatoes, then pass them through the medium-holed disk of a food mill to remove the seeds and establish consistency. Season the purée with the salt and cook until nappé.

3. Season with the pepper and add the basil and parsley chiffonade.

> **Nutritional Information per Serving (3 fl oz/90 mL):**
>
> 87 calories, 8 g fat, 1 g saturated fat, 0 mg cholesterol, 124 mg sodium, 4 g total carbohydrates, 1 g fiber, 2 g sugar, 1 g protein

Gremolata C D V H

Makes about 1 lb/454 g gremolata

8 oz/227 g chopped flat-leaf parsley

1½ oz/43 g finely shredded lemon zest

½ oz/14 g minced garlic

6 fl oz/160 mL olive oil

½ tsp/2 g kosher salt

Pinch freshly ground pepper, or as needed

1. In a medium bowl, combine the parsley, lemon zest, and garlic.

2. Add the oil and mix to combine. Season with the salt and pepper.

CHEF'S NOTE

This fragrant sauce can be used as a condiment, sauce, or even rubbed onto vegetables or proteins before cooking. It is best when served the same day it is made, or mixed to order.

> **Nutritional Information per Serving (1⅔ oz/45 g):**
>
> 150 calories, 15 g fat, 2 g saturated fat, 0 mg cholesterol, 95 mg sodium, 4 g total carbohydrates, 1 g fiber, 0 g sugar, 1 g protein

Gremolata on Braised Lamb Shanks (page 222)

Modified Rouille D V H

Makes 8 fl oz/240 mL rouille

3 fl oz/90 mL water

6 oz/170 g coarse fresh bread crumbs (preferably from a baguette, crust removed)

¾ oz/21 g garlic cloves

1 tsp/3 g coarse sea salt

1 tsp/2 g cayenne

3 fl oz/90 mL extra-virgin olive oil

1. In a medium bowl, combine the water and bread crumbs.
2. In a small bowl, mash the garlic into a paste with the salt. Add the moistened bread crumbs and continue to mash into a paste. Stir in the cayenne.
3. Add the oil in a slow stream and mix until well combined.

Nutritional Information per Serving (½ fl oz/15 mL):

80 calories, 6 g fat, 1 g saturated fat, 0 mg cholesterol, 220 mg sodium, 6 g total carbohydrates, 0 g fiber, 0 g sugar, 1 g protein

---

Onion Marmalade

 C D V H

Makes 16 fl oz/480 mL marmalade

2 lb/907 g thinly sliced red onions

3 fl oz/90 mL light agave syrup

4 fl oz/120 mL red wine vinegar

4 fl oz/120 mL red wine

1 tsp/3 g kosher salt

Pinch freshly ground black pepper, or as needed

1. Place all the ingredients in a medium pot over medium heat and bring the mixture to a boil.
2. Reduce the heat to low and simmer until the onions are tender and the marmalade has a syrupy consistency, 15 to 25 minutes. Season with the salt and pepper.
3. Cool and refrigerate for up to 1 week.

VARIATION

Roasted Red Pepper Marmalade

Replace 1 lb 8 oz/680 g of the onions with peeled and diced roasted red peppers. Replace the red wine vinegar with balsamic vinegar and the red wine with white wine.

Nutritional Information per Serving (1 fl oz/30 mL):

15 calories, 0 g fat, 0 g saturated fat, 0 mg cholesterol, 63 mg sodium, 3 g total carbohydrates, 0 g fiber, 1 g sugar, 0 g protein

---

Onion Marmalade, served with crostini and Parmesan cheese

Smoky Tomato Sauce C D V H

Makes 3 qt/2.88 L sauce

SMOKED TOMATOES

6 lb/2.72 kg plum tomatoes, stem ends removed

12 charcoal briquettes

8 oz/227 g hickory sawdust, dampened with
2 oz/57 water or whiskey

TOMATO SAUCE

8 oz/227 g small-dice onions

4 oz/113 g small-dice celery

6 oz/170 g small-dice carrots

½ oz/14 g minced garlic

4 fl oz/120 mL olive oil

12 oz/340 g tomato paste

1 Sachet d'Épices, made with 2 oz/57 g of herbs (see Chef's Note), plus peppercorns and bay leaves

Vegetable Stock (page 106), heated, as needed

1 tsp/3 g kosher salt

¼ tsp/.5 g freshly ground black pepper

1 oz/ 28 g chopped fresh herbs (see Chef's Note)

1. To make the smoked tomatoes, cut the tomatoes in half lengthwise and place them, cut side down, on a rack.

2. Place the charcoal briquettes in a sautoir and place in a salamander until red and glowing.

3. Place the rack of tomatoes on a sheet pan and place on the upper rack in a cold oven. Place the pan with the coals in the bottom of cold oven.

4. Sprinkle the dampened hickory dust on the coals and close the oven door.

5. Smoke the tomatoes for 45 to 60 minutes. Remove the tomatoes and coals from the oven. Heat the oven to 475°F/246°C and return the tomatoes to the hot oven.

Roast until the skins blister and turn golden. Cool and peel the tomatoes.

6. To make the tomato sauce, sweat the onions, celery, carrots, and garlic over medium heat in the oil until translucent, 8 to 10 minutes.

7. Add the tomato paste, smoked tomatoes, and sachet and simmer gently for 30 to 45 minutes, or cover and bake in the oven at 325°F/163°C.

8. Remove the sachet and pass the sauce through the large-holed disk of a food mill. Adjust the consistency with stock and season as needed with the salt and pepper. Sprinkle with the fresh herbs after plating.

CHEF'S NOTE

The herb selection varies depending on a specific application. The selection may include basil, oregano, chive, mint, tarragon, marjoram, lemon balm, or flat-leaf parsley.

A Sachet d'Épices can be used to flavor a variety of items including stocks, sauces, and soups. A standard sachet contains parsley stems, cracked peppercorns, dried thyme, and a bay leaf.

> **Nutritional Information per Serving (3 fl oz/90 mL):**
>
> 60 calories, 3 g fat, 0 g saturated fat, 0 mg cholesterol, 80 mg sodium, 7 g total carbohydrates, 2 g fiber, 4 g sugar, 1 g protein

Black Trumpet Mushroom Coulis [C] [D] [V] [H]

Makes 1 qt/960 mL coulis

1 lb/454 g dried black trumpet mushrooms

1 qt/960 mL hot water

1 lb/454 g thinly sliced white button mushrooms

3 oz/85 g butter

2 oz/57 g minced shallot

1 oz/28 g roasted garlic

2 fl oz/60 mL cognac

1 sprig thyme

1 tsp/2 g kosher salt

Pinch freshly ground black pepper

1. Rehydrate the black trumpet mushrooms in the hot water in a medium bowl until soft, about 20 minutes. Strain the mushrooms, and reserve the soaking liquid.

2. Slice the button mushrooms and combine in a medium bowl with the trumpet mushrooms.

3. Heat the butter in a medium pan over medium heat. Add the shallots and sweat until tender, 2 to 3 minutes. Add the roasted garlic and the mushrooms, cover the pot, and cook over medium heat until the mushrooms are tender, 10 to 12 minutes. Remove the lid and continue to cook until any accumulated liquid has evaporated.

4. Add the cognac and flambé. Add the thyme and stir in 8 fl oz/240 mL of the reserved soaking liquid. Simmer until the sauce develops a good flavor, about 10 minutes. Remove and discard the thyme.

5. Transfer the mixture to a blender or food processor and purée until the mixture is a smooth, coating consistency (nappé). Adjust the consistency, if needed, with additional soaking liquid. Season with the salt and pepper.

6. The sauce can be reheated and served, or chilled in an airtight container and refrigerated for up to 5 days and then reheated for service.

Nutritional Information per Serving (2 fl oz/60 mL):

41 calories, 3 g fat, 2 g saturated fat, 6 mg cholesterol, 146 mg sodium, 2 g total carbohydrates, 0 g fiber, 1 g sugar, 1 g protein

---

Red Pepper Coulis

....

Makes 1 qt/960 mL coulis

2 lb/907 g red bell peppers

4 oz/113 g onions, thinly sliced

3 fl oz/90 mL extra-virgin olive oil, plus more for the pan

½ fl oz/15 mL white balsamic vinegar

1 tsp/3 g kosher salt

Pinch freshly ground white pepper

1. Roast the red peppers directly over a flame or under the broiler, turning occasionally, until the pepper skins are blistered and blackened all over. Transfer the peppers to a bowl and let cool completely. Peel the peppers and discard the skins, seeds, and cores. Coarsely chop the peppers.

2. While the peppers are roasting and resting, gently sweat the sliced onions in olive oil over low heat until translucent and sweet to taste, but not browned.

3. In a food processor, combine the peppers with the sweated onions, olive oil, and vinegar, and purée until very smooth and no fibers remain. Season the coulis with the salt and white pepper.

4. The finished sauce may be adjusted with water or vegetable stock to the desired consistency. Additionally, the sauce may be strained if any stringy texture remains.

CHEF'S NOTE

This red pepper coulis may be refrigerated for up to 1 week. Bring to room temperature before serving.

....

> **Nutritional Information per Serving (1 oz/28 g):**
>
> 31 calories, 3 g fat, 0 g saturated fat, 0 mg cholesterol, 75 mg sodium, 2 total carbohydrates, 0 g fiber, 1 g sugar, 0 g protein

Yellow Pepper Coulis

....

Makes 10 portions

1 fl oz/30 mL olive oil

8 oz/227 g sliced onions

¼ oz/7 g sliced garlic

1 lb 8 oz/680 g seeded and chopped yellow bell peppers

4 oz/113 g trimmed, cored, and chopped fennel bulb

8 fl oz/240 mL water

1 tsp/3 g kosher salt

4 oz/113 g husked, washed, and quartered tomatillos

1 fl oz/30 mL lime juice

¼ tsp/1 g freshly ground black pepper

1. In a heavy-bottomed pot, heat the oil over medium heat. Add the onions and garlic and sweat until translucent, 8 to 10 minutes.

2. Add the peppers, fennel, water, and salt.

3. Cover the pot and simmer for 25 minutes, or until the bell peppers are soft.

4. Add the tomatillos and continue to simmer for 5 minutes more.

5. Transfer to a blender and purée until very smooth. Strain the purée through fine-mesh sieve.

6. Season with the lime juice and black pepper. Keep the coulis hot for service, or cool to 41°F/4°C and store in the refrigerator for up to 5 days.

> **Nutritional Information per Serving (2½ fl oz/75 mL):**
>
> 60 calories, 3 g fat, 0 g saturated fat, 0 mg cholesterol, 202 mg sodium, 8 g total carbohydrates, 3 g fiber, 3 g sugar, 1 g protein

USDA Serving Size and Food Group Association

FOOD	SERVING SIZE	FOOD GROUP ASSOCIATION	ASSOCIATED EQUIVALENTS
FRUITS			
APPLES	1 small	1 cup fruit	
BANANAS	1 large; 8 inches long	1 cup fruit	
GRAPEFRUIT	½ medium; 4 inches in diameter	½ cup fruit	
GRAPES	1 medium bunch; about 50 grapes	1½ cups fruit	
MANGOES	1 medium	1 cup fruit	
ORANGES	1 small	½ cup fruit	
PEACHES	½ large	½ cup fruit	
PLUMS	2 large; 2.5 inches wide	1 cup fruit	
RAISINS	¼ cup	½ cup fruit	
VEGETABLES			
Dark Green Vegetables			
ROMAINE LETTUCE	1 cup	½ cup dark green vegetables	
SPINACH	1 cup	½ cup dark green vegetables	
Starchy Vegetables			
CORN	½ cup	½ cup starchy vegetables	
POTATOES	1 medium	1 cup starchy vegetables	
Red and Orange Vegetables			
CARROTS	1 cup	1 cup orange vegetables	
SWEET POTATOES	1 large; 7.5 inches wide	1 cup orange vegetables	
TOMATOES	½ cup	½ cup other vegetables	
TOMATO JUICE	½ cup; 2⅝ inches wide by 3⅞ inches tall	½ cup other vegetables	
Other Vegetables			
CAULIFLOWER	½ cup	½ cup vegetables	
GREEN BEANS	½ cup	½ cup vegetables	
ICEBERG LETTUCE	1 cup 4⅜ inches wide	½ cup vegetables	
MUSHROOMS	½ cup	½ cup vegetables	
ONIONS	2 slices 3 inches wide	¼ cup vegetables	
ZUCCHINI	½ cup	½ cup vegetables	

Continued on page 344

FOOD	SERVING SIZE	FOOD GROUP ASSOCIATION	ASSOCIATED EQUIVALENTS
GRAINS			
Whole Grains			
BROWN RICE	1 cup	1 oz equivalent whole grains	
OATMEAL	½ cup	1 oz equivalent whole grains	
POPCORN	3 cups	1 oz equivalent whole grains	
WHOLE WHEAT BREAD	1 slice	1 oz equivalent whole grains	
WHOLE WHEAT CRACKERS	5 crackers	1 oz equivalent whole grains	
RTE Breakfast Cereals			
WHOLE WHEAT CEREAL FLAKES	1 cup	1 oz equivalent whole grains	
Refined Grains			
CORNBREAD	1 piece 2¼ by 2¼ by 1¼ inches high	2 oz equivalent refined grains	
CRACKERS	7 crackers	1 oz equivalent refined grains	
FLOUR TORTILLAS	1 tortilla, 8 inches in diameter	2 oz equivalent refined grains	
WHITE SANDWICH BUNS OR ROLLS	2½ oz	2.5 oz equivalent refined grains	
WHITE RICE	1 cup	2 oz equivalent refined grains	
RTE Cereals			
CORN FLAKES	1 cup	1 oz equivalents refined grains	
MEATS			
Lean Cuts			
BEEF	5 oz cooked weight	5 oz equivalents protein foods	
PORK	4 oz cooked weight without bone	4 oz equivalents protein foods	
Lean Ground Meats			
BEEF	Cheeseburger single patty	2 oz equivalents refined grains, 2 oz equivalents protein foods	¼ cup dairy
Lean Luncheon or Deli meats			
SLICED HAM	6 thin slices	2 oz equivalents protein foods	
Poultry			
CHICKEN	1 small breast half, cooked	3 oz equivalents protein foods	
BEANS AND PEAS			
BLACK BEANS	½ cup	2 oz equivalents protein foods	½ cup dry beans and peas
KIDNEY BEANS	½ cup	2 oz equivalents protein foods	½ cup dry beans and peas
PINTO BEANS	½ cup	2 oz equivalents protein foods	½ cup dry beans and peas

FOOD	SERVING SIZE	FOOD GROUP ASSOCIATION	ASSOCIATED EQUIVALENTS
NUTS AND SEEDS			
ALMONDS	1 oz; about 25 almonds	2 oz equivalents protein foods plus 2 tsp oil	
CASHEWS	1 oz; about 13 cashews	2 oz equivalents protein foods plus 2 tsp oil	
MIXED NUTS	1 oz	2 oz equivalents protein foods plus 2 tsp oil	
PEANUTS	N/A	2 oz equivalents protein foods and 3 tsp oil	
WALNUTS	1 oz; about 9 walnuts	2 oz equivalents protein foods and 2 tsp oil	
FISH			
Seafood			
SALMON	8 oz cooked weight	8 oz equivalents protein foods	
Shellfish			
SHRIMP	7 medium 2 oz cooked	2 oz equivalents protein foods	
Canned Fish			
TUNA		2 oz equivalents protein foods	
DAIRY			
Milk			
FAT-FREE SKIM	8 fl oz carton	1 cup dairy	
LOW-FAT 1 PERCENT		½ cup dairy	
Milk-based Desserts			
PUDDINGS	½ cup	½ cup dairy	
FROZEN YOGURT	1 small serving; about ½ cup	½ cup dairy	
Cheese			
CHEDDAR	½ cup shredded	1 cup dairy	
SWISS	2 slices; ¾ oz each	1 cup dairy	
YOGURT			
LOW-FAT	8 fl oz carton	1 cup dairy	
OILS			
CANOLA OIL	1 tbsp, 14 g , ½ oz		
OLIVE OIL	1 tbsp, 14 g, ½ oz		
VEGETABLE OIL	1 tbsp, 14 g, ½ oz		
BUTTER	1 tbsp		
SHORTENING	1 tbsp		

Cooking Ratios and Times for Selected Dried Beans and Legumes

LEGUMES	SOAKING TIME	COOKING TIME	COOKING METHODS/USES	FLAVORING SUGGESTIONS
BLACK BEANS	4–8 hours	1½ hours	Usually simmered Can be used in chilis, stews, soups, stuffings	Onion, garlic, cumin, oregano, Mexican herbs such as epazote and hoja santa
BLACK-EYED PEAS	Overnight	45 minutes to 1 hour	Usually simmered Can be used in chilis, stews, soups, stuffings In Southern U.S. cuisine	Onion, garlic; smoky flavors, mushrooms
CHICKPEAS	12–18 hours	2–2½ hours or more	Usually simmered Can be used in hummus, falafel, salads, pasta dishes	Lemon, rosemary, garlic, onion, fennel, cumin, coriander, curry
FAVA BEANS	12 hours	3 hours	Usually simmered Can be used in purées, succotash, salads, pasta dishes, falafel, stews	Olive oil, herbs such as tarragon, chervil, and chives, fennel, mushrooms, roasted peppers
GREAT NORTHERN/ CANNELLINI/ WHITE BEANS	4–8 hours	1 hour	Usually simmered Can be used in Tuscan-style beans, purées, soups	Garlic, onion, rosemary, oregano, basil, tarragon, herbes de Provence
KIDNEY BEANS; RED OR WHITE	4 hours	1 hour	Usually simmered Can be used in chilis, stews, salads, soups, stuffings	Latin and Mexican spice combinations; vinaigrettes
LENTILS*	N/A	30–40 minutes	Usually simmered Can be used in soups, purées Green lentils in salads or pilaf	Middle Eastern spice blends, curry, herbes de Provence, onion, garlic, walnuts, mushrooms, goat cheese
LIMA/BUTTER BEANS	4–8 hours	1–1½ hours	Usually simmered Can be used in succotash, soups, salads, stuffings	Butter, olive oil, herbs, onion, green onions, chives
NAVY BEANS	4 hours	2 hours	Usually simmered Can be used in chilis, stews, soups, stuffings, baked beans	Molasses, brown sugar, onion, garlic, all types of herbs and vegetables
SPLIT PEAS*	N/A	30 minutes	In soups, purées	Vegetables such as carrots, onion, leek, garlic; smoky flavors, cumin, mint, tarragon,
WHOLE PEAS	4 hours	40 minutes	In soups, stuffings, with rice, purées	Vegetables such as carrots, onion, leek, garlic; smoky flavors, cumin, tarragon, mint
PIGEON PEAS*	4 hours	30 minutes	Usually simmered Can be used in braised dishes, stews, soups, stuffings	Curry, herbs onion, garlic, carrots, celery, mushrooms
PINK BEANS	4–8 hours	1 hour	Usually simmered Can be used in chilis, stews, soups, stuffings, combined with rice	Latin and Mexican spice combinations, vinaigrettes
PINTO BEANS	4–8 hours	1½–2 hours	Usually simmered Can be used in chilis, stews, soups, refried, mashed In Southwestern and Southern U.S. cuisine	Latin and Mexican spice combinations, vinaigrettes, garlic, onions, smoky flavors
SOYBEANS; BLACK, GREEN, WHITE	12 hours	3–3½ hours	In homemade tofu, stuffings, stews, salads, chilis, soups,	Asian spices and sauces, all types of vegetables, sesame oil, ginger, green onions

*Soaking not necessary

Cooking Ratios and Times for Selected Pasta and Grains

TYPE	RATIO OF GRAIN TO LIQUID (CUPS)	APPROXIMATE YIELD (CUPS)	COOKING TIME
AMARANTH	1:2½ to 3	4	20 to 25 minutes
BARLEY, PEARLED	1:2	4	35 to 45 minutes
BUCKWHEAT GROATS (KASHA)	1:1½ to 2	2	12 to 20 minutes
WHOLE WHEAT COUSCOUS	1:1¼ to 1½	1½ to 2	5 to 10 minutes
FARRO	1:2	3	30 to 35 minutes
HOMINY, WHOLE†	1:2½	3	2½ to 3 hours
HOMINY GRITS	1:4	3	25 minutes
MILLET	1:2	3	30 to 35 minutes
OAT GROATS	1:2	2	45 minutes to 1 hour
POLENTA, FIRM	1:4	5	35 to 45 minutes
POLENTA, SOFT	1:5	6	35 to 45 minutes
QUINOA	1:2	3	15 to 20 minutes
RICE, CAROLINA	1:1½	3	25 to 30 minutes
RICE, LONG-GRAIN, BROWN	1:3	4	40 minutes
RICE, SHORT-GRAIN, BROWN	1:2.	4	30 to 35 minutes
RICE, WILD	1:4	5	40 to 45 minutes
RYE BERRIES	1:3½	4	1 hour
SPELT	1:2	3	40 minutes
WHEAT BERRIES	1:3	2	1 hour
WHEAT, BULGUR, SOAKED‡	1:4	2	2 hours
WHEAT, CRACKED§	1:2	3	20 minutes

†Grain should be soaked briefly in tepid water, then drained before it is steamed.

‡Grain should be soaked overnight in cold water, then drained before it is cooked.

§Grain may be cooked by covering it with boiling water and soaking for 2 hours, or by the pilaf cooking method.

STANDARD WEIGHT AND VOLUME MEASURE CONVERSIONS

Volume Measure Conversions

U.S.	METRIC
1 teaspoon	4.93 milliliters (rounded to 5)
1 tablespoon	14.79 milliliters (rounded to 15)
1 fluid ounce (2 tablespoons)	29.58 milliliters (rounded to 30)
2 fluid ounces (¼ cup)	59 milliliters (rounded to 60)
8 fluid ounces (1 cup)	236.64 milliliters (rounded to 240)
16 fluid ounces (1 pint)	473.28 milliliters (rounded to 480)
32 fluid ounces (1 quart)	946.56 milliliters (rounded to 950 milliliters or 0.95 liter)
128 fluid ounces (1 gallon)	3.79 liters (rounded to 3.75 liters)

Weight Measure Conversions

U.S.	METRIC
¼ ounce	7 grams
½ ounce	14 grams (rounded to 15)
1 ounce	28.35 grams (rounded to 20)
4 ounces	113.4 grams (rounded to 115)
8 ounces (½ pound)	226.8 grams (rounded to 225)
16 ounces (1 pound)	453.6 grams (rounded to 450)
32 ounces (2 pounds)	907.2 grams (rounded to 900)
40 ounces (2½ pounds)	1.134 kilograms (rounded to 1.15)

GLOSSARY

ACID A substance that tests lower than 7 on the pH scale. Acids have a sour or sharp flavor. Acidity occurs naturally in many foods, including citrus juice, vinegar, wine, and sour milk products. Acids also act as tenderizers in marinades, helping to break down connective tissues and cell walls.

ADULTERATED FOOD Food that has been contaminated to the point that it is considered unfit for human consumption.

AEROBIC BACTERIA Bacteria that require the presence of oxygen to function.

À LA CARTE A menu in which the patron makes individual selections from various menu categories; each item is priced separately.

À LA MINUTE Literally translated this French term means "at the minute." It refers to a restaurant production approach in which dishes are not prepared until an order arrives in the kitchen.

ALBUMEN The egg white. Makes up about 70 percent of the egg and contains most of the protein in the egg.

AL DENTE Literally translated this Italian term means "to the tooth." The term refers to an item, such as pasta or vegetables, cooked until tender but still firm to the bite, not soft.

ALKALI A substance that tests at higher than 7 on the pH scale. Alkalis are sometimes described as having a slightly soapy flavor and can be used to balance acids. Olives and baking soda are two of the few alkaline foods.

ALLUMETTE A vegetable cut usually referring to potatoes, which are cut into pieces the size and shape of matchsticks; ⅛ in by ⅛ in by 1 to 2 in/3 mm by 3 mm by 3 to 5 cm. Also called julienne.

AMINO ACIDS The building blocks of proteins. Of the twenty amino acids in the human diet, eight are called "essential" because they cannot be produced by the body and must be supplied through a person's diet.

AMOUNT PER SERVING Shows the number of calories found in a single food serving. Multiply this number by the serving size, and it should equal, or come close to, the total volume of the package.

AMUSE-GUEULE The term used for a chef's tasting; a small portion (one or two bites) of something exotic, unusual, or otherwise special that is served when the guests in a restaurant are seated. The *amuse* is not listed on a menu and is included in the price of an entrée. Also known as *amuse-bouche*.

ANAEROBIC BACTERIA Bacteria that do not require oxygen to function.

ANTIOXIDANTS Naturally occurring substances that retard the breakdown of tissues in the presence of oxygen. They may be added to food during processing or may occur naturally. They help to prevent food from becoming rancid or discolored due to oxidation.

ANTIPASTO Typically, a platter of hot or cold hors d'oeuvre served as part of an Italian meal that includes meats, olives, cheeses, and vegetables.

ARTIFICIAL FLAVORS Used in food labeling, this term can refer to any flavoring that is not derived from a natural food source. (*See* natural flavors.)

APERITIF A light alcoholic beverage consumed before the meal to stimulate the appetite.

APPAREIL A prepared mixture of ingredients used alone or in another preparation.

APPETIZER Light food served before a meal or as the first course of a meal. It may be hot or cold, plated, or served as finger food.

AQUACULTURE The farm raising of fish or shellfish in natural or controlled marine tanks or ponds.

ARBORIO A high-starch, short-grain rice, Arborio is traditionally used in the preparation of risotto. (*See* risotto.)

AROMATICS Ingredients, such as herbs, spices, vegetables, citrus fruits, wines, and vinegars used to enhance the flavor and fragrance of food.

ARROWROOT A powdered starch made from the root of a tropical plant of the same name. Used primarily as a thickener. It remains clear when cooked.

ASPIC A clear jelly made from stock (or occasionally fruit or vegetable juices) thickened with gelatin. Used to coat foods, or cubed and used as a garnish.

AS-PURCHASED (AP) WEIGHT The weight of an item as received from the supplier before trimming or other preparation, as opposed to edible-portion (EP) weight.

BACTERIA Microscopic organisms. Some have beneficial properties; others can cause food-borne illnesses when contaminated foods are ingested.

BAIN-MARIE The French term for a water bath used to cook foods gently by surrounding the cooking vessel with simmering water. Also, a set of cylindrical nesting pots used to hold foods in a water bath, or a pot with a single, long handle used as a double boiler. *Also,* steam-table inserts.

BAKE To cook food by surrounding it with dry heat in a closed environment, as in an oven.

BARBECUE To cook food by grilling it over a wood or charcoal fire. Usually some sort of marinade or sauce is brushed on the item during cooking. Also, meat that has been cooked in this way.

BATCH COOKING A cooking technique in which appropriately sized batches of food are prepared several times throughout a service period so that a fresh supply of cooked items is always available.

BÂTON/BÂTONNET Items cut into pieces somewhat larger than allumette or julienne; ¼ in by ¼ in by 1- to 2-in/6 mm by 6 mm by 3- to 5-cm. The French word for "stick" or "small stick."

BEURRE MANIÉ Literally, "kneaded butter." A mixture of equal parts by weight of whole butter and flour, used to thicken gravies and sauces.

BLANCH To cook an item briefly in boiling water or hot fat before finishing or storing it. Blanching preserves the color, lessens strong flavors, and helps remove the peels of some fruits and vegetables.

BLEND A mixture of two or more flavors combined to achieve a particular flavor or quality. Also to mix two or more ingredients together until combined.

BOIL A cooking method in which items are immersed in liquid at or above the boiling point (212°F/100°C).

BOUQUET GARNI A small bundle of herbs tied with string. It is used to flavor stocks, braises, and other preparations. Usually contains bay leaf, parsley, thyme, and possibly other aromatics wrapped in leek leaves.

BRAISE A cooking method in which the main item, usually meat, is seared in fat, then simmered at a low temperature in a small amount of stock or another liquid (usually halfway up the meat item) in a covered vessel for a long time. The cooking liquid is then reduced and used as the base of a sauce.

BRAN The outer layer of a cereal grain and the part highest in fiber.

BRAZIER/BRASIER A pan, designed specifically for braising that usually has two handles and a tight-fitting lid. It often is round but may be square or rectangular. It is also called a rondeau.

BRINE A solution of salt, water, and seasonings used to preserve or moisten foods.

BROIL To cook by means of a radiant heat source placed above the food.

BROILER The piece of equipment used to broil foods.

BROTH A flavorful, aromatic liquid made by simmering water or stock with meat, vegetables, and/or spices and herbs.

BROWN SAUCE A sauce made from a brown stock and aromatics and thickened by roux, a pure starch slurry, and/or a reduction; includes Sauce Espagnole, demi-glace, jus de veau lié, and pan sauces.

BROWN STOCK An amber liquid produced by simmering browned bones and meat (usually veal or beef) with vegetables and aromatics (including caramelized mirepoix and tomato purée).

BRUISE To partially crush a food item in order to release its flavor.

BRUNOISE Dice cut of ⅛-in/3-mm cubes. For a brunoise cut, items are first cut in julienne, then cut crosswise. For a fine brunoise of ¹⁄₁₆-in/1.5-mm cubes, cut items first in fine julienne.

BUTTERFLY To cut an item (usually meat or seafood) and open out the edges like a book or the wings of a butterfly.

BUTTERMILK A dairy beverage with a slightly sour flavor similar to that of yogurt. Traditionally, the liquid by-product of butter churning, now usually made by culturing skim milk.

CALORIE A unit used to measure food energy. It is the amount of energy needed to raise the temperature of 1 kilogram of water by 1°C.

CALORIES FROM FAT Food labels show Calories from Fat so you can limit the amount of fat you eat for a healthier diet. The rule of thumb is that no more than 30 percent of your daily calories should come from fat. Higher-fat foods should be eaten in smaller portions.

CANAPÉ An hors d'oeuvre consisting of a small piece of bread or toast, often cut in a decorative shape, garnished with a savory spread or topping.

CARAMELIZATION The process of browning sugar in the presence of heat. The caramelization of sugar occurs from 320° to 360°F/160° to 182°C.

CARBOHYDRATE One of the basic nutrients used by the body as a source of energy. Types include simple (sugars) and complex (starches and fibers).

CARBON DIOXIDE A colorless, tasteless, edible gas obtained through fermentation or from the combination of soda and acid, which acts to leaven baked goods.

CARRY-OVER COOKING Heat retained in cooked foods that allows them to continue cooking even after removal from the cooking medium. Especially important with roasted foods.

CELLULOSE A complex carbohydrate; it is the main structural component of plant cells.

CEPHALOPOD Marine creatures whose tentacles and arms are attached directly to their heads, such as squid and octopus.

CHIFFONADE Leafy vegetables or herbs cut into fine shreds or ribbons; often used as a garnish.

CHILE The fruit of certain types of capsicum peppers (not related to black pepper), used fresh or dried as a seasoning. Chiles come in many types (e.g., jalapeño, serrano, poblano, ancho) and varying degrees of spiciness.

CHILI A stewed dish flavored with chili powder, meat, and optional beans.

CHILI POWDER Dried chiles that have been ground or crushed, often with other ground spices and herbs added.

CHOLESTEROL A substance found exclusively in animal products such as meat, eggs, and cheese (dietary cholesterol) or in the blood (serum cholesterol).

CHOP To cut into pieces of roughly the same size. Also, a small cut of meat including part of the rib.

CHOWDER A thick soup that may be made from a variety of ingredients; usually contains potatoes.

CIGUATERA TOXIN A toxin found in certain species of fish, harmless to the fish, but causes illness in humans when eaten. The poisoning is caused by the fish's diet and is not eradicated by cooking or freezing.

CLARIFICATION The process of removing solid impurities from a liquid (such as butter or stock). Also, a mixture of ground meat, egg whites, mirepoix, tomato purée, herbs, and spices used to clarify broth for consommé.

COAGULATION The curdling or clumping of proteins, usually due to the application of heat or acid.

COARSE CHOP A type of preparation in which food is cut into pieces of roughly the same size. Also called "rough cut." Used for items such as mirepoix where appearance is not important.

COCOA The pods of the cacao tree, processed to remove the cocoa butter and ground into powder; used as a flavoring.

COLLAGEN A fibrous protein found in the connective tissue of animals, used to make glue and gelatin. Breaks down into gelatin when cooked in a moist environment for an extended period of time.

COMBINATION METHOD A cooking method that involves the application of both dry and moist heat to the main item (e.g., meats seared in fat then simmered in a sauce for braising or stewing).

COMPLETE PROTEIN A food source that provides all of the essential amino acids in the correct ratio so that they can be used in the body for protein synthesis. It may require more than one ingredient (such as beans plus rice to make a complete protein).

COMPLEX CARBOHYDRATE A large molecule made up of long chains of sugar molecules. In food, these molecules are found in starches and fiber.

COMPOSED SALAD A salad in which the items are carefully arranged separately on a plate, rather than tossed together.

CONCASSER To pound or chop coarsely. The result, a concassé, usually refers to tomatoes that have been peeled, seeded, and chopped.

CONDIMENT An aromatic mixture such as pickles, chutney, and some sauces and relishes that accompany food. Usually kept on the table throughout service.

CONDUCTION A method of heat transfer in which heat is transmitted through another substance. In cooking, when heat is transmitted to food through a pot or pan, oven racks, or grill rods.

CONSOMMÉ Broth that has been clarified using a raft. The raft, a mixture of ground meat, egg whites, and other ingredients, traps impurities, resulting in a perfectly clear broth.

CONVECTION A method of heat transfer in which heat is transmitted through the circulation of air or water.

CONVECTION OVEN An oven that employs convection currents by forcing hot air through fans so it circulates around food, cooking it quickly and evenly.

CONVERTED RICE Rice that has been pressure-steamed and dried before milling to remove surface starch and retain nutrients. Also known as parboiled rice.

CORNSTARCH A fine, white powder milled from dried corn; used primarily as a thickener for sauce and occasionally as an ingredient in batters.

COTTAGE CHEESE A fresh cheese made from the drained curd of soured cow's milk.

COULIS A thick purée of vegetables or fruit served hot or cold. Traditionally refers to the thickened juices of cooked meat, fish, shellfish purée, or certain thick soups.

COURT BOUILLON Literally "short broth." An aromatic vegetable broth that usually includes an acidic ingredient, such as wine or vinegar; most commonly used for poaching fish.

COUSCOUS Pellets of semolina or cracked wheat usually cooked by steaming, traditionally in a couscoussière. Also, the stew with which this grain is traditionally served.

COUSCOUSSIÈRE A set of nesting pots. Moroccan in origin, it is similar to a steamer, and is used to cook couscous.

CROSS CONTAMINATION The transference of disease-causing elements from one source to another through physical contact.

CRUSTACEAN A class of hard-shelled arthropods with elongated bodies, primarily aquatic, which include edible species such as lobster, crab, shrimp, and crayfish.

CAISSON Shallow poaching liquid, including stock, fumet, or other liquid, which may be reduced and used as a base for the poached item's sauce.

CURRY A mixture of spices, used primarily in Indian, Jamaican, and Thai cuisines. It may include turmeric, coriander, cumin, cayenne, or other chiles, cardamom, cinnamon, clove, fennel, fenugreek, ginger, and garlic. It may be dry or a paste. Also, the name for the stew-like dish seasoned with curry.

DAILY VALUES (DV) Standard nutritional values developed by the Food and Drug Administration for use on food labels.

DANGER ZONE The temperature range from 40° to 140°F/4° to 60°C; the most favorable condition for rapid growth of many pathogens.

DEBEARD To remove the shaggy, inedible fibers from a mussel. These fibers anchor the mussel to its mooring in its natural environment.

DECK OVEN An oven in which the heat source is located underneath the deck or floor of the oven and the food is placed directly on the deck instead of on a rack.

DEEP-FRY To cook food by immersion in hot fat; deep-fried foods are often coated with bread crumbs or batter before being cooked.

DEEP-POACH To cook food gently in enough simmering liquid to completely submerge the food.

DEGLAZE, DÉGLACER To use a liquid, such as wine, water, or stock, to dissolve food particles and/or caramelized drippings left in a pan after roasting or sautéing. The resulting mix then becomes the base for the accompanying sauce.

DEGREASE, DÉGRAISSER To skim the fat off the surface of a liquid such as a stock or sauce.

DEMI-GLACE Literally means "half-glaze." A mixture of equal proportions of brown stock and brown sauce that has been reduced by half. One of the "grand" sauces.

DICE To cut ingredients into evenly sized small cubes; ¼ in/6 mm for small, ½ in/1 cm for medium, and ¾ in/2 cm for large is the standard.

DIE The plate in a meat grinder through which foods pass just before a blade cuts them. The size of the die's opening determines the fineness of the grind.

DIRECT HEAT A method of heat transfer in which heat waves radiate from a source (e.g., an open burner or grill) and travel directly to the item being heated with no conductor between the heat source and food. Examples are grilling, broiling, and toasting; also known as radiant heat.

DREDGE To coat food with a dry ingredient such as flour or bread crumbs prior to frying or sautéing.

DRESSED Prepared for cooking. A dressed fish is gutted and scaled, and its head, tail, and fins are removed (same as pan-dressed). Dressed poultry is plucked, gutted, singed, trimmed, and trussed. Also, coated with dressing, as in a salad.

DRY SAUTÉ To sauté without fat, usually using a nonstick pan.

DURUM A very hard wheat typically milled into semolina, which is primarily used in the making of pasta.

DUSTING Distributing a film of flour, sugar, cocoa powder, or other such ingredients on pans or work surfaces, or on finished products as a garnish.

DUTCH OVEN A kettle, usually of cast iron or enameled cast iron, often used for stewing and braising on the stovetop or in the oven.

DUTCH PROCESS A method for treating cocoa powder with an alkali to reduce its acidity.

DUXELLES An appareil of finely chopped mushrooms and shallots sautéed gently in butter; used as a stuffing, garnish, or as a flavoring in soups and sauces.

EDIBLE-PORTION (EP) WEIGHT The weight of an item after trimming and preparation (as opposed to the as-purchased [AP] weight).

EGG WASH A mixture of beaten eggs (whole eggs, yolks, or whites) and a liquid, usually milk or water, used to coat baked goods to give them a sheen.

EMULSION A mixture of two or more liquids, one of which is a fat or oil and the other of which is water based, so that tiny globules of one are suspended in the other. This may involve the use of stabilizers, such as egg or mustard. Emulsions may be temporary, permanent, or semipermanent.

ENDOSPERM The largest portion of the inside of the seed of a flowering plant, such as wheat; composed primarily of starch and protein. This is the portion used primarily in milled grain products.

ESSENCE A concentrated flavoring extracted from an item, usually by infusion or distillation. Includes items such as vanilla and other extracts, concentrated stocks, and fumets.

ETHYLENE GAS A gas emitted by various fruits and vegetables; ethylene gas speeds ripening, maturing, and eventually rotting.

EVAPORATED MILK Unsweetened canned milk from which 60 percent of the water has been removed before canning. It is often used in custards and to create a creamy texture in food.

FACULTATIVE BACTERIA Bacteria that can survive both with and without oxygen.

FIBER, DIETARY FIBER The structural component of plants that is necessary to the human diet and is indigestible. Also referred to as roughage.

FILÉ A thickener made from ground dried sassafras leaves; used primarily in gumbos.

FINES HERBES A mixture of herbs, usually parsley, chervil, tarragon, and chives, which lose their flavor quickly. They are generally added to the dish just prior to serving.

FIRST IN, FIRST OUT (FIFO) A fundamental storage principle based on stock rotation. Products are stored and used so that the oldest product is always used first.

FISH POACHER A long, narrow pot with straight sides and possibly a perforated rack, used for poaching whole fish.

FIVE-SPICE POWDER A mixture of equal parts ground cinnamon, clove, fennel seed, star anise, and Szechwan peppercorns.

FLATFISH A type of fish characterized by its flat body and having both eyes on one side of its head (e.g., sole, plaice, flounder, and halibut).

FLAT TOP A thick plate of cast iron or steel set over the heat source on a range; diffuses heat, making it more even than an open burner.

FOLD To gently combine ingredients (especially foams) so as not to release trapped air bubbles (volume). Also, to gently mix together two items, usually a light, airy mixture with a denser mixture. Also, the method of turning, rolling, and layering dough over on itself to produce a flaky texture.

FOND The French term for stock. Also describes the pan drippings remaining after sautéing or roasting food. It is often deglazed and used as a base for sauces.

FOOD-BORNE ILLNESS An illness in humans caused by the consumption of an adulterated food product. For an official determination that an outbreak of food-borne illness has occurred, two or more people must have become ill after eating the same food, and the outbreak must be confirmed by health officials.

FOOD MILL A strainer with a crank-operated, curved blade. It is used to purée soft foods while straining.

FOOD PROCESSOR A machine with interchangeable blades and disks and a removable bowl and lid separate from the motor housing. It can be used for a variety of tasks, including chopping, grinding, puréeing, emulsifying, kneading, slicing, shredding, and cutting into julienne.

FORK-TENDER Degree of doneness in braised foods and vegetables; fork-tender foods are easily pierced or cut by a fork, or should slide readily from a fork when lifted.

FREE Used in food labeling, this term indicates that none of the substance cited (or only a negligible amount) is in the product. For instance, a calorie-free product must have fewer than 5 calories per serving, while fat-free and cholesterol-free foods should have less than half a gram per serving. Related words, such as "without," "no," and "zero," must meet the same standards. For example, suppose a food is labeled 95 percent "fat-free." This means that 5 percent of the total weight of the food is fat (which may not seem like much), yet a single

gram of fat contains nine calories compared to 4 calories in a gram of protein or carbohydrates.

FREE-RANGE Refers to livestock that is raised unconfined.

FRENCHING The process of cutting and scraping meat from rib bones before cooking.

FRESH Used in food labeling, this term means unprocessed, uncooked, unfrozen (for example, fresh or freshly squeezed orange juice). The washing and coating of fruits and vegetables is allowed. If a food has been quickly frozen, it can be described as fresh-frozen, which is commonly done with fresh fish.

FRUCTOSE A simple sugar found in fruits. Fructose is the sweetest simple sugar.

FUMET A type of stock in which the main flavoring ingredient is allowed to cook in a covered pot with wine and aromatics. Fish fumet is the most common type.

GARNISH An edible decoration or accompaniment to a dish or item.

GAZPACHO A cold soup made from vegetables, typically tomatoes, cucumbers, peppers, and onions.

GELATIN A protein-based substance found in animal bones and connective tissue. When dissolved in hot liquid and then cooled, it can be used as a thickener and stabilizer.

GELATINIZATION A phase in the process of thickening a liquid with starch in which the starch molecules swell to form a network that traps water molecules.

GERM The portion of the seed of flowering plants, such as wheat, that sprouts to form a new plant; the embryo of the new plant.

GLACE/GLACÉ Reduced stock (demi-glace); ice cream (glace); something frozen or glazed (glacé).

GLUCOSE A simple sugar found in honey, some fruits, and many vegetables. It has about half the sweetness of table sugar and is the preferred source of energy for the human body.

GLUTEN A protein present in wheat flour that develops through hydration and mixing to form elastic strands that build structure and aid in leavening.

GOOD SOURCE Used in food labeling, this term indicates that one serving of the food contains 10 to 19 percent of the daily value for a particular nutrient.

GRIDDLE A heavy metal cooking surface, which may be either fitted with handles, built into a stove, or heated by its own gas or electric element. Cooking is done directly on the griddle.

GRILL A cooking technique in which foods are cooked by a radiant heat source placed below the food. Also, the piece of equipment on which grilling is done. Grills may be fueled by gas, electricity, charcoal, or wood.

GRILL PAN A skillet with ridges that is used on the stovetop to simulate grilling.

GRISWOLD: A pot, similar to a rondeau, a brand made of cast iron; may have a single short handle rather than the usual loop handles.

GUMBO A Creole soup/stew thickened with filé or okra, flavored with a variety of meats and fishes and dark roux.

HAZARD ANALYSIS CRITICAL CONTROL POINT (HACCP) A monitoring system used to track foods from the time that they are received until they are served to consumers to ensure that the foods are free from contamination. Standards and controls are established for time and temperature, as well as for safe handling practices.

HEALTHY Used in food labeling, this term means the food may contain no more than 3 grams of fat (including 1 gram of saturated fat) and 60 milligrams of cholesterol per serving.

HIGH Used in food labeling, this term means that a product has more than 20 percent of the daily value of the nutrient state (example: high fiber).

HOMINY Corn that has been milled or treated with a lye solution to remove the bran and germ. Ground hominy is known as grits.

HOMOGENIZATION A process used to prevent the milk fat from separating out of milk products. The liquid is forced through an ultra-fine mesh at high pressure, which breaks up fat globules, dispersing them evenly throughout the liquid.

HORS D'OEUVRE Literally translated this term means "outside the work." It refers to an appetizer.

HOTEL PAN A rectangular metal pan with sides in any of a number of standard sizes, with a lip that allows it to rest in a storage shelf or steam table.

HYDROGENATION The process in which hydrogen atoms are added to an unsaturated fat molecule, making it partially or completely saturated and solid at room temperature.

HYDROPONICS A technique that involves growing vegetables in nutrient-enriched water rather than in soil.

HYGIENE Conditions and practices followed to maintain health, including sanitation and personal cleanliness.

INDUCTION BURNER A type of heating unit that relies on magnetic attraction between the cooktop and metals in the pot to generate the heat that cooks the foods in the pot. Reaction time is significantly faster than with traditional burners.

INFECTION Contamination by a disease-causing agent such as bacteria.

INFUSION Steeping an aromatic or other item in liquid to extract its flavor. Also, the liquid resulting from this process.

INSTANT-READ THERMOMETER A thermometer used to measure the internal temperature of foods. The stem is inserted in the food, producing an instant temperature read-out.

INTOXICATION Poisoning. A state of being tainted with toxins, particularly those produced by microorganisms that have infected food.

JULIENNE Vegetables, potatoes, or other items cut into thin strips; ⅛ in by ⅛ in by 1 to 2 in/3 mm by 3 mm by 3 to 5 cm is standard. Fine julienne is 1/16 in by 1/16 in by 1 to 2 in/1.5 mm by 1.5 mm by 3 to 5 cm.

JUS Juice. Refers to fruit and vegetable juices as well as juices from meats. Jus de viande is meat gravy. Meat served au jus is served with its own juice or jus lié.

JUS LIÉ Meat juice thickened lightly with arrowroot or cornstarch.

KASHA Buckwheat groats that have been hulled and crushed and roasted; usually prepared by boiling.

KOSHER Prepared in accordance with Jewish dietary laws.

KOSHER SALT Frequently used for general cooking as opposed to fine or iodized table salt. Pure, refined salt used for pickling, it is sometimes referred to as coarse salt or pickling salt.. Because it does not contain magnesium carbonate, it does not cloud brine solutions. Also used to prepare kosher items.

LACTOSE The simple sugar found in milk. This disaccharide is the least sweet among the natural sugars.

LEAN Used in food labeling, this term can be used to describe the fat content of meat, poultry, and seafood. To be called "lean," a serving of the product must have less than 10 grams of fat, 4.5 grams or less of saturated fat, and less than 95 milligrams of cholesterol. "Extra lean" has also been defined to mean less than 5 grams of fat, less than 2 grams of saturated fat, and less than 95 milligrams of cholesterol.

LEGUME The seeds of certain pod plants, including beans and peas, which are eaten for their earthy flavors and high nutritional value. Also, the French word for vegetable.

LIAISON A mixture of egg yolks and cream used to thicken and enrich sauces. Also loosely used to mean any appareil used as a thickener.

LIGHT Used in food labeling, this means that the food has half the fat and one-third the calories or half the salt of its regular counterpart. It can still be used to describe other properties like color or texture as long as the label makes the distinction clear (for example, "light brown sugar" or "light and fluffy").

LIQUEUR A spirit flavored with fruit, spices, nuts, herbs, and/or seeds and usually sweetened. Also known as cordials, liqueurs often have a high alcohol content, a viscous body, and a slightly sticky feel.

LOW Used in food labeling, this term may be used on products that do not exceed the dietary guidelines for fat, saturated fat, cholesterol, sodium, or calories. The criteria they must meet are: Low-fat: 3 grams or less per serving; low-saturated fat: 1 gram or less per serving,; low-sodium: 140 milligrams or less per serving; low-cholesterol: 20 milligrams or less of cholesterol and 2 grams or less of saturated fat per serving; low-calorie: 40 calories or less per serving.

LOW-FAT MILK Milk containing less than 2 percent fat.

LOZENGE CUT A knife cut in which foods are cut into small diamond shapes ½ in by ½ in by ⅛ in/1 cm by 1 cm by 3 mm thick.

MAILLARD REACTION A complex browning reaction that results in the particular flavor and color of foods that do not contain much sugar, including roasted meats. The reaction, which involves carbohydrates and amino acids, is named after the French scientist who first discovered it. There are low-temperature and high-temperature Maillard reactions; the high-temperature reaction starts at 310°F/154°C.

MANDOLINE A slicing device of stainless steel with carbon steel blades. The blades may be adjusted to cut items into various shapes and thicknesses.

MARBLING The intramuscular fat found in meat that makes it tender and juicy.

MARINADE An appareil used before cooking to flavor and moisten foods; may be liquid or dry. Liquid marinades are usually based on an acidic ingredient, such as wine or vinegar; dry marinades are usually salt based.

MARK ON A GRILL To rotate a food 90 degrees on the same cooking side after it has been on the grill for several seconds to create the cross-hatching marks associated with grilled foods.

MEDALLION A small, round scallop of meat.

MERINGUE Egg whites beaten with sugar until they stiffen. Types include regular or common, Italian, and Swiss.

MESOPHILIC A term used to describe bacteria that thrive in temperatures between 60° and 100°F/16° and 38°C.

METABOLISM The sum of chemical processes in living cells by which energy is provided and new material is assimilated.

MILLET A small, round, gluten-less grain that may be boiled or ground into flour.

MILLING The process by which grain is separated into germ/husk, bran, and endosperm and then ground into flour or meal.

MINCE To chop into very small pieces.

MINERAL An inorganic element that is an essential component of the diet. It provides no energy and is therefore referred to as a noncaloric nutrient. The body cannot produce minerals; they must be obtained from the diet.

MINESTRONE A hearty vegetable soup that typically includes dried beans and pasta.

MIREPOIX A combination of chopped aromatic vegetables—usually two parts onion, one part carrot, and one part celery—used to flavor stocks, soups, braises, and stews.

MISE EN PLACE Literally translated, the French term means "put in place." It refers to the preparation and assembly of ingredients, pans, utensils, and plates or serving pieces needed for a particular dish or service period.

MOLASSES The dark brown, sweet syrup that is a by-product of sugarcane and sugar beet refining. Molasses is available as light (the least cooked but sweetest), dark, and blackstrap (the most cooked and most bitter).

MOLLUSK Any of a number of invertebrate animals with soft, unsegmented bodies usually enclosed in a hard shell; mollusks include gastropods (univalves), bivalves, and cephalopods. Examples include clams, oysters, snails, octopus, and squid.

MONOSODIUM GLUTAMATE (MSG) A flavor enhancer derived from glutamic acid, without a distinct flavor of its own; used primarily in Chinese and processed foods. It may cause allergic reactions in some people.

MONOUNSATURATED FAT A fat with one available bonding site not filled with a hydrogen atom. Helpful in lowering the LDL cholesterol level (bad cholesterol). Food sources include avocados, olives, and nuts.

NAPPÉ From the French verb *napper*, this means to coat with thickened sauce. Often refers to the consistency of a sauce that will coat, or nap, the back of a spoon.

NATURAL FLAVORS The essential oil, oleoresin, essence or extractive, protein hydrolysate, distillate, or any product of roasting, heating, or enzymolysis, which contains a flavoring constituent derived from a spice, fruit, fruit juice, vegetable, vegetable juice, edible yeast, herb, bark, bud, root, leaf, or similar plant material; meat, seafood, poultry, eggs, dairy products, or fermentation products thereof whose significant function in food is flavoring rather than nutritional. This broad definition simply means that "natural flavors" are extracts from these non-synthetic foods.

NOISETTE The French word for hazelnut, it also refers to items that are hazelnut-colored. Also, a small portion of meat cut from the rib. Pommes noisette are tournéed potatoes browned in butter. Beurre noisette is browned butter.

NONBONY FISH Fish whose skeletons are made of cartilage rather than hard bone (e.g., shark, skate). Also called cartilaginous fish.

NUTRIENT A basic component of food used by the body for growth, repair, restoration, and energy. Includes carbohydrates, fats, proteins, water, vitamins, and minerals.

NUTRITION The process by which an organism takes in and uses food.

OBLIQUE CUT, ROLL CUT A knife cut used primarily with long, cylindrical vegetables such as carrots. The item is cut on a diagonal, rolled 180 degrees, then cut on the same diagonal, producing a piece with two angled edges.

OIGNON BRÛLÉ Literally translated this classic French term means "burnt onion." A peeled, halved onion is seared on a flat top or in a skillet and used to enhance the color of stock and consommé.

OIGNON PIQUÉ Literally "pricked onion." A whole, peeled onion to which a bay leaf is attached using a clove as a tack. It is used to flavor béchamel sauce and some soups.

OMEGA-3 FATTY ACIDS Polyunsaturated fatty acids that may reduce the risk of heart disease and tumor growth, stimulate the immune system, and lower blood pressure; they occur in fatty fish, dark, green leafy vegetables, and certain nuts and oils.

ORGANIC LEAVENER Yeast. A living organism acting to produce carbon dioxide gas, which will cause a batter or dough to rise through the fermentation process.

PAILLARD A scallop of meat pounded until thin; usually grilled or sautéed.

PALETTE KNIFE A small, long, narrow metal spatula with a rounded tip. May be tapered or straight, offset or flat.

PAN-BROILING A cooking method similar to dry sautéing that simulates broiling by cooking an item in a hot pan with little or no fat.

PAN STEAMING A method of cooking foods in a very small amount of liquid in a covered pan over direct heat.

PAPILLOTE, EN Refers to a moist-heat cooking method similar to steaming, in which items are enclosed in parchment and cooked in the oven.

PARCHMENT PAPER Heat-resistant paper used in cooking for such preparations as lining baking pans, cooking items en papillote, and covering items during the process of shallow poaching.

PARCOOK To partially cook an item before storing or finishing.

PARISIENNE SCOOP A small tool used for scooping balls out of vegetables or fruits and for portioning truffle ganache and other such preparations. Also called a melon baller.

PASTEURIZATION A process in which milk products are heated to kill microorganisms that could contaminate the milk.

PASTRY BAG A bag—usually made of plastic, canvas, or nylon—that can be fitted with plain or decorative tips and used to pipe out icings and puréed foods.

PATHOGEN A disease-causing microorganism.

PAYSANNE OR FERMIER CUT A knife cut in which ingredients are cut into flat, square pieces measuring ¼ in by ¼ in by ⅛ in/1 cm by 1 cm by 3 mm.

PEEL A paddle used to transfer shaped doughs to a hearth or deck oven. Also, to remove the skin from a food item.

PERCENT DAILY VALUE This section on a nutrition label tells you what percentage of the total recommended daily amount of each nutrient (fats, carbohydrates, proteins, major vitamins, and minerals) is in each serving, based on a 2,000 calorie per day diet.

PESTO A thick, puréed mixture of an herb, traditionally basil and oil. Used as a sauce for pasta and other foods and as a garnish for soup. Pesto may also contain grated cheese, nuts or seeds, and other seasonings.

PH SCALE A scale with values from 0 to 14 representing degree of acidity. A measurement of 7 is neutral, 0 is most acidic, and 14 is most alkaline. Chemically, pH measures the concentration of hydrogen ions.

PHYLLO/FILO DOUGH Very thin sheets of a flour-and-water dough Used in layered, flaky pastries often made with butter and/or bread or cake crumbs; similar to strudel.

PHYSICAL LEAVENER The leavening that occurs when steam is trapped in a dough through the introduction of air (versus a chemical leavener), expanding and causing the cake or bread to rise.

PHYTOCHEMICALS Naturally occurring compounds in plant foods that have antioxidant and disease-fighting properties.

PILAF A technique for cooking grains in which the grain is sautéed briefly in butter or oil, then simmered in stock or water with various seasonings until the liquid is absorbed. Also called pilau, pilaw, pullao, pilav.

PINCÉ Refers to an item caramelized by sautéing; usually refers to a tomato product.

PLUCHES The French word for whole herb leaves connected to a small bit of stem; often used as a garnish. Also called sprigs.

POACH To cook gently in simmering liquid that is 160° to 185°F/71° to 85°C.

POLENTA Cornmeal mush cooked in simmering liquid until the grains soften and the liquid is absorbed. Polenta can be eaten hot or cold, firm, or soft. The term can be used to describe other grains that are cooked in a similar fashion.

POLYUNSATURATED FAT A fat molecule with more than one available bonding site not filled with a hydrogen atom. Food sources include corn, cottonseed, safflower, soy, and sunflower oils.

PRAWN A crustacean that closely resembles shrimp; often used as a general term for large shrimp.

PRESENTATION SIDE The side of a piece of meat, poultry, or fish that will be served facing up. Usually the nicest side is selected before cooking and is often cooked first, as in "presentation side down" in a pan.

PRESSURE STEAMER A machine that cooks food using steam produced by heating water under pressure in a sealed compartment, allowing it to reach temperatures higher than boiling (212°F/100°C). The food is placed in a sealed chamber that cannot be opened until the pressure has been released and the steam properly vented from the chamber.

PROTEIN One of the basic nutrients needed by the body to maintain life, supply energy, build and repair tissues, form enzymes and hormones, and perform other essential functions. Protein can be obtained from both animal and vegetable sources.

PULSE The edible seed of a leguminous plant, such as a bean, lentil, or pea. Often referred to simply as legume. Also, the action of turning a food processor or blender on and off to control mixing speed and time.

PURÉE To process food by mashing, straining, or chopping it very finely in order to make it a smooth paste. Also, a product produced using this technique.

RAFT A mixture of ingredients used to clarify a stock as for consommé. The term refers to the fact that the ingredients rise to the surface and form a floating mass.

RAGOUT Stew of meat and/or vegetables.

RAMEKIN/RAMEQUIN A small, ovenproof dish, usually ceramic.

RECOMMENDED SERVING SIZE A standard measure of food. Serving size can be expressed in kitchen terms—cups, spoons, slices, ounces, and also in grams. Serving size refers to how much food makes up a single serving.

REDUCE To decrease the volume of a liquid by simmering or boiling; used to provide a thicker consistency and/or concentrated flavors.

REDUCED Used in food labeling, this term means that a nutritionally altered product contains at least 25 percent less of a nutrient or of calories than the regular product. A reduction: The product that results when a liquid is reduced.

REFRESH To plunge an item into, ice water or rinse it under, cold running water after blanching to prevent further cooking. The process is also known as shocking.

RISOTTO A rice dish in which rice (usually Arborio, Carnaroli, or Vialone Nano) is sautéed briefly in fat with onions and possibly other aromatics, then combined with stock, which is added in several additions and stirred constantly, to produce a creamy-textured dish with grains that are still al dente.

ROAST A dry-heat cooking method where the item is cooked in an oven or on a spit over a fire.

ROE Fish or shellfish eggs.

RONDEAU A shallow, wide, straight-sided pot with two loop handles often used for braising. It is also known as a brazier.

RONDELLE A knife cut that produces round or oval flat pieces; used on cylindrical vegetables or items trimmed into cylinders before cutting.

ROUND FISH A classification of fish based on skeletal type, characterized by a rounded body and eyes on opposite sides of its head. Round fish are usually cut by the "up and over" method.

ROUX An appareil containing equal parts of flour and fat (usually butter) used to thicken liquids. Roux is cooked to varying degrees, and characterized as white, blond, or brown, depending on its intended use. The darker the roux, the less thickening power it has, but the fuller the taste.

SACHET D'ÉPICES The French term literally translated means "bag of spices." Aromatic ingredients are encased in cheesecloth, and are used to flavor stocks and other liquids. A standard sachet contains parsley stems, cracked peppercorns, dried thyme, and a bay leaf.

SANITATION The maintenance of a clean food-preparation environment by healthy food workers in order to prevent food-borne illnesses and food contamination.

SANITIZE To kill pathogenic organisms by chemicals and/or moist heat.

SATURATED FAT A fat molecule whose available bonding sites are entirely filled with hydrogen atoms. These tend to be solid at room temperature and are primarily of animal origin, though coconut oil, palm oil, and cocoa butter are vegetable sources of saturated fat. Animal sources include butter, meat, cheese, and eggs.

SAUCE A liquid accompaniment to food, which is used to enhance the flavor of the food.

SAUTÉ To cook quickly in a small amount of fat in a pan over relatively high heat on the range top.

SAUTEUSE A shallow skillet with sloping sides and a single, long handle. Used for sautéing. Referred to generically as a sauté pan.

SAUTOIR A shallow skillet with straight sides and a single, long handle. Used for sautéing. Referred to generically as a sauté pan.

SAVORY Not sweet. Also, the name of a course (savory) served after dessert and before port in traditional British meals. Also, a family of herbs (including summer and winter savory) that taste like a cross between thyme and mint.

SCALD To heat a liquid, usually milk or cream, to just below the boiling point. It may also refer to blanching fruits and vegetables.

SCALE To measure ingredients by weighing, or to divide dough or batter into portions by weight. Also, refers to removing the scales from fish.

SCALER Tool used to scrape scales from fish. Used by scraping against the direction in which scales lie flat, working from tail to head.

SCALLOP A bivalve whose adductor muscle (the muscle that keeps its shells closed) and roe are eaten. Also a term for a small, boneless piece of meat or fish of uniform thickness. May refer to a side dish where an item is layered with cream or sauce and topped with bread crumbs prior to baking.

SCORE To cut the surface of an item at regular intervals to allow it to cook evenly, allow excess fat to drain, help the food absorb marinades, or for decorative purposes.

SEAR To brown the surface of food in fat over high heat before finishing by another method (e.g., braising or roasting) in order to add flavor.

SEA SALT Salt produced by evaporating seawater. Available refined or unrefined, crystallized or ground. Also known as sel gris (French for "gray salt").

SEASONING Adding an ingredient to give foods a particular flavor using salt, pepper, herbs, spices, and/or condiments. Also, the process by which a protective coating is built up on the interior of a pan.

SHALLOW POACH To cook gently in a shallow pan of simmering liquid. The liquid is often reduced and used as the base of a sauce.

SHEET PAN A flat baking pan, often with a rolled lip, used to cook foods in the oven.

SHELF LIFE The amount of time in storage that a product can maintain its quality.

SHELLFISH Various types of marine life consumed as food, including mollusks such as univalves, bivalves, cephalopods, and crustaceans.

SHERRY A fortified Spanish wine varying in color and sweetness.

SIEVE A container made of a perforated material, such as wire mesh, used to drain, rice, or purée foods.

SILVERSKIN The tough connective tissue that surrounds certain muscles. This protein does not dissolve when cooked and must be removed prior to cooking.

SIMMER To maintain the temperature of a liquid just below boiling. Also, to cook in simmering liquid. The temperature range for simmering is 185° to 200°F/85° to 93°C.

SIMPLE CARBOHYDRATE Any of a number of small carbohydrate molecules (mono- and disaccharides), including glucose, fructose, lactose, maltose, and sucrose.

SKIM To remove impurities from the surface of a liquid, such as stock or soup, during cooking.

SKIM MILK Milk from which all but 0.5 percent of the milk fat has been removed.

SLURRY A starch such as arrowroot, cornstarch, or potato starch dispersed in cold liquid to prevent it from forming lumps when added to hot liquid as a thickener.

SMOKE POINT The temperature at which a fat begins to break (and smoke) when heated.

SMOKE ROASTING A method for roasting foods in which items are placed on a rack in a pan containing wood chips that smolder, emitting smoke, when the pan is placed on the range top or in the oven.

SMOKING Any of several methods for preserving and flavoring foods by exposing them to smoke. Methods include cold smoking (in which smoked items are not fully cooked), hot smoking (in which the items are cooked), and smoke roasting.

SMOTHER To cook in a covered pan with little liquid over low heat. The main item is often completely covered by another food item or sauce while it braises.

SODIUM An alkaline metal element necessary in small quantities for human nutrition; one of the components of most salts used in cooking.

SORBET A frozen dessert made with fruit juice or another flavoring, a sweetener (usually sugar), and beaten egg whites, which prevent the formation of large ice crystals.

SOUFFLÉ Literally "puffed." A preparation made with a sauce base (usually béchamel for savory soufflés, pastry cream for sweet ones), whipped egg whites, and flavorings. The egg whites cause the soufflé to puff during cooking.

SPÄTZLE A soft noodle or small dumpling made by dropping bits of a prepared batter into simmering liquid.

SPICE An aromatic vegetable substance from numerous plant parts, usually dried and used as seasoning.

SPIDER A long-handled skimmer used to remove items from hot liquid or fat and to skim the surface of liquids.

STANDARD BREADING PROCEDURE The assembly line procedure in which items are dredged in flour, dipped in beaten egg, then coated with crumbs before being pan fried or deep-fried.

STAPHYLOCOCCUS AUREUS A type of facultative bacteria that can cause food-borne illness. It is particularly dangerous because it produces toxins that cannot be destroyed by heat. Staph intoxication is most often caused by transfer of the bacteria from infected food handlers.

STEAMER A set of stacked pots with perforations in the bottom of each pot. They fit over a larger pot that is filled with boiling or simmering water. Also, a perforated insert made of metal or bamboo that can be used in a pot to steam foods.

STEAMING A cooking method in which items are cooked in a vapor bath created by boiling water or other liquids.

STEAM-JACKETED KETTLE A kettle with double-layered walls, between which steam circulates, providing even heat for cooking stocks, soups, and sauces. These kettles may be insulated, fitted with a spigot, and/or tilting. The latter are also called trunnion kettles.

STEEP To allow an ingredient to sit in warm or hot liquid to extract flavor or impurities, or to soften the item.

STEW A cooking method nearly identical to braising, but stewing generally involves smaller pieces of meat and, hence, a shorter cooking time. Stewed items also may be blanched, rather than seared, to give the finished product a pale color. Also, a dish prepared by using the stewing method.

STIR-FRYING A cooking method similar to sautéing in which items are cooked over very high heat, using little fat. Usually this is done in a wok, and the food is kept moving constantly.

STOCK A flavorful liquid prepared by simmering meat bones, poultry bones, seafood bones, and/or vegetables in water with aromatics until their flavor is extracted. It is used as a base for soups, sauces, and other preparations.

STOCKPOT A large, straight-sided pot that is taller than it is wide. Used for making stocks and soups. Some have spigots. Also called a marmite.

STONE-GROUND A term used to describe meal or flour milled between grindstones. Because the germ of the wheat is not separated, this method of grinding retains more nutrients than other methods.

STRAIN To pass a liquid through a sieve or screen to remove particles.

SUPRÊME The breast fillet and wing of chicken or other poultry. Sauce suprême is chicken velouté enriched with cream. The term also refers to a section of citrus without its membrane covering.

SWEAT To cook an item, usually a vegetable, in a covered pan in a small amount of fat until it softens and releases its moisture but does not brown.

TABLE SALT Refined, granulated salt. May be fortified with iodine and treated with magnesium carbonate to prevent clumping.

TABLE WINE Still red, white, and rosé wines containing between 7 and 14 percent alcohol; usually served with a meal.

TEMPER To heat gently and gradually. It may refer to the process of incorporating hot liquid into a liaison, such as beaten eggs, to gradually raise its temperature. May also refer to the proper method for melting chocolate.

THERMOPHILIC The term means heat loving. It is used to describe bacteria that thrive within the temperature range from 110° to 171°F/43° to 77°C.

THICKENER An ingredient used to give additional body to liquids. Arrowroot, cornstarch, gelatin, roux, and beurre manié are examples of thickeners.

TILTING KETTLE A large, relatively shallow tilting pot used for braising, stewing, and occasionally steaming.

TOTAL FAT This equals the number of grams of fat per serving of the food. A heart-healthy diet limits foods containing saturated fats, trans fats, cholesterol, and sodium.

TOXIN A naturally occurring poison, particularly those produced by the metabolic activity of living organisms, such as bacteria.

TRANCHE A French term for a slice or cut of meat, fish, or poultry cut on a bias in order to visually increase the appearance of the cut.

TRICHINELLA SPIRALIS A spiral-shaped parasitic worm that invades the intestines and muscle tissue. Transmitted primarily through infected pork that has not been cooked sufficiently.

TRUSS To tie up meat or poultry with string before cooking it in order to give it a compact shape for more even cooking and better appearance.

TUBER The fleshy root, stem, or rhizome of a plant, able to grow into a new plant. Some, such as potatoes, are eaten as vegetables.

TUILE The French word literally translated means "tile." It refers to thin, wafer-like cookie, which resembles a roof tile in shape (or to food cut to resemble this cookie). Tuiles are frequently shaped while warm and still pliable by pressing them into molds or draping them over rolling pins or dowels.

UMAMI Describes a savory, meaty taste; often associated with monosodium glutamate (MSG) and mushrooms.

UNIVALVE A single-shelled, single-muscle mollusk, such as abalone and sea urchin.

UNSATURATED FAT A fat molecule with at least one available bonding site not filled with a hydrogen atom. These may be monounsaturated or polyunsaturated. They tend to be liquid at room temperature and are primarily of vegetable origin.

VEGETARIAN An individual who has adopted a specific diet (or lifestyle) that reduces or eliminates animal products. Vegans eat no foods derived in any way from animals. Lacto-ovo vegetarians include dairy products and eggs in their diet. Ovo-vegetarians include eggs in their diet.

VIRUS A type of pathogenic microorganism that can be transmitted in food. Viruses cause such illnesses as measles, chicken pox, infectious hepatitis, and colds.

VITAMINS Any of various nutritionally essential organic substances that do not provide energy but usually act as regulators in metabolic processes and help maintain health.

WASABI Root of an Asian plant similar to horseradish. It is used as a condiment in Japanese cooking.

WHIP/WHISK To beat an item, such as cream or egg whites, to incorporate air. Also, a special tool for whipping, made of looped wire attached to a handle.

WHITE MIREPOIX Mirepoix that does not include carrots and may include chopped mushrooms or mushroom trimmings and parsnips. It is used for pale or white sauces and stocks.

WHITE STOCK A light-colored stock made with bones that have not been browned.

WHOLE GRAIN An unmilled or unprocessed grain.

WHOLE WHEAT FLOUR Flour milled from the whole grain, including the bran, germ, and endosperm. Graham flour is a whole wheat flour named after Sylvester Graham, a nineteenth century American dietary reformer.

WOK A round-bottomed pan, usually made of rolled steel, which is used for nearly all cooking methods in Chinese cuisine. Its shape allows for even heat distribution and easy tossing of ingredients.

YAM A large tuber that grows in tropical and subtropical climates; it has starchy, pale-yellow flesh. The name yam is also used for the (botanically unrelated) sweet potato.

YEAST Microscopic fungus whose metabolic processes are responsible for fermentation. It is used for leavening bread and in the making of cheese, beer, and wine.

YOGURT Milk cultured with bacteria to give it a slightly thick consistency and sour flavor.

ZEST The thin, brightly colored outer part of citrus rind. It contains volatile oils, making it ideal for use as a flavoring.

BIBLIOGRAPHY

Anderson, Kenneth N., and Lois E. Anderson. *The International Dictionary of Food & Nutrition*. New York: Wiley, 1993.

Bittman, Mark. *Food Matters: A Guide to Conscious Eating with More Than 75 Recipes*. New York: Simon & Schuster, 2009.

Brand-Miller, Jennie, Thomas M.S. Wolever, Stephen Colagiuri, and Kaye Foster-Powell. *The New Glucose Revolution*. Emmaus, PA: Rodale, 2005.

Colbin, Annemarie. *Food and Healing*. New York: Ballantine Books, 1986.

———. *Food and Our Bones: The Natural Way to Prevent Osteoporosis*. New York: Plume, 1998.

Drummond, Karen E., and Lisa M. Brefere. *Nutrition for Foodservice and Culinary Professionals*. 8th ed. New York: Wiley, 2013.

Flaws, Bob, and Honora Wolfe. *Prince Wen Hui's Cook: Chinese Dietary Therapy*. Taos, NM: Paradigm Publications, 1985.

Fuhrman, Joel. *Eat to Live: The Amazing Nutrient-Rich Program for Fast and Sustained Weight Loss*. rev. ed. New York: Little, Brown and Company, 2011.

———. *Nutritarian Handbook & ANDI Food Scoring Guide*. Flemington, NJ: Gift of Health Press, 2012.

———. *Super Immunity: The Essential Nutrition Guide for Boosting Your Body's Defenses to Live Longer, Stronger, and Disease Free*. New York: HarperOne, 2011.

Harvard Medical School. *Diagnosis: Coronary Artery Disease*. Boston: Harvard Health Publications, 2013.

———. *Food Allergy, Intolerance, and Sensitivity*. Boston: Harvard Health Publications, 2011.

———. *Healthy Eating: A Guide to the New Nutrition*. Boston: Harvard Health Publications, 2011.

———. *Healthy Eating for a Healthy Heart*. Boston: Harvard Health Publications, 2011.

———. *Healthy Eating for Type 2 Diabetes*. Boston: Harvard Health Publications, 2012.

———. *Hypertension: Controlling the "Silent" Killer*. Boston: Harvard Health Publications, 2010.

———. *The Sensitive Gut*. New York: Fireside, 2001.

HRH The Prince of Wales. *The Prince's Speech: On the Future of Food*. Emmaus, PA: Rodale, 2012.

McGee, Harold. *On Food and Cooking: The Science and Lore of the Kitchen*. rev. ed. New York: Scribner, 2004.

Murray, Michael, Joseph Pizzorno, and Lara Pizzorno. *The Encyclopedia of Healing Foods*. New York: Atria Books, 2005.

National Restaurant Association. *ServSafe Essentials*. 6th ed. Upper Saddle River, NJ: Prentice Hall, 2012.

Pollan, Michael. *Food Rules: An Eater's Manual*. New York: Penguin, 2009.

Powers, Catharine, and Mary Abbott Hess. *Essentials of Nutrition for Chefs*. 2nd ed. Medina, OH: Culinary Nutrition Publishing, LLC, 2013.

Thompson, Janice, and Melinda Manore. *Nutrition: An Applied Approach*. 2nd ed. San Francisco: Benjamin Cummings, 2008.

Weil, Andrew. *Eating Well for Optimum Health: The Essential Guide to Bringing Health and Pleasure Back to Eating*. New York: William Morrow Paperbacks, 2001.

INDEX

Note: Numbers in *italic* indicate photographs.